Documents of Native American Political Development

Documents of Native American Political Development

1933 to Present

Edited by
DAVID E. WILKINS

OXFORD
UNIVERSITY PRESS

OXFORD
UNIVERSITY PRESS

Oxford University Press is a department of the University of Oxford.
It furthers the University's objective of excellence in research, scholarship,
and education by publishing worldwide. Oxford is a registered trade mark of
Oxford University Press in the UK and certain other countries.

Published in the United States of America by Oxford University Press
198 Madison Avenue, New York, NY 10016, United States of America.

CIP data is on file at the Library of Congress.

ISBN 978-0-19-021207-0

1 3 5 7 9 8 6 4 2

Printed by Sheridan Books, Inc., United States of America

Contents

Preface and Acknowledgments

In every respect this collection is a logical follow-up to its 2009 predecessor, and similarly named work, *Documents of Native American Political Development: 1500s to 1933*. I had no intention of compiling a second volume, as my goal had simply been to explore that earlier time. Native political and legal evolution during that long period had largely been ignored by political scientists, legal minds, and historians and it warranted attention. That volume was my attempt to correct that omission by chronicling the creative, intelligent ways Native nations adapted their governing systems as European colonial powers commenced unrelenting campaigns to dominate and coercively assimilate Indigenous peoples.

However, not long after that book's release, my good friend, Tom Holm (Cherokee/Creek), urged me to consider a second volume that would cover dramatic changes in Native governance, diplomacy, and intergovernmental relations from the New Deal era to the present. The idea made sense, but my writing table was already filled with other projects and I knew it would be some time before I could revisit the topic. Nearly a decade has elapsed and Native peoples have made enormous gains in exercising self-governing power and in finding strategic ways and means to wield their still-constrained inherent sovereign authority. And, while they continue to have both contentious and cooperative relations with one another, as well as with local, state, and the federal government—depending on the issue in question—we seem finally to have arrived at a point in history where there is a grudging acceptance by most non-native governments, particularly states, that tribal national governments are permanent polities that must be dealt with in a government-to-government manner. In ways that few could have foreseen, Native nations have become economic and social leaders.

This volume contains a bounty of documents, including new or modified constitutions, testimonials about the powers and duties of Indigenous governments, Native legal codes, ordinances and statutes, international Indigenous treaties and accords, and intergovernmental memoranda of understanding between Native governments and non-native governments. While many other items deserved inclusion, I selected these materials because together they tell a story that clearly demonstrates the ever-increasing vitality and maturity of modern Native societies and governments.

As is true of all my previous work, this book was inspired by the late Vine Deloria Jr. (Standing Rock Lakota), the indomitable intellectual prophet of Native sovereignty and self-governance. Vine was my mentor, my friend, and I had the good fortune of co-authoring two books with him. And I owe thanks to Tom Holm, noted earlier, for encouraging me to undertake this compilation. Several other individuals, including Kimberly TallBear (Sisseton-Wahpeton Oyate), Sarah Deer (Muscogee Creek), and Bill Zimmerman at the Bonneville Power Administration were generous with their time and expertise on specific documents. Tawa Ducheneaux, a dedicated librarian and archivist at Oglala Lakota College, helped me track down critical documents. I am especially grateful to Cecilia Fire Thunder, former president of the Oglala Lakota Nation, for sharing her fascinating political story with me.

Appreciation also goes to John Coleman, dean of the College of Liberal Arts at the University of Minnesota (UMN), Katherine Hayes, chair of the Department of American Indian Studies, and the outstanding reference librarians at the UMN main and law school libraries, particularly Vicente Garces. James Cook, my extremely patient editor at Oxford, who persevered through the project's dormancy, offered feedback that strengthened the book. Special thanks to the several reviewers who offered important suggestions and constructive criticisms that fortified the final manuscript.

As always, I'm grateful to my family: my late parents, Daniel and Thedis Wilkins, and brothers, Coskie and Webster, who all walked on too soon, as well as siblings remaining with me on this side—Roger, Deb, Michael, and Craig—and my kind and generous aunt, Faye D'Amico. Gratitude also to my children, Sion and his wife, Alyssa; Niltooli; and Nazhone; and most important, to my grandsons, Kai David and Levi Sion, who bring boundless energy and neverending smiles to my life.

Finally, to my wife, Shelly Hulse Wilkins, whose love, talent, and friendship inspire and enthrall me every day. Her skills helped bring this book to fruition after a long hiatus and much sooner than expected, given the constraints with which I was confronted. I love the adventures we have shared together and look forward to many, many more.

David E. Wilkins (Lumbee)
University of Minnesota

Referenced Native Peoples and Affiliations

1. Agua Caliente Band of Cahuilla Indians
2. Ak-Chin Indian Community
3. Alaska Natives
4. Apache Nations
5. Assiniboine (Fort Belknap)
6. Fort Peck Assiniboine and Sioux Tribes
7. Bad River Band of Lake Superior Chippewa Tribe
8. Blackfeet Nation
9. Blood Tribe (Kainai Nation, Alberta, Canada)
10. Bois Forte Band of Ojibwe
11. Buena Vista Rancheria of Me Wuk Indians
12. Caddo Nation
13. Cayuga Nation
14. Chehalis Tribe
15. Chemehuevi Indian Tribe
16. Cheroenhaka Nation (Nottoway)
17. Cherokee Nation of Oklahoma
18. Cheyenne River Sioux Tribe
19. Chickahominy Indian Tribe
20. Choctaw Nation
21. Citizen Potawatomi Nation
22. Cochiti Pueblo
23. Coeur d'Alene Tribe (Northern Idaho Tribes)
24. Colorado River Indian Tribes

25. Comanche Nation

26. Confederated Salish and Kootenai Tribes of the Flathead Nation

27. Confederated Tribes and Bands of the Yakama Indian Nation

28. Confederated Tribes of the Colville Reservation

29. Confederated Tribes of the Grand Ronde Community

30. Confederated Tribes of the Siletz Community

31. Confederated Tribes of the Umatilla Indian Reservation

32. Confederated Tribes of the Warm Springs Reservation

33. Consolidated Chippewa Agency

34. Coushatta Tribe of Texas

35. Coyote Valley Band of Pomo Indians

36. Creek Nation

37. Crow Tribe (Apsáalooke)

38. Crow Creek Sioux Tribe

39. Delaware Tribe of Indians

40. Eastern Band of Cherokee

41. Eastern Chickahominy Tribe

42. Eastern Shoshone Tribe of the Wind River Reservation

43. Fond du Lac Band of Lake Superior Chippewa

44. Forest County Potawatomi

45. Gila River Indian Community

46. Grand Portage Band of Lake Superior Chippewa

47. Grand Traverse Band of Ottawa and Chippewa Indians

48. Great Lakes Indian Agency

49. Gros Ventre Tribe (Fort Belknap)

50. Haudenosaunee Confederacy (Six Nations, Iroquois)

51. Hawaiian Natives

52. Ho-Chunk Nation

53. Hoh Tribe

54. Hopi Tribe

55. Hualapai Tribe

56. Hoopa Valley Tribe

57. Hopland Band of Pomo

58. Houlton Band of Maliseet Indians

59. Iñupiat

60. Isleta Pueblo

61. Jamestown S'Klallam Tribe

Documents of Native American Political Development

Introduction

In 1992 Vine Deloria Jr., the intellectual architect of modern Indigenous nationhood, was asked to write an afterword to a book edited by Alvin Josephy, *America in 1492: The World of the Indian Peoples Before the Arrival of Columbus*.[1] Marking the five hundredth anniversary of that fateful event, Deloria declared, "Increasingly, American Indians are understanding the European invasion as a failure. That is to say, in spite of severe oppression, almost complete displacement, and substantial loss of religion and culture, Indians have not been defeated."[2]

He went on to note, "Indeed, the hallmark of today's Indian psyche is the realization that the worst is now passed and that it is the white man with his careless attitude toward life and the environment who is actually in danger of extinction. The old Indian prophecies say that the white man's stay on these Western continents will be the shortest of any who have come here. From an Indian point of view, the general theme by which to understand the history of the hemisphere would be the degree to which the whites have responded to the rhythms of the land—the degree to which they have become indigenous. From that perspective, the judgment of Europeans is severe."[3]

Deloria was an astute analyst of the Indigenous condition and a clear-headed participant-observer of the complicated tensions between natives, the states, and the federal government. His bleak prognostications for the heirs of those European colonizers and the world they built at the cruel expense of Native peoples are proving to be eerily accurate. We now see the results of centuries of unrelenting destructive and extractive colonialist pressure upon Indigenous worlds, and are coming to understand that life, as we know it, will be impossible to sustain without a change in this ethos. The beings of land, water, air, and all other creatures contained within them have finally been pushed to the brink.

1. Alvin M. Josephy Jr. *America in 1492: The World of the Indian Peoples Before the Arrival of Columbus* (New York: Alfred A. Knopf, 1992).
2. Ibid., p. 429.
3. Ibid., p. 430.

3

It is fitting that Deloria was born in 1933, the very year in which this compilation commences, just months before Congress adopted the Indian Reorganization Act (IRA)[4] at the behest of newly appointed Commissioner of Indian Affairs, John Collier, and driven by the demands of a frustrated majority of Native nations and their allies.

Collier, a social scientist by training, was more familiar with Native cultures than any of his predecessors. He was ably supported by Felix S. Cohen, a young lawyer who initially served as his assistant solicitor. Together, they undertook the monumental task of reversing decades of heinous and erratic governmental policies that had, until that time, vacillated between ethnocide and coercive assimilation. Collier and Cohen created a plan to assist Tribal nations in the stabilization and reconstitution of their political systems and of their land bases, and then sought to help them revitalize their cultural traditions.

Passage of the IRA was the first step. Drafted by Cohen under the supervision of Collier, who had spent considerable time in New Mexico fighting for Pueblo land and water rights, the measure was meant to be an explicit Congressional rejection of the allotment policy and the harsh course of assimilation tactics that had been exercised by the Bureau of Indian Affairs (BIA) since the 1880s. The IRA had several essential objectives: to stop the loss of Tribal and individual Native lands, provide for the acquisition of new lands for Native nations and landless Indians, authorize Indigenous groups to organize and adopt constitutional or other forms of government, allow formation of corporations for business purposes, and establish a system of financial credit for Native governments and individual business entrepreneurs.

But, the measure was also beset by severe weaknesses. It did little to clarify the inherent political status of Native nations. It failed to devise any real constraints on federal power, particularly administrative power vis-à-vis tribal nations and their citizens. Nonetheless, it was a pivotal, if uneven, attempt by the federal government to rectify some of the damage caused by decades of horrific policies and laws imposed on Native nations.

The mixed results of the IRA continue to both help and hinder Tribal nations. Most dramatically and importantly, its passage put a halt to the rapid loss of Indigenous land. It also provided a powerful, codified reminder that these peoples were substantially different from other minority groups, as they continued to be political nations with inherent powers of self-governance and distinctive cultural and religious identities.

Yet, the IRA's avowed goal of energizing Native self-rule was not fully realized. While some nations made the decision to create constitutions and by-laws, their documents, at the insistence of federal officials, included clauses reminding Native leaders of the enormous discretionary authority of the Secretary of the Interior to dictate policy to Native governments or even overrule their decisions. Those reluctant to institutionalize their governing structures along federally suggested constitutional lines were sometimes pressured to acquiesce by Collier and his associates.

---

4. 48 Stat. 984.

Beyond the IRA

In 1945, the conclusion of World War II and John Collier's resignation as Commissioner of Indian Affairs signaled the beginning of another profound shift in federal Indian policy and law. For more than a dozen years, the government, as personified by Collier, had prioritized restoration of self-rule. The Cold War era focus changed completely, and termination of federal financial and legal trust obligations toward a number of Native nations became the goal. Termination was officially inaugurated as policy in 1953 by a joint resolution of Congress.

Ironically, there was bipartisan consensus regarding this new direction. Liberals supported termination as a means to free Indigenous peoples from racially discriminatory legislation and regulations, whereas conservatives viewed it as a means to relieve natives from effects of the IRA's policies, which they believed hampered Indian civil rights as American citizens. Whatever the ideological rationale, all viewed Natives as culturally stunted or, in the offensive parlance of the times, "retarded." They also agreed on the need to grow the federal budget and expand economic development in areas that had been protected by treaties.

Naturally, Native peoples had their own views. Some believed termination of the federal trust relationship would mean full emancipation and thereby create political and economic opportunities. Others suspected termination was nothing more than a stealth maneuver by which the United States would "legally" disavow its historic treaty and trust obligations in clear violation of the inherent rights of Indigenous peoples and the federal government's commitment to the rule of law. Unfortunately, the latter view was proven correct. Opportunities generally failed to materialize and, perhaps most tellingly, terminated reservations or other trust lands were targeted as priorities by those looking to exploit natural resources or acquire valuable real estate. Nations stripped of these assets went from the most socially and economically stable, such as the Menominee of Wisconsin and the Klamath of Oregon, to the poorest, but the scheme was a lucrative one for the federal government and private resource extraction companies.

This cycle now appears to be repeating sixty-five years later, with the Trump administration's fervid attack on Native resources and treaty rights. The administration seems determined to ride roughshod over all laws and sovereignty in its zeal to enrich private corporations seeking to extract short-term profits from hugely destructive and polluting resources like fossil fuels and uranium, regardless of the long-term environmental and human costs.

Adoption of termination set off a cascade of regressive policies in the 1950s and 1960s. The first was a relocation program that uprooted thousands of reservation Indians. Those selected were sent to designated urban areas where they formed segregated, tribally mixed communities in cities like Denver, Minneapolis, and Los Angeles. These urban Indians, removed from their homelands, relatives, and land-based culture, were promised jobs, education, and social and health services that never fully materialized in those foreign, often-hostile, environments. Perhaps, most difficult of all, many of these urban Natives were increasingly distanced—culturally speaking—from their traditional homes and ways and their situations raised troubling questions of belonging. As new generations were born into these urban communities, many of those who remained on traditional lands began to view their city-based relatives as outsiders, creating rifts that, in some cases, decades later would lead to disenrollment, the political disenfranchisement of otherwise bona fide natives. Thus, Native peoples themselves were shaped to become complicit in the colonizing government's removal process.

Congress also enacted Public Law 280,[5] which authorized several states to extend criminal and some civil jurisdiction over Natives and Indian Country. Local governments, many with a history of discrimination toward Natives, were now empowered as the legal authority. This was controversial and costly for all involved, as Indians were ill-served and local authorities were underpaid for the added responsibility. While the loss of jurisdiction was devastating for Native nations, PL 280 would later be amended to provide a means for the return, or retrocession, of these powers. A few nations have successfully engaged in the retrocession process in cooperation with their state legislatures. State Senator John McCoy (Tulalip-Washington) sponsored legislation in 2012 creating the process necessary for the retrocession of all or part of the powers PL 280 had taken from Tribes and given to the state. The Tulalip Tribes and Yakama Nation have since used the process to reclaim jurisdiction in some areas.

By the 1960s, grievances arising from termination, relocation, and extension of state jurisdiction had combined with the influences of the broader civil rights and environmental movements to fuel activism both in urban areas and on reservations. The resurgence of Native pride coincided with the appearance of a generation of legally trained Natives and shifts in key personnel in the US Supreme Court and in Congress to bring about a series of political, legal, and cultural victories in the struggle to regain a measure of self-determination.

Much of the 1960s Indigenous revival took shape through active resistance like the fishing rights battles of the Pacific Northwest and Great Lakes nations. In late 1972, the Trail of Broken Treaties caravan reached Washington, DC, drawing national attention. There were acts of reclamation, including the 1970 takeover of Seattle's Fort Lawton by a group of urban Indians belonging to the United Indian People's Council (later United Indians of All Tribes) led by Robert Satiacum (Puyallup). Participants included Bernie Whitebear and Randy Lewis (both Colville), Leonard Peltier (Anishinabe/Lakota), Grace Thorpe, daughter of athletic legend Jim Thorpe (Sauk and Fox), and actor Jane Fonda. Some had also taken part in the nineteen-month-long occupation of Alcatraz Island in 1969. Perhaps, the most well-known event was the 1973 Wounded Knee II occupation at Pine Ridge, South Dakota. Some of these actions were influenced by ideas generated at the American Indian Chicago conference in 1961 and gained energy from the birth and rapid expansion of the American Indian Movement (AIM) in 1968.

5. 67 Stat. 588.

Congress responded to these developments by enacting the Indian Self-Determination and Education Assistance Act in 1975,[6] and other concordant laws. But Native victories also engendered a vicious backlash among disaffected non-Indians and some lawmakers. A spate of congressional and judicial attacks attempted to further abrogate treaties and reduce financial support for Native programs, among other punitive measures.

The US Supreme Court also began to issue rulings that undermined tribal sovereignty, most notably *Oliphant v. Suquamish* (1978), which directly limited the law enforcement powers of Native governments over non-Indians committing crimes on tribal lands. Decades later, the devastating consequences of this jurisdictional void are still felt, particularly by Native women assaulted by non-Natives on reservation lands. Perpetrators have often gone unpunished as Tribal law enforcement lacked the authority to detain and prosecute them. The 2013 passage of the Violence Against Women Act (VAWA) finally began to address that issue, but dangers remain and statistics consistently show Native women are the most abused adults in the country. The high number of unsolved disappearances and murders of Native women have sparked activism.

Since *Oliphant*, Native nations have witnessed a parade of federal actions that at times supported Indigenous sovereignty (e.g., the Tribal Law & Order Act of 2010 and VAWA) and at other times significantly reduced Tribal powers, especially in relation to state governments (e.g., the Indian Gaming Regulatory Act of 1988). More distressing for Native nations was the Rehnquist Supreme Court's fairly consistent opposition to inherent Tribal authority, which has been continued by the Roberts Court in cases like *Carcieri v. Salazar* (2009), which limited the authority of the Secretary of Interior to place land purchased by a recently recognized nation, the Narragansett, into trust status.

Thus, Native governments' jurisdictional authority over portions of their lands and over non-Indians has been severely truncated, and the federal trust doctrine has been defined in a narrow manner that serves to reduce federal financial obligations to the nations and their citizens. Adding to the confusion, several of the US Supreme Court's decisions have elevated state governments to a more powerful position vis-à-vis tribal governments—and even the US Congress itself—while failing to either dislodge or reduce the long-entrenched idea of an absolute federal plenary power over Native peoples and their resources. The consistent pattern of federal policies toward Indian Country is its inconsistency.

Nevertheless, as the ensuing records show, the years since 1933 have also been dynamic. Many nations have made great strides in several notable arenas: cultural and language revitalization, land consolidation and expansion, and the development of more appropriate legal codes. Gaming revenues have provided a number with a small, but seemingly secure, foothold in the US political economy. Native peoples have also proven willing, through increased electoral participation, to engage in state and federal political processes in an effort to protect their inherent sovereignty and their limited natural resources. Increasingly, Indians have even begun to seek and hold elected office outside their nations, at the local, state,

6. 88 Stat. 2203.

and federal levels, such as former US Senator Ben Nighthorse Campbell (Northern Cheyenne/Colorado), Lieutenant Governor Byron Mallot (Tlingit) of Alaska, and dozens of state legislators.

The relationship between Native nations and the federal government, however, continues with incertitude. Further, because interracial and intercultural disputes are nearly always resolved in federal courts where spurious and ill-defined legal principles like plenary power, the discovery doctrine, and the trust doctrine still lurk within the cases and precedents, Indigenous nations rarely receive impartial or informed hearings. The United States has sometimes affirmed sovereignty while at other times it has acted to deny, diminish, or even terminate it.

Such indeterminacy does, however, accord imaginative Native leaders and non-Native leaders a degree of political and legal flexibility. Involved parties may successfully navigate difficult political terrain through careful selection of appropriate Indigenous statutes that best benefit their nations and citizens within a particular circumstance. But the ambiguity also deprives Native peoples, collectively, nationally, and individually, of clear and consistent standing regarding the powers and rights they may exercise. Overt hostilities may be a thing of the past, but cultural, philosophical, and political-legal tensions still cloud the relationships between Tribal nations and federal, state, and local governments.

Overview of the Book

The eight-and-a-half-decade-long period from 1933 to 2018 saw major transformation in the political, economic, legal, and cultural realities of Indigenous peoples living within the United States. Broadly, this span of time can be organized into four historical eras:

- resurgence and reorganization (1933–1940s),
- termination and relocation (1940s–1960s),
- revitalization and self-determination (1960s–1980s), and
- self-governance and resistance (1980s–Present).

Historians, educators, legal writers, economists, anthropologists, sociologists, and many others have studied the issues of these times and the strategies used by Native peoples to navigate through them. The exception to all this academic scrutiny is the field of political science. Political scientists have, until very recently, paid scant attention to the political dynamics operating within and without Indian Country. This dearth of material is extraordinary, given that there are more than 570 federally recognized Native nations functioning as independent polities within the boundaries of the United States. This volume, along with its predecessor, is an attempt to provide foundational material for those who wish to study this shamefully neglected area of political science.

Documents herein have been chosen because they were either generated by Native peoples or by non-Natives actively and legitimately engaged with them. Appropriation has taken many forms since initial colonial contacts, and those activities have been well chronicled. Nonetheless, Natives remain the authors of their own destinies, in spite of the efforts of those who would exploit them economically, physically, spiritually, or academically.

The predecessor to this volume concludes in 1933 with several Native constitutions adopted just prior to John Collier's appointment as Commissioner of Indian Affairs. That year was a turning point in Native political history, as Collier's tenure provided new opportunities for future intergovernmental relations. Collier, Assistant Solicitor Felix Cohen, and Solicitor Nathan Margold formed a powerful triumvirate bent on transforming federal Indian policy from the coercive assimilation of Native peoples to a policy that emphasized a strong measure of self-rule.

This second volume picks up the historical thread, commencing at the end of 1933 with records chronicling the development of the IRA and the political, legal, cultural, and economic revitalization of Native peoples during the so-called "Indian New Deal." The following year, nearly two hundred Native nations voted to adopt the IRA and a majority of these communities—well over one hundred—opted to draft formal constitutions and charters of incorporation as part of their political and economic reorganization. These were uncertain times, and the process of modern tribal constitutional development during this critical period is marked by this ambiguity. Many commentators have contended that Western-styled constitutions were forced on reluctant Tribal communities, thereby eclipsing extant traditional systems of governance, which, they argue, had survived all other preceding federal colonialist policies.

Some scholars, such as Elmer Rusco[7] and David E. Wilkins[8] have asserted, to the contrary, that while the Bureau of Indian Affairs and the Indian New Dealers led by Collier certainly would have preferred that Native peoples adopt Western European–style written constitutions, there is little evidence to support the notion that such systems were forced onto Tribal communities, as the Act became operative only after communities had adopted it through a vote of its members.[9]

All who study the question would agree with Collier's assessment that the pace of Native constitutional development during these early years was indeed remarkable. "These constitutions," he said, "were probably the greatest in number ever written in an equivalent length of time in the history of the world."[10]

7. Elmer Rusco, *A Fateful Time: The Background and Legislative History of the Indian Reorganization Act* (Reno: University of Nevada Press, 2000).

8. Felix S. Cohen, *On the Drafting of Tribal Constitutions*, ed. David E. Wilkins (Norman: University of Oklahoma Press, 2006).

9. It is true that Collier created a voting scheme that tipped the scales toward adoption of constitutions. He contrived a process whereby the IRA was to be considered adopted unless a majority of the adult Indian population voted against its application. Thus, for example, on the Santa Ysabel Reservation in California, while forty-three members voted against the IRA and only nine voted for it, the tribe still came under the Act's provisions because the sixty-two eligible tribal members who did *not* vote were counted as being in favor of the Act's adoption.

10. John Collier, *From Every Zenith: John Collier, A Memoir* (Denver: Sage Books, 1963), 177.

Although nearly sixty constitutions were operational across Indian Country prior to 1934, the Confederated Salish & Kootenai Tribes of the Flathead Reservation were the first to ratify an IRA Constitution in 1935. Many others have since chosen to form such governments; as of 2018 more than four hundred nations had organized under formal constitutions, and the majority of those trace back in some manner to the IRA.

Interestingly and importantly, this means that well over one hundred Native nations have chosen to govern without written constitutions. Instead they wield a variety of arrangements—from the theocracies of the Pueblo communities in New Mexico, to the General Councils of communities like the Arapahoe of Wind River, to the village and regional corporations in Alaska, to the Navajo Nation's three-branch government that operates from a 1938 formal code.

This compilation features a great many of these, but also includes other important records that exemplify the political, economic, and legal acumen of Native nations. All are surrounded by, or live adjacent to, counties, munici-palities, states, and, of course, the United States. The policies, procedures, laws, and activities of these polities and their leaders affect, either directly or indirectly, the ability of these nations to exercise self-determination. Thus, also included are a number of influential federal and state laws, court cases, policy pronouncements, speeches, and hearings that detail the frequently contentious, and occasionally cooperative, intergovernmental relations between Native and non-Native communities.

The materials are offered in their original, unedited forms so the reader will note minor errors and omissions in spelling, punctuation, and grammar. As these imperfections neither detract from nor diminish the meaning, I felt it im-portant to leave them as found in order to preserve the unvarnished historical record. They are important reminders that many Natives frequently found themselves in the double bind of using a foreign language or an unfamiliar formal dialect to operate within intimidating or even hostile cultural spaces, and that federal, state and local government officials and their staff assigned to these tasks were often rushed and uneducated about Native affairs. Each docu-ment is introduced to the reader by a descriptive and explanatory head note, and may generally be grouped into one of the following categories:

- *Native Constitutions*
- *Native Statutory and Judicial Documents*, such as legal codes, acts, court cases, charters;
- *Individual Native Nations Political Advocacy*, including testimonials, op-eds, briefs;
- *Collective Political Advocacy*, encompassing resolutions, ordinances, posi-tion papers;
- *International Treaties and Alliances*, of which the Anishinaabe Akii Protocol, United League of Indigenous Nations Treaty, and Northern Tribes Buffalo Treaty are examples;
- *U.S. Legislative, Executive, and Judicial Documents*, for example, Report to repeal the IRA, Termination of the Grand Ronde Community in Oregon, *Harjo v. Kleppe*;

- *Native Interest Group Activity*, comprised of documents such as the Testimony of Helen Peterson, Executive Director of the NCAI and Declaration of Sovereignty, 1974;
- *Intergovernmental Documents* such as compacts, memoranda of understanding, accords;
- *Miscellaneous*, including the Tulalip Tribes' Charter of Quil Ceda Village and a Virginia Attorney General opinion on applicability of state gaming laws to Native nations.

While no single book can incorporate every significant issue involving or affecting the more than 570 Native nations—and readers may rightly quibble with some of the document selections—every effort was made to ensure this collection would be comprehensive and representative. Some will note the absence of more recent, highly publicized events, such as the far-reaching 2009 Cobell settlement that addressed a century's worth of governmental mismanagement of trust funds. The decision was the result of the settlement of a large class-action lawsuit initiated in 1996, *Cobell v. Salazar*, with the late, indefatigable Elouise Cobell (Blackfeet) acting as lead plaintiff.

Another noteworthy event was the *Keepseagle v. Vilsak* case, filed in 1999 and settled in 2010, which acknowledged the US Department of Agriculture's systematic discrimination against Native farmers and ranchers who had sought loans from the agency. As such materials and related analyses are easily accessible, I judged it best to include lesser-known pieces that fill voids and add dimension to the arc of modern Native political history.

It is also important to acknowledge the reemergence of voices long silenced, as women, young people, and those who identify beyond Western European gender binary classifications step forward. The next volume of documents critical to Indian Country will undoubtedly chronicle their efforts to redefine what it means to be Indigenous, while rebuilding traditions and forging new coalitions. All perspectives are essential if we are to repair the damage done over the last five centuries and govern ourselves as people Vine Deloria Jr. would have recognized as fully mature Indigenous human beings responding to the rhythms of the land.

Finally, a bibliographic essay on Indigenous governance is included at the end of the book as a guide toward other resources about Native sovereignty and governance.

1

Expenses of the Northern
Cheyenne Indian
Tribal Council (1933)

In 1933, just before John Collier was appointed Commissioner of Indian Affairs, the Bureau of Indian Affairs, situated within the Department of the Interior, and the US Congress still dominated virtually every aspect of the lives and resources of Indigenous nations and their citizens. The concepts of self-determination and Tribal sovereignty, which had long been suppressed by federal lawmakers, remained unfamiliar to Congress as evidenced by the following Senate report detailing the contortions the Northern Cheyenne government had to go through to access and benefit from their own Tribal monies. This had been a common lament for a majority of Native nations since the 1880s and was one of the chief complaints motivating John Collier as he prepared to take the helm at the Bureau of Indian Affairs.

The Committee on Indian Affairs, to whom was referred the bill (H.R. 11896) to provide for expenses of the Northern Cheyenne Indian tribal council and authorized delegates of the tribe, having considered the same, report thereon with a recommendation that it do pass with the following amendment:

Line 3, strike out "the" and all to and including the word "expend" in line 4, substituting therefor "there is hereby authorized to be appropriated the sum of."

The amendment was adopted by your committee at the suggestion of the Secretary of the Interior.

The purpose of this measure is to authorize use of funds standing to the credit of the Northern Cheyenne Indians for the payment of expenses arising out of the activities of the tribal council and through the appointment of delegates who handle tribal business.

The bill was introduced at the request of the Indians concerned and has the approval of the Commissioner of Indian Affairs and the Secretary of the Interior in its amended form. The money is the property of the tribe and does not belong to the United States. It is customary to make this money available from time to time as needed and no new practice is established by the measure under consideration.

If the tribal council is to properly conduct its affairs it must have funds to meet the expenses which naturally arise. The money involved is the property of the Indians and disbursements will be under the supervision of the Secretary of the Interior. Your committee believes that the bill should be enacted and so recommends.

The favorable report of the Secretary of the Interior, transmitting a memorandum of the Commissioner of Indian Affairs recommending enactment, reads as follows:

Hon. Edgar Howard, Chairman Committee on Indian Affairs, House.

My Dear Mr. Chairman: In compliance with your request of May 7, 1932, for a report on H.R. 11896, to provide for expenses of the Northern Cheyenne Indian tribal council and authorized delegates of the tribe, I transmit herewith a memorandum on the subject that has been submitted by the Assistant Commissioner of Indian Affairs, to which attention is invited.

The department will offer no objection to the enactment of the bill if it be amended by striking out all of line 3 after the word 'That' and the first three words in line 4, and inserting in lieu thereof the following: 'there is hereby authorized to be appropriated the sum of.' In this connection, the Director of the Bureau of the Budget has advised us that the proposed legislation would not be in conflict with the financial program of the President if thus amended.

Very truly yours,
John H. Edwards, Acting Secretary

Source:

US Senate. "Expenses of Northern Cheyenne Indian Tribal Council." Report No. 1321. 72nd Cong., 2nd Sess. Washington, DC: Government Printing Office, Feb. 28, 1933.

---

2   *Indian Nations' Congressional Testimony (1934)*

After John Collier, Felix S. Cohen, and the Secretary of the Interior drafted the Indian Reorganization Act in 1934, Cohen convinced Collier that the measure should be presented in draft form to Native communities across Indian Country. A series of ten such "congresses" were held during which federal officials presented the bill and, in turn, received comments from Tribal individuals, both pro and con, as to the bill's merits. A sampling of the testimony from several of these gatherings shows how the concept of self-government was understood at the time by Native peoples. Also of interest is the wide range of reactions to the proposal that promised to radically alter the relationship between Native nations and the federal government.

Proceedings of the Plains Congress, Rapid City, South Dakota, February 8, 1934

Letter of Tribal Business Council of Standing Rock Sioux Reservation addressed to Mr. John Collier, Commissioner of Indian Affairs, handed to Chairman by Francis Red Tomahawk of Standing Rock.

Sir: We the Tribal Business Council of the Standing Rock Sioux Reservation of North and South Dakota, have the honor to submit the report of the action taken in connection with Circular dated January 20, 1934, Re "Indian Self-government" addressed to Superintendents, Tribal Councils and Individual Indians.

For the purpose of promoting the success of the proposed new policy outlined in the circular and to further the efforts of the administration to secure beneficial legislation which will enable it to realize its objective, the complete reconstructing of the whole Indian problem, we hereby endorse the plans contained in the above mentioned circular with certain reservations, which will be shown under the heading "Land Problems."

1. Evils of the Allotment System: After a thorough and comprehensive survey of the evils of the allotment system as we have experienced them on the Standing Rock Sioux Reservation we have listed the various sources of evils by which we have sustained losses in land sales and other benefits as will be seen in attached report dated February 7, 1934.

Land Problems

Under this heading we favor legislation positively prohibiting Indian land sales to outside parties, that no more patents be granted, that complicated heirship land and other heirship of like character be sold and purchased for the use of the tribe, that deeded lands located in areas predominated by Indian allotments be purchased for the use of the tribe, that timber lands lost to the tribe through land sales and opening of the Reservation be restored to original allottees wherever justifiable. The legislation to conform to the white man's land sale law be enacted and the present Indian land sale law be discarded for good.

We reserve all rights as to trust land owned by the original allottees and all heirship lands not complicated so long as they retain the status of "complicated heirship lands."

We believe that the plan to acquire land for the use of our tribe, landless and future generations, is one worthy of consideration by every Indian; the health improvement plan; the establishment of self-government and the stabilization of community life; the development and preservation of Indian land in Indian ownership; and the provision of opportunity for economic livelihood for Indian community life.

The action of the Tribal Business Council of the Standing Rock Sioux Reservation of the states of North and South Dakota is for all of the foregoing and for the express purpose of supporting the present administration in securing enabling legislation to better the status of the Indian, that in the end he may take his place in the economic life of the nation and not be a dead-weight economically.

As to the "program of Administration" and "Suggested Problems and Possible Solutions" we endorse the verdict of our sub-committee unanimously.

Respectfully submitted, Charles Ramsey, Chairman, Tribal Business Council, Francis Red Tomahawk, Secretary, Tribal Business Council, Fort Yates, North Dakota February 7, 1934.

Business Session of the Sub-Committee of the Tribal Business Council

The above-named subcommittee met at the Agency Hall and decided to organize by electing Edward Young Eagle as chairman, and Francis Red Tomahawk secretary.

The first matter taken up in connection with the Indian Office Circular in regard to "Indian Self-Government, dated January 20, 1934," was the "Evils of the Allotment System," which committee after careful survey of the land losses find as follows:

Opening of Reservation by Congress.

1. Allotment of Reservation.
2. Voluntary Land Sales.
3. Forced patents without knowledge of allottees.
4. Sale of heirship allotments.
5. Loss of large tracts of valuable grazing land through sales and plowing for agricultural purposes
6. Loss of timber allotments through land sales and opening of Reservation.
7. Loss of mineral lands through opening of Reservation and land sales.
8. Loss of land by granting school land to the States of North and South Dakota for school purposes.
9. Loss of land through tax sales.
10. Loss of land through mortgage foreclosures.
11. Loss of land through right of ways for railroad and Federal and State and County Highway.
12. Loss of land sale proceeds through present land sale law which calls for refund of all payments except the original 25 per cent and interest.
13. Loss of land by establishment of Government reserves.
14. Loss of land through grants to Missions and other Religious organizations.

Land Problems

We favor in the fullest degree the purchase of complicated heirship lands and other lands which will become complicated and deeded lands located in areas predominated by Indian allotments for the use of the tribe.

We favor the abolishment of the land division as operated on the Reservation as soon as suitable municipal or tribal means can be worked out to satisfactorily handle its work.

Program of Administration

We favor the program of the Administration as outlined in Indian Office Circular "Indian Self-Government, dated January 29, 1934" appearing on pages 3, 4, and 5, by unanimous vote.

Suggested Problems and Possible Solutions

In connection with this portion of the Commissioner's circular we agree and hereby vote unanimously in favor of the proposed plans as outlined in this section of the communication.

Proceedings of the Northwest Indian Congress, Chemawa, Oregon, March 8 and 9, 1934

Mr. Walter Woehlke: Congress will please come to order. It seems to me a lot of the delegation are staying out in the bright sunshine and enjoying it, but from what I can see of the dust on the roads you seem to need more rain here. The Chair has been informed that the delegates representing the largest tribe on the Taholah Reservation desire to leave early so as to be able to return to their business and they have requested to be heard out of their turn, so I will now like to hear some of the comments of the Taholah Reservation and I would also like to remind each speaker that his time is limited to five minutes because time is getting short. What was the name please?

Harry Shale: A meeting has been held by the Quinault tribe regarding this self-government matter. They held this meeting on the 21st day of February. The meeting was called by Superintendent Nicholson, who is in charge of that reservation, and he read the proposed bill regarding this self-government and explained it all and looked into it thoroughly and have decided that they did not care to accept this self-government so would not do so, as we are already self-governing. Years ago the Indians of Taholah won a case from the government regarding their fishing which is their main industry and is handled entirely by them. Their case has been handled by the Indian Office but we took it to the Court and it was decided in the Indians' favor.

Since then, the Indians of Taholah have elected their officers, such as a President, Vice- president, Treasurer and the committees who are in power by the tribe to act in all fishing cases and so far we have made a success of that self-government. We are getting along nicely.

Taholah is a self-supporting tribe and for that reason they object to your request to the people of Taholah. I have been represented here for them and to make the statement to you gentlemen who are here from Washington to confer with the Indians of the West. I merely state their opinion of the Quinaielt tribe and when I go back, I will also report to the tribe about these meetings, this conference, and will thank you good men from Washington for your aim to better the condition of the Indians in the West. Your problem for the Indians fits in many cases, but not in Taholah. For instance, I have heard a gentleman by the name of Williams who requested for some land and another gentleman has a reservation with nothing but gravel. Well, people like that are in need of this help and my request to you gentlemen who are here to better the conditions among the Indians is to recommend that strongly for them. I will admit the people of Taholah will not accept your offer but probably later on if we see other people make a success of that self-government, probably, we will. Thank you.

Mr. Woehlke: I wish you would tell your people that if they are organized now and governing themselves that they are doing something illegal. They are not allowed to do it under the law as it is now and the Indian Commissioner can abrogate your Organization any time he wants to. You are not allowed, according to the law to organize and it is only by permission of the Secretary of the Interior and the Commissioner of Indian Affairs that the law permits you to organize now. What we want to do in this law is to get you the right to organize that you do not have to depend on the Secretary or the Commissioner.

Mr. Shale: Our organization has been recognized at the Indian Office and all of the government officials have been advised by the Indian Office to have no voice in any of our fishing cases that may come upon the reservation.

Mr. Woehlke: That may be, but the law of the tribe is still illegal....

Now let us proceed with the statements and the speeches in English from the various delegates. We have not time for the various delegations to have the speeches interpreted because time is getting short, exceedingly short. We will now proceed with the program and we will limit the time of each speaker to seven minutes and we will begin from the beginning again. The Colville Spokesman.

Christine Galler: With your permission, may I use the stage to stand on? I thank you Mr. Chairman for the kind consideration you have given me and I thank you ladies and gentlemen. I have spoken many times before the white people; and I am sure I am going to speak to you, I suppose all that I have thought of and all that I have planned will be forgotten because I am self-conscious. [Everyone laughs]

Ladies and gentlemen: My education did not come to me on a silver spoon. I am one of seven children. We children were very, extremely poor. My mother and father were prejudiced against education. What I have learned was through the hard ways. I learned of my own free will and I am proud today to say that I learned the education of the white man's language and tongue. What little education I have I worked hard for it. And it was through the Indian school as a stepping stone. It was here that I first accomplished my education. I fought for 25 years for the cause of the Indian people. The reason I have fought for my people is this: I owe it to them, the old men and the old women of the Colville Indians. It is for their benefit that I speak for them today. I am a woman and you might think it funny that the Colvilles elect a woman for a delegate but the capacity of an Indian woman's head has the same amount as a man or a white man. Any woman can do what a man or a white man can do in any instance.

It is all up to you whether we will go back to the blanket. To those people who are not in favor of the bill, there is always a place for them. If they want to keep their allotments and their land they can ask the government for them. John Collier could take every foot of land, if they wish to, with the stroke of the pen according to law and we would lose every bit of ground we have. He has given us this privilege to find what kind of people we are. That is why he sent this Congress before you.

Someone said a while back that if it wasn't for the government we would be retarded back to an environment where our children would not have an opportunity like the white people.

Due to them, all over the Indian reservations there are schools that your children could attend, like Chemawa [Oregon]. There are schools for your children to go to. There is always a place for you if you don't want to be self-government and to pay your obligations of taxes and being a citizen of the United States, to direct in any way what you want done.

We have been driven. We have been led by the white people for 122 years since the white people came into this country. We have never been given the choice of our leaders. We have no voice in anything. And now you are opposed to the bill of Collier's. He has worked for 15 years for the Indians cause. You want to be driven to it because you are not accustomed to lead your people. Your people as a people, industrious and self-governing, can do just what you want if you have the Federal Court to back you in your cause.

Ladies and gentlemen: I hope that you don't think that I am like Emma Goldman or any other woman, but as an Indian, my heart is with the Indians. Let us hope that with this new form of government will not be imposing on our old people, that your younger men and women will have a voice in the government of the U.S. Let us try a new deal. It cannot be any worse than what it has been. You can say the government has stolen your land away from you. For the wagon, the implements, the government has given us direct compensation. That word "education" in exchange for the bow and arrow. That you can be thankful for. I thank you ladies and gentlemen. . . .

Mr. Woehlke: I think the speaker who has just finished spoke the truth. The thinking capacity of an Indian woman is equal to that of an Indian man's or a white man's. I would also like to say that a similar objection to this program was raised at the Great Plains Congress.

When it was said "This will set the Indians back 50 years," a Pine Ridge Sioux delegate rose and said: "I went to school with Henry Roe Cloud. We went to school together. Look at him now. Do you think it will set him back 50 years? Do you think he will ever go back to the blanket. . . ."

Proceedings of the Southern Arizona Indian Conference, Phoenix, Arizona, March 15–16, 1934

Mr. Woelke: This afternoon we are going to have a delegate from each different delegation [native delegates were present from the San Carlos Apache, White River Apache, Papago Nation, Colorado River tribes, and Truxton Canyon] sent to this meeting.

Randall Booth, Colorado River Delegation spokesman: Ladies and Gentlemen of the House: I have the pleasure to be spokesman of the Colorado River delegation from the Colorado River Indian reservation. I want to present to you briefly and pointedly in regard to Indian self-government. Now the Indian who lived along the Colorado River has always thought that he was self-governed before any white people arrived on the scene, and when the Mexicans came over and so called discovered this land, they found some human beings there and when they recognized that they were human beings they made an agreement with the Indians that where they lived that was their land. That was the grant which the Mexican Government granted to these Mohaves about eighty miles below Parker and to the Black Canyon where the dam now is today, and afterwards when the United States bought this country of ours they bought this country with all animals and human beings in it.

Of course the Mexican Government tried to show the United States Government that they recognized these human beings as Indians, and that they had inhabited this land long before the Spaniards came and the United States must honor that grant. With that agreement the United States bought this land. But when the United States got this country they ignored such lands and grants, and when this was taken up with the War department they passed a law and set aside this little piece of land, this executive order and they are kept there. So the people went to Washington, the chief of the people, and he was presented with this medal (shows a medal to the audience) and when the chief went to Washington he wanted to know why, when they risked their lives in behalf of their country, they should be allotted this land when actually it belonged to them already. So our organization of self-government extends away back over one hundred years ago, and the Indians of today have a record and they have a constitution and by-laws to carry out the best they can, the condition that existed away back there, and this is one of the main things that bill brings up, self-government.

Now the Allotment act of 1887—why didn't we know at the time that would be a detriment to the Indian, why didn't we know that it would not get us anywhere? Where was the voice of the Indians then? That is for you to answer. Now another law stands before us and we see that it not only deals with the Indians here but it deals with all the other tribes of Indians, and therefore that is why you must decide seriously. If we decide in favor of a bill or if we are opposed, probably we are doing an injury to some of our fellowmen, therefore we must think twice before we leap. I believe that this self-government is the only government and we know that we want to revise this Allotment act, so that we can have the whole land to ourselves. Now the most important thing to the Colorado River delegation is that we have land over there and they are building a dam right above us to give us water, as land without water is useless. If we have this land, more land, the point is this, the Secretary or the bill says that we want to have more land and then turns around and puts his hand in the pie and says if you don't need all of this land the Secretary has the right to sell what he thinks you don't need, that is our only objection to this bill. I believe now that it is up to you to oppose or support this bill.

This delegation says that we simply come here to understand fully and some kind of figure that this bill ought to be explained paragraph by paragraph. The first thing that this session took up and the bill read that has been the understanding of our people in a general way, but now they want to go back with this thought that they will go back and present this down among their own people and then voice the opinion of all their people to the Secretary. That is the wish of this delegation. This is my personal talk.

Proceedings of the Western Oklahoma Conference, Anadarko, Oklahoma, March 20, 1934

Statement by Henry Chapman of the Pawnee Agency, reading a resolution submitted by the Pawnee, Ponca, Kaw, Otoe and Tonkawa tribes:

We, the undersigned chairmen of the Tribal Business Committees for the Pawnee, Ponca, Kaw, Otoe, and Tonkawa tribes of Indians in Oklahoma, represent that our committees, after receiving Indian Office Circular dated January 20th, 1934, relative to a proposed so-called "Indian Self-Government" immediately called our tribes together for the purpose of considering the proposed program. We represent that at each of these tribal meetings the Indians in council assembled unanimously opposed the said program as outlined by our Commissioner of Indian Affairs, Mr. John Collier. We represent that these meetings were well attended by representative numbers of our Indian tribes, the educated and uneducated, and after a full discussion of the program, the opposition is unanimous. We represent that on March 16th, 1934, a general council of all five of the above tribes was held at the White Eagle Agency for the purpose of a joint discussion of the program referred to above, and of the bill which has been introduced in both Houses of Congress, titled, Indian Self-Government, by Senator Wheeler and Congressman Howard. Several hundred representative Indians from the five tribes attended this joint council and it was unanimously voted that the sentiment of the various tribes was opposed to this program and to the bill now before both Houses of Congress.

Therefore, we the chairmen of the five Tribal Councils under the jurisdiction of the Pawnee Indian Agency, and the chairman of the Inter-tribal Council representing the five aforesaid tribes, hereby express our protest against the program outlined by the Honorable Commissioner of Indian Affairs in his letter of January 20th, 1934, and further express our unanimous opposition to the aforesaid bill, "Indian Self-Government."

The sentiment expressed at the various tribal meetings indicates that our Indian people do not feel that they are capable of handling such a large undertaking and it was pointed out that practically all of the so-called competent Indians have demonstrated their lack of business ability in handling their own individual matters. It is admitted that the Indians have lost too much of their land which was due to a lack of their business ability and a mistake by the Department in permitting them, and in many instances compelling them, to take patents in fee for their homesteads.

We further represent that our people are opposed to the proposed change in our educational system. Facts will show that our children who have had the advantages of our splendid boarding schools are more advanced and better pre- pared to take their place in the white community than children who have missed a great deal of educational training by the attempt to have them attend the Reservation public schools. We recommend that the boarding schools be con- tinued that Indians may have the advantage of our splendid Indian educational institutions.

We recommend that the trust period on our trust land be extended for a period of fifty years and carry with it a non-saleable land provision. We recom- mend that the land be purchased for Indians who have disposed of their home- steads and that these homesteads purchased be protected with a restricted period of not less than fifty years.

We recommend what we understand to be one of the Commissioner's pol- icies of giving to qualified Indians preference to positions in the Indian Service. We commend the present policy of the non-sale of Indian land and the non- issuance of fee patents. We recommend the removal of all employees in the Indian Service now holding key positions who oppose the employment of Indians in the Indian Service.

Resolved, that a copy of this protest be filed with the Honorable Commissioner of Indian Affairs and the members of the entire Oklahoma delegation now in the House and Senate."

Proceedings of the Hayward Conference at Hayward, Wisconsin, April 23 and 24, 1934

Resolution introduced by John Pemberton—Twin Lakes White Earth:

"We the assembled delegation representing N 1/2 of White Earth Reservation comprising the following villages: Twin Lakes, Rice Lakes, Beaulieu, Pine Bend, Mahnomen, and Waubun, came here for the sole purpose of hearing discussions on the Wheeler-Howard Bill in order that we may clar- ify certain objectionable phrases of this bill—and after this hearing we may say that these phrases have been made so clear that we are in a position to accept the bill as a whole.

We wish to reserve the right to go back to our respective communities and have our people pass on the finding of this conference."

John Pemberton [White Earth]: I don't wish to take up any more time than is allotted me, but I just want to make a few remarks in regard to this bill. Since February 1 we have held our weekly councils in regard to this bill. There are a number of people in our community who have been misrepresenting this bill to a number of our older Indians—telling them not to accept it. So at our councils we held open house and challenged anyone to come and show us where it would be detrimental to accept this bill, and there has been no one who has been able to do so. As for the White Earth Indians, I do not see what we have to lose by accepting this bill.

Dr. Henry Roe Cloud: We will next hear from the Ponsford delegation.

John Broker, Ponsford, White Earth delegation: I just wish to make a few remarks. We represent about 900 people in our community and we were instructed by that community to favor this legislation. Also we were instructed to use our best judgment in formulating our opinions, and in going on record in favoring the bill, I just want to make a few statements and give a few reasons why.

We have been under the Indian Bureau for a good many years—going back 60 years. The system used under the bureau is becoming obsolete, and we desire a change. There has been legislation passed through Congress by unscrupulous politicians for the purpose of exploiting the Indians on these reservations. During all that time of legislation the Bureau has never made a protest in behalf of the Indians. It seems in a great many instances that it has been a party to the deal. This system we want to get away from, and through the new deal and the features of this bill we hope to provide that change. It gives us a better school system. It gives us more voice in the management of our affairs and in the expenditures of our money, and we have considered that bill to be very much favorable to our community. We recognize that there will be changes and amendments in this bill before it reaches final passage. We just merely want to go on record as favoring passage of the bill, but of course we want to have access to all new information that comes up on the bill. I believe that is about the extent of my statements now.

Arthur C. Beaulieu, White Earth: We were duly elected and sent here for the purpose of taking part in the discussion of this bill. We went pursuant to notice but were not instructed to accept or reject the bill, but to work in cooperation with other delegates coming from that section in taking the matter back to our people. In this decision there was only one dissenting vote—that of Edward L. Rogers.

Summary interpretation by Frank Smart.

Peter Graves, Chairman, Old Council, Red Lake delegation: We represent what they call the Chiefs' Council of Red Lake. Our delegation comprises 7 persons. Our instructions are to guard against the subdivision of the Red Lake Indian Reservation. Our instructions are also to guard against any unfavorable decision that the bill might impose upon the Red Lake Band of Indians. This Chiefs' Council of the Red Lake Band. is composed of the older Indians. We still maintain the belief that the greatest evil the United States Government ever perpetrated was to allot land in severalty to Indians in the United States. I don't like to have these different delegations think I am trying to advise them or anything like that. Our position is different from that of the allotted Indian, and it has not been an easy matter to have kept ourselves in the state to the present time.

There are many of us who still believe that if we once take our land in severalty on the Red Lake reservation, our doom is sealed. The bill that is in discussion at this time, known as the Wheeler Howard bill, is just the thing that the Red Lake Indians would want enacted so as to prevent them from dispossessing themselves of their homes.

I believe that one of the men who spoke here said it was a Christmas present. It certainly is more than a Christmas present, because at Christmas time we only give to each other little worthless trinkets, so to speak. Our delegation believes that we should accept this bill and urge Congress to have the bill enacted into law regardless of the opposition—opposition by those who in the future should never be called Indians. The old chiefs and old men that you profess to call ignorant in this day of civilization—those men had dreams of future men like Mr. Roe Cloud and Mr. Kershaw. They want to keep their reservations intact—keep their homes intact—make the future secure for their children. This dream of course is a bad dream. Very few will live up to be educated so that they can mix with the civilized races of this earth. I for one know that I am 99 percent behind what I should be now that I am grown up. I do not understand the action in instructing the delegates not to accept this bill at once after what the Indians have gone through, and in behalf of the Chiefs' Council we urge that this bill be enacted into law!

George Walters of White Earth delegation [speaking in Chippewa with translation by Frank Smart]: I want to say a few words in regard to the subject under discussion here. At the time the councils were held in my locality I did not know that these papers were in existence (referring to papers explaining the bill) until the time when I was elected a delegate. These papers were not presented to me. These other delegates here know all about this, but all the time as for myself, only five days before I started for this conference did I know something about this. I am located very near where they are, but they never notified me. And I kind of in a way understand that I as an Indian am being approached to ask these questions. On my account as an Indian the government is holding this conference, and I want to say at this time that I don't have a show at all at this conference. It is at this place that I hear of the contents of this bill for the first time, and there are Indians of my tribe at home that should hear this news. It is not right that individuals must be here personally to hear of this deal.

Why are we in such terrible and poor shape today? Am I responsible? The government is the cause of our privation. It is not the fault of the Commissioner of Indian Affairs we are in such privation. We are responsible for our own condition today. We did not follow the instructions of the Commissioner or the Government of the United States. I am the person that tried to hold back this person that wants to be a white man and there was not a single Indian that did not oppose me. The one that talked here previous he opposed me just the same. The White Indian is too susceptible to wrong doing. He always wants the money. That is the reason for such poverty. Our money in Washington is in very small amounts now and still we are writing the Government to ask them to give us some more. Isn't it a fact that future generations should be benefited by some of this money? What is being left for our children—for the future generation? And what then will they live on? All these allottees have sold their 160 acres and I don't believe any of them possess even a twig of a tree and I don't believe they have as much as one shot of gunpowder or a parcel of land!

Dr. Roe Cloud: Mr. Interpreter, will you tell him [George Walters] that the new bill will protect his land so that there need never be a loss, and also tell him it is safe for his children and grandchildren in future generations....

Mr. George Walters: That is all I want.

Paul H. Beaulieu, speaking for Young Council of Red Lake Band: Mr. Chairman, I have but very few words to say, and I want to start out by congratulating the old Red Lake Indians upon the stand taken in regard to this bill. The Young Council made its stand quite some time ago. That stand was forwarded to the Commissioner on January 27. We still stand on that same thing, and from that you can read between the lines that we had accepted the Indian Rights Bill as a whole, although there might be features we do not approve of. However, as a whole we do approve of the bill. That is our stand and I don't think there is a Red Lake Indian that wants an allotment. I just wanted to correct any impression that might have been created here in this respect.

Dr. Roe Cloud: You mean that you stand for the bill as a whole, but that there might be some features you do not approve of or that you are not yet familiar with?

Mr. Beaulieu: Yes, but we can thrash that out later at home.

Dr. Roe Cloud: It is interesting to note that these Red Lake people who have never been allotted and who have watched the experience of other tribes, now say they don't want to be allotted. I think that is exceedingly significant and important.

Sources:

Deloria, Vine, Jr., ed. *The Indian Reorganization Act: Congresses and Bills.* Norman: University of Oklahoma Press, 2002.

Rusco, Elmer R. *A Fateful Time: The Background and Legislative History of the Indian Reorganization Act.* Reno: University of Nevada Press, 2000.

---

3   *Authorizing Indians to Form Business Councils and Corporations (1934)*

This report summarized the key details of the Wheeler-Howard Act, also known as the Indian Reorganization Act (IRA). The measure was a clear admission on the part of the US that its policies of forced assimilation and individual allotment of lands had not worked, and that a new course was necessary; one designed to provide a dose of respect for the cultural, political, and legal sovereignty of Native nations. The IRA would prove controversial, however, as later documents reveal. While some Native lands were restored and federal trust protections were reinstated over remaining or newly acquired territory, the Secretary of Interior's discretionary power to deny or veto many political, legal, and economic decisions remained intact, thus thwarting true Indigenous self-determination.

———

The Committee on Indian Affairs, to whom was referred the bill (S. 3645) to conserve and develop Indian land and resources, to establish a credit system for Indians to provide for higher education for Indians, to extend towards Indians the right to form business and other organizations, and for other purposes, having considered the same, report thereon with recommendations that the bill do pass.

The purposes of the bill, briefly stated, are as follows:

1. To stop the alienation, through action by the Government or the Indian, of such lands, belonging to ward Indians, as are needed for the present and future support of these Indians.
2. To provide for the acquisition, through purchase, of land for Indians, now landless, who are anxious and fitted to make a living on such land.
3. To stabilize the tribal organization of Indian tribes by vesting such tribal organizations with real, though limited, authority, and by pre-scribing conditions which must be met by such tribal organizations.
4. To permit Indian tribes to equip themselves with the devices of modern business organization, through forming themselves into business cor-porations.
5. To establish a system of financial credit for Indians.
6. To supply Indians with means for collegiate and technical training in the best schools.
7. To open the way for qualified Indians to hold positions in the Federal Indian Service.

Under the operations of allotment, the land holdings of the Indians have steadily dwindled and a considerable number of Indians have become entirely landless. By section 1 of the bill, future allotment in severalty to Indians is pro-hibited and under section 2 the existing periods of trust on Indian lands are extended until otherwise directed by Congress.

When allotment was carried out on various reservations, tracts of surplus or ceded land remained unallotted and were placed with the Land Office of the Department of the Interior for sale, the proceeds to be paid to the Indians. Some of these tracts remain unsold and by section 3 of the bill they are restored to tribal use.

The existing allotted lands as a result of the multiplication of heirs of deceased allottees, frequently become so largely subdivided that their use by the Indians for their rental to whites is rendered impossible. Hence, in past years these lands have been sold to the highest bidder, practically always to whites. Section 4 of the act provides that the allotted lands of deceased allottees may be bequeathed only to the Indian tribe or corporation or to the individual Indian heirs, and that the allotted lands belonging to living and deceased allottees may be purchased by or for the Indian tribe. Likewise, section 4 authorizes exchanges of land where necessary for the proper consolidation of the Indian holdings.

To meet the needs of landless Indians and of Indian individuals and tribes whose land holdings are insufficient for self-support, section 5 of the bill authorizes the purchase of lands by the Secretary of the Interior, title to be vested in the United States in trust for the Indian tribe for which the land is acquired. There is authorized to be appropriated not to exceed $2,000,000 in any one fiscal year for such purchase of land.

The Secretary of the Interior is directed, by section 6 of the bill, to make rules and regulations for the management of Indian forestry units in accordance with the principle of sustained-yield management and for the prevention of soil erosion through overgrazing, and for like purposes of conservation.

The Secretary of the Interior is authorized by section 7 of the bill to proclaim new Indian reservations on the lands acquired, pursuant to section 5 of the bill.

By section 8 of the bill, Indian allotments for homesteads on the public domain are withheld from the various provisions of the bill.

By section 9 of the bill, any Indian tribe or tribes residing on the same reservation, are given the right to organize f or the common welfare. When a tribe shall have organized, in accordance with the procedures set down in section 9, the Secretary of the Interior may not abolish the organization without the consent of the Indians but the Indians may abolish it with the consent of the Secretary. Section 9 gives to such organized tribes various limited powers, all of which are at present enjoyed by some of the tribes under existing tribal organization.

Section 10 of the bill provide that on petition of at least one fourth of the adult Indians, the Secretary of the Interior may issue a charter of business incorporation to the tribe represented by the petitioners, subject to ratification by the tribe. The tribe so incorporated may be given power to own and manage property, including the power to buy the restricted allotted lands of its members and to issue to them, in exchange, interests in the corporate property. Such tribal corporation may have confirmed to it by the Secretary of the Interior the right, interest, or title in property held by the United States in trust, and it may have confirmed to it any liens held by the United States against members of the tribe, any claims of the tribe, and all liabilities of the tribe. The corporate charter may not be revoked or surrendered except by act of Congress.

Section 11 authorizes the appropriation of not to exceed $250,000 in any fiscal year, to be used in defraying the expenses of tribal organizations created under the bill. The inability, in the past, of Indians to make effective use of their land and their natural resources has been due in no small measure to the fact that access to financial credit has been denied them.

Section 12 of the bill authorizes to be appropriated $10,000,000, which shall be established as a revolving fund from which the Secretary of the Interior, under rules and regulations, may make loans to Indian tribes or chartered Indian corporations for the promotion of the economic development of such tribes or their members.

Under section 13 there is authorized to be appropriated not to exceed $250,000 annually for the payment of tuition and other expenses of Indians in recognized institutions of learning of high school and collegiate rank.

In section 14, the Secretary of the Interior is directed to establish standards of health, age, character, experience, knowledge, and ability for Indians who may be appointed, without regard to civil-service laws, to the various positions in the Federal Indian Service.

Section 15 of the act makes the provisions dealing with Indian corporations and Indian education applicable to Alaska and makes sections 2, 4, 7, 9, and 10 of the bill inapplicable to various tribes, named in the bill, resident in the State of Oklahoma.

Section 16 of the bill protects the Sioux benefits which, by existing law, are made contingent upon the receipt of land allotments by the Sioux.

Section 17 declares that nothing in the bill shall be construed to impair or prejudice any claim or suit by any Indian tribe against the United States and that no expenditures for the benefit of Indians made out of appropriations authorized by the bill shall be considered as offsets in any suit brought by Indians against the United States.

Section 18 of the bill defines the term "Indian" and other terms for purposes of the act.

The committee has given prolonged study to the subject matter of this bill. Its contents generally are in accord with the findings and recommendations made by the Indian investigation subcommittee of this committee across recent years. It is believed that Indian welfare will be genuinely served and Indian administration improved by the enactment of the bill.

Source:

US Senate. "Authorizing Indians to Form Business Councils, Corporations, and for Other Purposes." Report No. 1080. 73rd Cong., 2nd Sess. Washington, DC: Government Printing Office, May 10, 1934.

4

Memorandum on the Absolute Power of Congress over Tribes (1935)

The following is a letter from Raymond T. Bonnin (Yankton Sioux), the executive secretary of the National Council of American Indians (NCAI), a leading intertribal interest group established in 1926 to protect the rights of Indigenous peoples by lobbying for social justice and voting rights. Bonnin, a trained paralegal, represented the Yankton and other tribes in claims cases before the US Congress. He unsuccessfully battled John Collier, the Commissioner of Indian Affairs, as Collier pushed for the Indian Reorganization Act. Bonnin's wife was highly regarded author and activist Zitkala Sa (Yankton/White), also known as Gertrude Bonnin.

February 4, 1935

In 1928 a report was made by the Institute for Government Research, entitled "The Problem of Indian administration." The said report was of a survey made at the request of the Secretary of the Interior, which survey was made by 10 experts who visited practically every Indian reservation and boarding school in the United States. The said report was printed in a book of over 800 pages which quite severely criticizes the manner and method of handling Indian affairs. The opening sentence is as follows: "An overwhelming majority of the Indians are poor, even extremely poor, and they are not adjusted to the economic and social system of the dominant white civilization.

If an overwhelming majority of the Indians are extremely poor today, the blame must rest largely upon Congress because under the Constitution of the United States Congress has the exclusive and unfettered power over tribal Indians and their property. The legal status of Indians and Indian affairs is outlined in 22 Corpus Juris at page 529, as follows: "Under the Constitution of the United States Congress has the exclusive and unfettered power to regulate commerce with the Indian tribes and to extend that regulation to the individual members of the tribe, not only in the Indian country but through the states themselves wherever the Indians who belong to any tribal organization may be found, and to say with and on what terms they shall deal....The power of Congress is superior and paramount to the authority of the state within whose limits are Indian tribes. Such power does not cease when the Indians become citizens of the United States, when they become electors under state laws, or when their lands are allotted in severalty."

Congress has plenary power to deal with Indians and Indian lands and funds....The foregoing is amplified and supported by the act of June 30, 1926, entitled "An act to consolidate, codify, and set forth the general and permanent laws of the United States enforce December 7, 1925."

Title 25 of this code relates to Indians, and upon a careful study of this title containing the laws, court decisions, rules, and regulations promulgated by the president of the United States, the secretary of the interior, and the Commissioner of Indian affairs (for such rules and regulations have the force and effect of law in the eyes of the courts), it becomes clear that the Indians are completely and absolutely under the will and at the mercy of Congress.

The Indians are placed in this un-American position by a short clause in the Constitution of the United States, in the making of which Constitution the Indians had no part either directly or indirectly. The makers of that Constitution very likely never thought it would be interpreted any differently from what it would be interpreted in relation to foreign nations and among the several states, for the power over the Indians is given in section 8 of article 1, and reads as follows: "The Congress shall have power to lay and collect taxes, duties, imposts, and excises, to pay the debts and provide for the common defense and general welfare of the United States; but all duties, imposts, and excises shall be uniform throughout the United States to borrow money on the credit of the United States; to regulate commerce with foreign nations, and among the several States and with the Indian tribes."

Under this short phrase (which very likely was intended, at the time, to control the vast fur trade with Indian tribes), Congress later enacted legislation from time to time which has finally got the Indians into the plight in which we find them today, and against which some of them are complaining and protesting and asking for relief.

According to decisions of the Supreme Court of the United States, the matter of dealing with Indians and their property is a question of policy for Congress to determine. In the case of *Lone Wolf* v. *Hitchcock* (1903), the court held that the plenary power of Congress over tribal Indian property is such that the provisions of an existing treaty with the Indians could be abrogated without their consent, but that presumably such action would not be had without full consideration of justice, humanity, and public policy. It will be seen, therefore, that it is largely a question of policy for Congress to determine, and this gave rise to that further ruling by the same court in *Blackfeather v. United States* (1903), wherein it was held that the moral obligations of the government for the Indians offer Congress alone to recognize and that the courts can exercise only such jurisdiction over the subject matter as Congress passes from time to time may see fit to confer upon them.

The foregoing Supreme Court decisions are fair samples of the position taken by the federal courts and indicate the necessity for Congress to do its duty in such a manner as to give to the Indians the right of review in those matters over which the courts declare they do not now have any jurisdiction.

Under Title 25, United States Code, Chapter 1, section 2, we have what is entitled, "Duties of Commissioner—The Commissioner of Indian Affairs shall, under the direction of the Secretary of the Interior, and agreeably to such regulations as the President may prescribe, have the management of all Indian affairs and all matters arising out Indian relations...."

From the foregoing citations of the law and decisions of the courts, it is made clear that not only may the president of the United States adopt and promulgate rules and regulations, having the force and effect of statutes, which the courts take judicial notice of, but such rules and regulations can be initiated by subordinate officials of the government leading down, at least, to subagents.

From a practical knowledge of the administration of Indian affairs, it is well-known that "rules and regulations" are not initiated by the president nor the secretary of the interior nor the Commissioner of Indian Affairs, but by some subordinate person or persons. It is a physical impossibility for any one person to prescribe all the rules and regulations.

The positions of the president, secretary of the interior, and the Commissioner of Indian Affairs, together with their assistants, are political jobs, subject to change every four years, so the plans and policies of one administration may be abandoned by the one following and thus disrupt the lives and living conditions of the Indians each time. There is never any assurance of continuity of good plans or policies. The rules and regulations may be changed and have been changed from one administration to another.

No Indian tribe has a voice in formulating such rules and regulations nor in any manner are they recognized, excepting in so far as they may, in isolated cases, chance to influence Congress in the passage of legislation. The Indians' appearance before committees of Congress is very meager and limited. The expressed wishes of a whole tribe are too easily swept away by the statement of outsiders who may or may not have the best interest of the Indians at heart.

Selfish interests, who are vocal, have a great advantage over the silent Indians in influencing legislation regarding Indian matters.

Under a system adopted and adhered to by Congress, the Indian Bureau is given tremendous advantage over Indians, because its reports for or against legislation are usually controlling. Such reports often carry the endorsement of the Bureau of the Budget and the secretary of the interior and are accepted by Congress, regardless of the wishes or actual welfare of the Indians. Such a system may be applied to dumb animals with impunity, but to apply it rigidly to human beings who are involuntary wards is unfair. The following such a system too closely over the past years by Congress is largely responsible for the "extreme poverty" of the Indians today. The framers of the Constitution gave Congress the sole power "to regulate commerce with foreign nations and among the several states and with the Indian tribes." From that grant of power Congress has enacted laws from time to time, until the Indians are unable to do anything without the consent of Congress.

In February 1926, the National Council of American Indians, Inc., was established by Indians for the purpose of "helping Indians to help themselves." A month later, in March 1926, Senator King, of Utah, presented a 42-page typewritten petition of the National Council of American Indians to the Senate in which was set forth the manifold wrongs done to the Indians "in violation of the terms and the spirit of the said treaties and the Constitution of the United States" and asked for redress of their grievances. Under amendment one of the Constitution are the following words: "Congress shall make no law...abridging...the right of the people peaceably to assemble and to petition the government for a redress of grievances."

Senator King later introduced a resolution setting forth many of the wrongs done the Indians and in part provided for the appointment of a subcommittee of the Senate to investigate Indian affairs. The resolution eventually passed the Senate, and as a result extensive investigations have been made by that committee. Their printed reports of conditions found on Indian reservations cover some thirty-odd volumes, and it is the hope of the Indians that Congress will make proper use of the information gathered by its committee and render such relief as is necessary for the welfare of the Indians at an early date.

The presumption is that the administration measure known as the Wheeler-Howard Act is a preparatory step in the right direction, in that it purports to make land available to landless Indians and to establish a credit system for the benefit of Indians and to grant the tribes the right to manage their local affairs to some degree, along with other rights and benefits. Undoubtedly additional legislation will be necessary to perfect the policy which will fit Indians to become self- supporting, self-sustaining, with the rights and privileges equal to all other citizens of the United States.

Copies of the original petition of the National Council of American Indians, as printed in the *Congressional Record*, are available at the office of said organization and may be had for the asking.

In this connection attention is directed to Senate document No. 314,... entitled "Condition of in the United States," a speech made by the Honorable

William H. King, delivered in the Senate February 8, 1933....This 76-page document should be read by every member of Congress, inasmuch as Congress is finally to blame for the bad conditions among Indians, as told in unmistakable language by the Senator from Utah.

Had it not been for some measure of relief from the Public Works Administration, Federal Emergency Relief Administration, and Civilian Conservation Corps, many of the Indians might have starved to death, no appropriation having been made by Congress specifically to meet the urgent needs of the Indians.

The purpose of this short memorandum is to call attention to the fact that Congress is responsible for all the powers given to the Bureau of Indian Affairs or any official thereof, and Congress alone has absolute power to repeal its laws or to enact new laws, and to correct the evils complained. Only a few citations of Supreme Court decisions are herein given; however, the writer has compiled a comprehensive list of such citations, after careful study, and it can furnish them to committees or members of Congress if desired.

R.T. Bonnin, Executive Secretary, National Council of American Indians Washington DC

Sources:

US Congress. Conditions of Indians in the United States. Hearings Before the Committee on Indian Affairs. 74th Cong., 2nd Sess. On H.R. 8360. Pt. 1. Washington, D.C.: Government Printing Office, March 11, 1936.

Willard, William. "Zitkala Sa: A Woman Who Would Be Heard." *Wicazo Sa Review* 1, no. 1 (Spring 1985): 11–16.

Zitkala Sa. *American Indian Stories.* Washington, DC: Hayworth Publishing House, 1921; repr., Lincoln: University of Nebraska Press, 1985.

5   *American Indian Federation Documents (1935)*

The American Indian Federation (AIF) was one of several intertribal organizations created during the halcyon days of the Indian New Deal. Led by Joseph Bruner (Creek), this body challenged much of the policy architecture that Commissioner of Indian Affairs John Collier was intent on building through the Indian Reorganization Act. Its members viewed the law as retrogressive and a violation of the constitutional rights of individual Indians. The AIF used extremist right-wing rhetoric to attack Collier, urge his removal from office, and demand the termination of the Bureau of Indian Affairs. Bruner went so far as to call for complete integration of Native peoples into white society via a final cash settlement through congressional channels. The AIF ended operations in the mid-1940s, but its extremist positions were soon resurrected as foundational precepts to the termination policy Congress unleashed to devastating effect in the 1950s.

———

American Indian Federation Resolution

Whereas section I, article XIII, of the Constitution of the United States provides that "Neither slavery nor involuntary servitude, except as a punishment for crime whereof the party shall have been duly convicted, shall exist within the United States or any place subject to their jurisdiction;" and

Whereas the American Indian is the only race of people in the United States held in a position of slavery and involuntary servitude; and

Whereas article (amendment) V of the Constitution of the United States provides that "No person shall be deprived of life, liberty, or property, without due process of law;" and

Whereas the American Indian is the only race of people in the United States deprived of life, liberty, and property without due process of law; and

Whereas we are a group of American Indians convened in Washington in behalf of the interests of our race; and

Whereas article I (amendment) of the Constitution of the United States provides that "Congress shall make no law respecting an establishment of religion, or prohibiting the free exercise thereof or abridging the freedom of speech, or of the press; or the right of the people peaceably to assemble, and to petition the Government for a redress of grievances:"

Be it hereby *Resolved*, that we the undersigned Native American Indian leaders and duly elected delegates of our people have this day voluntarily associated ourselves for the purpose of forming an American Indian Federation; and be it hereby further

Resolved, that we bring this organization and its purposes to the attention of every Indian nation, council, tribe, pueblo, business committee, and other Indian organizations and individual Indians within the territorial limits of the United States.

In witness whereof we have hereby affixed our signatures on this eighth day of June 1934, at Washington DC.

The American Indian Federation Preamble:
Constitution Preamble

We, the members of the American Indian Federation, in this the first national convention duly assembled in the city of Gallup, N. M., this 28th day of August 1934, humbly invoking Divine guidance and pledging our allegiance to the American Government, do ordain and proclaim the objectives of this organization to be: a) To encourage intertribal relationship and cooperation in meeting and solving the problem of our future progress; b) To promote harmony and good-will among all mankind and brotherly love among ourselves; c) To provide for our common growth-materially, spiritually, and educationally and offensively and defensively; d) To foster and cherish a spirit of charity toward those in distress, want, and penury, and to this end our noblest and best efforts are dedicated; e) To preserve the noblest art and ideals of the red man and further to cultivate the new hopes and ambitions of an enlightened and awakened citizenship among our people; f) To teach and uphold American citizenship and civilization socially, economically, morally, and educationally; g) To stress the intrinsic value of health as a basis for our well-doing, and to this end consistently urge the establishment of such health agencies by the State or National Government; h) To cooperate wholeheartedly with any and all tribal councils of other Indian groups and State and Federal Governments in all progressive, constructive policies relative to the welfare of the Indian in securing equity and establishing justice; i) To establish and maintain a scientific system based upon a questionnaire relative to the qualifications of deserving Indians to officials in the so-called "Indian Service," regardless of political affiliation or tribal consideration, and to urge their appointment.

Article 1. Organization

The name of this organization shall be the American Indian Federation.

Article 2. Membership

All Indians of the United States and its Territorial possessions of legal age shall be eligible to membership provided that nothing in this article shall prohibit the eligibility of an intermarried citizen, with the exception of Orientals.

Article 3. Annual Meetings

The annual meeting of the American Indian Federation shall be held on the last Thursday, Friday, and Saturday of July, each year; the place for such meeting to be selected by the national federation president.

Article 4. Official Language

The official language of the American Indian Federation shall be the English language.

Article 5: Officers

Section 1. The officers of the American Indian Federation shall be national president, first and second vice presidents, national secretary, national treasurer, and a national chaplain.

Section 2. The above named officers shall be elected biannually by the national convention and shall hold their respective offices for a term of 2 years, or until their successors are elected and qualified.

Section 3. The national executive committee shall be composed of the officers named in section 1, article 5.

Article 6. Duties of Officers

Section 1. The national president of the American Indian Federation shall be its principle executive officer and shall preside at all annual and special called meetings. He shall appoint all committees as he deems necessary in conducting the work of the national organization; he shall have the privilege of participating in all discussions and shall perform such other duties as shall be required of him by the executive committee.

Section 2. The duties of the first and second national vice presidents shall be to assist at all times the national president and to perform such other duties as usually fall to such officers.

Section 3. The duties of the national secretary shall be to keep an accurate record of all proceedings of each annual convention or special meetings, and shall act as the secretary of the national executive committee; he shall also perform such other duties as the national president, in his wisdom, may direct.

Section 4. The duties of the national treasurer shall be to keep an accurate record of all money received and disbursed by this federation, and to install a modern accounting system under the direction of the national president.

Section 5: The duties of the national chaplain shall be to direct all devotional exercises and also to act as national patriotic instructor under the direction of the national president: also his duty shall be in the field of social service.

Section 6. The duties of the national executive committee shall be to hold themselves in readiness to serve in any emergency; to fill all vacancies which may be created by death or otherwise among the national officers and such other officers not otherwise provided for; they shall fix and provide a good and sufficient bond for all officers handling money, preferably by a reputable surety company, they shall have the power to remove for misconduct, inefficiency, and dishonesty, all officers or employees....

Article 11. Amendments

Amendments to the constitution may be made in either of two ways as follows: First. A two-thirds majority of the national executive committee may propose amendments to the constitution and if adopted by a majority of the delegates voting in a national convention, the same shall become a part and parcel of the constitution of the American Indian Federation.

Second. Any member may propose an amendment to the constitution and if adopted by a majority of the delegates to the national convention, the same shall become a part and parcel of this constitution. The national executive committee shall prescribe rules and methods in the premises.

Article 12. Special Meetings

Special meetings or conferences may be called by the national president, designating the time, place, and the purposes of said special meeting or conference.

Article 13. Expenditures and Accounting

Authority is hereby granted the national treasurer under direction of the national executive committee to expend such sums as they deem necessary in the promotion of the welfare of the American Indian. The national executive committee is hereby authorized to call for and take charge of all records, files, or other instruments of writing in possession of the national treasurer and secretary for the purpose of making an audit and report of the national convention through the national president.

Article 14. Rules of Order

In the absence of established rules, procedure shall be governed by Roberts' Rules of Order.

Joseph Bruner, National President American Indian Federation. February 7, 1935.

Sources:

Hauptman, Laurence M. "The American Indian Federation and the Indian New Deal: A Reinterpretation." *Pacific Historical Review* 52 (Nov. 1983): 378–402.

US Congress. "Constitution of the American Indian Federation." Hearings Before the Subcommittee on General Bills of the Committee on Indian Affairs. 74th Cong., 1st Sess. on H.R. 7781. Washington, DC: Government Printing Office, Feb. 11, 1935.

6   *Proposed Constitution of the Eastern Band of Cherokee Indians (1935)*

The Eastern Band of Cherokee had operated under a state corporate charter since 1889. In the fall of 1935, they drafted a constitution in an effort to come under the auspices of the Indian Reorganization Act. Although internal conflicts between various community factions led to defeat of ratification by a vote of 484 to 382, the document, nonetheless, merits attention, as it contains many clauses that were later adopted by many other Native nations able to approve formal constitutions.

Proposed Constitution of the Eastern Band of Cherokee

We, the people of the Eastern Band of Cherokee Indians, in the exercise of the right of local self-government, handed down to us by our fathers and confirmed by the State of North Carolina in a corporate charter... in order more clearly to define our relations to the Federal Government, do hereby adopt this Constitution.

Article I. Territory

The jurisdiction of the Eastern Band of Cherokee Indians shall extend to the lands within the Eastern Cherokee Indian Reservation, and to such other lands as may be held by the band as a tribe or corporation, and such other lands as may be hereafter added thereto.

Article II. Membership

The membership of the Eastern Band of Cherokee Indians shall consist as follows:

(a) All persons of Eastern Cherokee Indian blood lawfully enrolled upon the Eastern Cherokee Indian Reservation, and residing thereon, on June 8, 1935, shall be members of the Eastern Band of Cherokee Indians: Provided, that this section shall not affect any rights saved to members of the band under existing law.

(b) After one year from the date of adoption of this Constitution, the Council shall have power to deprive of membership any person who has not lived upon the reservation for at least one year during the preceding three years: Provided, that this section shall not affect any rights saved to members of the band under existing law.

(c) All children born to any member of the band who maintains a legal residence on the reservation at the time of the birth of said children shall be entitled to membership in the band, if said children shall be of at least one-sixteenth (1/16th) degree of Eastern Cherokee Indian blood.

(d) Persons of one-sixteenth (1/16th) degree or more Eastern Cherokee blood may be adopted as members of the band by a majority vote of the council, subject to the approval of the Secretary of the Interior, but no person shall be adopted as a member unless he shall have resided on the reservation for a probationary period of two (2) years.

Article III. Organization

Section 1. The seat of government of the Eastern Band of Cherokee Indians shall be at Cherokee Council Grounds, Swain County, North Carolina, until changed by the council....

Section 2. The officers of the Eastern Band of Cherokee Indians shall consist of a principal chief, an assistant (or vice) chief, twelve members of council, secretary, treasurer, interpreter, marshal of the band, and other officers as hereinafter provided....

Section 3. There shall be an executive council, which shall consist of the principal chief, assistant (or vice) chief and one associate, who shall be appointed by the principal chief and confirmed by the council, who shall receive the same compensation as is provided for members of council....

Section 4. There shall also be a business committee, which shall consist of the principal chief, assistant (or vice) chief, and the agency superintendent, as ex officio secretary of the council. This committee shall function at such times as the council is not in session, and have charge of all routine matters which may arise during such recess, including settling of disputes, caring for the poor and needy; enforcing the ordinances of the council, and such other matters as may be delegated to it by the council. The committee shall render a report to each regular and special sessions of the council.

Section 5. The council shall consist of twelve members elected from the towns and settlements as follows: From Yellow Hill settlement, Swain County, two members; from Big Cove settlement, Swain County, two members; from Birdtown settlement, Swain and Jackson Counties, two members; from Wolftown settlement, Jackson County, two members; from Painttown settlement, Jackson County, two members; from Cheoah settlement, Graham County, two members....

Section 6. The term of office of principal chief and assistant chief shall be four (4) years, and that of members of council two (2) years, and all other officers elected by the council shall hold until the first annual or grand council held after the election for members of council, and all officers of the band shall hold until their successors are duly qualified....

Article IV. Powers of Government

Section 1. The council shall have the authority to represent the band in all negotiations with the Federal, State, and local governments.

Section 2. The council shall have power to employ legal counsel, the choice of counsel and fixing of fees to be subject to the approval of the Secretary of the Interior.

Section 3. The council shall have power to prevent the sale, disposition, lease, or encumbrance of tribal land, interests in land, or other tribal assets without the consent of the band.

Section 4. The council shall have power to recommend the appropriation of tribal and other funds within the control of Congress or the Secretary of the Interior.

Section 5. The council of the Eastern Band of Cherokee Indians shall direct the management and control of all property, either real or personal, belonging to the band as a corporation; but no person shall be entitled to the enjoyment of any lands belonging to the Eastern Band of Cherokee Indians as a corporation or as a tribe, or any profits accruing therefrom, or any moneys which may belong to said band as a corporation or as a tribe, unless such person be of at least one-sixteenth (1/16th) of Eastern Cherokee blood, and in case that any money derived from any source whatever, belonging to the Eastern Band of Cherokee Indians, shall be distributed among the members thereof, the same shall be divided per capita among the members entitled thereto: Provided, that this section shall not be construed to affect any rights saved to members of the band under existing law....

Section 6. The said Eastern Band of Cherokee Indians is hereby fully authorized and empowered to adopt bylaws, and rules for the general government of the band, governing the management of all real and personal property held by the Eastern Band of Cherokee Indians as a corporation or as a tribe, and direct and assign among the members thereof homes in the Qualla boundary and other land held by them as a corporation or as a tribe, and is hereby vested with full power to enforce obedience to such bylaws and regulations as may be enacted by the council, through the marshal of the band....

Section 7. The council shall have power to appoint subordinate boards and officers and to prescribe their duties and powers....

Section 8. The council shall have power to appropriate out of available funds belonging to the band money for salaries of officials and other expenses of public business, including the support of the indigent and helpless.

Section 9. The council shall have power, subject to review by the Secretary of the Interior, to require members of the band to contribute labor for public works and enterprises, or to make money contributions in lieu of such labor.

Section 10. The council shall have power, subject to review by the Secretary of the Interior, to levy dues, fees, and taxes on members of the band.

Section 11. The council shall have power to remove or exclude from lands belonging to the band any nonmember whose presence may be injurious to the band or to the members thereof. This power shall not, however, extend to the removal or exclusion of Government officials, or other persons occupying reservation lands under lawful authority, and in all cases this power may be exercised only subject to review by the Secretary of the Interior.

Section 12. The council shall have power to promulgate ordinances for the purpose of safeguarding the peace and safety of residents of the Eastern Cherokee Indian Reservation and shall have power to adjudicate claims and disputes arising amongst the members of the band and to enforce the ordinances of the council. It shall have the further power to delegate to the business committee or to subordinate officers' jurisdiction over all offenses, disputes, or causes, subject to appeal to the council: Provided, however, that nothing contained in this section shall be construed to limit the existing jurisdiction of the courts of the State of North Carolina.

Section 13. Whenever it may become necessary, in the opinion of the council, to appropriate to school, church, or other public purposes, for the benefit of the band, any of the lands owned by the Eastern Band of Cherokee Indians as a corporation or tribe, and occupied by any individual Indian or Indians of the band, the council may condemn such land for the aforesaid purposes only by paying to the occupant of such land the value of such improvements and betterments as he may have placed or caused to be placed thereon, and the value of such improvements or betterments shall be assessed by a jury of not less than six competent persons, who are members of the band, to be summoned by the marshal of the band, under such rules and regulations as may be prescribed by the council....

Section 14. The council shall have power to provide for the general welfare of the members of the band by appropriate regulation of the disposition and use of property. It shall have the further power, subject to review by the

Secretary of the Interior, to regulate the business and trade of nonmembers with the members of the band on land belonging to the band as a corporation or tribe, and to institute a system of licenses and assessments for all trade and business conducted on the reservation.

Section 15. The council may, when necessary to protect the interests of the band or its members, regulate the activities of voluntary associations consisting of members of the band organized for purposes of cooperation or other purposes.

Section 16. The council shall have power, subject to review by the Secretary of the Interior, to prescribe rules of inheritance.

Section 17. The council shall have power to provide for the appointment of guardians for minors and mental incompetents, subject to review by the Secretary of the Interior.

Section 18. The council shall have power to appoint and supervise judges of elections in the several towns and settlements and to prescribe election rules and procedure. The council shall have the further power, except as otherwise provided in this constitution or in the bylaws, to regulate its own procedure....

Section 19. The council shall have power to determine questions of membership in the band, in accordance with the provisions of this constitution and the laws of the United States, and to determine questions of residence and absence arising under this constitution.

Section 20. Any resolution or ordinance which, by the terms of this constitution, is subject to review by the Secretary of the Interior, shall be presented to the superintendent of the reservation, who shall, within ten (10) days thereafter, approve or disapprove the same.

If the superintendent shall approve any ordinance or resolution, it shall thereupon become effective; but the superintendent shall transmit a copy of the same, bearing his endorsement, to the Secretary of the Interior, who may, within 90 days from the date of enactment, rescind the said ordinance or resolution for any cause, by notifying the council of such rescission. If the superintendent shall refuse to approve any ordinance or resolution submitted to him, within ten (10) days after its enactment, he shall advise the council of his reasons therefor. If these reasons appear to the council insufficient, it may, by a majority vote, refer the ordinance or resolution to the Secretary of the Interior, who may, within 90 days from the date of enactment approve the same in writing, whereupon the said ordinance or resolution shall become effective.

Section 21. The council may exercise such further powers as may be delegated to the Eastern Band of Cherokee Indians by the Secretary of the Interior or any other officer or agency of Government qualified to delegate such powers.

Section 22. Any rights and powers, not expressly referred to in this constitution, but heretofore vested in the Eastern Band of Cherokee Indians, in accordance with the law and Constitution of the United States, or by virtue of the organization of said band under Chapter 207, Private Laws of N.C., 1897, as amended, shall not be abridged by this article, but may be exercised by the members of the band through the adoption of appropriate bylaws and constitutional amendments.

Section 23. All ordinances or resolutions, pursuant to the exercise of any power enumerated in this article, shall be consistent with the laws and Constitution of the United States and of the State of North Carolina, so far as they may be applicable to an Indian tribe.

Article V. Bill of Rights

Section 1. All members of the band shall be accorded equal opportunities to participate in the economic resources and activities of the band.

Section 2. All members of the band may enjoy without hindrance freedom of worship, conscience, speech, press, assembly, and association.

Article VI. Elections

Section 1. The principal chief assistant (or vice) chief, and members of council shall be elected to their respective offices by the male and female members of the Eastern Band of Cherokee Indians who have attained to age of eighteen (18) years and who have been residents for ninety (90) days next preceding the date of an election in the districts in which they vote.

Section 2. Sixty (60) days before an annual election, the qualified voters of each township or settlement shall meet in convention in their respective townships or settlements and place in nomination candidates for each position wherein the town or settlement is entitled to have a representative. At those times when a chief is to be elected, these conventions shall also select delegates to attend the convention for nominating candidates for chief and assistant chief. Independent candidates desiring to enter any election contest must file a petition thirty (30) days before the election, which petition must be signed by ten (10) voters of the district in the case of candidates for the council, and fifty (50) voters in the case of candidates for the positions of chief and assistant chief. All nominations must be filed with the business committee. Votes for any candidate who has not complied with the requirements will not be counted but will be thrown out.

Section 3. The council shall, sixty (60) days preceding the election held for members of council, appoint two (2) judges for every Indian town and settlement that is entitled to a member of council, who shall hold the elections for such town and settlement shall certify the result of the same under such rules and regulations as may be prescribed by the council, to the next succeeding annual or grand council: Provided, however, That the candidates for principal and assistant chief, who shall have received a majority or plurality of the votes cast by the band, shall be declared by the said annual council to be the duly elected principal chief and assistant chief for the term of four (4) years, and the members of council who shall be certified by the said judges of election to be elected for that town or settlement shall be the duly elected members for the same and shall hold their offices for the term of two years....

Article VII. Vacancies

Section 1. In case of death, resignation, or disability of the principal chief, the assistant (or vice) chief shall become the principal chief until removal of disability or his successor be elected; or in case of death, resignation, or disability of the assistant (or vice) chief, the council may elect until removal of disability or his successor be elected....

Section 2. In case of death, resignation, or disability of any member of council a new member shall be elected by such town or settlement, under such rules and regulations as may be prescribed by the council....

Section 3. Any officer of the Eastern Band of Cherokee Indians who has violated his oath of office, or who has been guilty of any offense making him ineligible to hold said office, may be impeached by a two-thirds (2/3) vote of the council....

Article VIII. Referendum and Veto

Section 1. The members of the band shall have the right, by presentation of a petition signed by one-third (1/3) of the qualified voters, to demand a referendum on any question before the council and upon any act or resolution of the council. In such referendum the vote of those voting on such proposal shall be conclusive and binding on the council. The council shall have power to prescribe rules and regulations for conducting any such referendum election.

Section 2. The chief shall have the power to veto all acts and resolutions, etc., of the council, but his veto shall not prevail against a two-thirds (2/3) vote of the council, nor against the will of the people as expressed in a referendum election, as provided in the preceding section....

Article IX. Land

Section 1. The land now held by the Eastern Band of Cherokee Indians, and all lands which may be acquired in the future by the band or by the United States in trust for the band, shall remain tribal property, and shall not be divided up by allotment of any part to individuals or groups of individuals as private property, but assignment of land for private use may be made by the council, as in the past, in accordance with bylaws and ordinances that may be enacted from time to time.

Section 2. Tribal land which is not assigned for individual use may be used by the band for public purposes of any kind, or may be leased by the council in accordance with law, the proceeds of such leases to be used for the support of poor and any other public purposes of the band.

Article X. Amendments

This constitution and bylaws may be amended by a majority vote of the qualified voters of the band voting at an election called for that purpose by the Secretary of the Interior, provided that at least 30 percent of those entitled to shall vote in such election; but no amendment shall become effective until it shall have been approved by the Secretary of the Interior. It shall be the duty of the Secretary of the Interior to call an election on any proposed amendment at the request of the council, or upon presentation of a petition signed by one third (1/3) of the qualified voters, members of the band.

Source:

US Senate. "Tentative Draft of Constitution and By-Laws of the Eastern Band of Cherokee Indians of North Carolina." Hearings Before the Subcommittee of the Committee on Indian Affairs. 76th Cong., 1st Sess. Pursuant to Sen. Resolution 79 (70th Cong.) Pt. 37. Survey of Conditions of the Indians in the United States. Washington, DC: Government Printing Office, 1940.

7

Constitution of the Confederated Salish and Kootenai Tribes (1935)

For economic and political reasons, the Commissioner of Indian Affairs created several consolidated or confederated Native communities during the early period of the Indian Reorganization Act (IRA). In these cases, several culturally distinct Native peoples were merged together merely for legal and administrative convenience. In the present case, three Native nations—the Bitterroot Salish, Upper Pend d'Oreille, and the Kootenai, inhabiting the Flathead Reservation in Montana established by the 1855 Hellsgate Treaty—together created a single constitution under the IRA. This was the first of more than one hundred formally ratified constitutions written in accordance with the procedures outlined under the IRA of 1934.

Note the nearly dozen places in the document where the tribes' decisions are "subject to review by the Secretary of the Interior" or where their decisions are "subject to the approval of the Secretary of the Interior." The ubiquity of such constrictive language is a clear reflection of the fact that the secretary did not perceive Native governments as genuinely self-governing entities and that federal paternalism had not run its course. Such language was pervasive in many of the IRA constitutions and many such provisions are still embedded in Tribal organic charters.

Preamble

We, the Confederated Salish and Kootenai Tribes of the Flathead Reservation, Montana, in order to establish a more responsible organization, promote our general welfare, conserve and develop our lands and resources, and secure to ourselves and our posterity the power to exercise certain rights of self-government not inconsistent with Federal, State, and local laws, do ordain and establish this Constitution for the Confederated Tribes of the Flathead Reservation.

Article 1—Territory

The jurisdiction of the Confederated Salish and Kootenai Tribes of Indians shall extend to the territory within the original confines of the Flathead Reservation as defined in the Treaty of July 16, 1855, and to such other lands without such boundaries, as may hereafter be added thereto under any law of the United States, except as otherwise provided by law.

Article 2—Membership

Section 1. The membership of the Confederated Tribes of the Flathead Reservation shall consist as follows: All persons of Indian blood whose names appear on the official census rolls of the Confederated Tribes as of January 1, 1935. All children born to any member of the Confederated Salish and Kootenai Tribes of the Flathead Reservation who is a resident of the reservation at the time of the birth of said children.

Section 2. The Council shall have the power to propose ordinances, subject to review by the Secretary of the Interior, governing future membership and the adoption of members by the Confederated Tribes.

Section 3. No property rights shall be acquired or lost through membership in this organization, except as provided herein.

Article 3—The Tribal Council

Section 1. The governing body of the Confederated Salish and Kootenai Tribes of the Flathead Reservation shall be the Tribal Council.

Section 2. The Council shall consist of ten councilmen to be elected from the districts as set forth hereafter, and Chiefs Martin Charlo and Eneas Paul Koostahtah.

Section 3. Representation from the districts hereby designated shall be as follows: Jocko Valley and Mission Districts, two councilmen each; Ronan, Pablo, Elmo-Dayton, Hot Springs-Camas Prairie, and Dixon, one councilman each.

Section 4. The Tribal Council shall have the power to change the districts and the representation from each district, based on community organization or otherwise, as deemed advisable, such change to be made by ordinance, but the total number of delegates shall not be changed as provided for in section 2 of article III of this Constitution.

Section 5. The Tribal Council so organized shall elect from within its own number a chairman, and a vice chairman, and from within or without its own membership, a secretary, treasurer, sergeant-at-arms, and such other officers and committees as may be deemed necessary.

Section 6. No person shall be a candidate for membership in the Tribal Council unless he shall be a member of the Confederated Tribes of the Flathead Reservation and shall have resided in the district of his candidacy for a period of one year next preceding the election.

Section 7. The Tribal Council of the Confederated Tribes of the Flathead Reservation shall be the sole judge of the qualifications of its members.

Article 4—Nominations and Elections

Section 1. The first election of a Tribal Council under this Constitution shall be called and supervised by the present Tribal Council within 30 days after the ratification and approval of this Constitution, and thereafter elections shall be held every two years on the third Sunday prior to the expiration of the terms of office of the members of the Tribal Council. At the first election, five councilmen shall be elected for a period of two years and five for a period of four years. The term of office of a councilman shall be for a period of four years unless otherwise provided herein.

Section 2. The Tribal Council or an election board appointed by the Council shall determine rules and regulations governing all elections.

Section 3. Any qualified member of the Confederated Tribes may announce his candidacy for the Council, within the district of his residence, notifying the Secretary of the Tribal Council in writing of his candidacy at least 15 days prior to the election. It shall be the duty of the Secretary of the Tribal Council to post in each district at least 10 days before the election, the names of all candidates for the Council who have met these requirements.

Section 4. The Tribal Council, or a board appointed by the Council, shall certify to the election of the members of the Council within 5 days after the election returns.

Section 5. Any member of the Confederated Tribes of the Flathead Reservation who is 21 years of age or over and who has maintained a legal residence for at least one year on the Flathead Reservation shall be entitled to vote.

Section 6. The Tribal Council, or a board appointed by the Tribal Council, shall designate the polling places and appoint all election officials.

Article 5—Vacancies and Removal from Office

Section 1. If a Councilman or official shall die, resign, permanently leave the reservation, or be removed from office, the Council shall declare the position vacant and appoint successor to fill the unexpired term, provided that the person chosen to fill such vacancy shall be from the district in which such vacancy occurs.

Section 2. Any councilman who is proven guilty of improper conduct or gross neglect of duty may be expelled from the Council by a two-thirds vote of the membership of the Council voting in favor of such expulsion, and provided further, that the accused member shall be given full and fair opportunity to reply to any and all charges at a designated Council meeting. It is further stipulated that any such member shall be given a written statement of the charges against him at least five days before the meeting at which he is to appear.

Article 6—Powers and Duties of the Tribal Council

Section 1. The Tribal Council shall have the power, subject to any limitations imposed by the Statutes or the Constitution of the United States, and subject to all express restrictions upon such powers contained in this Constitution and attached Bylaws;

(a) To regulate the uses and disposition of tribal property, to protect and preserve the tribal property, wildlife and natural resources of the Confederated Tribes, to cultivate Indian arts, crafts, and culture, to administer charity; to protect the health, security, and general welfare of the Confederated Tribes.

(b) To employ legal counsel for the protection and advancement of the rights of the Flathead Confederated Tribes and their members, the choice of counsel and fixing of fees to be subject to the approval of the Secretary of the Interior.

(c) To negotiate with the federal, state, and local governments on behalf of the Confederated Tribes, and to advise and consult with the representatives of the departments of the government of the United States on all matters affecting the affairs of the Confederated Tribes.

(d) To approve sale, disposition, lease, or encumbrance of tribal lands and tribal assets which may be authorized or executed by the secretary of the interior, the Commissioner of Indian affairs, or any other agency of the government, provided that no tribal lands shall be sold or encumbered or released for a period in excess of five years, except for governmental purposes.

(e) To advise with the secretary of the interior with regard to all appropriations estimates for federal projects for the benefit of the Confederated Tribes, prior to the submission of such estimates to the Congress.

(f) To manage all economic affairs and enterprises of the Confederated Tribes in accordance with the terms of a charter to be issued by the secretary of the interior.

(g) To make assignments of tribal lands to members of the Confederated Tribes in conformity with article 8 of this Constitution.

(h) To appropriate for tribal use of the reservation any available applicable tribal funds, provided that any such appropriation may be subject to review by the secretary of the interior, and provided further, that any appropriation in excess of $5000 in any one fiscal year shall be of no effect until approved in a popular referendum.

(i) To promulgate and enforce ordinances, subject to review by the secretary of the interior, which would provide for assessments or license fees upon nonmembers doing business within the reservation, or obtaining special rights or privileges, and the same may also be applied to members of the Confederated Tribes, provided such ordinances have been approved by a referendum of the Confederated Tribes.

(j) To exclude from the restricted lands of the reservation persons not legally entitled to reside thereon, under ordinances which may be subject to review by the secretary of the interior.

(k) To enact resolutions or ordinances not inconsistent with article 2 of this Constitution governing adoptions and abandonment of membership.

(l) To promulgate and enforce ordinances which shall be subject to review by the secretary of the interior, governing the conduct of members of the Confederated Tribes, and providing for the maintenance of law and order and the administration of justice by the establishment of an Indian court, and defining its powers and duties.

(m) To purchase land of members of the Confederated Tribes for public purposes under condemnation proceedings in courts of competent jurisdiction.

(n) To promulgate and enforce ordinances which are intended to safeguard and promote the peace, safety, morals, and general welfare of the Confederated Tribes by regulating the conduct of trade and the use and disposition of property upon the reservation, providing that any ordinance directly affecting nonmembers shall be subject to review by the secretary of the interior.

(o) Two charter subordinate organizations for economic purposes and to regulate the activities of all cooperatives and other associations which may be organized under any charter issued under this Constitution.

(p) To regulate the inheritance of real and personal property, other than allotted lands, within the Flathead Reservation, subject to review by the secretary of the interior.

(q) To regulate the domestic relations of members of the Confederated Tribes.

(r) To recommend and provide for the appointment of guardians for orphans, minor members of the Confederated Tribes, and incompetence subject to the approval of the secretary of the interior, and to administer tribal and other funds or property which may be transferred or entrusted to the Confederated Tribes or Tribal Council for this purpose.

(s) To create and maintain a tribal fund accepting grants or donations from any person, state, or the United States.

(t) To delegate to subordinate boards or two cooperative associations which are open to all members of the Confederated Tribes, any of the foregoing powers, reserving the right to review any action taken by virtue of such delegated power.

(u) To adopt resolutions or ordinances to effectuate any of the foregoing powers.

Section 2. Any resolution or ordinance which by the terms of this constitution is subject to review by the Secretary of the Interior, shall be presented to the Superintendent of the Reservation who shall, within ten days thereafter, approve or disapprove the same, and if such ordinance or resolution is approved, it shall thereupon become effective, but the Superintendent shall transmit a copy of the same, bearing his endorsement, to the Secretary of the Interior who may, within 90 days from the date of enactment, rescind said ordinance or resolution for any cause, by notifying the Council of such action: Provided, that if the Superintendent shall refuse to approve any resolution or ordinance submitted to him, within ten days after its enactment, he shall advise the Council of his reasons therefor, and the Council, if such reasons appear to be insufficient, may refer it to the Secretary of the Interior, who may pass upon same and either approve or disapprove it within 90 days from its enactment.

Section 3. The council of the Confederated Tribes may exercise such further powers as may in the future be delegated to it by the Federal Government, either through order of the Secretary of the Interior or by Congress, or by the State Government or by members of the Confederated Tribes.

Section 4. Any rights powers heretofore vested in the Confederated Tribes but not expressly referred to in this Constitution shall not be abridged by this article, but may be exercised by the members of the Confederated Tribes through the adoption of appropriate bylaws and constitutional amendments.

Article 7—Bill of Rights

Section 1. All members of the Confederated Tribes over the age of 21 years shall have the right to vote in all tribal elections, subject to any restrictions as to residence as set forth in article IV.

Section 2. All members of the Confederated Tribes shall be accorded equal opportunities to participate in the economic resources and activities of the reservation.

Section 3. All members of the Confederated Tribes may enjoy without hindrance freedom of worship, speech, press, and assembly.

Section 4. Any member of the Confederated Tribes accused of any offense, shall have the right to a prompt, open, and public hearing, with due notice of the offense charged, and shall be permitted to summon witnesses in his own behalf and trial by jury shall be accorded, when duly requested, by any member accused of any offense punishable by more than 30 days' imprisonment, and excessive bail or cruel or unusual punishment shall not be imposed.

Article 8—Land

Section 1. Allotted lands. Allotted lands, including heirship lands, within the Flathead Reservation, shall continue to be held as heretofore by their present owners. The right of the individual Indian to hold or to part with his land, as under existing law, shall not be abrogated by anything contained in this Constitution, but the owner of restricted land may, with the approval of the Secretary of the Interior, voluntarily convey his land to the Confederated Tribes either in exchange for a money payment or in exchange for an assignment covering the same land or other land, as hereinafter provided. The Tribal Council shall have the right to exchange tribal lands for individual allotments when necessary for consolidation of tribal holdings and subject to approval of the Secretary of the Interior. Such exchanges should be based on the appraised value of the lands so exchanged, and the individual Indian shall hold the land so exchanged in the same manner as the original allotment.

Section 2. Tribal lands. The unallotted lands of the Flathead Reservation, and all lands which may hereafter be acquired by the Flathead Confederated Tribes or by the United States in trust for the Flathead Confederated Tribes, shall be held as tribal land, and no part of such land shall be mortgaged or sold. Tribal lands shall not be allotted to individuals but may be assigned to members of the Confederated Tribes, or leased, or otherwise used by the Confederated Tribes as hereinafter provided.

Section 3. Leasing of tribal lands. Tribal lands may be leased by the Tribal Council, with the approval of the Secretary of the Interior, for such periods of time as are permitted by law.

In the leasing of tribal lands preference shall be given, first, to Indian cooperative associations, and, secondly, to individual Indians who are members of the Confederated Tribes. No lease of tribal land to a nonmember shall be made by the Tribal Council unless it shall appear that no Indian cooperative association or individual member of the Confederated Tribes is able and willing to use the land and to pay a reasonable fee for such use. Grazing permits covering tribal land may be issued by the Tribal Council, with the approval of the Secretary of the Interior, in the same manner and upon the same terms as leases....

Article 9—Referendum

Section 1. Upon a petition of at least one-third of the eligible voters of the Confederated Tribes, or upon the request of a majority of the members of the Tribal Council, any enacted or proposed ordinance or resolution of the Council shall be submitted to a popular referendum, and the vote of a majority of the qualified voters voting in such referendum shall be conclusive and binding on the Tribal Council, provided that at least thirty percent (30 percent) of the eligible voters shall vote in such election.

Article 10—Amendments

Section 1. This Constitution and Bylaws may be amended by a majority vote of the qualified voters of the Confederated Tribes voting at an election called for that purpose by the Secretary of the Interior, provided that at least thirty percent (30 percent) of those entitled to vote shall vote in such election; but no amendment shall become effective until it shall have been approved by the Secretary of the Interior. It shall be the duty of the Secretary of the Interior to call an election on any proposed amendment, at the request of two-thirds of the Council, or upon presentation of a petition signed by one-third (1/3) of the qualified voters, members of the Confederated Tribes.

By-Laws

Article 1—The Tribal Council

Section 1. The Chairman of the Council shall preside over all meetings of the Council, perform all duties of chairman, and exercise any authority detailed to him, and he shall be entitled to vote on all questions.

Section 2. The vice chairman shall assist the chairman when called on so to do, in the absence of the chairman shall preside, and when so presiding shall have all the privileges, duties, and responsibilities of the chairman.

Section 3. The Council secretary shall forward a copy of the minutes of all meetings to the Superintendent of the Reservation and to the Commissioner of Indian Affairs.

Section 4. The duties of all appointed boards or officers of the organization shall be clearly defined by resolutions of the Council at the time of their creation or appointment. Such boards and officers shall report from time to time as required to the Council and their activities and decisions shall be subject to review by the Council upon petition of any person aggrieved.

Section 5. Newly elected members who have been duly certified shall be installed at the first regular meeting of the Tribal Council.

Section 6. Each member of the Tribal Council and each officer or subordinate officer, elected or appointed hereunder, shall take an oath of office prior to assuming the duties thereof, by which oath, he shall pledge himself to support and defend the Constitution of the United States and this Constitution and Bylaws. The following form of oath of office shall be given: "I, -------------, do solemnly swear (or affirm) that I will support and defend the Constitution of the United States against all enemies, to carry out faithfully and impartially, the duties of my office to the best of my ability; to cooperate, promote, and protect the best interests of my Tribe, in accordance with this Constitution and Bylaws...."

Section 8. Special meetings may be called by a written notice signed by the chairman or a majority of the Tribal Council and when so called the Tribal Council shall have power to transact business as in regular meetings.

Section 9. No business shall be transacted unless a quorum is present which shall consist of two-thirds (2/3) of the entire membership....

Section 11. It shall be the duty of each member of the Tribal Council to make reports to the district from which he is elected, concerning the proceedings of the Tribal Council.

Section 12. The Tribal Council may prescribe such salaries for officers or members of the Council as it deems advisable, from such funds as may be available.

Article 2—Ordinances and Resolutions

Section 1. All final decisions of the Council on matters of general and permanent interest to the members of the Confederated Tribes shall be embodied in ordinances. Such ordinances shall be published from time to time for the information and education of the members of the Confederated Tribes.

Section 2. All final decisions of the Council on matters of temporary interest (such as action on the reservation budget for a single year, or petitions to Congress or the Secretary of the Interior) or relating especially to particular individuals or officials (such as adoption of members, instructions for tribal employees or rules of order for the Council) shall be embodied in resolutions. Such resolutions shall be recorded in a special book which shall be open to inspection by members of the Confederated Tribes.

Section 3. All questions of procedure (such as acceptance of Committee reports or invitations to outsiders to speak) shall be decided by action of the Council or by ruling of the Chairman, if no objection is heard.

In all ordinances, resolutions or motions the Council may act by majority vote, but all matters of importance shall be fully discussed and a reasonable attempt shall be made to secure unanimous agreement.

Section 4. Legislative forms. Every ordinance shall begin with the words: "Be it enacted by the Council of the Confederated Salish and Kootenai Tribes—."

Section 5. Every resolution shall begin with the words: "Be it resolved by the Council of the Confederated Salish and Kootenai Tribes—."

Section 6. Every ordinance or resolution shall contain a recital of the laws of the United States and the provisions of this Constitution under which authority for the said ordinance or resolution is found.

Article 3—Ratification of Constitution and By-laws

This Constitution and the attached By-laws, when adopted by a majority vote of the voters of the Confederated Tribes voting at a special election called by the Secretary of the Interior, in which at least thirty (30) percent of those entitled to vote shall vote, shall be submitted to the Secretary of the Interior for his approval, and shall be inforce from the date of such approval.

Certificate of Adoption

Pursuant to an order, approved September 25, 1935, by the Secretary of the Interior, the attached Constitution and Bylaws were submitted for ratification to the members of the Confederated Salish and Kootenai Tribes of the Flathead Reservation and were on October 4, 1935, duly adopted by a majority vote of the members of said voting in an election in which over 30 percent of those entitled to vote cast their ballots in accordance with section 16 of the Indian Reorganization Act of June 18, 1934 (48 Stat. 984), as amended by the act of June 14, 1935 (Pub. No. 147, 74th Cong.).

Roy E. Courville, Chairman of Election Board

I, Harold L. Ickes, the Secretary of the Interior of the United States of America, by virtue of the authority granted me by the act of June 18, 1934 (48 Stat. 984), as amended, do hereby approve the attached Constitution and Bylaws of the Confederated Salish and Kootenai Tribes of the Flathead Reservation.

All rules and regulations heretofore promulgated by the Interior Department or by the Office of Indian Affairs, so far as they may be incompatible with any of the provisions of the said Constitution or Bylaws are hereby declared inapplicable to the Confederated Salish and Kootenai Tribes of the Flathead Reservation.

All officers and employees of the Interior Department are ordered to abide by the provisions of the said Constitution and Bylaws.

Approval recommended October 26, 1935.

Sources:

Fehey, John. *The Flathead Indians*. Norman: University of Oklahoma Press, 1971.

    Fuller, E. O. "The Confederated Salish and Kootenai Tribes of the Flathead Reservation." In *Interior Salish and Eastern Washington Indians*, 25–168. New York: Garland Publishing, 1974.

8   *Constitution of the Oneida Tribe of Wisconsin (1936)*

Of the original five (later six) nations composing the Haudenosaunee (Iroquois) Confederacy in New York, segments of one, the Oneida, known as "People of the Standing Stone," relocated to Wisconsin in a series of moves undertaken during the 1820s and 1830s. Other Oneidas remained and continue to reside in New York, while others live on the Six Nations Grand River Reserve in Ontario, Canada. The Wisconsin Oneida formally established their land base in 1838 by purchasing land from the Menominee Nation and their reservation now encompasses 2,500 acres. Many Oneida are Christian, but a number adhere to the Handsome Lake Code, a relatively recent religious tradition established by Seneca leader Handsome Lake in 1799, which blends traditional religious teachings with elements of Christianity.

Preamble

We, the people of the Oneida Tribe of Indians of Wisconsin, grateful to Almighty God for his fostering care, in order to reestablish our tribal organization, to conserve and develop our common resources, and to promote the welfare of ourselves and our descendants, do hereby ordain and establish this constitution.

Article I. Territory

The jurisdiction of the Oneida Tribe of Wisconsin shall extend to the territory within the present confines. of the Oneida Reservation and to such other land as may be hereafter added thereto within or without said boundary lines under any law of the United States, except as otherwise provided by law.

Article II. Membership

Section 1. The membership of the Oneida Tribe shall consist of (a) All persons of Indian blood whose names appear on the official annuity roll of the tribe as of October 7, 1935. (b) Any descendant of a member of the tribe who is of at least one quarter Indian blood, provided such member is a resident of the reservation at the time of the birth of the said descendant.

Section 2. The General Tribal Council shall have the power to promulgate ordinances subject to review by the Secretary of the Interior covering future membership and the adoption of new members.

Article III. Governing Body

Section 1. The governing body of the Oneida Tribe of Wisconsin shall be the General Tribal Council which shall be composed of all the qualified voters of the Oneida Reservation.

Section 2. All enrolled members of the Oneida Tribe of Wisconsin who are twenty-one years of age or over, and who have maintained continuous residence on the Oneida Reservation of not less than thirty (30) days, immediately preceding an election, shall be qualified voters, provided they shall present themselves in person at the polls on the day of election.

Section 3. The General Tribal Council shall elect from its own members by secret ballot (a) a chairman, (b) a vice chairman, (c) a secretary, (d) a treasurer, (e) and such other officers and committees as may be deemed necessary.

Section 4. The General Tribal Council shall meet on the first Monday of January and July. Within thirty days after the ratification and approval of this constitution and bylaws, a General Tribal Council shall be called by present Tribal Council for the purpose of electing the officers named herein, and it shall transact such other business as may be necessary. The officers elected at this meeting shall serve until the July meeting, at which time their successors shall be chosen. Thereafter officials shall be chosen at the July meeting. The chairman, or twenty-five (25) percent of the qualified voters, may by written notice, call special meetings of the General Tribal Council. One-third (1/3) of the qualified voters of the tribe shall constitute a quorum at any special or regular meeting.

Section 5. There shall be an executive committee, consisting of the chairman, vice-chairman, secretary, and treasurer of the General Tribal Council, which shall perform such duties as may be authorized by that Council.

Article IV. Powers of the General Tribal Council

Section 1. Enumerated Powers. The General Tribal Council of the Oneida Tribe of Wisconsin shall exercise the following powers, subject to any limitations imposed by the statutes or the Constitution of the United States:

(a) To negotiate with the Federal, State, and local governments.
(b) To employ legal counsel, the choice of counsel and fixing of fees to be subject to the approval of the Secretary of the Interior.

(c) To veto any sale, disposition, lease, or encumbrance of tribal lands, interests in lands or other tribal assets of the tribe.

(d) To advise with the Secretary of the Interior with regard to all appropriation estimates or Federal projects for the benefit of the Oneida Tribe of Wisconsin prior to the submission of such estimates to the Bureau of the Budget and to Congress.

(e) To manage all economic affairs and enterprises of the Oneida Tribe of Wisconsin in accordance with the terms of a charter that may be issued to the tribe by the Secretary of the Interior.

(f) To promulgate and enforce ordinances which shall be subject to review by the Secretary of the Interior, governing the conduct of members of the Oneida Tribe of Wisconsin providing for the manner of making, holding, and revoking assignments of tribal land or interests therein; providing for the levying of taxes and the appropriation of available tribal funds for public purposes; providing for the licensing of non-members coming upon the reservation for purposes of hunting, fishing, trading, or other business; and for the exclusion from the territory of the tribe of persons not so licensed and establishing proper agencies for law enforcement upon the Oneida Reservation.

(g) To charter subordinate organizations for economic purposes and to delegate to such organizations, or to any subordinate boards or officials of the tribe, any of the foregoing powers, reserving the right to review any action taken by virtue of such delegated power.

(h) To adopt resolutions not inconsistent with this constitution and the attached bylaws, regulating the procedure of the Council itself and of other tribal agencies, tribal officials, or tribal organizations of the Oneida Reservation.

Section 2. Future Powers. The General Tribal Council may exercise such further powers as may in the future be delegated to the Council by the Secretary of the Interior or any other duly authorized official or agency of the State or Federal Government.

Section 3. Reserved Powers. Any rights and powers heretofore vested in the Oneida Tribe of Indians of Wisconsin but not expressly referred to in this constitution shall not be abridged by this Article, but may be exercised by the people of the Oneida Tribe of Wisconsin through the adoption of appropriate bylaws and constitutional amendments.

Section 4. Manner of Review. Any resolution or ordinance which by the terms of this constitution is subject to review by the Secretary of the Interior shall be presented to the Superintendent of the Reservation, who shall, within ten days thereafter approve or disapprove the same. If the Superintendent shall approve any ordinance or resolution, it shall thereupon become effective, but the Superintendent shall transmit a copy of the same, bearing his endorsement, to the Secretary of the Interior, who may, within 90 days from the date of enactment, rescind the said ordinance or resolution for any cause, by notifying the Tribal Council of such decision. If the Superintendent shall refuse to approve any ordinance or resolution submitted to him within ten days after its enactment, he shall advise the Council of his reasons therefor. If these reasons appear to the Council insufficient, it may, by a majority vote, refer the ordinance or resolution to the Secretary of the Interior, who may, within 90 days from the date of enactment, approve the same in writing, whereupon the said ordinance or resolution shall become effective.

Article V. Amendment

This constitution and bylaws may be amended by a majority vote of the qualified voters of the tribe voting at an election called for that purpose by the Secretary of the Interior, provided that at least thirty (30) percent of those entitled to vote shall vote in such election; but no amendment shall become effective until it shall have been approved by the Secretary of the Interior. It shall be the duty of the Secretary of the Interior to call an election on any proposed amendment upon receipt of a petition signed by one-third (1/3) of the qualified voters of the tribe.

By-laws of the Oneida Tribe of Indians of Wisconsin

Article I. Duties of Officers

Section 1. Chairman of the Council. The chairman of the Council shall preside over all meetings of the Council, shall perform the usual duties of a chairman, and exercise any authority delegated to him by the Council. He shall vote only in the case of a tie.

Section 2. Vice Chairman of the Council. The vice chairman shall assist the chairman when called upon to do so and in the absence of the chairman he shall preside. When so presiding, he shall have all the rights, privileges, and duties, as well as the responsibilities, of the Chairman.

Section 3. Secretary of the Council. The secretary of the Tribal Council shall conduct all tribal correspondence and shall keep an accurate record of all matters transacted at Council meetings. It shall be his duty to submit promptly to the superintendent of the jurisdiction and the Commissioner of Indian Affairs copies of all minutes of regular and special meetings of the Tribal Council.

Section 4. Treasurer of Council. The treasurer of the Tribal Council shall accept, receive, receipt for, preserve, and safeguard all funds in the custody of the Council, whether they be tribal funds or special funds for which the Council is acting as trustee or custodian. He shall deposit all funds in such depository as the Council shall direct and shall make and preserve a faithful record of such funds and shall report on all receipts and expenditures and the amount and nature of all funds in his possession and custody at each regular meeting of the General Tribal Council and at such other times as requested by the Council or the executive committee. He shall not pay out or otherwise disburse any funds in his possession or custody, except in accordance with a resolution duly passed by the Council. The Treasurer shall be required to give a bond satisfactory to the Council and to the Commissioner of Indian Affairs.

Section 5. Appointive Officers. The duties of all appointive boards or officers of the community shall be clearly defined by resolutions of the Council at the time of their creation or appointment. Such boards and officers shall report, from time to time as required, to the Council, and their activities and decisions shall be subject to review by the Council upon the petition of any person aggrieved.

Article II. Ratification of Constitution and Bylaws

This constitution and these bylaws when adopted by a majority vote of the voters of the Oneida Tribe of Indians of Wisconsin, voting at a special election called by the Secretary of the Interior, in which at least 30 percent of those to vote shall vote, shall be submitted to the Secretary of the Interior approval, and shall be effective from the date of such approval.

Certification of Adoption

Pursuant to an order approved by the Secretary of Interior, the attached constitution and bylaws were submitted for ratification to the members of the Oneida Indian Tribe of the Oneida Reservation and were on —— duly —— by a vote of —— for and —— against, in an election in which over 30 percent of those entitled to vote cast their ballots, in accordance with section 16 of the Indian Reorganization Act of June 18, 1934, as amended by the act of June 15, 1935....

Sources:

Campisi, Jack, and Laurence M. Hauptman, eds. *The Oneida Experience: Two Perspectives.* Syracuse: Syracuse University Press, 1988.

Shattuck, George. *The Oneida Land Claims: A Legal History.* Syracuse: Syracuse University Press, 1991.

---

9   *Constitution of the Oglala Sioux Tribe (1936)*

The Oglala Lakota inhabit a one of the largest reservations contained within US borders. Among the first Native nations to accept the Indian Reorganization Act, they were already familiar with constitutional organization, as the community had adopted its first constitution in 1916. When problems ensued, another was adopted five years later. The 1921 document, however, was not approved by the Indian agent or the Bureau of Indian Affairs because, to their minds, it vested too much power in older, more traditionally minded Lakota leaders. Consequently, a third constitution was adopted in 1928, and endured until the Oglala's adoption of the IRA in 1934. The 1936 constitution below has never been accepted by all Oglala, largely due to ongoing tensions between elected Tribal officials and unelected leaders of more traditionally inclined Lakota. This balance of governance structures continues to pose challenges for this nation and some citizens are once again calling for constitutional reform.

Preamble

We, the Oglala Sioux Tribe of the Pine Ridge Indian Reservation, in order to establish a more perfect organization, promote the general welfare, conserve and develop our lands and resources, SECURE to ourselves and our posterity the power to exercise certain rights of home rule not inconsistent with Federal laws and our treaties, and in recognition of God Almighty and His Divine Providence, do ordain and establish this constitution for the Oglala Sioux Tribe.

Article I. Territory

The jurisdiction of the Oglala Sioux Tribe of Indians shall extend to the territory within the original confines of the Pine Ridge Indian Reservation boundaries, as defined by the act of March 2, 1889, and to such other lands as may be hereafter added thereto under any law of the United States except as may be otherwise provided by law for unrestricted lands.

Article II. Membership

Section 1. The membership of the Oglala Sioux Tribe shall consist as follows:

a) All persons whose names appear on the official census roll of the Oglala Sioux Tribe of the Pine Ridge Reservation as of April 1, 1935, provided that correction may be made in the said rolls within five years from the adoption and approval of this constitution by the tribal council subject to the approval of the Secretary of Interior.

b) All children born to any member of the tribe who is a resident of the reservation at the time of the birth of said children.

Section 2. The tribal council shall propose by-laws covering future membership and the adoption of new members.

Article III. Governing Body

Section 1. The governing body of the tribe under this constitution shall be a council which shall be composed of councilmen chosen by secret ballot by qualified voters of the tribe, which council shall hereafter be known as "The Oglala Sioux Tribal Council."

Section 2. Each community of the reservation as follows, shall be entitled to representation on the tribal council according to population as hereinafter provided....

Section 3. The tribal council shall have authority to make changes in the foregoing list according to future community needs, subject to the approval of the Secretary of the Interior.

Section 4. Each recognized community shall elect representatives to the tribal council in the proportion of one representative for each 300 members, or a remainder of more than 150: Provided, that each recognized community shall be entitled to at least one representative.

Section 5. Prior to the first election of the tribal council the membership of each community shall be determined by the superintendent and a committee consisting of one delegate from each community herein designated. Thereafter the membership of the various communities shall be determined by the communities, subject to review by the tribal council.

Section 6. The officers of the tribal council shall be a president and a vice president, elected by the members of the Oglala Sioux Tribe, at large, and a secretary, a treasurer, and such other officers as may be deemed necessary, elected by the tribal council from within or outside of its own number. Officers selected from outside the membership of the council shall have no vote in the council, except that the president shall vote in case of a tie.

Section 7. The first election of the tribal council hereunder shall be called and supervised by the Secretary of the Interior, or such persons as he may appoint.

Section 8. Members of the tribal council shall be elected for a term of two years.

Section 9. Elections to the tribal council, after the first election, shall be called by the tribal council at least sixty days prior to the expiration of office of its members.

Section 10. The Oglala Sioux Tribal Council shall be the sole judge of the constitutional qualifications of its own members.

Article IV. Powers of the Council

Section 1. Enumerated powers. The Oglala Sioux Tribal Council shall exercise the following powers, subject to any limitations imposed by the statutes or the Constitution of the United States and subject further to all express restrictions upon such powers contained in this constitution and attached by-laws.

(a) To negotiate with the Federal, State, and local governments, on behalf of the tribe, and to advise and consult with the representatives of the Interior Department on all activities of the Department that may affect the Pine Ridge Reservation.

(b) To employ legal counsel for the protection and advancement of the rights of the Oglala Sioux Tribe and its members, the choice of counsel and fixing of fees to be subject to the approval of the Secretary of the Interior.

(c) To approve or veto any sale, disposition, lease, or encumbrance of tribal lands, interests in land, or other tribal assets which may be authorized or executed by the Secretary of the Interior, the Commissioner of Indian Affairs, or any other authorized official or agency of government, provided that no tribal lands shall ever be leased for a period exceeding five years, sold, or encumbered except for governmental purposes.

(d) To advise the Secretary of the Interior with regard to all appropriation estimates or Federal projects for the benefit of the Pine Ridge Reservation prior to the submission of such estimates to the Bureau of the Budget and to Congress.

(e) To make assignments of tribal land to members of the Oglala Sioux Tribe in conformity with article X of this constitution.

(f) To manage all economic affairs and enterprises of the Oglala Sioux Tribe in accordance with the terms of a charter that may be issued to the tribe by the Secretary of the Interior.

(g) To appropriate for public purposes of the tribe any available tribal council funds, and subject to review by the Secretary of the Interior, any other available tribal funds.

(h) To levy taxes upon members of the Oglala Sioux Tribe and to require the performance of community labor in lieu thereof, and to levy taxes or license fees, subject to review by the Secretary of the Interior, upon nonmembers doing business within the reservation.

(i) To exclude from the restricted lands of the Pine Ridge Reservation persons not legally entitled to reside therein, under ordinances which shall be subject to review by the Secretary of the Interior.

(j) To enact resolutions or ordinances not inconsistent with article II of this constitution concerning membership in the Oglala Sioux Tribe.

(k) To promulgate and enforce ordinances, which shall be subject to review by the Secretary of the Interior, governing the conduct of members of the Oglala Sioux Tribe, and providing for the maintenance of law and order and the administration of justice by establishing a reservation court and defining its duties and powers.

(l) To purchase, under condemnation proceedings in courts of competent jurisdiction, land or other property needed for public purposes, subject to the approval of the Secretary of the Interior.

(m) To protect and preserve the property, wildlife, and natural resources—gases, oils, and other minerals, etc., of the tribe, and to regulate the conduct of trade and the use and disposition of property upon the reservation, provided that any ordinance directly affecting non-members of the tribe shall be subject to review by the Secretary of the Interior.

(n) To cultivate native arts, crafts, and culture, to administer charity and to protect the health and general welfare of the tribe.

(o) To charter subordinate organizations for economic purposes and to regulate the activities of associations thus chartered by the tribal council, or any other associations of members of the tribe, which are indebted to the tribe.

(p) To regulate the inheritance of property, real and personal, other than allotted lands, within the territory of the Pine Ridge Reservation, subject to review by the Secretary of the Interior.

(q) To regulate the domestic relations of members of the tribe.

(r) To provide for the appointment of guardians for minors and mental incompetents by ordinance or resolution subject to review by the Secretary of the Interior.

(s) To adopt resolutions regulating the procedure of the council itself and of other tribal agencies and tribal officials of the reservation.

(t) To delegate to subordinate boards or officers or to cooperative associations which are open to all members of the tribe any of the foregoing powers, reserving the right to review any action taken by virtue of such delegated power.

Section 2. Future powers. The council of the Oglala Sioux Tribe may exercise such further powers as may in the future be delegated to the council by members of the tribe or by the Secretary of the Interior, or any other duly authorized official or agency of the State or Federal Government.

Section 3. Reserved powers. Any rights and powers heretofore vested in the Oglala Sioux Tribe, but not expressly referred to in this constitution, shall not be abridged by this article but may be exercised by the people of the Oglala Sioux Tribe through the adoption of appropriate bylaws and constitutional amendments.

Section 4. Manner of review. Any resolution or ordinance which by the terms of this constitution, is subject to review by the Secretary of the Interior, shall be presented to the superintendent of the reservation, who shall, within ten days thereafter, approve or disapprove the same.

If the superintendent shall approve any ordinance or resolution, it shall thereupon become effective, but the superintendent shall transmit a copy of the same, bearing his endorsement, to the Secretary of the Interior, who may, within 90 days from the date of enactment, rescind the said ordinance or resolution for any cause, by notifying the tribal council of such decision.

If the superintendent shall refuse to approve any ordinance or resolution submitted to him within ten days after its enactment, he shall advise the Oglala Sioux Council of his reasons therefor. If these reasons appear to the council insufficient, it may, by a majority vote, refer the ordinance or resolution to the Secretary of the Interior, who may, within 90 days from the date of its enactment approve the same in writing, whereupon the said ordinance or resolution shall become effective.

Article V. Judicial Powers

Section 1. The judicial powers of the Oglala Sioux Tribe shall be vested in a court or courts which the tribal council may ordain or establish.

Section 2. The judicial power shall extend to all cases involving only members of the Oglala Sioux Tribe, arising under the constitution and bylaws or ordinances of the tribe, and to other cases in which all parties consent to jurisdiction.

Article VI. Community Organization

Each community established under this constitution shall elect, annually, a president and such other officers as may be advisable. The president shall call and preside over councils of the community whenever necessary for the consideration of matters of local interest. The various communities may consult with representatives of the Interior Department on all matters of local interest and make recommendations thereon to the tribal council or the superintendent or Commissioner of Indian Affairs, may undertake and manage local enterprises in furtherance of the purposes set forth in the preamble to this constitution, may levy assessments upon members of the community, may expend moneys in the community treasury for the benefit of the community, may keep a roll of those members affiliated with the community, and may exercise such further powers as may be delegated to communities by the tribal council. The actions of the community councils shall not be inconsistent with the constitution and bylaws, and ordinance of the tribe.

Article VII. Elections

Section 1. All members of the tribe, 21 years or over, who have resided on the reservation for a period of one year immediately prior to any election shall have the right to vote.

Section 2. The time, place and manner of nomination and election of councilmen and any other elective officers of the council shall be determined by the tribal council by appropriate ordinances.

Article VIII. Removal of Officers

Section 1. Any member or officer of the tribal council who is convicted of a felony or any other offense involving dishonesty shall forfeit his office.

Section 2. Any officer of the council or any councilman shall be subject to recall from office under due process of law for cause. Any complaint against any officer of the council or any councilman must be in writing and sworn to by the complainant. No person is to be impeached except by a two-thirds (2/3) vote of the council after the accused has had due notice of the charges against him and an opportunity to be heard in his own defense.

Article IX. Referendum

Section 1. Upon a petition by at least one-third (1/3) of the eligible voters of the Oglala Sioux Tribe, or upon the request of a majority of the members of the tribal council, any enacted or proposed ordinance or resolution of the council shall be submitted to popular referendum, and the vote of a majority of the qualified voters voting in such a referendum shall be conclusive and binding on the tribal council.

Article X. Land

Section 1. Allotted lands. Allotted lands including heirship lands, within the Pine Ridge Reservation shall continue to be held as heretofore by their present owners. It is recognized that under existing law such lands may be inherited by the heirs of the present owner, whether or not they are members of the Oglala Sioux Tribe. Likewise it is recognized that under existing law the Secretary of the Interior may, at his discretion, remove restrictions upon such land, upon application by the Indian owner, whereupon the land will become subject to State taxes and may be mortgaged or sold. The right of the individual Indian to hold or to part with his land, as under existing law, shall not be abrogated by anything contained in this constitution, but the owner of restricted land may, with the approval of the Secretary of the Interior, voluntarily convey his land to the Oglala Sioux Tribe either in exchange for a money payment or in exchange for an assignment covering the same land or other land, as hereinafter provided

Section 2. Purchase of land by tribe. Tribal funds may be used, with the consent of the Secretary of the Interior to acquire land under the following conditions: a) Land within the Pine Ridge Reservation or adjacent to the boundaries thereof which is not now in Indian ownership may be purchased by or for the Oglala Sioux Tribe. b) Land owned by any member of the tribe who desires to leave the reservation permanently may be purchased by the tribe, under such terms as may be agreed upon.

Article XI. Amendments

This constitution and bylaws may be amended by a majority vote of the quali-fied voters of the tribe voting at an election called for the purpose by the Secretary of the Interior, provided that at least thirty (30) percent of those entitled to vote shall vote in such election; but no amendment shall become effective until it shall have been approved by the Secretary of the Interior. It shall be the duty of the Secretary of the Interior to call an election on any proposed amendment, at the request of two-thirds (2/3) of the council, or upon presentation of a petition signed by one-third (1/3) of the qualified voters, members of the tribe.

Bylaws of the Oglala Sioux Tribe of the Pine Ridge Reservation of South Dakota

Article I. Duties of Officers

Section 1. It shall be the duty of the president to preside over all meetings of the Oglala Sioux Tribal Council and to carry out all orders of the council, unless prevented by just causes. All members of the council, within their re-spective districts, and all subordinate officers shall assist the president in all proper ways to carry out the orders of the council.

Section 2. The vice president shall perform the duties and execute the powers of the president in the absence of the president and shall assume the presidency in the event of a vacancy in the office.

Section 3. The council secretary shall keep a full report of all proceedings of each regular and special meeting of the tribal council and shall perform such other duties of like nature as the council shall from time to time by resolution provide, and shall transmit copies of the minutes of each meeting to the president of the council, to the superintendent of the reservation, to the Commissioner of Indian Affairs, and to all recognized communities of the reservation.

Section 4. The council treasurer shall be the custodian of all moneys which come under the jurisdiction or control of the Oglala Sioux Tribal Council. He shall pay out money in accordance with the orders and resolutions of the council. He shall keep accounts of all receipts and disbursements and shall make written reports of same to the tribal council at each regular and special meeting. He shall be bonded in such an amount as the council by resolution shall provide, and such bond to be approved by the Commissioner of Indian Affairs. The books of the council treasurer shall be subject to inspection or audit by the direction of the council or the Commissioner of Indian Affairs.

Section 5. There shall be an executive committee, which shall consist of the president, the secretary, and treasurer of the council, the superintendent of the agency, and a fifth member selected by the council. This committee shall act on behalf of the council at such times as the council is not in session and shall have charge of all routine matters which shall arise during such recess, including the administration of the land provisions of this constitution, and such other matters as may be delegated to it by the council. The committee shall make a report at each regular and special session of the council.

Section 6. The subordinate officers of the Oglala Sioux Tribal Council shall perform such duties as the council may by resolution from time to time provide.

Section 7. It shall be the duty of the tribal council and each member thereof to promote the general welfare of the Sioux of this reservation and to carry out the provisions and purposes of this constitution and by-laws.

Article II. Qualifications of Officers

Section 1. Any person elected as councilman must be a member of the Oglala Sioux Tribe and must be at least 25 years of age at the time of the election.

Section 2. No member of the council shall vote in any matter in which he may have an interest by reason of employment in the Federal service or by any private organization.

Article III. Oaths of Office

Section 1. Each member of the tribal council and each officer elected or appointed hereunder, shall take an oath of office prior to assuming the duties thereof; by which oath he shall pledge himself to support and defend the Constitution of the United States and this constitution and bylaws. (Oath) I, _, do solemnly swear that I will support and defend the Constitution of the United States against all enemies; carry out faithfully and impartially the duties of my office to the best of my ability; promote and protect the best interests of my tribe, the Oglala Sioux, in accordance with this constitution and by-laws.

Article IV. Salaries

Section 1. The salaries of the councilmen or other officers of the Oglala Sioux Tribe may be paid out of available funds of the tribe in accordance with ordinances duly enacted, provided that no council shall enact any ordinance increasing the salaries of councilmen during the existing term of office.

Section 2. No compensation shall be paid to any councilman, president, vice president, secretary, treasurer, tribal counsel, or any officer out of the tribal funds under the control of the Federal Government, except upon a resolution stating the amount of compensation and the nature of services approved by the Secretary of the Interior.

Article V. Meetings and Procedure

Section 1. Regular meetings of the council shall be four in each year, to be held during January, April, July, and October, on such days of such months as the council by resolution shall provide.

Section 2. Two-thirds (2/3) of the duly elected members must be present to constitute a quorum.

Section 3. Special meetings may be called by request of the president, or of a majority of the councilmen, in writing, and when so called, two-thirds (2/3) of said councilmen must be present to constitute a quorum, and the council shall have the power to transact business as in regular meetings.

Section 4. The order of business in any regular or special meeting of the council shall be as follows....

Article VI. National Sioux Council

Section 1. The tribal council may appoint delegates to represent the Sioux Tribe in national councils.

Article VII. Adoption of Constitution and Bylaws

Section 1. This constitution and the attached bylaws when approved by a majority of the adult voters of the Oglala Sioux Tribe voting in a special election called by the Secretary of the Interior in which at least thirty (30) percent of the eligible voters vote, shall be submitted to the Secretary of the Interior for approval and shall be effective from the date of such approval.

Certificate of Adoption

Pursuant to an order, approved December 11, 1935, by the Secretary of the Interior, the attached constitution and bylaws was submitted for ratification to the members of the Oglala Sioux Tribe of Indians of the Pine Ridge Reservation and was on December 14, 1935, duly approved by a vote of 1,348 for, and 1,041 against, in an election in which over 30 percent of those entitled to vote cast their ballots, in accordance with section 16 of the Indian Reorganization Act of June 18, 1934.

William Fire Thunder, Chairman of Election Board....

I, Harold L. Ickes, the Secretary of the Interior of the United States of America, by virtue of the authority granted me by the act of June 18, 1934, as amended, do hereby approve the attached constitution and by-laws of the Oglala Sioux Tribe of the Pine Ridge Reservation.

All rules and regulations heretofore promulgated by the Interior Department or by the Office of Indian Affairs, so far as they may be incompatible with any of the provisions of the said constitution and bylaws are hereby declared inapplicable to these Indians.

All officers and employees of the Interior Department are ordered to abide by the provisions of the said constitution and bylaws.

Approval recommended January 7, 1936. The Oglala Sioux Tribe is an unincorporated tribe and does not have a charter.

Sources:

Biolsi, Thomas. *Organizing the Lakota: The Political Economy of the New Deal on the Pine Ridge and Rosebud Reservations*. Tucson: University of Arizona Press, 1992.

Clow, Richmond. "The Indian Reorganization Act and the Loss of Tribal Sovereignty: Constitutions on the Rosebud and Pine Ridge Reservations." *Great Plains Quarterly* 7 (Spring 1982): 125–134.

Glover, John Henry. *Tribal Sovereigns of South Dakota: A Description of Contemporary Sioux Governments*. Rapid City, SD: Chiesman Foundation for Democracy, Inc., 2005.

---

10   *Testimony of Alonzo Hamblet (Tsimshian), Chair, Alaskan Native Brotherhood (1936)*

Alaska Natives had very little contact with non-Indians before or even after Russia "ceded" Alaska to the United States in 1867, an action, it should be noted, that Alaskan Natives protested. In fact, from 1741 to 1867, the Native communities retained their political independence, never signed any treaty with the Russians, and never sold land.

After the United States entered the picture, Alaskan Natives continued to live without any formal political arrangement with the federal government, but their political and legal status was comparable to that of Native peoples in the lower 48 states. The Indian Naturalization Act of 1924 expressly included the Eskimo, Aleut, and Indians of the Alaska territory. The Indian Reorganization Act (IRA) of 1934 partially included Alaskan Natives among its beneficiaries, declaring that "for the purposes of this Act, Eskimos and other aboriginal peoples of Alaska shall be considered Indians." An amendment to the IRA in 1936 extended all the law's original provisions to Alaskan Natives and many Indigenous groups organized politically under the IRA.

The Alaska Native Brotherhood was founded in 1912 to advocate for equality and human rights for all Alaskan natives. It is the oldest native interest group in the state. A comparable body, the Alaska Native Sisterhood was established in 1923 with similar goals for native women. The following statement expresses the concerns of the brotherhood with regards to their members' subsistence livelihood. The issues Mr. Hamblet raises here are still of concern today, as over-fishing and habitat destruction continue to threaten salmon populations upon which the Native peoples depend for physical and spiritual sustenance.

Gentlemen: When the First Lady of the Land was told about the pitiful outlook for the future of the natives of Alaska, she was deeply sympathetic and made careful inquiries into the question of the depletion of the salmon. The statements were not exaggerated and we are prepared to prove beyond a shadow of a doubt that red-salmon streams once teeming with shining sockeyes are now so nearly fished out that it does not pay to fish them with seine boats.

If the committee will go to these streams during the spawning season they will see very few sockeyes. And if the traps are not abolished altogether not only the sockeyes but all other salmon will be depleted to a mere fraction of the amount caught in former years.

This happened in Puget Sound so that the voters were compelled to vote the traps out to conserve the salmon supply and prevent the total extermination of every kind of salmon.

Six years ago, when Commissioner Henry O'Malley was Commissioner of Fisheries for Alaska, he made the statement to Congress: "We are doing everything to conserve the salmon; we have got to preserve them because otherwise they would be destroyed." But if it continues with these traps there, you are going to destroy the whole salmon industry."

The result of that report of Mr. O'Malley's was the passage of the White bill authorizing the Bureau of Fisheries to enforce more stringent regulations, to save the salmon from total depletion.

Evidently the law is not being enforced for the big fish traps are allowed to catch all the salmon possible and the seine boats are catching less and less for the traps get practically all the salmon.

When the great canneries of Puget Sound years ago saw that the sockeyes were being wiped out they sold their cannery stock to eastern people who knew nothing whatsoever about salmon, and these poor deluded people are still holding the bag.

When the sockeye salmon supply failed, Blaine, a city about the size of Ketchikan became a ghost town as far as salmon was concerned.

It is because we know what happened on Puget Sound and British Columbia that we are fighting for the total abolishment of fish traps in Alaska. We want the remedy applied before the salmon have entirely disappeared. We are asking for no new untried experiment for we have the concrete examples of Puget Sound and British Columbia.

British Columbia employees about three times the number of people to can 1 million cases of salmon that the Alaskan canneries do and yet British Columbia prospers. The salmon supply is building up and they are able to sell their product for the same price as the Alaska packs and still make a satisfactory profit.

So the abolishment of the fish traps will give employment to all in Alaska and would take the residents off the relief role.

On Puget Sound the seiners made a living wage last summer, and though there were all the seine boats in Shilshole Bay that had room to make a set, about 100 boats, there was such a large escapement that the spillway at the government ship dock at Ballard was too small to allow the salmon to go up to Lake Washington and Lake Sammamish to spawn. The attendants were compelled to open the big ship locks to allow the salmon to go to the spawning grounds.

It was the biggest salmon run in 30 years. A positive proof of what would happen here if the traps are abolished and enough salmon allowed to escape to replenish and again build up the streams that are now fished out.

Loring once had a population of 300, now abandoned because the Naha Creek is fished-out.

Another disputed question is, does the king salmon live on herring? All trollers are agreed that the king salmon does live on herring, and when the herring are fished out the king salmon disappears.

About 11 years ago Meyers Chuck was fished out by a big herring seiner and the king salmon disappeared. Three years ago the same man again started to clean out the herring but was ordered by the *Alert* to quit fishing out the herring, and now this year Meyers Chuck has more king salmon than any other creek in this district.

At this time in former years the sockeye or red salmon were running in large numbers in the dozen streams in the vicinity of Ketchikan, but if you'll go there now you find no fish. The streams are entirely depleted.

These streams can be protected and gradually restored to their former great production of red salmon, but it will have to mean a real enforcement of the rules and regulations by the Bureau of Fisheries.

The great cannery and trap corporations state that the fishing industry never has been in such good shape as it is at present, and point to the enormous packs of 6,000,000 cases in 1934 and other years.

Replying to that we will say that the trap owners have built larger and better traps that catch practically every salmon now, and that there are very few streams now that have any escapement of salmon for propagation at all. The streams near Ketchikan are among that number.

In the year 1927 there were 799 traps that caught 23,000,000 fish; in 1934 there were 459 traps that caught over 60,000,000 fish, according to the report of the Department of Commerce for the year 1934.

The general public and the seine fishermen have been led to believe that there has been a real reduction in trap gear, when the truth is that only the dummy traps that caught no fish have been abandoned, and the good traps have been improved and enlarged to such an extent that with one-half the number of traps—about 400 traps—twice the number of fish are caught as were caught in former years with 800 traps.

The Natives of Alaska are alarmed because they know the fish and they know that it will only be a short time when the waters of Alaska will be so depleted of salmon that they can no longer be able to make even a bare living.

And so we humbly pray and implore the Federal Government to...conserve the food salmon supply that means life and happiness to us, so that there will be salmon in Alaska so long as the Stars and Stripes wave over its waters.

The Alaskan Native Brotherhood, Camp 14, Ketchikan, Alaska

Sources:

Drucker, Philip. "The Native Brotherhoods: Modern Intertribal Organizations on the Northwest Coast." *Bureau of American Ethnology.* Bulletin 168. Washington, DC: Smithsonian Institution, 1958.

US Senate. Hearings Before a Subcommittee of the Committee on Indian Affairs. Survey of Conditions of the Indians in the United States. 74th Cong., 2nd Sess. Pt. 35. Metlakahtla Indians, Alaska. S. Res. 79 and 308. Washington, DC: Government Printing Office, 1939, 18422–18442.

11

Jacob C. Morgan (Navajo) on the Need for a Shiprock Agency Superintendent (1937)

After the end of their imprisonment in 1868 at Fort Sumner, New Mexico, the Navajo people were compelled to make substantial changes to their economic, cultural, and political systems. This included the gradual embrace of pastoralism that, after a time, became central to their economy and culture. In stark contrast to virtually every other Native people, their population and land base grew. Thus, by the early 1930s, the Navajo Nation was relatively well positioned and poised to reconsider means of diplomatic engagement and relations with other polities.

During that time, one of their leading political figures, Jacob Morgan, directly challenged the major political and cultural changes instigated by the federal government on behalf of his people. Morgan would later become chairman of the Navajo Tribal Council and his statements below give a sense of the contentious issues the Navajo people confronted—namely, the demand for separate federal agents to deal with Navajos living near Shiprock, New Mexico, and the urgent need to halt the disastrous federal program of forced livestock reduction that caused immense hardship for Navajo citizens. The repercussions of that disastrous and, arguably, vindictive governmental livestock policy are felt today as the Navajo are still fighting to regain physical, emotional, and economic security.

———

Morgan's Introductory Remarks

I do not believe it necessary to go into any detail here in presenting the request of the Navajo people of the northern jurisdiction, which is as follows: present condition of the Navajo people warrants an immediate reestablishment of a separate agent at Shiprock on the New Mexico side of the line. The change made in 1933 was not wanted by our people. Our people were disappointed in many ways when the superintendent was let out at Shiprock. This change has brought back, to a certain extent, the lawless days of the past. The idea of one central agency has never been approved by the Navajos, but the idea was forced upon them through and by a small hand-picked group (Council members) without proper consideration. We consider the plan above mentioned a failure. In former years, under separate agents, progress of every nature was made, and our people were satisfied.

We want reestablishment of the superintendent's office, a man with full and equal power and authority to help to check on gambling, drinking, and other evils now increasing on the reservation. Our people, especially the younger boys and girls, need protection; therefore we urge for a superintendent. I understand a few of the chapters [local governing units] have written Senator Thomas upon this very thing. I sincerely hope your honorable committee will consider this very important matter which my people, the Navajos, request of you....

Navajo Opposition to Sheep Reduction

In 1933 a wide reduction of sheep and goats was inaugurated. Of all resources, our people depend on for making a living for themselves and the only source of their income is their herds. At first some of the Navajo leaders thought Mr. [John] Collier's program might help out, so they rather favored it, but they soon found that that program was not safe; that is when they found a great many people became poor and hungry. According to an expert's figures, in 1931 the tribe as a whole owned 1,370,554 sheep and goats, but in the 1935 dipping it was found there were left 927,683 sheep and goats. The Navajo people know more about making proper reduction of their herds than any expert who came from the city of New York or other cities, for every year reductions are made of lambs, old sheep (ewes), and wethers; and not only this, but that during the year the family consumes (when they had plenty) anywhere from 40 to 60 sheep; consequently a family owning less than a hundred would have very little left at the end of each year. Of course, we understand the supposed purpose for the sheep reduction. It is said to save the grass of the range and to keep sheep from cutting up the soil with their hoofs to make ditches which cause erosion. We believe the Navajo knows more about their tribal matters and needs than the Soil Conservation people think they do, and we know that water development on all parts of the reservation is not only important but is absolutely necessary. Let not the minds of the people be confused on these matters, but that careful consideration might be given to them.

Navajo Tribal Council

The Navajo people, in general, are very much disappointed in the manner the Indian Bureau has interrupted the progress our people have made by a gradual climb in the past 70 years through all kinds and conditions of time until they arrived at the time when they really became happy and independent because of the fact that by their hand and hard struggles they obtained what they now have. Including these and other things, the Commissioner of Indian Affairs has torn down [much of the progress made] in a short period of 36 months.

In 1923 the Navajo people, by a general approval, a tribal council was organized with 12 delegates and 12 alternate delegates, all elected by the people in the six jurisdictions that were also established. The people were just getting used to every detail of the tribal government when Commissioner Collier came into office, and he immediately disapproved of and therefore abolished the six jurisdictions, with extreme regret to our people. Now the tribal council is about to be disorganized, because Mr. Collier said it has largely gone by default. We believe it important to continue the old order of the council, because it was with the understanding the council was to be the mouthpiece of the tribe in dealing with government officials on all tribal matters. We do not want any substitution for the council.

Agents or Superintendents

Up to 1933–34 we had superintendents on our reservation over six jurisdictions. The Navajo people were entirely in accord and satisfied with the old order of reservation affairs, with only needed employees under a competent superintendent. Our people knew what they were doing then. Now the Soil Conservation people and many others with titles as an "expert" or the "best brains" are actually running the reservation, disregarding all the tribal rights. When there were Superintendents—men who knew and sympathized with the Navajo people, who wanted schools and education—under such men in the past our people were satisfied with progress made by their boys and girls. Now, what do we have to guide and educate our people? Nothing. But the persons who had been playing second fiddle in their positions of stockman or Extension Service are now being elevated to positions as supervisors, whether they know anything about school work or not.

In this respect the Indian people again are much disappointed in the Bureau's program. Some of our boarding schools have been closed, and one of these school plants has run down, and it is a shame to see such a waste. There are over 40 day schools being built, costing to the taxpayers of the country from seventeen to sixty-five thousand dollars each. We do not object to any kind of education, but not the kind that is being offered to us now. We would like to see and will appreciate improvements of our boarding schools so that our boys and girls can, at least, get a high-school training. We know that Mr. Collier said at the beginning he would save about $6,000,000 a year for the Government by closing some of the schools; of course, we realize that saving is a good thing, but we deem it injustice to try to save money appropriated for education. With these things in view we believe one agent for forty-five or more thousand people is not going to lead our people anywhere, especially with the kind of man now holding that position. We believe he should be transferred, and in his place a man who is an educator be placed. We must have good schools, as well as good hospitals, under competent superintendents. So, for the good of the Navajo people, Mr. Fryer should be transferred.

Navajos Object to Land Management

Land management is a communistic plan, and for that reason we do not want to adopt it. It means more reduction of all animals we now have left; it means to us more unrest and confusion, more bitter suffering and humiliation, etc. We do not understand just why Mr. Collier, as a guardian of the Indians, should, without the consent or approval of the tribal council, have to allow the Soil Conservation people to draft plans for establishing more experiments on the reservation of 19 districts, with 19 supervisors over them. The matter of fact, as stated before, 3 years ago we had 6 useful plans of six jurisdictions and six superintendents. During the time we had this plan we really had gone forward in every line of work, but now, in the past 3 years, we have made no headway or improvements, but we have gone backward in bewilderment. For the reasons stated above, we object to this land management plan, with too many bosses. The minds of the people are confused bad enough now, so why make it worse? The Navajo people cannot afford to stand still, for they must move along without any interruption with too many plans by the "experts." Now, which is cheaper to the Government, 6 jurisdictions, with 6 superintendents, who, we suppose, received as their pay, 6 of them, at $300 per month, or $1800, or $21,600 per year; or 18 supervisors, at $300 per month, or $64,800 per year, as against the above amount? We think this new move of Mr. Collier is unprofitable to our Indian people.

Fruitland Irrigation Project

In this matter we regret to state that in all the years of understanding between our Indians and the Government there has never been a shameful treatment committed upon our people by any agent who has worked among us as we have received from the present agent at Window Rock. He has broken faith with our people by breaking promises made to our people in the Fruitland district concerning their lands. In the past 3 years our people were promised by the people representing the government that 20-acre plots of land were to be assigned to the head of the family under a new irrigation canal west of Farmington,N. Mex. Mr. A. L. Wathen, director of irrigation, Indian Service, in an article of July 15 1934, appearing in the *Indians at Work*, stated at follows: "All of the land is unallotted Navajo Reservation land. It is proposed that the entire area will be subdivided into small irrigable tracts of 20 acres each, which will be assigned to individual Indians and their families."

The new agent at Window Rock, who has been elevated from a ranch hand to a high position over the Navajo Tribe, has shown his iron fist, which means, in other words, his high dictatorial authority, in which he issued an order that the 20 acres of land promised to the Indians will not be given to them, but that if they wanted the land they could have 10 acres instead of 20 acres; that if they wanted 10 acres they can get rid of all their sheep. Our treaty of 1868 does not so provide. What we ask for is our right to our land. We see no reason why our people should be punished for what belongs to them. We ask that all promises made to us be fulfilled by the government; that is, we want the 20 acres as promised.

Navajo Boundary Bill

On this subject we realize it to be a big problem, but it must be met in some satisfactory manner. We believe that in order for the Navajo people to be satisfied with the result of the investigation they must have a voice in it. What I personally believe is that justice be given to our people. A just settlement must be made. I do hope that enough land that will prove adequate for the ever increasing tribe be considered without hurting the other party—the sheepmen—if in the future our Navajo people must be satisfied with the land for their future use.

I sincerely hope that the law of New Mexico, our native State, will allow all our young men and women, as fast as they are educated, full citizenship, so that they may in time come to help carry the burden of the State government.

I hope these incomplete points may help the committee to know what the Indians are thinking about.

Sincerely yours, J.C. Morgan

Sources:

Parman, Donald L. "J.C. Morgan: Navajo Apostle of Assimilation." *Prologue: The Journal of the National Archives* (Summer 1972): 4:83–98.

US Senate. "Navajo Boundary and Pueblos in New Mexico." Survey of Conditions of the Indians in the U.S. Hearings Before a Subcommittee of the Committee on Indian Affairs. 75th Cong., 1st Sess. Pt. 34. Washington: Government Printing Office, 1937, 18010–18013.

12   *Navajo Constitution,*
Proposed (1937)

Although the Navajo people narrowly rejected adoption of the provisions of the Indian Reorganization Act, they nonetheless decided to organize a constitutional committee of 250 leading Diné citizens tasked with the creation of an organic charter. Of that number, 70 were later tapped in 1937 to draft the following constitution. It was circulated but never approved by either the Secretary of the Interior or the Navajo people via referendum, out of fear that it would cause divisiveness within the nation. To this day, the Navajo Nation remains the largest Indigenous nation operating without a formal written constitution.

Proposed Constitution of the Navajo Tribe

In order to establish a tribal government and to promote the spiritual, social, and economic welfare of the Navajo people, this Navajo Constitution is proclaimed for the Navajo people.

Article I

Section 1. The Constitution of the United States of America with amendments thereto, and all Acts of Congress applicable to the Navajo affairs, including the treaty of 1868 between the Government and the Navajos, shall be the laws of the Navajo Tribe.

Article II

Section 1. Every Navajo who resides on the Navajo Reservation or individual trust allotment and is enrolled on the tribal census, and every individual who is at least one-quarter degree of Navajo blood and enrolled on the tribal census, shall be considered a member of the Navajo Tribe.
Section 2. No person shall be eligible for adoption into the Navajo Tribe unless he or she meets any of the qualifications provided for in the preceding section.

Article III

Section 1. Not inconsistent with any authority of the Federal Government or with any State laws, the jurisdiction of the Navajo Tribe and of the Navajo Council shall extend to the entire area within the outside boundaries of the existing reservation and to all trust allotments without such boundaries and to any area that may be added to the reservation by any Act of Congress.

Article IV

Section 1. The governing body of the Navajo Tribe shall be the Navajo Council.

Section 2. The Navajo Council shall consist of twenty delegates at large and fifty-four delegates, apportioned among the several land management districts as follows.... Provided, that the Navajo Council may change its membership to correspond with any increase that may occur in the population of any districts not exceeding one delegate for every six hundred Navajos.

Section 3. A delegate shall hold office for a term of six years which shall begin at noon on the first day of August of the year of his election: Provided, that terms of office of the first members of the Navajo Council shall be determined by the Constitution Assembly.

Section 4. No person shall be eligible for the office of a delegate unless he is a member of the Navajo Tribe, has attained the age of thirty years or over not exceeding seventy years, has resided upon the reservation or upon restricted allotment for a period of five years and in the elective precinct for a period of one year next preceding the election.

Section 5. No member of the Navajo Tribe holding any permanent position or employment under the authority of the United States, or of any State, shall be a member of the Navajo Council.

Section 6. No member of the Navajo Tribe holding membership in any organization or holding any position or employment for the purpose of influencing the Navajo Council shall be a member of the Navajo Council.

Section 7. If from any cause a vacancy should occur in the office of any delegate, the Navajo Council, or its authorized agency, shall order an election of a successor for the unexpired term of office.

Article V

Section 1. There shall be one president of the Navajo Tribe, and he shall hold office for only a term of six years, provided that no person shall serve as president for more than two terms.

Section 2. It shall be the duty of the president to take part in the sessions of the Navajo Council, to make recommendations to the Navajo Council, to advise and assist the government on any action or policy adopted by the Navajo Council, and to exercise any authority that may be vested in him by the Navajo Council.

Section 3. There shall be one vice president of the Navajo Tribe, and he shall hold office for only a term of six years, provided that no person shall serve as vice president for more than two terms.

Section 4. It shall be the duty of the vice president to preside over the sessions of the Navajo Council, and to exercise any authority that may be vested in him by the Navajo Council.

Section 5. No person shall be eligible for president or vice president of the Navajo Tribe unless he is a member of the tribe, has attained the age of 35 years or over, not exceeding 65 years, has resided upon the Navajo reservation for a period of five years next preceding the election.

Section 6. No person holding any position or employment under the authority of the United States, or of any state, shall be president, or vice president, of the Navajo Tribe.

Section 7. If from any cause a vacancy should occur in the office of the president, the vice president shall become president of the Navajo Tribe for the unexpired portion of the term of office.

Section 8. If from any cause a vacancy should occur in the office of the vice president, the Navajo Council shall appoint a successor for the unexpired portion of the term of office.

Article VI

Section 1. The election of president, vice president of the Navajo Tribe, and delegates of the Navajo Council, shall be governed by the By-laws of the Navajo Council.

Section 2. Any member of the Navajo Tribe, who has attained the age of 21 years or over and has resided on the Navajo Reservation or individual trust allotment for at least one year, shall have the right to vote in any election, except insane persons, idiots, persons under legal guardianship, and persons convicted of a felony and have not been restored to political rights.

Article VII

Section 1. Any delegate, who is accused of willfully misrepresenting or misinterpreting any measure or policy of the Navajo Council or accused of improper conduct or gross neglect of duty, shall be served with written charges against him at least 30 days before the date of the hearing set by the Navajo Council, and at the hearing, which shall be fair and complete, if the charges are proven, the accused may be expelled from the Council by the affirmative vote of two-thirds of the members of the Navajo Council.

Article VIII

Section 1. It shall be the permanent policy of the Navajo Council to preserve and promote the Navajo clan system of family and social organizations, to protect and conserve tribal property, natural resources, and wildlife of the Navajo Tribe; to cultivate Indian arts, crafts, and the best traditions and culture, to assist in administering charity; to protect and promote health, security, human and civil rights, and general welfare of the Navajo Tribe and members thereof.

Article IX

Section 1. The Navajo Council shall have the following powers:

a) To approve or veto any sale, disposition, lease, or encumbrance of tribal lands and tribal assets which may be authorized or executed by the Secretary of the Interior, the Commissioner of Indian Affairs, or any other agency of the government.

b) To improve or veto permits that may be granted for the establishment of religious missions on the reservation.

Section 2. The Navajo Council, in cooperation with the government, subject to the approval of the Secretary of the Interior, shall have the following powers:

a) To acquire by purchase, or otherwise, any property or property right of any member of the tribe and others on or off the Navajo Reservation.
b) To acquire by right of eminent domain any property or property right of any member of the tribe and others within the Navajo Reservation.
c) To cooperate with the government in the enforcement of existing grazing regulations as promulgated by the Secretary of the Interior.
d) To cooperate with the government in the enforcement of hunting, fishing, and wildlife regulations as promulgated by the Secretary of the Interior.
e) To regulate and control trading posts and trading practices on the reservation; to regulate, assess, and collect license fees for the privilege of selling, buying, exchanging, and trading merchandise and other articles of commerce on the reservation.
f) To employ legal counsel for the protection and advancement of the rights of the Navajo Tribe and members thereof.
g) To levy dues, fees, and taxes on members of the tribe and upon any property or property right of members of the tribe, within the reservation and other areas under the jurisdiction of the Navajo Council.
h) To provide and administer a revolving fund, from tribal funds and other sources, for the promotion of better housing facilities for the families of any members of the tribe.
i) To provide and maintain funds, from tribal and other funds or property, for the education and support of gifted Navajo boys and girls in universities, colleges, and other educational institutions.
j) To establish and maintain tribal saw mills, flour mills, and other tribal business enterprises, and to provide the necessary funds for these purposes.
k) To negotiate with the Federal, State, and local governments on behalf of the Navajo Tribe, and to advise and consult with the representatives of the departments of the government of the United States on all matters affecting the affairs of the Navajo Tribe.
l) To protect and control all prehistoric, archaeological, and scenic sites on the reservation not under the control of the National Park Service.
m) To adopt, promulgate, and enforce ordinances governing the conduct of members of the Navajo Tribe, and to provide for the maintenance of law and order and the administration of justice, and to establish Indian courts and to define their powers and duties.
n) To regulate the domestic relations of members of the Navajo Tribe not otherwise provided for under federal laws or under the laws of the states of Arizona, New Mexico, and Utah.

o) To regulate the inheritance of real and personal property, other than allotted lands, within the reservation and other areas under its jurisdiction.

p) To provide for the care and guardianship of orphans, incompetents, and minor members of the Navajo Tribe, and for this purpose to recommend the use and administration of tribal and other funds or property.

q) To create, and to provide for maintenance and administration of tribal funds from any source not inconsistent with the laws of the United States or rules and regulations of any department of the federal government.

r) To create, and to delegate any of the foregoing powers, to committees, commissions, boards, or cooperative associations, always reserving the right to review any action taken by virtue of any delegated power.

s) To provide for the compensation of the president, vice president, delegates of the Navajo Council, and other officials of the Council or tribe, for their services, and to provide for their traveling expenses when on official duty.

t) To adopt measures, resolutions, or ordinances in exercising any of the foregoing powers.

Section 3. Any measures or resolution or ordinance adopted by the Navajo Council shall take effect as soon as approved by the Secretary of the Interior.

Article X

Section 1. Any restricted allotment of land heretofore made to any member of the tribe on or off the Navajo Reservation shall remain in the individual ownership of the allottees unless sold or otherwise disposed of by the allottees to the tribe.

Section 2. The tribe shall have the first preference right, and any individual member of the tribe shall have the second preference right, to lease any restricted allotment of land for grazing or other purposes at a reasonable rate of annual compensation to the allottees.

Section 3. After the tribe and any member thereof have waived their preference rights, any restricted allotment of land may be leased by the allottees to anyone of any organization or any lawful purpose under the supervision of the Navajo Council.

Sources:

Iverson, Peter. *Diné: A History of the Navajos*. Albuquerque: University of New Mexico Press, 2002.

US Senate. Hearings Before a Subcommittee of the Committee on Indian Affairs. Survey of Conditions of the Indians in the United States. 76th Cong. 1st Sess. Washington, DC: Government Printing Office, 1940, 20960–20963.

David E. Wilkins. The Navajo Political Experience, 4th ed. Lanham, MD: Rowman & Littlefield, 2013.

13   *Senate Report on the*
                                        Wheeler-Howard Act (1939)

The Indian Reorganization Act, popularly known as the Wheeler-Howard Act, within its first five years attracted powerful and persistent opponents—including some Native leaders—who were intent on seeing the law repealed or at least substantially curtailed. Some leaders opposed it because they believed it had not gone far enough in freeing their nations from federal administrative control. Some federal lawmakers opposed it because they felt it had granted too much authority to Native governments and they feared it was resuscitating Tribal nationhood by encouraging Natives to rekindle their interest in culture, tradition, and religion.

The following report, prepared by Senator Dennis Chavez (NM) of the Committee on Indian Affairs, contains commentary describing the views of those in the federal government who held the law in great disdain. Resistance to the act continues to the present day, and although it has been amended several times, it has never been overturned. It remains one of the most important federal laws ever enacted related to Indian Country in that it provided a basis needed for the resurgence of Indigenous political, economic, and cultural sovereignty.

The Committee on Indian Affairs, to whom was referred the bill (S. 2103) providing for the repeal of the so-called Wheeler-Howard Act as amended by the act of June 15, 1935, having had the same under consideration, report thereon with the recommendation that it do pass with the following amendments: strike out all after the enacting clause and insert the following:

That section 13 of the act entitled "An Act to conserve and develop Indian lands and resources; to extend to Indians the right to form business and other organizations; to establish a credit system for Indians; to grant certain rights of home rule to Indians; to provide for vocational education for Indians; and for other purposes," approved June 18, 1934, as amended, is amended by adding at the end thereof following new paragraph:

"None of the provisions of this Act shall apply to 1) any Indian tribe on the Standing Rock Reservation located in the States of North and South Dakota; 2) the Pine Ridge Sioux Tribe of Indians of the State of South Dakota; 3) the Cheyenne River Sioux Tribe of Indians of the State of South Dakota; 4) the Yankton Sioux Tribe of Indians, of the Rosebud Agency of the State of South Dakota; 5) any Indian on any reservation or any Indian tribal group, located in the State of Nevada; 6) the Eastern Band of Cherokee Indians located in the State of North Carolina; 7) any Indian tribe, band, or group, located in the State of California; 8) any Indian or Indian tribe on the Colorado River Indian Reservation of the State of Arizona; or 9) the Navajo tribe located in the State of New Mexico."

Amend the title so as to read:

A bill to exempt certain Indians and Indian tribes from the provisions of the act of June 18, 1934, as amended.

Since the previous session of the Congress your committee have held many and extensive hearings on bills to amend the so-called Wheeler-Howard Act providing for the exclusion of certain Indians from certain provisions of said act, and on bills to repeal the entire act. During the past three years witnesses from various tribes and reservations have appeared before your committee and produced oral testimony, and statements and petitions have been submitted from tribes, groups, and individual Indians in support of said bills, which evidence has brought to the attention of your committee certain facts dealing with the legal aspects and attempted administration of said act. Evidence through these sources and information obtained by visiting various Indian reservations and communities throughout the United States, by a subcommittee of your committee making a survey of conditions among the Indians of the United States, have disclosed that certain general conditions prevail on all reservations and localities.

A summary of the evidence in various forms brought to the attention of your committee seems to reveal the following:

1. Four campaigns have been staged on the reservations by the Bureau of Indian Affairs, relative to the said act, viz.: a) campaign to secure Indian approval of the pending bill in 1934; b) campaign to secure Indian acceptance of the act itself, in elections held for that purpose; c) campaign to secure Indian acceptance of a constitution in elections held for that purpose; d) campaign to secure Indian acceptance of a charter in the elections held in those places where both the act and the constitution had been accepted.

2. Witnesses supporting the bills for repeal of the act were unanimous in their statements that unjustifiable amounts of federal appropriation for the Indian Bureau were used to conduct these four campaigns; that Indians were high pressured into accepting the act and adopting the constitutions and charters under authority of the act; that all local agency officials and Indians employed on Work Relief projects were ordered to campaign actively for the act and that, under threat of losing their positions, they did so campaign; that officials of the Washington office of the Indian Bureau and Indians from other reservations were brought into local areas to campaign and that Indians both from outside and within the local areas were paid a salary and traveling expenses for campaigning; that the Civil Service Commission has held that it cannot take action against Bureau employees who campaigned in these various elections because of authority conferred upon the secretary of the interior under the so-called Wheeler Act; that meetings were held with the Indians and they were promised practically unlimited credit to borrow money for industrial and agricultural purposes, for home, education, and other purposes; that Indians were promised self-government and lands which were to be purchased by the United States government;

that the elections had not been carried out by secret ballot as provided for in the act; and that in all the campaigns and the conduct of the elections, the press, the radio, the franking privilege of the Indian Bureau, government cars, gas and oil, publications, and other government facilities were freely used.

3. That the various campaigns conducted by Indian Bureau officials, local agency officials, and irresponsible agents of the Bureau, made promises that could not be kept, which have tended to stir up more ill feeling, factional disputes, and family troubles among the Indians than has ever existed at any previous time.

4. That those Indians who have refused to accept the act or have opposed the act, the program of the Bureau or any Indians who favored the act have been discriminated against in the distribution of work relief, rations, clothing, loans, and anything else which the local agency has jurisdiction to disburse or handle; and that some Indians lost their jobs because of such opposition.

5. That Indians opposing the act had been and are being threatened, coerced, and intimidated by either the Bureau employees or the local Indian officers will operate under the Wheeler-Howard Act, or a combination of both Bureau and Indian officials in the effort to force the program on the Indians. Indians have been arrested, fined, or jailed on trivial or false charges and been denied the right of trial by jury.

6. That individual rights of inheritance, private ownership of property, and private enterprise are being discouraged and destroyed by reason of some provisions of the act itself and the administration of the act.

7. That all efforts tend to force the Indians back into a primitive state; that tribal ceremonials, native costumes and customs, and languages are being both encouraged and promoted in the administration of this act; and that educational program of the Bureau of Indian affairs has been revised to accomplish this purpose in place of the regular school courses in white schools.

8. That the act is not administered in such a manner as to provide the self-government which was promised to the Indians, but provides for more mandatory power for the secretary of the interior and the program under the act has destroyed the self-governing rights which had previously been enjoyed. The constitutions prepared by the Indian Bureau officials for adoption by the Indians were so filled with the impositions of the department that there was little room for the ideas of the Indians, yet the constitutions were supposed to be Indian made. They provide for the reference of everything of importance to the secretary of the interior.

9. That generally the officers elected by the Indians when organizations are set up by virtue of the provisions of the so-called Wheeler-Howard Act, are, or become, employed by some government agency supervised by the Indian Bureau, or some other governmental function, and in the selection of lands and an extension of credits, many of such tribal officers have

secured advantages through their positions and in some cases advantages have been secured through fraud and malfeasance.

10. That the Indians were told that the act provided a means of repeal if they did not like it, yet not a tribe has yet been allowed to vote on repeal though some of them have presented petition after petition. In reply to such petitions they are told to revise the constitutions and that if they could not, they might vote on repeal.

11. That chaotic conditions prevail, due either to the ministration of the act or to legal complications which resulted from the application of the act to certain tribes; that individual initiative of the Indians is being destroyed; that no progress is being made; that conditions generally are worse, and great unhappiness, confusion, and despair among the Indians have resulted.

Arguments advanced against the Wheeler-Howard Act in general, can be summarized as follows:

1. Acceptance of the act changed the status of the Indians from that of involuntary wardship to voluntary wardship.

2. The act provides for continued wardship of the Indians and gives the Secretary of the Interior increased authority.

3. The act is contrary to the established policy of the Congress of the United States to eventually grant the full rights of citizenship to the Indians.

4. The act provides for only one form of government for the Indians, viz, a communal government, with all property, real and personal, held in common; and it compels Indians to live in communities segregated from the rest of American citizens.

5. The act itself and the administration of the act violates the rights of citizenship which the Indians have won through long years of efforts.

6. That the Indians prefer to be under the jurisdiction of the laws of the respective states where they reside.

Conclusion

Fundamentally the so-called Wheeler-Howard Act attempts to set up a state or nation within a nation which is contrary to the intents and purposes of the American Republic. No doubt but that the Indians should be helped and given every assistance possible but in no way should they be set up as a governing power within the United States of America. They should be permitted to have a part in their own affairs as to government in the same way as any domestic organization exists within a state or Commonwealth but not to be independent or apart therefrom.

Paradoxical as it may seem this act does not give them self-government and should not because that is the business of the state or nation. There should be no privilege to this group that any other group may not have within the limits of our Constitution. This act does not even provide that they may control their own property, either what they have inherited or may acquire by their own efforts or through the government. The Indians cannot well advance unless they are given responsibility and perhaps allowed to fail a few times as do other people, and thus learn to stand alone. They should be protected but not patronized.

There should be no plan that even savors of a state within a state or nation within a nation. In most places in this country they get along well with their white neighbors and a majority of the Indians want such associations and they realize their greatest advancement is with the white man and his civilization. They are gradually letting their own culture, so-called, go by. And, why not?

When the fact was brought to the attention of your committee in 1935, that an interpretation contrary to the intention of Congress had been made by the Interior Department of certain sections of the act, your committee recommended, and the Congress passed an act...amending the original act correcting the misinterpretation so as to further safeguard the Indians.

The bill, which finally became the so-called Wheeler-Howard Act, was introduced in the Senate by the then chairman of your committee, Mr. Wheeler, at the request of the Commissioner of Indian Affairs, Mr. John Collier. The bill as introduced was thereupon referred to your committee for consideration; thereafter your committee recommended the elimination of many provisions of said bill which it was not in sympathy with and recommended an amended bill which it was thought that all objectionable features had been stricken out, but it is the opinion of your committee that many of the objectionable features which your committee thought it had eliminated is now put into operation through its administrators.

Many tribes have voted to come under the said act, but few have adopted constitutions and accepted charters; that is, they have taken the first step necessary to come under the act, but refuse to go further. The tribes found that after they had gone through the long process of getting a constitution they still had another long grind to get a charter.

The purchase of land for the landless and the promise of the revolving loan fund to become available to those who come under the act were the greatest incentives to Indians to organize. The holding out of these promises drew the support of practically all Indians who had sold their allotments, lost, squandered, or dissipated the proceeds, and were landless. This class of Indians appeared to be mainly of the mixed-blood class and the educated full bloods who have been declared competent; these are the Indians who seem to be in control of the organizations.

The administration of the loan fund has been grossly mismanaged; books of rules and regulations have confused Indians and employees. Credit was intended for those who had no credit but did have character; but it has worked out that credit was for those who had bankable security, and those who have bankable security have been told to go to the bank for their loans.

Your committee is of the opinion that the most questionable methods were employed to obtain acceptance of this act by the Indians and that there is a determined effort being made to apply portions of the program, or all of the program provided by the act, to Indians who rejected the act entirely or refused to go fully into the program; and that no effort is being made by the department to use the lawful means provided in the act to evoke constitutions when the Indians so desire. It is a self-evident fact that the only method by which Indians can escape from the provisions of the act is by specific act of Congress excluding them therefrom.

Facts developed before your committee clearly established that the so-called Wheeler- Howard Act has resulted in increased Indian Bureau personnel and greatly increased appropriations. Your committee entertains a serious doubt that very much of these appropriations are actually benefiting the Indians. There is less Indian self-government now than ever has been. The attempt to set up a state within a state has failed. Tribes have bound themselves to the department and councils following the dictates of the local agencies.

The secretary of the interior has submitted his report on this bill and various other bills providing for the exclusion of certain reservations and tribes. These reports no doubt have been prepared by persons who are biased and prejudiced in favor of the retention of the so-called Wheeler-Howard Act. Your committee, however, does not concur in all the views expressed in these reports, nor do we agree as to certain facts stated therein as being a correct statement of the situation.

A copy of the secretary of the interior's report on S. 2103 and Senate bills...are attached hereto and made a part of this report, which reports are typical of reports submitted to your committee on similar bills which have been referred to your committee for consideration.

Source:

US Senate. "Repeal of the So-Called Wheeler-Howard Act," 76th Cong., 1st Sess. House Report No. 1047. Washington, DC: Government Printing Office, 1939.

---

14   *Navajo Loyalty Pledges to the United States (1940, 1942)*

Despite cross-generational, interracial conflict, citizens of Indigenous nations and individual Natives have voluntarily opted to serve directly in the US military service or have openly expressed support and allegiance to the US military when it has been engaged in global conflicts. Native people serve in the armed forces at the highest per capita rate of any other group. The Navajo people, who fought the US from the 1840s until they were captured and forcibly held as prisoners-of-war at Fort Sumner in the 1860s, are an example of a Native nation that has produced thousands of soldiers who have joined the US military and fought alongside Americans in several global conflicts. These documents evidence what Navajo political leadership was thinking in 1940 and 1942 at the start of World War II.

Resolution—Loyalty Pledge to the U.S., No. CJ-5-40 (June 4, 1940)

Whereas, the Navajo Tribal Council and the 50,000 people we represent, cannot fail to recognize the crisis now facing the world in the threat of foreign invasion and the destruction of the great liberties and benefits which we enjoyed on our reservation, and

Whereas, there exists no purer concentration of Americanism than among the First Americans, and

Whereas, it has become common practice to attempt national destruction through the sowing of seeds of treachery among minority groups such as ours, and

Whereas, we may expect such activity among our people,

Therefore, we hereby serve notice that any un-American movement among our people will be resented and dealt with severely, and

Now therefore, we resolve that the Navajo Indians stand ready as they did in 1918 to aid and defend our government and its institutions against all subversive and armed conflict and pledge our loyalty to the system which recognizes minority rights and a way of life that has placed us among the greatest people of our race.

Certification

I hereby certify that the foregoing resolution was considered and duly approved by the *unanimous* vote of the members of the Navajo Tribal Council at a regularly called meeting at Window Rock, Arizona, at which a quorum was present, on this fourth day of June, 1940.

J.C. Morgan, Chairman, Navajo Tribal Council

Resolution—Patriotism—Reaffirm Allegiance to the U.S. (January 12, 1942)

Whereas, on June 4, 1940, this body passed a resolution asserting our loyalty to the American way of life and our pledge to assist in its protection, and

Whereas, events have now transpired which have brought this nation into war against three major powers and lesser states of their domination, and

Whereas, the Navajo people stand ready to accept their responsibilities to their government and its authorized leaders,

Therefore, be it resolved, that we, the duly elected representatives of the Navajo people, and on their behalf, reaffirm our allegiance to the United States of America, to the president of the United States, and to other duly authorized leaders, to give our assistance where requested and at the times and in the manner deemed most necessary to the successful prosecution of the war at home and abroad until this nation shall achieve final, complete, and lasting victory.

Certification

I hereby certify that the foregoing resolution was considered and duly approved by the 64 to none vote of the members of the Navajo Tribal Council at a regularly called meeting at Window Rock, Arizona, at which a quorum was present, on this 12th day of January, 1942.

J.C. Morgan, Chairman, Navajo Tribal Council

Sources:

Holm, Tom. *Strong Hearts, Wounded Souls: Native American Veterans of the Vietnam War.* Austin: University of Texas Press, 1996.

Navajo Tribal Council Resolutions, 1922–1951. Window Rock, Arizona, 1952.

Riseman, Noah. *Defending Whose Country? Indigenous Soldiers in the Pacific War.* Lincoln: University of Nebraska Press, 2012.

---

15   William C. Reed, Uintah and Ouray Tribal Business Committee, Letter to Senator Burton Wheeler (1941)

A number of Native citizens and governments were unhappy with both the substance of the Indian Reorganization Act and the procedural manner by which it had been introduced in Indian Country. Treasurer Reed of the Uintah and Ouray here provides one example of the powerful discontent felt in some Indian circles. In his reply to this letter, Senator Wheeler informed Reed that he had only sponsored the measure at the request of the Indian Bureau and, in fact, he shared Reed's view that his nation should be able to opt out of the act's provisions. He then directed Reed to converse with Utah's two senators regarding conditions on the reservation, as Wheeler was no longer chairman of the Senate's Indian Affairs Committee. The reader should bear in mind that this strong, detailed letter was composed on a manual typewriter, so spelling and punctuation errors were not easily corrected by a typist with limited resources.

––––––––

Fort Duchesne, Utah.
June 16, 1941.
Hon.Burton K.Wheeler.
Washington, D.C.

Dear Senator;

In view of the fact that it was you who sponsored the Wheeler-Howard Bill (Indian Reorganization Act) in the congress, I wish to have you answer a few questions in connection there-with.

1. Was the Wheeler-Howard proposition designed to create a dictatorship by the Indian Office over the Indians?. If not, why does our superintendent tell our Tribal Business Committee "The governing body of our tribe" that, no matter what thier decision on any matter may be, he, "the superintendent, is the judge and has the final say."

2. Further, the superintendent says that it does not matter what the decision of our tribal judges is, he, "The superintendent," is the judge.

3. And further, he, "the superintendent," tells our Indians people who have gone to him with thier complaints and failed to get satisfaction, that it will do them no good to appeal to the tribal committee as the committee has no power to help them.

4. Why does our superintendent say that his decisions are final, in the matter of our Ute Indian labor and the amount of wages paid them, on our reservation.

5. Why does our superintendent say that he has the power to remove from our reservation, the livestock of our people, if he so desires.

6. And why does the superintendent say, that he controls our tribal funds accruing to the tribe here on our reservation, from the sale of timber, wood, grazing etc.

7. Why should the superintendent object to the use of intoxicants by our Indians, when it is a common practice for his white and other employes to have liquor on the reservation, in violation of the federal law.

8. Why does the superintendent say that our people have nothing to say about the transfer and replacement of employees, which we would consider in the best interests of our Indians.

9. And why is it against the policy of the Indian Bureau to employ our own educated Indians on our reservation.

10. Should there be reason for our tribal officials to fear reprisals from the Indian Office, should such officials defend the rights of our people against the Indian Office encroachments, if employed by the Indian Department,

11. Why does not the Indian Office in Washington D.C. advise or consult our tribal agent, CApt. R.T. Bonnin who is located in Washington, on all matters under consideration by the Indian Office, that concern our Ute people.

12. Why should our young Indians be required to enter the armed forces of the United States, to assist in the defence of this country against the possible invasionof it by the dictators of Europe, when we have a dictatorship over us by the Indian Office, as absolute as that exercised over the conquered nations of Europe by Hitler.

Honorable Senator, we would like to have the commissioner or some one in authority, come out here that we may have many of the things that I have refered to here-with straightened out, but if we fail to get satisfaction from the Indian Office we will not hesitate to take the matter to the congress or to the President of the United States, if such a course seems necessary.

Trusting that you will consider the fore-foing thoroughly, and advise us if it is what you wished to subject us to by sponsoring the Wheeler-Howard Bill.

Respectfully yours,

William C. Reed, Treasurer

Source:

Personal copy on file with the editor.

16

A Bill to Remove Restrictions on Indian Property Held in Trust (1943)

In 1943 federal officials once again began to entertain policy ideas that some believed essential for complete assimilation of Native peoples into mainstream American society. Much of this early termination language centered on the trust status of lands that are generally exempt from state taxation because of Tribal sovereignty and treaty language. The following bill, introduced by Senator E. H. Moore of Oklahoma, and the response to the measure in the form of a resolution by the Caddo Tribe and the Intertribal Indian Council of Oklahoma, highlight the significant divide that existed between those federal officials who wanted Native lands severed from trust protected status, and Native peoples who insisted on maintaining their tax-exempt status.

In 1948 Congress, in fact, amended the Indian Reorganization Act (IRA) by enacting an act (62 Stat. 236) that allowed individual Native land owners who held their lands in fee-simple title to sell their acreage to someone other than the tribal government, which had been disallowed under the IRA.

Be it enacted by the Senate and House of Representatives of the United States of America in Congress assembled, that all restrictions on alienation and encumbrance of lands now restricted as to sale and encumbrance, except with the approval of the secretary of the interior, allotted to individual Indians allottees living or dead, as their pro rata or distributive share, in whole or in part, of a tribal Indian estate, and all inherited interests therein, together with the proceeds, rents, royalties, and other revenue derived therefrom, including money in lieu of allotted land or the proceeds from the sale of allotted land; or moneys resulting from judgments for violated treaties, agreements, or acts of Congress, now in the hands of the federal government, are hereby removed, and the secretary of the interior is authorized and directed to forthwith execute and issue such certificates, patents, deeds, or other instruments as may be necessary to vest in said Indian allottees or their heirs, or heirs of heirs of said Indian allottees, unrestricted title in fee to such lands or inherited interests therein: Provided, that the secretary of the treasury is authorized and directed to forthwith pay to the said Indian allottees or their heirs, or heirs of heirs, of said Indian allottees, all proceeds, rents, and royalties derived from said land; money in lieu of land and the proceeds from the sale of allotted land, and moneys resulting from judgments for violated treaties, agreements, or acts of Congress, now in the hands of the federal government; and all moneys which may hereafter come into its hands from any and all sources whatsoever, due said Indian allottees or their heirs, or heirs of heirs of said Indian allottees: Provided further, that payment to heirs of deceased Indian allottees, or heirs of heirs of said Indian allottees, shall be upon heirship determination made final by the secretary of the interior or state court now having jurisdiction to determine heirs to lands and moneys due said Indian allottees and all inherited interests therein, down to and including the date of enactment of this act; payment subsequent to the date of enactment of this act, in case of death of said Indian allottees or their heirs, or heirs of heirs of said Indian allottees, shall be upon determination of heirs made by the respective state courts of the state in which said Indian allottees or their heirs, or heirs of heirs of said Indian allottees may be a legal resident at time of death, in accordance with the law of descents and distribution of such state: Provided further, that payment of money due a minor, heir of said Indian allottees, or heir of heirs of said Indian allottees, in an amount in excess of $300 shall be through a legal guardian appointed by the courts of the state wherein said minor may legally reside when payment is to be made; amount or amounts of $300 or less, in total, shall be made to the natural guardian of said minor having the care and custody of the minor at the time payment is to be made, or legal guardian in event no natural guardian then exists; that all money due mentally incompetent Indian allottees or their mentally incompetent heirs, or mentally incompetent heirs of heirs of said Indian allottees, shall be through a legal guardian appointed by the courts of the state wherein said mentally incompetent may legally reside when payment is to be made.

Section 2. Lands and moneys from which restrictions have been removed by this act shall be subject to taxation as though such lands and moneys were the property of persons other than said Indian allottees or their heirs, or heirs of heirs of said Indian allottees, except that said Indian allottees or their heirs, or heirs of heirs of said Indian allottees, who are of not less than one-half Indian blood, shall be entitled to and shall receive, annually, upon the real property in whole, from which restrictions on alienation or encumbrance are hereby removed, a homestead tax exemption of $1000 for a period of ten years from and after the date of enactment of this act, or upon alienation of said property or at the death of said Indian allottees or their heirs, or heirs of heirs of said Indian allottees recipients of said homestead tax exemption.

All acts or parts of acts in conflict herewith are hereby repealed.

Resolution (1944)

Whereas Senate Bill No. 1311, introduced by Senator E. H. Moore of Oklahoma, proposes to abolish all restrictions on the alienation of Indian lands and other Indian property in the United States; and

Whereas such an act of Congress with the approval of the president would be detrimental to the welfare of the Indians of the Caddo, Kiowa, Comanche, Apache, Delaware, and Wichita Indian Tribes of Oklahoma, under the jurisdiction of the Kiowa Indian Agency, at Anadarko, Oklahoma, and all other Indian tribes of said state, in that such action would result in the restricted lands and other property of a large number of the Indians of said tribes being sold and the proceeds from such sales dissipated thereby leaving such Indians without means for their support; and

Whereas many such Indians would be left dependent on public charity and on uncertain aid from state and county authorities; and

Whereas policies now in the course of operation and perfection by the Indian Bureau for the betterment of all Indians and for their education and training in agricultural and other economic undertakings for their general welfare and advancement in their efforts to become self-supporting and useful citizens would be nullified; and

Whereas tribal organization and Indian Association plans and purposes now being undertaken by the several tribes and Indian associations would be effectively disrupted, at great loss to both individual Indians concerned therein and to the United States in its advancement, by loans of large sums of money to promote such enterprises: Therefore be it

Resolved by the executive committee of the Caddo Indian Tribe of Oklahoma, in special session assembled, that the Intertribal Indian Council of Oklahoma in convention at the Huckins Hotel, in Oklahoma City, Oklahoma, on the 12th and 13th of May 1944, be and it is hereby requested to petition the Senators and members of Congress from the state of Oklahoma, in some appropriate manner, to use their greatest efforts to prevent the passage of said bill or of legislation of like character.

Done this 12th day of May 1944. Lloyd Tounwin, Chairman

Source:

US Senate. Hearings Before the Subcommittee of the Committee of Indian Affairs. Remove Restrictions on Indian Property. 78th Cong., 2nd Sess. On S. 1311. Washington, DC: Government Printing Office, 1944.

17

Resolution Submitted to the House Committee on Indian Affairs by the Confederated Salish & Kootenai Tribes (1944)

In 1944 House Resolution 166 was adopted by Congress. It authorized the Committee on Indian Affairs to conduct an investigation aimed at determining what the current status of Native peoples was in the US and to offer suggestions to improve their legal, social, and cultural conditions as a means to "advance the opportunity of the American Indian."

In the following resolution, the Confederated Salish & Kootenai Tribes, the first nations with a ratified IRA constitution, made clear their frustration with the degree of self-governance they had heretofore been allowed to exercise. They were deeply embittered by the bureau's refusal to support their self-determination and insisted that they were fully prepared to exercise self-governance if they could get the BIA to relinquish its paternalistic hold on their political affairs, natural resources, and trust funds.

The tribal council of the Confederated Salish and Kootenai Tribes of the Flathead Reservation, Montana, at the request of the subcommittee of the Committee on Indian Affairs, United States House of Representatives, at a hearing at Browning, Montana, August 4, 1944, do hereby submit the following statement in resolution form, covering major problems of the Indians and reservation, to wit:

Whereas numerous meetings have been held among the Indians throughout the reservation, said meetings being for the purpose of discussing all problems of the Flathead Reservation. It being found that the majority as well as the minority groups are in full accord and agreement with the contents of this resolution; and

Whereas the vast majority of the tribes are unalterably opposed to any act or procedure which would violate or abrogate the treaty of 1855 by and between the United States and the Confederated Flathead Nation. The vast majority of Indians also realize and agree that no one can better regulate and manage the affairs of their reservation than their own people; namely, a tribal business council elected by the Indians. The management of the affairs of the reservation to be carried on more economically than heretofore solely by the use of tribal funds derived from tribal assets; and

Whereas the so-called sustained yield program and numerous regulations governing the sale of tribal timber on the reservation hinders and prevents the most beneficial use of the timber. Timber being at the top of the critical war material list, operators are willing and anxious to continue timber purchases and cutting, but are prevented from doing so because of the regulations holding to an annual maximum cut of 14,000,000 feet per year. There being approximately one and one-half billion feet of merchantable tribal timber on the Flathead Reservation. The suggested solution being that timber be sold on a maximum cut per unit basis rather than the overall reservation basis; and

Whereas the extension program as carried out on the Flathead Reservation is not only detrimental to the Indians because of the long delays, red tape, and restrictions affecting credit loans to Indians, but is also a repetition of an identical office established in the county extension agent. It is generally felt that the tribal council could better administer through their own regulations the extension and credit program; and

Whereas this tribal council is formulating important postwar plans for jobs and rehabilitation of returning service men and women, utilizing and building up existing assets and revenue, an example being the use of our Blue Bay development on Flathead Lake as a veterans' hospital and rest camp. However, because of the control of our moneys and affairs of the reservation as exercised by the Indian Bureau, this council is reluctant to put much faith in carrying out such plans unless they can be made to meet the various requirements, ideas, and regulations of the various heads and their assistants of the Indian Bureau; and

Whereas the liquor question as applies to Indians is a serious question of considerable discussion. The majority of the Indians feel that if Indian boys are good enough to be drafted into the armed services and put through the horrors of war, they certainly should receive equal consideration to the white man in being allowed the white man's "fire water" if they so desire.

Thousands of the taxpayers' dollars are spent annually for liquor suppression which could well be saved. A study and survey made by the law and order committee of our council shows an almost unanimous voice of approval of allowing liquor to be sold to Indians; and

Whereas the so-called Indian irrigation service on the Flathead Indian Reservation has used tribal funds in an amount of over $2,000,000, and this amount being still owed the tribes, the irrigation service has also acquired lands for reservoir sites and canals without compensation to the tribes. Records actually show that Indians are being charged $1.50 per irrigated acre while white landowners are charged $1.20 per irrigated acre. This rate to Indians is set by the Indian Bureau, while the rate to non-Indians is set by the irrigation districts; and

Whereas the majority of the Confederated Salish and Kootenai Tribes are unalterably opposed to any act which may cause their lands or property to be taxable. It being clearly stated in the treaty of 1855 and subsequent acts and court decisions that Indians living on a reservation duly established by Presidential order or by act of Congress are exempt from taxation. To place Indian lands under taxation would ultimately result in the loss to the Indians of such land, as most lands are not of sufficient productive capacity to pay taxes. The fact, then, is evident that the economic structure of the counties would suffer a severe trend downward which would carry with it the social as well as economic structure of the Indians; and

Whereas there is being paid into the Treasury of the United States to the credit of the Confederated Salish and Kootenai Tribes an amount of nearly

$200,000 annually. This money must be appropriated back to and for use of the tribes. But such appropriations have heretofore been made only at the direction and under numerous regulations of the Indian Bureau, thus preventing the most beneficial use of the money by the tribes, although section 5 (h) of the Corporate Charter of the Confederated Salish and Kootenai Tribes, approved by the Secretary of the Interior and ratified by the tribes, April 25, 1936, reads:

"Corporate powers: (h) To deposit corporate funds, from whatever source derived, in any National or State bank to the extent that such funds are insured by a surety bond, or other security ..." The Indian Bureau has refused requests to recognize this part of the charter and to release these funds to a local tribal treasury for local use; and

Whereas the old-age assistance program as handled by the State of Montana and the Government of the United States for the Indians is not proving satisfactory to the Indians because the Indians are not in favor of liens being taken on heirship property to satisfy moneys paid out by the State and Government of the United States. A survey of these Indians receiving State and United States Government old-age assistance shows the Indians favoring a program using tribal funds for such assistance and handled by their tribal council; and

Whereas certain areas of the Flathead Reservation have been set aside without consent of or compensation to the tribes as bird refuges. These areas have proved to be a benefit to sportsmen but a direct detriment to the Indian stockmen as the areas reserved are some of the best grazing lands on the Flathead Indian Reservation and said Indian stockmen are not permitted to graze their stock on these refuges even though title to these refuges is still in trust for the tribes; and

Whereas it is the request of this tribal council having the approval and endorsement of the vast majority of the Indians on the reservation that they be permitted to exercise full authority to manage the affairs of the Confederated Salish and Kootenai Tribes of the Flathead Reservation, without restraint and interference by the Indian Bureau, on a trial basis for a period of 5 years, using tribal funds for said administration and subject to review and audit by the Congress of the United States or its designated committee; and

Whereas this council has endeavored time after time to prove itself capable of self- government by functioning for the direct betterment of the tribes social and economic program. However, it is found that unless the council follows or agrees exactly as directed by the Indian Bureau it is accused by them of not being capable of self-government which apparently promotes and promulgates the Indian Bureau. As requested by the Subcommittee of the Committee on Indian Affairs, United States House of Representatives, at the hearing at Browning, Montana, on August 4, 1944, an example of the cooperation received from the Indian Bureau on important matters is attached to and made a part of this resolution and is marked as exhibit A; and

Whereas it is obvious that the Confederated Salish and Kootenai Tribes has sufficient income from its numerous resources to pay from such income for its own hospitalization for its members as well as its proportionate share of the expense of education for Indian children, thus making a vast saving to the United States Government:

Now, therefore be it Resolved, that the Tribal Council of the Confederated Salish and Kootenai Tribes, acting on behalf of its people, the majority as well as minority groups, herby vigorously request that this resolution receive the immediate consideration and action of the Subcommittee of the Committee on Indian Affairs, United States House of Representatives. Investigation is invited on any or all statements contained herein, as all statements are substantiated by facts and figures of the Tribal Council of the Confederated Salish and Kootenai Tribes of the Flathead Reservation.

Respectfully submitted. S.C. De Mers, Chairman, Tribal Council.

Source:

US House of Representatives. "Investigate Indian Affairs." Hearings Before a Subcommittee of the Committee of Indian Affairs. 78th Cong., 2nd Sess., H.R. Resolution 166. Pt. 3. Washington, DC: Government Printing Office, August 4, 1944.

18

Relating to the Status of Keetoowah Indians of the Cherokee Nation (1945)

After the Cherokee people were forcibly resettled in Indian Territory in the first half of the nineteenth century, a secret society was established by some Tribal members. They adopted the name Nighthawk Keetoowah, and represented themselves as staunch cultural traditionalists. Over the following century, the Keetoowahs splintered into several segments, but by the 1930s the various groups coalesced and began pushing for political recognition of their autonomy, separate from the other two federally recognized Cherokee communities in the US: the Eastern Band of North Carolina and the Cherokee Nation of Oklahoma. The United Keetoowah Band, some 3,687 strong, eventually convinced the Secretary of the Interior of their legitimacy and the following report by Abe Fortas to Congress was sufficient to convince the legislature to recognize United Keetoowah's political distinctiveness.

———

Honorable Henry M. Jackson, Chairman, Committee on Indian Affairs,

My Dear Mr. Jackson: Reference is made to the request of the former chairman of your committee for a report on H.R. 341, a bill "relating to the status of Keetoowah Indians of the Cherokee Nation in Oklahoma, and for other purposes."

For the reasons hereinafter set forth, I recommend that this measure be enacted.

The purpose of the bill is to recognize the Indians who belong to the Keetoowah Society, as a separate band or organization of Cherokee Indians, so that it may organize under section 3 of the Oklahoma Indian Welfare Act (act of June 26, 1936).... This section provides that:

"Any recognized tribe or band of Indians residing in Oklahoma shall have the right to organize for its common welfare and to adopt a constitution and bylaws under such rules and regulations as the Secretary of the Interior may prescribe."

The word "Keetoowah" is closely interwoven in the fabric of Cherokee history. It was the name of the principal towns or seats of authority before the removal to Indian Territory. It is also the name applied to one of the two remaining dialects still spoken among the Eastern Band of Cherokees in North Carolina. It seems to have been the name by which, a century ago, the Cherokees spoke of themselves.

The Keetoowah Society formally came into existence in the years immediately preceding the Civil War. The preamble to the society's written constitution contains the statement that "on April 15, 1858, a small number of leading members of Keetoowahs got together and discussed the affairs of the Cherokees, the purpose and objectives for which they had always stood." This preamble also explains the reason behind the decision to organize the society. A written constitution prepared "in the dark of the night and in the woods" was adopted at a "general convention of the several districts" on April 29, 1859. This constitution provided that "only full- blood Cherokees, uneducated, and no mixed-blood friends, shall be...members." They distrusted and feared the growing power of their intermarried, non-Indian citizens and their offspring.

Further, "anything which may derive from English or white... the Keetoowahs shall not accept or recognize."

In later years, the Keetoowahs tried to prevent the allotment of the Cherokee tribal lands.

At the general election of January 31, 1899, to vote on the Dawes Commission terms, they counseled their followers to abstain from voting, and as a consequence the Dawes Commission was upheld by a comparatively narrow margin. They employed attorneys to prosecute the *Eastern Cherokee* cases in the proceedings of 1903–1906. When legislation was pending in Congress in 1905 to dissolve the tribal governments of the Five Civilized Tribes, the Keetoowahs applied for and received a charter of incorporation through the United States district court. The intention in this, as in all courses followed by the Keetoowah group, was that of keeping alive Cherokee institutions and the tribal entity.

In 1937 the Keetoowah Indians requested permission to organize under section 3 of the Oklahoma Indian Welfare Act on the grounds that the society was, in effect, a recognized band of Indians residing in Oklahoma. The Department was compelled to decline this request because it seemed impossible to make a positive finding that the Keetoowah Indians were and are a tribe or band within the meaning of the Oklahoma Indian Welfare Act. It remains true that the group is composed of individuals predominantly Indian who are interested in maintaining their identity, individually and as a group, as Cherokee

Indians. The organization has a recorded membership of 3,687 members, which represents nearly one-half of the Cherokees possessing one-half or more degree of Indian blood now residing in the territory known as the Cherokee Nation of Oklahoma, which is in the northeastern part of the state. The courts have regularly held that congressional recognition of a group of Indians as a band is conclusive. Legislative recognition of the Keetoowahs as a band would accordingly enable these Indians to secure any benefits, which, under the Oklahoma Indian Welfare Act, are available to other Indian bands or tribes.

H.R. 341 has been introduced, I understand, in response to a request of the leaders of the Keetoowah Indians. Its text seems to be sufficient to permit these Indians to organize for their common welfare and to adopt a constitution and bylaws. I urge that it be enacted.

The Bureau of the Budget has advised me that there is no objection to the submission of this report to your committee.

Sincerely yours,

Abe Fortas, Acting Secretary of the Interior.

Sources:

Slagle, Allogan. "United Keetowah Band." In *Native America in the Twentieth Century: An Encyclopedia*, ed. Mary B. Davis, 98–99. New York: Garland Publishing, Inc., 1996.

US House of Representatives. "Relating to the Status of Keetoowah Indians." House Report, No. 447. 79th Cong., 1st Sess. Washington, DC: Government Printing Office, 1945.

---

19   *Statement Opposing the Garrison Dam by Affiliated Tribes Chairman Martin T. Cross, Fort Berthold Indian Reservation (1945)*

In 1944 Congress enacted the Flood Control Act, popularly referred to as the Pick-Sloan Plan. It was an audacious engineering plan designed to tame the mighty Missouri River through the installation of a series of large dams. Some of these were projected to back up waters that would permanently flood land on several Indian reservations located within Great Plains states. Vine Deloria Jr., referred to the Pick-Sloan Plan as "the most destructive policy enacted by Congress" affecting Indigenous peoples. Many Tribal leaders desperately protested the impending ecological catastrophe. Martin Cross, chair at Fort

Berthold, was one such leader. Despite their efforts, the dams were constructed, submerging vast areas of Tribal land.

———

Mr. Cross: I am Martin T. Cross, a member of the Gros Ventre Tribe. I am chairman of the tribal business council of the Three Affiliated Tribes, residing on Fort Berthold Reservation at Elbowoods, North Dakota. I am also past commander of All Indian American Legion Post, Department of North Dakota, located at Elbowoods, North Dakota.

I am delegated here with three other men to voice the adverse disapproval of the construction of the proposed Garrison Dam. We wish to present evidence, testimony, and data in support, and substantiate our claim.

Most of our reservation, the best irrigable land, and about 370 well improved Indian homes will be in the flooded area. An unestimated amount of coal, timber, and wildlife will be destroyed.

The United States Army Engineer Corps, with the assistance of the State Water Commission, seem to think the Garrison Dam is the logical point for the construction of a water reservoir.

Lieutenant Colonel Goodall, of the Omaha District Office of the United States Army Engineer Corps, seems to think that the Indian land in the flooded area can be acquired by eminent domain if necessary. We question the legality of this process, on the ground that the treaty law between the United States Government and the Indians is binding and not subject to eminent domain.

Since I have no legal talent, I must rely on other authority to interpret this legal point. I want to raise that question to be considered, but I want to come out openly against the construction of the Garrison Dam, not only from the legal standpoint, but from destructiveness and the set back of our Indian people.

I believe that this group of men composing this honorable body are adamant foes of abuse and, being such, that they will not permit the Army engineers to carry out their program, their plan. And I want to have the Indian Department interpret the legal point of the treaty between the tribes and the Government.

The Chairman [Senator Joseph C. O'Mahoney, WY]: First, Mr. Cross, let me ask you, what are the names of the three Indian tribes who are affected by this proposed dam?

Mr. Cross: They are Gros Ventres, Mandans, and Arickaras. We call ourselves the Three Affiliated Tribes under the [Indian] Reorganization Act.

The Chairman: How many Indians are there?

Mr. Cross: There are 2,000 as of the latest census.

The Chairman: And where do you reside?

Mr. Cross: At Fort Berthold Reservation.

The Chairman: How large is the Reservation?

Mr. Cross: It is 600,000 acres.

The Chairman: I understand you to say that if the Garrison Dam were constructed, a large amount of that land would be flooded; is that right?

Mr. Cross: That is right.

The Chairman: How much?

Mr. Cross: About 221,000 acres.

The Chairman: I was correct, then, in my preliminary statement. In other words, the building of this dam would take about one-third of the land in the reservation?

Mr. Cross: That is right.

The Chairman: What is the character of the land which would be taken?

Mr. Cross: That would be the best land we have, along the river, the best irrigable land, and our homes are situated along this valley.

The Chairman: You say that the homes of the Indians are now built upon the land that would be flooded?

Mr. Cross: That is right.

The Chairman: How many homes are there?

Mr. Cross: Well, there are—I have available records—there are about 531 homes. Out of these, about 436 would be in the flooded area.

The Chairman: You mean there are five-hundred-plus homes on the entire reservation?

Mr. Cross: There are 500 homes, that is, entire homes, as we call it, on the reservation, and out of these homes there would be about 437 that would be in the flooded area.

The Chairman: Well, then, what you are saying is that three-fourths of the homes of the Affiliated Tribes would be flooded?

Mr. Cross: That is right....

The Chairman: Then the position you take is that this land is, from the point of view of the Indians, invaluable; that your homes are built upon this land; you do not want to abandon your homes; you do not want to sell the land, and you do not want to exchange it to go to live in the Bad Lands?

Mr. Cross: That is right.

Senator Moore: Or any other place?

Mr. Cross: Or any other place.

The Chairman: Are there any other questions?

Senator Langer: How long have your ancestors been living there? Pardon me, Senator Carville.

Senator Carville: That is the question I was going to ask. How long have your ancestors been living there?

Mr. Cross: From time immemorial we have been living there.

Senator Carville: Do you know the purpose of the proposed dam? What is the Government's idea—the engineers' idea?

Mr. Cross: The engineers' idea is, they seem to think it is the logical point to have a water reservoir for a flood menace.

Senator Carville: It is a flood-control project?

Mr. Cross: Yes, sir.

The Chairman: Garrison Dam, Senator Carville, was embraced in what was known as the Pick plan, developed by the Army Engineers. This Pick plan, together with the Sloan plan devised by the Bureau of Reclamation, were coordinated a year ago, and in the Flood Control Act of December 1944 Congress authorized the improvement of the Missouri Valley for purposes of flood control, navigation, irrigation and power. A preliminary appropriation for the initial work has been made, but no actual steps have been taken as yet, so far as I know toward the construction of the Garrison Dam. And this delegation of Indians are here to make their position clear....

Resolution of the Three Affiliated Tribes in Opposition to Garrison Dam

Whereas, at a special meeting of the subcommittee to the tribal council held at Elbowoods, North Dakota, on April 2, 1945, it was called to the attention of the council relevant to the proposed Garrison Dam, and having been carefully considered by the subcommittee: It is therefore,

Resolved by the subcommittee, for and on behalf of its constituent members, to wit, the Fort Berthold Indians, that the proposal of Garrison Dam would be not only injurious, but destructive, to the best interests of Fort Berthold Indians, whose estates are now being administered through the Federal Government; that a change of Fort Berthold Reservation by the Office of Indian Affairs of its supervision would, in effect, be a repudiation of treaty obligations assumed by the Federal Government in consideration of the surrender of vested land rights, in the past, and claims of Fort Berthold Indians; be it further

Resolved, that we hereby must request insertion of this resolution in the record of hearings pertinent to proposed Garrison Dam with attached memorial of a recent session addressed to Congress, and expressed what we believe are the sound and basic principles; be it further

Resolved, that copies of this resolution be sent to all officials and interested people of the United States.

Unanimously adopted by the subcommittee of the tribal council.

Martin T. Cross, Chairman, Tribal Business Council...

Resolution Further Opposing Garrison Dam

Whereas there is embodied in the proposed plan for development of the Missouri River construction of a dam at or near Garrison, North Dakota; and

Whereas construction of the proposed Garrison Dam at an approximate elevation of 1,850 feet would inundate 200,000 acres of the best irrigable land of our reservation; and

Whereas this will force approximately 200 families to move from their permanent homes, destroy or cause to be moved the houses and other farm buildings; and

Whereas it will flood or cause them to be useless, all Government buildings and improvements at Elbowoods, Nishu, Shell Creek, Independence, Beaver Creek, Lucky Mound, Charging Eagle, and Red Butte, including the hospital, school buildings, total value over $1,000,000, and other improvements, truck trails, dams, springs for livestock; and

Whereas cause to be either cut and removed all timber now growing along the bottoms, thus destroying natural shelter for the cattle and taking away the continual fuel supply of our people, and source of income from sale of timber, fence post, lumber, and firewood for Fort Berthold Indians; and

Whereas the unlimited supply of lignite in the hills and buttes and possibilities of lignite byproducts located near the river will be inundated to an extent that lignite will become useless for man; and

Whereas the cemeteries of our forefathers will be destroyed, and with it all our memories and kind remembrances of these burial places that have been held sacred for all; and

Whereas this large body of water will separate the reservation, which will make it difficult for the members to commute and transact the usual business, and the removal of the $250,000 bridge on the Fort Berthold Reservation; and

Whereas the members have recently contracted with the Federal Government to borrow money and cattle to develop a cattle program giving the members an opportunity to become self-supporting, and the program has been existing for nearly 2 years, and further contracted to with the Government, for repayment within 10 to 15 years, with privilege of extension of time, with the inundation of bottom lands makes it impossible to continue this program, and with an investment of $221,000 to repay the Government; and

Whereas and deprive approximately 250 boys from our reservation who are now serving in the armed forces of land rightfully theirs; and

Whereas the various treaties and executive orders have given the people of this reservation promise of a perpetual use of this land; further, the recent Indian Reservation Act gave indefinite extension of the trust status of the land;

Article IX—Land

"Section 1. Allotted lands, including heirship lands, within the Fort Berthold Reservation shall continue to be held as heretofore by their present owners. It is recognized that under existing laws such lands may be inherited by the heirs of the present owners, whether or not they are members of the Three Affiliated Tribes. Likewise it is recognized that under existing laws the Secretary of the Interior may, in his discretion, remove restrictions upon such land, upon application by the Indian owner, whereupon the land will become subject to State taxes and may be mortgaged or sold. The right of the individual Indian to hold or part with his land as under existing law, shall not be abrogated by anything contained in approval of the Secretary of the Interior, voluntarily convey this land to the Three Affiliated Tribes either in exchange for a money payment or in exchange for an assignment covering the same land, as hereinafter provided.

Section 2. The unallotted lands of the Fort Berthold Reservation and all lands which may hereafter be acquired by the Three Affiliated Tribes or by the United States in trust for the Three Affiliated Tribes, shall be held as tribal lands, and no part of such land shall be mortgaged, sold, or ceded. Tribal lands shall not be allotted to individual Indians but may be assigned to members of the Three Affiliated Tribes, or leased, or otherwise used by the tribes, as hereinafter provided."

Whereas we have permanently located on these lands, and our forefathers also have lived on these grounds and it is the hopes and plans to have our children and their children to occupy this land continuously forever; and money or exchange for other land will not compensate us for the land, landmarks, and sentimental attachments: Now, therefore, be it

Resolved by the tribal business council in a meeting duly and regularly called, a quorum being present, that we oppose the present plan of constructing a dam at Garrison, or any other plan which will destroy the flood areas in the Missouri Valley; also, we further

Resolve, to urge that the Bureau of Reclamation study and set up irrigation projects to irrigate our lowlands so as to furnish us feed for our cattle during the drought years to come. We hereby favor the original Sloan plan, diversion of water from Fort Peck Dam to Devil Lake, commonly called the Missouri-Souris unit; be it further

Resolved, Subcommittee has been appointed to execute draft of resolutions included in this memorial in opposition to the proposed Garrison Dam; be it further

Resolved, that copies of this memorial be sent to all officials and interested persons in the United States of America.

Respectfully submitted, Martin T. Cross, President, Tribal Business Council

Sources:

Lawson, Michael. *Dammed Indians: The Pick-Sloan Plan and the Missouri River Sioux, 1944–1980*. Norman: University of Oklahoma Press, 1982.

US Congress. "Protesting the Construction of Garrison Dam, North Dakota, by the Fort Berthold Indians." Hearing Before the Committee of Indian Affairs. 79th Cong., 1st Sess. on S.J. Res. 79. Washington, DC: Government Printing Office, October 9, 1945.

20   *William Zimmerman (BIA) Testimony Regarding Indian Bureau Withdrawal (1947)*

At the conclusion of World War II, federal officials overseeing Indian affairs geared up to introduce legislation to end the distinctive political and legal relationship between the federal government and Native nations. Their rationale was based on both economic and political grounds; as the costs of providing ongoing services and benefits were deemed too high and the popular solution of the time was to expedite assimilation of Native nations deemed capable of self-rule, notwithstanding treaties and the trust relationship. The federal government understood that not all Indian nations were equally prepared to have their political and legal standing so quickly eradicated, so Zimmerman organized federally recognized nations into three separate categories according to his own views of their readiness. Here he testifies before a congressional committee about the results of his analysis and proposal for termination of existing relations.

———

The Chairman: Mr. Zimmerman, the committee wanted certain data. Have you brought it?

Mr. Zimmerman: Mr. Chairman, as I understood the committee's request, you asked me to suggest certain procedures by which the personnel and expenses of the Indian Office might be reduced.

The Chairman: That is right.

Mr. Zimmerman: I have brought with me a number of proposals for specific steps which the Department and the Congress might take to bring about the results you have been seeking.

As I have said before, the personnel of the Indian Service is engaged in rendering a variety of services that provide education, medical service, building roads, developing irrigation systems, and generally developing Indian reservations, and assisting the Indians in bringing them into use.

Obviously, the cost of this service can be reduced. It is possible to curtail or eliminate any one of those. It would also be possible to reduce the number of Indians who are entitled to this service.

Now I take my point of departure from the report of the House committee to which I referred in previous testimony. I do not personally agree with all of the recommendations contained in that report.

The Chairman: You refer to the Senate report by Senators Chavez and Shipstead?

Mr. Zimmerman: No; the House committee.

The Chairman: What is the number?

Mr. Zimmerman: I previously referred to it, and the recommendations made by that committee are now in the record. I cannot give you the report number. I have prepared a list of the Indian groups, by their present jurisdictional units or reservations.I have broken that down into three parts. The first list included those which in my judgment could be denied Federal services immediately or in the future, whichever the Congress should decide.

In the second group there are a number of tribes who should be able to function with a small degree of Federal supervision, or no Federal supervision whatever, within 10 years. That second group includes some tribes for which a definite congressional policy should be established. The termination of Federal service would place the burden either on the Indians or on the States, and the termination of Federal service should not be brought about with full attention to that result.

Now, in the third group are the remaining tribes which, so far as can be foreseen today, would require a longer term than the 10-year term. I would like to point out in passing that the 10-year period is an arbitrary one. I selected it for two reasons, first because we had in the Indian Office prepared data, to which some reference has been made previously, on our so-called 10-year program, and the second reason is that the Indian Claims Commission has a 10-year period in which to make its findings on the claims of the Indians against the United States.

It is entirely possible that some of these tribes who have very substantial assets will receive substantial recoveries, and if, as a result of judgments paid by the United States they then have substantial assets, my judgment would be that the amount or degree of Federal supervision could be properly and probably immediately curtailed because those tribes would be in position then to finance their own functions.

Now, in the making up of these three groups of tribes, I took four factors into account. The first one is the degree of acculturation of the particular tribe. That includes such factors as the admixture of white blood, the percentage of illiteracy, the business ability of the tribe, their acceptance of white institutions and their acceptance by the whites in the community. The second factor is the economic condition of the tribe, principally the availability of resources to enable either the tribe or the individuals, out of their tribal or individual assets, to make a reasonably decent living. The third factor is the willingness of the tribe and its members to dispense with Federal aid. The last criterion is the willingness and ability of the State in which the tribe is located to assume the responsibilities.

Now, I submit for the record—I have this list of tribes. If the committee wishes, I shall be glad to read them and go into detail.

The Chairman: I wish you would.

Mr. Zimmerman: In the first group I have included these: the Flathead, the Hoopa, Klamath, Menominee, Mission, the Six Nations of New York, the Osage Tribe in Oklahoma, the Potawatomi in Kansas, and the Indians in northern California under the jurisdiction of the Sacramento Agency. Now, I have also in this first group, Mr. Chairman, tentatively placed the Turtle Mountain group in North Dakota, but I would like to discuss them a little later when I make the proposal to your committee that the State of North Dakota take over the Sacramento administration of the Indian affairs in that State.

The Chairman: Can you tell us about how many Indians there are in that group?

Mr. Zimmerman: Roughly, about 40,000 Indians. The second group is a rather longer group. I will just read these by name, and, Mr. Chairman, or any member of the committee, if you want to ask me about them, I shall be glad to explain why I think they belong in those groups [reading]: "Blackfoot, Cherokee, Cheyenne River, Colville, Consolidated Chippewa, Crow, Fort Belknap, Fort Peck, Fort Totten, Grand Ronde, Great Lakes, Northern Idaho, Quapaw (in part), Taholah (Tulalip), Tomah, Umatilla, Warm Springs, Wind River (in part), Winnebago (in part)."

Senator Thye: How many would be in that group, Mr. Zimmerman?

Mr. Zimmerman: In this second group?

Senator Thye: Yes.

Mr. Zimmerman: I have not totaled that, Senator Thye.

Senator Johnston: Could you estimate it?

Mr. Zimmerman: I would make a rough guess, at least 50,000 or 60,000.

Senator Thye: Between 50,000 and 60,000. Thank you.

Mr. Riley: Mr. Chairman, may I ask how many personnel that would be designed to release?

Mr. Zimmerman: In the first group I estimate at least 500 employees could be eliminated.

Mr. Riley: The first group?

Mr. Zimmerman: Yes, sir.

Mr. Riley: How much less budget would that require; do you know?

Mr. Zimmerman: I have not that figure tabulated. I can supply that very easily if you wish.

Mr. Riley: As much as $5,000,000, do you think?

Mr. Zimmerman: I think it should not be that high.

Senator Thye: Would you care to go on with your third group before you go back and answer questions on the No. 1 and No. 2—whichever would be more convenient to you, Mr. Zimmerman? If you would care to go on through and explain group No. 3 and then we will go back and have a couple of questions on No. 1 and No. 2, which, if you would prefer from the standpoint of your own fixed thoughts on that, I may defer.

Mr. Zimmerman: I shall be glad to answer any question now, Senator.

Senator Thye: From your No. 1 group here, you have completed classification No. 1, but are the tribes grouped in No. 1 able to assume the responsibility of their properties and proceed in an orderly manner and make their supervision and care for the elder groups or elderly people within their tribes? Of course we know that would have to be assumed under the fixed laws of the various States, both in old-age assistance and in other care that would be authorized, but they would be just exactly as the American citizen in that respect, and they are far enough advanced so they could be so accepted by the people and citizens in that group of States.

Mr. Zimmerman: I should like to state, even though this first group does not meet equally in all respects the four conditions that I used as measure—

Senator Johnston: What conditions did you use as measure, so the committee may have the benefit of that?

Mr. Zimmerman: The first one was the degree of acculturation; the second, economic resources and condition of the tribe; third, the willingness of the tribe to be relieved of Federal control; and fourth, the willingness of the State to take over. They are the tests that need to be applied in each case. They do not apply equally to all of these tribes, but as to some, the Flathead, Klamath, and the Osages, there are substantial tribal assets or individual assets.

Senator Thye: What could be done with the assets? Could that be turned over to the tribe and would the chiefs make allocation, or would they retain that and administer it as a tribal property?

Mr. Zimmerman: In the next part of my testimony I want to develop the answer to your question.

Senator Thye: That is the reason I asked whether you would rather carry right through. I think probably we had better let you proceed.

TABLE 20.1

Group 1			
Flathead	43	Osage	71
Hoopa	69	Potawatomi	19
Klamath	121	Sacramento*	27
Menominee	58	Turtle Mountain (conditionally)	118
Mission*	81		—
New York	8	Total	505**

Group 2—10 Years	
Blackfeet	Great Lakes (no resources)
Cherokee	Northern Idaho
Cheyenne River	Quapaw (in part, Wyandotte, Seneca)
Colville (subject to restoration of ceded lands)	Taholah, Tulalip (consolidation, in part)
Consolidated Chippewa	Tomah
Crow (special legislation)	Umatilla
Fort Belknap	Warm Springs
Fort Peck (irrigation and power)	Wind River (Shoshone only)
Fort Totten (no resources)	Winnebago (Omaha still predominantly full-blood)
Grand Ronde (no resources)	

Group 3	
Cheyenne and Arapaho	Rocky Boy
Choctaw	Rosebud
Colorado River	San Carlos
Consolidated Ute (claims recoveries)	Sells***
Crow Creek	Seminole
Five Tribes (Oklahoma policy and legislation)	Shawnee Fort Apache
	Sisseton
Fort Berthold	Standing Rock (re State's ability)
Fort Hall	Taholah, Tulalip (in part)
Hopi	Tongue River
Jicarilla	Truxton Cañon
Kiowa	Uintah and Ouray
Mescalero	United Pueblos
	(if sub-marginal lands are added to reservation and if franchise granted, then perhaps in class II)
Navajo	Western Shoshone
Pawnee	Wind River (Arapaho only)
Pine Ridge	Yakima
Quapaw (in part)	
Red Lake	

Mission and Sacramento as used here denote all California tribes served by those agencies
** *The total discrepancy in the totals is found in the original.*
****The peoples to whom Zimmerman refers as "Sells" are now known as the Tohono O'odham*

Mr. Zimmerman: If I may give you an idea of what I want to do?
Senator Thye: Yes.

Mr. Zimmerman: Let me say I have prepared a number of exhibits. Three of those are bills for the incorporation of specific tribes. There are different factors and conditions that have to be met, so in some cases I would recommend incorporation of a tribe by a bill. I have also prepared two tentative plans for State control, in the case of California and North Dakota, and the third proposal is a bill which would permit individuals to withdraw. So, it seems to me there are three possible approaches at the moment.

Mr. thye: I think, possibly, Mr. Zimmerman, you had better carry right straight through and make the presentation of your case to the committee, and we can go back and ask questions on the various phases of your presented report.

Mr. Zimmerman: First, I will present a tabulation of the third group for the record, as follows:

Indian tribes set out in groups, as submitted to the Senate Civil Service Committee by William Zimmerman, Jr., Acting Commissioner of Indian Affairs. Mr. Zimmerman recommended to the committee that group 1 could be released now from Federal supervision; group 2 in 10 years; and group 3, indefinite time.

Sources:

Philp, Kenneth R. *Termination Revisited: American Indians on the Trail to Self-Determination, 1933–1953*. Lincoln: University of Nebraska Press, 1999.

US Congress. House. Report with Respect to the House Resolution Authorizing the Committee on Interior and Insular Affairs to Conduct an Investigation of the Bureau of Indian Affairs. 82nd Cong., 2nd Sess. House Report 2503. Washington, DC: Government Printing Office, 1953: 161–165.

21

Constitution of Isleta
Pueblo (1947)

Isleta is one of nineteen Pueblos in present-day New Mexico. Its name, meaning "little island," comes from the Spanish missions San Antonio de la Isleta and San Augustin de la Isleta. By and large, all Pueblo governments derive from two distinct traditions, Native and Spanish. Indigenous traditional offices included the *cacique*, or head of the Pueblo, as well as war captains. These officials were also imbued with spiritual authority. At Isleta this was exemplified by the Corn Group leaders who had the authority to appoint the *cacique*. Thus, traditional Pueblo governance was of a theocratic nature.

The second set of traditions was coercively established by Spanish officials as early as the sixteenth century. Spanish-style officials operated alongside traditionally installed leaders and they generally dealt with church affairs and external matters. By the late 1890s severe factionalism arose within the community and war chiefs were called upon to serve as acting *caciques* for several decades. In the 1940s a major revolution split the community into distinct blocs. These conditions led BIA officials to propose the drafting of a constitution that was subsequently completed by three men from each of the three competing parties in 1947.

Preamble

We, the people of the Pueblo of Isleta, in order to establish a responsible and representative government, to promote the general welfare, to secure the blessings of liberty to ourselves and our posterity, to provide for our economic and social betterment through cooperative effort, industry and enterprise, to promote security and to provide for law and order, do establish this constitution for the Pueblo of Isleta.

Article I—Jurisdiction

This constitution shall apply within the exterior boundaries of the Isleta Pueblo Grant and within the exterior boundaries of such other lands as are now, or may in the future, be added by purchase, grant, lease, or otherwise acquired for use by the Pueblo of Isleta. No such lands shall ever be alienated from the Pueblo by action of any member of the Pueblo.

Article II—Membership

Persons of one-half or more degree of Isleta Indian blood and Isleta parentage shall be members of the Pueblo of Isleta, provided they have not renounced their right to membership. Other persons of Indian blood may become naturalized members of the Pueblo of Isleta.

All male members who are heads of families and male members who have attained the age of 21 and have established a separate household shall be eligible to vote in the general Pueblo elections provided that such members have established their eligibility by registration with the proper Pueblo official.

Article III—Executive Branch

Section 1. The Executive Branch of the Pueblo of Isleta shall consist of the Governor, First and Second Lieutenant Governors, Sheriff and Under-Sheriff, Secretary and Treasurer. These offices shall be chosen only from among the membership of the Pueblo of Isleta.

Section 2. These officers shall serve for a period of one year.

Section 3. The duties of the Governor shall be:

(a) To direct and be responsible for the administration of Pueblo affairs.
(b) To act officially for the Pueblo in its relation with other Pueblos, the States, other governmental agencies, individuals, and such other groups as may require the official action of the Pueblo.
(c) To co-sign with the Treasurer all checks drawn against the Pueblo of Isleta bank account.
(d) To be responsible for the maintenance of law and order within the Pueblo, and to require and direct such assistance in this regard as may be necessary.
(e) To attend all Council meetings.

Section 4. The duties of the First Lieutenant Governor shall be:

(a) To assist the Governor, as directed by him, in the performance of any or all of the Governor's duties.
(b) To maintain law and order at all times, under the direction of the Governor, if possible, but on his own initiative when necessary.
(c) To assume the governorship, and the duties thereof, in the case of death, resignation, or absence of the Governor.
(d) To attend all Council meetings.

Section 5. The duties of the Second Lieutenant Governor shall be:

(a) To assist the Governor, as directed by him, in the performance of any or all of the Governor's duties.
(b) To maintain law and order at all times, under the direction of the Governor, if possible, but on his own initiative when necessary.
(c) To assume the governorship, and the duties thereof, in the case of the death, resignation, or absence of the Governor and First Lieutenant Governor.
(d) To attend all Council meetings.

Section 6. The duties of the Sheriff and Under-Sheriff shall be:

(a) To maintain law and order at all times, under the direction of the Governor, when possible, but on their own initiative when necessary.
(b) To attend all Council meetings when requested.

Section 7. The duties of the Secretary shall be:

(a) To keep all records and files of the Pueblo and attend to such official correspondence as may be authorized.
(b) To register qualified voters and be responsible for the registration records.
(c) To attend all Council meetings, and act as interpreter on request.

Section 8. The duties of the Treasurer shall be:

(a) To keep all financial records and to be accountable for them.
(b) To issue and sign checks authorized to be drawn against the Pueblo of Isleta bank account and to submit these for all other necessary signatures.

Article IV—Legislative Branch

Section 1. The Legislative Branch of Isleta Pueblo shall consist of a Council of twelve, all of whom shall be chosen from among the eligible voters.

Section 2. The term of office of members of the Council shall be for a period of one year, but the Council shall stay in office until inauguration of their successors by the new Governor. In case of the death or resignation of any member of the Council, his successor shall be chosen by the officer who had selected him for office.

Section 3. The twelve Council members shall be selected as follows:

(a) Those candidates for Governor who receive the second and third greatest number of votes shall be the President and Vice-President of the Council, respectively.

(b) On the January 1 after an election, the new Governor, and the new President and new Vice- President of the Council shall meet to determine the other ten members of the new Council. The Governor shall select four members, and the President and the Vice-President shall each select three members.

(c) The Council shall, at its first meeting after election, choose one of its members as Council Secretary. The Council shall determine the special duties of its President, Vice-President, and Secretary. The Council shall also choose some qualified member of the Pueblo as Treasurer of the Pueblo, to serve in the executive branch.

Section 4. Council meetings shall be called by the Governor or by the President of the Council upon their own initiative, or by the President upon request of any three Council members. It is the duty of each individual Council member to be present at all Council meetings. A quorum of eight is necessary in order to transact official Council business, with a majority vote required.

Section 5. The duties of the Council shall be to pass ordinances for the Pueblo, and to determine generally the usage of Pueblo property. It shall be the further duty of the Council to appropriate such money, authorize employment and payment of such assistants or advisers and set up such rules and procedures as may be necessary for the proper administration of this Constitution and of all ordinances in effect.

Section 6. The Council shall enact no ordinances discriminating against individuals specifically named. The Council shall enact no ordinances abridging any of the following rights of the members of the Pueblo: freedom of religion, speech, and the press; freedom of the people to assemble and to request general or specific action from the Council or the officers; freedom from unreasonable searches and seizures; freedom from deprivation of liberty or property without due process of law; freedom, in all criminal prosecutions, to enjoy speedy, impartial and public trial with assistance of pertinent witnesses and defense counsel; freedom from excessive bail or fines and from cruel punishments. The enumeration in this constitution of certain rights retained by the people.

Article V—Judicial Branch

Section 1. The judiciary shall be composed of a Chairman and two other members appointed and sworn into office by the Governor and approved by the majority vote of the Council. Their term of office shall be one year but they shall serve until their successors have been chosen.

Section 2. The duties of the judiciary shall be:

(a) To pass on the constitutionality of ordinances when requested by any member of the Pueblo.

(b) To pass on the legality of the action of officers enforcing the ordinances.

(c) To handle all criminal and civil cases brought before it.

(d) To establish judicial methods and procedures within the framework of this Constitution and appropriate ordinances.

Section 3. The Council may, at its discretion, accept any appeals from action of the judiciary, and try these in its capacity as a superior court....

Article VII—Ratification

This Constitution, when adopted by a majority of the votes cast at a special election called by the Secretary of the Interior in which at least 30 percent of the members of the Pueblo 21 years of age or over shall vote, shall be submitted to the Secretary of the Interior, or his authorized representative, for approval and shall be effective from the date of such approval.

Certification of Adoption

Pursuant to an order approved March 7, 1947, by the Under Secretary of the Interior, the attached Constitution was submitted for ratification to the Indians of the Isleta Pueblo of New Mexico and was on March 23, 1947, duly adopted by a vote of 132 for, and 61 against, in an election in which over 30 percent of those entitled to vote cast their ballots, in accordance with Section 16 of the Indian Reorganization Act of June 18, 1934 (48 Stat. 984), as amended by the Act of June 15, 1935 (49 Stat. 378).

Remijo Jojola, Chairman, Election Board

Sources:

Ellis, Florence Hawley. "Isleta Pueblo." *Handbook of North American Indians.* Vol. 9, *Southwest,* edited by Alfonso Ortiz. Washington, DC: Smithsonian Institution, 1979, 361–365.

Pritzker. Barry M. *A Native American Encyclopedia: History, Culture, and Peoples.* New York: Oxford University Press, 2000.

22

Constitution and By-laws of the Crow Tribe (1948)

The Crow, who call themselves Absaroke or Apsáalooke, are a matrilineal society with a well-defined clan system. Once inhabiting over 38 million acres of land, by 1905 their landholdings had been reduced by treaties and congressional acts to about 2 million acres. Historically, their leadership consisted of a Council of Chiefs. They adopted a simple set of by-laws in 1922, but did not adopt a formal constitution until 1948, having rejected the Indian Reorganization Act in 1935. The document below entrenched the General Council–type of government whereby the entire adult population, constituting the legislative body of the nation, were to meet regularly. This constitution remained in effect until it was replaced by another in 2001.

Constitution

Preamble

The Crow Tribe of Indians, in an effort to enforce the respect of their basic human, constitutional and treaty rights, do hereby re-establish the Crow Tribal Council to represent, act and speak for the Crow Tribe in any and all tribal matters, and to promote the general welfare of the Crow Tribe, do adopt the following constitution and bylaws for the conduct of Crow Tribal matters in conjunction with the lawful right of the Bureau of Indian Affairs to conduct same.

Article I

The Crow Tribal Council shall be composed of the entire membership of the Crow Tribe.

Article II (Res. 62–11)

The council shall elect every two (2) years, in conformity to its rules of procedure, a Chairman, Vice-Chairman, Secretary and Vice-Secretary. The Chairman shall have no vote unless there be a tie vote before the council. The election for these officers shall be held the second Saturday of May every other year after May 12, then the first election shall be held under this constitutional change. Officials are to assume their duties July 1, after election.

Article III

Any duly enrolled member of the Crow Tribe, except as herein provided, shall be entitled to engage in the deliberations and voting of the council, provided the females are 18 years old and the males 21 years.

Article IV

All nominations for officers of the council and any other tribal matter before the council shall be by voice, standing, hand-raising or secret ballot, as the council shall elect at each of its meetings.

Article V

The Crow Tribe, through its tribal council, reserves unto itself the right to remove for cause any officer of the council, for misconduct or negligence or non-diligence in connection with the protection of the rights of the Crow Tribe in its relations with the Bureau of Indian Affairs or the local employees.

Article VI (Res. 62–11)

The Powers, Duties, and Functions of the Council:

1. The Council shall establish its own rules of procedure.
2. Meetings. There shall be regular tribal council meetings held each year on the second Saturday of January, the second Saturday of April, the second Saturday of July and the second Saturday of October, and as many additional meetings shall be held as tribal business may require. All meetings shall be called by the Chairman and the Committee....

Article VII

Status and Functions of the Council:

1. The Crow Tribal Council is the voice of the Crow Tribe.
2. The Crow Tribal Council is the medium, the body, the tribal organization through which the Crow Tribe speaks to the government and the general public.
3. The Council, representing the entire Crow Tribe, shall voice the opinions, wishes, sentiment, hopes and decisions in any and all tribal matters for the Crow people to the Congress and the Interior Department, by resolutions and through tribally elected delegates who shall, under instructions of the council, proceed to Washington or elsewhere to present in person such decisions and their own arguments and appeals in support thereof as the council shall direct by majority vote.
4. Subject to existing Federal law which endows the Congress with plenary powers over the Indians in their tribal state, and which in turn passes such authorities down the line to the Secretary of the Interior and the Commissioner of Indian Affairs, who by regulations based upon acts of the Congress, control the management of Indian Affairs subject to constitutional limitations. The Crow Tribal Council, without legal status as such, but being the mouth piece and the voice of the Crow people, will from time to time call to the attention of the Congress its views and wishes with respect to the administration of its rights, property and affairs by the Bureau of Indian Affairs.

5. Because of existing law governing Indian administration by the Congress herein pointed out, the Crow Council admits its limited authority in the administration of its own tribal matters, but also, understanding the constitutional limitations of the government in this same field, the Crow Tribal Council will sponsor all legislation with state, federal and local governments on behalf of the Crow Tribe, and will, through tribal council resolutions and elected delegates and representatives, consult with and otherwise deal with representatives of the department of the government of the United States on all matters affecting the interests of the Crow Tribe.

6. The Crow Tribal Council, which encompasses the entire membership of the Crow Tribe, so far as the Crow people are concerned, shall be supreme in determining by a majority vote of those attending, any course of action taken which is designed to protect Crow tribal interests....

By-Laws

Ratification of Constitution and Bylaws

This Constitution and the attached Bylaws, when adopted by a majority vote of those attending District Councils called to vote on accepting a Constitution and Bylaws shall be binding upon the Crow Tribe.

Certificate of Adoption

Pursuant to the constitutional election held on June 24, 1948, this Constitution and Bylaws of the Crow Tribal Council of Montana, was adopted by a vote of 295 for and 130 against in an election in which 425 votes were cast.
Robert Yellowtail, Chairman, Tribal Council

Source:

Lopach, James J., Margery Hunter Brown, and Richmond L. Clow. *Tribal Government Today: Politics on Montana Indian Reservations*, rev. ed. Niwot: University Press of Colorado, 1990.

23   *Toledo v. Pueblo de Jemez (1954)*

In *Native American Church v. Navajo Tribal Council* (1959), a federal court held that the Free Exercise Clause of the First Amendment did not apply to the

Navajo Nation, which had passed an ordinance making it illegal to use or possess peyote in Navajo country. Cases like this prompted some in Indian Country to pressure Congress to provide a remedy. Congress responded in 1968 by adopting the Indian Civil Rights Act (ICRA), which was the first piece of federal legislation to impose statutory versions of many of the provisions of the US Bill of Rights on the actions of Tribal governments vis-à-vis reservation residents—natives and non-natives.

The ICRA was a deeply intrusive law into the heart of Indian Country, yet its provisions are not explicit constitutional restrictions and frequently cannot be enforced by a private right of action in federal court. The only express remedy provided in the measure is a writ of habeas corpus (an order requiring a person to be brought before a judge or into a court to determine the lawfulness of their imprisonment), as was established in *Santa Clara Pueblo v. Martinez* (1978).

Since their first contacts with the Spanish in the seventeenth century, Pueblo communities have been heavily influenced by Catholicism. In the following case, the government of the Jemez Pueblo had refused to allow anyone except followers of the Catholic Church to be interred in its cemetery, denied missionaries of the Protestant faith the ability to proselytize, and refused Protestant adherents permission to build a church. The aggrieved Protestant Pueblo citizens filed this suit arguing that their constitutional rights had been violated. The district court disagreed, holding that the US Constitution's First Amendment protections did not apply to Pueblo community members.

———

Six Jemez Pueblo Indians, all of whom are members of various Protestant denominations, filed a complaint for a declaratory judgment for themselves and in a representative capacity, against the Pueblo de Jemez, a community of Pueblo Indians, in New Mexico, and the Governor of that Pueblo, charging that the Pueblo through its governing body and its Governor has subjected them to indignities, threats and reprisals because of their Protestant faith. All of the plaintiffs and those whom they represent are citizens of the United States.

Specifically, the plaintiffs complain that the Pueblo has refused them the right to bury their dead in the community cemetery; denied them the right to build a church of their own on Pueblo land; prohibited them from using their homes for church purposes; refused to permit Protestant missionaries freely to enter the Pueblo at reasonable times; deprived some of them of the right to use a communal threshing machine which threatened the loss of their wheat crop. They also allege that the officials of the Pueblo threatened them with loss of their birthrights, homes and personal property unless they accept the Catholic religion. All this was done, it is alleged, despite the fact that the Pueblo had validly adopted an ordinance recognizing that every member of the Pueblo should have freedom to worship as his conscience dictates and that no member of the Pueblo should be molested in person or property by the Pueblo on account of his or her mode of religious worship.

It is worthy of emphasis that the plaintiffs carefully acknowledge and allege specifically that the dispute is not between the Catholic and Protestant Churches or faiths as such but is one between the civil authorities of the Pueblo and the plaintiffs who adhere to various Protestant denominations.

The complaint is founded solely on alleged violations of the Civil Rights Act, Title 8, U.S.C.A. S.43 which reads: "Every person who, under color of any statute, ordinance, regulation, custom, or usage, of any State or Territory, subjects, or causes to be subjected, any citizen of the United States or other person within the jurisdiction thereof to the deprivation of any rights, privileges, or immunities secured by the Constitution and laws, shall be liable to the party injured in an action at law, suit in equity, or other proper proceeding for redress."

The jurisdiction of this court is alleged by the complaint to be based on Title 8, U.S.C.A. S.1343(3) which reads: "The district courts shall have original jurisdiction of any civil action authorized by law to be commenced by any person:...(3) To redress the deprivation, under color of any State law, statute, ordinance, regulation, custom or usage, of any right, privilege or immunity secured by the Constitution of the United States or by any Act of Congress providing for equal rights of citizens or of all persons within the jurisdiction of the United States."

The defendants filed motions to dismiss the complaint on the ground that this court has no jurisdiction for the reason that none of the actions complained of by the plaintiffs was taken under color of any statute, ordinance, regulation, custom or usage of any State or Territory.

Other grounds were contained in the motions to dismiss, but the one set out explicitly is the only one to which consideration need be given.

There is, therefore, presented a serious charge of invasion of religious liberty by a Pueblo Indian tribal government. The question for decision is not whether the tribal government has the right to interfere with the religious beliefs and practices of its members but whether or not the objectionable actions of the Pueblo come within the scope of the Civil Rights Act and whether this court has jurisdiction of this case as it is presented by the complaint.

There are some general allegations in the complaint that the actions of the defendants amounted to a violation of the First Amendment to the Constitution of the United States the guarantees of which it is said are among the privileges and immunities protected from state action by the Fourteenth Amendment. Likewise, in general terms, there are references to the Treaty of Guadalupe Hidalgo and to the *Kearney Code of Laws* of New Mexico. However, the heart of the whole case rests upon the question of whether or not the defendants acted under color of a law, statute, ordinance, regulation, custom or usage of New Mexico.

United States District Courts have only special or limited jurisdiction. They have only the jurisdiction that Congress has given them by statute. With jurisdiction so stringently narrowed, it is not every case that may be brought in this court no matter how serious a problem is presented nor how great the necessity for remedial action. Always this court must act within the scope of its jurisdiction. Otherwise, its action is of no validity.

For an action to succeed under the Civil Rights Statute which plaintiffs rely on, at least two conditions must exist. First, a person must be subjected to the deprivation of some right, privilege or immunity secured him by the Constitution and laws of the United States. Second, the action complained of must have been done under the color of a statute, ordinance, regulation, custom or usage of a state or territory. To bring themselves within the second condition the plaintiffs contend that by an 1847 Law of New Mexico, now carried as Section 54–1601, N.M. Statute 1941, Ann., all of the Pueblos of New Mexico, including the defendant, were constituted bodies politic and corporate with the right to sue and be sued in certain types of cases and that this is sufficient in and of itself to permit the court to conclude that the action of the defendants was under color of state law. However, the New Mexico Statute does not purport to vest any governmental powers, rights or duties in the Pueblos of New Mexico which are dependent Indian communities, Indian Tribes, under the guardianship of the United States. *United States v. Sandoval, United States v. Candelaria.* The Pueblo Lands Act, Act of June 7, 1924, 43 Stat. 636, is a statutory recognition of the guardianship of the United States over Pueblos or Pueblo Indians. Not to be ignored in this connection is Section 2 of Article 21 of the Constitution of New Mexico which provides that New Mexico disclaims all right to land within its boundaries owned or held by any Indian or Indian tribe, the right or title to which shall have been acquired through the United States or any prior sovereignty. Until the title of the Indian or Indian tribes has been extinguished said lands remain under the absolute jurisdiction and control of Congress. It is Congress and not the State of New Mexico that legislates for the Pueblos of New Mexico. At least since the *Sandoval* decision in 1913, it has been clear that the Pueblos do no derive their governmental powers from the State of New Mexico. It has, indeed, been held that the powers of an Indian tribe do not spring from the United States although they are subject to the paramount authority of Congress—*Talton v. Mayes* (1896). Their right to govern themselves has been recognized in such statutes as the Indian Reorganization Act, Act of June 18, 1934, 48 Stat. 984, as amended.

Consequently, there is no basis for holding that the conduct of the defendants of which the plaintiffs complain was done under color of state law, statute, ordinance, regulation, custom or usage.

In these circumstances the Court must conclude that since the defendants did not act under color of state law, statute, ordinance, regulation, custom or usage no violation of the Civil Rights Act has been alleged and the Court, therefore, has no jurisdiction of the case under Section 1343(3) of Title 28 U.S.C. A.

The complaint, therefore, will be dismissed.

Source:

Toledo v. Pueblo de Jemez, 119 F. Supp. 429 (March 8, 1954).

24

Termination of the Confederated Tribes of the Grand Ronde and the Confederated Tribes of the Siletz Communities (1954)

The federal policy of termination of the trust relationship with Native peoples was adopted in 1953 by congressional resolution. Designed with the dual purpose of saving federal dollars while intensifying the assimilation of Indigenous peoples into the body politic, the policy was rigorously applied in Oregon, wherein resided approximately 2,100 Tribal citizens belonging to sixty nations. Unsurprisingly, these documents evince the government's goals, but they also offer a poignant glimpse into the sentiments of Native communities in Oregon—sentiments that would prove woefully naive once the full impacts of the policy were felt. The Siletz Tribes were federally restored in 1977; the Grand Ronde Tribes were reinstated as federally recognized peoples in 1983.

Letter from Orme Lewis, Assistant Secretary of the Interior, to Richard Nixon, President of the Senate (Jan. 4, 1954)

My Dear Mr. President: There is transmitted herewith a draft of a proposed bill to provide for the termination of Federal supervision over the property of certain tribes and bands of Indians in western Oregon and the individual members thereof, and for other purposes.

The submission of the proposed bill is in accord with the policy of this department and the Congress as expressed in House Concurrent Resolution 108, 83d Cong., 1st session, to terminate relationships with tribes and groups of Indians as rapidly as the circumstances of each tribe or group will permit. It is requested that the proposed bill be referred to the appropriate committee for consideration.

We are also enclosing a section-by-section analysis of the proposed legislation, together with the report dated December 1953, and entitled "Proposed Withdrawal of Federal Responsibilities Over the Property and Affairs of the Indians of Western Oregon," by the Portland area office of the Bureau of Indian Affairs of this department, to provide relevant factual background material.

It is our belief that the Indians subject to the proposed bill no longer require special assistance from the federal government, and that they have sufficient skill and ability to manage their own affairs. Through long association and intermarriage with their white neighbors, education in public schools, employment and gainful occupations in order to obtain a livelihood, and dependence on public institutions for public services, the Indians have largely been integrated into the white society where they are accepted without discrimination. The services provided to them by the Bureau of Indian Affairs have been curtailed over the years and are now confined primarily to the disbursement of money from individual Indian money accounts, assistance in timber sales, management of the remaining trust property, and hospitalization of a few Indians from time to time. The Grand Ronde-Siletz Agency, which formerly served these tribes and groups, has been closed for several years and the remaining functions are now handled by the Portland area office.

The Indians include numerous small bands, tribes, and groups and number about 2,100 individuals in all. They reside at scattered locations in Western Oregon between the Cascade Mountain Range and the Pacific Ocean, from the Columbia River in the north to the California border in the south. About 800 of the Indians maintain no tribal organization and are not usually identified as tribal groups. Over 700 of the Indians are members of the Confederated Tribes of Siletz Indians, which are loosely organized to carry on tribal functions. The remainder of over 500 individuals organized as the Confederated Tribes of the Grand Ronde Community under the act of June 18, 1934, known as the Indian Reorganization Act.

Details concerning the status of these groups can be found in the enclosed report. In summary, there was a total of 13,596.84 acres of land still in the trust status, most of which is allotted to individuals. The status of the lands differs for the three main groups concerned. As the Indians of the Grand Ronde Community are organized under the Indian Reorganization Act, the trust period is, in accordance with section 2 of that act, extended indefinitely until otherwise directed by the Congress. The trust period on allotments held by the Siletz Indians was extended until 1964. For the public domain allotments, trusts have been extended by several executive orders, generally for a 25 year period, with the actual date depending on the year in which the previous trust expired.

The proposed bill has been drafted along the general pattern of terminal legislation submitted to the Congress in response to House Concurrent Resolution 108. While it is designed to accomplish the same purpose as H. R. 7489, introduced in the 82nd Congress, we believe that the proposed bill more nearly meets the legislative requirements for termination program. It provides for termination of Federal supervision of the real and personal property of the Indians, authorizes the disposition of federally owned property or facilities established for their benefit, and terminates all federal responsibility with respect to them except the responsibility the federal government assumes for its citizens in general.

The proposed bill will not, however, apply to the distribution of the judgments recovered by the Rogue River Indians, the Alcea Band of Tillamooks, and other bands of Indians in this area, all of whom are among the Indians affected by the bill. Under section 4 of the Jurisdictional Act of August 26, 1935, monies from these judgments may not be distributed without specific appropriation by the Congress....

The proposed bill in substantially its present form has been discussed at length with the various groups of Indians. While their reactions have generally been favorable, they have declined to take any positive action on these proposals until their judgment funds are distributed. It has also been discussed with state and county officials, who have indicated they have no objection to its enactment. Further reports on these discussions are included in the enclosed "withdrawal plan."

Since I am informed there is a particular urgency for the submission of the views of the department, this report is not been cleared through the Bureau of the Budget and, therefore, no commitment can be made concerning the relationship of the views expressed herein to the program of the president.

Sincerely yours,

Orme Lewis, Assistant Secretary of the Interior

Resolution of Approval Adopted by the Confederated Tribes of the Siletz Indians

Whereas we the members of the Confederated Tribes of the Siletz Indians feel that we have advanced in education, customs, and knowledge with the present age, have had a long association with the non-Indian population, our children are attending the public schools and we, ourselves, have attended public schools before them, and the English language is spoken by us universally; and

Whereas we feel that while our contacts and relationship with the personnel of the United States Bureau of Indian Affairs have been cordial, we feel that we are able, willing, and should assume the duties and responsibilities of full American citizenship and are competent to conduct our own business affairs without restrictions being placed as to the sale of timber on our lands, spending proceeds of such sales, and in conducting business generally in connection with our resources now held in trust by the federal government; and

Whereas we now feel that federal supervision has ceased to be necessary and it has in many cases, through antiquated regulations, become a burden to our people and no longer conducive to our welfare, present and future: Be it therefore

Resolved, That the federal government withdraw all restrictions and services now existing, in so far as the Indians of the Siletz Reservation are concerned, at the earliest practicable moment; that patents in fee be issued to the Confederated Tribes of the Siletz Indians, for all tribal property; that patents in fee be issued to Indian owners in case of all individual trust allotments, thus making all of these lands subject to state real property taxation; that health services now being extended by the Bureau of Indian Affairs be dispensed with and that all acts and functions necessary and required to eliminate each and every federal control of existing wardship as to the said Siletz Indians be performed; be it further

Resolved, That a roll of present members of the Confederated Tribes of the Siletz Indians be prepared by the Bureau of Indian affairs, for approval of the governing body of the said Confederated Tribes of the Siletz Indians, and that upon the withdrawal by the federal government of controls and supervision, the members whose names are listed on said roll, including their minor children and immediate families, shall thereafter be accorded full citizenship, including the right of obtaining and consuming intoxicants under state and federal laws, in the same manner and to the same extent as afforded other American citizens in the state in which they reside.

Done this 12th day of November, at regular meeting of the General Council of the Confederated Tribes of the Siletz Indians, held at Siletz, Oreon. Confederated Tribes of the Siletz Indians, Elmer Logan. Chairman.

Resolution of Approval Adopted by the Confederated Tribes of the Grand Ronde Community

Whereas the membership of the Confederated Tribes of the Grand Ronde community has, on two occasions, recently met, discussed, and voted on the proposition of early termination of selected activities and withdrawal of federal supervision over the Indians of Grand Ronde; and

Whereas the response of said membership has been a reluctance to accept said program of termination and withdrawal, on the grounds that no provision has been made therein to compensate the membership for loss of alleged rights to fish and hunt, believed to have been retained by the Indians when their lands were ceded by them, or when appropriated by the federal government without their consent; and

Whereas the following draft of bill has been discussed with this committee:

Section 1. It is the purpose of this act to provide for termination of Federal supervision over the trust and restricted property of Indian tribes, bands, and individual Indians that were formerly under the jurisdiction of the Grand Ronde and Siletz Agencies, Oregon, for the disposition of lands set aside for the use and benefit of such Indians, and for determination of the federal services furnished such Indians because of their status as Indians.

Section 2. In order to terminate federal supervision over the trust and restricted lands of Indian tribes and bands that were formerly under the jurisdiction of the Grand Ronde and Siletz Agencies, Oregon, and over lands set aside for the use and benefit of such tribes and bands, including improvements thereon, the secretary of the interior is here authorized—

- A. To issue patents in fee or deeds to such lands owned by or set aside for a tribe or band that incorporates or organizes under the laws of the state of Oregon with powers in the form of organization satisfactory to the secretary.
- B. To sell such lands upon such terms and conditions as he deems proper and distribute the proceeds of sale to the tribe or band or the members thereof: Provided, That no such lands shall be sold without the approval of the tribe or band if within a time prescribed by the secretary the tribe or band incorporates or organizes under the laws of the state of Oregon with powers in the form of organization satisfactory to the secretary.
- C. To remove restrictions from, sell, or otherwise dispose of trust or restricted personal property of such tribes or bands.

Section 3. In order to terminate federal supervision over the trust and restricted lands of individual Indians that were formerly under the jurisdiction of the Grand Ronde and Siletz Agencies, Oregon, the secretary is hereby authorized to issue to the Indian owners thereof without their consent patents in fee and orders removing restrictions unless within the time prescribed by the secretary the Indian owners request or consent to sale of the land pursuant to existing laws.

Section 4. When federal supervision over all or substantially all the trust and restricted property subject to the provisions of sections 2 and 3 of this act has been terminated, the secretary of the Interior shall proclaim that fact and the Indian tribes, bands, and individual Indians involved shall not be eligible thereafter for the educational, health, welfare, rehabilitation and other services extended by the United States to Indians because of their status as Indians.

Section 5. Upon issuance of the proclamation referred to in section 4 of this act the state of Oregon shall have civil and criminal jurisdiction over the persons and property of the Indian tribes, bands...and individual Indians formerly under the jurisdiction of the Grand Ronde and Siletz Agencies, Oregon, to the same extent the state has jurisdiction over the persons and property of other persons and property in the state; such Indian tribes, bands, and individual Indians shall have all the rights, privileges, immunities, and obligations possessed by other citizens of the state and the statutes of the United States applicable to the Indian country shall be inapplicable to such Indians and their property.

Section 6. The charter issued by the secretary of the interior under the provisions of the Indian Reorganization Act...to the Confederated Tribes of the Grand Ronde Community, Oregon, and ratified by the community on August 22, 1936, is hereby revoked, the revocation to become effective on the date of the proclamation referred to in section 4 of this act.

Section 7. Nothing contained in this act shall affect any claim hereto for or hereafter filed in accordance with the provisions of the act of August 13, 1946, but nothing in this act shall be made the basis for such a claim.

Whereas the business committee believes that it is the will and mandate of the membership, as evinced by actions previously taken as stated herein, that the federal government should withdraw its supervision over the Indians of the former Grand Ronde Reservation and that the draft of the bill set forth herein is satisfactory to said membership, with the exception of a portion of section 7: Therefore be it

Resolved, That the Confederated Tribes of the Grand Ronde Community does hereby approve the draft of the bill set forth herein, provided that section 7 thereof shall be amended by deleting the following words, immediately following "62 Stat. 1049": "but nothing in this act shall be made the basis for such a claim," and by substituting therefore the following: "and nothing contained in this act shall be construed to deprive any Indian of any hunting, fishing, or other right or privilege under federal law, treaty or agreement."

Adopted by the business committee of the Confederated Tribes of Grand Ronde Community in regular session, duly noticed and called, at which for members representing a quorum for conducting business were present, by an affirmative vote of four members and no dissenting votes, this 22nd day of August 1951, at Grand Ronde, Oregon.

Business Committee of Confederated Tribes of the Grand Ronde Community, Celia Smith, Chairman

Source:

US Senate. "Termination of Federal Supervision over Property of Certain Indians in Western Oregon." Rept. No. 1325. 83rd Cong., 2nd Sess. Washington, DC: Government Printing Office, May 12, 1954.

25
Navajo Nation Extradition Ordinance (1956)

Article 1 of the Treaty with the Navajo, negotiated in 1868, addresses the issue of criminal jurisdiction as it was to be resolved between the United States and the Navajo people. It formed the basis for this extradition ordinance in 1956 whereby the Navajo Nation declared that it would not release tribal defendants to other sovereigns unless in accordance with appropriate procedures. This law remained intact until it was amended in 2013.

Indian committing crime outside Indian Country—Apprehension on Reservation Whenever the President of the Navajo Nation is informed and believes that an Indian has committed a crime outside of Indian Country and is present in Navajo "Indian Country" and using it as an asylum from prosecution by the state, the President of the Navajo Nation may order any Navajo policeman to apprehend such Indian and deliver him or her to proper state authorities at the Reservation boundary.

Source:

Navajo Nation Code. Title 17. Law and Order. Section 1951.

26
Iron Crow v. The Oglala Sioux Tribe (1956)

This case dealt with two separate matters—adultery and tax assessment—involving three Oglala Sioux plaintiffs. The Tribal court claimed jurisdiction because two of the plaintiffs were enrolled members of the Oglala Nation and their alleged indiscretions had occurred on the reservation. The plaintiffs challenged the jurisdictional authority of the Oglala Sioux Tribal court. The Eighth Circuit Court of Appeals held the Tribal court had inherent authority to hear the case, although neither the US Constitution nor Congress had authorized the court's establishment.

Judge Vogel's opinion properly rested on the inherent sovereignty of the Oglala Sioux Nation to oversee both issues and the US Constitution's explicit "recognition" of that inherent sovereignty in key clauses such as the Commerce and Treaty provisions. Equally important, the court affirmed the inherent dignity and jurisdictional power of Tribal courts to exercise authority over all matters not taken over by the federal government.

———————

Inasmuch as the appellants' "statement of the case" is completely concurred in by the appellees, this court will adopt it as follows:

Marie Little Finger and David Black Cat, two of the plaintiffs herein, were tried and convicted in the Oglala Sioux Tribe. Jurisdiction was exercised under §§1 and 1.2 of said Code, they both being enrolled members of the Oglala Sioux Tribe and the crime having been committed on the Pine Ridge Reservation. The Tribal Court, after reaching a verdict of guilty, imposed fines on both the plaintiffs and sentenced David Black Cat to 30 days in jail, said jail sentence being suspended on condition of the payment of the fine and good behavior for one year. The fines have not been paid and the tribal authorities intend to proceed with the enforcement of the sentences.

These plaintiffs have brought this suit to enjoin the tribe and its officers from proceeding as intended, alleging that the Tribal Court did not have jurisdiction to try and convict them of the crime of adultery, and that enforcement of the sentences of the Tribal Court would deprive said plaintiffs of liberty and property without due process of law in violation of the Fifth Amendment to the Constitution of the United States.

The facts which were the basis for the verdict of guilty in the proceedings before the Tribal Court and the fairness of the procedures of the Tribal Court are not disputed or involved in this case.

The third plaintiff in this case, Thomas Iron Crow, is an enrolled member of the Oglala Sioux Tribe who possessed allotted land on the Pine Ridge Reservation, the title to which is held by the United States in trust for him. Originally all reservation lands were owned by the Oglala Sioux Tribe as a unit, but subsequently parcels of land, including that used by Thomas Iron Crow, were allotted to individual members of the tribe under applicable federal law. These separate tracts remained in trust status and still are classified as Indian country.

In past years, plaintiff has leased some of his land within the Pine Ridge Reservation for grazing purposes to nonmembers of the Oglala Sioux Tribe and he plans to continue this practice in the future. The Oglala Sioux Tribe has, under the provisions of Tribal Council Resolution 147–50, assessed a tax against plaintiff's lessee for the privilege of grazing stock on land within the reservation, and it in turn plans to continue to assess the tax in the future. Plaintiff now brings this action to enjoin the tribe from proceeding with that tax assessment.

Plaintiffs make two demands: (1) For an injunction prohibiting the Oglala Sioux Tribal Court from proceeding with the enforcement of the sentences against David Black Cat and Marie Little Finger; and (2) for an injunction to enjoin the tribe from proceeding with assessment and collection of the tax.

The court entered its findings of fact, conclusions of law, and judgment for the defendants and dismissed the action upon its merits. This is an appeal from these findings of fact, conclusions of law and the judgment. For purposes of convenience, the parties will be designated as they were referred to in the court below.

In dismissing this action, the trial court prepared an excellent and comprehensive memorandum which will be found in *Thomas Iron Crow v. Oglala*

Sioux Tribe. In the appeal to this court, the plaintiffs set forth six separate points which will be individually discussed. Plaintiffs claim:....

> The status of Indian tribes or nations first received important consideration in the case of *Cherokee Nation v. State of Georgia* (1831). The opinion, by Chief Justice Marshall, held that..."the acts of our government plainly recognize the Cherokee nation as a state, and the courts are bound by those acts," and that "an Indian tribe or nation within the United States is not a foreign state, in the sense of the constitution, and cannot maintain an action in the courts of the United States." The court stated, however, that "they may more correctly perhaps be denominated domestic dependent nations."

The proposition that the Constitution of the United States recognized the sovereignty of Indian tribes obtained greater acknowledgment in the case of *Worcester v. State of Georgia* (1832)...with Chief Justice Marshall again delivering an opinion of the court, wherein he stated: "The legislative power of a state, the controlling power of the constitution and laws of the United States, the rights, if they have any, the political existence of a once numerous and powerful people, the personal liberty of a citizen, are all involved in the subject now to be considered."

....

It would seem clear that the Constitution, as construed by the Supreme Court, acknowledges the paramount authority of the United States with regard to Indian tribes but recognizes the existence of Indian tribes as quasi sovereign entities possessing all the inherent rights of sovereignty excepting where restrictions have been placed thereon by the United States itself....

As late as 1940 the Supreme Court, in the case of *United States v. United States Fidelity & Guaranty Co.*, recognized the *quasi* sovereignty of Indian nations in holding that they possessed the sovereign exemption from suits and from cross-complaints excepting where authorized. Quoting from page 512..."The public policy which exempted the dependent as well as the dominant sovereignties from suit without consent continues this immunity even after dissolution of the tribal government. These Indian Nations are exempt from suit without Congressional authorization. It is as though the immunity which was theirs as sovereigns passed to the United States for their benefit, as their tribal properties did. Possessing this immunity from direct suit, we are of the opinion it possesses a similar immunity from cross-suits."

We accordingly are of the opinion that the plaintiffs cannot prevail on their second point. We hold that Indian tribes, such as the defendant Oglala Sioux Tribe of the Pine Ridge Reservation, South Dakota, still possess their inherent sovereignty excepting only where it has been specifically taken from them, either by treaty or by Congressional Act.

The court erred in its finding that defendants' courts are provided for under the federal constitution.

The plaintiffs would argue that there is found no provision in the Federal Constitution for Indian courts. None is necessary. As already indicated, the Constitution, by authorizing Congress to regulate commerce with the Indian tribes and by authorizing the making of treaties with them, while not in and of itself *establishing* the sovereignty of the tribes, nevertheless does *recognize* their sovereignty. As interpreted by the United States Supreme Court, that sovereignty is absolute excepting only as to such rights as are taken away by the paramount government, the United States. Under this view, not even a Congressional Act would be necessary to establish the legality of the Oglala Sioux Tribal Courts. However, regulatory powers over these judicial establishments have been exercised to promote uniformity, gradual assimilation and other ends.

The court erred in its findings that defendants' courts have been authorized by federal legislative action. ...That Indian courts are authorized by Congress under the foregoing section and companion sections as was held in *United States v. Clapox*. In the *Clapox* case, the defendants were charged with having broken into a reservation jail to free a prisoner confined therein while awaiting trial before a reservation court. The issue was whether the defendants were guilty of the federal offense of having freed a person committed for a crime against the United States. The court held that the general authority given by R.S. Section 463, 25 U.S.C.A. §2, and companion statutes authorized rules of government for the Indians on the reservation, including establishment of an Indian court and police for the enforcement of police regulations, to take cognizance of offenses designated as "Indian offenses," and gave authority to define such offenses....

In 1888, the Congress, in passing the Indian Department Appropriations Act, June 29, 1888, 25 Statute 233, provided for compensation for judges of Indian courts. Continuously since that time the Congress has made appropriations for maintaining law and order among Indians, *including pay and other expenses of judges of Indian courts*, Indian police and employees engaged in suppression of traffic in intoxicating liquors and deleterious drugs among the Indians.

The Bureau of Indian Affairs Authorization Act, 42 Statute 209, 1921, 25 U.S.C.A. §13, is particularly significant. It provided: "The Bureau of Indian Affairs, under the supervision of the Secretary of the Interior, shall direct, supervise, and expend such moneys as Congress may from time to time to appropriate***for the following purposes: 'For the employment of inspectors, supervisors, superintendents, clerks, field matrons, farmers, physicians, Indian police, Indian judges, and other employees.' "

This statute is still in effect and appropriations for the Indian Bureau are currently being made under its authority. That Congress specifically recognizes the authority of Indian Tribal Courts becomes patent from the provisions of Section 1152 of Title 18 U.S.C.A §1152. Laws governing. Except as otherwise expressly provided by law, the general laws of the United States as to the punishment of offenses committed in any place within the sole and exclusive jurisdiction of the United States, except the District of Columbia, shall extend to the Indian Country

"This section shall not extend to offenses committed by one Indian against the person or property of another Indian, nor to any Indian committing any offense in the Indian country who has been punished by the local law of the tribe, or to any case where, by treaty stipulations, the exclusive jurisdiction over such offenses is or may be secured to the Indian tribes respectively." We must conclude that the trial court was eminently correct in its statement, at page 19, that: "There can be little doubt *** that Congress has actually authorized the established and operation of the Ogallala Sioux Tribal Court." ...

Originally, and until 1885, all offenses committed by Indians within the confines of Indian country were under the jurisdiction of the Tribal Courts.

In 1885 Congress passed what is sometimes referred to as the "Seven Major Crimes Act." Therein, 23 Statute 362, 385, Mar. 3, 1885, Ch. 341, Sec. 9, 18 U.S.C.A. §548, Congress brought under federal jurisdiction the crimes of murder, manslaughter, rape, assault with intent to kill, arson, burglary and larceny. Subsequently three additional crimes were included, to-wit: incest, assault with a dangerous weapon and robbery. The clear inference is that Congress left to the Indian Tribal Courts jurisdiction over all crimes not taken by the federal government itself.... We accordingly hold that not only do the Indian Tribal Courts have inherent jurisdiction over all matters not taken over by the federal government, but that federal legislative action and rules promulgated thereunder support the authority of the Tribal Courts.

The court erred in its finding that the defendants have sovereign authority to set up a system of courts with civil and criminal jurisdiction over citizens of the United States of America, and the State of South Dakota.

This brings into the foreground the question of whether the granting of citizenship to the Indians has changed the status of Tribal Courts.

Prior to 1924 only some Indians possessed citizenship and that by reason of treaties between the United States and the Indian tribes or by special statute. The Act of June 2, 1924...provided as follows: "That all noncitizen Indians born within the territorial limits of the United States be, and they are hereby, declared to be citizens of the United States: Provided, That the granting of such citizenship shall not in any manner impair or otherwise affect the right of any Indian to tribal or other property."

Plaintiffs argue that as citizens of the United States they should have the right of free access to the courts of justice of the several states and that such right is, in its nature, independent of the will of any state. Plaintiffs claim that as citizens they "...have the right to prosecute and defend actions in the courts of the commonwealth according to the established rules of procedure...." The Supreme Court has answered this question in several cases. See *United States v. Nice* (1916). That case arose out of the prosecution of the defendant on a charge of having sold liquor to an Indian. The defense was that the Indian purchaser was a citizen. The lower court sustained a demurrer to the indictment and appeal was taken directly to the Supreme Court....

That Congress did not intend by the granting of citizenship to all Indians born in the United States to terminate the Indian Tribal Court system is patent from the fact that at the same session of Congress and at sessions continuously subsequent thereto funds have been appropriated for the maintenance of the Indian Tribal Courts. We hold that the granting of citizenship in itself did not destroy tribal existence or jurisdiction of the Indian Tribal Courts and that there was no intention on the part of Congress so to do....

Inasmuch as it has never been taken from it, the defendant Oglala Sioux Tribe possesses the power of taxation which is an inherent incident of its sovereignty. The tribe has seen fit to give orderly implementation to that power through the adoption of its constitution which, among other things, has specifically provided for the levy of taxes. Such action was taken in accordance with the provisions of the Indian Reorganization Act, 1934.

We conclude from the original precept of tribal sovereignty and the fact that the power of the Oglala Sioux Tribe to impose the tax or license in question has not been pretermitted by any federal statute or agency ruling thereunder, but, to the contrary, has been implemented by the Indian Reorganization Act, supra, that such power still exists. This case is in all things affirmed.

Source:

Iron Crow v. Oglala Sioux Tribe of Pine Ridge Reservation, 231 F. 2d 89 (8th Circ 1956).

27   *Embezzlement of Indian Tribal Organization Property (1956)*

The institutionalization of Native governments under the Indian Reorganization Act, along with access to a meager but steady federal revenue stream, precipitated a rise in the level of political corruption on some reservation communities. In response, the federal government created a new criminal sanction for the embezzlement or theft of the property of Indian Tribal organizations. What follows is the congressional testimony and committee discussion regarding this proposal.

Purpose:

The purpose of this legislation is to protect Indian tribal organizations from the actions of dishonest and corrupt tribal officials and from others who embezzle or steal tribal funds or property. It provides for the punishment of persons holding positions of trust in tribal organizations who abuse their responsibilities by diverting tribal funds to their own pockets or those of their friends. It also provides for the punishment of other forms of theft or embezzlement from Indian tribal organizations.

Statement:

The Indian Reorganization Act of June 18, 1934 (48 Stat. 984) deals with a wide variety of subjects, including land, credit, education, and Indian employment.

During the years since its adoption, situations have been encountered from time to time that involve the misuse or misappropriation of tribal funds and other improper actions by tribal officials and other persons. While many trust and other fiduciary positions have been created to take care of tribal business affairs and tribal moneys, corresponding safeguards in the Federal law or in the tribal codes have not kept pace with these activities. Even in those instances where criminal sanctions are provided in the tribal codes, tribal members in some instances have been reluctant to bring actions against apparently faithless tribal officials.

Under the authority of the Indian Reorganization Act, many Indian groups are qualified to obtain control of substantial sums of money derived from oil and gas leases, timber sales, and the like, to hold these funds in the tribal treasuries, and to expend them subject to the tribal constitutions and charters. In addition, under annual appropriation acts adopted by the Congress, tribal funds in the Treasury of the United States may be advanced to Indian tribes.

Under these circumstances, it is felt that adequate Federal penal safeguards are necessary to protect the tribal members and the public generally from actions of dishonest and corrupt tribal officials, and of other persons, including non-Indians, who commit these offenses involving tribal property.

This legislation has been requested by the Department of the Interior, and its executive communication, together with the views of the Department of Justice, are made a part of this report....

Honorable Sam Rayburn, Speaker of the House of Representatives, Washington, DC

My Dear Mr. Speaker: Enclosed is a draft of a proposed bill to amend Title 18, entitled "Crime and Criminal Procedure," of the *United States Code*, to provide a criminal sanction for the embezzlement or theft of the property of Indian tribal organizations.

We recommend that this proposed bill be referred to the appropriate committee for consideration, and we further recommend that it be enacted.

The principal objective of the proposed bill is to protect Indian tribal organizations, especially those created pursuant to the Indian Reorganization Act of June 18, 1934 (48 Stat. 984), from the actions of dishonest or corrupt tribal officials. It provides for the punishment of persons holding positions of trust in tribal organizations who abuse their responsibilities by diverting tribal funds to their own pockets or those of their friends. It also provides for the punishment of other forms of theft or embezzlement from Indian tribal organizations. The terms of the bill are modeled upon such existing criminal laws as sections 641, 656, and 660 of Title 18 of the *United States Code*.

The Indian Reorganization Act deals with a wide variety of subjects, including land, credit, education, and Indian employment. One of its chief designs was the development of Indian self-government. At the present time there are 195 tribes, bands, or identifiable groups under the act. Ninety-six of these groups have adopted constitutions and bylaws, and 73 of them have been granted charters permitting them to operate as chartered business organizations. In addition, there are some 77 tribes, bands, or identifiable groups which elected not to come under the Indian Reorganization Act but which are carrying on tribal affairs in some degree and are to some degree self-governing. A number of other Indian groups are organized under special laws pertaining to Oklahoma and Alaska.

During the years since the first group was organized under the Indian Reorganization Act, situations have been encountered from time to time that involved the misuse or misappropriation of tribal funds, the lack of adequate accounting records, or other improper actions by tribal officials. Occasionally, the same official has been guilty of repeated breeches of trust. Yet in most instances the creation of fiduciary positions has not been paralleled by corresponding safeguards in the law and order codes under which the tribes operate. Even in these instances where criminal sanctions are provided in the tribal codes, the tribal members have been extremely reluctant to bring actions in the tribal courts against apparently faithless tribal officials. The only practical recourse available to tribal members, therefore, has been to vote the malefactors out of office in the tribal elections.

Under authority of the Indian Reorganization Act, many Indian groups are qualified to obtain control of substantial sums of money derived from oil and gas leases, timber sales, and the like; to hold these funds in the tribal treasuries; and to expend them subject only to the limitations contained in the tribal constitutions and charters. In addition, under annual appropriation acts for the Department of the Interior and various special acts of Congress, tribal funds in the Treasury of the United States may be advanced to Indian tribes for such purposes as may be designated by the governing body of the particular tribe involved and approved by the Secretary of the Interior. In these circumstances, it is important that adequate penal safeguards be established to protect the tribal members from actions of dishonest or corrupt tribal officials and other types of peculation. This the proposed bill would do.

The Bureau of the Budget has advised that there is no objection to the submission of this proposed bill to the Congress.

Sincerely yours, Fred G. Aandahl, Assistant Secretary of the Interior....

Source:

US Congress. House of Representatives. "Embezzlement of Indian Tribal Organization Property." H.R. No. 2427. 84th Cong., 2nd Sess. Washington, DC: Government Printing Office, 1956.

28   *Amended Constitution of the Northern Cheyenne Tribe (1960)*

The Cheyenne refer to themselves as Tse-tsehese-staestsa, "the People." Today they are divided into two Nations, the Southern Cheyenne, residing in present-day

Oklahoma, and the Northern Cheyenne, who have lived on an executive-order reservation in southeastern Montana since 1884. Historically, the Cheyenne were governed by a Council of Forty-Four, a group comprised of forty peace chiefs (four from each of the ten bands) who each served for ten years. Another four leaders were always held over from the previous term to serve with the newly chosen forty, one of whom was called a Sweet Medicine Chief. Plaiting together the outgoing with the incoming leadership assured continuity and accountability. Under this leadership, several military or war societies maintained community discipline and carried out council recommendations. The Northern Cheyenne organized its first constitution in 1935 under the auspices of the Indian Reorganization Act. That document lasted until it was amended by the ensuing charter in 1960. Notwithstanding the Constitution, the Council of Forty-Four continues to have a role, although a modified one, in both Cheyenne communities.

———

Preamble

We, the members of the Northern Cheyenne Tribe of the Northern Cheyenne Indian Reservation in Montana, in order to establish a more unified tribal organization and to insure and promote the best interests of our society, industry, prosperity, and the general welfare of ourselves and our posterity do hereby establish this Constitution and Bylaws.

Article 1—Territory

The jurisdiction of the Northern Cheyenne Tribe under this Constitution and Bylaws shall extend to the territory within the confines of the Northern Cheyenne Indian Reservation boundaries as established by Executive Order dated November 26, 1884, under the administration of Chester A. Arthur and extended March 19, 1900, under the administration of William McKinley and to such other lands as may be hereafter added thereto by any law of the United States, except as otherwise provided by law.

Article 2—Membership

Section 1. The membership of the Northern Cheyenne Tribe shall consist of as follows:

  (a) All persons of Northern Cheyenne Indian blood whose names appear on the official census roll as of January 1, 1935, provided that by January 1, 1962, corrections shall be made in said roll by the Tribal Council, subject to approval of the Secretary of the Interior.
  (b) Each person of one-half (1/2) or more Northern Cheyenne Indian blood, regardless of residence, born heretofore or hereafter to any member or descendant of a member of the Northern Cheyenne Tribe whose name

was or is on the census roll referred to in Section 1(a) shall automatically be entitled to membership in the Northern Cheyenne Tribe.

(c) All children heretofore born to any member of the Northern Cheyenne Tribe who is a resident of the Northern Cheyenne Indian Reorganization at the time of the birth of said children.

Section 2. The Tribal Council shall have power to promulgate ordinances, subject to review by the Secretary of the Interior, covering future membership including adoptions and the loss of membership.

Article 3—Governing Body

Section 1. The governing body of the Northern Cheyenne Tribe under this Constitution and Bylaws shall be a council which shall hereafter be known as "The Tribal Council of the Northern Cheyenne."

Section 2. The Tribal Council shall consist of members elected from each of the following districts: Ashland, Birney, Busby, Muddy and Lame Deer in the proportion of one member for each two-hundred (200) population and an additional member for each major fraction thereof. The present Tribal Council shall designate the boundaries of each district named herein prior to the election of the first Tribal Council and the Tribal Council thereafter shall have power to change the boundaries of the districts.

Section 3. The officers of the Tribal Council shall be a President who shall be nominated and elected by popular vote as hereinafter provided; a Vice President and a Sergeant-at-Arms elected by the Tribal Council from within its own number; and a Secretary and a Treasurer appointed by the Tribal Council from outside its number. The Secretary and the Treasurer shall have no vote. Other officers and committees shall be appointed as provided for in the duties of the President....

Article 4—Powers of the Tribal Council

Section 1. Enumerated Powers.—The Tribal Council of the Northern Cheyenne shall exercise the following powers, subject to any limitations imposed by the applicable statutes of the United States and subject further to all express restrictions upon such powers contained in this Constitution and the attached Bylaws:

(a) To negotiate with the Federal, State, and local governments, on behalf of the Tribe, and to advise and consult with the representatives of the Interior Department on all activities of the Department that may affect the Northern Cheyenne Indian Reservation.

(b) To employ legal counsel for the protection and advancement of the rights of the Northern Cheyenne Tribe and its members, the choice of the counsel and fixing of fees to be subject to the approval of the Secretary of the Interior.

(c) To approve or prevent any sale, disposition, lease or encumbrance of tribal lands, interests in lands or other tribal assets, including minerals, gas and oil.

(d) To advise the Secretary of the Interior with regard to all appropriation estimates or Federal projects for the benefit of the Northern Cheyenne Tribe prior to the submission of such estimates to the Bureau of the Budget and to Congress.

(e) To engage in any business that will further the economic well-being of the members of the Tribe and to undertake any economic activity of any nature whatever not inconsistent with law or any of the provisions of this Constitution.

(f) To administer any funds within the control of the Tribe; to make expenditures from available funds for tribal purposes, including salaries and expenses of tribal officials or employees. All expenditures of tribal funds under control of the Tribal Council shall be by resolution duly approved by a majority of the Tribal Council in legal session and the amounts so expended shall be a matter of public record at all times. The Tribal Council, subject to the approval of the Secretary of the Interior, or his authorized representative, shall prepare annual budget requests for the advancement to the control of the Tribe such money as is now or may hereafter be deposited to the credit of the Tribe in the United States Treasury or which may hereafter be appropriated for the use of the Tribe.

(g) To levy taxes or assessments upon members of the Northern Cheyenne Tribe and to require the performance of community labor in lieu thereof, and to levy taxes or license fees, subject to review by the Secretary of the Interior, upon nonmembers doing business within the reservation.

(h) To exclude from the restricted lands of the Northern Cheyenne Indian Reservation persons not legally entitled to reside therein, under ordinances which shall be subject to review by the Secretary of the Interior.

(i) To promulgate and enforce ordinances, which shall be subject to review by the Secretary of the Interior, governing the conduct of members of the Northern Cheyenne Tribe and any other person or persons coming within the jurisdiction of the reservation, and providing for the maintenance of law and order and the administration of justice by establishing a reservation court and defining its duties and powers.

(j) To purchase, under condemnation proceedings in courts of competent jurisdiction, land or other property needed for public purposes, subject to the approval of the Secretary of the Interior.

(k) To protect and preserve the property, wildlife, and natural resources of the Tribe and to regulate the conduct of trade and the use and disposition of property upon the reservation, provided that any ordinance directly affecting nonmembers of the Tribe shall be subject to review by the Secretary of the Interior.

(l) To cultivate and preserve native arts, crafts, culture, and Indian ceremonials.

(m) To administer charity and to protect the health and general welfare of the Tribe....

Section 2. Future Powers.—The Tribal Council of the Northern Cheyenne Tribe may exercise such future powers as may in the future be given to the

Council by members of the Tribe through the adoption of appropriate Bylaws and Constitutional amendments.

Section 3. Reserved Powers.—Any right and powers heretofore vested in the Northern Cheyenne Tribe but not expressly referred to in this Constitution shall not be abridged by this article, but may be exercised by the people of the Northern Cheyenne Tribe through the adoption of appropriate Bylaws and Constitutional amendments.

Section 4. Manner of Review.—Any resolution or ordinance which pursuant to this Constitution is subject to review by the Secretary of the Interior, shall be presented to the Superintendent of the Reservation within ten (10) days of enactment by the Tribal Council; and the Superintendent shall, within ten (10) days after receipt, approve or disapprove same....

Article 5—Bill of Rights

Section 1. All members of the Tribe shall be accorded equal opportunities to participate in the economic resources and activities of the Tribe.

Section 2. All members of the Tribe may enjoy, without hindrance, freedom of worship, conscience, speech, press, assembly, and association as guaranteed by the Constitution of the United States.

Article 6—Elections

Section 1. All members of the Tribe eighteen (18) years of age or over shall have the right to vote at all reservation elections, except when the Federal law requires the voter to be twenty-one years of age or over....

Article 7—Removal From Office

Section 1. Forfeiture of Office.—

(a) Any officer or councilman found guilty of a felony in any tribal, county, State, or Federal Court shall automatically be removed from office and may not stand for election for three (3) years thereafter.

(b) Any officer or councilman found guilty of a misdemeanor involving moral turpitude in any court shall automatically be removed from office, but such member may stand for nomination and re-election.

Section 2. Removal from Office.—Any officer or councilman who shall fail to perform the duties assigned to him or shall be guilty of gross neglect may be removed by a two-thirds (2/3) vote of the Tribal Council, after affording the accused member a fair opportunity to be heard in his own defense. The decision of the Tribal Council shall be final.

Section 3. Any complaint against the President, a member, or officer of the Tribal Council must be in writing and sworn to by the complainant . . . .

Article 9—Land

Section 1. Allotted Lands.—Allotted lands, including heirship land, within the Northern Cheyenne Indian Reservation shall continue to be held as heretofore by their present owners. It is recognized that under existing law such lands may be inherited by the heirs of the present owner, whether or not they are members of the Northern Cheyenne Tribe. Likewise, it is recognized that under existing law the Secretary of the Interior may, in his discretion, remove restrictions upon such land, upon application by the Indian owner, whereupon the land will become subject to State taxes and may be mortgaged or sold. The right of the individual Indian to hold or to part with his land, as under existing law, shall not be abrogated by anything contained in this Constitution, but the owner of restricted land may, with the approval of the Secretary of the Interior, voluntarily convey his land to the Northern Cheyenne Tribe either in exchange for a money payment or in exchange for an assignment covering the same land or other land, as hereinafter provided....

Article 10—Amendments

This Constitution and Bylaws may be amended by a majority vote of the qualified voters of the Tribe, voting at an election called for that purpose by the Secretary of the Interior, provided that at least thirty (30) percent of those entitled to vote shall vote in such election, but no amendment shall become effective until it shall have been approved by the Secretary of the Interior. It shall be the duty of the Secretary of the Interior to call an election on any proposed amendment at the request of two-thirds (2/3) of the Tribal Council, or upon presentation of a petition signed by one-third (1/3) of the qualified voters of the Tribe.

Certificate of Adoption

Pursuant to an order, approved November 18, 1959, by the Assistant Secretary of the Interior, the attached amended Constitution and Bylaws was submitted for ratification to the members of the Northern Cheyenne Tribe of the Northern Cheyenne Indian Reservation, Montana, and was on April 12, 1960, ratified by a vote of 273 for, and 67 against, in an election which over 30 percent of those entitled to vote cast their ballots, in accordance with Section 16 of the Indian Reorganization Act of June 18, 1934 (48 Stat. 984), as amended by the Act of June 15, 1935 (49 Stat. 378).

John Wooden Legs, President, Northern Cheyenne Tribal Council
George Hiwalker, Jr., Secretary, Northern Cheyenne Tribal Council
Don T. Jensen, Supt., Northern Cheyenne Agency

Sources:

Author has a copy of this constitution.

Moore, John H., Margaret P. Liberty, and Terry Strauss. "Cheyenne." In *Handbook of North American Indians.* Vol. 13, *Plains.* Pt. 2, edited by Raymond J. DeMallie. Washington, DC: Smithsonian Institution, 2001, 863–885.

Powell, Peter J. *Sweet Medicine.* 2 vols. Norman: University of Oklahoma Press, 1969.

29   *Statement of George D. Heron, Seneca Nation President, In Opposition to Construction of the Kinzua Dam (1960)*

The Seneca Nation, one of the confederated nations of the Haudenosaunee Confederacy, faced a daunting challenge when the Army Corps of Engineers proposed construction of a massive dam to control flooding along the Alleghany River. The design of the $120 million structure was predicated on flooding more than 9,000 acres, nearly one third of Seneca reserved homelands. The 1794 Treaty of Canandaigua contained strong language affirming the ownership rights of the Six Nations, including the Seneca, to their aboriginal territories and the Corps' plan threatened both the letter and spirit of the historic treaty. Despite a strenuous, well-coordinated plan of action by the Seneca and many allies, the Kinzua Dam was eventually constructed, permanently inundating a large portion of Seneca territory, including burial grounds, a longhouse, and 150 Seneca family home sites.

President Heron's Statement

My name is George D. Heron. I live on the Allegany Reservation in New York, and I am president of the Seneca Nation of Indians. I appear before this subcommittee today as an official representative of my people to express once again their unaltered opposition to construction of the Kinzua Dam. As you know, this project will flood the heart of our reservation homeland, which we Seneca have peacefully occupied since the Treaty of November 11, 1794, under the protection of the United States, and will force the relocation of more than 700 members of the Nation.

Before starting the main part of my remarks this morning, I would like to clear up several misstatements which were made to this subcommittee during the hearings yesterday. My friends from Pennsylvania seem to believe that some Senecas are willing to sell their lands. I do not know where these witnesses got their information, although I suppose every group, even an Indian nation, contains a few unhappy people who will sell out their birthright. I do know that the overwhelming majority of my people, including every Councilman and other tribal leaders, both in and out of office, are trying desperately to save our reservation. The thought that we would freely give up the lands of our ancestors, which we are pledged to hold for our children yet unborn, is so contrary to the Seneca way of life that it is not even considered seriously.

Next my friends from Pennsylvania have said that the Treaty of November 11, 1794, was abrogated when all Indians became citizens in 1924. I would like to point out that the 1794 Treaty was signed by the *Seneca Nation*, not by individual

Seneca Indians, and the Nation has not yet become a citizen. It remains today exactly what it was 165 years ago—in the words of the courts as reported to us by our attorney, Mr. Lazarus, a "quasi-sovereign dependent nation." More important, our tribal lawyer tells me that the Supreme Court of the United States has held not once, but at least a dozen times, that the grant of citizenship does not affect any Indian treaty rights or in any other way change the special relationship of Indians and their property to the federal government. I am not an educated man, but it seems very strange to me that these lawyers from Pennsylvania are willing to say that the Supreme Court ruled against the Senecas, when it did not even hear the case, while at the same time they are ignoring a whole series of actual Supreme Court decisions which go against their arguments.

I am proud to be an American citizen, and have four years in the United States Navy to prove it. I am just as proud to be a Seneca Indian. And I do not see any reason why I cannot be both.

Now let me tell you a little bit about what the Kinzua Dam will do to my people. Our own census shows that over 700 members of the nation or more than half the population of the Allegany Reservation will be forced to move by the reservoir. On paper, this does not seem like very many people: other lands, substitute houses can be found say the supporters of the project. If you knew these Senecas the way I do, though, if you knew how much they love that land—the last remnant of the original Seneca country—you would learn a different story. To lose their homes on the reservation is really to lose a part of their life.

The Corps of Engineers will tell you that Kinzua Dam will flood only 9,000 out of the 29,000 acres within the Allegany Reservation. What the Corps does not say is that this 9,000 acres includes almost all of the flat lowlands and fertile riverbanks, while the remainder of the reservation is inaccessible and thus virtually uninhabitable mountainside. What the Corps also does not say is that during the dry season these 9,000 acres will not be a lake but rather muck and mud flats. What a pleasant yearly reminder, what an annual memorial to the breaking of the 1794 Treaty that will be!

Lastly, I know it will sound simple and perhaps silly, but the truth of the matter is that my people really believe that George Washington read the 1794 Treaty before he signed it, and that he meant exactly what he wrote. For more than 165 years we Senecas have lived by that document. To us it is more than a contract, more than a symbol; to us, the 1794 Treaty is a way of life.

Times have not always been easy for the Seneca people. We have known and we still know poverty and discrimination. But through it all we have been sustained by a pledge of faith, unbroken by the federal government. Take that pledge away, break our treaty, and I fear that you will destroy the Senecas as an Indian community.

The Seneca Nation always has taken the position that we will abandon our opposition to the Kinzua Dam if and when it is shown by competent evidence that the existing plans of the Corps of Engineers are better than any alternative plans. The facts are that Dr. Morgan's study has revealed an alternative, the Conewango Cattaraugus plan, which appears superior to the authorized project. For this reason, we urge that the committee pass H.J. Res. 703, which would provide an independent investigation of the merits of the two proposals.

On behalf of the Seneca Nation, may I thank you for granting us this hearing.

Sources:

Kinzua Project, Indian Committee, Philadelphia Yearly Meeting of Friends.
Kinzua Dam Controversy, A Peaceful Solution—Without Shame. Philadelphia:
Philadelphia Yearly Meeting of Friends, 1961.
    US Congress. House. "Kinzua Dam—Seneca Indian Relocation." Hearing
Before the Subcommittee on Indian Affairs. 88th Cong., 1st Sess. on H.R. 1794,
H.R. 3343, and H.R. 7354. Washington, DC: Government Printing Office, 1964.

---

30   *Declaration of Indian Purpose (1961)*

This important policy statement was created at a large intertribal gathering of Natives—nearly five hundred individuals from over ninety nations—who convened in Chicago to express their concerns about a number of issues bedeviling their peoples at the time: termination, inadequate education, poor economic conditions, and grave health concerns. The so-called American Indian Chicago Conference was organized by two non-Indian anthropologists, Sol Tax and Nancy Lurie, with strong support of leading Native interest groups like the National Congress of American Indians. The declaration resulting from the collaborative work at this meeting was presented to President Kennedy and other national political figures.

The American Indian Pledge:

1. We are steadfast, as all other true Americans, in our absolute faith in the wisdom and justice of our American form of Government.
2. We join with all other loyal citizens of our beloved country in offering our lives, our property and our sacred honor in the defense of this country and its institutions.
3. We denounce in emphatic terms the efforts of the promoters of any alien form of government to plant upon our shores or within any our institutions the ideology or way of life which inflicts slavery, trial and punishment without the sanction of a jury, denies free speech, abhors free choice of religious worship, or through force and fear threatens the peace and safety of mankind.
4. At this critical hour of human history the American Indians arise as one in pledging to the President of the United States and to our fellow citizens our assurance that upon these principles we and our children shall forever stand....

Statement of Purpose:

Whereas: The American Indian Chicago Conference was conceived and developed by voluntary effort. The steering committee composed of American Indians assisted by the University of Chicago endeavored to secure the interest and support of all American Indians, and

Whereas: Interest developed and drew to the conference some 460 Indians representing 90 tribes, and bands throughout the nation.

Therefore: in order to give recognition to certain basic philosophies by which the Indian People live, We, the Indian People, must be governed by principles in a democratic manner with a right to choose our way of life. Since our Indian culture is threatened by presumption of being absorbed by the American society, we believe we have the responsibility of preserving our precious heritage. We believe that the Indians must provide the adjustment and thus freely advance with dignity to a better life. In order to accomplish the general objectives of the creed adopted at this conference, we the Indian People herein assembled adopt as official the report herewith attached this date June 20, 1961....

Creed:

We believe in the inherent right of all people to retain spiritual and cultural values, and that the free exercise of these values is necessary to the normal development of any people.

Indians exercised this inherent right to live their own lives for thousands of years before the white man came and took their lands. It is a more complex world in which Indians live today, but the Indian people who first settled the New World and built the great civilizations which only now are being dug out of the past, long ago demonstrated that they could master complexity.

We believe that the history and development of America show that the Indian has been subjected to duress, undue influence, unwarranted pressures, and policies which have produced uncertainty, frustration, and despair. Only when the public understands these conditions and is moved to take action toward the formulation and adoption of sound and consistent policies and programs will these destroying factors be removed and the Indian resume his normal growth and make his maximum contribution to modern society.

We believe in the future of a greater America, an America which we were first to love, where life, liberty, and the pursuit of happiness will be a reality. In such a future, with Indians and all other Americans cooperating, a cultural climate will be created in which the Indian people will grow and develop as members of a free society.

Legislative and Regulatory Proposals

In order that basic objectives may be restated and that action to accomplish these objectives may be continuous and may be pursued in a spirit of public dedication, it is proposed that recommendations be adopted to strengthen the principles of the Indian Reorganization Act and to accomplish other purposes. These recommendations would be comparable in scope and purpose to the Indian Trade and Intercourse Act of June 30, 1834, the Act of the same date establishing the Bureau of Indian Affairs, and the Indian Reorganization Act of June 18, 1934, which recognized the inherent powers of Indian Tribes.

The recommendations we propose would redefine the responsibilities of the United States toward the Indian people in terms of a positive national obligation to modify or remove the conditions which produce the poverty and lack of social adjustment as these prevail as the outstanding attributes of Indian life today. Specifically, the recommendations would:

(1) Abandon the so-called termination policy of the last administration by revoking House Concurrent Resolution 108 of the 83rd Congress.
(2) Adopt as official policy the principle of broad educational process as the procedure best calculated to remove the disabilities which have prevented Indians from making full use of their resources.

It has been long recognized that one Commissioner cannot give the personal attention to all tribal matters which they deserve. He cannot meet all callers to his office, make necessary visits to the field, and give full attention to the review of tribal programs and supporting budget requests. In view of these conditions, we most urgently recommend that the present organization of the Bureau of Indian Affairs be reviewed and that certain principles be considered no matter what the organizational change might be.

The basic principle involves the desire on the part of Indians to participate in developing their own programs with help and guidance as needed and requested, from a local decentralized technical and administrative staff, preferably located conveniently to the people it serves. Also in recent years certain technical and professional people of Indian descent are becoming better qualified and available to work with and for their own people in determining their own programs and needs. The Indians as responsible individual citizens, as responsible tribal representatives, and as responsible Tribal Councils want to participate, want to contribute to their own personal and tribal improvements and want to cooperate with their Government on how best to solve the many problems in a business-like, efficient and economical manner as rapidly as possible.

It is, therefore, recommended that:

1. Area offices be abolished and their authority be given to the agency superintendents.
2. The position of reservation Superintendent be strengthened to permit broader exercise of responsibility and authority to act on significant and important matters of daily operations of Indian problems, preventing undue delays.
3. Position qualifications require the employment of Superintendents with courage and determination, among other qualities, to help with local problems and be willing to make without further referral to higher levels, decisions commensurate with the delegated authorities.

4. The Superintendent be charged with the responsibilities of cooperating with the local tribal governing bodies in developing the Federal Program and Budget for that particular tribe or reservation....

Concluding Statement:

To complete our Declaration, we point out that in the beginning the people of the New World, called Indians by accident of geography, were possessed of a continent and a way of life. In the course of many lifetimes, our people had adjusted to every climate and condition from the Arctic to the torrid zones. In their livelihood and family relationships, their ceremonial observances, they reflected the diversity of the physical world they occupied.

The conditions in which Indians live today reflect a world in which every basic aspect of life has been transformed. Even the physical world is no longer the controlling factor in determining where and under what conditions men may live. In region after region, Indian groups found their means of existence either totally destroyed or materially modified. Newly introduced diseases swept away or reduced regional populations. These changes were followed by major shifts in the internal life of tribe and family.

The time came when the Indian people were no longer the masters of their situation.

Their life ways survived subject to the will of a dominant sovereign power. This is said, not in a spirit of complaint; we understand that in the lives of all nations of people, there are times of plenty and times of famine. But we do speak out in a plea for understanding.

When we go before the American people, as we do in this Declaration, and ask for material assistance in developing our resources and developing our opportunities, we pose a moral problem which cannot be left unanswered. For the problem we raise affects the standing which our nation sustains before world opinion.

Our situation cannot be relieved by appropriated funds alone, though it is equally obvious that without capital investment and funded services, solutions will be delayed. Nor will the passage of time lessen the complexities which beset a people moving toward new meaning and purpose.

The answers we seek are not commodities to be purchased, neither are they evolved automatically through the passing of time.

The effort to place social adjustment on a money-time interval scale which has characterized Indian administration, has resulted in unwanted pressure and frustration.

When Indians speak of the continent they yielded, they are not referring only to the loss of some millions of acres in real estate. They have in mind that the land supported a universe of things they knew, valued, and loved.

With that continent gone, except for the few poor parcels they still retain, the basis of life is precariously held, but they mean to hold the scraps and parcels as earnestly as any small nation or ethnic group was ever determined to hold to identity and survival....

Sources:

Hauptman, Laurence M. "The Voice of Eastern Indians: The American Indian Chicago Conference of 1961 and the Movement for Federal Recognition." *Proceedings of the American Philosophical Society* 132 (1988): 316–329.

   The Voice of the American Indian. "Declaration of Indian Purpose." American Indian Chicago Conference. Chicago: University of Chicago, June 13–20, 1961.

31   *Helen L. W. Peterson (Oglala Lakota), Executive Director, National Congress of American Indians, on Native Rights (1961)*

Peterson (Cheyenne and Lakota) was born in 1915 and enrolled on Pine Ridge Reservation in South Dakota. A respected figure in Native politics for many years, she was the first female executive director of the National Congress of American Indians (NCAI). She served in that capacity from 1953–1961, a critical period encompassing adoption of P. L. 280 and the onslaught of federal termination policy—destructive measures she galvanized Indian Country to resist. It was under her leadership that NCAI drafted the Declaration of Indian Rights categorically rejecting termination. She went on to work as executive director of the Denver-based Commission on Community Relations, and later served in Washington, DC, as a special assistant to the Commissioner of Indian Affairs. Throughout her life, she remained unrelenting in her support of equal rights and encouraged natives to vote and become active at all political levels.

———

We have understood that a primary purpose of this investigation into constitutional rights for American Indians was to see how Indian citizens were faring in those areas where the Federal jurisdiction has been specifically transferred, by act of Congress, to five particular States, namely, Nebraska, California, Minnesota (Red Lake excepted), Wisconsin, and Oregon (with Warm Springs excepted in Oregon). We were pleased at this prospect since our organization has opposed such transfer of jurisdiction unless it had the consent of the tribe affected, and an important reason for this opposition on the part of our Indian constituency has been fear of what the States would do, or fail to do. In turn, this fear is based on experience with what some State and local law enforcement has done, or failed to do.

First, I should like to urge this committee to give careful consideration to the position of the National Congress of the American Indians [NCAI] in respect to Public Law 280, 83^d Congress, which brought about the specific transfers mentioned above. NCAI, by resolution of annual convention, has recommended amendment of Public Law 280 in such way as to require agreement by the particular State as well as by the particular tribes affected before jurisdiction may be transferred from the Federal to the State government. Furthermore, the NCAI-endorsed legislation would permit piecemeal transfer of jurisdiction, provided, of course, it is agreed to by the tribe and State concerned. Our bill would go further, however, and permit the undoing of specific transfers, again provided that the tribe and the State agree this should be done.

May I explain the last statement: When Congress, under Public Law 280, transferred jurisdiction to Nebraska that State was obviously unable or unwilling to accept its new responsibility. The Omaha and Winnebago tribes were without law enforcement for almost 8 years. Recently, we are informed, those Indian citizens and their non-Indian neighbors, with professional help, including research, from the University of Nebraska have finally gotten the State to assume this responsibility. The denial to these people of protection of the law for some 8 years, the energies expended to get for themselves what other citizens take for granted, the time, travel and other resources spent on this that should have gone into more constructive development programs are shameful to contemplate, particularly in view of the fact that the lands of the Omahas and Winnebagos have been taxed all along, that these two small tribes constitute a very small fraction of the State's total population and it can hardly be claimed that this is a case where the State can't afford to furnish the protection of the law.

We ask that our organization's resolution on the amendment of Public Law 280 and a copy of the proposed legislation be inserted for the record. Mr. Chairman, the reason for going into this in some detail is that, as these hearings opened and unfolded, it seemed that the emphasis developed on the notion that in some way Indian tribal councils are frustrating their members through denying such members their constitutional rights as citizens of the United States and of the States wherein they reside. We would like to go back to what has happened to Indians at the hands of States. We have pointed to one example in Nebraska—may I mention another? In 1956, a Sioux World War II veteran by name of Vincent Broken Rope was shot in the back and later died from the wounds over a minor incident in Gordon, Nebr., a town bordering the Pine Ridge Indian Reservation in South Dakota. A coroner's jury made a perfunctory examination and ruled that the town marshal was doing his duty but the general understanding was that this was a wholly unwarranted shooting. (The marshal was later shown to be an unstable person.) Within the same year, two white boys picked up a 15-year-old Indian girl and her brother on the highway; attacked the girl and when she fell or was pushed from the car, was killed on the highway. The boy responsible for that got 3 months in jail. In about 1956, there was a case of an Indian shot in the Platte Valley of Nebraska; only when courageous citizens in the valley persisted for months in the face of entrenched authorities did justice finally prevail. Then there were the instances when Sergeant Rice, in about 1950, and a Mr. Nash early this year, were refused burial in white men's cemeteries because they were Indians. Again, these occurred where white men, not Indian tribal councils, were responsible for justice and order in society. In Idaho a decade ago, some Indian boys were sentenced to 14 years for stealing sheep.

While these may not fit the classification of denials of civil rights exactly, they do indicate something of the attitudes of prejudice, and the quality of law enforcement in regard to Indians that exist under the white man's law enforcement and court systems where there is no connection whatsoever with any Indian tribal council or tribal court.

During this summer, I have seen a telegram sent by a California U.S. attorney asking a university professor where to get legal help for Indian citizens in Bishop, Calif. Your own committee has reported that some States are unwilling to admit Indians who are mentally ill, contending they are the special and even total responsibility of the Federal Government, yet at the same time patients are being discharged from St. Elizabeth's Federal hospital. And it is a well-known fact—though our organization doesn't have staff or resources to document the cases—that North Dakota and other States sometimes patently deny Indians equal access to State institutions.

The argument that Indian citizens do not now have the protection of law enforcement on their own reservations, and at the hands of their own tribal governments, but would do better at the hands of the States is simply not borne out by what we think we know. Whatever faults the tribal systems and the Federal Government may have, the complaints are far more in terms of inadequacy of law enforcement than denial of constitutional rights, and there is no evidence that the States would do as well, at least at this stage in history where most Indians will agree that there is prejudice and discrimination in the communities bordering their reservation homelands.

This leads to the second recommendation that Indian tribes and our organization have made in the past and we now make to this committee: that larger appropriations to provide more and better law enforcement officials be placed in the hands of the federal law enforcement officials and the tribal law enforcement agencies. We think the Bureau of Indian Affairs has been wrong in recent years in insisting to an extreme degree that such a large part of this burden be borne by the tribes themselves out of their own resources. Many of their resources are extremely limited, and their efforts to develop revenue are met with many frustrations. Great improvements in the quality and quantity of law enforcement can be brought about overnight with this obvious and direct kind of action, and your committee recommendations would be of great value toward this end....

As Congressman Arnold Olson and Commissioner-designate Nash have testified in this hearing, an essential element in improving law enforcement is communication with, and the confidence of, the Indian people themselves.

While we are painfully aware of our lack of resources for research and documentation, we do feel that our organization—being the only one on the national level of the Indians, by the Indians, for the Indians—can help your committee to gain more understanding of the strengths and advantages of the tribal law enforcement agencies and court systems. Having watched the obvious good will and concern of this committee for the Indian people and the subjects under consideration in these hearings, we know that you gentlemen of the committee could not but help be moved by many of the decisions of the Indian tribal judges and policemen. While their procedures or records may not be in the same form as those of the white man, nevertheless their deep concern for justice, for compassion, for determining the kind of punishment that will come closest to helping a man restore his dignity as a person, the appealing concern for the family of the defendant, the care that is taken to inform the defendant of the provisions of the tribal code in a way that the defendant truly understands (and where this involves explanations in an Indian language, with 150 different languages still spoken by the Indians today this is something the white man's court could hardly provide), these are truly attempts at justice that this committee will want to know about. They are among the positive things to be said for these Indian systems that, transitional or not, cannot but commend themselves to enlightened white men who search for better answers to the problems of what to do with offenders against society.

Mr. Chairman, is it not so that good citizens in the District of Columbia are shocked and fearful over the muggings, the yokings, the purse snatchings, the other crimes in the National Capitol, some of which go unapprehended and unpunished? Yet is it not also true that here in our Capitol there are those who drag their feet on appropriations that will come closer to meeting the needs for law enforcement? Well, so is it with Indian communities. We submit that there is not nearly so much denial by Indian systems of flaw of constitutional rights to Indian citizens as there is inadequacy of resources for law enforcement, for the training of Indian officials and judges, and for adult education of the general Indian community population as will bring about concern for, and observance of, the constitutional rights of Indians. Our organization has already demonstrated its grave concern for more and better law enforcement, for seeking the means to bring this about, for carrying on adult education programs within the tribal councils and among the Indian citizenry at large to bring about the community acceptance and demand for good law and order practices and compliance that are essential in any community for good results. Please notice the essays written by schoolchildren on the Pine Ridge Reservation on the subject "Laws Are Made To Protect Man." This was part of just one program we have carried on for which we have had to solicit the funds in order that we might work in this area.

The National Congress of American Indians stands ready at all times to step up its efforts to encourage and assist the tribal councils, the tribal law enforcement agencies and courts, the Bureau of Indian Affairs, the Congress of the United States, the State and county governments who truly wish to cooperate, and all others who will work sincerely with the Indian people to bring about improvements in this area. We are limited only by resources with which to work.

I would like the record to show that while the United States has despoiled tribes of their tribal lands, has violated treaties and agreements, and has put itself in the position of taking after taking of tribal property without just compensation in defiance of the fifth amendment, no single instance has been mentioned where a tribe has taken the property of a member without due process of law. Hundreds of claims of tribes against the United States have resulted over the years; they are now being processed by the Indian Claims Commission after the conscience of this country was appealed to because of the helplessness of tribes, as political entities, to gain access to the courts, as a result of which the Indian Claims Commission Act was adopted. But there is no similar backlog of demands against Indian tribes; tribal governments have been conservative in the extreme of tribal and individual property.

In only one instance whatever is there any demonstration of need for the United States to act. That is asserted in connection with freedom of worship—literally, the right of a group called the Native American Church to use the cactus button, peyote, in their religious celebrations. Now neither the National Congress of American Indians nor I wish to be understood as taking any position respecting peyotists; the organization has not acted upon any statement in this regard.

There have been many bills in Congress and State legislatures to ban the use of peyote and much testimony on one side and the other as to whether it should be classed with habit-forming drugs. Some Indian tribes have banned it. The contention seems to be that they have erred, though Congress would not be deemed to be in error if it chose to do the same thing. I would urge only that this matter be seen in perspective. The Indian tribes, before the white man came, governed themselves according to their own rights so as to satisfy their own cultural needs. Some measure of that aboriginal jurisdiction, that status of separateness and self-determination, remains to the tribes to this day. The question is not whether freedom of religion is satisfying as a concept to the white man; whether it meets the needs of his society. The question is whether our country is bold enough to permit the survival of governments which do not necessarily conform to the white man's concept of what is an ultimate good. Otherwise, the tribes could be stripped of the last vestige of their original total rights of self-determination, just to make them over in the image of the white man.

Lest another seemingly unrelated area not be brought to the attention of your committee, let us say that we hope you good gentlemen do not fail to consider the Indians' property considerations in all of these matters. The land, the oil, the water and water rights, the timber belonging to individual Indians (even in trust) and to the tribes has often been a reason for concern about the Indians in a covetous sort of way. Throughout history it is clear that following gold or oil or uranium discoveries, or as markets open up for more timber, or as water becomes scarcer, the movements to civilize, or integrate the Indians, or concern for their individual freedom and "right" to dispose of their property without interference or protection often result in programs or policies that lead to removal of his resources from his ownership. We trust that this good committee will not open more doors to easier exploitation of the remaining fragments of the Indians' land and resources in their sincere attempts to protect the rights of these very people.

Gentlemen of this committee, by your willingness to understand, by your deep and patient study, and then by your wise recommendations and follow-up, you can help greatly to straighten the American people out on their vast ignorance about the Nation's oldest inhabitants, actually the first Americans. You have an opportunity to help the poorest, least educated, least healthy group in the national society, for their problems of constitutional rights are all intertwined with their social and economic problems, and their cultural differences which could lend much to our increasingly materialistic national society. The Indian tribes have neither the financial resources nor the political strength to do very much about their problems, yet they nag at the conscience of thoughtful Americans. Most Americans simply do not understand and they don't know what to do to help. Now, in 1961, the whole world watches the United States of America and it may soon look much more closely to its relations with its native peoples. These relations may very well be of vital importance in winning the confidence of emerging native peoples and other nations all over the world. Together, let us all insist upon the means to find truly better answers to their problems and may we have guidance that we do not innocently blunder into further destroying their unique qualities and communities that lend refreshing variety and richness to our national society.

Source:

US Senate. "Statement of Helen L. Peterson." Hearings Before the Subcommittee on Constitutional Rights of the Committee on the Judiciary. 87th Cong., 1st Sess. on S. Res. 53, Pt. 1. Washington, DC: Government Printing Office, August 1962.

32   *Statement of Senator Sam Ervin (D-NC) on Indian Civil Rights (1961)*

In 1961, prompted by some Tribal citizens' complaints about their governments' abuse of civil rights, the Senate Judiciary committee, of which Ervin was a member, convened a series of hearings to examine the fraught constitutional status of Native individuals in the United States. Senator Church, as chairman of the Senate Subcommittee on Indian Affairs, was fairly familiar with the complex political and constitutional issues confronting Native nations and their citizens. These hearings culminated in 1968's Indian Civil Rights Act which formally imposed statutory versions of most of the US Constitution's first ten amendments onto Tribal governments.

———

Senator Church: Mr. Chairman and members of the committee, I would like to say at the outset of my remarks that you are to be commended for undertaking such an investigation into a very confused, difficult, and emotional subject area as that of the American Indian's relation to the constitutional guarantees accorded other citizens of our country. The entire area has been a nagging and persistent problem for some time and I am delighted to see action being taken.

During the past week my own Subcommittee on Indian Affairs has had before it a very serious Indian land problem that also presented a constitutional question. During these hearings, Mr. Bob Burnette, chairman of the Rosebud Sioux Reservation in South Dakota, stated that his tribal members had encountered many constitutional problems and they could get nothing done about them. Mr. Burnette further stated they had been presented to your committee and this was their only hope. I thought in bringing this out it would indicate to your committee how much depends on your investigation.

I feel personally that the American Indian is and has been the victim of a well-intended, but nevertheless unrealistic approach by the Federal Government. In the earliest days of our relations we were well aware of the fact that the Indian was not acculturated to our society and needed certain protections until such times as he became so. The laws that we passed and the measures we took to implement such safeguards were very necessary and worthwhile for that time and for those problems. We recognized that the Indian culture was different from ours and it would take quite a while for the acculturation process to work. We built, in effect, as a protective device, a cage into which we placed the Indian. The bars on that cage were composed of thousands of laws and regulations drafted to protect him. Literally, every action by an Indian was placed under some form of regulation. Now, as I have said, this was necessary at the time. It was this system we chose in trying to prepare him for full participation in our way of life.

During World War I, the American Indian made an exemplary record both on the battlefield and at home in defense work. As a result of this wonderful contribution, there was a belated, but successful, drive to make all Indians citizens of the United States. I might say at this point that many had been made citizens prior to 1924 by various treaties and other acts of Congress.

But when we did this we again allowed our, shall we say romantic, view of the Indian to prevail over the dictates of common sense. We gave the Indian citizenship, true, but for lack of anything else to call it, we gave him full citizenship, with a major geographic exception. By this I mean on the one hand we said, "You are now a full American citizen." And on the other hand we took no action to change the existing situation, which was, and is now, that the Indian tribes are not subject to Federal constitutional limitations in the Bill of Rights.

What did this mean to the Indian citizen? It meant he had all the constitutional rights of other citizens, except at one place. The one place where he lived. In effect, we said, "move away from home and you can have the protections of the Constitution too." Such is the action or inaction on the part of our Government that has raised the problem your committee is now confronted with. The inconsistency of our actions has risen to haunt us, for we have left a minority of our population without assurances of the basic constitutional rights which the majority enjoy. Let me reemphasize this point. While I realize the importance of your study of alleged violations of existing constitutional rights, I believe it is even more important that you look into the fact that some Indians under the Constitution just do not have the basic rights of other citizens. This situation arises because the prohibitions in the Constitution against State and Federal action do not necessarily apply to Indian tribal action. In the Department of the Interior's *Handbook of Indian Law* this is put in rather cogent terms as follows:

"...if an Indian desires protection in this respect, the members of an Indian tribe must write the guarantee they desire into tribal constitutions. Such guarantees have been written into many tribal constitutions that are now in force. In absence of such provisions, an Indian reservation may be, in some respects, a civil-rights no man's land where there is no relief against tribal oppressions because of the failure of Congress to make Federal civil-rights provisions, such as section 1343 (3) of the Judicial Code, applicable."

Senator Kenneth B. Keating: May I interrupt you, Senator?
Senator Church: Yes, indeed.
Senator Keating: So I am sure I understand your line of reasoning?

What you say is that an Indian, if he is on the reservation is not protected by the U.S. Constitution unless there is also in his tribal constitution or laws a complementary protection form?
Senator Church: Yes. And in this case his protection would derive from the provision in the tribal constitution, and in the absence of such provision there would be no restriction upon the tribal action that could be taken against him. So the normal, universal, application of constitutional restrictions that apply elsewhere do not necessarily apply on Indian reservations....

Source:

US Senate. Hearings Before the Subcommittee on Constitutional Rights of the Committee on the Judiciary. "Constitutional Rights of the American Indian." 87th Cong.,1stSess.S.Res.53,Pt.1.Washington,DC:GovernmentPrintingOffice,1962.

33

Testimony of Vine Deloria, Jr. (Standing Rock Sioux), Executive Director, National Congress of American Indians (1965)

Vine Deloria Jr. is now well known as the legendary leader and writer who best defined, and then tirelessly defended, Native sovereignty and self-determination. However, here, in 1965, he appeared before a Congressional committee as a young, untested head of the largest intertribal interest group, the National Congress of American Indians (NCAI). At that time, NCAI was ramping up efforts to assist Native peoples dealing with federal termination policy, aggressive state jurisdictional intrusions into Indian Country, attacks on treaty fishing rights, and other difficult struggles. The precise constitutional status of Native nations and their citizens was a leading topic of the day and Deloria's testimony clearly explained what needed to be done to improve Native rights and to support the residual inherent sovereignty of every nation.

———

Mr. Deloria: Thank you, Mr. Chairman. I would like to read this all the way through since it is very short. My name is Vine Deloria, Jr., I am the executive director of the National Congress of American Indians. I am very grateful for the opportunity to present testimony before this subcommittee of the Senate on these bills. The National Congress of American Indians wishes to express its thanks to this subcommittee for the hard work it has done on behalf of the Indian citizens of this country and for the insights it has brought to its task as seen in the legislation now under consideration.

The National Congress of American Indians endorses S. 963, S. 965, S. 967, and S. 968 as basically good bills which will provide for a more adequate protection of the constitutional rights of American Indians. S. 961, as presently written, does not spell out exactly what rights and responsibilities guaranteed by the U.S. Constitution would be applicable to either tribal governments or individual Indian citizens in relation to their tribal governments. Since many tribes have written a basic bill of rights into their tribal constitutions based upon the provisions of the U.S. Constitution, we feel that this bill, in most cases, is not needed. Until definite rights and responsibilities can be defined, we believe that this bill should not be considered further.

We believe that S. 962 should not be considered further as many tribes have or soon will have provisions for appellate procedures based upon their own needs and customs. We would like to comment specifically upon the provisions for a model code as contained in S. 964. A uniform model code would not, in all cases, promote justice as many tribal laws are built upon tribal customs, and all tribal customs are not the same. We would suggest that S. 964 be amended to provide only for the training of judges and to appropriate such sums as necessary to carry out a training course in legal procedures for Indian judges. It is more important for judges to receive continuing training in judicial procedures for the administration of tribal courts than for a uniform code to be introduced for the tribes.

We wholeheartedly endorse S. 966 and suggest the following amendment: The extent of such jurisdictions, either civil or criminal, shall be as agreed upon from time to time by the State and the tribe concerned, and may be extended or retracted by agreement of both the State and the particular tribe as experience proves practicable and planning may indicate to them advisable.

This amendment would allow for greater flexibility and common understanding of the problems involved in all areas in the relations between tribes and State governments.

We are aware that this country is presently groping for new forms of social understanding and participation. Governor Collins has called this the formation of the American soul. We feel that the passage of S. 966 would be a most significant step in the formation of a greater society. Much has been made of the contribution of the Iroquois League to the political understanding of the Founding Fathers of this country. We suggest that at nearly every point, social, economic, political, and patriotic American Indians can contribute their knowledge of cultural interaction and social concern that is needed today in this country.

This country has come to understand that a great society should provide for employment and education of all its citizens. Nearly every Indian tribe handles its resources to provide maximum employment and opportunity for its people. In the June 1 issue of *Look* magazine Atty. General Katzenbach advocates "substitute parents" as a means of handling juvenile delinquency. Indians have long had the kinship system whereby each member of the tribe had many relatives. In this social system there has been, until recently, no need for juvenile delinquency programs.

We point these things out for two reasons. First, tribal customs can best handle most of the problems that occur on the reservations and within the tribe. Passage of S. 966, with the amendment proposed, would allow tribes to continue to provide for their own people until there is sufficient understanding by all parties concerned to provide for Indian people under another legal and social system. The second reason is that much has been made of the so-called transitional nature of tribal government. We feel that tribal groups are indeed in transition, but to a new form of social understanding which, if understood by other people, would help solve some of the pressing social problems of today. We suggest that tribes are not vestiges of the past, but laboratories of the future. As we see the larger society beginning to adopt Indian social forms, we feel impelled to suggest that tribes be allowed maximum flexibility in developing their own economic, political, and human resources so that they might bring the best of the Indian understanding of life to the rest of this country. We urge passage of S. 966 with amendment as a good constructive beginning and as the application of the first principle of government—the consent of the governed....

Source:

US Senate. Hearing Before the Subcmte on Constitutional Rights of the Cmte on the Judiciary. 89th Cong., 1st Sess. S. 961 et al. Washington, DC: Government Printing Office, 1965.

---

34   Norman Hollow (Ft. Peck), Earl Old Person (Blackfeet), and Roger Jourdain (Red Lake Anishinaabe) Letter to President Johnson (1967)

Although presidential and congressional pronouncements were becoming more supportive of Native self-governance in the mid-1960s, bills continued to be introduced that attempted to undermine the economic progress of Tribal nations and threatened efforts to strengthen sovereignty. One such measure, the Indian Resources Development Act, was an omnibus bill deemed detrimental to Native interests. This joint letter by three leading Tribal politicians helped convince Congress to table the measure and sent a message that Indian Country leaders were determined to be heard when federal laws or policies threatened the well-being of their nations.

———

Dear Mr. President:

Upon presentation of and analysis by the delegates of this legislation, certain major titles and provisions thereof were rigorously opposed and unanimously rejected upon the grounds that they are inimical to, and incongruous with, the present needs, capabilities and conditions of the American Indians. Implementation of certain of the managerial techniques of the proposed legislation affecting mortgage, hypothecation and sale of Indian lands would render the Indian people immediately vulnerable to subversive economic forces, leading inevitably and inalterably to the prompt erosion and demise of the social and economic culture of the American Indian.

Enactment of this legislation by the Congress would constitute a breach of the trust comprehended under original Indian treaties, if not in word, then in the spirit of the same....

For other citizens government exists to serve them—as a matter of right and not of favor. It is time that government consistently recognize that it is our servant and not our master. Many of our difficulties today, we feel, lie in the unresponsiveness of public officials to our social and economic needs, despite the fact that adequate legislation exists to further Indian progress in many fields. The last major progressive policy and legislation was adopted in 1934—33 years ago. Today, we need a revision and updating of that policy. That policy saved our lands, insured our rights of limited self-government, and opened the door to financial credit for Indians.

Today, we need a reaffirmation of our rights to continue to occupy the lands remaining to us. Our very existence as a people is dependent on our lands. The tax status of Indian lands is founded on agreement by the Indians and the United States. This immunity is recognition that the Indian people paid more than adequate consideration when they gave up valuable land in exchange for smaller, less valuable parcels—today occupied by some 300,000 to 500,000 Indians.

Today, we are faced with threats of termination. We ask you to seek the repudiation of the idea behind Concurrent Resolution 108, adopted in 1953....

Mr. President, we wish to cooperate. With your understanding and consideration we will succeed....

Respectfully submitted, Chairman, Norman Hollow, Co-chairman, Earl Old Person, Co-Chairman, Roger Jourdain

Source:

Josephy, Alvin M. Jr., ed. *Red Power: The American Indians' Fight for Freedom.* New York: McGraw Hill, 1971; Lincoln: University of Nebraska Press, 1985.

35

Statement of Alaska State Lawmaker William L. Iġġiaġruk Hensley (Iñupiaq) (1968)

Alaska's Indigenous peoples have long enjoyed a unique political and legal status vis-à-vis the states and federal government. Having never signed treaties with the United States, nor with Russia, which occupied the territory for a short period of time, Alaska Natives' aboriginal rights to their homelands were largely ignored until oil was found on the North Slope in 1968. This discovery compelled the state, corporate America, and the federal government to finally attend to the proprietary and civil rights of Alaskan Natives. Willie Hensley established the Northwest Alaska Native Association in 1963 and has continued to be a leading advocate for the rights of all Alaskan Natives. He was elected to the Alaska House of Representatives from 1966–1970 and then served in the state senate. He would later become president of the Alaska Federation of Natives. His perspectives, such as the following testimony regarding Native land claims, contributed to Congress' 1971 enactment of the Alaska Native Claims Settlement Act, which comprehensively, if controversially, addressed the political and proprietary rights of Alaska's Indigenous peoples.

―――――

Mr. Chairman, members of the committee, other distinguished guests, ladies and gentlemen, my name is William L. Hensley. I am 26 years old. I live in Kotzebue and represent the 17th District in the Alaska Legislature. My district covers about 9,000 square miles, including two of the largest Eskimo villages in Alaska—Kotzebue and Barrow, both with a population of about 2,000 people. Ninety percent of the people are of Eskimo parentage.

I am the chairman of the land claims task force which drafted legislation now embodied in Senate bill 2906 which is the bill submitted with the support of the major regional native organizations. The State of Alaska—through its Governor—and with the presence and support of the Interior Department. In order that the committee may have the benefit of additional background, I am including in the record a copy of a paper I wrote in May 1966, entitled "What Rights to Lands Have the Alaska Natives."

Alaska was purchased by the United States in 1867. A resolution of the native claims has been neglected for a century. However, within the last 2 years, a major effort by the native groups around the State has resulted in the claims issue being the subject of prime attention in Alaska by the chief men in government and politics.

There are approximately 53,000 Alaska natives living in Alaska today— about 29,000 Eskimos—18,000 Indians—and 6,000 Aleuts. There are 177 communities in Alaska with the majority of inhabitants being Alaska native. There are about 75 communities with the majority of the population being non-native. These of course make up the major portion of the population of the State of Alaska.

Unlike the Indians of the lower States, there are few officially recognized tribal groups in Alaska. Except for the Indians of the Metlakatla Reservation, only the Tlingits and Haidas of southeastern Alaska have been recognized as a group. Natives feel that the areas they inhabit and occupy still belong to them—under Indian title, we feel that compensation would not be the answer to the problems that we are facing today—we feel that continued use and occupancy of large areas of land is necessary.

We also feel that if the law has developed and states that we own major portions of Alaska under Indian title—we feel that we have the right to request that the Government convey a certain amount of land to the Alaska native rather than to be paid completely in cash or in financial considerations.

Indeed—there are many groups throughout the State who would rather be assured of continued use and occupancy of their traditional lands rather than accept a penny from the Federal Government, the Alaska native realizes—however—that it will be very difficult to obtain fee title to the areas of land that he has used and occupied from time immemorial.

The Alaskan Indian—Eskimo—and Aleut—however feel that this is one of the last opportunities that the U.S. Government has to treat its aboriginal peoples in a fair and equitable manner.

We do not want to feel that a nation as rich as the United States will allow the Eskimo—Indian—and Aleut—to give up their lands without conveying a certain amount of land to them—or to be compensated for the lands taken at some date in the future.

Because there has been no regional tribal groups recognized by the Secretary of the Interior—the various regional groups around the State felt that in order to be stronger and effective regional associations were formed and many filed claims on the basis of use and occupancy of the land and villages within the region.

Initially—many of these claims were filed without the assistance of attorneys. In many cases the claims were filed simply because of rumor that they would not have another chance if the Secretary of the Interior did not accept their filing at some date in the future.

Other groups felt that this was the only method by which they could protect their use and occupancy from encroachment.

There were still other groups who felt that it was not necessary to file claims with the Bureau of Land Management since they felt that the land was theirs and nothing that can be done by the Federal or State governments could deny them use and occupancy of their lands.

The formation of regional native associations culminated in the formation of the statewide Alaska Federation of Natives which has led the Alaska natives in the attempt to obtain a resolution to the native land claims problem.

Under the Statehood Act—Alaska was given the right to select 103 million acres from the Federal lands. However—the Statehood Act also stated that the

State and its people agreed to disclaim all rights or title to any lands or other property—including fishing rights which may be held by any Indian, Eskimo, or Aleut—or lands that are held in trust by the United States for such Alaska natives.

As the new State proceeded with its selection—various groups in the interior of Alaska felt that the State was encroaching on their territory in making the statehood selections and they filed blanket claims with the Bureau of Land Management—which were accepted.

The Secretary of the Interior decided that no titles to land would be issued to third parties in areas claimed by the Eskimo, Indian, and Aleut.

The Alaska native no longer wants decisions to be made for him in Washington or in Juneau. We feel that every effort should be made to consult with the native groups in the State since we feel that in a democracy this is the prerogative of the people who will be affected and have to live under the decisions made by those in positions of authority.

I believe that this was the major error made by the Secretary of the Interior when his Department came forth with a bill designed to solve the native land claims problem in Alaska. It was quite obvious that the Secretary—in coming out with Senate bill 1964 was not aware of the political realities in the State of Alaska between the Alaska natives and the State at the time of the drafting of his legislation.

The Secretary's bill was absolutely opposed by all the regional groups in the Alaska Federation of Natives. The bill provided for only a small area of land around each community which no community of natives in Alaska would support. The Secretary's bill also provided hunting permits in certain areas which had a 25-year limitation—which we think is arbitrary.

The bill also provided for lands to be held in trust by a trustee who could do whatever he determined with the land—without consultation with the group for whom he is a trustee.

Furthermore—the Secretary's bill provided for termination of the trust within 25 years.

Very objectionable to the natives was the Secretary's arbitrary determination of 1867, as the date of taking, which was superfluous since most of Alaska—to this very day—has not been taken and therefore the takings would be in the future—rather than 100 years ago.

The Alaska Federation of Natives, formed in October 1966, had drafted a bill and was introduced by Senator Gruening in June 1967. The bill provided that the Court of Claims would determine which lands belonged to the natives of Alaska and would convey title to such lands claimed under Indian title.

It also provided that the Court of Claims would render judgments with regard to lands taken at the fair market value, needless to say—this bill was not supported by the State or the Interior Department and would have resulted in the ownership in fee of most of Alaska by the native groups in the State.

It was recognized that very little progress would be made in solving the land problem in Alaska unless it were possible for the natives, the State, and the Interior Department to get together in the support of a single bill.

Consequently, the Alaska Federation of Natives and other members selected by the Governor were appointed to attempt to come up with legislation which would be acceptable to the natives, the State, and the Interior Department. The State selected Edgar Paul Boyko, the attorney general of the State, to meet with the drafting committee of nine which were selected from the full task force by the chairman. Secretary Udall sent Under Secretary for Public Land Management, Robert Vaughn, to meet with the task force in the drafting of the proposed legislation.

Drafting sessions were held in early December, late December, and early January. The bill—Senate bill No. 2906—was the final result of the several drafting sessions between the natives, the State, and the Interior Department. The full task force unanimously approved Senate bill 2906 and the proposed complementary State legislation. The visit of Secretary Udall to Alaska in November contributed greatly to the creation of the task force and the suggestion of the Outer Continental Shelf revenues was considered one avenue by which the problem of the Alaska native land claims could be solved. This would provide the Federal lands for payment of future takings by the Government and would not necessitate appropriations of large sums by Congress.

The task force report of native land claims to the Governor is being made a part of this record. But there are certain objectives that the task force felt were important. The task force seeks to prevent years of litigation through the courts. We feel that not only will the State lose by lengthy litigation, but the natives would also be denied compensation for the lands taken and would not be able to utilize the funds due them for many years.

The need to utilize funds for economic development and building of homes and the advancement in education is necessary immediately.

Another objective in the route we have taken is to simplify the administrative process.

We feel that the objective of the Interior Department and the Bureau of Indian Affairs is to allow their clientele to be more self-sufficient.

Therefore, we felt that the creation of the Alaska Native Commission would enable the natives to be a part of the administrative process. The fact that the commissioners would be residents of Alaska would enable them to have a great deal more understanding of the problems of the native peoples and the State.

The task force feels that the benefits of the land settlement should be spread widely among the villages; yet we feel that we must also preserve the concept of private property.

The task force further believes that the use of a corporate form of organization would enable the village and regional groups to participate in modern economy.

The task force proposes a grant of land of 40 million acres to the village groups, allocated among the villages in proportion to the number of persons on their rolls.

We also propose and accept the Secretary's suggestion that 10 percent royalty interest in Outer Continental Shelf revenues in lieu of compensation for lands reserved or disposed of to third parties.

The task force also requests an initial grant of $20 million from the Federal Government.

Repayment would come from the Outer Continental Shelf revenues.

The task force also recommends a 5-percent royalty interest in State selected lands, but excluding current revenue sources from State lands and beginning only upon the early lifting of the land freeze and resumption of the State selections.

Very important to the native groups is the recommendation that the natives be allowed to use the surface of lands used and occupied by the natives, if the use to which the land is put is not incompatible with such use.

I personally feel that the majority of Alaskans today would like to see a just and equitable solution to the Alaska native lands claims problem.

Alaskans should recognize that a State such as Alaska will remain economically and socially healthy only if its major groups progress in a fairly equal manner.

Therefore, if an equitable settlement is made, the present drastic economic imbalance will not persist. Furthermore, capital generated out of this settlement will circulate in those regions of the State presently without capital for economic development purposes.

The Alaska native feels today that he has met the challenge of attempting to resolve the very difficult, very complex, lands problem. We feel that if given the opportunity we shall be able to develop the leadership and the educated person who will enable the village and regional corporations to succeed in managing resources that will be his under the settlement.

The Alaska native seeks not to isolate himself from the State—but to become a moving and dynamic part of the State—and we feel that a resolution of the lands problems will enable us to participate in the development of the State, rather than be a burden in the progress that we see on the Alaskan horizon.

We sincerely appreciate your coming to Alaska to spend time taking testimony which will assist you in passing legislation which we hope can be accomplished within a relatively short time. Thank you.

Sources:

Hensley, William Iggiagruk. "Why the Natives of Alaska Have a Land Claim." In *The Alaska Native Reader: History, Culture, Politics*, ed. Marla Shaa Tlaa Williams. Durham, NC: Duke University Press, 2009, 192–201.

US Senate. Hearings Before the Committee on Interior and Insular Affairs. "Alaska Native Land Claims." 90th Cong., 2nd Sess. S. 2906. Washington, DC: Government Printing Office, 1968.

36   *Arizona ex rel. Merrill v. Turtle (1969)*

In the 1950s, the Navajo Nation adopted a series of laws reflecting its sovereign authority. One such law was a 1956 resolution that allowed for extradition, but only to the three states into which the reservation's lands extended—Arizona, Utah, and New Mexico. In this federal case, a Cheyenne Indian living on Navajo land faced extradition to Oklahoma. The Ninth Circuit Court of Appeals held the Navajo Nation was not required to honor Oklahoma's request because their extradition law did not apply to that state. Oklahoma then sought Arizona's intervention but the Court held that Arizona also lacked extradition authority. This decision affirmed the integrity of the 1868 Navajo Treaty and the Nation's freedom from state jurisdictional authority.

———

Appellee, a Cheyenne Indian who resides with his Navajo Indian wife on the Navajo Reservation in Arizona, is sought by the State of Oklahoma for trial on a charge of second degree forgery. Oklahoma apparently first applied to the Navajo Tribal Council for appellee's extradition. Appellee was thereafter brought before the Navajo Tribal Council, but following a hearing, that court ordered him released, apparently on the ground that Navajo tribal law provided for extradition only to the three neighboring states of Arizona, New Mexico and Utah.

After the Navajo Tribal Court declined to extradite appellee to Oklahoma, Oklahoma made demand upon the Governor of Arizona to secure appellee for extradition, and the Governor issued his warrant of extradition pursuant to Arizona law. The sheriff of Apache County, Arizona, thereupon executed the Arizona Governor's warrant by arresting appellee on the Navajo Reservation and confining him at the tribal jail facility to await removal to Oklahoma. Before Oklahoma authorities arrived to take custody of him, appellee sought a writ of habeas corpus from the United States District Court for the District of Arizona, on the ground that the State of Arizona had no authority to arrest him on the Navajo Reservation.

The District Court after hearing ordered issuance of the writ on the grounds that the Arizona authorities had exceeded their jurisdiction in arresting appellee on the Navajo Reservation. The District Court made no formal findings and wrote no opinion. The State of Arizona urges here, as it did in the District Court, that Article IV, Section 2 of the United States Constitution requires that the state retain extradition jurisdiction over Indian residents of the Navajo Reservation. We affirm the decision of the District Court.

The relationship between the Navajo Tribe, the United States and the State of Arizona has previously been considered by the Supreme Court in *Williams v. Lee* and by this court in *Littell v. Nakai*. The history reviewed by the courts in these cases discloses that historically the Indian tribes were regarded as distinct political communities, protected by treaty from the laws of any state and subject only to the plenary power of Congress over Indian Affairs. Over the years this original concept of tribal sovereignty has been modified to permit application of state law to reservation Indians in matters not considered essential to tribal self-government, but the basic principle that the Indian tribes retain exclusive jurisdiction over essential matters of reservation government, in the absence of specific Congressional limitation, has remained. "Essentially, absent governing Act of Congress, the question has always been whether the state action infringed on the right of reservation Indians to make their own laws and be ruled by them" (*Williams* v. *Lee*).

In *William* v. *Lee*, the Supreme Court considered the question whether the Arizona state courts had authority to entertain civil suits against Indian residents of the Navajo Reservation arising out of commercial transactions on the Reservation. In holding that Arizona courts did not have such authority, the Supreme Court emphasized the broad independence retained by the Navajo Tribe since its formal recognition by the United States in the Treaty of 1868. In characterizing the nature of the tribal sovereignty recognized by this treaty, the court said at p. 221–222: "Implicit in these treaty terms, as it was in the treaties with the Cherokees involved in *Worcester v. State of Georgia*, was the understanding that the internal affairs of the Indians remained exclusively within the jurisdiction of whatever tribal government existed."

The court went on to point out that Congress in the intervening years has not acted to limit the authority of the Navajo Tribe over governmental affairs within the Reservation. The court noted that, to the contrary, since the Treaty of 1868 "Congress and the Bureau of Indian Affairs have assisted in strengthening the Navajo tribal government and its courts.... The Tribe itself has in recent years greatly improved its legal system through increased expenditures and better-trained personnel."

In *Littell v. Nakai*, supra, this court, following the rationale of the *Williams* decision, held that a federal court sitting in a diversity case was likewise without jurisdiction over an action alleging tortious interference with contractual rights, the situs of which interference was the Navajo Reservation, brought by a non-Indian against an Indian resident of the Reservation. Noting that "a strong Congressional policy to vest the Navajo Tribal Government with responsibility for their own affairs emerges from the decision in *Williams*," this court concluded that exclusive jurisdiction over such a suit remained in the Navajo tribal courts. Ibid. at p. 489 of 344 F.2d.

The initial question presented by this case, then, is whether Arizona's claim to extradition jurisdiction over Indian residents of the Navajo Reservation is subject to the tests of non- interference with the right of the tribal self-government laid down in *Williams*, or is free from those limitations by reason of Article IV, Section 2 of the Constitution.

Article IV, Section 2, read literally, purports to impose upon the governor of each State a duty to deliver up fugitives charged with a crime in a sister state. The constitutional mandate requires exercise of the state's lawful jurisdiction in responding to the extradition demands of sister states, but it does not itself attempt to define the reach of that jurisdiction. We have found no authority bearing directly upon the relationship between Article IV, Section 2, and treaty-protected Indian lands and conclude that with regard to the exercise of extradition jurisdiction over Indian residents of the Navajo Reservation, the constitutional mandate must be interpreted in light of the Treaty of 1868 and the long history of the principle of retained tribal sovereignty.

As indicated above, the historical development of this principle down to its contemporary formulation in *Williams* prohibits the State of Arizona, in the absence of specific Congressional authorization, from extending its laws or process to the Navajo Reservation if to do so would interfere with tribal self-government or impair a right granted by federal law. We have been referred to no specific Congressional action limiting the power of the Navajo tribal government to deal with the extradition of Indians resident within the Reservation or granting to the State of Arizona the authority to exercise extradition jurisdiction over such residents. In these circumstances, Arizona's right to exercise the jurisdiction claimed must be determined in light of whether such exercise would "infring[e] on the right of the reservation Indians to make their own laws and be ruled by them," or, as the *Williams'* test was characterized by the court in *Kake, Organized Village of v. Egan*, "whether the application of that law would interfere with reservation self-government."

Applying these considerations, we conclude that Arizona's exercise of the claimed jurisdiction would clearly interfere with rights essential to the Navajo's self-government. The essential and intimate relationship of control of the extradition process to the right of self-government was recognized long ago in *Kentucky v. Dennison*, holding that there is no power, state or federal, to compel a state to perform its constitutional duty of extradition.

Furthermore, the right of the Navajo Tribe to exercise power over Indian residents of its reservation appears to have been recognized by the federal government from the outset by the terms of the Treaty of 1868. Article I of the Treaty provides in relevant part:

"If bad men among the Indians shall commit a wrong or depredation upon the person or property of any one, white, black, or Indian, subject to the authority of the United States and at peace therewith, the Navajo Tribe agree that they will, on proof made to their agent, and on notice by him, deliver up the wrongdoer to the United States, to be tried and punished according to its laws; and in case they willfully refuse so to do, the person injured shall be reimbursed for his loss from the annuities or other moneys due or to become due to them under this treaty, or any others that may be made with the United States...."

These provisions recognized a jurisdiction in the Navajo Tribe over inter-sovereign rendition, at the time the relationship between the United States and the Tribe was originally defined. This jurisdiction was apparently intended to be exclusive, for only a damage remedy was provided for the wrongful refusal to extradite.

In 1956 the Navajo Tribal Council, the tribal legislative body, adopted a Resolution providing procedures for Indian extradition. While this tribal extradition law by its terms specifically provides for extradition only to the states of Arizona, Utah, and New Mexico, it has been approved by the Commissioner of Indian Affairs as provided for by federal law and is now part of the *Navajo Tribal Code*. 17 *N.T.C.*, Sections 1841–42. The Tribe has thus codified and does now exercise its extradition power. This power cannot now be assumed by or shared with the State of Arizona without "infring[ing] on the right of reservation Indians to make their own laws and be ruled by them" (*Williams* v. *Lee*).

This conclusion does not frustrate the State of Arizona in carrying out the constitutional mandate of Article IV, Section 2. It simply recognizes that Arizona has no authority, and hence no duty, to exercise jurisdiction over Indian residents of the Navajo Reservation. Affirmed.

Source:

Arizona ex rel. Merrill v. Turtle, 413 F.2d 683 (1969).

37

Senate Committee on the Judiciary Report: "Protecting the Rights of the American Indian" (1969)

With Congressional adoption of the Indian Civil Rights Act (ICRA) in 1968, modified versions of several of the US Constitution's Bill of Rights were made applicable to Tribal governments. This was a profound intrusion of federal law into Indian Country and it caused great consternation within many Indigenous governments. A great deal of discussion and testimony was required to prevent damage to Tribal nations, even when the proposals were well intentioned. The measure presented here is one example of modifications that were called for in the wake of the ICRA that, while seemingly helpful, could have had unintended negative consequences for Indian County.

———

The Committee on the Judiciary, to which was referred the bill (S. 2173) to amend an act "An act to prescribe penalties for certain acts of violence or intimidation," and for other purposes approved April 11, 1968, having considered the same, report favorably thereon without amendment and recommends that the bill do pass.

The purpose of the bill is to amend titles II and III of the act entitled "An act to prescribe penalties certain acts of violence or intimidation, and for other purposes," approved April 11, 1968.... This amendment is intended to make it plain that the provisions of title II of the 1968 act... Shall not be construed to affect any tribal property rights secured by law or treaty or to dilute the sovereignty of the tribal governments except to the extent of the prohibitions set forth in the present section 202 of the 1968 act. The bill would also extend from July 1, 1968, until July 1, 1973, the deadline before which the Secretary of the interior is required to complete the Model Code of Indian Offenses provided for in title III of the 1968 act, and would provide that such Model Code would apply only to those Indian tribes that have adopted such code through the action of the body exercising the legislative powers of the tribe.

Statement:

In 1961, the subcommittee began its preliminary investigation of the legal status of the Indian in America and the problems Indians encounter when asserting constitutional rights in their relations with state, federal, and tribal governments. This research, the first such study ever undertaken by Congress, demonstrated a clear need for further congressional inquiry and legislation.

S. 961 through S. 968 and Senate Joint Resolution 40 of the 89th Congress were introduced in response to the findings of the subcommittee based on these hearings and investigations.... These proposals were consolidated to one ... and it received unanimous approval of the Senate on December 7, 1967, after which it was sent to the House of Representatives where no action was taken.... Briefly, these titles provide the following protections for Indians in their relationships: with Indian tribes:

Title II constitutes a bill of rights for American Indians. It provides that Indian tribes exercising powers of self-government shall be subject to many of the same limitations and restraints that are imposed on federal, state, and local governments by the Constitution of the United States. It thus assures adequate protection of the basic rights of individual Indians who are members of tribes whose tribal constitutions now permit governmental action that would be unconstitutional if undertaken by federal, state, or local government.

Title III directs the secretary of the interior to prepare and recommend to the Congress a model code governing the administration of justice by courts of Indian offenses on Indian reservations.

Title IV repeals section 7 of Public Law 83–280 which confers civil and criminal jurisdiction over Indian country to certain states and gives consent to all other states to assumed jurisdiction at any time. Title IV repeals the section and permits states to assert civil and criminal jurisdiction in Indian country only after acquiring the consent of the tribes in the state.

Title V amends the Major Crimes Act of 1885 by adding the crime of "assault resulting in serious bodily injury," to the list of serious crimes ... which, under that act, can be prosecuted in federal courts although committed by an Indian in Indian country.

Title VI remedies the problems Indian tribes have had in securing Interior Department approval of contracts or legal assistance by providing that if an application made by a tribe for approval of contracts for the employment of legal counsel is neither approved nor denied by the secretary or by the Commissioner of Indian Affairs within 90 days of the date of filing, approval is deemed to have been granted.

Title VII authorizes and directs the secretary of the interior to revise and publish on a current annual basis Senate Document No. 319, 58th Congress, containing treaties, laws, executive orders and regulations relating to Indian affairs, to compile and maintain on an annual basis the official opinions of the solicitor of the department of the interior relating to Indian affairs, and to pre-pare a revised edition of the treatise entitled "Federal Indian Law."

Need for Legislation: S. 2173

The present bill deals only with titles II and III of the Civil Rights Act of 1968. Since its enactment, misapprehensions have arisen among individual Indians and Indian tribes that the two titles go beyond the language in which they are couched and affect rights of property of Indian tribes in tribal lands and abridge the powers of self-government of Indian tribes in a manner incon-sistent with the language of titles.

S. 2173 makes it plain that title II does not affect the property rights of any Indian tribe in its tribal lands or abridge any of the rights of self-government of any Indian tribe except to the extent of the prohibitions upon governmental action expressly set forth in title II.

Also, S. 2173 makes it clear that the model code enumerated in title III of the act will not become applicable to any tribe unless it is first adopted by the tribal council or other governing body of the tribe.

These amendments were introduced as a result of hearings conducted in Albuquerque, New Mexico, on April 11, 1969.... These amendments are designed merely to obviate these misapprehensions of the Pueblos and other Indian tribes; as far as committee is able to determine, there is no opposition to this measure.

Source:

US Senate. "Protecting the Rights of the American Indian." Senate Report No. 91–294. 91st Cong., 1st Sess. Washington, DC: Government Printing Office, 1969.

38

American Indian Task Force Statement, "We Speak as Indians," Presented to Vice President Spiro Agnew (1969)

The American Indian Task force was made up of some forty-two prominent Native leaders, including Earl Old Person, Dennis Banks, John Belindo, and Peterson Zah. Formed in response to Edgar Cahn's polemic *Our Brother's Keeper*, about the dire social and economic conditions in Indian Country, members focused on Cahn's assertion that federal policies had ultimately failed to protect the rights and resources of Native nations. They prepared the following strong statement outlining a shared vision for genuine Native self-determination.

We speak as Indians who care about what has happened to our people. We speak out because every individual must, and there must be some who are willing to start a process. We do not view ourselves as "chosen leaders" or an "Indian elite," though we come from various backgrounds and diverse tribes. But we do claim to be a cross-section of concerned and non-establishment Indians.

We came together initially to assist in providing information for the book *Our Brother's Keeper* and to state whether, within our own personal knowledge, it spoke the truth.

The national concern aroused by *Our Brother's Keeper* cannot be allowed to dissipate. One of the main points made by this book is that, unlike most Americans, the Indians have little or no forum for redress of grievances and wrongs committed against them. The Task Force believes that there must be a direct channel of communication so that Indian voices are not lost in the Bureau of Indian Affairs, the Department of the Interior, the Bureau of the Budget, Congressional Committees, or other parts of the bureaucratic and political maze in which Indians are now trapped. We are, therefore, proposing a process which could provide a way in which Indians could speak directly to the government of the United States, both to seek a redress of grievances and to initiate and shape Indian policy....

The Task Force proposes that a process of dialogue be initiated in all areas which shall coincide with the eleven area offices of the Bureau of Indian Affairs.

Each of these eleven areas is partially represented by individual members of the Task Force but it would be the responsibility of the entire Task Force, working with others, to expand in each area to insure that it included a broad spectrum of representation from numerous tribes, tribal chairmen, local organizations, individual spokesmen involved in issues, and representatives of urban Indians from cities within each area. Thus, the Task Force will establish separate and broadly representative Boards of Inquiry which would conduct hearings, receive grievances, and generate recommendations in the manner set forth below.

1. That a working meeting of the Task Force, with the National Council on Indian Opportunity [NCIO], be convened to determine the best way to present the idea of conferences and hearings.
2. That further area conferences be held to explain the need to begin the hearing process with each area's representatives to the Task Force and NCIO to discuss ways to expand the concept and lay groundwork for the hearings.
3. That there be hearings in each of the eleven areas—these hearings are to take testimony in open meetings from groups, tribes, and individuals about the needs and situations of the various people and to call for specific recommendations from the people. We urge federal agencies to attend the hearings as observers.
   (a) After the hearings, there will be continued input into the process by having a local center or person to take complaints in each local community. A "circuit rider" is to be hired by the local Board of Inquiry who will take the complaints and make recommendations about solutions.

(b) Red ribbon "grand juries," composed entirely of Indians, should be convened in order to investigate and report upon deprivations of rights, charges of inaction or unresponsiveness by officials, lack of effectiveness of educational, health, and other services—and...where the facts appear to warrant it, the red ribbon "grand jury" shall not only come forward with findings of fact, but should also, by prior arrangement with the U.S. Attorney, present an "indictment" which the U.S. Attorney or (in the event of conflict of interest) a lawyer provided by the government shall be called upon to investigate such charges and represent Indians in such a manner as to protect their rights and make government programs genuinely responsive to the desires and needs of Indians.

4. The Boards of Inquiry in the eleven areas are to meet again to evaluate the first round of hearings, include the continuing complaints, consider the circuit rider's findings, and take recommendation from another round of testimony to deal particularly with proposals and recommendations.

5. From each of the hearings and Boards of Inquiry, there is to be a National Board of Inquiry, composed of three members from each of the eleven areas to meet and make national recommendations. These members are to be chosen by an elective process by Indians. Finally, the entire process will result in the creation of a permanent ongoing local watchdog on bureaucratic programs. We make this proposal because as Indians, we choose to go beyond talking about process and dialogue and consultation and to try to think through what would be a process that would be honest and would give Indians a genuine opportunity to be heard, to seek a redress of grievances, and to take the initiative in shaping government policy.

We propose that the Task Force, supplemented by additional Indians from additional tribes and organizations, form a core of a group which would contract to implement this proposal. We believe that the time has come, not only for Indians to be consulted, but for them to design and implement a process of consultation whereby they can speak out their own grievances as they know them, articulate their problems, shape proposals, draft recommendations, circulate proposed legislative or administrative action for widespread discussion among Indian peoples.

We believe that such functions should be performed by Indians—that there is no question here as to whether qualified Indians exist when this proposal has come from Indians—and we believe there is a clear statutory duty to contract this function to Indians under 36 Stat. 861. We submit that this is not only desirable—but that it would be a major symbolic break with the past practice where no Indians have been the ones paid to become Indian experts, while Indians served as volunteer educators for non-Indians.

We do not come here to blame this administration for the failures of the past—it is our hope that by implementing a listening process, that another group like this, in some future time, will not be needed because this administration failed to hear the Indian peoples.

Source:

Josephy, Alvin M., Jr., ed. *Red Power: The American Indians' Fight for Freedom.* New York: McGraw-Hill, 1971; Lincoln: University of Nebraska Press, 1985.

39   *Constitution of the Zuni Tribe (1970)*

The Zuni, also known as the A:Shiwi, are culturally related to other Pueblo peoples but they speak a unique language referred to as Zunian. Some ten thousand strong, they were historically a theocratic society led by a council of priests who provided the community spiritual and physical protection. The 640-square-mile reservation established in 1877 is home to fifteen matrilineal clans that are the foundation for their communal religious system. The Zuni adopted the Indian Reorganization Act in 1934 but did not choose to develop a constitution until 1970.

———

Preamble

We, the members of the Zuni Tribe, Zuni Indian Reservation, New Mexico, in order to secure to us and to our posterity the political and civil rights guaranteed to us by treaties and by the Constitution and statutes of the United States; to secure educational advantages; to encourage good citizenship; to exercise the right of self-government; to administer both as a municipal body and as a proprietor of our tribal affairs; to utilize, increase and protect our tribal resources; to encourage and promote all movements and efforts leading to the general welfare of our tribe; to guarantee individual rights and freedom of religion; and to maintain our tribal customs and traditions; do ordain and establish this constitution.

Article I—Jurisdiction

The jurisdiction of the Zuni Tribe, Zuni Indian Reservation exercised through the Zuni Tribal Council, the Executive Department and the Judicial Department, acting in accordance with this constitution and the ordinances adopted in accordance herewith, shall extend to all tribal lands included within the present boundaries of the Zuni Indian Reservation and to such other lands as may hereafter be added thereto, unless otherwise provided by law. This jurisdiction shall apply to and be for the benefit and protection of all Indians who now, or may in the future, reside on the Zuni Reservation. The name of this organization shall be the Zuni Tribe.

Article II—Membership

Section 1. Membership of the Zuni Tribe, Zuni Indian Reservation, shall consist of the following:

   a. All persons enrolled on the Zuni Agency census roll of April 1, 1963; provided the roll may be corrected at any time by the tribal council, subject to the approval of the Secretary of the Interior.
   b. All descendants of such persons, provided such descendants shall have not less than one-quarter (1/4) Zuni Indian blood.
   c. The membership roll of the Zuni Tribe shall be kept current by striking therefrom the names of persons who have relinquished in writing their membership in the tribe; and of deceased persons upon receipt of a death certificate or other evidence of death acceptable to the Zuni Tribal Council, and by adding thereto the names of persons who meet the membership requirements and who comply with the procedure for enrollment as members of the tribe. The membership roll will be maintained by the tribal secretary....

Article III—Bill of Rights

Section 1. Subject to the limitations prescribed by this constitution, all members of the Zuni Tribe shall have equal political rights and equal opportunities to share in tribal assets, and no member shall be denied freedom of conscience, speech, religion, association or assembly, nor shall he be denied the right to bear arms.

Section 2. The Zuni Tribe, in exercising its powers of self-government, shall not:

   a. Make or enforce any law prohibiting the free exercise of religion, or abridging the freedom of speech, or of the press, or the right of the people peaceably to assemble and to petition for a redress of grievances;
   b. Violate the right of the people to be secure in their persons, houses, papers, and effects against unreasonable search and seizures, nor issue warrants, but upon probable cause, supported by oath or affirmation, and particularly described the place to be searched and the person or thing to be resized;
   c. Subject any person for the same offense to be twice put in jeopardy;
   d. Compel any person in any criminal case to be witness against himself....

Article IV—Organization of the Government of the Zuni Tribe

Section 1. The government of the Zuni Tribe shall consist of a Legislative, and Executive, and a Judicial department.

Article V—The Legislative Department: Composition and Qualification

Section 1. The legislative authority of the Zuni Tribe shall rest in the Zuni Tribal Council, hereinafter sometimes called the tribal council, which shall hold its sessions at Zuni, New Mexico.

Section 2. The tribal council shall consist of eight (8) members, including a governor and lieutenant governor, all elected at large by popular vote as hereinafter provided....

Article VI—Authorities of the Tribal Council

Section 1. The Zuni Tribal Council, as the Legislative body of the tribe, shall exercise the following authorities subject to any limitations imposed by statues of the United States applicable to Indians or Indian tribes, and subject to all expressed restrictions contained in this constitution.

   a. To regulate its own procedures; to appoint subordinate boards, committees, officials and employees not otherwise provided for in this constitution and to prescribe for in this constitution and to prescribe their salaries, tenure and duties, provided that the tribal council shall, by appropriate ordinance, establish the personnel policies and procedures of the tribe, including a requirement that a statement of qualifications and standards be developed and published for all personnel employed by the tribe;
   b. To establish tribal corporations, associations and other subordinate organizations for economic and other purposes, and to transfer assets of the tribe thereto for management and control;
   c. To borrow money for tribal purposes;
   d. To represent the tribe, and to act in all matters that concern the welfare of the tribe....

Article XI—The Executive Department

Section 1. The governor, lieutenant governor and the treasurer shall comprise the executive department of the tribal government, exercising the authorities set forth in this constitution, and such other authorities as the tribal council may, from time to time, by appropriate ordinance, delegate to the executive officers.

Section 2. The governor and lieutenant governor shall be elected as provided in this constitution.

Article XII—Duties of the Executive Officers

Section 1. The Governor of the Zuni Tribe shall exercise the following authorities as the chief executive officer of the tribe; and such other authorities as the tribal council may assign.

   a. The governor shall preside over meetings of the Zuni Tribal Council;
   b. The governor shall appoint all non-elected officials and employees of the executive department of the tribal government and shall direct them

in their work, subject only to applicable restrictions embodied in this constitution or in enactments of the tribal council established personnel policies or governing personnel management;

c. The governor, subject to the approval of the tribal council, may establish such boards, committees or subcommittees as the business of the council may require, and shall serve as an ex-officio member of all such committees and boards....

Article XIV—The Judicial Department

Section 1. The tribal court shall consist of a chief judge and two associate judges, appointed by the Governor of the Zuni Tribe, with the concurrence of the tribal council. Any one of the judges may hold court as determined by the chief judge.

Section 2. By ordinance, subject to approval by the Secretary of the Interior, the tribal council shall establish a court of appeals.

Section 3. The tenure of trial judges shall be six (6) years. Their salary shall be established by ordinance of the tribal council.

Section 4. No person shall be appointed to the office of trial judge unless he is at least thirty (30) years of age and not more than seventy (70) years of age; nor shall any person be appointed as a trial judge who has ever been convicted of a felony or, within one year, a misdemeanor....

Article XVI—Oath of Office

All newly elected officers and members of the Zuni Tribal Council shall be required to take an oath of office, as shown below at the time of their installation. Such oath shall be administered by the Head Cacique of the Pueblo and his aides.

Oath of Office

"Into your care we entrust our land and our people. Regardless of whether you are poor, or lack the oratory to express yourself fluently, you will, to the best of your ability, be the protector, impartially, for your people. The stranger who comes into our land will become as one of your people, regardless of race, color, or creed, and you will give unto them the same protection and rights as you would your own. You will cherish and protect all that contains life; from the lowliest crawling creature to the human. By hasty work or deed you will refrain from hurting the feelings, both mentally and physically, of our people. In times when you, to the best of your ability and judgment, have resorted to every peaceful means of bringing reason to an individual, on a matter, and that individual, through stubbornness, remains contrary to the point of disrespect for the office you hold, and would, through his action, be a bad example to his fellowmen, you will question him four times if he will continue to set aside peaceful intelligent reasoning. If his answer is yes the four times, then you may strike him with the flat of your hand, and four times if necessary...."

Article XVIII—Inherent Powers of the Zuni Tribe

Section 1. No provision of this constitution shall be construed as a limitation of the inherent residual sovereign powers of the Zuni Tribe. Any such powers, not delegated to the representative tribal government by this institution are retained for direct exercise by the people through referendum, as provided for herein, or for exercise by the tribal government following amendment of the constitution....

Article XXI—Ratification

Section 1. This constitution, when adopted by majority vote of the qualified voters of the Zuni Tribe, voting at an election authorized for that purpose by the Secretary of the Interior, in which at least 30% of those entitled to vote shall cast their ballot, shall be submitted to the Secretary of the Interior for his approval, and shall be effective from and after the date of his approval.

Approval

I, Harrison Loesch, Assistant Secretary of the Interior of the United States of America, by virtue of the authority granted to me by the Act of June 18, 1934 (48 Stat. 984), as amended, do hereby approve the attached Constitution of the Zuni Tribe, Zuni Reservation, Zuni, New Mexico....

Sources:

Crampton, Gregory C., *The Zunis of Cibola*. Salt Lake City: University of Utah Press, 1977.

Ladd, Edmund J. "Zuni Social and Political Organization." In *Handbook of North American Indians*. Vol. 9, *Southwest*, edited by Alfonso Ortiz, 482–491. Washington, DC: Smithsonian Institution, 1979.

40   *Groundhog v. W.W. Keeler (1971)*

Descendants of several enrolled members of the Cherokee Nation of Oklahoma sought a judgment to nullify the process whereby their principal chief was selected, not by Tribal members, but by the US president. Principal Chief W.W. Keeler had been originally appointed in 1949 and over the subsequent twenty years had been reaffirmed by the president with no official Tribal consent or consultation. Plaintiffs argued that Keeler's continued empowerment was illegal on two grounds: first, that Congress lacked the authority to allow the president to make the appointment because it violated the 5th and 14th amendments of the Constitution; and because they claimed Keeler was not a citizen by blood and was therefore ineligible for office in the first place. Circuit Judge Phillips turned aside both arguments, claiming the court had no jurisdiction to hear internal Tribal disputes and that the Constitution's provisions had no application to Native nations unless they were related to the commerce clause or had been made directly applicable by an act of Congress.

———

This is declaratory judgment action brought by Groundhog, Blair, Guess, Tanner and Proctor, descendants of enrolled citizens of the Cherokee Nation, against Keeler, who now holds, and since 1949 has held, the office of Principal Chief of the Cherokee Nation....

We turn first to the plaintiffs' claim that the appointment of Keeler as Principal Chief of the Cherokee Tribe was illegal. The plaintiffs predicate that claim on two grounds:

1. That Congress had no power to authorize the President to appoint the Chief of the Cherokee Tribe, because so to do violated the Fifth and Fifteenth Amendments to the Constitution of the United States; and
2. That Keeler was not a citizen by blood of the Tribe and therefore was not eligible for appointment as Chief of the Tribe....

Plaintiffs also urge that the due process clause of the Fifth Amendment and the equal protection and due process clauses of the Fourteenth Amendment and the provisions of the Fifteenth Amendment, by the passage of 25 U.S.C. § 1302(8) of the Indian Bill of Rights, have been made applicable to the Cherokee Tribe.

The provisions of the Constitution of the United States have no application to Indian nations or their governments, except as they are expressly made so by the Constitution (the Commerce Clause), or are made applicable by an Act of Congress.

We think the legislative history of the so-called Indian Bill of Rights refutes the contentions of plaintiffs stated above....

The summary of the report of the Subcommittee was endorsed and adopted by the Senate Committee on the Judiciary. Such report makes it clear that Congress intended that the provisions of the Fifteenth Amendment, certain procedural provisions of the Fifth, Sixth, and Seventh Amendments, and in some respects the equal protection requirement of the Fourteenth Amendment should not be embraced in the Indian Bill of Rights.

It is also clear from such report that Congress was concerned primarily with tribal administration of justice and imposition of tribal penalties and forfeitures, and not with the specifics of tribal structure or office-holding. By its stated intentional exclusion from the Act of the provisions of the Fifteenth Amendment, any basis of federal court jurisdiction over tribal elections was definitely eliminated....

When consideration is given to the fact that the summary of the bill, referred to above, stated the equal protection clause in § 1302(8) of the Indian Bill of Rights was not as broad as the equal protection clause of the Fourteenth Amendment, we are of the opinion the allegations of the complaint do not state facts showing a violation of such clause in the Indian Bill of Rights.

Indeed, we would reach that conclusion if the Fourteenth Amendment provision was applicable in the instant case, which it is not....

Source:

Groundhog v. *Keeler*, 442 F.2d 674 (1971).

---

41   *Senate Concurrent Resolution Regarding a National American Indian Policy (1971)*

In 1970 President Richard Nixon issued a policy statement that emphasized his administration's plan to emphatically move away from federal termination of Native peoples and toward a policy stance that supported Tribal self-determination. The following proposed concurrent resolution was Congress's initial and very positive response to Nixon's plan.

———

Resolution Purpose:

The primary purpose of the resolution is to replace the national Indian policy set forth in House Concurrent Resolution 108 [the infamous Termination policy]...adopted on August 1, 1953. In addition, Senate Concurrent Resolution 26 embraces the principles of maximum Indian control and self-determination and seeks to strengthen and improve the delivery of services to Indian people wherever they may reside.

Senate Concurrent Resolution 26 is based upon the premises that American Indians stand in a unique legal, social, and economic relationship to the federal government and that this relationship is the basis for federal responsibility to protect Indian lands, resources, and rights, as well as to provide basic community services to American Indians residing on reservations and in other areas considered to be within the scope of the trust relationship.

The concurrent resolution also recognizes that Indians are entitled to share and participate fully in all federal, state, and local social and economic development programs. It states further that the federal government is responsible for assuring that the aforementioned rights are fulfilled and that the eradication of adverse conditions which prevent any American from achieving a life of decency and self-sufficiency is a national priority goal.

The concurrent resolution declares it to be the sense of Congress that:

1. A government-wide commitment shall be made to enable Indians to determine their own future to the maximum extent possible;
2. This statement policy replaces that set forth in House Concurrent Resolution 108 approved by the 83rd Congress on August 1, 1953;
3. Indian self-determination and development shall be a major goal of our national Indian policy;
4. There should be a recognition of federal responsibility to assure that Indians residing beyond the areas served by special Indian programs receive equal consideration as other citizens for services through other Federal, state, and local agencies;
5. Indian property and identity will be protected and Indians shall be brought to a social and economic level of full participating citizens;
6. The Office of Management and Budget should submit an annual report to Congress showing government expenditures on behalf of Indians; and
7. "American Indian" or "Indian" is defined to include "Alaska Natives."

Background:

Throughout the history of our nation, the basic posture of our government toward American Indians has assumed a variety of forms. In the most sweeping terms, these have ranged from according tribes the full dignity and respect as separate and sovereign nations to treating the Indians in a demeaning and paternalistic guardian-ward relationship.

Underlying these various relationships is a large and still growing body of treaties, court decisions, and laws. They provide the judicial basis and historical background which supports the long-standing and unique relationship between Indians and the federal government.

Although this relationship has sometimes been criticized by the Indian community and others, it, nevertheless, carries with it certain benefits which Indians value, and even consider critical to the continued survival of their culture and their identity as a people. These benefits are, first, the federal government's special responsibility for the protection of Indian lands, resources, and rights; and, second, the provision of basic community services to Indians under specified conditions.

A more recent congressional expression on national Indian policy was embraced in House Concurrent Resolution 108 of the 83rd Congress. This resolution was cast in terms of granting Indians their rights and prerogatives as American citizens. Its stated purpose was to free them from federal control and supervision and make them subject to the same laws and entitled to the same privileges as other citizens. What this meant, however, to many in the Indian community was an end to their unique relationship with the federal government along with its attendant benefits, protection, and services. It was from this policy era that the word "termination" was added to the Indians' vocabulary. As a consequence, this policy statement has become a symbol and has been resented and resisted by the Indian community.

Need:

A new national Indian policy that is compatible with the Indians' unique relationship with the federal government is needed to restore the confidence of Indian people in the government to permit them to work together to resolve the adverse social and economic conditions which beset Indian reservations and communities. House Concurrent Resolution 108 contributed significantly to the loss of such confidence and continues to be viewed with suspicion by the Indian community.

The status of life of Indian people when compared with other citizens underscores the need for prompt congressional approval of a new national Indian policy designed to improve Indian living conditions. This status is illustrated by the following:

1. The infant mortality rate for Indians is 30.8 deaths per 1,000 live births compared to 20.7 for all races;
2. The average age at death for Indians is 46.1 years compared to 65.0 years for all races in the nation;
3. The average Indian family of five or six lives in a one or two room house, 24 percent of which lack running water and adequate sanitation facilities;
4. Fifty percent of Indian students drop out of school before graduation, and the average number of years of schooling completed by Indians is 8.4 compared to the national average of 10.6;
5. Unemployment among Indian people is many times the national average, and runs as high as 60 percent on some reservations during the winter months; and
6. In 50 percent of the Indian households, the annual income is under $2,000, well below the poverty level established by the federal government.

While these statistics are only illustrative of the total social circumstances of Indian people, they represent the conditions which must be overcome through a new positive dynamic national Indian policy if Indian people are to share social and economic equality along with other Americans.

Committee Comments:

As a result of history and events American Indians are no longer confined exclusively to reservations and Indian communities. The Department of the Interior reports that of the 827,000 American Indians enumerated in the 1970 census, approximately 50 percent now live outside reservations.

At present 488,000 American Indians reside on or near reservations and continue to look to the special Federal Indian service programs of the Bureau of Indian Affairs and the Indian Health Service in partial response to their diverse social and economic needs. Included in this number are Indian people residing in former reservation areas of Oklahoma and the natives of Alaska—Indians,

Aleuts, and Eskimos. However, in California only those Indians who were clearly identified as living on or near reservations or Indian trust land are included in this count. The Bureau of Indian Affairs reports that there are approximately 21,000 rural Indians throughout California whose entitlement to the special Federal Indian service programs is unclear at this time. These groups are currently endeavoring to clarify their federal relations status in order to qualify for the programs and services of the Bureau of Indian Affairs and the Indian Health Service.

The committee wishes to emphasize to the executive branch of government that the thrust of Senate Concurrent Resolution 26 is inclusive rather than exclusive. None of the language of the resolution is intended to diminish the responsibility of the federal government, including the Bureau of Indian Affairs and the Indian Health Service, to provide appropriate programs and services to Indian people who continue to maintain federal relations with the government. In addition, a responsibility shall continue to exist for federal protection of the land, resources and rights of Indian people who come within this category.

Conversely, none of the language of the resolution should be interpreted by the executive branch to deny Indian citizens their rightful entitlement to the programs and services of other federal, state, and local units of government. These resources are important to the well-being of the thousands of Indian people who now reside in urban areas....

Source:

US Senate. "National American Indian Policy." Senate Report No. 92–561. 92nd Cong., 1st Sess. Washington, DC: Government Printing Office, 1971.

42

Vine Deloria, Jr. on Restoration of Constitutional Treaty-Making Authority (1973)

Preeminent political theorist Vine Deloria Jr. drafted this unpublished essay on the federal government's response to Native activists' calls for the restoration of treaty-making between Indigenous nations and the United States. He worked closely with Hank Adams (Sioux-Assiniboine), a highly respected and gifted political strategist who in 1972 drafted the pivotal "Twenty Point Proposal," a blueprint for improvement of Native status and intergovernmental relations. Together, Deloria and Adams championed the treaty process as the most fair and legitimate means by which Native nations could engage in diplomacy with the federal government and better exercise their inherent governing authority.

Although Vine Deloria Jr. has walked on, Hank Adams has harnessed the power of social media to continue his work on these foundational issues, particularly with regard to the tension between the concepts of consultation and consent.

———

On November 3–9, 1972, nearly a thousand American Indians in the caravan known as the Trail of Broken Treaties arrived in the nation's capital to present Twenty Points, which they had designed as a partial solution to the pressing problems of the American Indian community. The events of that desperate week overshadowed the real issues of the caravan, which were highlighted in the Twenty Points and discussion since the incident has focused on the destruction of some government records and partial damage to the headquarters of the Bureau of Indian Affairs.

During the negotiations between the people of the Trail of Broken Treaties and the people representing the administration, the people representing the federal government promised to consider the Twenty Points and to report their responses within sixty days. On January 9, 1973, a response to the Twenty Points was released from the White House under the signatures of Leonard Garment and Frank Carlucci. The response was hardly adequate for the issues raised.

Among the Twenty Points were several (Points one, two, four, five, six, seven, and eight) that involved the restoration of the authority to make treaties with Indian communities, with the need to enforce treaty provisions for the protection of Indian individuals, and for the need to place all Indian people under a new general category of status to be known as "treaty relations."

The treaty points were most strenuously rejected by members of the administration task force on vague grounds that the Indian Citizenship Act of 1924 had precluded the United States from dealing with Indian tribes by treaty because the individual members thereof happened to be United States citizens.

The following is the administration's response to the first point of the Twenty Points, which involved a restoration of the constitutional authority to make treaties. This response generally characterizes the approach of the administration and seems to mean that the subject has been rejected without much consideration of the value of the proposal for contemporary times and in the context of the world situation today.

Over one hundred years ago the Congress decided that it was no longer appropriate for the United States to make treaties with Indian tribes. By 1924, all Indians were citizens of the United States and of the states in which they resided. The citizenship relationship with one's government and the treaty relationship are mutually exclusive; a government makes treaties with foreign nations, not with its own citizens. If renunciation of citizenship is implied here, or secession, these are wholly backward steps, inappropriate for a nation which is a Union.

Indians do need to "represent their own interests" and Indian tribes, groups, and communities are finding increasingly effective ways of expressing these interests. There are several active and vocal nationwide Indian organizations; there are many tribal governments and these are being strengthened with full Administration support and endorsement. The President has even proposed that the administration and control of most BIA and HEW Indian programs be transferred to Indian tribal governments, at the latters' option, but the Congress has not yet approved this legislative proposal. The President has proposed the creation of an Indian Trust Counsel Authority to represent Indian interests in the vital field of natural resources rights, but the Congress has not enacted this legislation.

The White House and every Department in this Administration meets frequently with Indian leaders and groups, listens to and pays attention to Indian recommendations and, as for example in the development of the Alaska Native Claims legislation, works with Indian representatives on matters vitally affecting Indian people. We will continue to go forward with these many, close relationships.

It is singularly unfortunate that the authors of the White House response to the Twenty Points had such a lack of understanding of the history of the relationship between the United States and the aboriginal Indian tribes of the North American continent. Laying aside the early period of exploration by the European powers, and taking only the recent years of American history as a guideline, the policy of the United States with respect to the Indian tribes has been one of expediency grounded only in the political considerations of the moment and without any lasting understanding of the nature of peoples, laws, governments, or responsibilities.

The result of this fluctuation from allotment to I.R.A. to termination to self-determination to Indian Claims Commission to Poverty Programs to the National Council on Indian Opportunity has been the tremendous rise in federal expenditures without many visible results, the creation of numerous liabilities of the United States toward the Indian tribes with whom they have a relationship, hundreds of cases of needless litigation, and not one solid or concrete path by which either the United States or the Indian tribes can understand the nature of their relationship or find a way to finally conclude their business with each other on mutually satisfactory grounds.

The fact that there are a multitude of accounting claims in the Indian Claims Commission in which Indian tribes are suing the American government for inadequate trust activities when supervising tribal lands and funds, and the fact that claims against the United States are continuing to grow should be sufficient for any responsible official of the government to at least consider an alternative plan for defining a new relationship with the Indian tribes. It is useless and stupid to refuse to solve the problems which exist between the United States and the Indian tribes in one generation only to throw the problem into a claims commission two generations later and compensate the descendants of those injured while never thinking of a final resolution of the conflict.

The following paper does not make any pretense to be a final statement of the legal and moral issues involved in the present situation. It is written specifically for one purpose—to demonstrate to the people in Congress and the present administration that the proposal to reopen the treaty-making procedure is far from a stupid or ill-considered proposal but rather one which would place the United States in the forefront of civilized nations in its treatment of the aboriginal peoples of the continent—a problem which even Japan and the Soviet Russian Union have yet to solve.

Moreover by illuminating some of the twists and turns of the policies of the past perhaps a better understanding of the status of the American Indian tribes can be seen in a world-historical perspective—a perspective which the recent Viet Nam war indicates is sadly lacking in contemporary American political understanding. The Twenty Points specifically asked that all Indians be placed under treaty relations. In order to do that Congressional hearings of great length should be held to determine exactly what relationships do exist between American Indians and the United States government. This paper is thus designed particularly to justify such hearings before the Senate Foreign Relations Committee and other Senate and House committees which are willing to open their eyes to a broader understanding of the world than is encompassed in the narrow rules and regulations which now bind and block the relationship between American Indians and the federal government and which appear to isolate American Indians and their situation from the situation of other aboriginal peoples of the globe.

The Claim of the United States of America to North America:

The Indian treaties from 1778 to 1842, many of which were demonstrative of the initial contact between the United States and the respective Indian tribe and the subsequent relationship that ensued from such contact, are contained in Volume Seven, United States Statutes at Large. The editor of that volume purports to exhibit "the general principles which have been recognized by the Supreme Court of the United States in relation to the Indian tribes, the Indian title to the lands occupied by them, and the effect of treaties with them upon their claims to these lands."

Citing the case of *Johnson and Graham's Lessee v. William M'Intosh* (1823) the editor summarizes the theory under which the lands of the Indian tribes came under scrutiny by the European nations: "On the discovery of this immense continent, the great nations of Europe were eager to appropriate to themselves so much of it as they could respectively acquire. Its vast extent offered an ample field to the ambition and enterprise of all; and the character and religion of its inhabitants afforded an apology for considering them as a people over whom the superior genius of Europe might claim an ascendency. The potentates of the old world found no difficulty in convincing themselves that they made ample compensation to the inhabitants of the new, by bestowing on them civilization and Christianity, in exchange for unlimited independence. But, as they were all in pursuit of nearly the same object, it was necessary, in order to avoid conflicting settlements, and consequent war with each other, to establish a principle, which all should acknowledge as the law by which the right of acquisition, which they all asserted, should be regulated as between themselves. This principle was, that discovery gave title to the government by whose subjects, ore by whose authority, it was made, against all other European governments, which title might be consummated by possession.... "

The editor then reviews the ventures of the various European nations who contested for the lands of North America bringing his brief history up to the American Revolution, each time remarking that as the respective European nations ceded lands in North America to each other they rarely occupied or possessed those lands but owned the exclusive right which was recognized by the other European nations to extinguish the land title of the original inhabitants. Of the American Revolution, the editor concludes: "By the treaty which concluded the war of our revolution, Great Britain relinquished all claim, not only to the government, but to the "propriety and territorial rights of the United States," whose boundaries were fixed in the second article. By this treaty the powers of government, and the right to soil, which had previously been in Great Britain, passed definitively to these states. We had before taken possession of them, by declaring independence; but neither the declaration of independence, nor the treaty confirming it, could give us more than that which we before possessed, or to which Great Britain was before entitled. It has never been doubted, that either the United States, or the several states, had a clear title to all the Lands within the boundary lines described in the treaty, subject only to the Indian right of occupancy, and that the exclusive power to extinguish that right, was vested in that government which might constitutionally exercise it."

The United States, in the exercise and claim of dominion over the lands conceded to it by Great Britain following the Revolutionary War, does not hold absolute fee to the lands of the interior of the continent. It holds a definite and limited fee as follows: a title recognized by European nations which allows it to extinguish the aboriginal title held by the inhabitants of the land free from the hostile interference of European nations, and a title limited in a severe manner by the outstanding title of the aboriginal peoples who can only sell their title to the United States, rather than another European nation, but who, if they wish not to sell their lands to the United States, must be protected by the United States as against the possible future failure of recognition of the United States' right to extinguish aboriginal title by a member of the European national coalition which has recognized discovery rights.

This basic complex of relationship which defines the right of the United States to recognition of its lands by the other nations of the world incorporates those lands still held by aboriginal nations into one balanced complex. That is to say, the title of the United States receives its legality in the world scheme of legality because it is a purchase of lands allotted to nations of the world through a procedure recognized and approved by European nations in whose eyes the world system of land titles receives its validity. Since the United States at no point makes acquisition of lands through conquest the basis for its title, the presently existing lands of the American Indian nations must still have a validity in the world legal scheme if only that they are remnant lands of the planet surviving from the lands declared eligible to be discovered.

The fundamental question raised by the Trail of Broken Treaties concerning the restoration of Indian treaty rights and recognition of Indian land rights concerns the possibility of converting both the Indian aboriginal title and the United States purchased and protective title to recognizable present titles and establishing the logical conclusion of four hundred years of indeterminable interests on both types of land title. That is to say, at what point is the title of the United States defensible on any present theory except that of military and economic force. And at what point does the Indian aboriginal title shed its protectorate status in an active trust exercised by the United States government and become a title fully cognizable in federal and international law.

Since the world is no longer open to "discoveries" by the nations of European peoples and since the days of colonization have been superseded by cessions of sovereignty back to the aboriginal peoples of Africa and Asia by European nations such as Great Britain and France, Germany, Sweden, Holland, and Denmark, the title of the American Indian tribes to their lands recognized by the nations of the civilized world community must now be restored....

The orientation of the United States government and its policy making people has not been focused on the realities of the world situation. Nor has it been focused on the fact of history, the movement of peoples around the globe in historical times and in the more recent movements toward self-government. True, people in the last two administrations have spoken about "self-determination" of the Indian tribes. But the phrase has had a hollow ring. These people cannot believe that cultural differences exist except as a side attraction for tourists.

The situation of the world today is that mankind must finally face itself, must finally define a world standard of morality for all men, and must recognize the yearnings of peoples to be themselves in spite of the dogmas and doctrines concerning the meaning of history promulgated by western men. Of all the nations taking or accepting a trusteeship over smaller and weaker nations the United States has been singularly inept in its treatment of the Indian nations. Even the smaller islands such as Malta and Cyprus have gained an independence for themselves after centuries of domination by outsiders. The Jews have come back to their homelands after a period of exile of nearly two thousand years.

Yet American Indian communities, protected according to legal doctrines against the invasions of the Europeans by the United States, do not have the right to sit on school boards to determine what the education of their children shall be. Nauru gains its independence because of its phosphate reserves. Yet the Crow, Northern Cheyenne, and Navajo tribes between themselves have two-thirds of the remaining soft coal on the continent and are virtually without power to decide how it shall be used.

There are numerous reasons for the Senate Foreign Relations Committee to hold open congressional hearings on the current state of Indian treaties. We have listed many of those reasons above. A number of other treaties have been kept in the past which involved nations much smaller than Indian tribes. We see no reason for the present distortion of legal doctrines to continue to preclude any discussion of Indian tribes as having a status and an identity in the world of today.

The fact that American Indians also hold citizenship in the United States is not a sufficient reason to withhold recognition of tribal existence in terms of the world community of nations. The Cook Islanders have dual citizenship with New Zealand, Lichtenstein has dual citizenship with Switzerland (which is smaller than the Navajo reservation itself), and the citizens of Monaco have rights with respect to France. Citizenship itself is not a sufficient barrier to recognition of national existence.

The argument continues to rebound that the United States is one nation and that "we are all one people" but the facts of social existence in the United States today disclaim that contention as headlines of murders, broken laws and treaties, and violations of trust by the United States abound. If we are truly one nation then the Indian treaties, signed and ratified under the provisions of the Constitution, should be enforced. They are not enforced.

The responsibility of any nation and the particular responsibility of elected officials of any nation is not to justify what has passed for legality but to antic- ipate the conditions and problems of tomorrow and attempt to deal with them. The current confusion and violence in Indian country is a result of the failure to do so by generations of elected officials in this country. To continue to per- petuate myths about American Indians which have no basis in fact or in law is merely avoiding the larger issues confronting the nations of the world. What is the basis for individual or national existence?

We would urge the members of the Senate Foreign Relations Committee and all citizens interested in justice and a solution to some of the pressing problems of our time to consider the points of this paper and to call for hearing on the current state of Indian treaty rights and their enforcement in the immediate future.

Sources:

Adams, Hank. *The Hank Adams Reader: An Exemplary Native Activist and the Unleashing of Indigenous Sovereignty.* Edited by David E. Wilkins. Golden, CO: Fulcrum Publishing, 2011.

Deloria, Vine, Jr. *Behind the Trail of Broken Treaties: An Indian Declaration of Independence.* Austin: University of Texas Press, 1974, 1985.

43   *Declaration of Sovereignty (1974)*

The National Congress of American Indians (NCAI) had served as the major intertribal interest group since the 1940s, but with the surge of Indigenous ac- tivism in the late 1960s and early 1970s, it had been relegated to a secondary position—at least in the minds of many young Native activists and elders— behind more activist organizations such as the American Indian Movement (AIM) and the National Indian Youth Council (NIYC). This "Declaration," drafted under the leadership of highly respected Northwest leader Mel Tonasket (Colville), was intended to remind Native peoples and the federal and state governments of NCAI's importance and its intention to be fully engaged in the critical developments of the time.

The National Congress of American Indians assembled at the Royal Inn in San Diego, California for the Thirty First Annual Convention during the period of October 21–25, 1974, hereby declares:

1. The Sovereign Aboriginal American Indian Nations and the United States of America, from time to time, subsequent to the year 1776 A.D., did negotiate and did enter into solemn treaties to exchange territorial rights for the mutual benefit and welfare of both parties to the negotiated treaties, and that,

2. The Sovereign Aboriginal American Indian Nations through said direct binding relations, whether written or implied by the sacred treaties, Constitution of the United States of America, or by Executive, legislative, or judicial action, did believe and do hereby further declare that,

3. The Government of the United States of America in negotiating said solemn treaties, did recognize Aboriginal sovereignty and by its sacred honor, did agree to honor, preserve, protect and guarantee to other states and nations and to the Aboriginal Tribes and nations those inherent sovereign rights and powers of self-government and self-determination afforded every sovereign nation of the world, and

4. The government of the United States of America did accept an obligation to assume a Trust Responsibility to honor, enforce, preserve, protect, and guarantee, without interference, the inherent sovereign rights and powers of self-government to the recognized and specified Aboriginal American Indian Nations, and,

5. The government of the United States of America, by acceptance and assumption of Trust Responsibility, did obligate itself to provide and to establish the necessary Federal Governmental instrumentalities required to honor, enforce, preserve, protect, and fulfill the treaty obligations and the general constitutional obligations pursuant thereto, and

6. The government of the United States of America is, by the conditions of said treaties and other agreements, and by legislation, and by results of litigation, required to assist in the management, development, preservation, protection, and guarantee of sovereign status of all of the Exclusive rights of the Aboriginal American Indian Nations to their Aboriginal or Treaty Territorial Domain, to the assets of natural resources of the surface, subsurface, and above-surface, to include but not limited to, hunting, fishing rights, land, water, air, wild rice, minerals, and timber, and

7. The government of the United States of America is further required to insure adequate Federal facilities and services, to be staffed with sufficient professional and qualified technical personnel for Health, Education, Welfare, and personal services to be commensurate with the predominant society, and

8. The National Congress of American Indians hereby States that the Government of the United States of America, in performance and recognition of its treaty obligations and responsibilities, has Failed and Neglected:

    a. To fully recognize inherent Aboriginal American Indian sovereignty and the rights and powers of self-government and self-determination, and

    b. To provide and fulfill its Trust Obligations and Responsibilities to establish Independent Governmental Instrumentalities, free from conflicts of interest, to insure inherent rights and powers of self-government as guaranteed by the negotiated treaties with Aboriginal American Indian Nations, and

    c. To honor, preserve, protect, and guarantee the Aboriginal American Indian Tribes and Nations' territorial integrity and other rights guaranteed by treaties which under article six of the Constitution of the United States of America is the supreme law of the land, and therefore,

9. The National Congress of American Indians declares and hereby petitions the Congress of the United States of America to initiate and implement immediate corrective legislation to:

    a. Honor and recognize the sovereignty and rights of Aboriginal American Indian Tribes and Nations, whether they exist by treaty or non-treaty, and

    b. Re-establish those independent Aboriginal American Indian Tribes and Nations which were terminated by executive order or legislative action without the consent of the Tribe or Nation, and

    c. Establish a Single, Independent, Federal Governmental Instrumentality with Concurrence of the Majority of the Recognized Aboriginal American Indian Tribes and Nations, in order to implement and guarantee the treaty responsibilities and Trust Obligations of the United States of America under Article Six of the Constitution of Said Nation.

    d. We, the assembled members of the National Congress of American Indians and of various tribes do hereby adopt this declaration and pledge our honor toward instituting its intent to the end that the Indian people shall enjoy the fruits of liberty, justice and the right to maintain their culture and religious heritage.

Certification

At a duly called meeting of the National Congress of American Indians held in San Diego, California, on October 24, 1974, the foregoing declaration was passed by a unanimous vote for passage of said declaration.

    Mel Tonasket, President

Source:

"Declaration of Sovereignty,", 1974. Records of the NCAI, 1933–1990. Box 22; National Museum of the American Indian Archive Center Smithsonian Institution. http://nmai.si.edu/sites/1/files/archivecenter/AC010_ncai.pdf.

44

Declaration of Continuing Independence by the First International Indian Treaty Council at Standing Rock (1974)

In the summer of 1974, members of the American Indian Movement (AIM), with support from traditional Native leaders, convened a large international gathering of Natives from throughout the Western Hemisphere. They united on the Standing Rock Sioux Reservation to outline the philosophy of the recently established International Indian Treaty Council (IITC). Unlike the National Congress of American Indians with its focus on national developments, the IITC's avowed purpose was to represent and support the interests of Native peoples at the global level. In 1977 it became the first Indigenous organization to achieve consultative status as a nongovernmental organization with the Economic and Social Council of the United Nations. IITC continues to advocate for Indigenous peoples and communities worldwide.

Preamble:

The United States of America has continually violated the independent Native Peoples of this continent by Executive Action, Legislative fiat and Judicial decision. By its actions, the U.S. has denied all Native people their International Treaty rights, Treaty lands and basic human rights of freedom and sovereignty. This same U.S. Government which fought to throw off the yoke of oppression and gain its own independence has now reversed its role and become the oppressor of sovereign Native people.

Might does not make right. Sovereign people of varying cultures have the absolute right to live in harmony with Mother Earth so long as they do not infringe upon this same right of other peoples. The denial of this right to any sovereign people, such as the Native American Nations, must be challenged by truth and action. World concern must focus on all colonial governments to the end that sovereign people everywhere shall live as they choose, in peace with dignity and freedom.

The International Indian Treaty Conference hereby adopts this Declaration of Continuing Independence of the Sovereign Native American Indian Nations. In the course of these human events, we call upon the people of the world to support this struggle for our sovereign rights and our treaty rights. We pledge our assistance to all other sovereign people who seek their own independence....

The First International Treaty Council of the Western Hemisphere was formed on the land of the Standing Rock Sioux Tribe on June 8–10, 1974. The delegates, meeting under the guidance of the Great Spirit, represented 97 Indian tribes and Nations from across North and South America.

We, the sovereign Native Peoples recognize that all lands belonging to the various Native Nations are clearly defined by the sacred treaties solemnly entered into between the Native Nations and the government of the United States of America.

We, the sovereign Native Peoples charge the United States of America with gross violations of our International Treaties. Two of the thousands of violations that can be cited are the "wrongful taking" of the Black Hills from the Great Sioux Nation in 1877, this sacred land belonging to the Great Sioux Nation under the Fort Laramie Treaty of 1868. The second violation was the forced march of the Cherokee People from their ancestral lands in the state of Georgia to the then "Indian Territory" of Oklahoma after the Supreme Court of the United States ruled the Cherokee treaty rights inviolate. The treaty violation, known as the "Trail of Tears" brought death to two-thirds of the Cherokee Nation during the forced march.

The Council further realizes that securing United States recognition of treaties signed with Native Nations requires a committed and unified struggle, using every available legal and political resource. Treaties between sovereign nations explicitly entail agreements which represent "the supreme law of the land" binding each party to an inviolate international relationship.

We acknowledge the historical fact that Independence of the Peoples of our sacred Mother Earth have always been over sovereignty of land. These historical freedom efforts have always involved the highest human sacrifice.

We recognize that all Native Nations wish to avoid violence, but we also recognize that the United States government has always used force and violence to deny Native Nations basic human and treaty rights.

We adopt this Declaration of Continuing Independence, recognizing that struggle lies ahead—a struggle certain to be won—and that the human and treaty rights of all Native Nations will be honored. In this understanding the International Indian Treaty Council declares:

The United States Government in its Constitution, Article VI, recognizes treaties as part of the Supreme Law of the United States. We will peacefully pursue all legal and political avenues to demand United States recognition of its own Constitution in this regard, and thus to honor its treaties with the Native Nations.

We will seek the support of all world communities in the struggle for the continuing independence of Native Nations.

We the representatives of sovereign Native nations unite in forming a council to be known as the International Indian Treaty Council to implement these declarations.

The International Indian Treaty Council will establish offices in Washington, D.C. and New York City to approach the international forces necessary to obtain the recognition of our treaties. These offices will establish an initial system of communications among Native Nations to disseminate information, getting a general consensus of concerning issues, developments and any legislative attempt affecting Native Nations by the United States of America.

The International Indian Treaty Council recognizes the sovereignty of all Native Nations and will stand in unity to support our Native and international brothers and sisters in their respective and collective struggles concerning international treaties and agreements violated by the United States and other governments.

All treaties between the Sovereign Native Nations and the United States Government must be interpreted according to the traditional and spiritual ways of the signatory Native Nations.

We declare our recognition of the Provisional Government of the Independent Oglala Nation, established by the Traditional Chiefs and Headmen under the provisions of the 1868 Fort Laramie Treaty with the Great Sioux Nation at Wounded Knee, March 11, 1973.

We condemn the United States of America for its gross violation of the 1868 Fort Laramie Treaty in militarily surrounding, killing, and starving the citizens of the independent Oglala Nation into exile.

We demand the United States of America recognize the sovereignty of the Independent Oglala Nation and immediately stop all present and future criminal prosecutions of sovereign Native Peoples. We call upon the conscionable nations of the world to join us in charging and prosecuting the United States of America for its genocidal practices against the Sovereign Native Nations; most recently illustrated by Wounded Knee 1973 and the continued refusal by the United States of America to sign the United Nations 1948 Treaty on Genocide.

We reject all executive orders, legislative acts and judicial decisions related to Native Nations since 1871, when the United States unilaterally suspended treaty making relations with Native Nations. This includes, but is not limited to, the Major Crimes Act, the General Allotment Act, the Citizenship Act of 1924, the Indian Reorganization Act of 1934, Indian Claims Commission Act, Public Law 280 and the Termination Act. All treaties between Native Nations and the United States made prior to 1871 shall be recognized without further need of interpretation.

We hereby ally ourselves with the colonized Puerto Rican People in their struggle for Independence from the same United States of America.

We recognize that there is only one color of Mankind in the world who are not represented in the United Nations. And that is the indigenous Redman of the Western Hemisphere. We recognize this lack of representation in the United Nations comes from genocidal policies of the colonial power of the United States.

The International Indian Treaty Council established by this conference is directed to make application to the United Nations for recognition and membership of the sovereign Native Nations. We pledge our support to any similar application by any aboriginal people.

This conference directs the Treaty Council to open negotiations with the government of the United States through its Department of State. We seek these negotiations in order to establish diplomatic relations with the United States. When these diplomatic relations have been established, the first order of business shall be to deal with violations of treaties with the Native Indian

Nations, and violations of the rights of those Native Indian Nations who have refused to sign treaties with the United States.

We, the People of the International Indian Treaty Council, following the guidance of our elders through instructions from the Great Spirit, and out of our respect for our sacred Mother Earth, all her children, and those yet unborn offer our lives for our International Treaty Rights.

Source:

Anaya, S. James. *Indigenous Peoples in International Law*, 2nd ed. New York: Oxford University Press, 2004.

45   *Harjo v. Kleppe (1976)*

In this important case, Allen Harjo, a local leader who had lost a recent election bid for principal chief, argued in federal court that the newly created Creek Nation was illegal and that the lawful government instead was encapsulated within the traditional Tribal towns as they were organized under the 1867 Constitution and recognized in various treaties. District Judge Bryant agreed with Harjo and characterized the usurpation of Tribal authority by the Bureau of Indian Affairs over a period of seventy years as "bureaucratic imperialism." This case carefully laid out the Creek Nation's historical experiences under federal policies and legislation that generally applied to all of the so-called "Five Civilized Tribes," which had been removed to territory that later became Oklahoma. Tor the Muscogee (Creek) Nation, who call themselves Este Mvskokvlke, this decision was key in strengthening their self-determination.

———

Introduction

This matter is now before the Court on the parties' cross-motions for summary judgment.

The parties have stipulated that no genuine issues of material fact exist. Plaintiffs in this action seek declaratory and injunctive relief against the policy and practice of the Interior Department in recognizing and dealing with defendant Cox, Principal Chief of the Creek Nation, as the sole embodiment of the Creek tribal government, and in refusing to recognize, facilitate, or deal with a Creek National Council as a coordinate branch of the tribal government responsible for certain legislative and financial functions.

The Creek Nation is one of the Five Civilized Tribes of Oklahoma. Each of the four plaintiffs is a resident of Oklahoma, a citizen of the United States, and a Creek Indian who is a citizen of the Muskogee (Creek) Nation and of a Creek Tribal Town. Each of the plaintiffs is a duly qualified elector under the laws or customs of his or her respective tribal town and under the laws of the Creek Nation, as to the election of tribal town representatives to the Creek national legislature. Each of the male plaintiffs is also a duly qualified elector under the original laws and 1867 Constitution of the Creek nation as to the election of the Principal Chief and Second Chief of that Nation. In addition, named plaintiff Allen Harjo is an elected representative of Fish Pond Tribal Town. Harjo has also twice run unsuccessfully for Principal Chief of the Creek....

Primarily at issue is the legitimacy of Cox's authority to disburse tribal funds and enter into contracts on behalf of the Creek Nation without the approval of the Creek National Council. Specifically, the first cause of action alleges: (1) Article 1 of the 1867 constitution of the Creek Nation lodges the lawmaking power of that Nation in the Creek National Council; (2) The Constitution of the Creek Nation places the financial affairs of the Nation exclusively under the control of the Creek National Council; (3) Congress, between 1866 and 1906, on several occasions specifically recognized the Creek National Council as the ultimate repository of power within the Creek national government; (4) Under the terms of the Act of 1906, 34 Stat. 137, and the Treaties of 1856 and 1866 Congress imposed on defendants the duty to respect and follow the provisions of the constitution of the Creek Nation; and (5) Federal defendants have approved the disbursement of tribal funds by defendant Cox on behalf of the Creek Nation and have paid federal funds to Cox contrary to the intent of Congress.

Defendants argue that (1) This Court lacks jurisdiction over the action; (2) The action is a nonjusticiable controversy; (3) The Court should dismiss the action due to the absence of certain indispensable parties; (4) Various congressional acts have relieved the Creek Nation of sufficient authority that it has been rendered incompetent to handle the affairs of the tribe under the 1867 Constitution; (5) Congress was aware of the fact that the affairs of the Five Civilized Tribes (Creeks, Cherokees, Choctaws, Chickasaws, and Seminoles) were being administered by Principal Chiefs or Governors and therefore ratified this form of government when it enacted the Act of October 22, 1970, 84 Stat. 1091....

The Central issue to be resolved in this case is whether the tribal government of the Creek Nation has survived statutory dismemberment, and if so, whether the federal government is acting legally in recognizing the Principal Chief as the sole embodiment of that government. Phrased differently, the question is whether the federal government may permit funds belonging to the Creek Nation to be expended solely on the authority of the Principal Chief, or whether Creek and federal law require the participation of the Creek National Council in the tribe's financial decision-making.

After extensive investigation and careful consideration, aided by the able written and oral presentations of counsel, the Court has arrived at the inescapable conclusion that despite the general intentions of the Congress of the late nineteenth and early twentieth centuries to ultimately terminate the tribal government of the Creeks, and despite an elaborate statutory scheme implementing numerous intermediate steps toward that end, the final dissolution of the Creek tribal government created by the Creek Constitution of 1867 was never statutorily accomplished, and indeed that government was instead explicitly perpetuated....

In summary, then, it is clear that with the passage of the Curtis Act, the territorial sovereignty of the Creek Nation had been seriously eroded. Territorial sovereignty, however, is not the issue in this case; the issue here is much narrower. The relevant question is whether or not the tribal government of the Creeks had been stripped of its power to deal with tribal affairs as such. While the tribe had clearly lost much of its authority in a territorial sense, or in the sense that a state has sovereignty, it is equally clear that the tribal government remained authoritative—in legal contemplation—as to matters of tribal organization and management, including control of tribal funds....

Conclusion

The plaintiffs' claim in this case has been that the federal defendants, through their policies and practices, have acted illegally in recognizing the Principal Chief as the sole embodiment of the government in the Creek Nation, and that according to existing federal and Creek law tribal funds may not be disbursed by the federal defendants for general tribal purposes without the approval of the Creek national legislature. The federal defendants' responsive argument has been that either the Creek national government has, by Congressional action, been rendered incompetent to handle the tribe's financial decision-making, or in the alternative that Congress in enacting a 1970 law stripping the Interior Department of any power to appoint the Principal Chief of the tribe somehow impliedly abolished the entire federal and tribal legal scheme theretofore defining the form and scope of the tribal government.

The defendants' first argument has withstood neither logical, historical, nor legal analysis. If the Creek government had been rendered incapable of allocating its own funds, then the Interior Department would have been unable to implement or justify the policy which has in fact most recently been in force, i.e. recognition of the Principal Chief as the embodiment of Creek government responsible for and capable of making those decisions. By its very policies the Department demonstrates that a functioning and competent Creek government in fact continues to exist; the historical record demonstrates moreover that a competent legislative-executive government has persisted throughout more than half a century of the most adverse conditions imaginable.

Indeed, plaintiffs do not challenge the Department's recognition that a functioning Creek government continues to exist, but rather contend that by law the Department may not confine its recognition of that government solely to one of its constituent institutions, the Principal Chief. Therefore the Department's argument that the Creek government has been rendered incompetent to handle Creek affairs is logically irreconcilable with its actual policies and practices, and must fall on that ground alone. However even had the defendants argued—as they have not in this Court, despite the use of such arguments by the Department over the course of the preceding seventy years—that Congress had somehow replaced the Creek constitutional form of government with an imposed government consisting of the Principal Chief, their position would have been legally and historically unsupportable. For such an argument to prevail, the Congress would have had to both terminate the authority of the Creek National Council to initially determine the tribal purposes for which Creek funds would be spent and also to invest the Principal Chief with that authority.

Congress undoubtedly has the power to do any of those things, or to terminate the existence of the tribe entirely. However, because such an abolition of the Creek constitutional government would have been tantamount to a total repudiation of the tribe's right, solemnly guaranteed to it by treaty after treaty, to determine its own form of organization and government—and indeed a final repudiation of tribal sovereignty itself—familiar principles of statutory construction in general and of interpretation of federal Indian law in particular mandate that such congressional action be clear and explicit; where the statutes and their legislative histories fail to clearly establish such an intent, the Court may not supply one by judicial interpretation. As the Supreme Court recently noted, courts "are not obligated in ambiguous circumstances to strain to implement [an assimilationist] policy Congress has now rejected, particularly where to do so will interfere with the present congressional approach to what is, after all, an ongoing relationship.... [T]he Court also goes on to indicate that present federal policy has returned to an intention to strengthen tribal self-government."

This is not, in any event, a case of statutory ambiguity. As this Court's examination of the relevant statutes and history makes clear, not only did Congress not terminate the sovereign status of the tribe, it expressly reaffirmed that status. Nothing in the Acts of 1898, 1901, and 1906 or any other legislation abolished the Creek National Council or stripped it of its power to determine the uses to which tribal funds are to be put, except with respect to certain mandatory expenditures and uses connected with the allotment and equalization program, and with the abolition of the tribe's territorial jurisdiction in the process of organizing the Indian Territory for statehood. These limitations have long since become irrelevant to tribal affairs, leaving the elected legislature created by the 1867 constitution (and effectively re-established at least twice thereafter) the authoritative body for initial allocation of tribal funds. While Congress has limited the overall duration of legislative sessions in any one year, and has explicitly specified the procedures through which such legislative actions become final, it has equally explicitly recognized and preserved the authority of the national legislature and the basic form of government established by the 1867 constitution.

A necessary corollary to that conclusion is that Congress has not replaced that form of government with a government consisting exclusively of the Principal Chief. This conclusion is not only a logical necessity, but is also the only conclusion possible after an examination of the relevant statutes and history. None of those statutes had either the intent or the effect of investing the Principal Chief with the authority to determine the purpose to which tribal funds should be put; that he has now come to perform that function results wholly from the Interior Department- Bureau of Indian Affairs' determined use of its raw power over the tribe to bring about that result. And finally, for the reasons stated in the Court's earlier discussion of the issue, the Act of 1970 carried with it no congressional intent to abolish the existing legal situation and to replace it with government by Principal Chief alone.

In conclusion, plaintiffs have asked the Court to vindicate certain legal rights guaranteed them by solemn promises of the United States, given over the course of a century and a half.

While the credibility of these promises has been gravely undermined by various federal actions, culminating in the abolition of the tribe's territorial sovereignty, the essence of those promises, that the tribe has the right to determine its own destiny, remains binding upon the United States, and federal policy in fact now recognizes self-determination as the guiding principle of Indian relations. Plaintiffs' claim is, at bottom, simply an assertion of their right to democratic self-government, a concept not wholly alien to American political thought. Plaintiffs have demonstrated a clear legal entitlement to have these rights vindicated, and the Court cannot honorably do otherwise....

Sources:

Debo, Angie. *The Road to Disappearance: A History of the Creek Indians.* Norman: University of Oklahoma Press, 1941; repr., 1989.

   Harjo v. *Kleppe*, 420 F. Supp. 1110 (1976).

---

46   Pacific Northwest Fishing Intergovernmental Memorandum of Understanding (1976)

This important memorandum was negotiated during a critical moment in Northwest history as all Native fishers inched closer to securing their full treaty right to fish "at all their usual and accustomed places" through the US judicial system. Although some important lower court rulings had affirmed these rights for some Nations, most notably the famous ruling *United States v. Washington* (1974)—also known as the "Boldt Decision," after its author, Judge George H. Boldt—not every Native nation was represented in that case.

What follows is the formula for cooperation between several Indigenous groups from Washington, Oregon, and Idaho, the governors of those states, and the Bonneville Power Administration (BPA). The BPA is the entity responsible for the system of massive dams on the Columbia River lethal to salmon populations. The alliance forged herein was based on the realization that the natural resources of the Pacific Northwest depended on cooperation of all parties if utter depletion and degradation were to be avoided. While it has since been superseded by a series of statutes, court cases, and other memoranda, this state-ment clearly reflects a more pragmatic, collegial relationship than is usually enjoyed between Native leaders and non-Native governments and institutions.

————

Preamble

One of the most priceless assets and precious natural resources of the Pacific Northwest is the anadromous fishery of the Columbia River and its tributaries. The gradual depletion of this great resource is of grave concern to a broad range of Northwest interests, be they social, cultural, economic, environmen-tal, recreational, or governmental. The preservation and restoration of the fish-ery has long been a common goal of dedicated, albeit fragmented, efforts on the part of numerous agencies, organizations, and individuals.

The parties to this Memorandum of Understanding are committed to the premise that decisive action is essential if further deterioration of the fishery is to be forestalled. They are equally committed to the concept of solving a regional problem on a coordinated regional basis.

The signatories to this Memorandum of Understanding represent the follow-ing parties: the Nez Perce Tribe of Idaho, the Confederated Tribes of the Umatilla Indian Reservation, the Confederated Tribes of the Warm Springs Reservation of Oregon, the Confederated Tribes and Bands of the Yakima Indian Nation (herein-after collectively referred to as "The Tribes"), the Bonneville Power Admin-istration (hereinafter referred to as "BPA"), and the Pacific Northwest Regional Commission, consisting of the Governors of the States of Idaho, Washington and Oregon and the Federal co-chairman (hereinafter referred to as "PNRC").

Community of Interest

The Parties hereto each have compelling reasons for jointly participating with each other and with other interests in a regional program to assure protection and enhancement of the fishery, and for entering into this Memorandum of Understanding.

The Tribes have a deep-rooted cultural and economic concern for the well-being of the resource. The BPA and the PNRC recognize that The Tribes have governmental powers which are reinforced by judicial decisions which recog-nize their salient interests with regard to the equitable sharing of the resource. It is further recognized that Federal court decisions have specifically estab-lished that The Tribes have treaty rights to an equitable share of the Columbia Basin fishery resource, and to restraints on fluctuations in river levels which would interfere with their harvest of the resource.

BPA recognizes that operation of the Federal Columbia River Power System (FCRPS) may be subject to restraints on peaking and rates of flow for the protection of the fishery resource, even though such restraints may reduce power generation. Any fishery improvement programs which would permit greater FCRPS power production would directly benefit users of BPA power.

As the marketing agent, BPA collects, and under Federal law may make authorized expenditures from, revenues from the power generated at the projects of the FCRPS. The investment to date in fishery mitigation programs and facilities authorized as part of these projects is approximately $300 million. Currently some $19.5 million annually is allocated for repayment from power revenues to cover operation and maintenance costs and interest and amortization on this investment.

As a bureau of the U.S. Department of the Interior, BPA recognizes the special trust and treaty responsibilities vested in the Secretary of the Interior with regard to Indian Tribes.

Additionally, BPA has indicated its responsiveness to a recent joint proposal by the Governors of Oregon, Washington, and Idaho that BPA expand its participation in a regional program of fishery mitigation through whatever entity (hereinafter called the designated entity) may be designated by the three Governors acting in their joint capacity as members of the PNRC, and concurred in by The Tribes and BPA.

PNRC is a joint State/Federal commission with responsibility for economic development and resource program coordination in the Pacific Northwest. PNRC or its designated entity shall consult and coordinate with the other parties hereto and other resources and user groups in identifying and implementing projects and in assessing their results.

Other parties share with The Tribes, BPA, and PNRC a common concern for and dedication to the restoration of the fishery. These include other Federal, State, and local government agencies, other Indian tribes, sports and wildlife associations, river and marine commercial fisheries, environmental, business and labor organizations, and many thousands of concerned individuals. These groups may recommend fish restoration activities for implementation hereunder.

Statement of Purpose

The purpose of this Memorandum of Understanding is to forge a partnership among The Tribes, BPA, and PNRC for undertaking coordinated programs aimed at helping to restore the Columbia River anadromous fishery, in coordination with all other fishery interests for the betterment of the region as a whole.

Objectives

The objectives of this joint program are:

   A. To assure that programs approved compliment and strengthen those
      carried out by other resource agencies;

B. To develop funding procedures that can support a flexible ongoing program;
C. To assure The Tribes and all concerned agencies, groups and individuals equitable participation in the preparation of regional fisheries restoration programs and policies;
D. To identify initially a specific pilot project or projects which promise measurable results in the near term (2–4 years) and which are compatible to a regional program;
E. To consult and coordinate with other resources and user entities in identifying and implementing projects, and in assessing their results;

Agreement

With the foregoing principles in mind, the parties hereto agree as follows:

1. BPA agrees, within the limits of its authority, to participate in funding a regional program of Columbia River Fisheries Restoration. In the event it is determined that BPA lacks the administrative authority to provide such funding, BPA will use its best efforts to obtain legislative funding authority.
2. BPA will exert its best efforts to improve the fishery without involving itself in the regulation or user apportionment of the resource.
3. The parties hereto will identify specific projects which promise measurable results and which are compatible to a regional program.
4. BPA will be responsible for the final approval of the expenditure of all BPA funds pursuant to this agreement.
5. All programs and projects developed under this agreement will be administered by and through the PNRC or its designated entity after consultation with the parties hereto and with the appropriate State resource management agencies.

The parties to this Memorandum of Understanding jointly commit their good faith and best efforts to seeking the restoration of the anadromous fishery of the Columbia River and its tributaries. We welcome the advice, assistance, and cooperation of all interested parties in pursuing this goal on a coordinated regional basis. Nothing in this agreement prevents the parties from seeking minimum stream flows consistent with maintaining the integrity of fish and wildlife habitat. This Memorandum replaces the original agreement signed by The Tribes and the BPA on October 13, 1976, and strengthens the concepts and goals stated in that agreement by the addition of the PNRC.

This Memorandum of Understanding is hereby executed in nine duplicate original copies on this 29th day of November, 1976.

Nez Perce Tribe of Idaho, Bonneville Power Administration, Pacific Northwest Regional Commission, Confederated Tribes of the Warm Springs Reservation of Oregon, Confederated Tribes of the Umatilla Indian Reservation, Confederated Tribes and Bands of the Yakima Indian Nation.

Source:

Nez Perce Tribe of Idaho, Bonneville Power Administration, Pacific Northwest Regional Commission, Confederated Tribes of the Warm Springs Reservation of Oregon, Confederated Tribes of the Umatilla Indian Reservation, and the Confederated Tribes and Bands of the Yakima Indian Nation, "Memorandum of Understanding," 1976.

47

Report on the Feasibility of Alternative Native Governing Arrangements (1976)

The American Indian Policy Review Commission was established for a period of two years by Congress in 1975 at the behest of Senator James Abourezk (D-SD). The commission, a bipartisan assemblage of eleven members, was dually tasked with investigating the rise of Indigenous activism and with proposing improvements to the federal/Indigenous relationship. To this end, the commission created eleven task forces, each focused on a distinct topic such as the trust relationship, Tribal government, administration, jurisdictional matters, and urban and rural/non-reservation Indians. Task Force Three examined the federal administration of Indian affairs, and in this report excerpt members identify and discuss the strengths and flaws of alternative governing arrangements on Native political and economic status.

———

Feasibility of Alternative Indian Elective Bodies Eligibility of Tribes and Indians for Federal Services

A. The Status of Indian Tribes and People

1. *Legal Status of Indian Tribes*

(A) INDIAN NATIONS AND TRIBES AS INDEPENDENT NATIONAL ENTITIES

Anthropologists and historians have estimated that over one million Indians, making up over 600 societies, lived in what is now the United States before the first landing of Europeans. A complex trade economy and highly structured governments were found wherever European explorers traveled. Indians exercised all the governmental powers necessary to maintain social, economic and political stability. There can be no doubt that the numerous distinct governments checker-boarding the continent were nations. These Indian Nations were dealt with by all of the early European countries who established colonies in the New World, and then by the United States. In all, there were over 800 formal and informal treaties with Indians through 1871. Such treaties covered the full range of relations between nations, including trade, social intercourse, land cessions and the ending of war. By definition and by example of international relations, Indian tribes fully met the qualifications of nationhood. The treaties concluded among themselves and with European nations and the United States carried the full weight of law. This point was explained by Justice Marshall when the Supreme Court held: "The words 'treaty' and 'nation' are words of our own language, selected in our diplomatic and legislative proceedings by ourselves, having each a definite and well-understood meaning. We have applied them to other nations of the earth. They are applied to all in the same sense."

That treaties were concluded between sovereign Indian nations and the United States is supported by the position taken by U.S. Attorney General William Wirt, who said, in 1828:

> "If it be meant to say that, although capable of treating, their treaties are not to be construed like the treaties of nations absolutely independent, no reason is discerned for this distinction in the circumstance that their independence is of limited character. If they are independent to the purpose of treating, they have all the independence that is necessary to the argument. The point, then, once conceded, that Indians are independent to the purpose of treating, their independence is, to that purpose, as absolute as that of any other nation."

Indian nations had the capacity to govern themselves, make war and peace, and form alliances with other nations. Having such capacities, and having those capacities recognized by other Indian nations and European nations, firmly establishes their sovereign nationhood. The independent national character of each Indian nation was secured among the family of nations.

Even as treaties placing certain Indian nations under the protection of various kings and potentates were concluded, the nature of Indian sovereignty remained unaltered. As Justice Marshall concluded in *Worcester v. Georgia* (1832): "... the settled doctrine of law of nations is that a weaker power does not surrender its independence—its right to self-government, by associating with a stronger, and taking its protection. A weak state, in order to provide for its safety, may place itself under the protection of one more powerful, without stripping itself of the right of government, and ceasing to be a state."

Though the United States dealt with Indian nations according to protocols similar to those of European nations, its motivations were decidedly different. The Continental Congress concluded its first treaty with the Delawares [1778] for the purposes of defining boundaries between the Colonies and Indian Territory and forming a military alliance. In this instance, no land cessions were made. However, after the war with Great Britain, the United States sought treaties with Indian nations for the main purpose of land cessions. A major provision typically contained in treaties spoke to a perpetual relationship arising out of compensation for land purchased by the United States. The basic motivation of the United States in its treaty-making emerged—the taking and securing of land. In spite of this, Indian nations retained their independence and their right to govern.

(B) INDIAN NATIONS AS "DOMESTIC DEPENDENT NATIONS"

The United States and its citizens moved rapidly into ceded Indian territories and purchased land. The forced removal of Indians to lands west of the Mississippi had opened large tracts of land previously occupied by Indian nations. Though the act of forced removal was in violation of treaties with Indian nations and therefore a violation of international law, the United States was not held back. Justice and fairness were not principles to guide the U.S. in its dealings with Indian nations. Destruction and expedience became the means to secure land, wealth and new opportunities for the United States. In its wake, the U.S. left death, destruction, and a disrupted economy among the Indian nations.

Whole Indian tribes and communities were forced out of their original territories or surrounded by white communities. It was the isolated Indian Territory that became the subject of a U.S. Supreme Court decision which rendered a whole new concept by which Indian nations and tribes could be described. The court held that Indian nations could be "denominated domestic dependent nations."

In a recent analysis of this decision, the Institute for the Development of Indian Law noted: "...it is important to know that the 'domestic dependent nations' doctrine was a compromise between the political realities of the time and views of several judges that Indian tribes were indeed independent nations....A strong decision supporting the complete independence of Indian nations would have been more in line with the facts. Chief Justice Marshall's decision had the effect of defining a U.S. responsibility to protect Indian nations and tribes against encroachments by states and recognized the weakened condition—brought on by the destructive militarism of the United States—of the Indian nations requiring U.S. protection. This decision did not in fact reduce the tribes' authority; but it did serve as the means by which the U.S. government justified extension of federal power over Indian governments."

It remains a settled legal doctrine to this day that Indian nations and tribes are "dependent nations" of people; dependent on the greater power of the United States for their protection and survival. This condition of dependence does not reduce the national powers of an Indian tribe or nation, though as a practical reality, tribes have reduced their own powers by entering into treaties and agreements with the United States. Tribal powers have further been reduced by unilateral usurpations without the consent of tribes, by the United States. Nevertheless, to have such reductions in national power does not diminish the national character of an Indian tribe.

The legal status of Indian tribes as "domestic dependent nations" was used to refer to "political dependency in the international sense," of a lesser power taking the protection of a greater power. U.S. federal authority to regulate Indian affairs ends at tribal borders. It can be said, therefore, that the United States has the authority to control the external affairs of Indian nations and tribes, but it does not have the authority to supervise, regulate, or control their internal affairs unless consent is given to do so.

2. *Political Status of Indian Nations and Tribes*

Indian tribes and nations do not have a role as political entities, either as members of the family of Indian nations, or as political units within the federal Union that makes up the United States. Their political status has been characterized as "unique" though no specific interpretation of uniqueness has been developed, except in terms of the relationship between Indians and the United States—likened to that of a ward/guardian relationship. But, nowhere else is there a comparable relationship except perhaps the relationship between the Micronesia Islands in the Pacific and the United States. This possible comparison is discussed in Section E.

(A) Indian Nations as States in the Union

Early in the history of the United States, attempts were made to include Indian nations as formal members of the federal Union. Such attempts are reflected in the first treaty concluded by the Continental Congress with the Delaware Nation. Contained in the treaty was a proposal for the creation of an Indian state "...where the Delaware Nation shall be the head, and have a representation in Congress." In the treaty of 1785 with the Cherokee Nation, it was provided that, "they shall have the right to send a deputy of their choice, whenever they think fit, to the Congress." Public sentiment in support of Indian nations becoming states within the Union continued for one hundred years, but no direct actions were taken to implement the treaty provisions just mentioned or actions to respond to public opinion.

The United States continued to deal with each Indian nation and tribe as separate political entities having no political affiliation with each other nor with the United States, except as expressly stated in treaties and agreements, until 1871, when Congress enacted the Appropriation Act of March 3, 1871 containing a rider for the termination of treaty-making with Indian tribes. The hearings regarding the "rider" reflect that the House of Representatives felt that the Senate, being the only house to confirm a treaty, was committing a funding requirement without any House participation. This rider was for procedural purposes rather than a direct intent to change the political status of Indian tribes. Though this Act did not prevent the process of treating with Indians by agreement, it has served to diminish the tribal national character which had been commonly recognized since the Europeans first placed settlements on the continent. The 1870's marked the first decade in the history of U.S./Indian relations in which the growth of federal Indian law was entirely a matter of legislation rather than a treaty.

(B) Indian Nations as Territories

Though no legislation was enacted, nor specific agreements made between Indian tribes and the United States to change the separate status of Indian nations and tribes, the nature of tribal political status took on the character of territories in the minds of legislators and administrators. In a case concerning the authority of an administrator appointed by a probate court of the Cherokee

Nation, the Supreme Court held: "...In some respects they bear the same relation to the federal government as a territory did in its second grade of government, under the ordinance of 1787. Such territory passed its own laws, subject to the approval of Congress, and its inhabitants were subject to the Constitution and Acts of Congress.... It is not foreign, but a domestic territory, —a territory which originated under our Constitution and laws. As separate political entities, dependent nations and then Indian territories, the Courts had held to the doctrine passed down by the Supreme Court in *Worcester v. Georgia*, that: "They and their country are considered by foreign nations, as well as by ourselves, as being so completely under the sovereignty and dominion of the United States that any attempt to acquire lands, or to form a political connection with them, would be considered by all as an invasion of our territory and an act of hostility." Such a status was clearly never contemplated by tribes as they entered into treaties with the United States.

(c) Indian Nations as Colonies

The present political status of Indian nations and tribes has been characterized as one of colonies under the denomination and rule of a "government department" of the United States. The "colonial status" of Indian nations began with the unilateral termination of treating with Indians and the assumption of agreements and legislation. The colonial character of Indian nations and tribes today stems from the United States imposing rules over all aspects of Indian life. From birth to death, the Indian individual and nation are subject to totalitarian authority of the United States. The United States imposes its form of education, which attempts to alienate the Indian child from his/her parents and culture.

The second International Indian Treaty Conference, Yankton Lakota Sioux Reservation, South Dakota, June 13–20, 1976 declared: "The United States has imposed a foreign form of government on the Indians and recognizes that government...not a traditional, legitimate government. The United States maintains that no Indian nation's law is effective without United States approval. It imposes its criminal law, foreign trade, currency, postal service, radio, television, and air transport regulations or reservations....An Indian nation is not even allowed to sign contracts or to hire a lawyer without the permission of the United States. Any self-government left to Indian nations by the United States is, it is made clear, left only by the grace of the United States Congress. The United States maintains it has a right to, at any time, pass a law and make it applicable to Indians on their reservations whether or not the laws conform to treaties with Indians, to international law, or to the United Nations Charter."

As two hundred years of Indian/U.S. relations have evolved, the question of Indian political status remains unresolved. Indians, as a people, do not fully exercise the right of self-government nor do they have the right to participate as Indian nations and tribes in the decisions which affect their lives and welfare. This state of affairs has given rise to frustration and violence in various parts of Indian Country. Indians have discussed among themselves and publicly stated alternative approaches to settling the question of Indian political status.

Some have urged that all of the Indian nations and tribes ought to be joined politically to form an Indian State, a fifty-first state of the Union. Others have urged the United States to recognize the sovereignty and independence of Indian nations and tribes. Such views reflect the wide diversity in the positions of tribal governments regarding Indian political status. It is clear, despite of this diversity that any determination of Indian political status must evolve from the Indian people and their respective governments and not as a result of U.S. unilateral action. The latter approach most surely will not settle the question of Indian political status because of the increasing disinclination of Indian nations and tribes to take direction from the United States and their greater inclination to define a status as a result of inter-tribal negotiations. An imposed political status rather than an agreed-upon status which is a product of bilateral negotiations can do nothing more than bind Indian nations and prevent self-governance and diminish the chances of an emergent self-sufficiency....

ALTERNATIVE INDIAN ELECTIVE STRUCTURES

The notion that there could or should be a national Indian elective body which represents the interests of Indian nations, tribes and their people in relations with the United States is not a new one. Thirty-two years ago in Denver, Colorado, representatives of 50 Indian nations met together for just that purpose. The result of those formative efforts was the creation of the National Congress of American Indians, which today includes a membership of over 100 Indian nations. Despite its substantial successes since 1944, the NCAI has never had as its membership all Indian nations and tribes, nor has it functioned with the direct participation of the majority of individual tribal members. Though the Indian Congress has a membership of perhaps 5,000 individual Indians in addition to tribal governments, it can hardly be said to represent each individual. It is, however, clearly the only successful national constituent Indian organization.

The National Congress of American Indians is by no means the only national Indian organization. Many others of a specialty or professional nature have either "spun off" of the Indian Congress or developed on their own in answer to a specialized need. Among these national organizations are the National Indian Youth Council, National Tribal Chairmen's Association, American Indian Movement, National Indian Education Association, National Indian Businessmen's Association, and many others....

In a workshop specifically arranged for the purpose of the Task Force on Federal Administration and Structure of Indian Affairs, eighteen Indian scholars and tribal leaders were asked to examine the question of tribal political status and national Indian elective bodies' alternatives. Their conclusions were as follows:

1. It is not politically feasible to create a national Indian elective body at the present; but it may be feasible in the future if the subject is thoroughly discussed throughout Indian Country and the United States provides economic assistance to tribes and nations to facilitate the process.

2. There are potentially several feasible alternatives for national Indian elective bodies which may be considered by Indian nations and tribes. Among these are:

Election of an Indian Congressional Delegation. This approach includes two senators and three or more representatives elected by Indians to represent Indians in the U.S. Congress. Direct election of an Indian Congressional delegation would require an amendment to the U.S. Constitution and a formal introduction of Indian Country into the Union as a state with a form of government not unlike that of the other states. The trust relationship would have to be substantially modified. This option has been considered in the past by the Delawares, Cherokee of Oklahoma and the Navajo—as single Indian tribes and not as multiple tribes.

Union of Indian Nations. This approach would establish an Indian legislative body with tribal delegations from each Indian nation or tribe elected by popular vote among the adult population. The elected delegates would be directly accountable to the Indian constituency. Each tribal government may reserve the right to ratify actions taken by its elected delegation or actions taken by the Union of Indian Nations. The Union of Indian Nations would serve as elected Indian voice which works directly with the Congress in the development of Indian policy. Individual tribes would naturally have unimpeded access to Congress. The Union of Indian Nations would require formal ratification by a majority of the tribes before it could be established. Financial support would be provided by the trustee, United States.

Indian Board of Representatives or Commissioners. Through direct election by the Indian population and appointment by the president the Indian Board would define U.S. policy toward Indian nations; and oversee and coordinate the program activities of federal agencies as they relate to Indian interests.

As a guide to the establishment of any Indian elective body, the following objectives were thought to be controlling:

1. *Provide real Indian input into the budgetary process taking place in both the legislative and executive branches of the U.S. government.* This would include program definition, line item control and development of rules and regulations for the administration....
2. *Provide a constant review of the activities of the executive and legislative branches.* The intent is to identify areas where the executive branch changes the intent of Congress, to make Congress aware of these inconsistencies and to take follow-up actions to correct them.
3. *Provide accountability of the United States to tribes and tribal representatives to their people.*
4. *Provide a method for enhancing tribal self-government and strengthening the trust responsibility of the United States government.*

The workshop on Indian Legislative Institutions concluded its review with the consensus being that such a review can only be considered an academic exercise since the feasibility of any concept of Indian elective bodies can only be determined by tribal governments and the Indian people as a whole. Any other conclusions, it was thought, would violate the rights of Indian people to determine their own form of government through a process that permits full and complete participation.…

Source:

US Congress. American Indian Policy Review Commission. "Report on Federal Administration and Structure of Indian Affairs. *Final Report to the American Indian Policy Review Commission.* Task Force Three. Washington, DC: Government Printing Office, 1976.

48   *Red Lake Band of Chippewa Indians v. Minnesota (1976)*

The Red Lake Band of Anishinaabe is the only federally recognized Native nation in Minnesota to have retained a significant portion of their original homelands—more than 500,000 acres. Incredibly, their lands were never subject to the individualization process mandated by the General Allotment Act of 1887, nor to the Nelson Act of 1899. Moreover, Red Lake was spared subjugation to the 1953 P. L. 280 measure that extended state jurisdiction over every other Indigenous nation located within Minnesota. Thus, given their relatively strong, independent position, Tribal leaders' enactment of their own motor vehicle registration and licensing ordinance should not have surprised state officials. This case affirmed the nation's right to adopt its own ordinance and required Minnesota to accept the decision.

———

In January, 1974, the Tribal Council of the Red Lake Band of Chippewa Indians enacted a motor vehicle registration and licensing ordinance. The Red Lake Band requested that the commissioner of public safety and the State of Minnesota recognize the validity of these registration and licensing procedures by extending reciprocity recognition to them and by granting exemptions from state motor vehicle registration and license plate fee requirements to Red Lake Band members who were registered under the Red Lake Band ordinance. The state refused and informed the band that members who drove on roads outside the Red Lake Indian Reservation in vehicles without Minnesota vehicle registrations and license plates would be subject to arrest. The Red Lake Band then sought judicial relief.... On November 20, 1974, the court issued the order for declaratory judgment and permanent injunction. We affirm the order and the judgment entered accordingly for these reasons....

The motor vehicle registration license ordinance adopted by the Red Lake Band on January 16, 1974, and approved by the Secretary of the Interior on March 5, 1974, imposes a substantial annual registration fee on all motor vehicles using the public streets or highways of the Red Lake reservation; provides for the issuance of certificates of title to the owners of registered vehicles; requires the maintenance of records of license applications and certificates of title, establishes procedures for the recording of transfers and proving of security interests; and prescribes the form of registration plates and the manner of their display. This ordinance approved by the Secretary of the Interior is an appropriate exercise of governmental authority vested in the Tribal Council of the Red Lake Band. The states does not contend otherwise....

Two principles of law to be derived from the decisions of the United States Supreme Court and the Supreme Court of the State of Minnesota are accepted by the parties: First, the State of Minnesota has no authority to govern the affairs of persons within the territorial boundaries of the Red Lake reservation except as specifically authorized to do so by Congress. No such authorization exists with respect to the licensing of motor vehicles within the reservation.

Second, the State of Minnesota does have authority to require that persons subject to the jurisdiction of the Red Lake Band submit to the governing authority of the State of Minnesota with respect to activities occurring within the territorial limits of Minnesota and without the territorial boundaries of the reservation.

To these accepted principles we believe that continued maintenance of good relations between the State of Minnesota and the Red Lake Band requires a recognition of a third principle not previously articulated in our decisions: Apart from the requirements of the Federal Constitution, the State of Minnesota, as a matter of state policy and with due regard for the unique status of the Red Lake Band of Chippewa Indians under the laws of the United States and of this state, should not, in the absence of some compelling state interest, impose burdens upon persons subject to the governing authority of the Red Lake Band when such burdens will undermine the effectiveness of the band's efforts to achieve effective self-government....

Minn. St. 168.181, subd. 1, provides: "Notwithstanding any provision of law to the contrary or inconsistent herewith the registrar of motor vehicle ... is hereby empowered to make agreements with the duly authorized representatives of the other states, District of Columbia, territories and possessions of the United States or arrangements with foreign countries or provinces exempting the residents of such other states, districts, territories and possessions ... using the public streets and highways of the state from the payment of any or all motor vehicle taxes or fees imposed by Minnesota Statutes...."

Minn. St. 168.187, subd. 1, provides: "It is the policy of this state to promote and encourage the fullest possible use of its highway system by authorizing the making of agreements, arrangements, and declarations with other jurisdictions, for reciprocal recognition of vehicle registrations...."

We assume that the legislature did not intend when it adopted Minn. St. 168.181, subd. 1, to include the Red Lake Indian Reservation within the scope of its language, although argument to the contrary has been made. We make this assumption because of the unlikelihood that the problem with which we are now confronted was ever considered one way or the other by the legislature when the statute was enacted. Had the problem been considered, more precise language would have been used.

The motor vehicle registration ordinance adopted by the Red Lake Band will be rendered ineffective if owners of vehicles subject to its terms are required to have an additional license from the State of Minnesota as a condition for use of Minnesota's highways. Except for the symbolism involved, the motor vehicle licenses issued to the Red Lake reservation would be of little value to the registrants if the State of Minnesota were to refuse to recognize their validity beyond the territorial limitations of the reservation....

The Red Lake Band ordinance provides: [for exemption from tribal registration of persons from reciprocal jurisdictions.]....

In addition, the admitted facts suggest that a grant of reciprocity to the Red Lake Band is consistent with Minnesota's governmental interest: The State of Minnesota law enforcement personnel do not patrol the lands encompassing the Red Lake Indian Reservation. The Red Lake Band has its own law enforcement personnel and justice system to enforce its civil and criminal code. The 275 miles of roads on the Red Lake reservation were constructed and are maintained by the Red Lake Band with the assistance of the United States Department of the Interior, Bureau of Indian Affairs, although 65 miles of state trunk highways running through the reservation are maintained by the state. The Red Lake Band receives no payments from the State of Minnesota for maintenance and construction of roads on the reservation, nor does it share in the Minnesota motor vehicle license fees or gasoline taxes. Owners of motor vehicles registered in the State of Minnesota and elsewhere are free to use these roads maintained and constructed by the Red Lake Band, without duplicate license.

The burden on Minnesota's highways resulting from the use of motor vehicles owned by residents of the Red Lake reservation is no greater than that resulting from like use of automobiles by residents of neighboring states or residents of the Canadian provinces. The advantages of reciprocal recognition of vehicle registration by the state of Minnesota and the Red Lake band are at least as great as the advantage of such reciprocal recognition by this state and other states, territories, possessions, and foreign countries.

Minnesota, by the adoption of Minn. Stat. 168.181 and 168.187, subd. 1, has declared that our state interests are best served by the recognition of the validity of automobile registration license issued by other "jurisdictions." Had this policy not been established and carried into effect, Minnesota would not be obligated to recognize the validity of the Red Lake Indian Reservation licenses on vehicles being driven on our public thoroughfares. But, having granted the privileges contemplated by §168.181 and 168.187 to other comparable governmental entities, the denial of those privileges to the residents of the Red Lake reservation is unacceptable.

Under these circumstances, we hold that to deny to the Red Lake Band reciprocity accorded to other jurisdictions is an indirect interference with the internal government of the Red Lake Band not justified on the facts disclosed by the record before us.

Affirmed.

Sources:

Lawrence, William J. "Tribal Injustice: The Red Lake Court of Indian Offenses." *North Dakota Law Review* (Summer 1974): 48:639–659.

Red Lake Band of Chippewa v. State and Another, 311 Minn. 241 (December 10, 1976).

49   *Plan for the Bureau of Indian Affairs Presented by Mel Tonasket, President, National Congress of American Indians (1977)*

Tonasket, a respected Colville leader, provided testimony at this Senate oversight hearing before the Select Committee on Indian Affairs as Congress sought advice on how to improve the Carter Administration's effectiveness in administering and managing the federal government's handling of Indian affairs. Part of his statement included an NCAI resolution of recommended reforms for the BIA that had been approved by the NCAI Executive Council. A plan titled, "Transition Proposal for the Administration: A Management Model for Indian Affairs," had been presented to the Executive Council, and this accompanying resolution was adopted.

————

Whereas, there have been 76 management studies of the Bureau of Indian Affairs in the past 25 years; and

Whereas, continued studies is a substitute for immediate action; and

Whereas, a transition proposal for a management model for Indian affairs has been presented to the new Administration (Indian self-government "An Alternate to Rule by a Federal Department"); and

Whereas, the principles in that proposal have been continuously supported by the Indian tribes; and now therefore, be it

Resolved, That the National Congress of American Indians in Executive Council Assembled in Washington, D.C., adopts and supports the following general principles in a new Bureau of Indian Affairs Administration:

1. That an Indian Management team be selected which is prepared to implement an action plan.
2. That the BIA budget process become a tribal budget process with the BIA participation emphasizing Indian needs.
3. That the BIA Management information and automatic data processing system be overhauled to provide for tribal use and terminals with full access to the BIA/Tribal budget information.
4. That a new organizational structure be proposed to transfer authority to the tribal level.
5. That the twelve Area Offices of the BIA be immediately divested of their line authority and those authorities be delegated to the agency and tribe.
6. That a General Counsel be immediately created by the Secretary of the Interior to relieve serious conflicts of interest.
7. That the Secretary of the Interior administratively create an Assistant Secretary for Indian Affairs immediately.

And be it further resolved, that continued necessary studies be conducted in an action context with the philosophy of implementation....

Source:

US Senate. Hearing Before the Senate Select Committee on Indian Affairs. Oversight on the Organization of the BIA. 95th Cong., 1st Sess. Washington, DC: Government Printing Office, 1978.

50

The Tribal-State Compact Act with Statement by Delfin J. Lovato, Chairman, All Indian Pueblo Council (1978)

Beginning in the late 1960s and continuing into the 1970s, congressional policies generally favored Native governmental and economic development by promoting a measure of Tribal sovereignty. This encouragement fortified Indigenous initiative to attain political and legal confirmation of their rights to property and resources.

Even with federal governmental backing, Native nations often ran headlong into confrontations with state and local governments and experienced major judicial losses particularly when challenging state authority. States also found themselves in a serious dilemma. While under political pressure to resist Indian claims, they, too, had often fared poorly in federal court battles with Tribal nations. Thus, by the late 1970s, it was apparent to all that a formal, alternative, and non-adversarial dispute resolution mechanism might afford both parties a more amicable, cost-effective means by which to address their conflicts.

The idea for a formal negotiation mechanism of tribal-state compacts reached Congress's agenda in the late 1970s with the introduction of Sen. James Abourezk's (D-SD) Tribal-State Compact bill. The measure was not written to alter the basic framework within which the Tribes, states, and the United States exercised authority, nor did it purport to authorize a state or Native Nation to enter agreements at odds with their constitutions and laws. It would have neither enlarged nor diminished the governmental powers of states or Tribal nations, but simply would have allowed those entities to allocate between themselves certain governmental responsibilities.

Despite its apparent worth, the window of opportunity that made debate of the measure and succeeding versions possible closed in 1982. In part, because of growing Native concerns that under such an act the long-standing principle of federal oversight of Indian affairs would be seriously eroded. From the states' perspective, the compacting process may have been allowed to lapse because, with the advent of the Reagan years and the ideological rightward shift of the Supreme Court, the states sensed that their power position vis-à-vis Tribes would be enhanced. This view was subsequently borne out in a number of Supreme Court decisions rendered in favor of states over Native nations and individual Indians in the areas of water rights, natural resource issues, taxation, and religious freedom cases.

Included here is a statement by Delfin J. Lovato, chairman of the All Indian Pueblo Council, that, while supportive of the overall idea of a more constructive Native/state relationship, withheld support for the bill out of a deep concern about states' commitments to recognizing the inherent sovereignty of Native nations.

A Bill to Authorize the States and the Indian Tribes to Enter into Mutual Agreements and Compacts Respecting Jurisdiction and Governmental Operations in Indian Country

Be it enacted by the Senate and House of Representatives of the United States of America in Congress assembled, that this Act may be cited as the "Tribal-State Compact Act of 1978."

Findings

Sec. 2. (a) The policy of Congress toward the Indian tribes throughout the history of this Nation is marked by great inconsistency and vacillation. The jurisdictional controversies which surround the relationships between Indian tribes and the States today are the logical consequence of this historical vacillation and inconsistency.

(b) The absence of a flexible mechanism providing for mutually accepta- ble divisions of authority and governmental responsibility between the States and the Indian tribes has led to continuing conflict between the Indian tribes and the States characterized by increasing litigation in Federal and State courts. Such court decisions have reaffirmed the legal relationship which exists be- tween the United States and the Indian tribes, and have affirmed the right of self- government of the Indian tribes. They have also, through the judicial con- struction of Public Law 83–280, raised questions as to the capacity of tribal and State governments to voluntarily enter into intergovernmental arrange- ments based on the consent of both parties which could potentially resolve existing jurisdictional disputes to the benefit of both of the parties.

(c) It is evident that the judicial process itself does not provide the flexibil- ity necessary to address the issues presented by the varying capacities, needs or desires of the various tribal and State and local governments. The jurisdictional issues between the tribes and the State and local governments and the solution which the parties would desire vary significantly. This variance in local cir- cumstances also precludes resolution of jurisdictional issues between the States and the tribes on any one statutory formula. The issues are local in nature and should, wherever possible, be resolved at the local level on the basis of mutual consent and agreement of the governments involved.

(d) In recent years, there have been cooperative agreements between States and tribes regarding the operations of their governments, and there are increas- ing expressions of interest from State and tribal authorities to enter into com- pacts and agreements respecting their mutual authorities and responsibilities. It is the responsibility of the Congress to facilitate this process.

Declaration of Policy

Sec. 3. The Congress hereby declares that it is the policy of this Nation to con- tinue to preserve and protect the tribes of the American Indian people. The policy of this Nation is premised on the status of tribal governments as a con- tinuing part of the American political fabric. Accordingly, the United States has a responsibility to establish a legal framework which will enable the tribes and the States to achieve maximum harmony and facilitate their cooperative efforts in the orderly administration of their governments. Federal enabling authority for the establishment of viable intergovernmental agreements between the tribes and the States based on mutual consent must be established....

Title I—Authorization of Compacts and Agreements

Sec. 101. (a) Notwithstanding the Act of August 15, 1953 (67 Stat. 588), as amended, or any other Act transferring civil or criminal jurisdiction over

Indians within Indian country from the United States to the various States, or establishing a procedure for such transfers, and notwithstanding the provisions of any enabling Act for the admission of a State into the Union, the consent of the United States is hereby given the States and the Indian tribes and the same are hereby authorized to enter into compacts and agreements between and among themselves on matters relating to (1) the enforcement or application of civil, criminal, and regulatory laws of each within their respective jurisdictions, and (a) allocation or determination of governmental responsibility over specified subject matters or specified geographical areas, or both, including agreements or compacts which provide for the allocation or determination of jurisdiction on a case-by-case basis, and agreements which provide for concurrent jurisdiction between the States and the tribes.

(b) Such agreements and compacts shall be subject to the prior approval of the Secretary of the Department of the Interior, and shall be subject to revocation by either party upon six months written notice to the other unless a greater period of time is agreed upon in the agreement or compact. The Secretary shall have sixty days after notification to review any such agreements or compact or any revocation thereof and unless the Secretary disapproves the same, such agreement, compact, or revocation thereof shall become effective. The Secretary shall not approve any such agreements or compacts which authorize or provide for the alienation, financial encumbrance, or taxation of any real or personal property, including water rights, belonging to any Indian or any Indian tribe, band, or community that is held in trust by the United States or is subject to a restriction against alienation imposed by the United States.

(c) Upon approval of such agreement, compact, or revocation thereof, or upon such agreement, compact, or revocation becoming otherwise effective, the Secretary shall cause such agreement, compact, or revocation to be published in the Federal Register.

(d) Such agreements, compacts, or revocation thereof shall not affect any action or proceeding over which a court has already assumed jurisdiction and no such action or proceeding shall abate by reason of such agreement, compact, or revocation unless specifically agreed upon by all parties to the agreement or compact.

(e) Nothing in this Act shall be construed to either enlarge or diminish the jurisdiction over civil or criminal matters which may be exercised by either State or tribal governments except as expressly provided in this Act.

Funding and Implementation—Federal Assistance

Sec. 102. (a) In any agreement or compact between an Indian tribe and a State authorized under this Act in which one of the parties assumes an obligation which it would not otherwise be legally obligated or entitled to perform, or would not be obligated to perform at the standard established in the agreement or compact, the United States, upon agreement of the parties and the Secretary, shall provide financial assistance to such party for costs of personnel or administrative expenses in an amount up to 100 per centum of costs actually incurred as a consequence or such agreement or compact, including indirect costs of administration which are clearly attributable to the services performed under the agreement or compact.

(b) Whenever a party to such agreement or compact seeks financial assistance from the United States to offset their costs, such party shall prepare a detailed statement of the projected costs; a copy of such statement shall be supplied to the Secretary at the time said agreement or compact is tendered to him for his approval.

(c) In any agreement or compact in which one of the parties qualifies for Federal assistance, the other party shall be supplied with copies of all vouchers for payment at the time they are submitted and shall be fully informed of all payments made by the United States to the recipient party. The books and records of the party receiving Federal assistance which are relevant to the agreement or compact shall be open to inspection and copying by authorized representatives of the other party and by the United States.

(d) In the funding of governmental operations authorized under this Act, the Secretary may enter into agreements or other cooperative arrangements with any and all other Federal departments, agencies, bureaus, or other executive branches for transfers of funds or contributions of funds appropriated for programs within the category of the functions to be performed by the parties under such agreements or compacts, and such departments, agencies, bureaus are hereby authorized to use such funds in the implementation of this Act.

(e) All Federal departments, agencies, and other executive branches are authorized to provide technical assistance and material support and assign personnel to aid tribal and State authorities in the implementation of the agreements or compacts they may enter into under the terms of this Act.

(f) The Secretary is hereby authorized to promulgate such rules and regulations as may be necessary to carry out the purposes of this Act.

(g) There are authorized to be appropriated $20,000,000 during fiscal year 1980; and such sums thereafter as may be necessary during each subsequent fiscal year in order to carry out the purposes of this title. Such funds shall be expended by the Secretary only after determination that there are no funds available from alternative sources as provided in subsection (d) of this section.

Title II—Planning and Monitoring Boards

Sec. 201. (a) The Secretary is hereby authorized and directed to encourage the tribes and the States to establish councils, committees, boards, or task forces between the States and individual tribes, or on a statewide or regional basis, to discuss and confer upon jurisdictional questions which exist between the parties, and to provide Federal representatives from his Department as may be useful at such conferences.

(b) In furtherance of this objective, the Secretary is authorized and directed to provide adequate representation of tribal members at such conferences, and such further conferences among the tribe as may be necessary for their separate deliberations, and to participate in the payments of expenses in employment or

reporters, transcription of statements, and preparation of report as in his judgment may be appropriate.

(c) There are authorized to be appropriated $1,000,000 during fiscal year
1980; and such sums thereafter as may be necessary during each subsequent
fiscal year in order to carry out the purposes of this title.

Statement of Delfin J. Lovato, Chairman, All Indian Pueblo Council, Before the Temporary Select Committee on Indian Affairs on S. 2502

Thank you, Mr. Chairman and members of the Committee, for giving us
this opportunity to present testimony on S. 2502, the "Tribal-State Compact
Act of 1978."

My name is Delfin Lovato, I am Chairman of the All Indian Pueblo Council,
representing the nineteen (19) New Mexico Pueblos. I am accompanied today
by Governor Joe A. Quintana of Cochiti Pueblo; Governor Gilbert Pena of
Nambe Pueblo; Governor Valentino Garcia of Santo Domingo; and, Councilman
Harold Sando representing Jemez Pueblo.

Mr. Chairman, the nineteen (19) Pueblos of New Mexico have, on numerous
occasions, advocated the concept of cooperative dialogue and agreements on
problems of mutual concern between state and tribal governments. We do so in
the firm belief that the problems facing state and tribal governments are rooted in
the political, social, and economic structure of our local communities and state.
As such, the solutions to these problems must be resolved at the local level and
cannot be legislated by Congress, or for that matter, the state legislature. Our
support is conditioned on the proposition that cooperative agreements will work
only if both parties recognize and respect the other's legal existence, powers and
authority. This has not always been possible to obtain from state governments.
We have made it known in our state that while we support the concept, we will
not negotiate such agreements at gun point or under threat of adverse legislation.

While we wholeheartedly support the Declaration of Policy contained in
S.2502, it is our firm belief that there is sufficient flexibility and authority
under existing federal laws which allow for cooperative agreements between
state governments and Indian tribes. For this and other reasons which are presented herein, we seriously question the need for this legislation. Though well
intended, we questions its usefulness in bringing about a working relationship
between state governments and Indian tribes.

In addition, S.2502 provides for publication in the Federal Register and
requires that the Secretary of the Interior approve all compacts and agreements
which may be negotiated between tribal governments and states, counties, or
municipal governments. This legislation would in effect make such agreements
a matter of federal law. Any agreements under this Act allowing for state jurisdiction within tribal lands could result in the same thing as an implementation
of P.L.280, the only difference being that such relinquishing of jurisdiction
would be subject to revocation by either party provided six months' notice is
given. However, even a revocation is subject to secretarial approval, and,

therefore, revocation by a tribe of state jurisdiction under a previous compact could theoretically be refused, leaving the tribe under state jurisdiction. Besides, six months seems like a long period of time for simply adequate notice.

Secondly, Section 102(a) allows for either state or tribal governments to receive federal monies to cover the cost of administrative expenses implementing such compacts. If this is to be done, it would be easier for tribes to simply contract directly with the federal government to administer their own needs, thus, limiting the need for any such compacts. If no state monies are involved, there seems to be little need for state involvement.

Also, we strongly feel that the success or failure of any compacts between tribal and state governments will depend upon the extent of responsibility and resources each is willing to provide to such an effort. Total federal subsidation of such efforts may not be the answer in view of our position that state and local governments have a responsibility to provide essential services to the Indian community as substantial tax paying citizens. We strongly feel that while state governments are seeking more jurisdiction over Indian people and their resources, they do not have the capability or the desire to use existing state resources to accomplish this objective.

The Pueblo tribes have dealt with the question of joint powers agreements and/or compacts for the past three years. We have had open discussions and have had bills introduced in the New Mexico Legislature, only to find that opponents of Indian sovereignty are unwilling to accommodate cooperative efforts. Attached is a copy of H.B. 312 introduced in this year's legislature which was killed by the New Mexico State Senate. Therefore, we strongly feel that we need some positive assurances that the state governments are not only interested in supporting the concept enunciated in S.2502, but that such a concept will develop into true joint powers agreements, rather than slow, relinquishment of tribal jurisdictional powers. At present, we strongly feel that states and tribal governments have sufficient flexibility to initiate joint agreements outside of binding federal laws, and, we view S.2502 as not warranted at this time. A less binding and legally final federal framework might be more appropriate and less potentially dangerous to the self-governing rights of the Indian communities. Perhaps, a joint resolution of the United States Congress expressing its intent and recommendations for joint cooperative efforts between state, local governments, and Indian tribes would be more appropriate.

Aside from the tribal concerns there may be some practical legal problems that might need further clarification. The State of New Mexico has a disclaimer clause in its Enabling Act over jurisdiction of Indian lands. Though the state has contended that this goes only to the land itself and not activities of non-Indians on those lands, a disclaimer is still a part of their state constitution. The question is, would a federally legislated "Tribal-State Compact Act" supersede the state disclaimer, or would state action be necessary to amend their constitution to accommodate the compacts?

The second question is, are these agreements to be viewed as joint powers agreements or simply contracts subject to approval of the trustee of Indian governments? And if they are viewed as contracts, will they be subject to cancellation by the Secretary of the Interior, in light of the United States Constitutional Prohibition of Interference with contracts? And, finally, would any compact cession of jurisdiction to a state, even though temporary on its face, supersede P.L.280, or would the safeguard provisions of P.L.280 as found in the Amendment of 1968 supersede any compact provisions?

If these questions cannot be adequately answered at this point, we would suggest that more research may be necessary, before we are convinced that all our governmental rights are properly, and strongly safeguarded. . . .

Sources:

Wilkins, David E. "Reconsidering the Tribal-State Compact Process." *Policy Studies Journal* 22, no. 3 (Autumn 1994): 474–488.

US Senate. Hearings Before the Senate Select Committee on Indian Affairs. "Tribal-State Compact Act of 1978." 95th Cong., 2nd Sess. on S. 2502. Washington, DC: Government Printing Office, 1978.

51

Affirmation of Sovereignty of the Indigenous Peoples of the Western Hemisphere (1978)

The period from 1969–1978 produced a series of congressional laws, judicial opinions, and presidential directives that comported with the Red Power movement's push for greater support of Native sovereignty, treaty rights, and Indigenous cultural revitalization. However, these developments provoked a caustic, anti-Indian backlash, and several congressional bills were introduced that threatened those tenuous new political and legal gains—including treaty enforcement. These malicious measures inspired a cross-country march and gathering of thousands of Native activists and their supporters—the February–July 1978 trek from San Francisco to Washington, DC, that came to be known as The Longest Walk.

The walk culminated with a major rally held on July 25 at the Washington Monument and the issuance of a manifesto challenging assaults on Native treaty rights and sovereignty. Ultimately, none of the eleven pending anti-Native bills were adopted into law. The Longest Walk was the last major Native demonstration of this halcyon period. This affirmation of sovereignty was read and submitted by Native youth for this event.

We are the sovereign and free children of Mother Earth. Since before human memory, our people have lived on this land. For countless generations, we have lived in harmony with our relatives, the four-leggeds, the winged beings, the beings that swim, and the beings that crawl.

For all time our home is from coast to coast; from pole to pole. We are the original people of this hemisphere. The remains of our ancestors and of our many relatives are a greater part of this land than any other's remains. The mountains and the trees are a part of us—we are the flesh of their flesh. We are the Human Beings of many nations, and we still speak many tongues. We have come from the four directions of this Turtle Island. Our feet have traveled our Mother Earth over many thousands of miles. We are the evidence of the Western Hemisphere, the carriers of the original ways of this area of the world, and the protectors of all life on this Turtle Island.

Today we address you in the language of the oppressor, but the concepts predate the coming of the invaders. The injustice we speak of is centuries old, and has been spoken against in many tongues. We are still the original people of this land. We are the people of The Longest Walk.

For many generations we have been seeking justice and peace from the European refugees, and their descendants who have settled on our sacred Turtle Island. It has been an incredibly long struggle. We have entered into many agreements for peace and friendship with the governments of these people, and yet we have received neither peace nor friendship. Most of our original home-lands have been illegally taken from us. Our people have been, and continue to be, mercilessly hunted and slaughtered to serve the needs of corporations, governments, and their agents.

Today, the conditions in Central and South America are identical to the condi-tions in this country during the 19th Century. The process of annihilation and destruction are carried on with money, sophisticated weapons, missionaries, wide-spread sterilization, so-called developmental programs, CIA and FBI organized training of terrorists and provocateurs that are sponsored and provided by the United States. We can find no other words for the description of these acts other than murder and terrorism. This process is hidden from the peoples of the world by a conscious suppression of information coming from the offending countries.

Our people are often forced to leave their beloved homelands and are sent to lands where they greatly suffer. Our grandfathers and grandmothers were forced to walk many times in front of the guns of the invaders. Today we have been forced to walk, again in front of guns and the threat of destruction that comes from words in legislation.

The guns of today are not held by the Seventh Cavalry but are in the hands of the FBI, the Federal Marshals, and other persons who are supposedly up-holding the laws of the United States. These guns and many other sophisticated weapons have been used to continue a campaign of legalized murder, terror-ism, torture, mutilation, and oppression of our people. All of these weapons have been used in direct violation of international laws concerning the use of weapons against civilian populations.

Our Mother Earth feeds, clothes, and shelters us, as she does all life, but those who have embraced Western values do not realize the value of the Creation. They are exploiting our Mother Earth and all our relatives who walk and grow with us. This is not right.

For countless generations the cycles of life have been guarded and respected by our people. In the short span of five centuries, the people who invaded these lands have caused an unbelievably massive annihilation of all life forms of the Western Hemisphere. We indigenous people recognize and understand the Natural Balance of these life cycles and assert the right to live within this natural order.

Most of our original homelands have been taken from us. We have been allowed access to only a tiny fraction of the land which remains and it, too, is being destroyed against our will. Our lands hold natural resources that are coveted by huge transnational corporations. These organizations are very powerful. In many ways, the United States government has acted as a direct agent of these organizations.

We know that the present attacks on our lands and sovereignty will, unless halted, ultimately benefit the interest of corporations which seek coal, uranium, water and other parts of our Mother Earth. We understand that the attack on our existence originates with these interests. The land speculators of the last century have been replaced by the oil refineries and the ore processors of this century. The United States government failed to protect our interest against land speculators, who were far less powerful than the transnational corporations we face today. The present day racism against our people is fueled by the organizations, and the denial of our rights will open up our air, water and lands to a ruthless exploitation unparalleled in history. Uncontrolled Western development will destroy our ways of life, and will threaten all life on this Turtle Island.

The Creator gave to us our original instructions telling us how to walk about on this Earth as protectors and relatives to all life. As long as the sun rises, the grasses grow, and the cycles continue, we are to carry on this duty. Around us a people who act in a way that will bring about the total destruction. The transnational corporations destroy life in the waters, air, and land. Huge trawlers attack our relatives in the sea, giant machineries strip our Mother Earth's skin bare, factories and vehicles fill the sky with tons of poison. The recent rush to use nuclear power poses the most potent threat to ending all life in one generation.

In order to further satisfy the greed of these corporations, members of our communities have been seduced to aid their processes. Our resistance to these processes is strongly oppressed by the United States government, agencies and corporations. Much to our dismay, we find this process being promoted and used against us by the corporations of newly liberated areas. We call for a stop to these practices, and we seek real assistance from liberated people.

Our people gathered together on the western coast of this Turtle Island and discussed actions that could be taken to stop these many threats to the dignity and permanence of Life. It was decided that we should join together and begin this walk across our beloved land, starting at Alcatraz, our symbol of our continuing resistance. It also serves as the symbol of our unity as the original people of this land, and starting from this symbol we decided to bring to the American people, and the people of the world, the message that we are still a People. We carried with us our babies on cradle boards, and the little ones who run about on the Earth. We came with our young men and women, and we came with our elders and wise people. We are carrying with us our spiritual ways, and we have planted our prayers and sacred things all along our journey.

We have come to seek justice and to deliver a message to the leaders and the people of the United States and the world. Our journey has indeed been The Longest Walk.

Why are we the only people of this hemisphere whose land and resources can be stripped from us by governmental decree? Formal agreements between our sovereign and separate nations and the occupying governments always become nullified, abrogated or violated and we have no legal recourse or protection from these illegal actions. Only to the indigenous people of this hemisphere does this happen. The oppression of indigenous populations is an automatic characteristic of Western Civilization. The United States' Bureau of Indian Affairs is one prime example of how that oppression becomes an institution of these people.

How do we explain to the American people that we love our Mother Earth and ways of life? How can we state we do not need the United States government to tell us how to be indigenous people? What will it take to convince the U.S. government to allow us to live in peace? How do we convince the U.S. government to simply leave us alone to live according to our ways of life?

The federal system has tried many programs for the so-called improvement of our lives.

There have been an endless procession of such programs: the BIA, the Dawes Act, the 1924 Citizenship Act, the 1934 Indian Reorganization Act, the Indian Claims Commission, Termination, Relocation, Self-determination, Housing, and on and on. Our conditions have not improved.

There are those of our people who have been destroyed by words and promises of a better way of life through the American system. The American government chooses to see them as leaders of indigenous people. They form corporations and committees. But a corporation is not a nation!

On many of our territories, we are subjected to governments created under the Indian Reorganization Act of 1934, or the fostering of dissidents who are willing to sell out for an American sanctioned position. The Indian Reorganization Acts was created as a part of a long range plan to terminate indigenous nations. The Indian Reorganization Act and other United States policies created governments which supposedly have the power to sell or lease away indigenous lands and resources, but the power is not recognized as a legitimate power by the majority of indigenous people. Those governments were created largely to implement United States policies that are contrary to the beliefs and laws of our people. They were given recognition by the United States government as having power to negotiate away our inherent rights. They were intended to give the appearance that those negotiations possess some legitimacy from the indigenous people. From the beginning these puppet governments have brought the wishes of the federal government to the indigenous people. They have never been able to effectively bring the wishes of the indigenous people to Washington. These governments are the clearest manifestation of federal policy in the indigenous communities. They do not, and cannot, effectively represent the people. They represent a policy which, when advocated by indigenous individuals, presents what can best be described as a kind of self-destruction. The United States government has divided, subdivided

214 DOCUMENTS OF NATIVE AMERICAN POLITICAL DEVELOPMENT

and allotted our land, and then directed the most desired parcels to those among us who shift alliances from traditional leaders to government agents. It has then termed much of the remainder of our sacred Mother Earth as excess to give it away to non-Indians.

In order for our people to be happy, healthy, and productive, we must have access to all of our relatives and the self-esteem, respect, affection, and a sense of belonging we receive from them. There are many policies and regulations that remove our many relatives from us. Our relatives in the waters are being removed by millions of sports fishermen and commercial fishing fleets. Our relatives, the four-legged creatures, are being hunted, trapped, slaughtered, driven away, and forced into extinction. Our relatives in the sky are faced with the same problems and have the same threats upon them. This indiscriminate barbarism is beyond the reason of our people. Our people only took the lives of those other beings when it was necessary for our survival and not the mere "sport" of it. Our Grandmother, the Moon, has been molested and a part of her being has been removed.

As we look about us we find it hard to believe that other two-leggeds can act in such a way. Zoos act as reservations for the other members of the natural World. In every way the process of Western civilization commits a genocide toward all living things. This disruption of the natural cycles cannot continue without serious consequences, as we seek to protect and continue the original instructions of our people, we must now take actions to protect and preserve all those that help to form all the cycles of the Natural World.

Among us we find many people, agencies, and institutions actively removing the young people who run about the Earth. Daily, hundreds of those who are our closest relatives are torn from their communities. The transfer of the children from one group to another is recognized, by international law, as an act of genocide. This mass removal is rationalized in the laws and values of Western civilization, and by not recognizing our traditional institutions and systems. Western civilization can practice assimilation processes that have as their goals the disappearance of our people as a unique way of life. We are here to say that these practices are going to stop.

Our cultures are structured for Human Beings. They are based on principles of respect and responsibility for everyone and everything. The manner in which the people are to live is described to the people through our religious teachings. These religious teachings were given to the Creation by the Creator in order to insure our existence in this world. To remove our children from our communities, and to deny them access to these original instructions leads to the collapse of our families, societies, and nations. It is our commitment to reverse this process and rebuild our country.

We understand that self-esteem derives from the things that people do every day. Our elder people teach a respect for one another and the respect for all the things of this place, including Mother Earth, the Grasses, the Waters, and the many things which support our lives.

We have a high regard for the affection of our people. In our ways, we are taught our relationship to the generations yet unborn, to those who have gone before us, and to our nations of people.

We are deeply rooted in the land and our people's roots draw sustenance from our Mother Earth. We, the traditional people, are instructed in the old ways and every day we still live these instructions.

Every day we must struggle to protect our right to carry on our way of life. In every way we are met with an interference. Our healing cultures are ridiculed, and laws are passed to keep us in the American healing systems. Laws exist which forbid the practice of our healing cultures.

The occupiers' border defining the settler regimes of Mexico, the United States and Canada divide our territories and peoples. Each of these regions seeks to impose fake identities of being Mexican, American or Canadian. Border policies inhibit the free flow of the members of our nations and break up the cultural continuity and integrity of our peoples. The national laws of these regimes function uniformly in the destruction and exploitation of our peoples. Land laws in Mexico force our people from their lands, and force them northward to seek survival. The immigration laws of the United States deny entrance to the indigenous people coming from Mexico. Yet, these same laws are distorted to allow for a legalized kidnapping of our children from the Canadian area. Throughout the hemisphere, immigration laws have historically been used to bring in large groups of immigrants to further the colonization and destruction of our Mother Earth and People. Since those immigrants are coming to this hemisphere to occupy our lands, we are asserting our right to determine who enters our lands and asserting our right to deport those people who we determine to be illegal aliens.

In our own country the leadership of our people evolves from the natural cycles of the Creation. The quality of leadership is one that is in harmony with the Universe. It is a leadership that genuinely arises from the people, responds to the people, and does not seek to dominate either people or the Natural World. It is a leadership whose vision is constantly trained on the well-being and survival of present and future generations. These are the people who are of the Longest Walk.

It is the common knowledge of many people that the American theories of democracy were derived from indigenous people. Among our people were the inspirations for Franklin, Washington and Jefferson. Today, it is in our minds that the Western people have never escaped the need to have a single king-like figure to be their leader. Throughout the history of the United States, the Western people have always chosen leaders who successfully led the process of genocide against our people and other indigenous people throughout the world.

So we have watched the process of American government, and we are shocked that American leaders have little or no accountability to their people. President Carter has come to office talking strong words about "Human Rights." To us, these words have a hollow ring when applied to our people. We call upon all people of the world to confront President Carter on the question of United States' honor of Human Rights for the indigenous people of this land.

One specific problem of Human Rights violations is the problem of political prisoners in America. Our children are political prisoners of American compulsory education laws. Our women are political prisoners through health practices that force sterilization upon them. Entire communities are political prisoners when our right to protect our communities from violent and destructive forces is ignored.

There can be no amnesty for all the political prisoners of the United States and the Western civilization, for all things—the air, the trees, the four-legged beings, the ones in the oceans, as well as the two-legged beings—are political prisoners. All types of life are prisoners of a political system which has no respect for human or natural rights—a system only interested in protecting corporate financial interests. And at what cost is this done? Survival?

Today, many brothers and sisters from sovereign indigenous nations are being held in prisons as prisoners of war, because they dared to defend their rights given to them by the Creator and acknowledged by treaties made in good faith with the United States government.

We as sovereign indigenous people demand the release of our people from your inhuman jails and behavior modification units. We do not want a "pardon" or "amnesty"—only the complete and total release of our people, for we have committed no crimes. We have only acted in defense to protect the sacred gifts of this Creation and her children. We are under attack and forced into a state of war for our land and resources.

We never had jails. Our leaders had no need of weapons to protect them from their own people, because they truly are servants of the people. But today we see these problems placed upon us. We do not want jails on our lands, nor do we want our people or ways imprisoned within them. No one was meant to live that way and no man has the right to make that decision.

We know and understand how our leaders and warriors have been locked away, as well as murdered to steal the land we live upon, to silence our voices and to destroy our survival. This has been so since your arrival. Your laws were made to protect, not your people, but the greed of the wealthy. So there is no respect in your laws and no justice in your courts. We do not recognize your self-appointed control over our lives and freedom.

As a people we have the right to gather together to give a greeting and thanksgiving to the Creation. We have the right to live in peace and tranquility. We have the right to the fruits of our owl lands to feed, shelter and clothe our people. We have a right to conceive and to give birth according to our natural ways. We have the right to educate our children to our ways of life. We have the right to protect ourselves and our lands against abuses and to settle disputes that arise within our own territories. We have the right to clean air, clean water and the peaceful usage of our lands. We have the right to be a people. These are inherent rights. All people possess these rights under the laws of the Universe, as well as man-made laws. These are rights that cannot be given to or denied by one group of people over another. As the traditional people, we recognize and understand that these rights came from the Creator and not by actions of humans.

The United States has claimed to confer U.S. citizenship upon our people. Even that act has been used as a weapon against our people. It may be true that the United States has the power to confer citizenship upon whoever seeks it, but it has no right to deny our citizenship to our own nations. Today it comes to our ears that we are "privileged citizens" and that the treaties should be "abrogated" in order that we may be equal to United States citizens.

We are not United States citizens. We have treaties with the United States, and the U.S. does not make treaties with its own citizens. We protested the 1924 Citizenship Act. We do not claim U.S. citizenship. Nothing the U.S. has done in its relations with us has moved us to change that position.

The Indigenous people of the Western Hemisphere are the most oppressed of any people in these lands. Every facet of our lives are regulated and interfered with by the institutions of the people who invaded our territories. In every way the lives of our people are disrupted. The hospitals sterilize our women, the bureaucracies aid in the theft of our lands, resources and waters. But the most outrageous aspect of this oppression is the Western people's fetish for disturbing our ancestors.

In the name of science and academics, the archeologists and other grave robbers roam the countryside eagerly seeking the remains of our people.

To our people, one's passing from this world to the next is as significant as birth. At the time our spirit starts its journey to the Creator's world, we have completed our cycle within the many cycles of the Universe. At that time we balance the many lives it has taken to provide for our continuance.

The passing into the next world and the process of burial are very dignified and sacred events in the lives of our people. But that dignity and sacredness are severely disrupted by the activities of the Western grave robbers among our people; we provide our relatives with the necessities of their journey and return our relatives to the bosom of our Mother Earth dressed in their finest clothes. We place their bodies throughout our lands, and they act as constant reminders of the cycles we live within.

Our ancestors' right to be at peace is not respected by the invaders. In many areas the grave robbers have a free hand to desecrate the resting places of our people. The objects we gave them for their journey and their clothes end up on display in side shows and museums. Further insult is added when such displays are rampant with misinformation about our people. The people of the United States are encouraged to support these outrages through contributions and tax dollars. Daily, thousands of children are herded through these buildings and are taught to believe that these practices are normal and acceptable.

Many of our sacred burial sites have been desecrated by the construction of dams, housing tracts, industries and other land destroying processes of the West. Laws have been passed, forcing our people to follow alien and contradictory burial rites.

All of these practices are genocidal in nature and are heaped upon our people, consequently promoting the destruction of the spiritual health of our people. The original intents are clear. They are part of the Western desire to practice forced assimilation. If this is denied by you, then prove it by taking action to end these practices.

We call upon all museums, collectors and other hobbyists for the return of our sacred items, the remains of our people and items of our material heritage for proper reinterment. We call for the return of those items not taken from graves, but from our people, to be returned for their continued use in our ways of life.

We call for the restoration of all lands illegally removed from our protection. We call for the payment of war reparations due to us, for the reconstruction of our nations.

We call for an end to the confusing situation regarding state and federal jurisdiction, and direct America's attention to our treaties and agreements which define the relationship of our countries.

We call upon organized religion to become allies in the process of liberation, and to stop their competition for our "souls."

We are here to make it clear to the American government and the people of the world that there is only one definition of who we are as a people. That definition arises from our religions, governments and the ways of life that we follow. No one else on the Mother Earth has the right to attempt to define us or our existence.

We feel these are simple things to carry out. If the processes that affect us today are allowed to continue, in thirty or fifty years our nations and communities will be as destroyed as the areas that America occupies. At this time in history, we, as the original people of the hemisphere, are the only ones living in this part of the world left with any direction on how to be a human being in harmony with the Universe. Yet this is the greatest gift we could offer to all humanity.

In closing, the young people of The Longest Walk want our elders to know that we cannot thank you enough for carrying on the traditional ways. If it were not for our elders, we would not be speaking and thinking this way today. We, the young people, want our elders to know that as long as there is breath left in our bodies, that we commit ourselves to never allow your teachings to be forgotten. We commit ourselves to carrying on these peaceful traditional ways....

Sources:

"Affirmation of Sovereignty of the Indigenous Peoples of the Western Hemisphere." Akwesasne Notes 10, no. 3 (Summer 1978): 14–16.

Deloria, Vine, Jr. *Behind the Trail of Broken Treaties: An Indian Declaration of Independence.* Austin: University of Texas Press, 1985.

Johnson, Troy. *The Occupation of Alcatraz Island: Indian Self-Determination and the Rise of Indian Activism.* Urbana: University of Illinois Press, 1996.

US Congressional Record. House. 95th Cong., 2nd Sess. Vol. 124–Pt. 12. Pgs. 23134–23136.

---

52   *Itti̱-kāna-ikbi "Peacemaker" Court (1978)*

Peacemaking is a non-adversarial cultural process that long predates the arrival and imposition of the Western legal tradition that evolved from a more confrontational rubric. While Native peacemakers were outlawed by federal policy and law in the late nineteenth century, they continued to function clandestinely until the law was changed a century later. Indigenous peacemaking is based on the use of traditional dispute resolution techniques that involve consensus, respect for both victims and offenders, reconciliation, and community justice. As compared with Western models, it is more informal and conducted without the need for lawyers and judges. Several Native nations now operate full-time peacemaking processes—Grand Traverse Band of Ottawa and Chippewa, Organized Village of Kake, Navajo Nation, Seneca, and the example cited here, the Mississippi Band of Choctaw Indians.

Title XXIV: Choctaw Peacemaker Code: Choctaw Itti-Kāna-Ikbi Code

Chapter 1. Choctaw Peacemaker Code

SECTION 24–1–1: ITTI-KĀNA-IKBI COURT CREATION AND PURPOSE (GENERAL)

1) The spelling for this term (Itti-kāna-ikbi) is in accordance with Mississippi Band of Choctaw Indians (MBCI) Tribal Council Resolution 42–81 (A). All references to the Choctaw Peacemaker Code appearing in any other ordinances or codes are deemed to refer to the Choctaw Itti-kāna-ikbi Code as stated.
2) There is hereby established a Choctaw Peacemaker Court known as the Choctaw Itti-kāna-ikbi Court as a division of the Tribal Court, which shall operate in accordance with provisions of this Chapter.
3) The purpose of the Choctaw Itti-kāna-ikbi Court is to provide a forum for the use of traditional Choctaw methods of peacemaking to resolve disputes in a fair, informal and inexpensive manner. Any ambiguity in the Itti-kāna-ikbi Code shall be liberally construed to carry out its purpose of encouraging traditional Mississippi Band of Choctaw Indians (MBCI) methods of dispute resolution without formal court proceedings.
4) The Senior Itti-kāna-ikbi shall supervise the activities of the Itti-kāna-ikbi Court and shall exercise supervisory control over any Itti-kāna-ikbi pursuant to this Cod....

SECTION 24–1–4: USE OF TRIBAL TRADITIONS AND CUSTOMARY LAW

The Itti-kāna-ikbi aliha shall have the authority to use tribal cultural teachings and customs, including present-day religious teachings in the peacemaking process if the Itti-kāna-ikbi reasonably believes that such will further the objective of voluntarily resolving a dispute....

SECTION 24–1–6: LIMITATIONS ON ITTI-KANA-IKBI ALIHA AUTHORITY

Itti-kāna-ikbi aliha shall not have the authority to force the parties to resolve the disputed matter, nor shall Itti-kāna-ikbi aliha have the authority to adjudicate a matter which the parties cannot resolve through voluntary agreement.

SECTION 24–1–7: PROCEDURE FOR INITIATING AN ACTION
IN THE ITTI-KĀNA-IKBI COURT

All parties to a dispute may file a written request with the court clerk asking that their dispute be heard in the Itti-kāna-ikbi Court. The complaint may be informal and handwritten and it may be made either on a form provided by the court or in any written form which provides the court with the following information:

1) the name, address and phone number of the person requesting the peacemaking;
2) the names of the parties involved in the dispute and their mailing address and place of residence;
3) a short statement of the type of dispute involved in the action;
4) the reason the party desires the action to be heard in the Itti-kāna-ikbi Court;
5) the names and addresses of any persons other than the parties, that the party believes might have information useful to an Itti-kāna-ikbi in resolving the action; and
6) if known, information as to whether each party is non-Indian or Indian, and if Indian, the party's Tribal affiliation and membership, if any.

SECTION 24–1–12: ENFORCEMENT OF JUDGMENTS

1) A judgment entered pursuant to this chapter shall be enforceable in the same manner as other judgments of the tribal court.
2) The Itti-kāna-ikbi may give full faith and credit or comity to judgments, orders, decrees of the tribal court or courts of foreign jurisdiction.

SECTION 24–1–16: METHOD/BASIC RIGHTS

The Itti-kāna-ikbi permitted to use any reasonable method of working with people to solve their problems, as long as there is not force, violence or violation of an individual's basic rights. This Code is intended to provide guidance, in writing, to the MBCI traditional method of resolving disputes.

SECTION 24–1–17: MISCELLANEOUS

1) The Itti-kāna-ikbi Judge may adopt standard forms for the implementation of these rules.
2) Information or plain language for explanations of the Itti-kāna-ikbi Court peacemaking process may be published by the clerk of the Itti-kāna-ikbi Court for the use of persons before the Itti-kāna-ikbi Court. The provisions of this chapter shall prevail over any inconsistencies between the provisions of this chapter and any plain language explanations that may be published.

Sources:

Costello, Nancy A. "Walking Together in a Good Way: Indian Peacemaker Courts in Michigan," *University of Detroit Mercy Law Review* 76, 875–890, 1999.

http://www.Choctaw.org/government/court/peace.html.

Nielson, Marianne O., and James W. Zion, eds. *Navajo Nation Peacemaking: Living Traditional Justice.* Tucson: University of Arizona Press, 2005.

Quan, Julio, and Maralise Hood Quan. *Model of the Natural History of Conflict.* San Jose, Costa Rica: United Nations University for Peace, 1987.

53   *Mutual Protection and Law Enforcement Agreement (1979)*

The following agreement was initiated at the local level between the Ak-Chin Indian Community and Pinal County in Southern Arizona. It was an effort to clarify lines of jurisdictional authority between the parties in the wake of the US Supreme Court's 1978 ruling *Oliphant v. Suquamish,* where the court held that Native governments no longer had criminal jurisdiction over non-Indians who committed crimes on Tribal land. Ak-Chin had already built a decent working relationship with state and local governments, and this law enforcement agreement was meant to formally reestablish and reaffirm those political ties.

This agreement entered into as of the first day of July, 1979, by and between Ak-Chin Indian Community, hereinafter referred to as the "Community," and the County of Pinal, State of Arizona, hereinafter referred to as "Pinal,"

Whereas, the parties hereto are desirous of providing for the mutual protection and preservation of the public peace and for the general welfare of the residents of the parties hereto; and

Whereas, it is to the mutual benefit of the parties hereto that they enter into an agreement of mutual protection and assistance in the field of law enforcement, and will greatly benefit by their mutual cooperation and mutual assistance in the area of law enforcement;

Whereas, Pinal and the Community, by resolution, a true certified or authenticated copy of each attached hereto, have approved this joint exercise of powers;

Now, therefore, the County of Pinal...and the Ak-Chin Community, by virtue of and pursuant to the authority contained under Article 8, section 1...of the Articles of Association of the Ak-Chin Indian Community,...do hereby enter into this agreement in order to more efficiently and economically facilitate their capabilities to provide for the maximum amount of protection for the public health, safety and welfare of their citizens;

Now, therefore, it is hereby mutually agreed by the parties hereto:

1) That commencing July 1, 1979, for a period of three years, and until June 30, 1982, Pinal and Community agree to cooperate and assist each other to their mutual benefit in the field of law enforcement.

2) The Community, through its duly designated and employed tribal police officers, agrees to assist and aid the officers of Pinal in the area of Maricopa, Pinal County, Arizona, when called upon so to do by a duly commissioned and regularly employed officer of Pinal when said call does not conflict with his then present duties on the Indian reservation of the Community.

3) Pinal, through its duly designated and employed law enforcement officers, agrees to assist and aid the Community on the Ak-Chin Indian Reservation, Pinal County, Arizona, when called upon so to do by a duly commissioned and regularly employed officer of the Community, and when said call does not conflict with their then present duties.

4) That upon the duly authorized request of the officer of the Community to an officer of Pinal for aid, the officer of Pinal shall assist in law enforcement for the Community in relation to all crimes set forth in the Law and Order Code, 1975....

5) That upon the duly authorized request of the officers of Pinal to an officer of the Community for aid the officer of the Community shall assist in law enforcement for Pinal in relation to all crimes of the state of Arizona as set forth in Arizona revised statutes, 1956, as amended.

6) The Community agrees to hire and pay the entire salary of the tribal police officers without compensation from Pinal, and Pinal agrees to hire and pay the salaries of the duly commissioned officers of Pinal without compensation from the Community in the exercise of any of the provisions of this Agreement.

7) Officers of either party shall not have the authority to make arrests within the jurisdiction of the other party, unless under the direct supervision, direction or control of a duly authorized officer of the jurisdiction where the offense occurs and unless otherwise allowed by law; however, the officer of Community may have the authority to issue summons to traffic offenders on the reservation to non-Indians to appear before the justice court having jurisdiction of the offense; said summons shall be on the Arizona traffic complaint form.

8) The officers of the Community shall be assigned a call number on the radio frequency of the Pinal County Sheriff's office; said officers shall utilize said radio frequency; however, the Community shall furnish and pay for the purchase price, installation costs and repair of any radio equipment to be utilized by the officers of the Community in his patrol vehicle.

9) The Community shall be allowed the use of the facilities at the Maricopa branch of the Pinal County Jail for the incarceration of persons

arrested within the jurisdiction of the Community, and over which the Community has exclusive jurisdiction, but the Community shall reimburse Pinal for all expenses incurred by Pinal in caring for persons incarcerated in the Maricopa branch of the Pinal County Jail for any violation of the Law and Order Code of the Ak-Chin Indian Community; such expenses shall include, but not be limited to, meals, medical services and similar personal services rendered to the prisoners.

10) Nothing contained herein shall be construed as an employment contract of individual officers of either Pinal or Community by the other, and when an officer of either party acts under the authority or on behalf of the other party, it shall be under the direct control and supervision of the party having jurisdiction of the offense, except as otherwise specifically provided herein.

11) This agreement may be canceled or terminated by either party at any time upon 30 days written notice by registered mail....

12) This agreement shall become effective 10 days after the filing of this Agreement with the Secretary of State, and after approval by the Attorney General as provided by law.

Witness our hands the day and year first written above.

Ak-Chin Indian Community, by Wilbert J. Carlyle, Tribal Chairman

Pinal County, Arizona, by Jimmie B. Kerr, Chairman, Pinal County Board of Supervisors

Source:

US Senate. "Tribal-State Compact Act of 1979." Hearing Before the Select Committee on Indian Affairs. 96th Cong., 1st Sess., on S. 1181. Washington, DC: Government Printing Office, 1979.

54

Standing Rock Sioux Tribal Attorney Reid Peyton Chambers's Statement on Extension of the Statute of Limitations for Claims (1979)

Prior to 1966 there was no limit on the time in which the US could bring an action for damages, either for itself or on behalf of a Native nation. That year, Congress established a six-year limit for claims, except for actions to establish titles to lands. It was amended in 1972 to add five years to the time in which actions could be brought, and again with the addition of another two and one-half years. When the Department of the Interior finally conducted a search in 1979, they reported an astonishing backlog of approximately 9,768 claims, with the potential for 5,000 more. Reid Peyton Chambers here testifies that Congress, as the tribes' principal trustee, should never impede efforts of Native peoples to secure justice with regard to their lands and resources.

My name is Reid Peyton Chambers. I am an attorney in private practice here in Washington. I represent the Standing Rock Sioux Tribe of North and South Dakota, the Assiniboine and Sioux Tribes of the Fort Peck Indian Reservation in Montana, the Shoshone Tribe of the Wind River Indian Reservation in Wyoming and the Houlton Band of Maliseet Indians in Maine. These tribes are all seriously impacted by the running of the statute. The Tribes believe that at a minimum, the statute of limitations in 28 U.S.C. 2415 must be extended. More basically, under current circumstances, we submit that the statute of limitations should not be applied at all to bar actions brought by the United States as trustee for Indians.

The need for congressional action on this problem begins with the Act of July 18, 1966, which for the first time established a statute of limitations upon certain actions commenced by the United States seeking money damages against private persons. The most important claims, for our purposes, covered by the statute were actions to recover damages for trespass to lands of the United States and for conversion of property of the United States. The original period of this statute was six years. And while the statute's intent was to subject the United States to a statute of limitations when suing to protect its own property interests, the 1966 Act also pertains to trespass to trust or restricted Indian lands.

This application of the statute to Indian claims went unnoticed by the Interior and Justice Departments and by Indian tribes and their lawyers until the six-year period was nearly up. Then, at the last moment, Indian groups, with Interior Department support, presented the problem to Congress, and Congress extended the statute for five additional years. In 1977, it was hoped that extensions would provide sufficient time to investigate and bring all historic claims for trespass to Indian lands. This hope has gone unfulfilled. While many actions have been filed, many others have not, and there is still a vast number of claims remaining to be investigated, or as yet undiscovered. I served as Associate Solicitor for Indian Affairs at the Interior Department from 1973 to 1976, and I accept the censure due for my part in the failure of the Government to identify and prosecute all these potential claims. The problem, I submit, is not simply insufficient time—it is the extreme lack of resources to service the immense needs, legal and otherwise, of American Indians.

The United States as trustee for the Tribes, has the responsibility for managing, conserving and protecting all trust lands and resources from outside encroachment. But the trustee has clearly not devoted sufficient legal resources to fulfill its responsibility. Over the last decades, as Indians looked to the courts to protect their rights, Indian litigation has rightly multiplied. There are six divisions in the Interior Solicitor's office in Washington—the Indian Division is the smallest now, as it was in 1972, although it handles a larger caseload (both quantitatively and surely in terms of the nature of its cases) than most other Divisions. The section in the Justice Department responsible for prosecuting these cases has far fewer lawyers than another Justice section charged with defending the United States in the Indian Claims Commission cases against the Indians.

In addition, there is frequent conflict and competition for natural resources within the Interior and Justice Departments between Indians and agencies like the Bureau of Reclamation, Bureau of Land Management, Forest Service, Army Corps of Engineers, and Fish and Wildlife Service. A great deal of lawyers' time is devoted to administrative controversies, and it is often no easy matter for tribes or for their advocates within the Government to get controversial cases filed. Legal manpower in the Solicitor's Office and Justice Department has been insufficient to meet all these needs—both in Washington and in Indian country. The same is true of the Bureau of Indian Affairs. The Tribes fear that these dire shortages of manpower and other resources will continue.

While federal resources have been limited, the task required is massive. To assure that all valid claims are brought, reservation lands must be surveyed, tract by tract, to discover unlawful encroachments. Aerial photographs should be compared with section lines and metes and bounds descriptions. In addition, federal agencies have in their possession (generally deep in archival vaults around the country) papers, records and accounts concerning trust property.

These must be searched, and the validity of each existing land use on Indian reservations should be analyzed. On the Standing Rock Reservation, for example, over 3,000 allotments were made after the opening of the reservation. From 1910 to 1921 several hundred allottees were illegally forced to take fee patents without consent. The records of all the Reservation's allotments must now be reviewed to determine where valid trespass claims exist following a forced patent. The task has been rendered all the more difficult because the records are not located at Standing Rock, but have been dispersed to various other BIA offices. It is certain that the searching of records will turn up major, valid claims.

Several years ago attorneys for the Native American Rights Fund in researching 19th century documents happened to discover an invalid railroad right-of-way across the Walker River Reservation in Nevada. The United States and the Tribe brought suit against the railway, and with a favorable decision by the court of appeals, the Tribe stands to recover a substantial sum. The title to every right-of-way grant in Indian country should be similarly searched and reported to the tribes and their attorneys before any statute of limitations is imposed.

There are doubtless hundreds of encroachments in Indian country as yet undiscovered. It is the responsibility of the United States to uncover these claims, notify the tribes of their existence, and bring litigation if necessary. Failure to do so before the expiration of a statute of limitations could subject the United States to massive liability for failure to bring valid claims for its Indian beneficiaries. In any event, the Indians should not be penalized and lose their property rights because the trustee did not know what property it manages and what claims it has, or because no action is taken by the trustee to learn and prosecute their rights.

We suggest that a statute of limitations against the United States is eminently reasonable where *only* the property of the United States is involved, and the United States with all of its resources has slept in its rights. That is not the situation here. The United States is trustee for Indian property rights, the United States manages and administers the property. But the trustee has no inventory of the property it manages, reservation-by-reservation and tract-by-tract, or of the use of this property. It has never reported all possible reasonable claims to its trust beneficiaries. A statute of limitations in these circumstances shifts the loss from private trespassers to the Indians where the Indians have never been fully informed by their trustee. That the trustee has not had sufficient manpower or resources does not diminish the unfairness of making the Indians bear this loss.

To be sure, it is possible that all of the actions necessary to inform Indians of their claims *could* be taken by the United States during a fixed period of time if the statute were extended to another set deadline. But given the other needs and priorities facing American Indians in the immediate future, the Tribes question the wisdom of having a statute of limitations applied at all to claims regarding Indian trust property and of utilizing the large amount of resources that would be necessary to make a complete parcel-by-parcel inventory of all uses of trust lands on Indian reservations, and report the findings of such an inventory to the tribes and to Congress.

For this reason, the Tribes would prefer an amendment holding the statute inapplicable to Indians over another limited extension. It goes without saying, however, that the Tribes would greatly prefer a fixed extension to the running of the statute on April 1, 1980.

Sources:

Sutton, Imre, ed. *Irredeemable America: The Indians' Estate and Land Claims*. Albuquerque: University of New Mexico Press, 1985.

US House. "Statute of Limitations for Indian Claims." Oversight Hearing Before the Subcommittee on Administrative Law and Governmental Relations of the Committee on the Judiciary. 97th Cong., 2nd Sess. Washington, DC: Government Printing Office, 1982.

US Senate. "Statute of Limitations." Hearing Before the Select Committee on Indian Affairs. 96th Cong., 1st Sess. Washington, DC: Government Printing Office, 1980.

Wilkins, David E. *Hollow Justice: A History of Indigenous Claims in the United States*. New Haven, CT: Yale University Press, 2013.

55

Testimony of Billy Frank, Jr., Chairman, Northwest Indian Fisheries Commission, Against Sen. Slade Gorton's Steelhead Trout Protection Act (1981)

Native nations located within the boundaries of what is now Washington State have relied on steelhead trout, salmon, and other species for cultural and physical sustenance since time immemorial. But, as the state was settled by a majority Anglo population, pressure mounted to restrict Native access to fish and other natural resources. Billy Frank, Jr., a Nisqually citizen, was a beloved, iconic figure in the Northwest beginning with his courageous leadership in the Indian fishing rights battles of the 1950s until his passing in 2014. Famous for his sense of humor, Billy often referred to himself as the "getting-arrested-Indian," because of the more than fifty arrests he endured as he sought to exercise his treaty rights. When the federal courts concluded that Natives were entitled to half the fish in the 1974 *U.S. v. Washington* (the Boldt Decision) and other contemporaneous decisions, Frank became the chairman of the Northwest Indian Fisheries Commission (NWIFC), a powerful consortium of Native nations who together coordinate regional fisheries management.

Despite the major judicial victories affirming Native treaty rights, Tribal nations occasionally had to confront legislative attacks like the Steelhead Trout Protection Act that Frank, on behalf of the NWIFC, here testifies against. Interestingly, the act, which subsequently failed, was sponsored by Washington senator Slade Gorton—dubbed the "Last Indian Fighter" by his detractors. He and Billy Frank had famously clashed before, as prior to his election to the Senate, Gorton was the Washington state attorney general who had also been unsuccessful in arguing against the Tribes' treaty right to fish in *U.S. v. Washington* (the Boldt Decision). The fight outlined here in Frank's testimony was one of many skirmishes in the decades-long battle over treaty rights between these seasoned antagonists.

———

I am Bill Frank, Jr., Chairman of the Northwest Indian Fisheries Commission, speaking for the Commission and its 19 member Tribes on Puget Sound and the Washington Coast. Other Commissioners and tribal representatives will provide detail on concerns in their specific treaty areas and are available to help answer questions you may have regarding our testimony.

The Northwest Indian Fisheries Commission is authorized by its member Tribes to represent and coordinate their fisheries management policies. The

Commission functions as the Tribes' voice in dealing with ocean fisheries management, Canadian treaty negotiations and other general fisheries matters.

Senator [Slate] Gorton, while we appreciate the Committee's stated concern for steelhead conservation in Washington State, we must state our opposition to this bill as we have to previous similar legislation. The attempts to legislate away the Tribes' reserved fishing right to steelhead have through the years been consistently rejected by a Congress which will not permit the immoral unilateral abrogation of treaties, especially for the benefit of a selfish special interest group advocating single-purpose use of a public resource. We believe this unsuccessful series of legislation targeted at revoking the Tribes' fishing rights is nothing more than a political device and shallow response to pressure from a few. Senator, today we see the same people and hear the same tired rhetoric.

The 1980 Salmon and Steelhead Conservation and Enhancement Act provides an impetus for the state and tribal governments to formulate a comprehensive plan to manage steelhead and salmon. Your effort to exclude steelhead from the joint comprehensive fisheries and management package would ensure the failure of this important work. The 1980 law holds the promise of finally resolving some of the problems in management facing the salmon and steelhead resource in the Pacific Northwest.

Your bill reflects no sensitivity to the importance these fish have for Indian people. With limited resources on their small reservations, the Tribes depend almost entirely upon fishing for salmon and steelhead as an economic base. Steelhead is a vital resource to Indian communities during winter and spring months when salmon are not available. To some Tribes, steelhead is more important than salmon. For coastal Tribes, especially, steelhead is often their "bread-and- butter" fishery. For example, 70 percent of the Hoh Tribe's annual fishery income is derived from steelhead.

At least as important as the Tribes' economic dependence on fishing is the continuation of a way of life. Salmon and steelhead fishing represents both a cultural value to the Tribes' religious beliefs and a sustenance value in the health and sustenance of the Indian people. Indian communities continue as always to hold ceremonies and celebrations tied to fish and fishing.

Before the 1974 *U.S. v. Washington* ruling the treaty Tribes were prevented from participating in the management of salmon and steelhead fisheries in off-reservation waters. Little was done by the State of Washington's Department of Game to acquire the data needed to properly manage the resource, to conduct research on steelhead spawning escapement requirements, or to collect other information essential to management.

Steelhead management today has benefited from the Tribes' increased participation. The advantages of the Tribes' work in steelhead research, enhancement and in protection of the spawning habitat is evident.

The Tribes have, in the past five years, reared and released more than 1,685,000 steelhead. Tribal hatchery steelhead production has risen to more than 300,000 annually. Projections for 1983 indicate that the Tribes will release 2.5 million steelhead which will contribute to both treaty and sports fisheries. Further, the Tribes are active in the collection and preservation of brood stock native to western Washington river systems.

The Tribes are conducting surveys to assess spawning escapement needed to determine total run size and to evaluate the success of management programs. Research on juvenile steelhead provides information on timing of outmigration, abundance habitat requirements, and freshwater survival. All of this information is vital to predicting future returns and evaluating needed enhancement and habitat restoration work.

Precise and effective management result from the Tribes' in-season catch data collection. Figures from the sport harvest alone do not provide timely or reliable data on which to manage.

The Tribes are active in habitat protection. The treaties provide a unique remedy-at-law for ensuring protection of the fisheries habitat. Through state and federal governments' treaty obligation to refrain from approving or participating in activities potentially destructive to the habitat, the resource will be protected and the people of Washington State can enjoy a clean and healthy environment.

This legislation proposes an irresponsible use of taxpayers' dollars in many ways—the cost of this and further hearings; the proposals to have the Tribes file damages with the court of Claims; and the attempt in essence, to draw funding away from working tribal steelhead management and enhancement programs. Federal tax dollars would be more productively used for fisheries management, enhancement and research programs to improve the steelhead resource.

If Tribes are prohibited from the commercial harvest of steelhead, the loss will not only be monetary but will also affect other factors—employment; the upset of tribal enterprise; the usurping of tribal self-determination; and the disruption of the cultural value of fish and fishing to maintaining tribal identity and lifestyle.

The allegation in your bill that decommercialization of steelhead is necessary for conservation is without foundation. The Federal courts have consistently found that there is a total lack of credible data that treaty fisheries have caused a decline on the steelhead resource. Recognizing that no method is inherently damaging if properly managed, the Tribes carefully regulate their fisheries in accordance with the biological needs of the resource.

The proposal that the Tribes may profit more serving as guides and licensing non-Indians to fish on reservation mistakenly views the importance of the Tribes' reserved fishing right to steelhead as merely economic. It further purports to grant as a privilege a right that the Tribes have always possessed, and that is already exercised by many Washington Tribes.

The impact of your bill, Senator Gorton, goes beyond the decommercialization of steelhead—which is itself an unlawful taking of a property right for private rather than public use. It would also give Washington State regulatory powers on-reservation, which is a major intrusion on the Tribes' right to self-determination.

Not once did you contact the Tribes during development of your bill for information or confirmation of steelhead data. It has been the practice of members of Congress to rely on the Northwest Indian Fisheries Commission and tribal staffs for statistical and historical information relating to fisheries and tribal management. We urge that kind of communication, and will welcome your questions here today.

Thank you....

Sources:

Cohen, Fay G. *Treaties on Trial: The Continuing Controversy over Northwest Indian Fishing Rights.* Seattle: University of Washington Press, 1986.

US Senate. "Steelhead Trout Protection Act." Hearing Before the Select Committee on Indian Affairs. 97th Cong., 1st Sess. on S. 874. Washington, DC: Government Printing Office, 1981.

Wilkinson, Charles. *Messages from Frank's Landing: A Story of Salmon, Treaties, and the Indian Way.* Seattle: University of Washington Press, 2000.

56 Position of the Haudenosaunee Grand Council of Chiefs Regarding the "Ancient Indian Land Claims Settlement Act" (1982)

In the late 1970s, a number of Native communities in the eastern United States, having long-endured enormous land losses, began to push for justice. They utilized the 1790 Non-intercourse Act as their principal legal tool. Lawsuits were filed and some negotiated settlements were forged that led to the restoration of some territory for several small Native nations in Maine. Other native communities vigorously pushed forward on land claims. These actions prompted a virulent backlash against Native claims that culminated in a 1992 bill titled the "Ancient Indian Land Claims Act." Proposed by the Senators from New York and South Carolina, it ostensibly sought to "establish a fair and consistent national policy for the resolution of ancient Indian land transfers and to clear the titles of lands subject to such claims." In spite of its benign moniker, the act would have disastrously dealt with Native land claims, first by validating all prior land transfers and then allowing Native claimants only a right to sue for monetary damages. During the congressional hearing on June 23, 1982, a cavalcade of congressional officials, state leaders, county officials, and non-Indian citizens supported the bill, while Native governments and individuals anxiously and powerfully testified in opposition. The leadership of the Haudenosaunee Confederacy, also known as the Iroquois Confederacy or Six Nations, provided this statement.

———

To: Representative Morris Udall, Chairman House Committee on Interior and Insular Affairs
From: Grand Council of Chiefs of the Haudenosaunee (Iroquois Confederacy).

Re HR–5494 "Ancient Indian Land Claims Settlement Act."

Chairman Udall, members of the Committee, members of Congress, representatives of the branches of the United States government, the Grand Council of Chiefs of the Haudenosaunee (Iroquois Confederacy) wish to extend to you greetings on behalf of our people.

Also on behalf of all of our people; our ancestors, those who walk the Earth today, and especially our future generations, we wish for who will read this to understand clearly our feelings and positions regarding this legislation before you.

The Haudenosaunee, or Iroquois Confederacy, has existed on this land since the beginning of human memory. Our culture is among the most ancient continuously existing cultures in the world. We still remember the earliest doings of human beings. We remember the original instructions of the Creators of Life on this place we call Etenoha—Mother Earth. We are the spiritual guardians of this place. We are the Ongwhewhowhe—the Real People.

It may seem strange, at this time, that we are here asserting the obvious fact of our continuing existence. For countless centuries the fact of our existence was unquestioned, and for all honest people, it remains unquestioned today. We have existed since time immemorial. We have always conducted our own affairs from our territories, under our own laws and customs.

We have never, under those laws and customs, willingly or fairly surrendered either our territories or our freedoms. Never, in the history of the Haudenosaunee have the People or the government sworn allegiance to a European sovereign. In that simple fact lies the roots of our oppression as a People, and the purpose of our journey here, before this Committee.

In the beginning we were told that the human beings who walk about the Earth have been provided with all the things necessary for Life. We were instructed to carry a love for one another, and to show a great respect for all of the beings of the Earth. We were shown that our Life exists with the Tree of Life, that our well-being depends on the well-being of the Vegetable Life, that we are close relatives of the Four-Legged Beings. In our ways, spiritual consciousness is the highest form of politics.

Ours is a Way of Life. We believe that all living things are spiritual beings. Spirits can be expressed as energy forms manifest in matter. A blade of grass is an energy form manifested in matter-grassmatter. The spirit of the grass is that unseen force which produces the species of grass, and it is manifest to us in the form of real grass.

All things of the world are real, material things. The Creation is a true, material phenomenon, and the Creation manifests itself to us through reality. The spiritual universe, then, is manifest to the Humans as Creation, the Creation which supports Life. We believe that Humans are real, a part of the Creation, and that their duty is to support Life in conjunction with the other beings. That is why we call ourselves Ongwhewhowhe—Real People.

The original instructions direct that we who walk about on the Earth are to express a great respect, an affection and a gratitude toward all the spirits which create and support Life. We give a greeting and thanksgiving to the many supporters of our lives—the corn, beans, squash, the winds, the water, the sun, all living beings who work together on this land. When people cease to respect and express gratitude for these many things, then all Life will be destroyed, and Human Life on this planet will come to an end.

Our roots are deep in the lands where we live. We have a great love for our country, for our birthplace is there. The soil is rich from the bones of thousands of our generations. Each of us were created in these lands, and it is our duty to take great care of them, because from these lands will spring the future generations of the Ongwhewhowhe. We walk about with a great respect, for the Earth is a very sacred place.

We are not a people who demand or ask anything of the Creators of Life, but instead, we give greetings and thanksgiving that all the forces of Life are still at work. We deeply understand our relationship to all living things. To this day, the territories we still hold are filled with trees, animals and the other gifts of the Creation. In these places we still receive our nourishment from our Mother Earth.

Since the beginning of the invasion, more than 400 years ago, the development and evolution of our civilizations have taken a radical turn for the worst. Since the beginning of the process of the colonization of our lands we cannot look back and identify one year in which we can say that we enjoyed peace and harmony with the settlers.

From the beginning of its existence the United States has conducted a reign of terror in the Haudenosaunee territory. Colonial agents entered our country between 1784 and 1842 and returned to Washington with treaties for cessions of land fraudulently obtained with persons not authorized to make land transfers. The Grand Council of the Haudenosaunee, which is the only legitimate body authorized to conduct land transactions, never signed any agreements surrendering the territories.

The United States entered into solemn treaties with the Haudenosaunee, and each time has ignored virtually each and every provision of the treaties which guarantee our rights as a separate nation. Only the sections of the treaties which refer to land cessions, sections which often were fraudulently obtained, have validity in the eyes of the United States courts or governments.

The mechanism for the colonization of the Haudenosaunee territory is found in legal fiction, in the United States Constitution. That document purports to give Congress power to "regulate commerce with foreign nations and among the several States, and with Indian tribes." Congress has expanded that section to an assertion of "plenary power," a doctrine which asserts absolute authority over our territories. This assertion has been repeatedly urged upon our people, although we have never agreed to that relationship, and we have never been conquered in warfare. The Haudenosaunee are vassals to no people—we are a free nation, and we have never surrendered our rights as free people.

Somehow, the United States takes the position that the Haudenosaunee ceased to exist by the year 1784, although the longhouse has continued to this day. There is ample evidence that all the nations continue to participate in the matters of the Grand Council, the legislative body of the Confederacy. None of the nations of the Confederacy has ever declared themselves separate from the Confederacy. The Oneidas whose reputed allegiance to the United States was based on the existence of Oneida mercenaries, continued to send their delegates to the Council, and the Tuscarora remain firmly attached to the Confederation.

The Onondagas, Senecas, Cayuga and Mohawks continue to hold their positions within the Confederation. Although the Haudenosaunee has been severely disrupted by the Westward expansion of the United States, the subsequent surrounding of our lands, and the attempts to devour our people, the Confederacy continues to function. Indeed, today its strength continues to be increasing.

By pretending that the Haudenosaunee government no longer exists, both the U.S. and Britain illegally took Haudenosaunee territories by simply saying the territories belong to them. The Haudenosaunee territories are not, and have never been part of the U.S. or Canada. The citizens of the Haudenosaunee are a separate people, distinct from either Canada or the U.S. Because of this the Haudenosaunee refuse to recognize a border drawn through our lands by a foreign people.

The policy of the dispossession of North American Native peoples, first by the European kingdoms, and later by their settler heirs, began with the first contact. Dispossession took a number of approaches: the so-called "just warfare" was a strategy by which Native nations were deemed to have offended the Crown and their elimination by fire and sword was justified. That was followed by the Treaty Period in which Native nations were "induced" to sell their lands and move westward. The Treaty Period was in full swing at the beginning of the 19th Century. By 1815, the governor of New York was agitating for the removal of all Native people from the state for "their own good."

While the infamous Trail of Tears was removing Native peoples from the Southeast to Oklahoma, New York State was lobbying for a treaty in 1838, which was intended to remove the Haudenosaunee, who were on lands the state wanted, away to an area of Kansas. The principal victims were to be the Senecas.

Like the Termination Era a century later, the Removal Policy was eventually abandoned due in part to the bad press received from the Cherokee removal of 1832. During the process of their removal thousands of Cherokee men, women, children and elders were subjected to conditions which caused them to die of exposure, starvation and neglect.

In 1871, the U.S. Congress passed an act which included a clause that treaties would no longer be made with "Indian Nations." It was at this time that official U.S. policy toward Native people began to shift to a new strategy. Reports to the Congress began to urge that the Native people be assimilated into U.S. society as quickly as possible. The policy of fire and sword simply became less popular with a significant percentage of the U.S. population. The principal hindrance to the assimilation of the Native peoples, according to its most vocal adherents, was the Indian land base. The Native land base was held in common and this was perceived as an uncivilized and un-American practice. The Congressional supporters of assimilation urged that if every Indian family owned its own farmstead, they would more readily acquire "civilized" traits. Thus the Dawes Act of 1887 ordered the Native nations stripped of their land base, resulting in the transfer of millions of acres to European hands.

There was consistent pressure in the New York legislature to "civilize" the Haudenosaunee. To accomplish this, all vestiges of Haudenosaunee nationality needed to be destroyed. This is the 19th Century origin of the policy to "educate" the Indian to be culturally American. It was thought that when the Indian was successfully Americanized, he would no longer be distinct and separate, and that there would no longer be an indigenous people with their own customs and economy. At that point, the Indian could be simply declared to have assimilated into the U.S. or Canadian society. The net effect would dispense with the entire concept of Native nations, and that would extinguish the claims of those nations to their lands. The report of the Whipple Committee to the New York Legislature in 1888 was clear: "Exterminate the Tribe."

In 1924, the Canadian government "abolished" Haudenosaunee government at the Grand River territory. The Oneida and Akwesasne territories were invaded and occupied by Canadian troops in order to establish neo-colonial "elective systems" in the name of democracy. Also in 1924, the United States government passed illegal legislation declaring all "American Indians" to be U.S. citizens.

The 1924 Citizenship Act was an attempt to deny the existence of Native nations, and the rights of these Native nations to their lands. The denial of the existence of Native nations is a way of legitimizing the United States' claim to our homelands. This concept is furthered by the imposition of non-Native forms of government. This also serves to fulfill the United States' need to destroy any semblance of Native sovereignty. The actual process of taking lands can be accomplished when the Native nation no longer exists in its original context—when it is less a nation.

With all semblance of a Native nation's original context destroyed, Canada and the U.S. can rationalize that integration has occurred. With this rationale in hand, both governments have set out to enact their final solutions to the "Indian Problem."

The Haudenosaunee vigorously objected to the Citizenship Act and maintains to this day that the People of the Longhouse are not citizens of Canada or the U.S., but are citizens of their own nations of the Confederacy. To underline this position our government has issued its own passports to those of our people travelling abroad. To date, we entered 18 countries with our passports.

The Termination Acts of the 1950s were efforts to simply declare that the Native nations no longer exist and to appropriate their lands. The acts were so disastrous that they caused something of a national scandal. "St. Regis", the European name for Akwesasne, was one of our territories targeted by the Bureau of Indian Affairs as "ready for integration."

The B.I.A. based its recommendation on the fact that many of the Mohawk people had acquired at least some of the material conditions which made their community outwardly indistinguishable from the white communities. In fact, however, Akwesasne was, and is, very different from the small towns in the area surrounding it. We have only recently finished 2 ½ years of armed siege resisting New York State's efforts to destroy the Traditional Mohawk government and their distinctiveness.

Termination submerged as an official policy in the late 1960s. But Termination is simply a means to an end. The objective is the economic exploitation of a people and their lands. The taking of lands and the denial and destruction of Native nations are concrete and undeniable elements in the colonization process as it is applied to Native people. Tools to accomplish this end include guns, disease, revised histories, repressive missionaries, indoctrinating teachers, and these things are often cloaked in codes of law. In the 20th Century, the taking of land and the destruction of cultures and Native economy serve to force Native peoples into roles as industrial workers, just as in the 19th Century the same processes forced Native peoples into roles as landless peasants.

The Haudenosaunee over a period of 375 years met every definition of an oppressed nation. It has been subjected to raids of extermination from France, England and the United States. Its people have been driven from their lands, impoverished, and persecuted for their Haudenosaunee customs. It has been the victim of fraudulent dealings from these European governments which have openly expressed the goal of the extermination of the Haudenosaunee. Our children have been taught to despise their ancestors, their culture, their religion and their traditional economy. Recently it has been a U.S. government sponsored fad to have "bi-lingual/bi-cultural" programs in the schools of the settlers. These programs are not sincere efforts to revitalize the Haudenosaunee, but exist as an integrationist's ploy to imply their "acceptance" of our ways.

Some American historians have cloaked the past in a veil of lies. The national and local governments of the Haudenosaunee have been suppressed and usurped by the U.S. authorities, and have been aided by Indian helpers, to carry out policies of repression in the name of democracy. Generation after generation has seen the Haudenosaunee land base, and therefore its economic base, shrink under the expansionist policies of the U.S. and Canada.

The world is told by the U.S. government's propaganda machines that the Haudenosaunee are simply victims of "civilization and progress." The truth is that we are victims of a conscious and persistent effort of destruction directed at us by the former European colonizing governments and their heirs in North America. The Haudenosaunee is not suffering a terminal illness of natural causes—it is being deliberately strangled to death by those who would benefit from its death.

Although treaties may often have been bad deals for the Native nations, the U.S. chose not to honor those which exist because to do so would require the return of much of the economic base and sovereignty to the Haudenosaunee. The Treaties contain the potential for independent survival of the Native people. The dishonoring of treaties is essential to the goal of the U.S. vested interests which are organized to remove any and all obstacles to their exploitation of the Earth and her peoples.

Today as we sit in this room we clearly see that we continue to be the victims of an unchanged attitude that has prevailed throughout the United States' 206 years. Representative Gary Lee continues the traditions of racism and demagoguery that have been the hallmarks of the relations between our two nations. Only one American leader has ever been held in esteem by our people—your first president, George Washington. In all of our years it is only from him that we felt we heard words of truth, and now, Representative Lee is working hard to crush those words as they are set in the treaties.

Because of Congress' mistaken belief that you have "plenary power" over our lives, and the irrefutable lessons of history, we have taken our case to the world at large. Since 1924, our leaders have been actively seeking allies and friends amongst the other nations of the world. This work has gained us many supporters in other countries; gained us access to various commissions of the United Nations; and gained us political support, most notably from Western European countries. How Congress chooses to act on this so-called "Ancient Indian Claims Settlement Act" will not be done in isolation.

The very serious questions of our rights to our homelands will not go away with the swipe of a pen. We continue to exist, and the lands that the Creators of Life gave to us continue to exist. As long as this is a reality, and as long as the American government continues to act in a racist and genocidal manner, the problem will never be over.

The Traditional People recognize that the injustices perpetrated upon our people, and indeed many of the peoples of the world, are the major factor destroying the Spirituality of the Human Race. Peace and unity are the foundations of the Spiritual Way of Life of our peoples. But, peace and unity are not companions to injustice.

We never were, nor are we now, nor ever intend to be "citizens" of the U.S. or Canada. We are Haudenosaunee determined to make a future for our people based on our own constitution, the "Great Law of Peace," our religion, and the message of the Gai wiio....

Sources:

Sutton, Imre, ed. *Irredeemable America: The Indians' Estate and Land Claims.* Albuquerque: University of New Mexico Press, 1985.

US Senate. "Ancient Indian Land Claims." Hearing Before the Select Committee on Indian Affairs. 97th Cong., 2nd Sess. on S. 2084. Washington, DC: Government Printing Office, 1982.

Vescey, Christopher, and William A. Starna, eds. *Iroquois Land Claims.* Syracuse, NY: Syracuse University Press, 1988.

57   *Kerr-McGee Corp. v. Navajo Tribe (1985)*

Kerr-McGee, a major multinational corporation, had exploited the abundant uranium and coal reserves of the Navajo Nation since the 1950s and paid virtually no taxes to the Nation. As the Navajo government's infrastructure matured in the 1970s, its leaders decided to create a taxing program for larger businesses as a way to generate much-needed revenue. Kerr-McGee challenged the Navajo's right to impose taxes without having first secured approval from the Secretary of the Interior. The Supreme Court, however, held that the Navajo Nation did not need such approval as the Tribe had not organized its government under the Indian Reorganization Act (1934)—having rejected that act in national referendum—and thus no language in its governing law, a tribal code, required such a sanction.

The Opinion of the Court

We granted certiorari to decide whether the Navajo Tribe of Indians may tax business activities conducted on its land without first obtaining the approval of the Secretary of the Interior.

In 1978, the Navajo Tribal Council, the governing body of the Navajo Tribe of Indians, enacted two ordinances imposing taxes known as the Possessory Interest Tax and the Business Activity Tax. The Possessory Interest Tax is measured by the value of leasehold interests in tribal lands; the tax rate is 3 percent of the value of those interests. The Business Activity Tax is assessed on receipts from the sale of property produced or extracted within the Navajo Nation, and from the sale of services within the nation; a tax rate of 5 percent is applied after subtracting a standard deduction and specified expenses. The tax laws apply to both Navajo and non-Indian businesses, with dissatisfied taxpayers enjoying the right of appeal to the Navajo Tax Commission and the Navajo Court of Appeals.

The Navajo Tribe, uncertain whether federal approval was required, submitted the two tax laws to the Bureau of Indian Affairs of the Department of the Interior. The Bureau informed the Tribe that no federal statute or regulation required the Department of the Interior to approve or disapprove the taxes.

Before any taxes were collected, petitioner, a substantial mineral lessee on the Navajo Reservation, brought this action seeking to invalidate the taxes. Petitioner claimed in the United States District Court for the District of Arizona that the Navajo taxes were invalid without approval of the Secretary of the Interior. The District Court agreed and permanently enjoined the Tribe from enforcing its tax laws against petitioner.

The United States Court of Appeals for the Ninth Circuit reversed.... Relying on *Southland Royalty Co.* v. *Navajo Tribe of Indians* (1983), it held that no federal statute or principle of law mandated Secretarial approval.

We granted certiorari ... We affirm. ...

In *Merrion* v. *Jicarilla Apache Tribe* (1982), we held that the "power to tax is an essential attribute of Indian sovereignty because it is a necessary instrument of self-government and territorial management." Congress, of course, may erect "checkpoints that must be cleared before a tribal tax can take effect." Id., at 155. The issue in this case is whether Congress has enacted legislation requiring Secretarial approval of Navajo tax laws.

Petitioner suggests that the Indian Reorganization Act of 1934...is such a law. Section 16 of the IRA authorizes any tribe on a reservation to adopt a constitution and bylaws, subject to the approval of the Secretary of the Interior. The Act, however, does not provide that a tribal constitution must condition the power to tax on Secretarial approval. Indeed, the terms of the IRA do not govern tribes, like the Navajo, which declined to accept its provisions.

Many tribal constitutions written under the IRA in the 1930's called for Secretarial approval of tax laws affecting non-Indians. See, e.g., Constitution and Bylaws of the Rosebud Sioux Tribe of South Dakota, Art. 4, 1(h) (1935). But there were exceptions to this practice. For example, the 1937 Constitution and By-laws of the Saginaw Chippewa Indian Tribe of Michigan authorized the Tribal Council, without Secretarial approval, to "create and maintain a tribal council fund by levying taxes or assessments against members or non-members." Art. 6, 1(g). Thus the most that can be said about this period of constitution writing is that the Bureau of Indian Affairs, in assisting the drafting of tribal constitutions, had a policy of including provisions for Secretarial approval; but that policy was not mandated by Congress.

Nor do we agree that Congress intended to recognize as legitimate only those tribal taxes authorized by constitutions written under the IRA. Long before the IRA was enacted, the Senate Judiciary Committee acknowledged the validity of a tax imposed by the Chickasaw Nation on non-Indians....And in 1934, the Solicitor of the Department of the Interior published a formal opinion stating that a tribe possesses "the power of taxation [which] may be exercised over members of the tribe and over nonmembers."...The 73d Congress in passing the IRA to advance tribal self-government, see *Williams* v. *Lee* (1959), did nothing to limit the established, pre-existing power of the Navajos to levy taxes.

Some tribes that adopted constitutions in the early years of the IRA may be dependent on the Government in a way that the Navajos are not. However, such tribes are free, with the backing of the Interior Department, to amend their constitutions to remove the requirement of Secretarial approval. See, e.g., Revised Constitution and Bylaws of the Mississippi Band of Choctaw Indians, Art. 8, 1(r) (1975).

Petitioner also argues that the Indian Mineral Leasing Act of 1938... requires Secretarial approval of Navajo tax laws. Sections 1 through 3 of the 1938 Act establish procedures for leasing oil and gas interest on tribal lands. And Sec. 4 provides that "[a]ll operations under any oil, gas, or other mineral lease issued pursuant to the [Act] shall be subject to the rules and regulations promulgated by the Secretary of the Interior." Under this grant of authority, the Secretary has issued comprehensive regulations governing the operation of oil and gas leases....The Secretary, however, does not demand that tribal laws taxing mineral production be submitted for his approval.

Petitioner contends that the Secretary's decision not to review such tax laws is inconsistent with the statute. In *Merrion*, we emphasized the difference between a tribe's "role as commercial partner," and its "role as sovereign." The tribe acts as a commercial partner when it agrees to sell the right to the use of its land for mineral production, but the tribe acts as a sovereign when it imposes a tax on economic activities within its jurisdiction....Plainly Congress, in passing 4 of the 1938 Act, could make this same distinction.

Even assuming that the Secretary could review tribal laws taxing mineral production, it does not follow that he must do so. We are not inclined to impose upon the Secretary a duty that he has determined is not needed to satisfy the 1938 Act's basic purpose—to maximize tribal revenues from reservation lands....Thus, in light of our obligation to "tread lightly in the absence of clear indications of legislative intent," *Santa Clara Pueblo* v. *Martinez* (1978), we will not interpret a grant of authority to regulate leasing operations as a command to the Secretary to review every tribal tax relating to mineral production.

Finally, we do not believe that statutes requiring Secretarial supervision in other contexts...reveal that Congress has limited the Navajo Tribal Council's authority to tax non-Indians. As we noted in *New Mexico* v. *Mescalero Apache Tribe* (1983), the Federal Government is "firmly committed to the goal of promoting tribal self-government."...The power to tax members and non-Indians alike is surely an essential attribute of such self-government; the Navajos can gain independence from the Federal Government only by financing their own police force, schools, and social programs....

II

The Navajo Government has been called "probably the most elaborate" among tribes. The legitimacy of the Navajo Tribal Council, the freely elected governing body of the Navajos, is beyond question. We agree with the Court of Appeals that neither Congress nor the Navajos have found it necessary to subject the Tribal Council's tax laws to review by the Secretary of the Interior; accordingly, the judgment is Affirmed.

Sources:

Kerr-McGee Corporation v. *Navajo Tribe*, 471 U.S. 195 (1985).

Reno, Philip. *Navajo Resources and Economic Development.* Albuquerque: University of New Mexico Press, 1981.

Smith, Sherry L., and Brian Fehner, eds. *Indians and Energy: Exploitation and Opportunity in America's Southwest.* Santa Fe, NM: School for Advanced Research Press, 2010.

---

58   *Voices of Alaska Natives in Response to the 1971 Alaska Native Claims Settlement Act (1985)*

In 1983, Canadian jurist Thomas R. Berger was tapped by members of the Inuit Circumpolar Conference (an international organization of Inuit from Greenland,

Canada, and Alaska) and the World Council of Indigenous Peoples to review the potential problems and possibilities of the 1971 Alaska Native Claims Settlement Act (ANCSA) on Native lives and resources. ANCSA had provided Natives 962.5 million dollars and title to 44 million acres of land. It had also established thirteen regional corporations for Alaskan natives, with members defined as shareholders. The law was written so that in 1991 shares in the corporations could be sold to anyone, including non-Natives. Also, after that date, the state would be given authority to tax Native land, even in cases where the land did not generate revenue for the Native landowner.

Berger traveled across Alaska in 1983 and 1984 to hear what Alaskan Natives thought of ANSCA and what the future might hold. Below are some of the comments they offered.

———

Marie Schwind (Kotzebue): "I think that we are really fortunate to be given the time to speak up and address how we feel, how we personally feel, even though for a lot of us and I can say that for myself, is really hard to come up and try to address your personal feelings."

Tom Fields (Kotzebue): "Might say, that this is a good vehicle, a good time for us to say our feelings to the rest of the people in the region; where we are now and what we can do about it."

Dennis Tippleman (Kotzebue): "I don't look at Mister Berger as a person that is going to miraculously turn things around. He can only rephrase what, ultimately, all of us as individuals and collectively decide is going to happen next in how we view our world. That world can be as small and narrow as we interpret it, or as wide as the worldview that we have or the universal view that we have."

Lester Erhart (Yukon River): "This is a good start, anyway. It's a good, truthful start, just to find out what everybody thinks and do something that's going to be productive for all of us; not only us but the ones after us and everything, to keep it intact."

Richard King (Klukwan): "I'm glad at least I talk a little bit that you hear me, you hear me saying what I think. Thank you very much."

Sheila Aga Theriault (Larsen Bay): "I think this thing with having people come from the other Native villages is just fantastic because here we are in Larsen Bay, and we think our problems must be the only ones like them any place, but I know in every other village we're all doing with the same thing, and if we get our heads together periodically and talk about it among ourselves and decide what to do and then back that decision up all the way, I don't think it's too late."

Andrew Gronholdt (Sand Point): "This is the first concrete thing I've seen of somebody really come in here and talking to people about it. I think when you leave here, I think whoever came to this meeting here will understand it so much better." . . .

Lonnie Strong Hotch (Klukwan): "Sovereignty derives from the people.... Well, we, the people, are still here, and we still have our sovereignty. We can't wait for Washington, D.C., or Juneau. We should start acting like sovereigns. Why can't we pass our own laws?"

Virginia Commack (Shungnak): "Inupiat values...traditional councils have these values as backbones....Our Inupiat values are respectable. Our IRA's and the statewide tribes of Alaska are valuable and respectable—our key to survival."

Mike Albert (Tununak): "The Yup'iks had their own government for many years before the IRA was introduced. Yup'iks had their own instructions from way back, you know. That was government. The IRA has that and that's its job. And that whole idea is powerful and can be defined by one word by the White men: sovereignty." ...

Sources:

Berger, Thomas R. *Village Journey: The Report of the Alaska Native Review Commission.* New York: Hill & Wang, 1985.

Case, David S., and David A. Voluck. *Alaska Natives and American Law*, 2nd ed. Fairbanks: University of Alaska Press, 2002.

59   *Coyote Valley Band of Pomo Indians v. United States (1986)*

A decade into the Tribal self-determination era, increasing numbers of Native nations sought to exercise their sovereignty by amending or significantly rewriting their constitutions to better meet the needs of their populations and to more authentically reflect their own understanding of nationhood. In some cases, the Bureau of Indian Affairs and the Secretary of the Interior attempted to stymie these efforts, claiming the Tribes were not fully prepared to wield genuine self-governance. In this case, several California Tribes and an individual Native citizen successfully challenged the government's efforts to suppress their sovereignty.

———

Plaintiffs are an individual Native American, Wanda Carrillo, and three Native American tribes, Coyote Valley Band of Pomo Indians, Hopland Band of Pomo Indians, and Karuk Tribe of California. All three tribes are federally recognized tribal entities which have a government-to- government relationship with the United States and are eligible for programs administered by the Bureau of Indian Affairs (BIA).

On April 9, 1984, plaintiffs brought this action seeking declaratory and injunctive relief against the United States of America, the Secretary of the Interior, and various officials of the BIA. Plaintiffs allege that defendants acted arbitrarily, capriciously, and in direct violation of federal law and their trust responsibility to plaintiffs by (1) unreasonably delaying the calling of secretarial elections on their draft constitutions under the Indian Reorganization Act of

1934 (IRA); (2) establishing an unwritten policy requiring BIA review and approval of IRA draft constitutions prior to authorizing elections; (3) failing to adopt uniform standard for reviewing and approving IRA constitutions; and (4) refusing to provide BIA benefits and services to plaintiffs until after the calling of IRA elections.

In their cross-motions for summary judgment, the parties present a question of first impression which requires the court to interpret provisions of the IRA as well as various regulations promulgated pursuant to that Act. At the heart of this controversy is the proper interpretation of 25 U.S.C. § 476 which authorizes any recognized Indian tribe to organize for its common welfare and to adopt an appropriate constitution by a majority vote of the adult members of the tribe. Tribal ratification of a draft constitution in such a manner cannot be accomplished until the Secretary of the Interior authorizes a special election.

Plaintiffs challenge the Secretary's practice of withholding authorization of special elections until after the completion of a lengthy process for the review and modification of proposed tribal constitutions by the BIA. They contend that the Secretary has delayed authorization of elections for several years from the time of the tribes' initial request for elections because the tribes did not willingly incorporate the BIA's suggested modification into their draft constitutions.

Plaintiffs maintain that, in order to be consistent with the statutory policy in favor of tribal self-government, section 476 of the IRA must be interpreted to impose upon the Secretary a mandatory, nondiscretionary duty to authorize election within a reasonable time after a final request from an eligible tribe. It is their view that, while defendants may offer recommendations for the modification of draft constitutional provisions prior to elections, the Secretary has the discretion to approve or disapprove the constitution only after an election has been held and the constitution officially ratified by the majority vote of tribal members. Plaintiffs therefore assert that the Secretary's failure to call elections at this stage of the process violates defendants' trust responsibility to them under 25 U.S.C. § 476 of the IRA, regulations promulgated thereunder, and 5 U.S.C. § 706(2)(A) of the Administrative Procedure Act ("APA"). They also assert that the BIA's failure to publish its existing procedure for the preelection review and approval of draft constitutions violates 5 U.S.C. §§ 552 and 553 of the APA.

Defendants take the position that the Secretary has broad, unreviewable discretion to approve the draft constitution in all particulars before he authorizes an election under section 476. In the alternative, if secretarial discretion is reviewable, defendants argue that the Secretary's decision to withhold elections was neither arbitrary nor capricious. They maintain that section 476 authorizes the Secretary only to conduct elections on "appropriate" constitutions, i.e., those with provisions which conform with his interpretation of federal law. Elections, they argue, are too costly and should not be called unless the tribal constitution has received prior approval from the Secretary. Otherwise the election would be a meaningless formality because the Secretary would certainly disapprove the constitution after tribal members had ratified it....

Conclusion

The Court finds that defendants' failure to call elections within a reasonable time after plaintiffs' final requests for elections is unlawful under 5 U.S.C. § 706(2)(A) of the APA. Defendants' conduct contravenes the procedures described in 25 U.S.C. § 476 and the accompanying administrative regulation, 25 C.F.R. § 81.5(a). The language of section 476, the policies underlying the statute, and defendants' own administrative regulations all support the conclusion that the Secretary has a mandatory duty to call elections upon a request from an eligible tribe.

Since the court has decided that defendants' current practice of requiring secretarial approval of draft constitutions prior to elections is contrary to law, it is not necessary to address plaintiffs' additional contention that defendants violated the APA by failing to publish that invalid procedure.

In light of the foregoing, it is ordered:

1. That plaintiffs' motion for summary judgment is granted; and
2. That defendants' motion for summary judgment is denied....

Sources:

Coyote Valley Band of Pomo Indians v. *United States*, 639 F. Supp. 165 (1986).

Jaranko, Timothy W., and Mark C. Van Norman. "Indian Self-Determination at Bay: Secretarial Authority to Disapprove Tribal Constitutional Amendments." *Gonzaga Law Review* 81 (1993–1994). 29 Gonz. L. Rev. 81–103n88.

60

Oglala Sioux Nation President Joe American Horse and Senator Bill Bradley (D-NJ) on the Sioux Nation Black Hills Act (1986)

The eight member nations of the Great Sioux Nation—Oglala, Cheyenne River, Rosebud, Standing Rock, Lower Brule, Crow Creek, Santee Sioux of Nebraska, and Fort Peck Sioux Tribe of Montana—negotiated one of the last great multinational treaties with the United States: the Fort Laramie Treaty of 1868. Less than a decade after the treaty's ratification, they saw their immense reserved lands illegally invaded and overwhelmed by gold-diggers, silver miners, and unauthorized military personnel led by Lt. Col. George A. Custer.

When Custer and his troops were killed in 1876 by a large force of Lakota, led by Sitting Bull and Crazy Horse, the US Congress, incensed and aroused by the defeat, attached a legislative rider to the 1876 Indian Appropriation Act that unjustly denied Native citizens their appropriations and treaty annuities unless they agreed to sell the Black Hills to the United States.

The US then sent another treaty commission to the Tribes charged with securing the signatures of three-fourths of the adult males as required by the 1868 treaty. While they were able to secure only about 10 percent of the requisite signatures, Congress nonetheless ratified the agreement into law in 1877. Upon passage of this measure, 7.7 million acres of Native lands were confiscated by the federal government; a unilateral violation of Lakota sovereignty and property and an abrogation of key provisions of the 1868 treaty.

The decades that followed were marked by further violations of Lakota sovereignty and greater loss of lands. Tribal nations were forced onto ever-smaller tracts. In 1920, the Nations were finally able to pursue legal redress for their immense property losses when Congress enacted a special statute allowing them to do so. In 1923 a lawsuit, filed in the Court of Claims, asserted the US had taken the Black Hills unlawfully and in violation of the Fifth Amendment.

This lawsuit was unsuccessful as were subsequent legal efforts until 1974, when the Indian Claims Commission held the Black Hills had, indeed, been unconstitutionally taken and Tribal nations, while not entitled to a land return, were due $17.5 million plus interest. The decision was upheld by the Court of Claims in 1979 and by the US Supreme Court in *U.S. v. Sioux Nation* in 1980.

By that time, the eight Lakota nations had each adopted resolutions expressing their unequivocal opposition to a monetary settlement, insisting the land should be returned. The situation remained at an impasse until 1985, when Sen. Bill Bradley (D-NJ) introduced the Sioux Nation Black Hills Act which called for payment *plus* restoration of about 1.3 million acres owned by the federal government in the Black Hills. At the bill's hearing, Bradley gave his rationale for the measure and Tribal leaders responded, including Joe American Horse of the Oglala Lakota Nation. While supported by all the Lakota leaders, the bill was never embraced by the South Dakota congressional delegation, governor or lawmakers and ultimately failed to pass.

The 1980 judgment of $17.5 million plus interest, which at that time amounted to $104 million, remains untouched in the US Treasury where it is held on behalf of the nations. As of 2018, although the total amount has grown to more than $1.2 billion, the Lakota nations refuse to accept anything less than the return of the Black Hills and acknowledgment of their treaty rights.

Statement of Bill Bradley, U.S. Senator from New Jersey

Thank you very much, Mr. Chairman and Senator Inouye. Thank you very much for the chance to come before the committee, and let me express my appreciation to you, Mr. Chairman, for scheduling this hearing. I think it is important that you have demonstrated the seriousness with which you treat this issue by scheduling the hearing and allowing the representatives of the Sioux Nation to come before the committee today, as well as other interested parties, to offer their views of this legislation.

Mr. Chairman, the legislation considered today has a simple purpose: to right a wrong committed by the United States more than 100 years ago. The bill would restore to the Sioux Tribes a portion of the lands awarded to them by the 1868 treaty and subsequently illegally taken from them.

In 1851—and some of this history you have gone over—the Sioux Nation signed a treaty that established a large Sioux reservation including all of the present state of South Dakota as well as parts of Nebraska, Wyoming, North Dakota, and Montana. However, in its deliberations, the U.S. Senate added amendments which were rejected by the Sioux, and the treaty was never finally ratified.

The result was the Powder River War of 1866–67. The war ended in a second treaty, signed at Fort Laramie on April 29, 1868, and later ratified by the Senate. It established the Great Sioux Reservation which included approximately half of South Dakota, essentially everything west of the Missouri River, and authorized extensive hunting grounds covering large parts of North Dakota, Wyoming, Colorado, Kansas, and Nebraska. The United States "solemnly agreed" that no unauthorized persons "shall ever be permitted to pass over, settle upon, or reside in this territory."

Prior to signing the treaty, both the U.S. Government and the Sioux knew that at least small deposits of gold existed in the Black Hills, the western-most portion of the Great Sioux Reservation. In 1874, following rumors of large deposits, Lt. Col. George Custer led an expedition into the Black Hills which confirmed the existence of gold. Despite the terms of the treaty requiring the U.S. government to keep non-Indians out of the reservation, prospectors swarmed into the region. In 1875, President Grant unilaterally decided to abandon the treaty obligations.

The Government attempted to buy the land in 1876 from the Sioux for about $6 million but the Sioux dismissed this offer. Negotiations broke down, leading to further violence which culminated in the Sioux victory over Custer at Little Big Horn.

That victory was short-lived, however. The Sioux were soon defeated and were deprived of horses and weapons. They were returned to the reservation and became dependent on the government for their survival.

The Government threatened the Sioux with starvation unless they ceded the Black Hills back to the federal government. Another commission was sent to negotiate with the Sioux, but the negotiations consisted of presenting the Sioux with a prepared treaty text which the tribes had no choice but to accept. The Sioux were forced to give up all rights to the Black Hills as well as to their hunting grounds in lands outside the reservation.

Since 1877, the Sioux have contested this taking in a number of lawsuits. In 1974, the Indian Claims Commission found the Sioux claims to be legitimate and awarded the Sioux $17 million, the value of the land in 1877, plus interest which amounted to $88 million. In 1980, the Supreme Court affirmed the award of the commission, citing in its conclusion that "a more ripe and rank case of dishonorable dealing will never, in all probability, be found in our history."

The Fort Laramie Treaty had provided that none of the lands set aside for the Sioux could be ceded back to the government without consent of three-quarters of all adult males. The 1877 Treaty was signed by only about 10 percent of adult males. Ignoring this, Congress enacted the agreement into law, and it is this law that the Supreme Court found unconstitutional in 1980.

The $105 million—$17 million plus interest since 1877—was appropriated in 1980 and is drawing interest in an account at Treasury. That fund now amounts to approximately $160 million.

The Sioux have maintained that the Black Hills should not be sold. They have argued that their claims to their ancestral lands should not be relinquished. The Black Hills have a deep religious significance for the Sioux Nation, a significance this government should respect. As others at this hearing can eloquently testify, to the Sioux, the Black Hills are sacred. They call the Black Hills "the heart of everything that is," and later testimony will elaborate on that point.

The bill we consider today is a recognition of the errors of the past. The claims courts could only award monetary compensation for the illegal taking of the Sioux land. It is within the power of Congress to mitigate the wrong in another way, by restoring some of the land.

Of the 7.3 million acres taken from the Sioux in 1877, this bill would return up to 1.3 million acres. The bill would cede to the Sioux Nation only those portions of the Black Hills region that are still federally owned and not all Federal land would be ceded. For example, Mount Rushmore would not be touched. Land for court houses, buildings, rights-of-way, and military bases would not be affected. No private or State-owned lands would be transferred.

In addition, the bill provides that nothing shall deprive any person or government of any valid existing right to access mineral leases, timber leases, grazing rights, permits, or contracts. As compensation to the Sioux for having been deprived of the use of these lands since 1877, the bill would award them the amount of money already appropriated and drawing interest in the Treasury. Finally, the bill establishes a Sioux National Park to be owned and operated by the Sioux Nation and open to all.

Mr. Chairman, history will judge us by our deeds. We now have an opportunity to write a new chapter in the history of our deeds dealing with the Sioux people. This new chapter could, indeed, be one of honor and of understanding, and I hope we do not allow this opportunity to slip away....

Statement of Joe American Horse, President, Oglala Sioux Tribe

Mr. Chairman and members of the Committee

My name is Joe American Horse. I am President of the Oglala Sioux Tribe. The Tribe is one of the eight Lakota tribes which formerly comprised the Sioux

Nation recognized by the United States in many treaties. The Tribe occupies the Pine Ridge Indian Reservation, which was once a part of the Great Sioux Reservation set aside for the Sioux Nation by the Fort Laramie Treaty of April 29, 1868. We appreciate the opportunity to testify before the committee on this important piece of legislation.

The Oglala Sioux Tribe was instrumental in organizing and supporting the Black Hills Steering Committee in a unified effort of the various Sioux tribes to develop legislation for the return of the federal land in the Black Hills to the Sioux Nation. The bill that was introduced by Senator Bill Bradley of New Jersey, S. 1453, is essentially the bill that was developed through this organized effort. We therefore support S. 1453 and urge the committee and the United States Congress to support the return of the federal lands in the Black Hills to the Sioux Nation. The bill corrects a century old wrong against the Lakota people caused by the United States taking of the Black Hills in violation of the 1868 Treaty and the United States Constitution.

The history of the federal government's takeover of the Black Hills and the tribes' attempts to recover this sacred area is long and complex. The Black Hills were at the heart of the Lakota territory recognized under the Treaty of September 17, 1851, which included all of the present state of South Dakota, and parts of what is now Nebraska, Wyoming, North Dakota and Montana. Repeated unlawful incursions into the Lakota territory led to the Powder River War of 1866–1867 in which the Sioux tribes, led by the great chief, Red Cloud, were undefeated by federal troops. The tribes' successes in the war led to the Fort Laramie Treaty of 1868, considered by some commentators to have been a complete victory for Red Cloud and the Sioux. One commentator describes the treaty as "the only instance in the history of the United States where the government has gone to war and afterwards negotiated a peace conceding everything demanded by the enemy and exacting nothing in return."

The Fort Laramie Treaty established the Great Sioux Reservation, which included approximately half the area of what is now the state of South Dakota, including all of the state west of the Missouri River save for a narrow strip in the far western portion. The reservation also included a narrow strip of land west of the Missouri and north of the border between North and South Dakota. The United States pledged that the reservation would be "set apart for the absolute and undisturbed use and occupation of the Indians herein named." The government "solemnly agreed" that no unauthorized persons "shall ever be permitted to pass over, settle upon, or reside in this territory." The Sioux also retained hunting rights outside the reservation and north of the North Platte River. In return, the Indians agreed to not oppose the building of railroads that did not pass over their reservation lands, not to engage in attacks on settlers, and to withdraw their opposition to the military posts and roads that had been established south of the North Platte River....

The 1868 Treaty brought relative peace to the Dakotas, until the greed of non-Indians for the gold in the Black Hills caused the United States government to breach its promise to the Sioux people. Prior to the Treaty, both the United States government and the Sioux people knew that at least small deposits of gold existed in the Black Hills. In 1874, following rumors of large deposits,

Lieutenant Colonel George Armstrong Custer led a military and exploratory expedition into the Black Hills in violation of the Fort Laramie Treaty. The expedition confirmed the existence of large deposits of gold in the Black Hills, creating an intense popular demand for the opening of the Hills for settlement by non-Indians.

Initially, the United States Army made some feeble attempts to exclude prospectors and settlers from trespassing on lands reserved to the Indians, as it was obligated to do under the Fort Laramie Treaty. At the same time, however, the Army supported the extinguishment by Congress of the Indian title to the land....

Settlement of the Black Hills increased once the Army had stopped excluding trespassers. The Sioux Nation refused an offer by a federal commission to buy the Black Hills for $6 million, due to the religious value of the land to the Sioux people. Subsequently, in the winter of 1875–1876, the secretary of the interior declared Indians hunting off the reservation in the exercise of their hunting rights under the Fort Laramie Treaty "hostiles" and turned them over to the jurisdiction of the War Department. Despite Crazy Horse's famous victory over Custer's forces at Little Big Horn, the Indians soon surrendered to the Army and were returned to the reservation and deprived of their weapons and horses, leaving them completely dependent for survival on government rations.

Defeated and impoverished by the United States, the Lakota were unable effectively to resist the conditions imposed on them in a so-called "agreement" enacted into law as the Act of February 28, 1877. Under this statute, the Sioux were deprived of their rights to the Black Hills and other lands west of the 103rd meridian, and their rights to hunt in the unceded territories, in exchange for subsistence rations for as long as they would be needed to ensure their survival. Article 12 of the Fort Laramie Treaty, requiring that any cession of lands within the Great Sioux Reservation be joined by three-fourths of the adult males, was ignored by the federal government and violated by the Congress when it enacted the statute. The agreement was presented only to the Sioux Chiefs and their leading men and signed by only 10 percent of the adult male Sioux population....

Despite the illegality of the government's actions, the Sioux were without a forum in which to present their claims until Congress passed a special jurisdictional statute in 1920. In 1923, pursuant to that statute, the Sioux Tribe's filed a petition with the Court of Claims alleging that the government had taken the Black Hills without just compensation in violation of the Fifth Amendment. The court dismissed the claim on jurisdictional grounds in 1942. In 1950, attorneys for the tribes resubmitted the Black Hills claim to the Indian Claims Commission, pursuant to the Indian Claims Commission Act of 1946. In 1975, the Court of Claims ruled against the Tribes' argument that the taking was unconstitutional, on the grounds that the Tribes have already lost that issue in the 1942 decision. Subsequently, Congress passed Public Law 95–254 in 1978, directing the Court of Claims to decide the case de novo without regard to the 1942 decision. The court subsequently found for the Tribes, and an award of $17.1 million plus simple interest was affirmed by the Supreme Court in 1980.

The Oglala Sioux tribe chose not to refile the Black Hills case under P.L. 95–254, deciding instead to seek the restoration of federal lands in the Black

Hills to the Sioux Nation. The Tribe filed suit in 1980 in federal district court arguing that the United States, in taking the Black Hills, unconstitutionally exercised its power of eminent domain because the land was taken for private rather than a public purpose. The Eighth Circuit affirmed the district court's dismissal of this case, holding that the Indian Claims Commission Act provided the Tribe with an effective and exclusive remedy for the alleged wrongful taking of the Black Hills....

Despite the decision of the Eighth Circuit and the award over $100 million with interest to the Sioux Tribes in the Black Hills, the Oglala Sioux Tribe has not and will not accept money as compensation for the illegal and unconstitutional taking of the sacred Black Hills. The Black Hills were never and will never be for sale. To demonstrate how adamant our people are in seeking land restoration, I would like to point out that Shannon County, located entirely within the Pine Ridge Indian Reservation, is listed by the Bureau of Census as the poorest county in the United States. Yet our people continue to reject the money and demand a return of federal land.

The Sioux claim for a return of the Black Hills is based on a combination of factors not present in other Indian land restoration efforts. The principal elements are 1) the Supreme Court has ruled that the government illegally confiscated the land through a "ripe and rank case of dishonorable dealings;" and 2) land is sacred to the Sioux people. On two prior occasions, Congress has returned federal land containing sacred religious sites to Indian tribes. In 1970, Congress returned Blue Lake, the most sacred shrine to the Taos Pueblo since the early fourteenth century.... Similarly, in 1978 Congress returned Zuni Salt Lake, a sacred shrine of the Zuni Tribe and the site of annual pilgrimages, to the Zuni Tribe....

The claim for the Black Hills is even more compelling than were these claims because it also involves the illegal taking of the land by the federal government. Moreover, because of the unique combination of illegal taking by the federal government and the religious significance of the land, granting the Black Hills claim will not necessarily set a precedent for other possible tribal land claims where such factors are not present.

Finally, the proposed legislation protects the interests and rights of non-Indians. The bill would return only federal lands, not private or state lands. Section 8 provides that title to and use of state and private lands within the reestablished area shall not be disturbed. Section 16 preserves valid existing rights of use or possession in lands conveyed to the Sioux Nation currently held by any individual or government. That section protects the rights of persons holding mineral leases, grazing permits, timber leases, [and] permits or contracts from the federal government.

The Oglala Sioux Tribe urges this committee and the Congress to correct a long-standing wrong committed by the United States government in illegally confiscating the Black Hills in 1877 against the will of the Sioux people, in a series of events which the Court of Claims has characterized as a "ripe and rank case of dishonorable dealings," in a decision affirmed by the US Supreme Court. The return of federal land would be in keeping with the wishes of the Indian people for return of our land rather than a monetary settlement, while recognizing the existing rights of non-Indians to lands within the restored area....

Sources:

Deloria, Vine, Jr. "Reflections on the Black Hills Claim," *Wicazo Sa Review* 4, no. 1 (Spring 1988): 33–38.

Dunbar Ortiz, Roxanne. *The Great Sioux Nation: Sitting in Judgment on America: An Oral History of the Sioux Nation and Its Struggle for Sovereignty.* New York: Moon Books/Random House, 1977.

Orr, Raymond I. *Reservation Politics: Historical Trauma, Economic Development, and Intratribal Conflict.* Norman: University of Oklahoma Press, 2017.

US Senate. "Sioux Nation Black Hills Act." Hearing Before the Select Committee on Indian Affairs. 99th Cong., 2nd Sess. on S. 1453. Washington, DC: Government Printing Office, 1986.

61

Earl Old Person, Blackfeet Nation Chairman, Statement on Indian Tribal Taxation (1987)

Earl Old Person, a long-time hereditary chief of the Blackfeet Nation of Montana, also served as chairman of his nation from 1964–2008. An advocate of Tribal education and economic development, he served on numerous national organizations, including the National Advisory Council on Aging. In the testimony below, he urged Congress not to support S. 1039, which was designed to review and determine the impact of Tribal taxation on reservations and their Native and non-Native residents. Old Person and the Tribal council wanted, instead, to shift attention to state and federal taxation levels, which he argued were more onerous than Tribal taxes. Tribal governments had begun to focus more on the development of taxation programs to provide much-needed revenue, but such programs were interpreted as causing distress for some. Non-Indian individuals, non-Indian businesses, and local and state governments were lobbying strenuously against any expansion of Tribal taxation.

Mr. Chairman, thank you for the opportunity to appear before this Committee and voice my opinion on Senate Bill 1039 which has been introduced by Senator Melcher and Senator Baucus from my home state of Montana, along with Senator Simpson from Wyoming.

Mr. Chairman, the Blackfeet Tribal Business Council has carefully reviewed, considered and discussed Senate Bill 1039. The Tribal Council subsequently passed Tribal Resolution No. 40–88 which opposes Senate Bill 1039 and instead urges that the focus of any review for the adverse impact of taxation on Indian Reservations be shifted to an examination of the levels of federal and state taxation, which far exceed the level of tribal taxation.

The power to levy and collect taxes is an inherent aspect of the retained sovereignty of Indian tribes. This is a power which, until relatively recently, was not exercised for a number of reasons. Tribes have sufficient alternative sources of income to continue to meet the demand for the delivery of goods and services which are constantly placed on tribal government. On my own reservation, prices were high, which meant more revenues from my tribe. Cattle prices are good, which meant that our ranchers would make a living on their own terms without having to rely on the tribe. The timber industry was active and the tribe as a result was realizing revenues from this industry. The tribe was able to lease its own land to Indian and non-Indian farmers and ranchers and realized even more revenues. In summary the level of tribal revenues was sufficient to satisfy the demands which were placed on the Tribal Council in which the Tribal Council expected to satisfy.

Meanwhile, the federal government and state government all along have taxed individuals and commercial activities on the reservation, to the exclusion of tribal taxation. The typical attitude of the state of Montana has been that the state will continue to tax whatever they want. The result has been litigation, and the tribe has been successful in every lawsuit concerning the state's authority to tax the tribe and tribal members. Today, we are faced with the situation where tribal revenues are not sufficient to satisfy the demands of the residents at the Blackfeet Indian reservation. In 1982, for example, total tribal revenues were $7,911,436. In 1984, tribal revenues decreased to $4,693,918. For fiscal year 1988, tribal revenues are projected at $4,085,188.

The Blackfeet Tribe is continuing to supply Congress and Reservation non-Indians proof of services (although we are proud that we can prove that we provide such a wide range of services—I've attached documents to demonstrate this proof of services—I might point out that the state does not have to supply this information when they impose a tax on the reservation).

The tribe is pursuing an economic model which will benefit all residents of the Blackfeet Indian Reservation. The Tribe is majority stakeholder in the Blackfeet Indian Writing Company, which manufactures and markets writing instruments. The Blackfeet National Bank recently began operations as a federally chartered, Tribally-owned bank to serve the reservation and enhance the local economy. The Blackfeet Tribe recently purchased 100 percent of the capital stock of Advertising Corporation of America, a company active in the specialty advertising industry. This company will be relocated to the Blackfeet Reservation so that more employment opportunities can be provided. Also, the tribe has had a principal role in the establishment of Heart Butte Industries, a Tribally-owned clothing industry on the Reservation which has negotiated major contracts with Commonwealth Edison of Cincinnati, Ohio. This industry is currently employing about forty people.

The point I'm making is that the Blackfeet tribe has taken the predominant, if not the sole, role in advancing the lifestyle of Reservation residents.

State taxation has historically served as a negative factor because the truth is that the state and counties have not put back into the Reservation any amount of funds near the amount of taxes which have been collected from Reservation residence and Reservation businesses. Further, the levels of federal and state taxation are in turn disproportionate to the actual level of Tribal taxation. For example, total state taxation on oil and gas production is approximately 22–25 percent. This compares with the Tribe's level of taxation at 4.25 percent. Yet, the natural resource being taxed belongs to the Tribe or the Tribal members in most instances. This is an unfairness which is never addressed or proposed to be addressed, by Senate Bill 1039, or any other act of Congress. Someone should tell the Blackfeet tribe and the other Indian tribes what is improper about limiting federal and state taxation on Indian reservations so that the reservation economies can truly sustain themselves. That is where true progress can be made so that a true reservation economy will be dynamic enough to be self-sustaining.

The Blackfeet Tribe and other Indian Tribes do not want a continued fostering of the creation of an artificial economy. That is what an authorization of $525,000,000 under Senate Bill 1039 does. We who live on the reservations have said for years and years that the true answer to the proper exercise of sovereign powers is the establishment of strong Indian sovereigns who possess the capacity and professional judgments to make well considered, fair-minded decisions. A continued strong reliance on the federal government is not the answer. Besides, the $525,000,000 is merely an authorization, and not an actual appropriation. Appropriations in this era of balanced budget mandates is simply not guaranteed by Senate Bill 1039, nor is it an attractive concept.

With respect to the argument that tribal taxation without representation is occurring, I would point out a number of things. First, the Blackfeet Tribal Business Council has adopted a policy regarding tribal ordinances in general, and commercial and tax ordinances in particular. The policy mandates a public hearing with due notice to all affected parties. This is the policy and it has been closely adhered to.

Second, the Tribe often mandates a specified period of time for public comment, frequently in the form of written comment. The Tribe had followed a pattern of publishing an entire piece of Tribal legislation in the local newspaper, holding public hearings and soliciting written comments. This proved to be too costly, so the Tribe has made individual copies of the proposed legislation available to the public well in advance of the hearing date. Thus, anyone had the opportunity to review the legislation and express their views. The copies are provided at Tribal expense.

If these methods of public input are insufficient, affected parties are always welcome to appear before the Tribal Council and express their concerns and recommendations. In my years of serving on the Council, I have found many non-Indians pursue this avenue. Not once have they been denied the right and opportunity to discuss matters with the Council directly. I would go so far as to say that the individual who lives on the Blackfeet Reservation has more access to the Tribal government than any other government because of the frequency with which we meet.

I fail to understand the rationale behind arguments that the Blackfeet tribe and other Indians are practicing taxation without representation. Tribal taxation is a legitimate exercise of a sovereign nation's authority to generate revenues. For instance, if I travel to a state where a sales tax has been enacted I must pay this tax. I have no choice not to pay, nor do I have the right to vote. I have subjected myself to that sovereign's jurisdiction as long as I remain within its territory. The same principle applies when non-Tribal members come to the territory of an Indian Tribe. So the concept of sovereign taxation is not unique when the sovereign exercise of power and authority to tax occurs amongst Indian tribes.

The sad fact of the matter is that the Blackfeet Tribe and other Indian Tribes cannot afford to operate at a deficit. The Tribes must retain the inherent authority to tax in order to sustain the quantitative and qualitative standards of the delivery of goods and services to the residents of the Blackfeet Indian Reservation. Senate Bill 1039 would stop the process of Tribal sovereign development and reduce Indian Tribes to what they had historically been, totally dependent on the federal government for minimal survival. We don't want this. We want to continue to experience the opportunities of self-development, and we want to take our rightful place in the national and international arena of sovereign-to-sovereign relations and relationships. For these reasons, the Blackfeet Tribe opposes Senate Bill 1039. Thank you.

Source:

US Senate. "Indian Tribal Taxation." Hearing Before the Select Committee on Indian Affairs. 100th Cong., 1st Sess. on S. 1039. Washington, DC: Government Printing Office, 1988.

62   *Testimony of Joseph B. Delacruz, Chairman, Quinault Indian Nation (1987)*

On December 2, 1987, Senator Daniel Inouye (D-HI) introduced S. Con. Res. 76, "a resolution to acknowledge the contribution of the Iroquois Confederacy of Nations to the development of the United States Constitution and to reaffirm the continuing government-to-government relationship between Indian tribes in the United States as established in the Constitution." This was a controversial measure, and the hearing brought together numerous voices to discuss the Iroquois' contributions to the federal Constitution, as well as to discuss and attempt to clarify the actual political status of Native nations vis-à-vis the US.

Joseph Delacruz, who walked on in 2000, was a well-respected leader of his Pacific coastal nation and served as president of NCAI from 1981–1984. He gave testimony that focused on his tenure with the latter and highlighted some of the distinctive traits of Indigenous political, legal, and cultural authority.

———

I appreciate the privilege and honor to testify today before the Senate Select Committee on Indian Affairs…I certainly hope this Congressional Resolution will serve to educate the American public as to American Indian tribal sovereignty as embodied in the U.S. Constitution and create meaningful improvements in the relationship between American Indian tribes and the United States.

I recently participated in a forum hosted by the Alliance of American Indian Leaders and the Indian Rights Association in Philadelphia, in commemoration of the Bicentennial of the Constitution to explore the topic: "In Search of 'A More Perfect Union:' American Indian Tribes and the United States Constitution." It was an enlightening and saddening experience to refresh my knowledge of the United States and American Indian Tribes at the time of the Constitution and the historic relationship established between sovereign nations. American Indian people have suffered, endured, and survived over the last 200 years despite the assurances of the Constitution, the Northwest Ordinance of 1787, and solemn agreements between leaders of nations.…

American Indian tribal governments are unique to the federal system by virtue of their treaty-trust relationship with the United States. Unfortunately, the historical evolution of the United States-Tribal relationship has allowed a dominating federal bureaucracy to permeate and control most aspects of tribal government operations.

American Public Needs to Be Educated About American Indian Treaties, Governments, and Cultures

The Congress, federal bureaucrats, and the general American public have minimum knowledge about American Indian Tribal governments, their distinct cultural heritages, their sovereign status as dependent nations, their contributions to society, the meaning of their treaties, and their clear legal right to existence in modern society. Generally, we are understood in the context of Hollywood and the brief historical anecdotes included in high school American history textbooks.

This limited public knowledge creates obvious opportunities for political mischief and negative racism. In the Congress, we are constantly involved in the education process whether promoting positive policies or opposing negative legislation in Indian affairs. With the federal bureaucracy, we daily confront policies, regulations, and program requirements promulgated for the general system of governments, which negatively impact our sovereign tribal status. And, the general public is most susceptible to an ever-present network of anti-Indian hate groups fed by greed and racism whose public agenda is to destroy Tribal treaty rights and steal Tribal resources. As Tribal governments have more assertively protected their rights and resources in Congress and the courts in recent years, these anti-Indian organizations have grown proportionately spreading negative misinformation. Sadly, there continues to be politicians at all levels most willing to capitalize on these negative elements within their constituencies.

I am heartened in my travels to experience general public interest and support for American Indian people when they are informed on the issues. In Washington State many misunderstandings have been resolved and a spirit of mutual respect and cooperation is prevailing due to a process of public dialogue and education. I believe Senate Concurrent Resolution 76 should serve as the cornerstone to fully inform the American public through research, media, and public forums as to our rightful place in history and in the modern world....

Self-sufficiency among Indian peoples means that Indian nations are able to govern their country and peoples without external interference; Indian peoples can renew their natural creative abilities to feed themselves, house themselves, and clothe themselves, relying on their own labor and natural resources; Indian peoples can freely decide how to best serve their social and health needs; and, as self-sufficient societies Indian nations expect the United States of America to uphold its agreements and treaties to "preserve, protect and guarantee the rights and property" of Indian nations against encroachments and fraud. Clearly, Indian nations believe self-sufficiency must lead to their perpetual existence as distinct social, economic, and political societies....

As NCAI President, I proposed in a speech before the Fortieth Annual Convention...in 1983 "that we make a decisive departure from the recurring issues that divert our attention from the most important priorities of initiatives necessary to establish meaningful government-to- government relations with the United States." I proposed to Indian leaders that we take "the next logical step beyond the Indian Self-Determination Act" with the enactment of a *Tribal-Grant-In-Aid* act to include:

> "The act would authorize five-year financial agreements between Indian nations and the United States, negotiated to cover Tribal government operations, economic development, housing, health and human services, and other tribally-determined needs. The Grant-In-Aid would require a line item appropriation from Congress for each Indian government concluding an agreement with the U.S. as disbursed through the Department of the Treasury. The Act would include a transition clause allowing Tribal governments a supportive bridge from P.L 93–638 contracting to grant-in-aid management. Each agreement, of course, would provide that the trust relationship and obligations of the U.S. will be upheld"

Although a Tribal Grant-in-Aid Act has not been achieved, I believe substantial progress has been made in the Senate Indian Self-Determination Act Amendments of 1987 to streamline the contracting process....

I firmly believe it is appropriate for American Indian Tribal leadership, the federal government, and Congress to begin consultation and dialogue on the possible restructuring of the federal management of American Indian affairs. I don't expect that a new federal mechanism to protect the trust responsibility and deliver resources or services to be a major expansion of federal expenditures. I envision that an independent, separate, or autonomous federal structure would consolidate functions and resources, reduce the size of the Indian affairs bureaucracy, increase appropriations and management capacities at the Tribal government level, and maximize the utilization of federal appropriations designated for Indian country. This new federal Indian affairs structure, designed by American Indian leadership and established through formal agreement between Indian Tribes and the United States, could feasibly accommodate the broad spectrum of development needs in Indian Country from those Tribes most dependent on the federal presence to Tribal governments seeking the greatest degree of self-government....

Indian leaders over the last 100 years have sought an array of federal structures with cabinet-level status to manage Indian affairs. In 1974, the National Congress of American Indians unanimously endorsed a position paper entitled, *Proposal for Readjustment of Indian Affairs* ... which urged the "establishment of independent federal governmental machinery to replace the Bureau of Indian Affairs." ...

Obviously, any restructuring of the federal management of Indian Affairs will require extensive dialogue, debate, and negotiation to achieve a mutually agreeable strategy and structure. I urge consideration of establishing a formal consultation process between Tribes, the succeeding United States administrations, and Congress. It is literally essential that Tribal leadership is directly involved in improving the federal administration of Indian Affairs. Tribal governments and their leaders, when directly involved in the development of agreements, have proven the importance of their direct involvement. A recent example is the ratification and implementation of the US-Canada Pacific Salmon Treaty ratified by Congress in 1985. Twenty-four Pacific Northwest Tribal representatives were substantively involved in the treaty negotiation process involving the departments of State, Commerce, and Interior; the States of Washington, Oregon, and Alaska; and Canadian representatives. Tribal representatives, as included in the Treaty, served on the Commission and Fisheries panels.

In the State of Washington, the Timber-Fish-Wildlife Agreement also involved negotiations between Washington State Tribes, private industry, and Washington State to conclude agreements to protect, preserve, and rehabilitate the environment.

As the Senate Select Committee on Indian Affairs initiates field hearings on Senate Concurrent Resolution 76, Tribal witnesses will offer enlightening concepts and ideas to improve the management of Indian Affairs. Hopefully, these hearings will prove most instructive on the importance of involving American Indian people in the policy and programmatic decision-making processes affecting their quality of life....

Source:

US Senate. "Iroquois Confederacy of Nations." Hearing Before the Select Committee on Indian Affairs. 100th Cong., 1st Sess. on S. Con. Res. 76. Washington, DC: Government Printing Office, December 2, 1987.

63

Statement of Chief Judge George Aubid (Mille Lacs Band of Ojibwe) (1988)

The Tribal courts, first established in 1883, were largely federally sponsored institutions designed to weaken, and eventually destroy, Indigenous cultural identity. It was not until the Indian Reorganization Act of 1934 that modern Tribal courts began to appear on some reservations. Since then, they have proliferated throughout Indian Country and provide a forum for Tribal governments and individuals—Native and non-Native—to address many issues.

The Indian Civil Rights Act (ICRA) of 1968 imposed statutory versions of several of the U.S. Constitution's first ten amendments, the Bill of Rights, onto Tribal courts and governments and required Native nations to provide basic civil liberties protections to all persons and entities within Indian Country. This was a significant federal imposition of constitutional benefits upon Native nations and citizens not generally bound by US or state constitutions' provisions.

In 1988 the Senate Select Committee on Indian Affairs held this hearing to provide Tribal court officials, Tribal politicians, and their allies an opportunity to comment on the status of Tribal court systems, their relations with other courts, and the manner in which the ICRA had affected these court systems. George Aubid, a Mille Lacs Band Tribal judge, testified regarding the merit and vitality of Tribal courts and encouraged federal lawmakers to keep their distance.

As Chief Judge of the Non-Removable Mille Lacs Band of Chippewa Indians, I am devoted to the inherent right of bands, tribes and individuals to resolve disputes in tribal court.

The Mille Lacs Reservation is located in central Minnesota. Over six years ago we decided to adopt the separation of powers form of government. Our government features an executive, legislative and judicial branch.

There is a fair and equitable system of checks and balances among the three branches. The Band Assembly is the legislative branch of our government; all appropriations originate in the Band Assembly and all laws are written by the Assembly. The executive branch includes a chief and several commissioners who execute and enforce our laws. The judicial branch is responsible for the interpretation of our laws and the adjudication of disputes.

Each branch is dependent upon the other two and our government cannot operate properly if the powers of any branch are diminished. Therefore, any attack upon the judicial branch is an attack upon our government as a whole. Any attack upon our government is an attack upon our sovereignty. Sovereignty is our right and ability to control our own destiny. We existed as a sovereign nation prior to the existence of the United States and we retain and vigorously defend our sovereign status.

As a sovereign nation, we have the inherent right to be self-governing. The Supreme Court has consistently upheld our right to have a court system, and operate under our own system of laws....

Beginning in 1962, Congress began holding hearings about possible abuses of discretion in tribal courts. To remedy these alleged abuses, Congress passed the Indian Civil Rights Act in 1968. This act provided tribal court litigants with most of the rights guaranteed in the first ten amendments to the U.S. Constitution....

All of these rights are provided for in the Band Code of the Mille Lacs Chippewa. Most of the guarantees are found in Chapter 5 of our Code which deals exclusively with civil rights....

The Mille Lacs band feel strongly that the ICRA remedied any problems tribal courts were having and that any additional legislation would infringe on the bands right to be self-governing.

Again, the Supreme Court upheld the right of Indian tribes to adjudicate disputes in *Santa Clara Pueblo v. Martinez*. That case interpreted the ICRA as meaning that when a tribe violates a person's rights, that person can seek federal review only if he is being wrongfully detained. This is in accordance with section 1303 of the act....

Hence, the intent of Congress, as interpreted by the Supreme Court, was to only get involved in the decisions of Indian courts if someone is wrongfully jailed. Any amendments to the ICRA would be a disservice to Indian tribes. In 1968, Congress achieved two goals by passing the ICRA. First, it imposed upon the Tribes parameters for their court systems. Second, it guaranteed the right of tribal courts to exist into perpetuity.

It is the position of the Mille Lacs Band that any compromise of these two initial goals would be an egregious error by Congress. The ICRA struck a nice balance, Congress got its civil rights laws into tribal court. The Tribes got the right to permanently operate their court systems.

Should Congress impose more civil rights laws upon tribal court, it will be infringing on the tribal right to self-government which is a cornerstone of federal-tribal relations. Should Congress attempt to eliminate tribal courts, it will have broken a promise to the Indians.

It was our impression that breaking promises to Indians was out of fashion in this century. As a people, we have different folkways and mores from the predominant white society. Consequently, we have cultural and traditional matters which can only be heard in our court system. No other tribunal in the world can make decisions which interpret our ancient laws and age-old traditions.

We believe that mankind constantly searches for truth. We as a people need some tribunal in our midst to seek truth. If you remove the court from the community, you remove the community's ability to ferret out truth and purge itself. We also believe that mankind seeks justice. We enjoy the right to dispense justice. Many of our band members don't believe justice is possible in the white man's court. We believe our Band Court satisfies the need for justice among our people.

Therefore, the Mille Lacs Band court is in complete compliance with the ICRA, and the court is a fundamental element of our government as well as our best forum for seeking truth and justice. Further legislation is not needed and we will oppose any further restrictions on our court system and our right to be self-governing. In addition, the Mille Lacs Band court concurs with the testimony given by David Getches. We support the concept of a National Indian Justice Center which would train our judges and staff. We support the amelioration for judicial funding by the BIA, we feel the need for greater funding on a daily basis and urge Congress to instruct the BIA to place our needs at a higher position on the list of priorities. We support the increasing of criminal jurisdiction by tribal courts. A mechanism which would allow us to retrocede Public Law 280 with greater ease is needed. We support a Tribal–State Cooperative Jurisdiction Act. We would like to work with the state of Minnesota and be assured that our courts are shown the proper respect by the state. We agree that CFR courts should be eliminated. Finally, we agree that the federal government must curtail its plenary powers and respect the sovereignty of the Indian tribes and bands.

Source:

US Senate. "Tribal Court Systems and the Indian Civil Rights Act." Hearing Before the Select Committee on Indian Affairs. 100th Cong., 2nd Sess. Washington, DC: Government Printing Office, 1988.

64   *Centennial Accord Between Federally Recognized Tribes and the State of Washington (1989)*

In 1989, 100 years after the founding of Washington State and following decades of contentious, often dangerous, political and legal battles, leaders in Washington State and twenty-six federally recognized Native nations decided to explore cooperation, negotiation, and arbitration to see if those approaches would improve relations.

In January of that year, Governor Booth Gardner had issued a proclamation formally recognizing the government-to-government relationships between the state and the Nations located within its borders. On August 4, representatives from the Tribes and the state met to produce the *Centennial Accord*. The negotiated document codified commitments to implement and institutionalize the governor's proclamation for the purposes of achieving mutual goals, including delivery of services to Native communities. Tribal and state officials agreed to meet once a year, thereafter, to report on the status of their efforts. Each state agency assumed responsibility for implementation of the principles laid out in the accord. Tribal leaders agreed to communicate with appropriate state agencies in conjunction with the accord's goals.

A decade later, Governor Gary Locke and the Tribes reaffirmed these commitments with the *Millennium Agreement*, in which the leaders pledged, among other things, to improve channels of communication, promote education, and develop a consultation protocol. An *Out of State Accord* was also implemented, which formalized similar arrangements with Oregon- and Idaho-based Tribal nations with reserved treaty rights in Washington.

The government-to-government protocols formalized in 1989 continue to the present and improve with scrutiny and use. The parties, including Tribal leaders, the governor, and directors from each state agency, meet annually to report problems and progress. As a result of the *Centennial Accord*, meaningful consultation has become an integral part of tribal-state relations. This precedent-setting agreement has now been emulated in several other states, including Oregon, New Mexico, Arizona, California, and Minnesota.

The Centennial Accord

I. Preamble and Guiding Principles

This Accord dated August 4, 1989, is executed between the federally recognized Indian tribes of Washington signatory to this Accord and the State of Washington, through its governor, in order to better achieve mutual goals through an improved relationship between their sovereign governments. This Accord provides a framework for that government-to-government relationship and implementation procedures to assure execution of that relationship.

Each Party to this Accord respects the sovereignty of the other. The respective sovereignty of the state and each federally recognized tribe provide paramount authority for that party to exist and to govern. The parties share in their relationship particular respect for the values and culture represented by tribal governments. Further, the parties share a desire for a complete Accord between the State of Washington and the federally recognized tribes in Washington reflecting a full government-to-government relationship and will work with all elements of state and tribal governments to achieve such an accord.

II. Parties

There are twenty-six federally recognized Indian tribes in the state of Washington. Each sovereign tribe has an independent relationship with each other and the state. This Accord provides the framework for that relationship between the state of Washington, through its governor, and the signatory tribes.

The parties recognize that the state of Washington is governed in part by independent state officials. Therefore, although, this Accord has been initiated by the signatory tribes and the governor, it welcomes the participation of, inclusion in and execution by chief representatives of all elements of state government so that the government-to-government relationship described herein is completely and broadly implemented between the state and the tribes.

III. Purposes and Objectives

This Accord illustrates the commitment by the parties to implementation of the government-to-government relationship, a relationship reaffirmed as state policy by gubernatorial proclamation January 3, 1989. This relationship respects the sovereign status of the parties, enhances and improves communications between them, and facilitates the resolution of issues.

This Accord is intended to build confidence among the parties in the government-to-government relationship by outlining the process for implementing the policy. Not only is this process intended to implement the relationship, but also it is intended to institutionalize it within the organizations represented by the parties. The parties will continue to strive for complete institutionalization of the government-to-government relationship by seeking an accord among all the tribes and all elements of state government.

This Accord also commits the parties to the initial tasks that will translate the government-to-government relationship into more-efficient, improved and beneficial services to Indian and non-Indian people. This Accord encourages and provides the foundation and framework for specific agreements among the parties outlining specific tasks to address or resolve specific issues.

The parties recognize that implementation of this Accord will require a comprehensive educational effort to promote understanding of the government-to-government relationship within their own governmental organizations and with the public.

IV. Implementation Process and Responsibilities

While this Accord addresses the relationship between the parties, its ultimate purpose is to improve the services delivered to people by the parties. Immediately and periodically, the parties shall establish goals for improved services and identify the obstacles to the achievement of those goals. At an annual meeting, the parties will develop joint strategies and specific agreements to outline tasks, overcome obstacles and achieve specific goals.

The parties recognize that a key principle of their relationship is a requirement that individuals working to resolve issues of mutual concern are accountable to act in a manner consistent with this Accord. The state of Washington is organized into a variety of large but separate departments under its governor, other independently elected officials and a variety of boards and commissions. Each tribe, on the other hand, is a unique government organization with different management and decision-making structures.

The chief of staff of the governor of the state of Washington is accountable to the governor for implementation of this Accord. State agency directors are accountable to the governor through the chief of staff for the related activities of their agencies. Each director will initiate a procedure within his/her agency by which the government-to-government policy will be implemented. Among other things, these procedures will require persons responsible for dealing with issues of mutual concern to respect the government-to-government relationship within which the issue must be addressed. Each agency will establish a documented plan of accountability and may establish more detailed implementation procedures in subsequent agreements between tribes and the particular agency.

The parties recognize that their relationship will successfully address issues of mutual concern when communication is clear, direct and between persons responsible for addressing the concern. The parties recognize that in state government, accountability is best achieved when this responsibility rests solely within each state agency. Therefore, it is the objective of the state that each particular agency be directly accountable for implementation of the government-to-government relationship in dealing with issues of concern to the parties. Each agency will facilitate this objective by identifying individuals directly responsible for issues of mutual concern.

Each tribe also recognizes that a system of accountability within its organization is critical to successful implementation of the relationship. Therefore, tribal officials will direct their staff to communicate within the spirit of this Accord with the particular agency which, under the organization of state government, has the authority and responsibility to deal with the particular issue of concern to the tribe.

In order to accomplish these objectives, each tribe must ensure that its current tribal organization, decision-making process and relevant tribal personnel is known to each state agency with which the tribe is addressing an issue of mutual concern. Further, each tribe may establish a more detailed organizational structure, decision-making process, system of accountability, and other procedures for implementing the government-to-government relationship in subsequent agreements with various state agencies. Finally, each tribe will establish a documented system of accountability.

As a component of the system of accountability within state and tribal governments, the parties will review and evaluate at the annual meeting the implementation of the government-to- government relationship. A management report will be issued summarizing this evaluation and will include joint strategies and specific agreements to outline tasks, overcome obstacles, and achieve specific goals.

The chief of staff also will use his/her organizational discretion to help implement the government-to-government relationship. The office of Indian Affairs will assist the chief of staff in implementing the government-to-government relationship by providing state agency directors information with which to educate employees and constituent groups as defined in the accountability plan about the requirement of the government-to-government relationship. The Office of Indian Affairs shall also perform other duties as defined by the chief of staff.

V. Sovereignty and Disclaimers

Each of the parties respects the sovereignty of each other party. In executing this Accord, no party waives any rights, including treaty rights, immunities, including sovereign immunities, or jurisdiction. Neither does this Accord diminish any rights or protections afforded other Indian persons or entities under state or federal law. Through this Accord parties strengthen their collective ability to successfully resolve issues of mutual concern.

While the relationship described by this Accord provides increased ability to solve problems, it likely will not result in a resolution of all issues. Therefore, inherent in their relationship is the right of each of the parties to elevate an issue of importance to any decision-making authority of another party, including, where appropriate, that party's executive office.

Signatory parties have executed this Accord on the date of August 4, 1989, and agreed to be duly bound by its commitments.

Sources:

Annual Report (Olympia: Northwest Indian Fisheries Commission, 1989)

"Centennial Accord Between the Federally Recognized Indian Tribes in Washington State and the State of Washington." In *Fostering State-Tribal Collaboration: An Indian Law Primer*, by Andrea Wilkins. Lanham, MD: Rowman & Littlefield, 2016.

http://www.goia.wa/gov/Government-to-Govenment/Data/Centennial Accord.htm.

---

65   *Testimony of Director Denis Turner (Rincon Band of Luiseno Indians) of the Southern California Tribal Chairman's Association (1989)*

California is home to more Native nations than any other US state, with over 100 Indigenous groups still residing in their original homelands. Most of these Tribes have fewer than 250 citizens and their geographic range is wide, from the mountains, to the deserts, to the Pacific Ocean. Native peoples in this area were ravaged by Spanish colonialism and its mission system. Diseases wreaked incalculable havoc. Then, in the 1840s, after the Treaty of Guadalupe Hidalgo was signed between Mexico and the US, Americans learned of California's significant gold deposits, triggering another horrific period of death and loss of land.

While eighteen treaties were signed with various nations in 1851 and 1852, the US Senate refused to ratify the documents on the grounds that the planned reservations contained lands deemed too valuable to California. As a result of this craven non-action, for nearly a century, those Native peoples were rendered virtually landless

Many Native nations were also formally terminated in the 1950s and suffered immensely. While all, save for one, have been restored to federally recognized status, they are still plagued by serious problems that this hearing was designed to explore and address. Denis Turner here offers his organization's perspective on the issues.

Southern California Tribal Chairmen's Association (SCTCA) Inc., was established in 1975 for a mission and purpose of supporting and advocating quality socioeconomic growth on Southern California Indian reservations.

The SCTCA Board of Directors are Tribal chairpersons who are community-based at each reservation. The SCTCA currently provides services to twenty-two reservations within five counties in Southern California.

The SCTCA believes more than ever before, the 1990s will require tribal people and their leaders to be more innovative and creative planning and developing for successful socioeconomic growth on reservations in the Southern California area.

In this effort of preparing and planning for the next decade, tribal leaders and tribal representatives are setting goals clear, and achievable, realistic and supported by its tribal membership.

The necessary socioeconomic changes on reservations in all the Southern California and the rest must be accompanied by its relationship with the Bureau of Indian affairs (BIA) required by law. The BIA acts as an incoherent clearinghouse process, which has been viewed and seen by tribal leaders. The BIA efforts to assist tribes from the area and central offices levels are nil and marginal at best.

The sources and character of confusion surrounding the tribes of Southern California and some other seventy tribes in Central and Northern California, have been the BIA agency, area and central agency officials inconsistency and inability to help carry out initiatives and opportunities planned and developed by tribal leaders in a timely manner. The specific problem is line of authority for approval and other times at the agency depending upon project and dollar amounts of the proposal from tribe to tribe and how the funds might be used, with inconsistency from agency to agency.

We believe the first thing the Senate Select Committee must remember about the California situation is ninety-six or more tribes are provided BIA services with funding being the lowest of low, for all states, coupled with a lack of staff and adequate resources as well as residual supports for tribal projects. It doesn't take much imagination as to why Indian people avoid BIA when trying to resolve issues that face tribal governments.

We urge the committee to convene at least the Office of Technical Services to obtain firsthand knowledge of the potential permanent long-term endangerment to the tribes' social economic conditions, which are caused by the critical backup BIA funding base.

We believe tribal conditions with the BIA office situation in California can be changed by reviewing the following recommendations:

1. Develop a local Advisory Committee composed of two tribal representatives from the Northern, Central and Southern agency to provide impact into BIA budget and policy decisions at the area office level. Representatives could be selected at the annual IPS meeting.
2. BIA line of authority to change in California to provide agency level officers to approve all contracts and grants, and agreements with tribes in tribal organizations.
3. Provide a tribal base funding equitable or practical to support tribal government operations, which are consistent to tribal operation needs, which are guaranteed by the Constitution of the United States.
4. Provide an updated tribal representative report of 1985 California Indian Task Force Report.

However, this testimony is only a reflection of tribal people's needs and conditions on the Southern California reservations, it may provide a better understanding of the complex issues of ninety-six tribes in California with some insight into the intertwined conditions between tribes and federal agencies.

We understand and realize your committee has millions of things to do, but the single most important thing you can do is help provide an increase in base funding small tribes of California.

The tribal leaders, federal agencies, state officials, and knowledgeable people working with Indian tribes in California, have said for the last ten years, without increased funding to adequately make change, taxpayer money is wasted on the fruitless fiduciary effort of government authorities.

The Senate Select Committee must go on Congressional record to support the following action recommendations provided by the Southern California tribal leaders.

Thank you for providing us the opportunity to testify before your committee on the subject that is of great concern to the tribal leadership of Southern California.

Source:

US Senate. "Issues of Concern to Southern California Tribes." Hearing before the Select Committee on Indian Affairs. 100th Cong., 1st Sess. Washington, DC: Government Printing Office, April 27, 1989.

66

Testimony of Chairman W. Ron Allen (Jamestown S'Klallam) on Proposed Amendments to the Self-Determination Act (1989)

In 1975 Congress enacted the Indian Self-Determination and Education Assistance Act designed to provide Tribes a greater role in the administration of their own sovereignty and self-governing capabilities. However, Native nations soon learned that federal agencies, especially the Bureau of Indian Affairs, were unwilling to surrender authority to Native communities, contending that they were not fully competent to manage their own affairs.

The proposed 1988 Amendments to the original act were an attempt by Congress to acknowledge the difficult position in which Native peoples found themselves. W. Ron Allen, a well-respected leader in Indian Country, here offers testimony that reflects the tensions between his nation and the BIA and the Indian Health Service and he offers his perspectives on what needed to occur in order to rectify the situation.

———

Mr. Chairman and committee members, my name is W. Ron Allen and I'm the chairman and Executive Director of the Jamestown S'Klallam Tribe. I would like to thank you for inviting me to this hearing to address this critical issue of developing the regulations for the Self-Determination and Education Assistance Act of 1988.

The spirit and intent of this act is to provide the tribes with improved administrative authorities and mechanisms to carry the self-determination and self-sufficiency goals forward. These amendments are also directed at improving the political/bureaucratic environment to administer the P.L. 93–638 Act consistent with the president's "Government-to-Government" policy. Carrying out our governmental responsibilities, tribes are becoming more stable, skilled, efficient, and effective at managing their governmental affairs. The passage of P.L. 93–638 has assisted tribes at becoming proficient and skilled at managing their own programs. Yet, over these last few years we have been extremely frustrated with the overly bureaucratic maze that we have to navigate to accomplish the objectives.

The current system and consultation process has never been conducted consistent with the "Government-to-Government" policy. We have our unique governmental status, sovereignty, treaty rights, and jurisdictional obligations to serve our people, but the system still treats the tribes as a constituency. The tribal constituency which the bureaucracy attempts to manage as if we do not have the skills, competence, capability, education, and/or experience to manage the trust resources or other governmental functions such as education or social services without a considerable amount of oversight. This paternalistic disposition of the BIA and IHS agencies is the most objectionable aspect of the government-government-relationship from the Tribes' perspective.

We consistently find that the current bureaucratic system is deeply rooted in a subtle mentality of self-protection. Subsequently, the tribes not only find that we have to spend an excessive amount of energy making the current system work for us, but fight the Bureau for the precious dollars that Congress makes available to the tribes.

The competitive reality juxtaposing over the destiny of the BIA or IHS relative to the independence and self-sufficiency of tribes is at the root of our current dilemma. The 1988 amendments to P.L. 93–638 provide the opportunity for the development of new regulations to implement Self-Determination. How this regulatory development process is to be logically conducted consistent with the legislative purposes is the primary theme of my testimony.

In 1988 when the tribes were working with the Senate Select Committee and the House Committee on Interior and Insular Affairs in developing the "638" amendments, we were addressing a number of issues to improve the conditions for tribal "638" contractors. One of the key issues was our effort to change the system of "consultation" with the tribes on the development of policy, rules, and regulations to "participation." In our judgment, this means that in the context of the "Government-to-Government" relations, tribes would now negotiate as equals with the federal government the conditions of "638" contracts. The tribes commenced to work with the BIA and IHS in developing the regulations for this law with this fundamental shift in participatory involvement embedded in the law.

We felt that if the Bureau and IHS would sincerely work with us in developing the regulations, the tribes would be walking over the threshold of an opportunity to spend less time and effort fighting the bureaucracy and more of the resources carrying out the purpose of the Indian Self-Determination Act.

In the early phase of the development of the regulations, the BIA and IHS were attempting to draft the regulations within the schedule outlined in the law. Unfortunately, the communication was poor between the agencies and the tribes and the tribes objected to the process of developing the regulations without our direct participation. This initial bureaucratic process caused considerable alarm from the tribes because we knew that the Bureau did not wholeheartedly support the 1988 amendments and that the IHS appealed to the president to veto the amendments.

The tribes sought support from this committee and the House Committee on Interior and Insular Affairs to delay the proposed schedule for the development of the regulations to assure our substantive involvement. We were successful in that effort and with the support of IHS and the reluctant disposition of BIA, we scheduled two workshops to "jointly" draft a single set of regulations for both BIA and IHS. These workshops were viewed by the tribes as legitimate process to address the regulatory needs and resolve conflicts and disagreements.

Tribes were extremely disappointed that the Bureau was dragging its feet in participating in the process. BIA officials kept asserting that the tribes did not fully understand how the regulations were to be developed. They also presented a position that the environment of 250 tribal leaders, lawyers, and technicians is an unfair situation to allow them to argue for their views. We acknowledge that the tribal representatives outnumbered the BIA and IHS personnel, yet we consistently pointed out that if their positions were reasonable or consistent with the law they would find support from the tribes.

From the beginning of the process, the BIA would not accept the concept of negotiating these regulations with the tribes consistent with the principle of the "Government-to-Government" relationship. They rarely came to the workshop with their positions developed and were not prepared to work out differences when such differences arose.

The two first meetings, referred to as the Regulation Drafting Workshop initiated by the Indian Health Service were conducted in Nashville and Albuquerque. At first the Bureau would not state whether or not they would acknowledge this process, but in the second meeting said that they only considered the process another form of consultation. They consistently vacillated back and forth regarding their involvement in the process and then finally settled on a position of drafting their own version of the regulations.

We want to point out to the committee that the 250 tribal participants represented over 450 tribes, Alaska villages, and California Rancherias. The Bureau on the other hand, would take the position that because there were some tribes, villages, and rancherias not present, that we did not represent all of Indian Country. This position we feel is a smokescreen why they would have to draft regulations to "protect" those tribes not present. Every time we presented an argument or a position in trying to get the BIA to commit to a position, they would shift to a non-committed posture apparently to leave their options open for deliberation in their close environment where no trouble representatives would be present to challenge their position.

The Bureau has argued that regulations cannot be developed with such a large group. We pointed out, however, that the effort worked in the first two sessions and that we were only asking for one more national session to resolve the disagreements. We then proposed that the final phases could be coordinated through the steering committee forum. The steering committee, which had been initiated by IHS, was established to provide a small workable group of Indian leaders who represented each of the twelve regions. This committee was to negotiate the final problem or conflict areas. It was embraced by the tribes as a compromise approach to have a smaller group negotiate the final details of regulations with the departments.

Another example of our frustrating experiences with the Bureau is its unwillingness to accept the Indian leaders on the steering committee as the point of tribal contact in this process. The BIA has asserted various reasons for not accepting the steering committee; all of which boil down to the fact the committee was generated by IHS and not the BIA.

A key problem with the Bureau has been their attitude. During the workshop meetings they have consistently said that this issue or problem will not get past OMB. The tribes would respond by saying why can't we work these issues out with OMB? In our judgment, BIA sadly did not want the tribes in a position to talk to upper level department or OMB personnel regarding the process because of the influence of our logic and consistency with the law and the president's policy.

The development of the schedule to complete the regulation is another area that has reflected the Bureau's unwillingness to cooperate. It has taken us months to get the Bureau to cooperate in the development of a joint schedule; they have consistently been publishing a different schedule than IHS even after we thought that an agreement was reached in the steering committee.

The way the process is emerging, we feel the strategy of the Bureau is to posture their position so as to not commit to the ideas of negotiating with the tribes and in the end draft their version of the regulations referred to as "Notice of Proposed Rulemaking." This strategy would result in reverting back to the old system with the tribes in a position of attempting to modify regulations that have been developed internally by the BIA. We feel that their regulations would be implicitly aimed at the BIA retaining control over tribes.

One of the ironic observations of the process is that IHS has conducted itself more in the context of a trustee than the Bureau. There are a number of problems in IHS, but they are not as major as within the Bureau of Indian affairs. Within the top level of the IHS there is exhibited concern about their commitment to work with the tribes in the final phases including the clearance process.

My comments have been directed at the political and policy aspect of the process to promote a Congressional awareness of the importance of changing this process and the relationship of the administration with the tribes in administering Indian programs. I have other more technical comments to supplement and complement those views that you will receive today and would like the opportunity to provide them within the next week.

In conclusion, I would like to urge this committee to assist the tribes in influencing the administration to implement this policy consistent with the "Government-to-Government" policy. It would be a grave disappointment if we are not able to persuade the administration to adjust to the intent of the P.L. 100–472 and regress back to the status quo situation. A situation where the bureaucracy will prevail in the hope of self-determination fades into the night....

Source:

US Senate. "Implementation of Amendments to the Indian Self-Determination Act." Hearing Before the Select Committee on Indian Affairs. 100th Cong., 1st Sess. Washington, DC: Government Printing Office, June 9, 1989.

---

67   *Statement on Self-Governance by Principal Chief Wilma Mankiller of the Cherokee Nation (1991)*

In 1988, at the behest of several Tribal nations, including the Cherokee Nation of Oklahoma, Congress adopted an experimental Tribal self-governance project aimed at providing Native nations with a greater degree of political and economic autonomy than they had experienced under the Indian Self-Determination and Education Assistance Act of 1975. As one tribal leader put it: "Self-Governance is fundamentally designed to provide Tribal governments with control and decision-making authority over the federal financial resources provided for the benefit of the Indian people." This original experimental policy had proven quite successful for the twenty nations that opted-in, so Congress began to consider extending the policy a while longer and increasing the number of eligible Native nations. Mankiller, the first female principal chief of the Cherokee Nation, testified boldly in favor of both proposals.

After the law was approved in 1991, it was amended again in 1994 to create a permanent self-governance program throughout the Interior Department and with the Indian Health Service. It was amended yet again in 2000 when the program was expanded to include the Department of Health and Human Services.

Mr. Chairman and members of the Senate Select Committee, I am very pleased to have the opportunity to testify today on S. 1287, the Tribal Self-Governance Demonstration Project Act and the Cherokee Nation's experience with its own Self-Governance Compact. Our nation recently submitted to the Assistant Secretary for Indian Affairs a semiannual report on our self-governance project, a copy of the primary text is attached as background for my testimony.

I enthusiastically support this concept. By way of background, it is interesting to note the continued discussion and effort to reorganize the administration of Indian affairs to make the federal government more responsive. While I support the initiative, I believe the self-governance authorization contained in the Indian Self-Determination Act Amendments in 1988 and the self-governance process may do more to reform federal administration. I believe the federal government and the Tribes have the best opportunity of the century to finally bring about a mature relationship between our governments which has often been promised but up until now, only a dream. The challenge for the federal and tribal governments is to use this opportunity properly and chart a wise course for the future.

Since colonial times, the Cherokee Nation has continued a government to government and trust relationship with the United States. Our first treaty of peace, friendship, and protection was in 1785. Since then we have engaged in over twenty treaties and numerous agreements ratified by the Senate and passed by both the Senate and the House. Last summer we negotiated a compact of self-governance with the Secretary of Interior and the Congress was notified pursuant to the authorizing federal law. The Cherokee Nation views the compact as our newest "treaty" with the United States of America. The Cherokee Nation has faith that the federal government will honor this treaty compact in utmost good faith. Of course our faith in the federal government must be tempered by our actual experience between the federal government and Indian tribes. Hopefully, we can be more optimistic about the future having learned the lessons of history.

I am advised the committee is particularly interested that I address four questions. First, should the Congress extend the self-governance authorization for the self-governance demonstration project for several years? Second, should additional tribes beyond the number of twenty be authorized to participate? Third, should an Indian tribe be required to go through a grant planning process prior to negotiating a compact with the Department of Interior? Fourth, what has been the Cherokee Nation's experience with the self-governance compact process?

In answer to the first question, the Cherokee Nation's experience under self-governance has been successful and therefore, we endorse an extension of the self-governance demonstration authority. The project should be given adequate time for everyone involved to assess the experience.

The Cherokee Nation's compact was destined to be successful because it is consistent with our long-sought goal of self-determination. I recommend that the self-governance authorization be made permanent with the Cherokee Nation and for any other tribe already participating in the demonstration project which has determined by its own achievements that the project is a success and is comfortable with the arrangement. At the same time, I respect the other tribes may want and need a longer demonstration to be comfortable with making this assessment.

An additional point is there are a number of ways to fashion self-governance projects and measure their success. I suppose what constitutes success of a particular project could be debated from various viewpoints. I hope the Congress and executive branches recognizes that some flexibility must be instilled in the process to accommodate the diversity in ways and means Tribes may desire to self-governance. The bottom line should be that the Tribe, guided by responsible governmental leadership, has demonstrated sustained stability, efficient and satisfactory delivery of services, and financial integrity.

As to the second question, if additional tribes express an interest in participating, the federal government should make every effort to accommodate them. The current participating tribes had to meet acceptable standards of governmental and financial accountability. Additional tribes can also demonstrate the maintenance of these standards. If they desire to participate, they should not be denied because of limited authorization of the total number allowed.

I believe there are many tribes ready, willing, and able to be successful compacting partners with the federal government. Leaders of tribes and their memberships need to be confident in their government's ability to administer independently the additional responsibilities.

It is also important that the department be required to state its reasons for declining tribal governance project requests. Those reasons should be limited to specific criteria. Any determination by the department not to compact should be supported by evidence that shows beyond doubt that a tribe is not ready, for example, because it had not observed acceptable financial standards over a reasonable period of time. Another example, if it was absolutely clear and evident that a tribal government was unstable and failed to be accountable to its members through the established tribal institutions of government then it should not be allowed to participate. In both cases, the criteria should be very clear and easily understood.

In response to the third question, relative to whether an Indian tribe should be required to go through a grant planning process prior to becoming a self-governance participant. The Cherokee Nation did not have the benefit of a grant prior to entry. While it might be useful and helpful, the judgment to do so should be the decision of the tribal leadership. As long as it is evident that the applicant tribe has a record of sustained accountability of its tribal systems and the tribal government ensures the rule of law, a deserving tribe should be able to proceed directly to the negotiation of its compact with the department.

In answer to the fourth, the Cherokee Nation's very positive experience with self-governance is summarized in the attached semiannual report. Our recent tribal election is a testament to the support of the Cherokee Nation's membership for our self-governance project and its continued success.

As a final point, the Self-Governance Project is in essence an important acknowledgment by the Department of the Interior that it is the Cherokee Nation which represents and serves the Indians residing within the Cherokee's original Treaty lands in the Indian Territory that today comprises the fourteen Northeast Counties in Oklahoma. The foundation of the Cherokee Nation's Self-Governance Compact is the numerous treaties and statutes acknowledging the Cherokee Nation as the tribal governing authority in Cherokee territory. I hope the committee will work with the secretary to take whatever action, if any, is needed to make the compact a permanent bilateral agreement for self-governance between the United States and the Cherokee Nation....

Sources:

Strommer, George D., and Stephen D. Osborne. "The History, Status, and Future of Tribal Self-Governance Under the Indian Self-Determination and Education Assistance Act." *American Indian Law Review* 39 (2014–2015): 1–80.

US Senate. "Tribal Self-Governance Demonstration Project Act." Hearing before the Select Committee on Indian Affairs. 102nd Cong., 1st Sess. on S. 1287. Washington, DC: Government Printing Office, July 18, 1991.

68   Tribal-State Gaming Compact between the Red Lake Band of Chippewa and the State of Minnesota (1991)

Three years after Congress enacted the Indian Gaming Regulatory Act (IGRA) in 1988, the Red Lake Band negotiated its compact with Minnesota, as required by law. The act was ostensibly intended to balance the inherent right of Tribal governments to regulate economic activity within their borders with states' concerns about the alleged negative impacts of Indian gaming outside Indian Country with regards to crime, addictive gambling, and increased traffic.

IGRA defines three types of gaming: Class I, Class II, and Class III. Within Class I are social games and as such are not subject to regulation under IGRA. Class II gaming includes bingo and other games of chance that are subject to IGRA regulation and Tribal control. Class III comprises all other forms of gaming, such as slot machines, blackjack, roulette, and other table games. This level of gaming is only allowed if a Tribe adopts an ordinance, secures federal approval, and negotiates a compact with the state. Importantly, IGRA does not give the state authority to tax Indian gaming revenue.

The Red Lake government opened the Lake of the Woods Casino, now known as Seven Clans Casino Warroad, in 1991 and it quickly became the area's major tourist industry. The Nation now operates three casinos on its land.

————

Whereas, the state of Minnesota (hereinafter "State") and the Red Lake Band of Chippewa, (hereinafter "Band") are separate sovereigns, and each respects the laws of the other; and

Whereas, the Band exercises governmental authority within the Red Lake Reservation (hereinafter "Reservation"), which, for purposes of this compact, means those tribal trust lands located in Warroad, Roseau County and specifically described as Lot 1 ... and

Whereas, the Congress of the United States has enacted the Indian Gaming Regulatory Act (hereinafter "IGRA"), ... creating a mechanism through which the several states and Indian tribal governments may allocate jurisdiction and control of Class III gaming activity which occurs on their lands; and

Whereas, the Band is a federally recognized Indian tribal government which is duly qualified to conduct certain types of Class III gaming on its lands;

Whereas, the State of Minnesota pursuant to Minnesota Statute Section 3.9221 (1990), authorizes the governor's representatives to negotiate with regard to compacts with the several Indian tribal governments in the state of Minnesota; and

Now Therefore, in consideration of the mutual undertakings and agreements hereinafter set forth, the Band and the State enter into the following compact.

Section 1. Findings and Declaration of Policy

1.01 Findings. As the basis for this compact, the State and the Band have made the following findings:

1.02 This compact shall govern the licensing, regulation and play of the banking card game of "Blackjack" or "Twenty-One" ... within the reservation.

1.03 The purpose of this compact generally are to provide the Band with the opportunity to offer Blackjack in a way that will benefit the Band economically that will ensure their operation of the game and that will minimize the possibilities of corruption and infiltration by criminal influences.

1.04 The Band has the right to license and regulate gaming activity on its lands in accordance with the IGRA and this compact.

1.05 A principal goal of federal Indian policy is to promote tribal economic development, tribal self-sufficiency, and strong tribal government.

1.06 The State and the Band find it to be consistent with the IGRA, and the public health, safety and welfare to regulate Blackjack pursuant to this compact.

1.07 The Band as operating various forms of Class II gaming, will operate Class III video games of chance pursuant to a Tribal-State compact, and has implemented controls satisfactory to the Band for the responsible operation and regulation of the games.

1.08 The Band will operate Blackjack pursuant to this compact and contemporaneously with its Class II and Class III gaming operations.

1.09 Nothing herein shall in any way affect or alter the terms of the Tribal-State compact for control of Class III video games of chance on the Red Lake Reservation in Minnesota, executed by the Band and the State in 1991 and approved by the secretary of the interior.

1.1 Declaration of Policy

1.2 The State recognizes the positive impacts that gaming may provide to the Band. The Band may utilize gaming generated financial resources to fund programs that provide various vital services to Band residence. These programs may include education, health and human resources, housing development, road construction and maintenance, sewer and water projects, and economic development. The State also recognizes that the positive economic effects of such gaming enterprises may extend beyond tribal governments to the tribe's neighbors and surrounding communities and may help to foster mutual respect and understanding among Indians and non-Indians.

1.3 The Band and the State, through this compact and the regulations incorporated herein, shall attempt, in good faith, to address the legitimate common concerns of both parties....

Section 9. Effectiveness Contingent upon Federal Court Judgment

This compact and obligations hereunder shall be contingent upon 1) the Bois Forte, Fond du Lac, Grand Portage, Leech Lake, Mille Lacs, Red Lake, and White Earth Bands of Chippewa Indians, and the Prairie Island, Shakopee, Mdewakanton, and Upper Sioux Communities intervening as plaintiffs in the lawsuit entitled *Lower Sioux Indian Community v. State of Minnesota*;... and 2) the court in the above *Lower Sioux* lawsuit entering a Consent Judgment incorporating the compact and its terms; and 3) the court in the above *Lower Sioux* lawsuit determining that consideration of the Report and Recommendation of Magistrate Bernard P. Becker, dated December 20, 1990, is unnecessary.

Section 10. Effect of Breach

In the event that any federally recognized Indian tribal government bound by the consent judgment described in section 9 breaches the consent judgment or compact incorporated therein, the state That shall direct any legal action at the breach in tribal government only, and such action shall not affect the validity of the remaining compacts between the state and any non-breaching party.

Red Lake Band of Chippewa (June 11, 1991)

State of Minnesota (May 8, 1991)

Assistant Secretary of the Interior (September 25, 1991)

Sources:

Cattelino, Jessica R. *High Stakes: Florida Seminole Gaming and Sovereignty.* Durham, NC: Duke University Press, 2008.

Mason, W. Dale. *Indian Gaming: Tribal Sovereignty and American Politics.* Norman: University of Oklahoma Press, 2000.

US Federal Register. "Notice of Approved Tribal-State Compact." Vol. 56, no. 192. Thursday, October 3, 1991.

69

Constitution of Ka Lāhui Hawai'i (1993)

Hawaiian Natives maintained active diplomatic relations with several European powers and the US prior to their 1893 forced annexation by the US federal government with the overthrow of Queen Lili'uokalani.

Once Hawaii acquired statehood, Natives were under even more pressure to assimilate and have since struggled to retain and reestablish their sovereignty. The US created two Native land trusts, the Hawaiian Homeland Trust of 1920 and the Ceded Land Trust of 1959, ostensibly in attempts to better conditions for Hawaiian Natives. In the 1970s and 1980s, as federal policy shifted and began to reflect greater respect for Indigenous self-determination, Hawaiian Natives, like mainland Native peoples, began to demand recognition of their rights of self-governance. They called for reparations for the profound losses endured since the late 1890s, and pushed for greater clarity of their status as a sovereign people in relation to both the state of Hawaii and the federal government.

The following draft constitution, based upon the one first drafted in 1987, democratically formalizes the distinct political autonomy of Native Hawaiians as a modern-polity, but it also establishes clear links with their own unique history by including provisions for traditional chiefs who are charged with providing advice to the legislature on important cultural matters.

Constitution of Ka Lahui Hawai'i

Na Ke Alma (Nā Akua) hath all nations of people been made to dwell on the Earth, in unity, peace, and righteousness. Na Ke Akua (Nā Alma) hath certain rights also been bestowed alike on all people and alaka'i of all lands.

These are some of the rights which Ke Akua (Nā Akua) hath given alike to every person and every alaka'i: life, liberty, freedom from oppression, to have the earnings of one's hands and the productions of one's mind.

Na Ke Akua (Nā Akua) hath the people been given the wisdom and knowledge to establish government and to rule or the purpose of peace. In making laws for Ka Lāhui Hawai'i, it is not proper to enact laws for the enrichment or protection of alaka'i only, without the enrichment and protection of the people. There shall be no laws enacted which are at variance with these principles, nor shall there be laws enacted which would result in the people of Ka Lāhui Hawai'i being left homeless or laws enacted which would result m the suffering of the children of Ka Lāhui Hawai'i.

Preamble

He Hawai'i makou and with our descendants we are, the traditional occupants and kahu (guardians) of the land, water, sea, mineral, and all other resources as farmers, fishermen, hunters, manufacturers, miners, tradesmen, professionals, and residents, who discovered, settled and nurtured the Hawaiian Archipelago.

He Hawai'i makou and with our descendants we have inhabited and occupied this archipelago and exercised our traditional, religious and access rights since time immemorial to sustain and maintain our culture and primordial interests, regardless of other governments exercising jurisdiction over the Hawaiian Archipelago.

Our sacred queen, Keōpūolani, on her deathbed on September 15, 1823 expressed to Liholiho (Kamehameha II): E mālama mai nei ika 'aina iloa' amai kou makuakane. Eho'omaluhia i nā po'eme ke aloha, 'o nā ' ōiwi. (Take care of the land which you have received from your father. Exercise a tender care over the people.)

In 1843, Kauikeaouli (Kamehameha III) reaffirmed the Hawaiian principle of governance that had been in place since time immemorial: "Ua Mau Ke Ea 0 Ka 'Āina I Ka Pono" (The Life and Sovereignty of the Land is Perpetuated in Righteousness).

On August 19, 1850, the Kingdom of Hawai'i through Kauikeaouli (Kamehameha III), entered into a treaty of friendship, commerce and navigation with the United States of America and thereafter, other nations, thereby declaring perpetual peace and amity between the Kingdom of Hawai'i and these nations.

The United States of America has recognized Native Hawaiians and their lands in the Hawaiian Homes Commission Act of 1920 (Act of July 9, 1921, 42 Statute 108, Chapter 42, as amended; Act of March 18, 1959, Public Law 86–3, 73 Statute 4, Section 4) and the State of Hawai'i Admissions Act of 1959 (Act of March 18, 1959, Public Law 86–3, 73 Statute 4, Section 5[f1]). Two public land trusts were thereby created for the betterment of conditions for Native Hawaiians and their heirs.

We, the citizens of Ka Lāhui Hawai'i, state our natural and cultural native claims which may never be alienated as follows:

(A) The minerals and other natural and cultural resources of the lands and submerged lands of the archipelago, the airspace above the archipelago, as well as the plant and animal life forms, aquatic and terrestrial, which dwell therein, belong to Ka Lāhui Hawai'i and shall never be alienated. However, permission may be given by law for the leasing and development of same.

(B) The lands, airspace and waters of the archipelago as herein described, are declared nuclear free and independent zones.

(C) The historical and cultural sites and places of Native Hawaiians and their descendants shall be perpetuated and preserved as a living part of our community life to ensure future generations a genuine opportunity to appreciate and enjoy the rich heritage of Ka Lāhui Hawai'i. The 'Aha 'Ōlelo Kānāwai (Legislature) shall establish and maintain a National Registry of all Prehistoric and Historic Places along with supporting documentation locating, describing, and establishing the significance of each site identified. The 'Aha 'Ōlelo Kānāwai shall initiate measures to protect historical sites, structures, artifacts, objects, and ecosystems of cultural, religious, and archaeological significance.

Now, therefore, he Hawai'i makou and with our descendants, hereby adopt this Constitution for Ka Lāhui Hawai'i in exercise of our right to self-determination; to build a Nation upon established traditions; to form an orderly and representative government; to provide for citizenship; to promote the welfare of our citizens and children; to exercise certain rights of home rule; to secure the blessings of freedom and liberty; to develop our trust resources and to conserve our trust assets; and to dedicate ourselves and our Nation to disarmament, peace, and absolute faith in equity and justice.

Article I

Bill of Rights

SECTION 1. FREEDOM OF RELIGION, SPEECH, PRESS, RIGHTS OF ASSEMBLY AND PETITION:

There shall be separation of Church and Government, but there shall be no separation of Culture (native Hawaiian culture) and Government and no law shall be enacted respecting the establishment of religion or prohibiting the free exercise thereof. No person shall discourage or suppress the practice of traditional native Hawaiian religion or beliefs. No law shall be enacted abridging the freedom of speech or of the press, or the right of people to peacefully assemble, and to petition the Government for a redress of grievances.

SECTION 2. NO DEPRIVATION OF LIFE, LIBERTY, OR PROPERTY WITHOUT DUE PROCESS:

No person shall be deprived of life, liberty, or property without due process of law, nor shall private property, native Hawaiian trust lands or their resources be negotiated for public use by Ka Lāhui Hawai'i without just compensation.

SECTION 3. PROTECTIVE POLICY:

The Government of Ka Lāhui Hawai'i and its constituent agencies accept as a sacred trust, the obligation to promote to the utmost, the well-being of the inhabitants of Ka Lāhui Hawai'i, and to this end its policy is:

(A) To ensure, with due respect for the culture of the people concerned, their political, economic, social, and educational advancement, their just treatment, and their protection against abuses;

(B) To develop self-government, to take due account of the political aspirations of the people, and to assist them in the progressive development of their free political institutions, according to the particular circumstances of each district, its people and their best interests;

(C) To further internal peace and security;

(D) To promote constructive measures of development, research, and cooperation with one another and, when and where appropriate, with specialized agencies and bodies of other nations and states with a view toward the realization of social, economic, and scientific purposes as set forth in this Section;

(E) To protect and increase the land base of Ka Lāhui Hawai'i. To also ensure that Hawaiian lands shall not be utilized by another nation, by any nations' military forces, or by civilian business organizations with military contract; and

(F) To protect Native Hawaiians and their descendants from alienation of their traditional ancestral lands and destruction of the Hawaiian way of life and language, contrary to their best interests. Such legislation as may be necessary shall be enacted to protect the lands, culture, customs, and traditional Hawaiian family organization. Business enterprises by Native Hawaiians and their descendants shall be encouraged. No change in law respecting the alienation or transfer of trust lands or any interest relating thereto, nor alienation of the traditional ancestral rights, shall be lawful.

SECTION 4. DIGNITY OF THE INDIVIDUAL:

The dignity of the individual shall be respected and every person is entitled to protection of the law against malicious and unjustifiable public attacks on the name, reputation, or honor of himself or his family.

SECTION 5. PROTECTION AGAINST UNREASONABLE SEARCHES AND SEIZURES:

The right of the people to be secure in their persons, houses, papers and effects, as well as protected against unreasonable searches and seizures, shall not be violated. No warrant shall be issued, except upon probable cause, supported by oath or affiliation, particularly describing the place to be searched, and the persons or things to be seized. Evidence obtained in violation of this Section shall not be admitted in any court.

SECTION 6. RIGHTS OF AN ACCUSED:

No person shall be subject for the same offense, to be twice put in jeopardy of life or liberty, nor shall he be compelled in any criminal case to be witness against himself; and the failure of the accused to testify shall not be commented upon nor taken against him. For all criminal prosecutions, the accused shall have the right to a speedy and public trial, the right to be judged by a jury of his peers, to be informed of the nature and cause of the accusation and to have a copy thereof, to be confronted with the witnesses against him, to have compulsory process for obtaining witnesses in his favor, and to have the assistance of counsel for his defense. Every person is presumed innocent until pronounced guilty by law. No act of severity which is not reasonably necessary to secure the arrest of an accused person shall be permitted. All persons shall be bailable by sufficient sureties except where judicial authorities shall determine the presumption is great that an infamous crime, which charge shall include murder, rape, and violent crimes, has been committed and that the granting of bail would constitute a danger to the community. Bail shall be set by such judicial authorities. Excessive bail shall not be required, nor excessive fines imposed, nor cruel and unusual punishment inflicted.

SECTION 7. HABEAS CORPUS:

The writ of habeas corpus shall be granted without delay and free of costs. The privilege of the writ of habeas corpus shall not be suspended.

SECTION 8. QUARTERING OF MILITIA:

No soldier or member of the militia shall, in time of peace nor in time of war, except in a manner prescribed by law, be quartered upon native Hawaiian trust lands nor in any house without the consent of the owner or the lawful occupant.

SECTION 9. IMPRISONMENT FOR DEBT:

There shall be no imprisonment for debt except in cases of fraud.

SECTION 10. SLAVERY PROHIBITED:

Slavery shall not exist in Ka Lāhui Hawai'i.

SECTION 11. TREASON:

Treason against Ka Lāhui Hawai'i shall consist of: violating the Oaths of Loyalty to Ka Lāhui Hawai'i; levying war against it; adhering to its enemies or giving them aid and comfort. No person shall be convicted of treason except on the testimony of not less than two (2) witnesses to the same overt act, or by confession in open court.

SECTION 12. SUBVERSIVES INELIGIBLE TO HOLD OFFICE:

Any person who advocates, aids, or belongs to any party, organization, or association which advocates the overthrow of Ka Lāhui Hawai'i shall not be qualified to hold office in the Government of Ka Lāhui Hawai'i.

SECTION 13. RETROACTIVE LAWS AND BILLS OF RETAINER:

No bill of retainer, ex post facto law, nor any law impairing the obligation of contracts shall be passed.

SECTION 14. HEALTH, SAFETY, MORALS, AND GENERAL WELFARE:

Laws shall be enacted for the protection of the health, safety, morals, and general welfare of the people of Ka Lāhui Hawai'i.

SECTION 15. EDUCATION:

The Government shall operate a system of free and nonsectarian education. The Government shall also encourage and aid qualified persons including Kūpuna (Elders) to acquire further education in Hawaiian culture and language, as well as in the general and technical fields locally and abroad, to aid in the development of Ka Lāhui Hawai'i.

SECTION 16. LAND AND NATURAL RESOURCES:

Ka Lāhui Hawai'i shall enact laws for the protection, conservation and management of its natural resources within the Hawaiian archipelago.

SECTION 17. UNSPECIFIED RIGHTS, PRIVILEGES, AND IMMUNITIES:

The enumeration of certain rights in this Constitution shall not be construed to impair or deny other rights retained by the people. No law shall be made nor enforced that abridges any privileges or immunities of the citizens of Ka Lāhui Hawai'i.

SECTION 18. CUSTOMARY AND TRADITIONAL RIGHTS:

(A) General:
   1. Domain of Customary and Traditional Rights: The domain of customary and traditional rights shall extend through the entire Hawaiian archipelago and shall include the air over the archipelago and oceans surrounding the archipelago extending outward from it for two hundred (200) miles. The domain shall also include subterranean, surface, and subsurface minerals found therein.
   2. Konohiki Rights: The traditional and customary konohiki rights of Native Hawaiians and their descendants shall not be abridged.
   3. Rights of Access: Native Hawaiians and their descendants shall be allowed free access to the mountains, caves, seas, and sites of religious and cultural importance for personal, subsistence, religious and cultural purposes.

4. Kānāwai Mamala Hoe (Law of the Splintered Paddle): Native Hawaiians and their descendants shall be free to traverse the archipelago and shall be entitled to safe passage upon the roads and highways of the archipelago.

5. Birth and Burial Rights: In harmony with Article II nature and Ke Alma (Nā Akua), the people are born from the land. The life of the land and its people is maintained in righteousness. The right of Native Hawaiians, their descendants, and possessions, to be buried on the land of their Hawaiian ancestry shall not be denied. Hawaiian burial sites shall not be disturbed. Ka Lāhui Hawai'i shall provide and designate lands for this purpose and shall acknowledge the responsibility of the decedent's 'ohana to care for and maintain such burial sites.

6. Definition: Subsistence applied herein, means use for personal consumption, or use which provides a basis for the economic support of the immediate family, the ahupua'a (land division extending from the uplands to the sea), or the larger Hawaiian community according to culturally appropriate practices.

(B) Law of the Land and Fresh Water:

1. General: Lands used by Native Hawaiians and their descendants for the cultivation of traditional food staples shall be entitled to water in sufficient quantities so as to maintain customary and traditional agricultural practices including, but not limited to, the cultivation of kalo, la'i or ki, aho, and medicinal plants for subsistence, cultural, and religious purposes. Kuleana rights shall not be abridged. Native Hawaiians and their descendants shall have full indigenous rights of gathering for subsistence, medicinal, cultural, and religious purposes. All other land use on native Hawaiian trust lands shall employ culturally appropriate or Ka Lāhui Hawai'i-sanctioned practices.

2. Water: The customary and traditional rights possessed by Native Hawaiians and their descendants to harvest, cultivate, and propagate from the streams and their ecosystems, traditional food staples including but not limited to, hihiwai, ' ōpae, 'o'opu, ho'i'o, and limu shall not be abridged. The right to maintain stream flows and watercourses of the archipelago for subsistence, medicinal, cultural, and religious purposes shall not be abridged. Native Hawaiians and their descendants shall also have the right to drinking water, running water, groundwater and rain water, and this shall be free to all who are citizens of Ka Lāhui Hawai'i on all lands of the archipelago.

3. Landlords' Titles Subject to Tenants' Use: Where landlords have obtained, or may hereafter obtain, allodial title to their lands, Native Hawaiians and their descendants shall not be deprived of their right to take building materials, medicinal or other plants, and minerals from the ahupua'a within which they live, for their own use, including but not limited to: firewood, timber, stones, aho, thatch, la'i or ki.

   4. Land-Locked Bodies of Water: Traditional and customary rights
      shall extend to all lakes, anchialine ponds, and punawai (water
      springs) of the archipelago.
(C) The Law of the Shore to the Depth of the Ocean: The traditional and
    customary rights of Native Hawaiians and their descendants to fish,
    gather, and harvest, including but not limited to the right to spear fish,
    to throw and lay net in the waters and shorelines of the archipelago, to
    cultivate its resources for personal subsistence, medicinal, cultural,
    and religious purposes shall not be abridged.
(D) Fishponds: The traditional and customary rights of Native Hawaiians
    and their descendants to propagate and harvest in the loko wai (fresh-
    water fishpond), loko i'a kalo, loko kuapā, and other types of fish
    ponds shall not be abridged. Fishponds shall be maintained by cultur-
    ally appropriate practices.
(E) Rules and Regulations: Ka Lāhui Hawai'i shall protect and provide
    for the above rights in the exercise of its powers and duties, and in the
    promulgation of rules and regulations to provide administration of its
    lands, the airspace above those lands, all bodies of water within and
    surrounding its domain.

Article II

Ho'okupa (Citizenship)

SECTION 1. ENROLLMENT:

Native Hawaiians and their descendants may enroll as citizens of Ka Lāhui Hawai'i.

SECTION 2. NOTICE OF MAILING ADDRESS:

Citizens of Ka Lāhui Hawai'i shall have either a post office box, a residence
address, or a forwarding address registered for official correspondence.

SECTION 3. CITIZENSHIP RIGHTS AND DUTIES:

The full rights, privileges, and duties as prescribed by the Constitution of Ka
Lāhui Hawai'i shall extend to each citizen.

(A) Voting Qualifications: Any Hawaiian who is and has been a citizen of
    Ka Lāhui Hawai'i for a period of one (1) year, who has resided in his
    elective Mokupuni (Island), and who is the age of eighteen (18) years
    or older, shall have the right to vote.
(B) Voting Registration: The Lukānela Kia'āina (Lieutenant Governor,
    Deputy Prime Minister) shall enact procedures to ensure that Hawaiians
    register to vote.
(C) Conflict of Interest: No person vacating an elected position with the
    U.S. Federal, State, or County governments shall be eligible to run for
    elective office in Ka Lāhui Hawai'i until the second Ka Lāhui Hawai'i
    election following their departure from such U.S. Federal, State, or

County office, provided that said candidate has been a registered citizen of Ka Lāhui Hawai'i for five (5) consecutive years.

SECTION 4. HONORARY CITIZENSHIP:

There shall be honorary citizens of Ka Lāhui Hawai'i who are not of Hawaiian ancestry. Such citizens shall not be entitled to the rights and privileges afforded the Native Hawaiian and Hawaiian citizens of Ka Lāhui Hawai'i. Procedures for conferring citizenship shall be enacted by the 'Aha 'Ōlelo Kānāwai.

Article III

Mokuna Ali'i Nui

SECTION 1. ALI'I NUI:

In accordance with the appointment of Kalokuokamaile II, the Ali'i Nui shall be Kalokuokamaile III. Kalokuokamaile III shall be Noa Ka' ipoho' ohuaamauwaokalanikupuapa 'ikalaninui DeGuair, grandson of Kalokuokamaile II.

SECTION 2. DUTIES AND RESPONSIBILITIES:

The Ali 'i Nui shall symbolize Ka Lāhui Hawai'i, represent Ka Lāhui Hawai'i in all matters requiring protocol and consult with the 'Aha Ali'i and the 'Aha Kūkā o Ke Ali'i Nui on matters of cultural tradition. The Ali'i Nui shall hold no other office under this Constitution.

SECTION 3. KUHINA NUI:

Ka Lāhui Hawai'i recognizes that Kalokuokamaile II did duly appoint Owana Ka'ohelelani as the Kuhina Nui to oversee the office of Ali'i Nui until such time as Kalokuokamaile III is twenty-one (21) years of age or is prepared to assume the office of the Ali'i Nui of Ka Lāhui Hawai'i.

SECTION 4. SUCCESSORSHIP:

The Ali'i Nui shall appoint a successor from among the 'Aha Ali'i or from his issue. Should there be no appointment, the decision shall rest with the 'Aha Ali'i.

SECTION 5. 'AHA ALI'I:

The Ali'i Nui shall assemble an 'Aha Ali'i, with the assistance of each Island Caucus, comprised of various chiefly clans from each Mokupuni. The eligibility criteria for the 'Aha Ali'i shall be as follows:

(A) Genealogy which proves Ali'i lineage; and
(B) Knowledge of culture, traditions and protocol as established by Kiipuna or other recognized authorities. The Ali'i Nui shall appoint all traditional ranks and assign duties within the 'Aha Ali'i.

SECTION 6. 'AHA KŪKĀ O KE ALI'I NUI:

The Ali'i Nui shall assemble the 'Aha Kūkā O Ke Ali'i Nui, with the assistance of each Island Caucus, to be composed of citizens who are specialists, Kūpuna and Maka'āinana, who shall advise the Ali'i Nui in matters of history, genealogy, Hawaiian language, social, and cultural traditions for the purposes of protocol and education.

SECTION 7. COMMUNICATION WITH OTHER BRANCHES:

The Ali'i Nui shall be kept informed by all branches of the Ka Lāhui Hawai'i government as to the affairs of the Nation.

Article IV

Ka Mana O Ka Mokuna O Ka 'Aha 'Ōlelo Kānāwai
A Me Nā Ho'okupa (Legislative Power)

SECTION 1. LEGISLATIVE AUTHORITY:

The Legislative authority of Ka Lāhui Hawai'i shall be vested in the 'Aha 'Ōlelo Kānāwai (Legislature) consisting of one chamber. The voting citizens reserve for themselves the power to propose laws and amendments to the Constitution, to enact or reject the same at the polls, independent of the 'Aha 'Ōlelo Kānāwai, through exercise of their reserve powers, and to approve or disapprove at the Rolls any act, item, Section, or part of any act passed by the 'Aha 'Ōlelo Kānāwai.

SECTION 2. RESERVED POWERS OF THE PEOPLE:

The voting citizens shall have the exclusive right to initiate petition for the enactment or rejection of laws and the recall of elected officers and Luna Kānāwai (Judges) as provided below.

(A) Initiative:
  1. The citizens may enact laws and Constitutional amendments independent of the 'Aha 'Ōlelo Kānāwai. The power of the citizens to enact laws shall be by petition pursuant to the following rules:

(a) Petition to Enact a Law: The laws to be enacted shall be set forth at length in clear language (Hawaiian or English) which shall include a statement concerning the purpose of the law. The petition shall be signed by seven percent (7 percent) of the number of votes cast for Kia'āina in the preceding election. The registered voters who sign the petition must come from twofifths (2/5) of the districts of Ka Lāhui Hawai'i. The petition shall be filed with the Kākau 'Ōlelo of Ka Lāhui Hawai'i at least four (4) months before the next General Election. The same law, in form or substance, shall not be submitted to the citizens by initiative petition more often than once every two (2) years. If conflicting measures are submitted to the citizens at the same election, the measure receiving the highest number of affirmative votes shall become law as to all conflicting provisions.

(b) Petition to Enact a Constitutional Amendment: The law to be enacted shall be set forth at length in clear language which shall include a statement concerning the purpose of the law. The petition shall be signed by ten percent (10 percent) of the number of votes cast for the Kia'aina in the preceding election. The registered voters who sign the petition must come from two-fifths (2/5) of the districts of Ka Lāhui Hawai'i. The petition shall be filed with the Kākau 'Ōlelo at least four (4) months before the next General Election. The Kākau 'Ōlelo of Ka Lāhui Hawai'i shall refer the matter to the election officer for submittal to the citizens of Ka Lāhui Hawai'i for approval or disapproval at the next General Election. The same law, in form or substance, shall not be submitted to the citizens by initiative petition more often than once every three (3) years. If conflicting measures are submitted to the citizens at the same election, the measure receiving the highest number of affirmative votes shall become law as to all conflicting provisions.

> 2. The constitutional limitations that pertain to the scope and subject matter of statutes enacted by the 'Aha 'Ōlelo Kānāwai shall apply to those enacted by initiative.

(B) Referendum:

The citizens may revoke, in whole or in part, any act of the 'Aha 'Ōlelo Kānāwai, subject to the following limitations. The citizens may not revoke any law which appropriates money to Ka Lāhui Hawai'i nor to any institution in existence at the time of passage, nor shall the citizens revoke emergency acts for the immediate preservation of the public peace, health, and safety. The power of the citizens to revoke legislation shall be by petition pursuant to the following rules:

1. The petition shall be signed by five percent (5 percent) of the number of votes cast for the Kia'āina in the preceding election. The registered voters who sign the petition shall come from twofifths (2/5) of the districts of Ka Lāhui Hawai'i. The petition shall be filed with the Kākau 'Ōlelo of Ka Lāhui Hawai'i not less than ninety (90) days after the adjournment of the 'Aha 'Ōlelo Kānāwai which enacted the measure. The petition shall set out in clear language the title of the act against which the petition is invoked or, where applicable, the specific Sections or portions of the act against which the referendum is invoked.
2. When referendum is invoked as provided for in Section 2(B)(1) above, the Kākau 'Ōlelo of Ka Lāhui Hawai'i shall refer the matter to the elections officer for submittal to the citizens of Ka Lāhui Hawai'i for approval or disapproval at the next General Election held not less than thirty (30) days after the petition is filed with the Kākau 'Ōlelo.

(a) Initiative and Referendum, Base Number of Votes, Veto, Election Returns, Constitutional Amendments, Non-Partisan Ballot:

I. The veto power of the Kia'āina shall not extend to measures initiated by or referred to the citizens.
II. In determining the percentage of registered voters needed to sign a petition in Section 2(A) and Section 2(B) above, the base number for

which the number of signatures shall be computed as the whole of votes cast for the Kia'āina in the preceding election.

   i. A measure will be enacted or amend the Constitution as the case may be, if it receives the majority of the votes cast and it receives at least thirty-five percent (35 percent) of the total votes at the election to which it was submitted.

   ii. The vote on initiative and referendum measures shall be returned and canvassed in the manner prescribed by law. Measures enacted by initiative and referendum shall become law, or cease to be law, as the case may be. The Kia'āina shall make a declaration on the voting not less than ten (10) days after the official canvas of the votes has concluded.

   iii. The method of adopting amendments to the Constitution provided in this Article shall be supplemental to that prescribed in Article VIII Section 3 of the Constitution entitled, "Amendments to the Constitution."

   iv. The provisions regarding initiative and referendum shall be self-executing, but the 'Aha 'Ōlelo Kānāwai may enact provisions to facilitate their operation.

   v. When a proposition is submitted, it shall be submitted in a non-partisan manner and there shall be no marking on the ballot indicating its endorsement or censure by a political party of organization.

   vi. Only the title or proper descriptive words of a measure shall be printed on the ballot and when two (2) or more measures have the same title, they shall be numbered consecutively in the order of filing with the Kākau 'Ōlelo of Ka Lāhui Hawai'i. Such number shall be followed by the name of the first petitioner on the corresponding petition.

(b) Recall: An elected officer or Luna Kānāwai (Judge) may be recalled by petition. Upon receipt by the Lukānela 'Kia'āina (Lieutenant Governor, Deputy Prime Minister) of a petition signed by ten percent (10 percent) of the voters eligible to vote for that elected officer or Luna Kānāwai, it shall be the duty of the Lukānela Kia'āina to call a Special Election on the question of recall. Such Special Election shall be called and held within a period of sixty (60) days after the receipt of the petition. No elected officer or Luna Kānāwai may be recalled except by a majority vote in an election in which at least thirty-five percent (35 percent) of the eligible voters of Ka Lāhui Hawai'i have voted.

SECTION 3. LEGISLATIVE JOURNAL, VOICE VOTE, OPEN DOORS:

The 'Aha 'Ōlelo Kānāwai shall keep a journal of its proceedings and publish them, to include the yea and nay votes for each member on any question, except such parts as may require confidentiality. All votes shall be by voice. The doors of the 'Aha 'Ōlelo Kānāwai and of the Standing Committees shall be open at all times, with the exception of any executive sessions.

SECTION 4. STYLE OF BILLS, MAJORITY NECESSARY FOR PASSAGE:

The style of all bills shall be: "Be it enacted by the people of Ka Lāhui Hawai'i…" No law shall be enacted except by bill. No bill shall be passed by the 'Aha 'Ōlelo Kānāwai unless by vote of a majority of all elected members and the yea and nay votes on the question of final passage of any bill shall be entered upon the journal.

SECTION 5. BILLS AND RESOLUTIONS READ BY TITLE, BILLS TO CONTAIN
ONE SUBJECT, SIGNING OF BILLS:

Every bill and resolution shall be read by title when introduced. A printed copy shall be provided to each member and the bill and all amendments shall be read at-large before the vote is taken upon its final passage. No bill shall contain more than one subject and the same shall be clearly expressed in the title. No law shall be amended unless the bill contains the Section or Sections to be amended. The Kia'āina, or the Lukānela Kia'āina, if acting as presiding officer, shall sign in the presence of the 'Aha 'Ōlelo Kānāwai, while the same is in session and capable of transacting business.

SECTION 6. ACTS TAKE EFFECT AFTER THREE (3) MONTHS,
EMERGENCY BILLS, PUBLICATION OF SESSION LAWS:

No act shall take effect until three (3) calendar months after the adjournment of the session at which it passed, unless in case of emergency, as expressed in the Preamble or body of the Act. All laws shall be published within sixty (60) days after the adjournment of each session and distributed in such manner as the 'Aha 'Ōlelo Kānāwai may provide.

SECTION 7. ELECTIONS:

(A) General Election:

1. Executive: Beginning with the General Election in February 1990, and every four (4) years thereafter, all voting citizens shall elect a Kia'āina (Governor, Prime Minister), Lukānela Kia'āina, Kākau 'Ōlelo, and Pu'uku Lāhui (National Treasurer, Minister of Finance) of the Mokuna Ho'okō (Executive Branch).

2. District Representatives: Each district shall elect a Chair, a Vice-Chair, a Secretary, and representatives for the Health, and for the Land and Natural Resources concerns for the district. The elected District Chair, the Health, and the Land and Natural Resources representatives shall sit on the Island Caucus. The elected Chairs of the eight (8) districts of Hawai'i, Maui, and Kaua'i shall represent those districts in the 'Aha 'Ōlelo Kānāwai of Ka Lāhui Hawai'i. For the Mokupuni of Ni'ihau and Lana'i, the elected district officers and one person elected at-large shall sit in the 'Aha'Ōlelo Kānāwai of Ka Lāhui Hawai'i, for a total of eight (8) Alaka'i (legislators). For the

Mokupuni of O'ahu, the four (4) district Chairs and four (4) people elected at-large shall sit in the 'Aha 'Ōlelo Kānāwai of Ka Lāhui Hawai'i, for a total of eight (8) Alaka'i. For the Mokupuni of Moloka'i, the three (3) District Council Chairs, the three (3) District Council Vice-Chairs, and two (2) people elected at-large shall sit in the 'Aha 'Ōlelo Kānāwai of Ka Lāhui Hawai'i, for a total of eight (8) Alaka'i. Such elections shall be by majority vote.

(B) Special Election: In the event an elected official is removed by recall, censure, impeachment, arrest, death, or disability, the vacant seat shall be filled by Special Election. The procedures of the Special Election shall be defined by the 'Aha 'Ōlelo Kānāwai.

SECTION 8. DISTRICT COUNCILS:

There shall be a District Council created in each district of Ka Lāhui Hawai'i. The elected Chair, Vice-Chair, Secretary, and District Chairpersons of the Standing Committees shall comprise a District Council. Other committees may be added to the District Council. Each district will conduct meetings on a regular basis so that information and concerns may be solicited from citizens of the district and forwarded to the Island Caucus and the 'Aha 'Ōlelo Kānāwai for appropriate action, and to be informed of the affairs of Ka Lāhui Hawai'i.

(A) District Council Standing Committees: There shall be not less than two (2) District Council Standing Committees for each district of Ka Lāhui Hawai'i: (1) Health; and (2) Land and Natural Resources. A Committee shall consist of not less than three (3) members who shall consider, investigate, and take action on certain matters or subjects in regard to the aforesaid District Council Standing Committees.

SECTION 9. ISLAND CAUCUSES:

(A) Establishment of The Island Caucuses: There shall be an Island Caucus for every Mokupuni of Ka Lāhui Hawai'i. The Island Caucus shall be composed of the chairpersons and representatives of the Standing Committees of each district and elected district representatives. The 'Aha 'Ōlelo Kānāwai and the Mokuna Ho'okō (Executive Branch) shall utilize the Island Caucus to present information on the affairs of Ka Lāhui Hawai'i for involvement and action by the Island Caucuses, District Councils, and the citizenry.

1. The Island Caucus shall elect an Island Po'o to conduct Island Caucus meetings on a regular basis so that information and concerns may be solicited island-wide for appropriate action.
2. The Island Caucus shall also elect an Island Treasurer. The Island Treasurer shall be a citizen of Ka Lāhui Hawai'i and of Hawaiian ancestry. He shall be not less than twenty-five (25) years of age on the date of his election. The Island Treasurer must be knowledgeable of Generally Accepted Accounting Principles (GAAP). The Island Treasurer shall be the chair of the respective Island Budget and Finance Committee. He shall keep full and accurate books of account of

receipts, disbursements, vouchers, and other records of the Island and Districts. He shall, on behalf of the Island or District, and with the approval of the Island Caucus as appropriated by the Island Caucus Budget, endorse all checks, warrants, bills payable and negotiable instruments of or for the Island. He shall make disbursements and deposit all monies and other valuables in the name and to the account of the Island Caucus in such banks or other depositories as may be designated by the Island Caucus. He shall render an accounting of his transactions, together with the official records thereof, to the Pu'uku Lāhui (National Treasurer), the Island Caucus, and the respective Island Po'o for their examination and approval as often as the Pu'ukn Lāhui, the Island Caucus, or the Island Po'o may require. In addition, the Island Treasurer is required to make a full financial report annually, of which a copy must be provided to the Pu'uku Lāhui. Such an annual report may be subject to audit. The Island Treasurer shall perform other duties as incident to his office, as prescribed by law, or assigned by the Pu'uku Lāhui. A vacancy of the office of the Island Treasurer shall be filled by two-thirds (2/3) vote of the respective Island Caucus.

3. The Island Caucus shall also elect an Island Education Chair. The Island Education Chair shall be a citizen of Ka Lāhui Hawai'i and be of Hawaiian ancestry. He shall be not less than twenty-five (25) years old on the day of his election. The Island Education Chair shall be knowledgeable of the Constitution of Ka Lāhui Hawai'i and shall be responsible for the facilitation of Sovereignty (Self-governance) workshops. The Island Education Chair shall make himself available to the National Education Chair for any duties deemed necessary by the National Education Committee.

4. The Island Caucus shall elect a Health Chair and a Land and Natural Resources Chair.

(B) Island Caucus Standing Committees: There shall be not less than five (5) Island Caucus Standing Committees for each of the Mokupuni of Ka Lāhui Hawai'i: (1) Budget and Finance; (2) Education; (3) Enrollment; (4) Health; and (5) Land and Natural Resources.

1. Island Budget and Finance Committee:

   (a) The Island Budget and Finance Committee shall be chaired by the respective Island Treasurer. The Committee shall be composed of a minimum of four (4) other members who shall be appointed by the respective Island Po' o promptly after the first Legislative Session, to consider, investigate, and take action upon certain matters in regard to the finances of Ka Lāhui Hawai'i . It shall be the duty of each Island Budget and Finance Committee to prepare an Island budget for the fiscal year beginning the first day of January, and to submit it to the Island Caucus for review. The Committee shall then submit the reviewed budget to the National Budget and Finance Committee for its approval no later than two (2) months prior to the second Legislative Session. The Island Budget and Finance Committee may periodically submit supplements to the budgets for the current fiscal year.

(b) An Island Budget shall be developed by the respective Island Budget and Finance Committee, reviewed by the Island Caucus and approved by the National Budget and Finance Committee. The role of the Island Budget shall be two-fold: (1) to allow the Island Caucus to prioritize the financial goals, including revenue generating activities, of the Island in accordance with the National Budget Act; and (2) to support daily governmental operations and related expenses at the National and Island levels as well as other National priorities of Ka Lāhui Hawai'i.

(c) The Island Budget and Finance Committee shall implement National revenue enhancement activities at the Island level. The Committee shall also develop, implement, monitor, and evaluate Island revenue enhancement activities, and have the authority to propose amendments to any District revenue enhancement proposals. All Island and District revenue enhancement proposals must be approved by the National Budget and Finance Committee before implementation.

(d) There shall be performed an internal audit of all of Ka Lāhui Hawai'i Island Treasuries within ninety (90) days after the close of business of each fiscal year, and said reports shall be made available by the respective Island Budget and Finance Committee to the citizens for inspection.

2. Island Education Committee:

(a) The Island Education Committee shall be chaired by the Island Education Chair who shall be elected by the respective Island Caucus, and be composed of a minimum of four (4) other members who shall be appointed by the respective Island Po'o promptly after the first Legislative Session. It shall be the duty of the Island Education Committee to establish a calendar of events for the year beginning the first of January, to be submitted to the National Education Committee for review and approval.

(b) The Island Education calendar shall reflect the National priorities as set forth according to the laws established by the 'Aha 'Ōlelo Kānāwai. The National Education calendar shall also reflect the Island priorities as established by the respective Island Caucus.

3. Island Enrollment Committee:

There shall be an Enrollment Committee on each Island that shall work with the Kākau 'Ōlelo to implement the Ka Lāhui Hawai'i citizen enrollment, register, and information system. Each Committee shall coordinate the enrollment of citizens and shall appoint one (1) person to maintain a computer database for the respective Island. All Island database persons shall designate one (1) person from its group to maintain a National Ka Lāhui Hawai'i citizen roll. A copy of the National Ka Lāhui Hawai'i citizen roll shall also be on file with the Office of the Kākau 'Ōlelo. Each Island database person shall take the Nōkali Oath of Confidentiality.

SECTION 10. TREATY RATIFICATION:

The 'Aha 'Ōlelo Kānāwai of Ka Lāhui Hawai'i shall have the exclusive power to ratify or amend any treaty or convention between the Government of Ka Lāhui Hawai'i and other states, governments, nations, or peoples. The vote for Convention or treaty ratification or amendment shall be by two-thirds (2/3) vote of the 'Aha 'Ōlelo Kānāwai.

Article V

Mokuna 'Aha 'Ōlelo Kānāwai (Legislative Branch)

SECTION 1. LEGISLATIVE DISTRICTS:

(A) Nā Mokupuni (Islands) Identified: Nā Mokupuni of Ka Lāhui Hawai'i shall be Kaua'i, Ni'ihau, O'ahu, Maui, Moloka'i, Kaho'olawe, Lana'i, and Hawai'i.

(B) Legislative Districts of Nā Mokupuni: There shall be thirty-three (33) legislative districts as follows:

1. Hawaii: Ka'u, South Kona, North Kona, Kohala, Harnakua, Keaukaha-North Hilo, Hilo, Puna;
2. Maui: Ke'anae/Wailuanui, Kahului, Lahaina, Wailuku, Kihei, Makawao, Pa'ia, Hana;
3. Moloka'i: West, Central, East;
4. Lana'i: Lana'i;
5. O'ahu: Ko'olau, Leeward, Kona, Central;
6. Kaua'i: Hanalei, Anahola, Kapa' a, Lihu'e, Koloa, Kalaheo, Waimea, Napali
7. Ni'ihau: Ni'ihau
8. Kaho'olawe: See Section (l)(E) herein.

(C) Number Of Alaka'i (Legislators): The Legislative districts shall have the following number of Alaka'i: Mokupuni of Hawai'i, eight (8); Mokupuni of Maui, eight (8); Mokupuni of Moloka'i, eight (8); Mokupuni of Lana'i, eight (8); Mokupuni of O'ahu, eight (8); Mokupuni of Kaua'i, eight (8); Mokupuni of Ni' ihau, eight (8); and Mokupuni of Kaho'olawe, see Section (l)(E) herein. Not less than one-half (1/2) of the Alaka'i of each Island shall be Native Hawaiians of fifty percent (50 percent) blood quantum or more and shall be elected by Native Hawaiians. The remaining Alaka'i of each Island may be of any blood quantum and shall be elected by Hawaiians of less than fifty percent (50 percent) blood quantum. The provisions of this Section shall be subject to the provisions of Article IV, Section 7.

(D) Redistricting And Apportionment: The 'Aha 'Ōlelo Kānāwai shall enact laws to provide for redistricting and apportionment based on data obtained from a national census which shall be conducted every five (5) years beginning in 1987.

(E) Kaho'olawe Representation: Until Hawaiians reside on Kaho'olawe or until the 'Aha 'Ōlelo Kānāwai resolves the residency requirement and Kaho'olawe may elect their own Alaka' i, Ka Lāhui Hawai'i shall maintain a Kaho'olawe Caucus.

1. Kaho'olawe Caucus: The purpose of the Kaho'olawe Caucus is to assure the concerns of Kaho'olawe are properly represented and protected. There shall be no limit on the number of members of the Kaho'olawe Caucus; however a member must meet all of the following requirements:

   (a) Demonstrate at least three (3) years of involvement with the Mokupuni of Kaho'olawe through active participation in projects and activities relating to the advancement of aloha 'aina;
   (b) Citizenship in Ka Lāhui Hawai'i (voting or thereof, or any Country during the term for which he shall have honorary) for not less than one (1) year; and

(c) Actively participate in the Kaho'olawe Caucus. Failure to adequately participate actively shall result in removal from the Caucus. Any person removed from the Caucus may be replaced by a person satisfying all aforementioned requirements.

2. Kaho'olawe Representation in the 'Aha 'Ōlelo Kana Wai: The Kaho'olawe Caucus shall function as any other Island Caucus and shall be empowered to nominate and elect eight (8) non-voting representatives to sit in the 'Aha 'Ōlelo Kānāwai of Ka Lāhui Hawai'i. To be nominated, a person must meet all of the following requirements:

(a) Demonstrate at least five (5) years of involvement with the Mokupuni of Kaho'olawe through active participation in projects and activities that pertain to the advancement of aloha 'aina;
(b) Be a voting citizen of Ka Lāhui Hawai'i; and
(c) Be an active member of the Kaho'olawe Caucus.

SECTION 2. LEGISLATIVE SESSIONS:

(A) The 'Aha 'Ōlelo Kānāwai shall consist of not more than sixty-nine (69) members and not less than thirty (30) members. The sessions of the 'Aha 'Ōlelo Kānāwai shall be held twice annually except as otherwise provided by law.
(B) Emergency sessions of the 'Aha 'Ōlelo Kānāwai shall be convened at the request of a majority of the members of the Executive Board (Cabinet), provided that one (1) week notice be given.

SECTION 3. 'AHA 'ŌLELO KĀNĀWAI, TERMS, ELECTION:

At the General Election to be held on February 1990, one-half (1/2) of the members of the 'Aha 'Ōlelo Kānāwai that accrue the highest number of populace votes shall be elected for a term of four (4) years, and the remainder for a term of two (2) years, and thereafter all members shall be elected for a term of four (4) years, with the manner of such election to be determined by the 'Aha 'Ōlelo Kānāwai. Each member shall be nominated and elected in a non-partisan manner and without any indication on the ballot that he is affiliated with or endorsed by any political party or organization.

SECTION 4. QUALIFICATIONS AND REMOVAL OF ALAKA'I:

(A) A person shall be eligible to seek Legislative office if on the date of the General Election at which he is elected, or on the date of his appointment he is a registered voter, and has at least attained the age of twenty-one (21) years. He shall have resided within the district from which he is elected for at least two (2) years preceding such election, with the exception of absences for the public business for Ka Lāhui Hawai'i. No person who is elected to Legislative office shall hold such office after he moves away from said district.
(B) Alaka'i shall be citizens of Ka Lāhui Hawai'i.

SECTION 5. DISQUALIFICATION OF ALAKA'I:

No person holding office under the authority of the United States, or any lucrative elective office under the authority of the State of Hawai'i shall be eligible to, or have a seat in the 'Aha 'Ōlelo Kānāwai. No person elected or appointed to the 'Aha 'Ōlelo Kānāwai shall receive any civil appointment to a foreign government office while holding membership in the 'Aha 'Ōlelo Kānāwai or while the 'Aha 'Ōlelo Kānāwai is in session. All such elected or appointed Alaka'i shall be disqualified.

SECTION 6. PRIVILEGE OF MEMBERS:

No member of the 'Aha 'Ōlelo Kānāwai shall be liable in any civil or criminal action whatever for words spoken in debate.

SECTION 7. CONFLICTS OF INTEREST, STANDARDS:

No member of the 'Aha 'Ōlelo Kānāwai or any national officer shall have a conflict of interest, as defined by the 'Aha 'Ōlelo Kānāwai, directly or in any contract with the United States of America and the State of Hawai'i, or any county or municipality been elected or appointed, or within one (1) year after the expiration of such term. The 'Aha 'Ōlelo Kānāwai shall prescribe standards and definitions for determining the existence of such conflicts of interest in contracts, and it shall prescribe sanctions for enforcing this Section.

SECTION 8. LEGISLATIVE SESSIONS, QUORUM, RULES OF PROCEDURE, EXPULSION OF MEMBERS, DISRESPECTFUL BEHAVIOR, PENALTY:

(A) Beginning with the year 1990, regular sessions of the 'Aha 'Ōlelo Kānāwai shall be held biannually, commencing in the months of June and November. The duration of regular sessions shall not exceed ten (10) Legislative days unless extended by a vote of four-fifths (4/5) of all voting members elected to the 'Aha 'Ōlelo Kānāwai. Bills and resolutions under consideration by the 'Aha 'Ōlelo Kānāwai upon adjournment of a regular session may be considered at the next regular session, as if there had been no such adjournment.

(B) The Kia'āina shall preside, but shall vote only when the 'Aha 'Ōlelo Kānāwai is equally divided.

(C) A majority of the voting members elected to the 'Aha 'Ōlelo Kānāwai shall constitute a quorum.

(D) The 'Aha 'Ōlelo Kānāwai shall determine the rules of its proceedings. No member shall be expelled except by a vote of twothirds (2/3) of all voting members elected to the 'Aha 'Ōlelo Kānāwai. The 'Aha 'Ōlelo Kānāwai may punish by imprisonment any person not a member thereof who shall be guilty of disrespect to the 'Aha 'Ōlelo Kānāwai by disorderly or contemptuous behavior in its presence, but no such imprisonment shall extend beyond twenty-four (24) hours at one time, unless the person shall persist in such disorderly or contemptuous behavior.

SECTION 9. IMPEACHMENT PROCEDURE:

The 'Aha 'Ōlelo Kānāwai shall have the sole power of impeachment, but a majority of the voting members elected must concur. Upon the adoption of a resolution of impeachment, a notice of an impeachment of any officer, other than a Pono Kānāwai (Justice) of the 'Aha Kānāwai Ki'eki'e (High Court), shall be forthwith served upon the Pono Kānāwai Ki'eki'e (Chief Justice of the High Court) by the Clerk of the 'Aha 'Ōlelo Kānāwai, who shall thereupon call a session of the 'Aha Kānāwai Ki'eki'e to meet at the Capitol within ten (10) days after such notice to try the impeachment.

A notice of any impeachment of the Pono Kānāwai Ki'eki'e orany Pono Kānāwai of the 'Aha Kānāwai Ki'eki'e shall be served by the Clerk of the 'Aha 'Ōlelo Kānāwai, and upon any Luna Kānāwai (Judges) of the judicial district within which the Capitol is located. The Clerk shall notify all the Luna Kānāwai of the 'Aha Kānāwai Mokupuni (Island Courts) of Ka Lāhui Hawai'i to meet with him within thirty (30) days at the Capitol. All the Luna Kānāwai shall thereby sit as an 'Aha Kānāwai (Court) to try such impeachment, which such 'Aha Kānāwai shall organize by electing one of its number to preside.

No person shall be convicted without the concurrence of two thirds (2/3) of the voting members on the 'Aha Kānāwai of impeachment. Judgment in cases of impeachment shall not extend further than removal from office and disqualification to hold and enjoy an office of honor, profit, or trust, in Ka Lāhui Hawai'i. No officer shall exercise his official duties after he has been impeached and notified. The party impeached, whether convicted or acquitted, shall nevertheless be liable to prosecution and punishment according to law.

***Article VI

Mokuna Ho'okōlokolo (Judicial Branch)

SECTION 1. MANA LUNA KĀNĀWAI (JUDICIAL POWER):

The Mana Luna Kānāwai shall be vested in the 'Aha Kānāwai Ki'eki'e (High Court), the 'Aha Kānāwai Mokupuni (Island Courts) and such other 'Aha Kānāwai (Courts) as may from time to time be established by the 'Aha 'Ōlelo Kānāwai of Ka Lāhui Hawai'i.

SECTION 2. INDEPENDENCE OF THE 'AHA KĀNĀWAI:

The Mokuna Ho'okōlokolo of Ka Lāhui Hawai'i shall be independent of all other mokuna (branches) of government. The Constitution of Ka Lāhui Hawai'i shall be the supreme law of the land and the 'Aha Kānāwai Ki' eki'e shall be the final arbiter of the Constitution. The 'Aha Kānāwai Ki'eki'e shall also declare any law unconstitutional if found to be in contravention of the Constitution.

SECTION 3. JURISDICTION:

The 'Aha Kānāwai Mokupuni shall be courts of limited jurisdiction vested with authority over cases or controversies arising under the Constitution and laws of the 'Aha 'Ōlelo Kanawal of Ka Lāhui Hawai'i. The 'Aha 'Ōlelo Kānāwai of Ka Lāhui Hawai'i shall be empowered to create and expand the jurisdiction of the 'Aha Kānāwai Mokupuni and such other 'Aha Kānāwai as may from time to time be created. The 'Aha Kānāwai Ki'eki'e shall have appellate jurisdiction over final judgments of the Kānāwai Mokupuni and such othe rcourts as may be created. The 'Aha Kānāwai Ki'eki'e shall have original jurisdiction over disputes between the Islands and in matters of admiralty. The 'Aha 'Ōlelo Kānāwai of Ka Lāhui Hawai'i shall not have authority to alter the jurisdiction of the 'Aha Kānāwai Ki'eki'e. The jurisdiction of the 'Aha Kānāwai Ki'eki'e may be changed only by constitutional amendment. The 'Aha Kānāwai Ki'eki'e shall promulgate rules of procedure and conduct governing all courts of Ka Lāhui Hawai'i as well as the licensing of public advocates. Jurisdictional authority shallremain with the appropriate U.S. Federal and State courts until such time as the 'Aha 'Ōlelo Kānāwai of Ka Lāhui Hawai'i shall delegate jurisdictional authority to the Mokuna Ho'okōlokolo (Judiciary) of Ka Lāhui Hawai'i.

SECTION 4. ELECTION OF LUNA KĀNĀWAI (JUDGES), APPOINTMENT OF PONO KĀNĀWAI (HIGH COURT JUSTICES):

The Luna Kānāwai Mokupuni (Island Court Judges) shall be elected by a majority vote of the citizens of each Island. The Kia'aina shall be vested with authority to appoint, from the pool of Luna Kānāwai Mokupuni, five (5) candidates to the 'Aha Kānāwai Ki'eki'e. Each appointment to the 'Aha Kānāwai Ki'eki'e must be ratified by a two-thirds (2/3) vote of the 'Aha 'Ōlelo Kānāwai of Ka Lāhui Hawai'i. In the event an appointed Luna Kānāwai Mokupuni fails to receive the requisite two-thirds (2/3) vote, the Kia'āina shall appoint another Luna Kānāwai Mokupuni for consideration tothe 'Aha Kānāwai Ki'eki'e. Oncea Luna Kānāwai Mokupuni is ratified by the 'Aha 'Ōlelo Kānāwai, the title of Pono Kānāwai shall be conferred. The five (5) Pono Kānāwai (High Court Justices) of the 'Aha Kānāwai Ki'eki'e shall in tum elect a Pono Kānāwai Ki'eki'e (Chief Justice of the High Court).

SECTION 5. QUALIFICATION OF LUNA KĀNĀWAI MOKUPUNI (ISLAND COURT JUDGES) AND PONO KĀNĀWAI (HIGH COURT JUSTICES):

All Luna Kānāwai Mokupuni and Pono Kānāwai of Ka Lāhui Hawai'i shall be citizens of Ka Lāhui Hawai'i for at least one (1) year, have attained the age of thirty (30) years, and have resided on the island from which he is elected for two (2) years preceding his election unless he shall have been absent on public business of Ka Lāhui Hawai'i. All Luna Kānāwai and Pono Kānāwai must have necessary experience in conflict resolution and shall be persons of good moral character. No person holding an elected position in either Ka Lāhui Hawai'i or the U.S. Federal, State, and county governments shall be eligible to serve in judicial positions. No judge shall sit in any proceeding in which he has a personal interest either directly or indirectly. The 'Aha 'Ōlelo Kānāwai of Ka Lāhui Hawai'i shall pass all laws regarding qualifications of Luna Kānāwai Mokupuni and Pono Kānāwai.

SECTION 6. NUMBER OF LUNA KĀNĀWAI MOKUPUNI:

The number of Luna Kānāwai Mokupuni and the length of term for all Luna Kānāwai shall be decided by the ʻAha ʻŌlelo Kānāwai elf Ka Lāhui Hawaiʻi.

SECTION 7. INABILITY TO PERFORM LUNA KĀNĀWAI DUTIES:

(A) Luna Kānāwai Mokupuni: In the event a Luna Kānāwai Mokupuni is permanently unable to perform his judicial duties, the person with the next highest number of votes for that position in the last election will serve the duration of that term. In the event there are no candidates available to replace the Luna Kānāwai Mokupuni, the Pono Kānāwai Kiʻekiʻe of the ʻAha Kanawai Kiʻekiʻe shall appoint another Luna Kānāwai Mokupun1 for the duration of the term.

(B) Pono Kānāwai: In the event any Pono Kānāwai is permanently unable to perform his judicial duties, the Kiaʻāina shall nominate a Luna Kānāwai Mokupuni for consideration to the ʻAha Kānāwai Kiʻekiʻe and submission to the ʻAha ʻŌlelo Kānāwai of Ka Lāhui Hawaiʻi for ratification.

SECTION 8. PUBLIC ADVOCATES:

Ka Lāhui Hawaiʻi shall provide public advocates to offer free legal representation to indigent citizens of Ka Lāhui Hawaiʻi. All public advocates shall be citizens of Ka Lāhui Hawaiʻi, have necessary experience in conflict resolution, and be persons of good moral character.

SECTION 9. ʻAHA KŪKĀ O NĀ KŪPUNA (COUNCIL OF ELDERS):

Any citizen of the Nation may submit any controversy or claim for hoʻoponopono (a traditional Hawaiian conflict resolution technique) to the ʻAha Kūkā O Nā Kūpuna pursuant to the procedures established by the ʻAha Kūkā O Nā Kūpuna, provided that the resolution of any claim or controversy shall be binding and shall not be appealed to any level of the Mokuna Hoʻokōlokolo of Ka Lāhui Hawaiʻi. Each Island shall form their respective ʻAha Kūkā O Nā Kūpuna.

Article VII

Mokuna Hoʻokō (Executive Branch)

SECTION 1. KIAʻĀINA (GOVERNOR), PRIME MINISTER:

The executive power shall be vested in the Kiaʻāina. The Kiaʻāina, whose title shall also be Prime Minister, shall take care that the laws of Ka Lāhui Hawaiʻi are faithfully executed. His primary duties shall be as follows: have the power *to* veto legislation, which veto may be overridden by not less than a two thirds (2/3) vote of the ʻAha ʻŌlelo Kānāwai; and have co-custody of all funds of the National Treasury with the Puʻukū Lāhui (National Treasurer). The term of office for the Kia'āina shall be four (4) years, but shall not exceed two (2) consecutive terms. He shall have been a Hawai'i resident for not less than three (3) years, a citizen of Ka Lāhui Hawai'i, of Hawaiian ancestry, and shall not be less than thirty (30) years of age on the date of his election.

SECTION 2. LUKĀNELA KIA'ĀINA (LIEUTENANT GOVERNOR), DEPUTY PRIME MINISTER:

The Lukānela Kia'āina, whose title shall also be Deputy Prime Minister, shall be responsible for General and Special Elections of Ka Lāhui Hawai'i. He shall also perform such other duties as prescribed by law or assigned by the Kia'āina. The term of office for the Lukānela Kia'āina shall be four (4) years, but not to exceed two (2) consecutive terms. He shall have been a Hawai'i resident for not less than three (3) years, a citizen of Ka Lāhui Hawai'i, of Hawaiian ancestry, and shall not be less than thirty (30) years of age on the date of his election. The Lukānela Kia'āina shall have powers and duties of the Kia'āina in the event the office of Kia'āina is vacated for any of the following reasons: death, disability, recall, impeachment, or temporary absence. In the event the office of the Kia'āina is permanently vacated, the Lukānela Kia'āina shall serve as Kia'āina until such vacated office is filled by a Special or General Election.

SECTION 3. KĀKAU 'ŌLELO, SECRETARY TO GOVERNMENT:

The primary duties of the Kākau 'Ōlelo, whose title shall also be Secretary to Government, shall be as follows: record-keeping for all proceedings of Ka Lāhui Hawai'i, which minutes and records therefrom shall be made available to the citizens upon request; he shall keep on file all committee reports; conduct the general correspondence of Ka Lāhui Hawai'i; keep on file the Ka Lāhui Hawai'i Citizen Roll; shall have the power of oversight to develop, maintain and update a citizen enrollment information system; and shall have supervisory authority over the Island Enrollment Committees. He shall also perform such other duties as prescribed by law or assigned by the Kia'airia. The term of office for the Kākau 'Ōlelo shall be four (4) years, but not to exceed two (2) consecutive terms. He shall have been a Hawai'i resident for not less than three (3) years, a citizen of Ka Lāhui Hawai'i, of Hawaiian ancestry, and shall not be less than twenty-five (25) years of age on the date of his election. The Kākau 'Ōlelo shall have powers and duties of the Lukānela Kia'āina in the event the office of Lukānela Kia'aina is vacated for any of the following reasons: death, disability, recall, impeachment, or temporary absence. The Kākau 'Ōlelo shall continue to serve as Lukānela Kia'āina until such vacated office is filled by a Special or General Election. Vacancy of the office of Kākau 'Ōlelo shall be filled by a two-thirds (2/3) vote of the 'Aha 'Ōlelo Kānāwai.

SECTION 4. PU'UKŪ LĀHUI (NATIONAL TREASURER), MINISTER OF FINANCE:

The primary duties of the Pu'ukū Lāhui, whose title shall also be Minister of Finance, shall include the following: chair the National Budget and Finance Committee; exercise the power of oversight of the National and Island Budget and Finance Committees; have co-custody of all funds of the National Treasury with the Kia'āina; keep full and accurate books of account receipts, disbursements, vouchers, and other records of the National Treasury; subject to the approval of the National Budget and Finance Committee or as mandated by the National Budget Act, co-endorse with the Kia'āina , all checks, drafts, warrants and bills payable, and negotiable instruments of the National Treasury; make disbursements and deposit all monies and other valuables in the name and to the account of the National Treasury in such banks or other depositories as may be designated by the 'Aha 'Ōlelo Kānāwai; render an accounting of such transactions and official records thereof to the National Budget and Finance Committee and to the Kia'āina; and provide a full annual financial report, which copy must be submitted to the Kia'āina and the National Budget and Finance Committee, said annual report may be subject to an internal or external audit. The Pu'ukū Lāhui shall also perform other duties incident to his office, as prescribed by law, or assigned by the Kia'āina.

The term of office for the Pu'ukū Lāhui shall be four (4) years, but not to exceed two (2) consecutive terms. He shall have been a Hawai'i resident for not less than three (3) years, a citizen of Ka Lāhui Hawai'i, of Hawaiian ancestry, and shall not be less than twenty-five (25) years of age on the date of his election. He shall be knowledgeable of Generally Accepted Accounting Principles (GAAP). Vacancy of the office of Pu'ukū Lāhui shall be filled by a two-thirds (2/3) vote of the 'Aha 'Ōlelo Kānāwai.

SECTION 5. EXECUTIVE BOARD (CABINET):

The Executive Board shall be composed of the Kia'āina, the Lukānela Kia'āina, the Kākau 'Ōlelo, the Pu'ukū Lāhui, appointed Ministers, Chairs of each of the National Standing Committees, and all Island Po'o. It shall be the duty of the Executive Board to conduct the business of Ka Lāhui Hawai'i.

SECTION 6. SECURITY:

The Kia'āina may summon the posse commitatus or call out the militia to prevent or suppress violence, invasion, insurrection, or rebellion.

SECTION 7. EXECUTIVE REGULATIONS:

The Kia'āina shall have the power to issue executive regulations not in conflict with laws of Ka Lāhui Hawai'i.

SECTION 8. SUPERVISION AND CONTROL BY KIA'ĀINA:

The Kia'āina shall have general supervision and control of all executive departments, agencies, and instrumentalities of the Government of Ka Lāhui Hawai'i.

SECTION 9. ANNUAL REPORT:

The Kia'āina shall make an official report of the transactions of the Government of Ka Lāhui Hawai'i and the 'Aha 'Ōlelo Kānāwai within ninety (90) days after the close of each fiscal year.

SECTION 10. PARDONING POWER:

The Kia'āina, and the Aha 'Ōlelo Kānāwai by a two-thirds (2/3) vote, shall have the power to remit fines and forfeitures, commute sentences, and grant reprieves and pardons after conviction for offenses against the laws of Ka Lāhui Hawai'i.

SECTION 11. RECOMMENDATION OF LAWS:

The Kia'āina shall provide information to the 'Aha 'Ōlelo Kānāwai on the state of Ka Lāhui Hawai'i and recommend for its consideration such measures as he may deem necessary and expedient. He may attend or deputize another person to represent him at meetings of the 'Aha 'Ōlelo Kānāwai, and may express his views on any matter before that body.

SECTION 12. APPOINTMENT OF OFFICIALS:

With the exception of elected officials and those which are otherwise provided for in the Constitution, the Kia'āina shall appoint the following officials of the Government of Ka Lāhui Hawai'i including, but not limited to, the following:

(A) Minister of Foreign Affairs: Upon investiture into office, the Minister of Foreign Affairs shall also be known as Minister Extraordinary and Ambassador Plenipotentiary and as directed by the Ka Lāhui Hawai'i Executive (Kia'āina, Lukānela Kia'āina, Kākau 'Ōlelo, or Pu'ukū Lāhui) shall have duties and powers as follows:

1. Establish diplomatic relations for and on behalf of Ka Lāhui Hawai'i;
2. Make official communications with any state, government, nation, or peoples;
3. Receive official communications from any foreign state, government, nation, or peoples in the name of the Government of Ka Lāhui Hawai'i and transmit such communication to the Executive Board; and
4. Initiate treaty negotiations and other agreements of diplomatic recognition by and between the Government of Ka Lāhui Hawai'i and all friendly states, governments, nations, or peoples, which treaties and agreements shall become effective upon their ratification by the 'Aha 'Ōlelo Kānāwai of Ka Lāhui Hawai'i.
5. He shall also submit a budget proposal for the fiscal year beginning the first of January to the National Budget and Finance Committee for approval.
   (a) Minister of Justice: Upon investiture into office, the Minister of Justice shall represent the Government in all claims on behalf of or against the Government brought by the citizens or the 'Aha 'Ōlelo Kānāwai of Ka Lāhui Hawai'i. He shall have no power or authority over the Judicial Branch of the Government. He shall also submit a budget proposal for the fiscal year beginning the first of January to the National Budget and Finance Committee for approval.
   (b) Minister of Home Affairs: Upon investiture into office, the Minister of Home Affairs shall work in conjunction with the National Standing Committees to institute a system of education, health,

and maintenance of land and natural resources, to perpetuate, preserve, and promote the lands within the domain of Ka Lāhui
Hawai'i, the Hawaiian culture, and its people.

SECTION 13. REMOVAL OF OFFICERS, POWERS AND DUTIES OF OFFICERS:

The Kia'āina may appoint or remove any officer whose appointment is not otherwise provided for. All officers shall have such powers and duties as may be
conferred or imposed upon them by law or by executive regulation of the
Kia'āina not consistent with any law.

SECTION 14. PUBLICATION OF LAWS:

The Kia'āina shall make provisions for the publication of laws within sixty
(60) days after the close of each session of the 'Aha 'Ōlelo Kānāwai for distribution to public officials and for sale to the public.

SECTION 15. NATIONAL STANDING COMMITTEES OF KA LĀHUI HAWAI'I:

There shall not be less than four National Standing Committees of Ka Lāhui
Hawai'i as follows: (A) Budget and Finance; (B) Education; (C) Health; and
(D) Land and Natural Resources.

(A) National Budget and Finance Committee:

1. The National Budget and Finance Committee shall be chaired by the Pu
'ukil Lāhui and be composed of a minimum of four (4) other members who
shall be citizens of Ka Lāhui Hawai'i. Such members shall be appointed by the
Kia'āina upon recommendation of the Pu'ukū Lāhui and the 'Aha 'Ōlelo
Kānāwai promptly, after the first Legislative Session, to consider, investigate,
and take action upon certain matters or subjects in regard to the finances of Ka
Lāhui Hawai'i. It shall be the duty of the National Budget and Finance
Committee to prepare a National Budget for the fiscal year beginning the first
day of January, and to submit it to the 'Aha 'Ōlelo Kānāwai for approval at the
next Legislative session. The National Budget and Finance Committee may
periodically submit supplements to the budget for the current fiscal year. The
National Budget and Finance Committee shall have the authority to approve or
disapprove any Island or National Standing Committee budget proposal.
2. A National Budget shall be developed by the National Budget and Finance
Committee and approved by the 'Aha 'Ōlelo Kānāwai. The role of the National
Budget shall be twofold:

(a) To allow the 'Aha 'Ōlelo Kānāwai to prioritize the financial goals, including revenue generating activities of Ka Lāhui Hawai'i in accordance
with the National Budget Act; and
(b) To support daily governmental operations and related expenditures
and National priorities of Ka Lāhui Hawai'i.

3. Budget proposals from each Island Treasurer, the National Standing
Committees, and the Executive Board shall be submitted to the National

Budget and Finance Committee for approval no later than two (2) months prior
to the second Legislative Session. The National Budget and Finance Committee
shall present the National Budget Bill to the 'Aha 'Ōlelo Kānāwai at the second
Legislative Session of each year. The 'Aha 'Ōlelo Kānāwai shall discuss and
vote on motions and amendments to the National Budget Bill for enactment, to
be effective on the first of January of the following year.
4. The National Budget and Finance Committee shall develop, implement,
monitor, and evaluate National revenue generating activities. The Committee
shall also review and make recommendations to all Island Budget and Finance
Committees for revenue generating activities, and shall have authority to approve or disapprove any Island proposals for revenue generation.
5. An internal audit of the Ka Lāhui Hawai'i National Treasury shall be performed within ninety (90) days after the close of business of each fiscal year,
and reports of said internal audit shall be made available by the National
Budget and Finance Committee to the citizens for inspection.

(B) National Education Committee:

1. The National Education Committee Chair shall be appointed by the
   Kia'āina. The National Education Committee shall be composed of not
   less than four (4) other members who shall be appointed by the National
   Education Committee Chair promptly after the first Legislative Session.
   It shall be the duty of the National Education Committee to establish a
   National calendar which shall encompass all Island calendars for the
   year beginning the first of January.
2. Establishment of the National Education Calendar: Education calendars
   will be submitted by each Island Education Chair and by the Executive
   Board to the National Education Committee not less than two (2) months
   prior to the second Legislative Session. Education calendars for each
   Island shall be compiled to assure that no conflicts exist between any
   scheduled Island or national activities. Upon review and approval by the
   National Education Committee. The National education calendar shall
   be submitted to the Kākau 'Ōlelo for distribution to the Executive Board
   and the Island Education Chairs. Amendments to the National calendar
   may be considered, provided no scheduling conflicts exist.
3. The National Education Committee shall also develop, implement,
   monitor, and evaluate all functions that pertain to education as recommended by the Executive Board.

Article VIII

Nā Mea Like 'Ole (Miscellaneous Provisions)

SECTION 1. OFFICERS:

For public convenience and to ensure continuity in the operation of Ka Lāhui
Hawai'i, all officers of Ka Lāhui Hawai'i shall, subject to the right of resignation

or removal as may be provided for by law, continue to hold their respective offices until the expiration of the time for which they were respectively elected or appointed.

SECTION 2. EXISTING LAWS:

All laws of Ka Lāhui Hawai'i consistent with this Constitution shall continue to be in force until they expire by their limitation, or are altered or repealed by competent authority.

SECTION 3. AMENDMENTS TO THE CONSTITUTION:

Amendments to this Constitution may be made as follows:

(A) Any amendment to this Constitution may be proposed to the 'Aha 'Ōlelo Kānāwai, and if agreed to a three-fifths (3/5) vote of all voting members of the 'Aha 'Ōlelo Kānāwai, such proposed amendment shall be entered on the journals, with the yea and nay votes taken thereon. The Kia'āina shall then be requested to submit the proposed amendment to the elections officer for submittal to eligible voters at the next General Election. Amendments approved by a majority of votes cast shall be incorporated into the Constitution.

(B) Constitutional amendments may be made at a Constitutional Convention which shall be held within two (2) years from the date of passage of the original Constitution, thereafter at three (3) years thereafter at five (5) years, and thereafter at ten (10) year intervals to review, amend, or revise the Constitution as may be appropriate. The Convention shall be held as provided by law.

(C) Amendments may also be made pursuant to the provisions of Article IV, Section 2(A)(1)(b) and Article IV, Section 2(A)(2) which provides constitutional amendments by initiative.

SECTION 4. EXISTING RIGHTS AND LIABILITIES:

Except as otherwise provided for in this Constitution, all existing actions, writs, suits, proceedings, civil or criminal liabilities, prosecutions, judgments, decrees, sentences, orders, appeals, causes of action, contracts, claims, demands, titles and rights shall continue unaffected notwithstanding any and all amendments to this Constitution.

SECTION 5. OATHS OF LOYALTY:

(A) Citizen Oath of Loyalty: All citizens of Ka Lāhui Hawai'i shall take and subscribe to the following oath:

I, (Name), of (District of Residence), do solemnly affirm that I will advocate and support and defend the Constitution of Ka Lāhui Hawai'i to all emissaries, foreign and domestic; that I will bear truth, faith and allegiance to the same; that I take this obligation freely; and that I will uphold the laws of Ka Lāhui Hawai'i.

(B) Officer and Legislator Oath of Loyalty:

I, (Name), of (District of Residence), do solemnly affirm that I will support and defend the Constitution of Ka Lāhui Hawai'i against all enemies foreign and domestic; that I will bear true faith and allegiance to the same and will not endorse any other entity claiming Hawaiian sovereignty. I take this obligation freely, without any mental reservation or purpose of evasion, and that I will well and faithfully discharge the duties of the office on which I am about to enter, and that I will well and faithfully uphold the laws of Ka Lāhui Hawai'i.

SECTION 6. DEFINITION OF NATIVE HAWAIIAN:

Native Hawaiian is defined as any descendant of not less than one-half (1/2) part of the blood of the races inhabiting the Hawaiian Islands previous to 1778.

SECTION 7. DEFINITION OF HAWAIIAN:

Hawaiian is defined as any individual whose ancestors were native to the area which comprised the Hawaiian Islands prior to 1778.

SECTION 8. CONSTRUCTION:

Titles in this Constitution shall not be used for the purposes of construction and wherever any personal pronoun appears it shall be construed to mean either gender. In this Constitution, a special or particular provision shall control a general provision should there be any inconsistency between a special or particular provision and a general provision.

SECTION 9. PROVISIONS SELF-EXECUTION:

The provisions of this Constitution shall be self-executing to the fullest extent that their respective natures permit.

SECTION 10. SEAT OF GOVERNMENT:

The seat of Government shall be in Hilo, Hawai'i.

SECTION 11. FLAG OF KA LĀHUI HAWAI'I:

The flag of Ka Lāhui Hawai'i shall be the star constellation known as the Makali' i (Pleiades). The rising of the Makali' i shall serve as an eternal reminder to po'e Hawai'i of the Kumulipo, a creation chant of the native people and one most relevant source of their primordial origins. The symbolic representation of the Makali'i shall be a flag which is a field of royal blue with seven (7) large stars in white and several small stars in white.

SECTION 12. HAWAIIAN GOVERNMENT TITLES:

The following Hawaiian titles, along with their definitions, shall be created and used in the Government of Ka Lāhui Hawai'i:
(A) Legislative Titles
Mokuna 'Aha 'Ōlelo Kānāwai—Legislative Branch
Ka Mana O Ka Mokuna O—Legislative Power

Ka 'Aha 'Ōlelo Kānāwai—Legislative Power
A Me Na Ho'okupa—Legislative Power
'Aha 'Ōlelo Kānāwai—Legislature
Alaka'i—Legislators
Island Po'o—Chair of the Island Caucus
Pu'ukū Mokupuni—Island Treasurer
(B) Executive Titles
Mokuna Ho'okō—Executive Branch
Kia'āina—Governor, Prime Minister
Lukānela Kia'āina—Lieutenant Governor, Deputy Prime Minister
Kākau 'Ōlelo—Secretary to the Governor
Pu'ukū Lāhui—National Treasurer, Minister of finance
(C) Judicial Titles
Mokuna Ho'okōlokolo—Judicial Branch
Mana Luna Kānāwai—Judicial Power
'Aha Kānāwai Ki'eki'e—High Court
Pono Kānāwai Ki'eki'e—Chief Justice of the High Court
Pono Kānāwai—High Court Justices
'Aha Kānāwai Mokupuni—Island Court
Luna Kānāwai Mokupuni—Island Court Judges
'Aha Kānāwai—Court
Luna Kānāwai—Judge
'Aha Kukā o Nā Kūpuna—Council of Elders
(D) Other Titles and Terms
Nā Ke Akua—From God
Nā Akua—From the Gods
Ke Akua—God
Nā Akua—The Gods
Ke Akua (Nā Akua)—God (the Gods)
Kūpuna—Elders
Ho'okupa—Citizenship
Maka' āinana—Citizen
Nōkali—Registrar
Mokuna—Branches of Government
Na Mokupuni—Islands
Nā Mea Like 'Ole—Miscellaneous Provisions

SECTION 13. OFFICIAL LANGUAGES:

The official languages of Ka Lāhui Hawai'i shall be 'Ōlelo Hawai'i (Hawaiian) and English.

SECTION 14. MELE (SONG) OF KA LĀHUI HAWAI'I: (RESERVED)
SECTION 15. EFFECTIVE DATE:

This Constitution shall be effective as of the date of its passage at the first Constitutional Convention on March 15, 1987, and as amended on August 20, 1989, and on July 5, 1992.

SECTION 16. 'AHA KŪKĀ O NĀ KŪPUNA (COUNCIL OF ELDERS):

There shall be a council of elders known as the 'Aha Kūkā ONā Kūpuna, comprised of Kūpuna of the districts of Ka Lāhui Hawai'i. They shall advise Ka Lāhui Hawai'i on matters pertaining to the significance of 'Ōlelo Hawai'i, mo'olelo (oral and written literature, including history) and other ethical, social, traditional, and cultural values of Ka Lāhui Hawai'i. The 'Aha Kūkā O Na Kūpuna shall also have the authority to resolve conflicts as provided for in Article VI, Section 9.

SECTION 17. DONATION OF LANDS PROHIBITED:

Lands under the control of Ka Lāhui Hawai'i shall never be donated to companies, private corporations, or individuals. There shall be enacted laws to prohibit the sale of all Hawaiian lands to non-citizens.

SECTION 18. LAND TRUSTS, DEFINITIONS:

(A) Native Hawaiian Land Trusts:
    The Native Hawaiian Land Trusts refers to lands identified by the Hawaiian Homes Commission Act of 1920 (Act of July 9, 1921, 42 Statute 108, Chapter 42, as amended; Act of March 18, 1959, Public Law, 73 Statute 4, Section 4) and the State of Hawai'i Admissions Act of 1959 (Act of March 18, 1959, Public Law 86–3, 73 Statute 4, Section 5[f]).
    (B) Hawaiian Land Trusts: The Hawaiian Land Trusts refers to lands of the following private land trusts: The Kamehameha Schools/Bishop Estate, Queen Emma Foundation, Queen's Medical Center and Health Care System, Lunalilo Trust, Queen Lili'uokalani Children's Trust, and Kapi'olani Women's and Children's Medical Center.

SECTION 19. OFFICIAL SYMBOLS OF KA LĀHUI HAWAI'I:

The official flower of Ka Lāhui Hawai'i shall be the 'Ohi'a Pua Lehua.
    The official trees of Ka Lāhui Hawai'i shall be the 'Iliahi and Kukui.
    The official marine mammal of Ka Lāhui Hawai'i shall be the Nai'a (Porpoise).
    The Seal and Coat of Arms (Reserved).
    The official bird of Ka Lāhui Hawai'i shall be the 'Io (Native Hawaiian Hawk).

SECTION 20. OFFICIAL HOLIDAYS OF KA LĀHUI HAWAI'I:

(A) Ka Lāhui Hawai'i Independence Day shall be March 15 of each year. It shall be a remembrance day for Mitsuro Uyehara, and a national holiday to recognize this man, the first Honorary Citizen of Ka Lāhui Hawai'i and a founder of this Nation.
(B) Other Holidays (Reserved)

Sources:

Goodyear-Ka'opua, Noelani, Ikaika Hussey, and Erin Kahunawaika'ala Wright, eds. *A Nation Rising: Hawaiian Movements for Life, Land, and Sovereignty.* Durham, NC: Duke University Press, 2014.

Kauanui, J. Kehaulani. *Hawaiian Blood: Colonialism and the Politics of Sovereignty and Indigeneity.* Durham, NC: Duke University Press, 2008.

US Senate. "Native Hawaiian Reparations Community-Based Mental Health Initiative." Hearing Before the Select Committee on Indian Affairs. 100th Cong., 2nd Sess. Washington, DC: Government Printing Office, 1989.

70

Acknowledgement of the Overthrow of the Hawaiian Kingdom (1993)

In January 1993, some 50,000 people attended the 'Onipa'a Centennial Commemoration, a reenactment of the US invasion of Hawaii that had taken place a century earlier. This and other events that year were followed by Congressional approval of Joint Resolution 19, the Apology Resolution, which declared that "the indigenous Hawaiian people never directly surrendered their claims to their inherent sovereignty as a people" and it affirmed that, "Congress...apologizes to Native Hawaiians on behalf of the people of the United States for the overthrow of the Kingdom of Hawaii...and the deprivation of the rights of Native Hawaiians to self-determination." It should be noted, that the resolution, while calling for reconciliation, did not return any lands or powers of government to the Hawaiian people.

———

Joint Resolution 19

To acknowledge the 100th anniversary of the January 17, 1893 overthrow of the Kingdom of Hawaii, and to offer an apology to Native Hawaiians on behalf of the United States for the overthrow of the Kingdom of Hawaii.

Whereas, prior to the arrival of the first Europeans in 1778, the Native Hawaiian people lived in a highly organized, self-sufficient, subsistent social system based on communal land tenure with a sophisticated language, culture, and religion;

Whereas, a unified monarchical government of the Hawaiian Islands was established in 1810 under Kamehameha I, the first King of Hawaii;

Whereas, from 1826 until 1893, the United States recognized the independence of the Kingdom of Hawaii, extended full and complete diplomatic recognition to the Hawaiian Government, and entered into treaties and conventions with the Hawaiian monarchs to govern commerce and navigation in 1826, 1842, 1849, 1875, and 1887;

Whereas, the Congregational Church (now known as the United Church of Christ), through its American Board of Commissioners for Foreign Missions, sponsored and sent more than 100 missionaries to the Kingdom of Hawaii between 1820 and 1850;

Whereas, on January 14, 1893, John L. Stevens (hereafter referred to in this Resolution as the "United States Minister"), the United States Minister assigned to the sovereign and independent Kingdom of Hawaii conspired with a small group of non-Hawaiian residents of the Kingdom of Hawaii, including citizens of the United States, to overthrow the indigenous and lawful Government of Hawaii;

Whereas, in pursuance of the conspiracy to overthrow the Government of Hawaii, the United States Minister and the naval representatives of the United States caused armed naval forces of the United States to invade the sovereign Hawaiian nation on January 16, 1893, and to position themselves near the Hawaiian Government buildings and the Iolani Palace to intimidate Queen Liliuokalani and her Government;

Whereas, on the afternoon of January 17, 1893, a Committee of Safety that represented the American and European sugar planters, descendants of missionaries, and financiers deposed the Hawaiian monarchy and proclaimed the establishment of a Provisional Government;

Whereas, the United States Minister thereupon extended diplomatic recognition to the Provisional Government that was formed by the conspirators without the consent of the Native Hawaiian people or the lawful Government of Hawaii and in violation of treaties between the two nations and of international law;

Whereas, soon thereafter, when informed of the risk of bloodshed with resistance, Queen Liliuokalani issued the following statement yielding her authority to the United States Government rather than to the Provisional Government:

"I Liliuokalani, by the Grace of God and under the Constitution of the Hawaiian Kingdom, Queen, do hereby solemnly protest against any and all acts done against myself and the Constitutional Government of the Hawaiian Kingdom by certain persons claiming to have established a Provisional Government of and for this Kingdom.

"That I yield to the superior force of the United States of America whose Minister Plenipotentiary, His Excellency John L. Stevens, has caused United States troops to be landed at Honolulu and declared that he would support the Provisional Government.

"Now to avoid any collision of armed forces, and perhaps the loss of life, I do this under protest and impelled by said force yield my authority until such time as the Government of the United States shall, upon facts being presented to it, undo the action of its representatives and reinstate me in the authority which I claim as the Constitutional Sovereign of the Hawaiian Islands."

Done at Honolulu this 17th day of January, A.D. 1893;

Whereas, without the active support and intervention by the United States diplomatic and military representatives, the insurrection against the Government of Queen Liliuokalani would have failed for lack of popular support and insufficient arms;

Whereas, on February 1, 1893, the United States Minister raised the American flag and proclaimed Hawaii to be a protectorate of the United States;

Whereas, the report of a Presidentially established investigation conducted by former Congressman James Blount into the events surrounding the insurrection and overthrow of January 17, 1893, concluded that the United States diplomatic and military representatives had abused their authority and were responsible for the change in government;

Whereas, as a result of this investigation, the United States Minister to Hawaii was recalled from his diplomatic post and the military commander of the United States armed forces stationed in Hawaii was disciplined and forced to resign his commission;

Whereas, in a message to Congress on December 18, 1893, President Grover Cleveland reported fully and accurately on the illegal acts of the conspirators, described such acts as an "act of war, committed with the participation of a diplomatic representative of the United States and without authority of Congress" and acknowledged that by such acts the government of a peaceful and friendly people was overthrown;

Whereas, President Cleveland further concluded that a "substantial wrong has thus been done which a due regard for our national character as well as the rights of the injured people requires we should endeavor to repair" and called for the restoration of the Hawaiian monarchy;

Whereas, the Provisional Government protested President Cleveland's call for the restoration of the monarchy and continued to hold state power and pursue annexation to the United States;

Whereas, the Provisional Government successfully lobbied the Committee on Foreign Relations of the Senate (hereafter referred to in this Resolution as the "Committee") to conduct a new investigation into the events surrounding the overthrow of the monarchy;

Whereas, the Committee and its chairman, Senator John Morgan, conducted hearings in Washington, D.C., from December 27,1893, through February 26, 1894, in which members of the Provisional Government justified and condoned the actions of the United States Minister and recommended annexation of Hawaii;

Whereas, although the Provisional Government was able to obscure the role of the United States in the illegal overthrow of the Hawaiian monarchy, it was unable to rally the support from two-thirds of the Senate needed to ratify a treaty of annexation;

Whereas, on July 4, 1894, the Provisional Government declared itself to be the Republic of Hawaii;

Whereas, on January 24, 1895, while imprisoned in Iolani Palace Queen Liliuokalani was forced by representatives of the Republic of Hawaii to officially abdicate her throne;

Whereas, in the 1896 United States Presidential election, William McKinley replaced Grover Cleveland;

Whereas, on July 7, 1898, as a consequence of the Spanish-American War, President McKinley signed the Newlands Joint Resolution that provided for the annexation of Hawaii;

Whereas, through the Newlands Resolution, the self-declared Republic of Hawaii ceded sovereignty over the Hawaiian Islands to the United States;

Whereas, the Republic of Hawaii also ceded 1,800,000 acres of crown, government and public lands of the Kingdom of Hawaii, without the consent of or compensation to the Native Hawaiian people of Hawaii or their sovereign government;

Whereas, the Congress, through the Newlands Resolution, ratified the cession, annexed Hawaii as part of the United States, and vested title to the lands in Hawaii in the United States;

Whereas, the Newlands Resolution also specified that treaties existing between Hawaii and foreign nations were to immediately cease and be replaced by United States treaties with such nations;

Whereas, the Newlands Resolution effected the transaction between the Republic of Hawaii and the United States Government;

Whereas, the indigenous Hawaiian people never directly relinquished their claims to their inherent sovereignty as a people or over their national lands to the United States, either through their monarchy or through a plebiscite or referendum;

Whereas, on April 30, 1900, President McKinley signed the Organic Act that provided a government for the territory of Hawaii and defined the political structure and powers of the newly established Territorial Government and its relationship to the United States;

Whereas, on August 21, 1959, Hawaii became the 50th State of the United States;

Whereas, the health and well-being of the Native Hawaiian people is intrinsically tied to their deep feelings and attachment to the land;

Whereas, the long-range economic and social changes in Hawaii over the nineteenth and early twentieth centuries have been devastating to the population and to the health and well-being of the Hawaiian people;

Whereas, the Native Hawaiian people are determined to preserve, develop and transmit to future generations their ancestral territory, and their cultural identity in accordance with their own spiritual and traditional beliefs, customs, practices, language, and social institutions;

Whereas, in order to promote racial harmony and cultural understanding, the Legislature of the State of Hawaii has determined that the year 1993 should serve Hawaii as a year of special reflection on the rights and dignities of the Native Hawaiians in the Hawaiian and the American societies;

Whereas, the Eighteenth General Synod of the United Church of Christ in recognition of the denomination's historical complicity in the illegal overthrow of the Kingdom of Hawaii in 1893 directed the Office of the President of the United Church of Christ to offer a public apology to the Native Hawaiian people and to initiate the process of reconciliation between the United Church of Christ and the Native Hawaiians; and

Whereas, it is proper and timely for the Congress on the occasion of the impending one hundredth anniversary of the event, to acknowledge the historic significance of the illegal overthrow of the Kingdom of Hawaii, to express its deep regret to the Native Hawaiian people, and to support the reconciliation efforts of the State of Hawaii and the United Church of Christ with Native Hawaiians;

Now, therefore, be it Resolved by the Senate and House of Representatives of the United States of America in Congress assembled,

Section 1. Acknowledgment and Apology.

The Congress -

(1) on the occasion of the 100th anniversary of the illegal overthrow of the Kingdom of Hawaii on January 17, 1893, acknowledges the historical significance of this event which resulted in the suppression of the inherent sovereignty of the Native Hawaiian people;

(2) recognizes and commends efforts of reconciliation initiated by the State of Hawaii and the United Church of Christ with Native Hawaiians;

(3) apologizes to Native Hawaiians on behalf of the people of the United States for the overthrow of the Kingdom of Hawaii on January 17, 1893 with the participation of agents and citizens of the United States, and the deprivation of the rights of Native Hawaiians to self-determination;

(4) expresses its commitment to acknowledge the ramifications of the overthrow of the Kingdom of Hawaii, in order to provide a proper foundation for reconciliation between the United States and the Native Hawaiian people; and

(5) urges the President of the United States to also acknowledge the ramifications of the overthrow of the Kingdom of Hawaii and to support reconciliation efforts between the United States and the Native Hawaiian people.

Section 2. Definitions.

As used in this Joint Resolution, the term "Native Hawaiians" means any individual who is a descendent of the aboriginal people who, prior to 1778, occupied and exercised sovereignty in the area that now constitutes the State of Hawaii.

Section 3. Disclaimer.

Nothing in this Joint Resolution is intended to serve as a settlement of any claims against the United States.

Approved November 23, 1993

Source:

Joint Resolution 19, U.S. Public Law 103–150, 103rd Cong., 1st Sess. (November 23, 1993).

71
President William Clinton's Government-to-Government Relations Memorandum (1994)

Bill Clinton received wide support across Indian country as a candidate, and he showed his support for Tribal nations by hosting over three hundred Native leaders on the White House lawn on April 29, 1994. This was considered a historic event, as it was the first time a president had requested a meeting with all US-based Indigenous leaders. Within a week he issued the following memorandum in which he and the executive departments and agencies under his leadership pledged to support treaties, recognize tribal sovereignty, and follow a more collaborative approach in dealing with Native peoples.

The United States Government has a unique legal relationship with Native American tribal governments as set forth in the Constitution of the United States, treaties, statutes, and court decisions. As executive departments and agencies undertake activities affecting Native American tribal rights or trust resources, such activities should be implemented in a knowledgeable, sensitive manner respectful of tribal sovereignty.

Today, as part of an historic meeting, I am outlining principles that executive departments and agencies, including every component bureau and office, are to follow in their interactions with Native American tribal governments. The purpose of these principles is to clarify our responsibility to ensure that the Federal Government operates within a government-to-government relationship with federally recognized Native American tribes. I am strongly committed to building a more effective day-to-day working relationship reflecting respect for the rights of self-government due the sovereign tribal governments.

In order to ensure that the rights of sovereign tribal governments are fully respected, executive branch activities shall be guided by the following:

(a) The head of each executive department and agency shall be responsible for ensuring that the department or agency operates within a government-to-government relationship with federally recognized tribal governments.

(b) Each executive department and agency shall consult, to the greatest extent practicable and to the extent permitted by law, with tribal governments prior to taking actions that affect federally recognized tribal governments. All such consultations are to be open and candid so that all interested parties may evaluate for themselves the potential impact of relevant proposals.

(c) Each executive department and agency shall assess the impact of Federal Government plans, projects, programs, and activities on tribal trust resources and assure that tribal government rights and concerns are considered during the development of such plans, projects, programs, and activities.

(d) Each executive department and agency shall take appropriate steps to remove any procedural impediments to working directly and effectively with tribal governments on activities that affect the trust property and/or governmental rights of the tribes.

(e) Each executive department and agency shall work cooperatively with other Federal departments and agencies to enlist their interest and support in cooperative efforts, where appropriate, to accomplish the goals of this memorandum.

(f) Each executive department and agency shall apply the requirements of Executive Orders Nos. 12875 ("Enhancing the Inter-governmental Partnership") and 12866 ("Regulatory Planning and Review") to design solutions and tailor Federal programs, in appropriate circumstances, to address specific or unique needs of tribal communities.

The head of each executive department and agency shall ensure that the department or agency's bureaus and components are fully aware of this memorandum, through publication or other means, and that they are in compliance with its requirements.

This memorandum is intended only to improve the internal management of the executive branch and is not intended to, and does not, create any right to administrative or judicial review, or any other right or benefit or trust responsibility, substantive or procedural, enforceable by a party against the United States, its agencies or instrumentalities, its officers or employees, or any other person.

The Director of the Office of Management and Budget is authorized and directed to publish this memorandum in the Federal Register.

William J. Clinton

[Filed with the Office of the Federal Register, 3:49 p.m., May 2, 1994]

Source:

US Weekly Compilation of Presidential Documents. April 29, 1994, 936–937.

---

72   *Executive Accord between the Mississippi Band of Choctaw Indians and the State of Mississippi (1997)*

The Mississippi Band of Choctaw are one of two federally recognized Choctaw communities; the other being the Choctaw Nation of Oklahoma. Their original homelands were located within what is now the state of Mississippi. In 1830 some citizens were parties to the Dancing Rabbit Creek Treaty in which they agreed to relocate to what was soon to become Indian Territory (present-day Oklahoma). Their trek to the west has been referred to as their Trail of Tears, in which a great many suffered due to exposure, maltreatment, and disease.

A small segment of Choctaw chose to remain in their traditional territory and came to be known as the Mississippi Band. In 1918 they received federal funds to buy lands that today form their land base. Under the long-term leadership of Chief Phillip Martin, beginning in the 1970s, well before the Indian gaming boom, the Tribe was comparatively well off economically, engaging in various industrial and manufacturing enterprises, including electronics, automobile assembly, and plastics.

Although the two modern-day Choctaw communities are located within different states and operate separate governments, according to Clara Sue Kidwell, they are beginning to establish a sense of shared history. This accord is evidence of the maintenance of those historical and kinship bonds.

Whereas, the Mississippi Band of Choctaw Indians is a federally recognized Indian tribe retaining its rights of sovereignty as recognized by treaty, federal and state law, and federal and state court decisions; and

Whereas, the territory of the Mississippi Band of Choctaw Indians is located in Mississippi, and citizens of the Mississippi Band of Choctaw Indians residing in Choctaw Indian country located in Mississippi are also citizens of the State of Mississippi; and

Whereas, there exists an interdependent relationship between the government of the Mississippi Band of Choctaw Indians and the government of the State of Mississippi; and

Whereas the executive branch of the Mississippi Band of Choctaw Indians and the executive branch of the government of the State of Mississippi, on a regular basis, work and cooperate with each other on numerous and varied governmental programs; and

Whereas, in working with each other, it is proper, necessary, and beneficial that the executive branches of the Mississippi Band of Choctaw Indians and the State of Mississippi act in a manner that will continue to build upon and improve the delivery of governmental services and in a manner that is cognizant of, respectful of and consistent with the sovereignty of the Mississippi Band of Choctaw Indians and the sovereignty of the State of Mississippi; be it therefore

Resolved and agreed that the executive branch of the Mississippi Band of Choctaw Indians and the executive branch of the State of Mississippi will, in the future, at all times, work with each other on the government-to-government basis, and in furtherance of this relationship, will develop memorandums of understanding between the executive departments of the Mississippi Band of Choctaw Indians and the executive departments of the State of Mississippi setting forth the procedures and guidelines to ensure that programs affecting both entities are effectively implemented while the sovereignty of both entities is properly respected; and be it

Resolved and agreed that the parties hereto have entered into this Accord for the sole purpose of enhancing government-to-government cooperation between the executive branch of the Mississippi Band of Choctaw Indians and the executive branch of the State of Mississippi. This Accord does not, and shall not be construed to, change, enlarge, diminish, or waive the sovereignty or jurisdiction of either party, or the rights, privileges, or immunities of any person. In addition, this Accord is not, and shall not be construed any right to administrative or judicial review, or any other right, benefit or responsibility, substantive or procedural, enforceable by any person against the executive branch of the Mississippi Band of Choctaw Indians, the executive branch of Mississippi, their officers or employees, or any other person.

Executed on this the 24th day of November 1997.

Sources:

http://www.choctaw.org/government/court/accord.html.
    Kidwell, Clara Sue. *The Choctaws in Oklahoma: From Tribe to Nation, 1855–1970.* Norman: University of Oklahoma Press, 2007.

73

The Anishinaabe Akii Protocol (1998)

The following protocol is an early example of an intertribal treaty negotiated across international borders. The agreement was reached between the eleven Anishinaabe member nations of the Great Lakes Indian Fish and Wildlife Commission located within the US and Canadian-based First Nations represented by the Kabapikotawangag Resources Council, an aboriginal non-profit organization which provides advisory and technical services to its member nations. These Native nations signed treaties with the US in 1836, 1837, 1842, and 1854 in which they reserved hunting, fishing, and gathering rights in their reserved and ceded territories.

The protocol was intended to reflect the shared history, respect, and urgency of the relationship between this broad-based, yet culturally aligned, set of peoples and their sacred lands, waterways, and resources. One of the first modern international/intertribal treaty-type accords, it has been followed by several other such arrangements, verifying the inherent sovereignty of the Nations involved and displaying a recognition of the concerted cooperation required to protect the interwoven ecosystems that sustain Native peoples.

The Anishinaabe Akii Protocol

Knowing that our sacred grandfather, Saagima Manitou, placed us here upon grand mother Earth under the sky; in the forest hills and valleys; in the lakes, rivers, and islands of our ancestors; and Bound by common origin in territory; clan and blood; history and tradition; language and custom; we are brothers and sisters, leaders and warriors of the sovereign Anishinaabe Nation; and Reaffirming our sacred trust to protect the natural environment and resources for all peoples and generations yet unborn, we hereby covenant and agree to work jointly and actively in

1. The conservation, control, and prudent use of the land, air, water, and all resources including rock, soil, minerals, fish, flora, fauna and all other life within our traditional territory;
2. Strategic planning and management of all natural resources as the basis for sustained and balanced self-governed economies within our tribal communities in territory;
3. Mutual support and respect regarding the recognition, fulfillment and faithful implementation of treaties and sovereign prerogatives;
4. Education, training and human resource development in natural resources;
5. Technical and scientific development, data collection, analysis and advocacy;
6. Vetting of national and other international initiatives in respect of natural resources;
7. Finance and enterprise development strategies within Anishinaabe territory;
8. The exercise of the inherent tribal and national right of political, economic, social, and cultural self-determination; and
9. Any action with respect to national and territorial integrity.

Being of one mind on these covenants, we affixed our signatures, on behalf of our members and constituencies, at Madeline Island this ninth day of September, 1998.

Great Lakes Indian Fish and Wildlife Commission, Tom Maulson, Chairman Kabapikotawangag Resources Council, Chief Wesley Big George, Chairman....

Sources:

Author has copy of the Protocol.

Nesper, Larry. *The Walleye War: The Struggle for Ojibwe Spearfishing and Treaty Rights.* Lincoln: University of Nebraska Press, 2002.

Norrgard, Chantal. *Seasons of Change: Labor, Treaty Rights, and Ojibwe Nationhood.* Chapel Hill: University of North Carolina Press, 2014.

74

Challenges to Relations between Washington State and Native Nations (1999)

Despite a decade of improved intergovernmental relations inaugurated by the Centennial Accord in 1989, Washington State and the twenty-nine federally recognized Tribes residing there continued to struggle to find common ground on many issues. The following report details some of the major concerns as expressed by Natives and non-Natives, as well as a series of recommendations aimed at generating a more cooperative and collegial approach. This snapshot of that moment in time shows that, while considerable progress has been made over the last twenty years with regard to improved government-to-government relations and the mandatory inclusion of Tribal history and culture in the state's public school curriculum, many contentious issues remain, particularly those of water rights, taxation, salmon and shellfish habitat loss, and political exploitation of anti-Native sentiments.

Challenges to Relations between Washington and Native Nations

A. Introduction

The purpose of this report is to document concerns about relations between State and Tribal governments in the State of Washington. Although the report also includes suggestions offered by individuals interviewed for the project, this is not its primary focus. Instead, the report is intended to summarize various perspectives and concerns in advance of a November 1999 meeting to assist State and Tribal leaders in identifying opportunities for strengthening Tribal-State Relations. The report was prepared by an independent fact-finder, under contract with the Office of the Attorney General and with guidance from the Planning Committee on Tribal-State Relations (see the Appendix for a list of Planning Committee members)....

B. General Governance

FINDING 1: COMMUNICATIONS BETWEEN STATE
AND TRIBAL GOVERNMENT LEADERS NEED IMPROVEMENT.

State leaders expressed a desire to work with Tribes in a government-to-government relationship to ensure there is mutual respect, that racial bigotry problems are addressed, economic opportunities increased and natural resources preserved for future generations. Tribal leaders generally expressed a similar desire. Most State and Tribal leaders said they were looking forward to the November summit as an opportunity to be productive, re-energize State/Tribal relations and put Washington in the forefront in government-to-government relations.

Many interviewees said that strong, respectful Tribal/State relations are especially important today in light of the trend toward more management responsibility for States and Tribes, and less for federal agencies. Almost all interviewees acknowledged that maintaining effective Tribal/State communications is also extremely challenging due to the complexity of State government, regular turnover in State and Tribal leadership and/or staff, and the large number and diversity (in terms of location, size, and economic situation) of Tribes.

Tribal leaders generally commented that Tribal/State relations reached a high point with the 1989 signing of the Centennial Accord. Many of them noted that, since then, communications have improved in some respects and worsened in others, with considerable tension and uneasiness characterizing the relationship today, despite general good will between the Tribes and the current leadership of the State's executive branch. The level of concern about communications was considerably higher in certain issue areas than in others. Some leaders on both sides said that working together has become increasingly painful, time-consuming and unproductive in certain issue areas. Several State leaders suggested both sides need to restore and foster respect. One interviewee described relations between the State and the Tribes as "mature, but conflicted and contentious," due to the difficulty of the issues they must address together and the lack of an institutional framework for resolving differences.

While most interviewees focused on relations between the Tribes and the executive branch of State government, many noted that communications and relations with the legislature are more problematic. Some Tribal leaders also expressed serious concern about their working relationships with local governments, while others said their working relationships with local government are better in many respects than with the State.

Major Concerns Identified by Interviewees

Level of Communication
Many Tribal leaders expressed a desire to work more directly with Governor Locke and other elected leaders. This was seen as important, among other reasons, because Tribal leaders' broad range of responsibilities is more comparable to the Governor's than to that of other State officials who may not appreciate the pressures and demands on Tribal leaders. Some Tribal leaders noted that the Tribes need to avoid sending staff representatives to meetings with high-level State officials.

State leaders similarly expressed a strong desire to work with Tribal chairs on important policy matters rather than with Tribal staff who are not authorized to speak for Tribes, or whose perspective may be relatively narrow. Senior State leaders said that, on some highly important occasions (e.g., during shellfish negotiations), they were very disappointed that Tribes sent technical staff to critical high level negotiations. Some State leaders added that effective government-to-government relations must also include Tribes' working with field staff on many matters and that senior State officials cannot be available for personal consultation on all issues.

Both State and Tribal leaders complained about frequent reliance on lower level staff by the other side, yet both acknowledged the frequent need to rely on staff due to extraordinary demands on the time of senior officials and the need to bring in technical expertise on many issues.

Manner of Communication and Consultation:

Most interviewees expressed a desire for collaborative relationships between the State and Tribes. Both State and Tribal leaders said collaboration is usually the most successful approach but that, unfortunately, issues are all too often turned over to lawyers who focus on problems and details that make agreement difficult if not impossible. Interviewees did not agree, however, on who is responsible for this trend. Each tended to blame the other. It was generally acknowledged, however, that both sides play a role. Many leaders noted that, historically, when progress has been made, legal issues have been set aside while agreement is reached on shared goals and basic principles. Interviewees had many different interpretations of what is or should be required for "co-management" or "cooperative management." [Note: Co-management issues are discussed in more detail in the Natural Resources section of this report.]

Many interviewees noted that differences in Indian/non-Indian communication styles can present challenges during meetings of State and Tribal officials. For example, Tribal leaders generally stressed the importance of personal relationships, putting issues in long-term future and historical context, and recognizing interrelationships among issues. Many State leaders, in contrast, stressed the importance of focusing on specifics and efficiency in achieving closure. Some Tribal leaders felt that State officials often expect Indians to behave like non-Indians and do not appreciate the importance of native culture and traditions related to meeting protocol.

Some State leaders said that Tribal leaders tend to make rhetorical statements about past problems rather than seeking solutions that can be implemented now. Several interviewees noted that State and Tribal attendees too often leave a meeting with different impressions of the outcome. One State leader also said that, when meeting with more than one Tribe, State officials are repeatedly asked the same question, making discussions with Tribes more time-consuming than with other parties.

Many Tribal leaders were concerned about the manner and means for routine State agency consultation with Tribes. (Specific concerns are mentioned throughout this report, particularly in the natural resources section.) Tribal leaders often noted that State officials do not appreciate the limits on Tribal resources or the extent of demands on them by federal and local agencies, as well as the many different State agencies. The volume of paperwork coming into Tribal offices makes written correspondence, especially use of fax and regular mail, an ineffective means to communicate or consult with most Tribal leaders on urgent matters. Some Tribal leaders felt that State agencies claim to have consulted but they have instead made haphazard or perfunctory, often undocumented, contact with Tribes. Some noted that one contributing factor is that non-Indians, including State employees, seem reluctant to visit reservations, when in fact Tribes welcome such visits as a way to improve understanding and trust.

State leaders noted that Tribes are increasingly requesting formal MOUs and detailed "legalistic" documentation. This approach was seen by senior State leaders as an insurmountable barrier to reaching timely decisions when events are moving quickly. In addition, this was often seen as counterproductive to more desirable collaborative approaches. Some State leaders noted that Tribes tend to be more formal in documenting decisions than State agencies and the State could do better in accommodating this difference, even as the parties work to avoid letting minutia get in the way of progress.

Some State and Tribal leaders noted that communication among State agencies and Tribes is most effective when it is multifaceted, with links to both Tribal leaders and staff at appropriate points and a combination of both regular meetings (perhaps through Tribal consortia or established advisory committees) and special issue-oriented conferences when appropriate. However, several State agency leaders noted that they have been provided no federal or State funding to consult or coordinate with Tribes and therefore must take resources from already under-funded program activities to do so. State officials also noted that Tribes often do not appreciate the limits on State agency resources or the costs associated with consultation on a multitude of issues with each of the Tribes. Some State leaders said they would be interested in working more often with Tribes on a regional or treaty-by-treaty basis. Some interviewees suggested the multifaceted Tribal outreach and communications efforts of DSHS could be a model for other State agencies. (While several interviewees had suggestions for improving DSHS' Tribal interactions, a significant number noted that DSHS has perhaps the best and most improved system of all State agencies.) However, some State leaders noted that, unlike some other State agencies, DSHS' jurisdiction and relationships with Tribes are tightly defined by federal law, leaving relatively little room for dispute compared to natural resource, taxation, and other issues.

Group versus Individual Communications:
State leaders noted that Tribes often ask the State to deal with them individually but, at the same time, a single Tribe may prevent all other Tribes from reaching agreement with the State. State leaders suggested that Tribes need to find better ways to communicate collectively and work toward consensus (both among themselves and with other parties). State leaders, especially those at the highest level, said they have been unable to obtain quick decisions from Tribes. State leaders recognized that this is partly because Tribal governments are "spread too thin" and cannot maintain well-informed staff with the time and ability to build consensus among Tribes. Nevertheless, State leaders saw this as a challenge Tribes must strive to meet in order to participate effectively in State policy-making.

Both State and Tribal leaders noted that Tribal consortia, such as the Northwest Indian Fisheries Commission, appear to be less successful in facilitating Tribal consensus than in the past. This was attributed by some to the increasing economic strength of some Tribes and the change in focus of some Tribal leaders from traditional issues (e.g., natural resources) to emerging issues (e.g., gaming and business development).

Many Tribal leaders acknowledged that Tribes could do a better job of communicating and working to build consensus among themselves to expedite constructive interaction with State and federal authorities. Some expressed strong support for existing special issue consortia and for an effective, general interest consortium (such as the Association of Washington Tribes) to track important high level State executive and legislative developments. However, a few Tribal leaders expressed deep concern that consortia represent a threat to Tribal sovereignty and that unelected consortia members and staff should not be involved in policy-making. These leaders also pointed out that larger, wealthier Tribes often dominate consortia because they are better able to participate. Many Tribal leaders expressed concern about the expense to Tribes of supporting consortia.

Dispute Resolution:
Both Tribal and State interviewees lamented the need to resolve important issues through litigation. Many deplored the costs, delays, and hard feelings involved.

State leaders expressed a strong desire to find better ways to negotiate with Tribes so that issues can be settled out of court, but said that differences among Tribes sometimes prevent successful settlement of issues, even when almost all Tribes are willing to agree. State officials said that certain settlement negotiations with Tribes have been unsuccessful because no one is able to speak for the Tribes or persuade Tribes to accept an offer from the State, even when that offer is very advantageous to the Tribes. Some State officials said that they would like to be able to negotiate with Tribes individually to speed settlements in cases where this is possible, but they are concerned that any concession made to a Tribe in negotiations becomes a floor for future negotiations with other Tribes, thereby making negotiation with all Tribes necessary in virtually every situation. These State officials were also concerned that, for the same reason, it is often not possible to negotiate reasonable tradeoffs with a Tribe that has several issues with the State (e.g., a natural resource and a taxation issue).

Many Tribal leaders similarly expressed a desire to avoid litigation whenever possible but felt that State leaders sometimes fail to acknowledge the legal correctness of Tribal positions due to pressure from non-Indian constituents. As a result, Tribes feel they must litigate. Others expressed a desire to work more often with the State on a policy basis, but saw the State as often relying on narrow, legalistic interpretations (e.g., about States' rights or jurisdiction) rather than using State discretion to interpret the gray areas of the law in favor of Tribal interests. They said this compels them to turn to their own lawyers for help. Tribal leaders also pointed out that State agencies generally do not coordinate well with one another, making tradeoffs among issues difficult, if not impossible.

Some interviewees suggested that litigation is occasionally pursued even though an issue could be settled or the State's lawyers know they will lose in court, at least partly because this helps placate non-Indian special interests.

(Shellfish and slot machine cases were cited as examples.) Some interviewees said a dispute resolution process is needed and most were willing to consider such a process, although there was some skepticism on both sides and a wide range of views about how to structure an appropriate forum. Some interviewees suggested strongly that a single forum or process would be unwieldy and that several subject-area forums are needed, perhaps under a single umbrella organization.

Suggestions Offered by Interviewees

1. Tribal leaders invited the Governor to visit as many Tribes as possible. They said such visits would help demonstrate his personal relationship with Tribal leaders and send a message to both Indians and non-Indians that a good relationship with Tribes is a State priority. State officials at all levels were encouraged to visit Tribes.

2. Seek to agree in advance on the appropriate level of State and Tribal leadership needed at face-to-face meetings and remain flexible about meeting with technical staff where that will serve the purpose.

3. Evaluate the following options that might help strengthen the State's infrastructure for working with Tribes:

   a) Review institutional arrangements in other states to help understand what may or may not work.
   b) Consider establishing a commission on Tribal relations, made up of Tribal and State leaders, to facilitate discussion and help resolve disputes (recognizing that defining the membership, jurisdiction and authority of such a commission would be key to its effectiveness). Consider including both large and small Tribe representatives elected by the Tribes, and both legislative and executive branch leaders from the State. Perhaps, provide for consideration of Tribal/local as well as Tribal/State issues, and offer both binding and non-binding dispute resolution. [Note: Some state and tribal leaders did not support a commission because they felt it would further insulate the governor's office from direct interaction with Tribes, could not realistically decide critical issues in a timely way, and/or would be unable to make its decisions binding on both the state and Tribes.]
   c) Support establishment of a State legislative committee on Indian Affairs to help assure that the effect of legislation on Tribes is identified and considered before a vote is taken and to give Tribes a forum for expressing their views. Seek ways to assure that such a committee would include important legislative leaders and that membership on it is not seen as politically undesirable.
   d) Appoint a distinguished, preferably nonpartisan, person (such as a retired Supreme Court Justice) to serve as permanent special liaison between Tribes and the State, provide continuity when State leadership changes, and help maintain State commitment to its past agreements with Tribes.

e) Further invigorate the hardworking Governor's Office of Indian Affairs to, among other things, better facilitate communications between State agencies and Tribes, serve as a "barometer" on Tribal/State relations for the Governor, maintain current directory materials, and educate State agency personnel on Tribal cultures and history. Assign the Office responsibility for organizing a regular, annual meeting between State elected officials and Tribal leaders. Consider establishing a Tribal advisory group for the Office. Give the Office more "clout" to hold agencies accountable for progress and consultation. [Note: Some interviewees thought the Office should serve as an advocate for native people within state government, while others thought this would be inappropriate or unrealistic.] The Governor's recent actions to strengthen the Office are appreciated.

f) Fully implement relevant provisions of the 1989 Centennial Accord, require State agencies to report regularly on their progress in this regard, and hold agency heads accountable for meeting their obligations. Possibly issue an order defining minimum procedural rules for accomplishing consultation.

g) Where this has not already been done, establish Tribal liaison positions within State agencies.

Consider elevating existing liaison positions, some of which are now seen by Tribes as "buried" in State agencies or insufficiently staffed, to build trust and handle real-time communication with Tribes. Establish Tribal advisory committees for appropriate Agency programs where this has not already been done. Possibly establish a reporting relationship for Tribal liaisons with the Governor's Office of Indian Affairs.

4. Evaluate the following options to strengthen the ability of Tribes to communicate with State government.

a) Support forming a strong organization of Tribes to serve as a point of communication with elected officials on high priority and rapidly emerging issues of importance to many Tribes (taking care to respect the sovereignty of individual Tribes). Consider supporting such an organization with Tribal and State funds (similar to the county and city associations) and/or work together to obtain federal funding.

b) Recognizing that larger Tribes may tend to dominate such an organization, find ways to give special support to smaller Tribes which face unique challenges, perhaps by providing funds from the State and/or larger Tribes to help smaller Tribes participate or form their own separate organization.

c) Where this has not already been done, identify State or State agency liaisons within Tribes to handle communications when Tribal chairs are not available.

d) Offer training for Tribal officials and staff on the organization and functions of State government (perhaps with the assistance of the Governor's Office on Indian Affairs).

5. Consider how the State and Tribes might work more on a regional basis when concerns differ on a geographic basis and consensus across the State is difficult to achieve.

6. Make better use of electronic communications. For example, use E-mail more often and link State and Tribal web sites to demonstrate the government-to-government relationship to others.

FINDING 2: CULTURAL MISUNDERSTANDING, INTOLERANCE AND HARASSMENT AGAINST INDIANS APPEAR TO BE INCREASING IN SOCIETY GENERALLY

Many Tribal leaders noted that while prejudice against Indians may have declined in recent decades, intolerance and racial bigotry are currently on the rise. They expressed concern that the situation will worsen as population growth and loss of natural resources lead to more competition and resentment against the exercise of Tribal hunting and fishing rights. They were also concerned that tension has increased because Tribes have had to rely on so-called "sin businesses" such as gaming and sales of liquor, cigarettes, and fireworks, to provide economic opportunity for Indian people. In addition, both State and Tribal leaders noted that Tribal economic development is leading to resentment from non-Indian competitors (or perceived potential competitors) as well as non-Indians in rural areas who are experiencing economic downturns of their own. Senior state leaders noted that intolerance against all minorities seems to be increasing throughout society and indicated that this is also a matter of grave concern to them.

Major Concerns Identified by Interviewees

Racist rhetoric during the Makah whale hunt, including letters to editors published in local newspapers, was frequently cited as one obvious example of a deterioration in relations between Indians and non-Indians. However, Tribal leaders gave other examples of threats or hate-related incidents directed at Indians in their geographic areas. Some noted that Indians have recently armed or said they will arm themselves in light of threats directed at their people. Governor Locke's action in calling out the National Guard during the whale hunt was noted with approval. However, the atmosphere of tension was seen by many Tribal leaders as requiring continuing attention.

Some State leaders also said they have seen evidence that anti-Indian sentiment and harassment are on the rise. Others were not aware of the apparent trend, but did not doubt that it exists. State agency leaders generally viewed themselves and their own programs as fair and supportive of Indian rights, although many indicated that some racial prejudice exists or may exist among State agency field staff. A few stressed the importance of trust and focusing on the important substantive issues at the leadership level.

Although Tribal leaders generally viewed the Governor, the Attorney General and other leaders in the executive branch as respectful of Tribes, Tribal leaders and some State leaders noted that some politicians in State and federal government have found it politically advantageous to "campaign against"

Tribes, thus helping to stir up anti-Indian bias. Several Tribal leaders suggested that to help counter this incitement to prejudice, Tribes need to step up efforts to inform the general public about their contributions to the State as a whole. As well, they said the Governor and others in State government could exert more powerful moral leadership through public statements and actions. One Tribal leader, speaking of national politics in the 1990s, said "Too many amoral judgments are made based on economic concerns alone." Another said he hoped the State could avoid "pragmatic political balancing" when issues of equity are involved. Tribal leaders said it helps when State leaders speak out on what is morally right. Some Tribal leaders said that it is important to consider the history of exploitation of Tribes, failure to honor treaties with Tribes, and mistreatment of Indian people. This is the context within which Tribal leaders must deal with their own people on a daily basis and affects many aspects of their dealings with others. Some Tribal leaders noted that although there are many good people in State government, State leaders may be "in denial" about the bias of some State bureaucrats against Indian people. For example, one Tribal interviewee said that State employees often conduct themselves as if to say "Why can't you be more like us? Why do you hold on to your culture?" Tribal leaders expressed concern about cuts in funding for training State agency personnel (especially field staff working regularly with Tribes) on Tribal history and culture.

State leaders said they respect the rights of Tribes and deplore racism, hate letters and harassment. However, they cannot always support decisions Tribes make in exercising their rights and believe Tribes sometimes misinterpret or mischaracterize respectful disagreement as racial or cultural bias. Senior State leaders also questioned whether their public statements could have been effective in easing tensions. For example, in the case of the whale hunt, many people simply disapproved of the decision to kill a whale, even if they agreed that the Tribe had a legal right to do so. While they generally said they understand the Tribes' concerns about intolerance, State leaders suggested that Tribes sometimes make choices that predictably bring on anger from those who disagree with their actions. Some State leaders said that Tribes sometimes cite treaty rights and/or their need for economic development to justify actions that have adverse impacts on others in society (sale of dangerous fireworks that are illegal in the State, for example). In some cases, State officials said, Tribal decisions that bring on anger from others also appear to be unwise in terms of the health and safety of Tribal communities. Several State officials expressed the hope that when Tribes diversify economically, some of these "hot button" issues will fade away. However, State officials were concerned that Indian hunting and fishing for threatened and endangered species could exacerbate tensions in rural areas where non-Indian hunting and fishing are restricted.

Most interviewees saw education as a key to overcoming racial and cultural tensions. One Tribal interviewee said that "Tribes should inform; the State should not misinform." Several Tribal interviewees said with frustration, that educating non-Indians is a "never-ending process." Almost all Tribal interviewees and many State officials stressed the importance of such education to the future well-being of the State and the Tribes. Over the long term, education about Tribes in the public schools was seen as essential. One State leader stressed the need to start this education in the early grades because it may be too late to reverse intolerance at the high school level. Tribal leaders said it was important that such education not be guilt-producing, and instead focus on being informative and forward-looking.

Suggestions Offered by Interviewees

Governor Locke and other State leaders should consider making strong statements to non-Indian groups inside and outside the State (e.g., to NGA, NAAGS, NACO, WGA, and industry groups), as well as the general public, in support of respect for Tribal treaty rights, the value of Tribal economic and cultural contributions to the State, and the importance of understanding the history and cultures of the Tribes. For example, the Governor's State of the State address presents a regular opportunity to demonstrate leadership on good relations between native and non-native people.

Tribes should consider ways to continue and expand their efforts to inform the general public about Tribal culture and contributions.

The State should consider ways to help enhance public school education about the Washington Tribes, including support for development of a curriculum for K through 12 public schools that is forward-looking and informative about treaties and Tribal contributions. Tribes should participate in developing the curriculum, partly to help assure an appropriate recognition of the oral history traditions of native people.

The State should consider ways to support public education about Tribes through agency programs. For example, the Parks and Recreation Department is considering providing informative displays and interpretive kiosks to educate park visitors about the original native inhabitants of ceded park lands.

The Governor's Office of Indian Affairs should reinstate its program to train State employees on Tribal culture and history, and, possibly train State and Tribal staff together, using role-playing and other techniques to build understanding and trust.

C. *Natural Resources*

FINDING 1: SALMON RESTORATION IS A PRIORITY FOR THE STATE
AND TRIBES, BUT THE EFFECTIVENESS OF COOPERATION BETWEEN
THE STATE AND TRIBES HAS BEEN DISAPPOINTING.

Almost all interviewees who addressed natural resources, including almost all Tribal leaders, agreed that the State currently lacks an effective plan and implementation measures to protect and restore salmon and saw this as an extremely urgent challenge. State leaders noted that society generally is very divided over protection of endangered species, and that the issues are particularly sensitive for Tribes because they are seen as champions of resource protection even as some of them wish to harvest scarce resources in listed areas. Tribal leaders said the loss of salmon fisheries is a major blow to their economic, social, religious and cultural well-being. It was suggested that the State should declare an emergency and take very strong action to address the problem. Tribal leaders feared the State will "run away" from the salmon issue due to the political controversy and potential hardships involved in addressing the problem. Some state leaders feared Tribes were not as united and committed to salmon restoration as in the past.

State natural resources leaders also expressed deep concern about past losses and current threats to salmon runs, especially the impacts of growth in western Washington and the need to build a public and political commitment to salmon restoration (including but not limited to meeting the mandate of the Endangered Species Act). Almost all interviewees who were familiar with recent developments expressed concern and regret about the outcome of the last State legislative session. Most Tribal leaders were frustrated by the State's failure to work closely with Tribes to develop an effective strategy. One Tribal interviewee said the State tended to "talk to the 'important people' first, and then to Tribes." State leaders were frustrated by limits on their ability to work quickly with Tribes to react to fast-moving developments during legislative deliberations. Both State and Tribal leaders expressed an urgent desire to work together to develop a more effective approach for the upcoming legislative session.

Major Concerns Identified by Interviewees

Co-management, Cooperation, and Consultation:

Individual State officials and Tribal leaders used the terms co-management, cooperative management and consultation in many different contexts and with a broad array of meanings. Many Tribal leaders expressed concern that, although the State gives "lip service" to cooperative management, there is no agreement on the meaning of co-management or the means for implementing it. Tribal leaders said they did not assert a veto right over State management decisions, such as land use, but emphasized the need to jointly establish policies and general rules. Some Tribal leaders said they believe State leaders fear sharing any management decisions with Tribes. Tribal leaders also noted that in order for the State to provide certainty to regulated parties, it will be necessary to involve Tribes more effectively. Tribal leaders generally acknowledged that the State faces a challenge in dealing with the diverse views of the various Tribes. One Tribal leader pointed out that "there is no such entity as 'The Tribes.' "

State officials generally said they hope to work with Tribes to develop an effective salmon restoration program. However, some noted that co-management is not a legal doctrine, although Tribes tend to see it that way. They said that while co-management is an agreed-upon approach for harvest and hatcheries management, it is not applicable to management of fish populations or habitat— responsibilities for which joint recovery plans must be developed, involving many parties, including Tribes. Some State leaders noted that Tribes' refusal to "come to the table" with other parties sets them apart when important deliberations are underway and that Tribes, in effect, expect a veto power afterward, rather than participating in policy-making. Some State officials noted that the State cannot give one group, such as Tribes, decision-making authority over other groups in society; yet that seems to be the expectation of Tribes. State leaders indicated that an appropriate, effective forum for Tribal participation has not yet been devised by the parties and that this has contributed to the current "stalemate." A key concern of State leaders was that, even if a forum is identified, the Tribes may not be able to empower an effective, knowledgeable spokesperson to facilitate consensus among Tribes and speak with the confidence of Tribes when quick decisions are needed. They noted that it is impossible for State officials to slow the process to give Tribes time to "catch up."

Several Tribal leaders said that co-management as a concept is not "broken" but needs to be "brought back into play." Several Tribal leaders expressed deep concern that the Governor's office drafted the salmon recovery plan without consulting Tribes and then tried to compel Tribes to concur with it. Some Tribal leaders characterized co-management as a fifty-fifty division of responsibility for managing forest, shore and aquatic lands, not necessarily as "cooperative" in implementing day-to-day responsibilities. Some said co-management means that in carrying out their respective responsibilities, the State and Tribes will carefully consider each other's needs. Some State leaders said they implement co-management by managing "with Tribes" through consultation. Tribal leaders described their dealings with the many relevant State agencies, including DOE, DNR, DFW, and DOT, as "exhausting." (For example, DFW now insists on yearly rather than five-year agreements on fisheries management.) Some Tribal and State leaders complained that staff lawyers on both sides tend to impede progress in policy deliberations because of jurisdictional worries.

A number of State leaders said the State has historically failed to reach out to Tribes and has pursued an "ill-advised policy" of apparently acknowledging that Tribes have co-management rights while at the same time making it necessary for Tribes to litigate to exercise those rights. Some State leaders suggested it would be helpful for Tribes to define more specifically what they (the Tribes) envision in achieving co-management. Many State leaders noted that the State cannot give up its authority over land use management. With regard to harvest and hatcheries, State leaders noted that they are attempting to "reinvent" existing co-management processes, which were designed to address problems that existed 25 years ago, before the tremendous upheavals of the Endangered Species Act listings, the shellfish decision, and other recent developments.

One interviewee noted that Tribes spend as much as 50% of their revenue on natural resources management, whereas the State invests only one-half of 1%. Several Tribal leaders viewed State water quality, fisheries and habitat protection programs as weaker than Tribal programs and suggested that, at a minimum, the State should do as much on its lands as the Tribes are doing on their lands. Several Tribal leaders said the State's approach to watershed management is not coherent and pointed to specific cases in which the State has failed to implement or enforce its existing laws and regulatory programs to protect water quality, fish and game stocks, and habitat. A few interviewees noted that, unfortunately, declines in fisheries have led some Tribal governments to disinvest in natural resource programs and shift funding to more economically productive programs, such as gaming. Most Tribal leaders, however, said they are continuing or increasing their historic investments in natural resources protection, especially salmon habitat protection and fisheries management. There was agreement that Tribes are playing a more important role, with State assistance in some cases, in water quality monitoring and the establishment of water quality standards. Tribes were acknowledged as leaders in conducting stock assessments and habitat inventories, as well as managing hatcheries and protecting habitat.

Senior State leaders said they were very disappointed that a "one-Tribe veto" in the U.S.-Canada salmon treaty process prevented all Tribes from receiving payments above market value for fish not caught. In contrast, some Tribal leaders expressed concern about how negotiations on the U.S.-Canada salmon treaty were handled. In particular, one Tribal leader said that the Tribe's fishery resources were sacrificed by U.S. negotiators. Several Tribal leaders expressed grave concern about the move in the U.S. Senate to condition Tribal funds under the treaty on waiving rights to sue the State.

Endangered Species Act Issues
Both Tribal and State leaders acknowledged that the need to coordinate with several federal agencies (NMFS, FWS and EPA) on salmon restoration has made the process even more cumbersome. Some State officials were interested in learning more about the Tribes' strategy in dealing with federal agencies and were concerned about the "triangulation" of negotiations. Generally, interviewees agreed that the State, federal agencies, and Tribes need to work together to be effective. However, Tribal leaders said they are generally not interested in "pre-negotiating" issues with the State when three-way negotiations are required (e.g., in the case of DNR's habitat protection plan). State leaders said they were concerned that Tribes had negotiated with federal agencies (deciding that the 50/50 rule would extend to all species, not just salmon), and then simply delivered the decision to the State without consultation. They said the State should ensure that Tribes are at the table with federal officials and Tribes should do the same for the State.

Some Tribal leaders oppose the ESA approach to individual species protection, while others see the ESA as valuable but want it to be implemented with a better appreciation of ecological systems. One Tribal leader noted that federal funding provided to the State to implement the ESA was passed through to counties. Although Tribes may be able to obtain some assistance from the counties, the funds are very limited and inadequate for most Tribes to carry out the ESA. Many Tribes also lack resources to implement related programs, such as water quality, land use, and agricultural initiatives.

Several interviewees expressed concern about how the ESA affects Tribal treaty rights and said that litigation is likely over whether the ESA "trumps" Tribal rights. Some Tribal and State officials also noted that if hatchery fish were considered, some salmon listings would be eliminated. However, NMFS was said to be unyielding on this issue, making it more likely that litigation will be pursued. Some Tribes expressed concern that the State wants to redefine harvest standards in a way that unfairly shifts conservation burdens to Tribes. While State officials acknowledged that the Tribes did not create the problems adversely affecting salmon runs, they questioned the logic of some Tribes who wish to continue fishing in listed areas, thus speeding the extinction of certain species.

Some Tribal and State interviewees noted that resentment against Tribal treaty rights by non-Indians who are affected by ESA listing will be exacerbated by these issues. There was hope expressed on both sides that the State will show leadership on restoration. Many Tribal leaders said they will continue their voluntary commitment to salmon restoration, for example in continuing their past voluntary restraint in fishing certain species even when they are very important to Tribal subsistence and culture. They expressed concern, however, about a "paternalistic" attitude toward Tribes regarding fishery science and a failure to credit Tribes for their extensive knowledge and understanding of their own watersheds. Some Tribal leaders said the State is too conservative on "jump-starting natural production" and impedes Tribal recovery efforts.

Suggestions Offered by Interviewees
Seek a way for the State and Tribes to work together without delay to develop an agreed upon salmon restoration program to present to the legislature this fall. Consider whether the Governor's office can exercise stronger leadership with legislators and how the Tribes can help. Consider whether Tribes might designate a delegation to work with the Governor's office and the legislature, perhaps with the general blessing of the Tribes for purposes of negotiating (even though the delegation could not commit each Tribe on all specific issues).

The State and Tribes should work toward a better understanding of the meaning of co-management and consultation and how they can be implemented in the context of salmon recovery. A key aspect may be to improve understanding of the State's authority and obligations to all affected parties, including Tribes.

Work to agree on specific performance measures that will help direct funding to the most effective implementation strategies. Focus on long term cycles and take advantage of the wisdom of people who live close to the land, not just the biologists.

Recognize the value of the Northwest Indian Fisheries Commission as a clearinghouse for information and facilitator of Tribal consensus on salmon restoration; consider how the NWIFC might be more effective.

Rely more on electronic communications among Tribes and between the State and Tribes, especially when a quick turnaround is required, for example to help respond to deliberations in the legislature.

Consider the following to better protect salmon habitat: Develop an MOU between the State and Tribes on forest practices. [Note: One State official said such an MOU could not legally establish more stringent standards for fee lands than for other state lands.]

Increase State enforcement to prevent pollution, clean up waste sites, implement sports and commercial fishing limits, and enforce other natural resources protection laws.

Increase the pace of developing plans to restore impaired waters under Section 303(d) of the Clean Water Act and work closely with relevant Tribes in establishing TMDLs.

Provide more effective Tribal liaison positions in individual State natural resource agencies (e.g., DNR). Reserve judgment on the need to breach dams to aid salmon restoration until relevant evidence is collected and evaluated.

FINDING 2: THE STATE'S WATER ALLOCATION PROGRAM NEEDS REFORM, BUT TRIBES ARE NOT OPTIMISTIC ABOUT THE STATE'S CURRENT EFFORTS TO IMPROVE THE PROGRAM.

Major Concerns Identified by Interviewees

Tribal leaders' main concern is that water is over-allocated in the State. Many Tribal leaders cited the water allocation program as a longstanding and important source of friction between Tribes and their non-Indian neighbors. They cited recent efforts to reform the State's program without Tribal involvement as an example of how the program is often managed to serve the interests of powerful economic interests rather than assuring fairness to all State citizens. Tribal leaders suggested that DOE should not have agreed to the legislatively-directed reform process without Tribal involvement and noted that this has diminished many of the good things DOE has attempted to do to improve the program. They noted that Tribal water rights predate the State's program. Some Tribal leaders noted that certain localities are working to become purveyors of water for economic gain in the long term and that the State is not resisting this trend or fully implementing its own laws. Tribes saw water allocation as a major economic battle for the future.

Some State leaders agreed that the State's historic allocation process has been a failure. They noted that although there is an adjudication process, no one wants to use it. State officials acknowledge that Tribes were excluded from the watershed model process but indicated that the legislature established a process for review of the water allocation program which unfortunately did not include Tribes. Senior State officials noted that the Governor vetoed the most onerous aspects of the legislation because Tribes were not included. Some State officials noted that the result of the watershed model process is an improvement that will benefit Tribes, even though it is understandable that Tribal leaders, not having been involved, may not recognize the improvement. State agency officials acknowledge that they need to better inform Tribes about how to work with local planning organizations.

Suggestions Offered by Interviewees

Work together on legislation to reform the water allocation program.

Consider ways to improve State implementation and enforcement of current allocation laws.

Explore ways for the Tribes and Department of Health to work together to better assure the health and safety of Tribal water supplies.

FINDING 3: TRIBAL AND STATE LEADERS ARE VERY CONCERNED ABOUT
DISAGREEMENTS RELATED TO THE EXERCISE OF TRIBAL TREATY
RIGHTS TO HUNT AND FISH ON NON-TRIBAL LANDS.

Recent arrests of Tribal members for alleged hunting violations were cited by several Tribal leaders as fueling racial tensions in some rural communities. State leaders said the hunting disputes were leading to "troubling" tensions between Tribes and county leaders. Several Tribal leaders expressed a desire to work with the State to resolve the disagreements that led to these arrests and indicated that the Inter-Tribal Hunting Committee is working to develop a Tribal position on hunting rights.

Tribal leaders expressed concern that declining fish and game lead to resentment against Indians partly because Tribal hunting and fishing seasons may be longer than State seasons. Tribal leaders also noted that some non-Indians believe that Indians take more fish and game than they actually do take. Indians are therefore sometimes blamed for declining resources, even though they have no responsibility for the far more significant impacts of pollution, land uses, and water diversions. State and Tribal leaders indicated that talks are now underway on hunting issues.

Some Tribal leaders noted that the process for developing the Tribal/State MOU on hunting was a good model for the State in working with Tribes.

Major Concerns Identified By Interviewees

Tribal leaders indicated that they believe some Tribal members have been prosecuted for hunting within territory covered by Tribal treaty rights. Some indicated that the State and Tribes disagree on the definition of ceded land. This issue may need to be resolved through litigation if the parties cannot reach agreement soon. Some Tribal leaders suggested that the definition of "usual and accustomed" hunting areas may need to be redefined by the courts because there are no places to hunt in some ceded areas due to economic and population development. Urban Tribes were seen as particularly hard hit. Some State leaders expressed a desire to find innovative solutions to this problem. Others suggested that there may be no satisfactory solution and that Tribes may need to accept the consequences of specific treaty terms.

Suggestions Offered by Interviewees

The hunting rights issue needs to be resolved soon, if possible through agreement among State and Tribal leaders.

Consider how to define "ceded" lands for purposes of Tribal hunting rights.

Possibly consider "trading" land on which Treaty hunting rights may be exercised as one way to ensure that hunting occurs only in areas that are appropriate. [Note: One state official pointed out that State trust lands could be traded only if this would benefit the trust beneficiaries.]

Consider whether game might be made available to Tribes from damage control hunts or other sources.

Consider ways to collect better information on causes of the downturn in elk populations on the Olympic Peninsula.

D. Economic Development

FINDING 1: STATE AND TRIBAL LEADERS AGREE ON THE NEED
FOR AN ECONOMIC DEVELOPMENT STRATEGY FOR TRIBES.

Several interviewees noted that the decline in natural resources and Tribal businesses based on forestry and fishing has led to a growing reliance on gaming
and sales of gasoline, cigarettes, liquor and fireworks. Some Tribal leaders said
the State needs to consider how better to share the State's increasing prosperity
with Tribes. State officials were similarly interested in exploring ways to support Tribal economic development and wanted to learn more about the economic
development goals and strategies of the Tribes. Both State and Tribal officials
noted that the economic vitality study recently conducted by the Governor's
Office of Indian Affairs was a good first step and that the next steps suggested
by the study need to be pursued. Some State and Tribal interviewees said the
study may need refinement to be more useful in dealing with bankers and business people as well as State legislators. However, senior State leaders said it is
more important to move forward now on specific strategies to help attract new
businesses to Tribal communities.

Many Tribal leaders pointed out that Tribal economic growth has been
good for the State and localities and that this is not well understood or appreciated by the non-Indian community or the legislature. However, they noted that
the most impoverished areas in the State are still Tribal lands and that non-
Indians misperceive the extent to which gaming has solved the Tribes' economic
problems. While some gaming Tribes now have full employment, unemployment in the State's Indian population is still very high, with some Tribes experiencing levels of up to 90% unemployment. Some Tribal leaders noted that
gaming is a good economic strategy for Tribes in the I-5 corridor, but not elsewhere. Others pointed out the social disadvantages of the so-called "sin businesses" for Tribal members and the criticism that Tribes face from non-Indians
because of the types of businesses they pursue. One Tribal leader said that
non-Indians generally do not understand that gaming revenues go to Indian
communities rather than to individual business people. State leaders generally
expressed the hope that Tribes will be able to reduce their dependence on gambling and tobacco sales, but they did not fault the Tribes for pursuing these
businesses. Several Tribal leaders pointed out that many Tribes are "location
disadvantaged" and so have had to attract outsiders to their reservations by offering special incentives, including taking advantage of "loopholes" in certain
laws and sales taxes.

It was noted that Tribes generally lack a tax base and therefore become
entrepreneurs to support Tribal government and their communities. Tribal leaders noted that even where they have the authority to tax, doing so "on top of"
State and local taxes would only discourage business. The differences among
Tribes in terms of economic status, location, and size are considerable and Tribal
leaders had a wide range of suggestions about steps the State could take to support Tribal economic development, not all of which were seen as important or
even attractive to other Tribes. For example, some Tribes are major employers

of both Indians and non-Indians, while others restrict employment to Tribal members. Generally, Tribal leaders said their goals were to assure safe and healthy communities for Indian people, to assure sustainability of their economic enterprises through good relations with their neighbors, and to attract visitors who will spend money in Indian country and invest in Tribal enterprises. Several Tribal leaders noted that they are working to develop specific proposals for an Economic Development Strategy, including such things as objective criteria for tax credits and other development incentives.

Major Concerns Identified By Interviewees

Tobacco and Fireworks Enforcement
Some Tribal leaders complained strongly that aggressive enforcement against non-Indians who purchase cigarettes or fireworks from Indian businesses constitutes an attempt by the State to limit Indian economic prosperity or to protect non-Indian competitors. State officials noted that enforcing the cigarette tax was seen by the legislature as a revenue issue involving the potential loss of $104 million. They also noted that public safety was paramount in enforcing restrictions on the sale of dangerous fireworks. State officials agreed that non-Indian competitors (or potential competitors) often pressure State legislators and other officials to assure that Tribal entrepreneurs not receive "special treatment," and that non-Indians' understanding of Tribal economic conditions and contributions is very limited.

Gaming
Tribal leaders said that even though Tribal economic development is beneficial to both Tribal and non-Indian local economies, the State has historically blocked or attempted to neutralize Tribal enterprises. For example, the State's legislation on mini-casinos was seen as an attempt to set up competition with Indian gaming. Some Tribal leaders also complained of State "hypocrisy" on the impropriety of gaming, especially given that Tribal casinos attract mostly middle-income customers, while the State lottery attracts mostly low-income individuals.

Senior State officials noted that gaming Tribes are competing with one another for the most favorable terms in their compacts with the State. State leaders suggested that a fairer, more efficient approach would be to negotiate compacts collectively, with separate provisions only as needed to deal with anomalies in Tribal circumstances. State officials also said they need more flexibility in their compacting authority but the legislature has "stymied" the Governor's efforts in this regard. Some Tribal leaders specifically objected to the requirement for gubernatorial approval of Tribal links for a progressive gaming operation. One Tribal leader indicated that the Tribes will soon seek such approval.

Taxation and Revenue Sharing
Tribal leaders were also concerned about policies related to taxation of gasoline sold by Tribal members and taxation of fee lands on reservations. They noted that although these taxes are collected by the State and localities, public

services (e.g., highway construction and water and sewer services) are not provided by States and localities to reservations. Several Tribal leaders noted that the State shares revenue with localities, but not with Tribes. State leaders were generally interested in ways to reach agreement with Tribes on taxation and revenue sharing issues by, for example, exploring legislative initiatives to assure that State taxes would be backed out when Tribes impose their own sales taxes. At least one Tribal leader suggested that if the legislature will not act affirmatively to address these inequities, litigation may be necessary.

Tourism

Tribal leaders were also concerned that the State has not been working with Tribes to promote tourism, even though the State often uses Tribal culture and symbols to attract tourists. Several State leaders also identified tourism as an area of potential successful cooperation. One State leader specifically discussed promotion of "eco-tourism" as a potentially lucrative, non-consumptive use of natural resources that could benefit Tribes.

Planning

Some Tribal leaders were concerned that the State's transportation corridors are delineated without adequate consultation with Tribes whose interest in expansion or vision for development may conflict with the State's plans. Some noted that the Growth Management Act may limit Tribal development involving fee lands on reservations. Some noted that State agencies affecting Tribal economic development (e.g., DOR, the Department of Licensing, The Liquor Control Board) do not always get along well with one another, making comprehensive planning difficult.

Collaboration

Many State leaders expressed a strong interest in finding ways the State can help promote Tribal economic development. Senior State leaders noted that business development usually depends on strong, collaborative, non-adversarial relationships. They said they look forward to partnering with Tribes in an atmosphere of trust and supporting the Tribes in developing strong partnerships with neighboring local communities.

Federal grants

Many Tribal leaders expressed concern about how Tribal set-asides in State grants are managed. Several noted that, contrary to popular belief, the federal government now spends considerably less per capita on Indians than on non-Indians. Others said that State agencies do not always keep Tribes informed about the availability of set-asides for Tribes. Some Tribal leaders suggested that an economic development strategy for the Washington Tribes should include ways the State would support Tribes in obtaining more federal assistance (e.g., for infrastructure development and maintenance) and making that assistance available in a more rational way (e.g., through consolidation of the multitude of small grants that entail considerable reporting and management burdens for Tribes).

Suggestions Offered by Interviewees

Decide whether to refine the report on Tribal economic vitality; pursue the next steps envisioned therein.

Work together to establish a joint Economic Development Strategy for Tribes in Washington State.

Work together to help address Tribal infrastructure problems, such as transportation, water supply, sewer services and fiber-optics, possibly through revenue sharing legislation and promoting local partnerships, as well as other means.

Consider developing a model compact on apportionment of tax revenues.

Work together to address differences on State and local taxation of products sold by Tribes and Indian businesses.

Reduce costs and delays by streamlining State requirements and procedures (e.g., in licensing Indian-owned businesses and casino employees, in providing grants to Tribes).

Consider how the State can help with long-term, low interest loans, creative financing and technical assistance for new Tribal and Indian-owned economic enterprises. (Note: Potential new enterprises mentioned by Tribal leaders as currently in need of assistance include aquaculture, shellfish, nurseries for trees to be used in watershed restoration, marinas, campgrounds, gasoline stations, mini-marts and agriculture.)

Find ways the State can support the Tribes in obtaining greater federal assistance, e.g., through Tribal set-asides in State grants, and improve communications to Tribes about assistance that is available.

Seek ways that Tribes can join with the State and localities to attract new businesses, (e.g., through fast track development, enterprise zones, partnerships and tax incentives). Consider offering a tutorial to Tribes on attracting businesses to their communities.

Consider ways that the compacting process can be improved and streamlined to reduce "dickering" and provide for more comprehensive economic planning for Tribes.

Develop a joint strategy on tourism that will help attract visitors to Tribal communities.

Promote employment of Tribal members by State agencies and contractors by, among other things, providing for hiring preferences for Tribal members in appropriate cases, supporting vocational training, and assisting Tribal members in becoming bonded.

Promote the purchase of Tribal products by State agencies and contractors by, for example, providing more preferences for use of Tribal forest products and gravel mined by Tribes and by informing potential buyers of the economic advantages of purchasing these materials from nearby Tribes during public works construction.

Improve understanding of the economic realities affecting Tribes. For example, consider ways to estimate the total taxes paid by Tribal members to the State and localities and the total revenues from the State and localities that are returned to the Tribes.

Seek ways to assist Tribes in obtaining development grants from local planning organizations.

Evaluate and learn from successful economic initiatives of Tribes in other States (e.g., the Mississippi Choctaw, the Wisconsin Oneida).

E. Social, Cultural, Education and Law Enforcement Issues

FINDING 1: ALTHOUGH THE RELATIONSHIP BETWEEN THE STATE
AND TRIBES ON HEALTH AND SOCIAL SERVICES IS GENERALLY GOOD,
THIS IS AN AREA OF ENORMOUS CHALLENGE
AND REQUIRES CONTINUOUS IMPROVEMENT.

Many Tribes face tremendous challenges in assuring the social stability, health, and well-being of their communities. One interviewee noted that the Congressional Research Service estimates that unemployment for Tribal members nationally is between 70 and 75%. Rates of disease and premature death are far higher among Indian people than in the general population. In recent years, federal funding for Tribal health and social services has not kept pace with increases for non-Indians.

Pursuant to the Centennial Accord of 1989, DSHS established a director for Indian policy and support services. Both State officials and Tribal leaders said that, since then, DSHS has made good strides in communicating effectively with Tribes through, among other means, its Tribal advisory committee and regional representatives. Tribal leaders indicated that there is agreement on the mission and objectives of DSHS programs. State officials believe that the agreed upon approach for triage of issues and concentric circles to identify concerns has helped overcome barriers and increase respect and understanding. Generally, DSHS has a Tribe-by-Tribe approach to services and this was seen as appropriate.

Several Tribal leaders noted that the Indian Child Welfare Act has been an important step and is generally working well in assuring that Indian children remain in their own communities and culture. State leaders said they were pleased to have been the first State to assume responsibility for implementing the Act and transferring authority to the Tribes.

Major Concerns Identified By Interviewees

Funding

Many Tribal leaders noted that funding for Indian welfare and health programs goes to the State and that their long term goal is for these funds to be passed through to Tribes. State officials noted that they are responsible for providing services to non-affiliated Indians as well as to Tribal members. Both the State and the Tribes acknowledged concerns about the data used to determine whether the appropriate funding levels are in fact going to Indian people. Several Tribal leaders especially questioned whether adequate mental health funding is being provided to Tribal members, noting that addiction and other mental health problems are very serious on the reservations. Tribal leaders also noted that Tribes desiring to implement federal social programs, such as the Older Americans Act and Welfare Reform, have serious problems building the needed governmental infrastructure to do so. [Note: This problem was said to exist in virtually all program areas, although social programs were mentioned most often in the interviews.]

Working Relationships with DSHS

Some Tribal leaders noted that, despite DSHS' improved communications and the current director's personal relationship with Tribal officials, working with DSHS is "like dancing with an elephant; it's easy to get stepped on." Some Tribal leaders expressed disappointment that the Tribal interface function has recently been given less access to upper management through organizational change.

Others noted that although they have a good relationship with their DSHS liaison, that person is often overruled by supervisors.

Welfare Reform

With regard to Welfare Reform, both State and Tribal leaders said their main concern is to find ways to assure that those losing welfare benefits do not "fall through the safety net." They saw a need for the State and Tribes to work together on employment opportunities and vocational training for these individuals. Several Tribal leaders expressed concern about the State's failure to consult with Tribes on design of the Work First program and designate Tribes as program partners with DSHS. One Tribal leader said that the Work First program excludes Tribal casinos from receiving incentives for hiring, even though other employers (including other Tribal businesses and non-Indian cardrooms) do receive such incentives. An important concern for leaders of rural Tribes was that the Work First program could undermine the stability of Tribal communities if Tribal members are forced to leave their reservations to seek employment in urban areas. State officials were also concerned about this potential unintended impact and agreed that not consulting with Tribes earlier had been a "blunder."

Health Services

Several Tribal leaders were concerned that non-Indians have the impression that Indians are well-cared for by the federal government. Those in rural areas especially saw economic deterioration in the larger community as increasing competition for available assistance and causing non-Indians to be less sympathetic to the problems Tribes are facing. Tribal leaders also noted that the history of Indian health services needs to be better understood by non-Indians and help provided in educating Tribal members about how to use health services. (Generally, the medical establishment had refused to treat Indians because of their inability to pay and Indians learned to distrust and avoid medical treatment. As health services have become more available, some Indian people are still learning when they do and do not need to take advantage of them, in some cases leading to overuse or underuse.) In addition, it was noted that mental health facilities that take Indian cultural traditions into account are likely to be more successful for Indian people. One Tribal leader was very concerned that, because the Indian Health Service is not funded for long term care, Tribal elders are referred to the State for such care and the State has been attaching their land (including trust land) for payment.

Relations with the Department of Health

One State official observed that the Department of Health has few contacts with Tribal Councils, but deals almost exclusively with Tribal health directors. This official questioned whether there needed to be more contact and attention to health issues from Tribal Councils. One specific area of concern mentioned was the safety of Tribal drinking water supplies.

Tobacco

A variety of views were expressed about the States' settlement with the to-bacco industry. Tribal leaders noted that Indian people have higher rates of tobacco-related illness than the general population. State leaders indicated that, recognizing Tribes' sovereignty, the States lacked the authority to settle Tribal claims and so did not address them, even though the tobacco companies would have preferred that they do so. One Tribal leader expressed concern that the State had proposed an allocation of its share of the settlement without consult-ing Tribes and said the Tribes should have received a share of the allocation. Other leaders expressed an interest in bringing a Tribal class action against the tobacco companies. Some State leaders expressed regret that a local Tribe is apparently beginning to manufacture cigarettes. Some State and Tribal leaders expressed concern about how best to discourage Indian youth from smoking, while some Tribal leaders said they were already implementing aggressive pro-grams to discourage youth smoking. State leaders expressed interest in estab-lishing a partnership with Tribes to reduce youth smoking. They would support using monies from the national foundation established in the agreement and State tobacco control programs for these efforts, and would encourage the Tribes to dedicate their revenues from tobacco sales for these programs. (Some Tribes are already doing this.)

Child Welfare

One Tribal leader spoke of his personal experience as a child placed temporar-ily in a non-Indian home and said he was very troubled by this practice and its continuing adverse impact on many Indian people. Some Tribal leaders noted that improvements are still needed to assure rapid return of Indian children to their communities, while others acknowledged that the Indian Child Welfare Act initially had "an agonizing impact" on some non-Indian families. Some State officials expressed particular concern about neglect of some Indian children by their parents and said they hope the State and Tribes can make progress to-gether on this problem. One official noted that alcoholism was seen as the main cause of child neglect in the past, but gambling addiction is a growing cause.

Suggestions Offered by Interviewees

Continue to work together to address the causes and treatment for addiction, diabetes and other serious health problems on reservations. Consider ways to improve services to Indian patients through methods that work better for Indians than traditional western techniques (for example, using shamanic counseling techniques and providing sweat lodges in recovery facilities).

Consider how DSHS can continue to hire more native people in its programs for Indians.

Work together to provide opportunities for those leaving welfare through the Work First program (e.g., by providing vocational training and employment opportunities), and assure than these individuals are not required to leave their reservations to find employment.

Consider ways to provide more health clinics to serve Tribal members, especially in rural areas.

Consider whether the State and Tribes could work together to better reduce youth access to tobacco products on reservations.

Work to better inform Tribes about how to participate in the Children's Health Insurance Program.

Continue to work toward improvement in DSHS communications with Tribes and cultural education for DSHS employees.

Seek ways to streamline DSHS programs affecting Tribal members (e.g., returning children under the Indian Child Welfare Act).

FINDING 2: TRIBAL GOVERNMENTS SEEK STATE SUPPORT IN MEETING THE DIFFICULT CHALLENGES OF CRIME PREVENTION AND LAW ENFORCEMENT, EVEN THOUGH JURISDICTIONAL ISSUES ARE COMPLEX AND TROUBLESOME.

Many Tribal and State officials noted that crime rates are higher on reservations than in neighboring communities but also observed that offenders are often non-Indians. Tribes vary in the extent to which they cross-deputize or are cross-deputized by local law enforcement agencies, and counties have inconsistent policies about the requirements for cross-deputizations and the law enforcement services they provide. The State patrol develops policies on a Tribe-by-Tribe basis but meets regularly with the Northwest Tribal Enforcement Officers Association to communicate about policies and matters of mutual concern. Generally, for non-Indians on reservations, Tribes are responsible for civil law enforcement and the State or counties are responsible for criminal law enforcement.

Major Concerns Identified by Interviewees

Tribal leaders had a number of concerns about law enforcement against Indians but also acknowledged that, at times, illegal conduct by some Indian people is a problem. They noted that non-Indian offenses on Tribal lands are a significant problem for many Tribes. Many concerns of Tribal leaders related to jurisdictional issues and disagreements over limits on treaty rights. Tribal leaders generally said their ultimate goal is to obtain full recognition of Tribal jurisdiction over all activities on reservations and full faith and credit for Tribal courts. However, for the most part, Tribal leaders focused their comments on immediate concerns.

Cross-Deputization

The most common concern raised by Tribal leaders related to cross-deputization of Tribal law enforcement officers. They noted that some, but not all, counties are refusing to cross-deputize Tribal law enforcement officers because these officers have not been trained at the State's facility. (Tribal leaders said these counties still expect and receive backup from Tribal officers.) Some Tribal leaders noted that, with the assistance of the Bureau of Indian Affairs, their officers are trained at arguably superior federal law enforcement facilities and counties should give full credit for this training. Other Tribal leaders noted that Tribal officers at one time could attend the State's training facility under scholarship, but local governments have objected to this practice. They said scholarships are no longer available and many Tribes cannot afford to pay for State training. This was a very important source of friction between some Tribes and their neighboring counties. Tribes generally said cross-deputization is a key to improved understanding between Tribal communities and their neighbors. Gaining the respect of local authorities and citizens for Tribal jurisdiction was seen as requiring a long struggle and almost daily interaction with sheriffs and other officials (for example, to gain respect for Tribal arrests and warrants).

Tensions between Indians and non-Indians
Several Tribal leaders said that anti-Indian harassment has increased and that, more and more, Tribal members are arming themselves. One Tribal leader noted that Tribal fisheries officers were being seriously harassed by non-Indians. State law enforcement officials agreed that anti-Indian harassment seems to be on the rise.

Relations with Local Prosecutors
Tribal leaders suggested that the Attorney General's Office could do more to provide leadership to local prosecutors to encourage them to work more constructively with Tribes. State leaders said that local prosecutors similarly complain that the Attorney General's Office does not exert enough leadership with Tribes. It was noted that the AG's Office is supporting pilot projects that may be helpful. Some State leaders said that Tribes could do a better job of policing themselves and that this is a source of ill-will toward Tribes from local law enforcers.

Local Law Enforcement
Some Tribal leaders said that law enforcement by local authorities against non-Indians (including non-U.S. citizens) committing crimes on the reservation is seriously inadequate in some areas. Response is slow or nonexistent in some cases. Some Tribal leaders believe that local authorities do not want to enter (or resent having to enter) reservations. At the same time, several Tribal leaders recognized that there is not enough funding for law enforcement and noted that local law enforcement authorities are asking the Tribes to pay higher fees for their services. Not all Tribes are able to pay more. One Tribal leader said a Tribe is paying fees that are clearly exorbitant considering the number of incidents on Tribal lands compared to the rest of the county, but this Tribe does receive good service in return. One State official said some Tribes have indicated they are getting too much attention from local law enforcement.

State Law Enforcement

Several Tribal leaders expressed concern that State law enforcement is more vigorous against Indians than against non-Indians (for example in enforcement of hunting and fishing limits, as noted above). Several Tribal leaders expressed frustration over the fact that State funding for enforcement of cigarette tax laws has been greatly increased, while funding for social services is declining. One Tribal leader raised concern that State patrol officers will not write tickets to Tribal courts and another said that State patrol officers seem to be afraid to come onto reservations, except when there is a major accident. State officials expressed frustration that Tribal law enforcement directors who interact with State and local law enforcement do not always reflect the wishes of Tribal Councils (e.g., regarding writing traffic tickets on county roads).

Detention Facilities

Several Tribal leaders expressed concern about the inadequacy of State detention facilities, and especially about the State's refusal to accept Indian youths convicted in federal court. One Tribal leader questioned whether the per capita distribution of natural resources payments to Tribal members must continue to be confiscated by the State when a Tribal member is incarcerated.

Full Faith and Credit

Tribal leaders said that full faith and credit for court orders needs to be "a two-way street." Tribal leaders said that a system is needed to ensure proper conversion of State and local court orders into Tribal court orders. For example, one Tribal leader noted that when a Tribe is served with a garnishment order for non-Indian employee wages, the Tribe will execute the order only if it is first converted to a Tribal court order. The number of such orders is said to be increasing. Other examples included child custody orders and orders under the Violence against Women Act.

Suggestions Offered by Interviewees

State and Tribal leaders may wish to identify ways to improve relations between Tribes and local prosecutors and law enforcement officers.

The State should consider how to improve training on Tribal treaty rights for personnel involved in enforcement of fishing and hunting limits.

The State should consider whether it can facilitate cross-deputization by funding participation by Tribal law enforcement officers in the State's training program. [One option might be to offer scholarships to economically distressed localities as well as Tribes. An alternative might be to persuade counties to recognize the federal training that Tribal officers receive.]

Consider ways the State can help improve incarceration facilities to meet the needs of Tribes and Indian prisoners. In particular, seek better ways to accommodate Indian youth and support Tribes that are interested in constructing their own incarceration facilities.

State leaders could help Tribes by telling the President and the Secretary of Interior that federal funding for Tribal law enforcement is a priority.

Consider whether the State can help fund or support federal funding specifically for less expensive law enforcement equipment, such as cell phones for officers, when Tribes cannot afford to do so.

Work together to develop a system for speedy conversion of court orders.

FINDING 3: STATE AGENCIES COULD SHOW MORE RESPECT FOR TRIBAL CULTURE AND TRADITIONS THROUGH CERTAIN SPECIFIC IMPROVEMENTS.

As noted above, both State and Tribal leaders acknowledged the need for better public education and training for State employees on Tribal culture and history. Also, as noted above, sensitivity to Indian traditions in the provision of social services is an ongoing challenge. The following additional points were made on this subject by interviewees.

DOT needs to find better ways to respect Indian archaeological sites.

It is important to Tribes that State officials not romanticize or disrespect Indian culture but instead focus on how Tribal communities are faring.

State employees need to recognize the importance of use of certain resources (e.g., cedar logs and certain species of salmon), in religious and traditional ceremonies. These are more than just economic resources for the Tribes.

The Parks and Recreation Department needs to make better progress on repatriation of artifacts (now that some funding is available for this effort).

Important Tribal traditions need to be respected in State policies affecting employees and prisoners (e.g., time off for funerals).

FINDING 4: IMPROVING EDUCATION FOR INDIAN CHILDREN IS A HIGH PRIORITY, ESPECIALLY GIVEN HIGH DROPOUT RATES.

While interviewees were not specifically invited to comment on education programs, several Tribal leaders raised this as a critical concern. (As noted above, public education about Tribes was also an important concern.) The following points were made:

State leaders should assure full funding of the Indian Education Office.

Statewide, the school dropout rate for Indian children is between 60 and 80%. It is important to the future of the State and the Tribes to make education more relevant and more useful to Indian children.

Keep expectations high for Indian students and help publicize their successes, but be sure that those who are not college bound have options for realistic vocational training.

The State should not fine grandparents of Indian children who are truants. The grandparents, who often serve as guardians because of social or health problems in the family, cannot afford the fines and it does not work as a way to get the kids to school.

Tribal leaders should continue to train Indian youth to be more resource-ful, have better self-esteem, and move past concerns about racism and histori-cal inequities.

Source:

Prothro, Martha. "Preliminary Report: Challenges to Relations Between the State of Washington and the Washington Tribes." Seattle: Ross & Associates Environmental Consulting, Ltd., October 11, 1999.

75

Presidential Executive Order 13175: Consultation and Coordination with Indian Tribal Governments (2000)

President Bill Clinton, more often than most contemporary US presidents, used the executive order power of his office to recognize the inherent sover-eignty of Native Nations, support their religious expressions, and improve the broader relationship between the executive branch and Tribal governments. In 1998 he issued an executive order (executive order 13084 "Consultation and Cooperation with Indian Tribal Governments") that called upon every agency of the federal government to establish a process of consultation with Native nations when it appeared policies or goals might impact Tribes.

In 2000 he expanded upon his earlier order by stipulating anew in this executive order that federal agencies be more proactive in consulting and col-laborating with Native governments before implementing rules or policies that might do harm to those communities or their resources.

———

By the authority vested in me as President by the Constitution and the laws of the United States of America, and in order to establish regular and meaningful consultation and collaboration with tribal officials in the development of Federal policies that have tribal implications, to strengthen the United States govern-ment-to-government relationships with Indian tribes, and to reduce the imposi-tion of unfunded mandates upon Indian tribes; it is hereby ordered as follows:

Section 1. Definitions.

For purposes of this order:

a. "Policies that have tribal implications" refers to regulations, legislative comments or proposed legislation, and other policy statements or actions that have substantial direct effects on one or more Indian tribes, on the relationship between the Federal Government and Indian tribes, or on the distribution of power and responsibilities between the Federal Government and Indian tribes.

b. "Indian tribe" means an Indian or Alaska Native tribe, band, nation, pueblo, village, or community that the Secretary of the Interior acknowledges to exist as an Indian tribe pursuant to the Federally Recognized Indian Tribe List Act of 1994, 25 U.S.C. 479a.

c. "Agency" means any authority of the United States that is an "agency" under 44 S.C. 3502(1), other than those considered to be independent regulatory agencies, as defined in 44 U.S.C. 3502(5).

d. "Tribal officials" means elected or duly appointed officials of Indian tribal governments or authorized intertribal organizations.

Section. 2. Fundamental Principles.

In formulating or implementing policies that have tribal implications, agencies shall be guided by the following fundamental principles:

a. The United States has a unique legal relationship with Indian tribal governments as set forth in the Constitution of the United States, treaties, statutes, Executive Orders, and court decisions. Since the formation of the Union, the United States has recognized Indian tribes as domestic dependent nations under its protection. The Federal Government has enacted numerous statutes and promulgated numerous regulations that establish and define a trust relationship with Indian tribes.

b. Our Nation, under the law of the United States, in accordance with treaties, statutes, Executive Orders, and judicial decisions, has recognized the right of Indian tribes to self-government. As domestic dependent nations, Indian tribes exercise inherent sovereign powers over their members and territory. The United States continues to work with Indian tribes on a government-to-government basis to address issues concerning Indian tribal self-government, tribal trust resources, and Indian tribal treaty and other rights.

c. The United States recognizes the right of Indian tribes to self-government and supports tribal sovereignty and self-determination.

Section 3. Policymaking Criteria.

In addition to adhering to the fundamental principles set forth in section 2, agencies shall adhere, to the extent permitted by law, to the following criteria when formulating and implementing policies that have tribal implications:

a. Agencies shall respect Indian tribal self-government and sovereignty, honor tribal treaty and other rights, and strive to meet the responsibilities that arise from the unique legal relationship between the Federal Government and Indian tribal governments.

b. With respect to Federal statutes and regulations administered by Indian tribal governments, the Federal Government shall grant Indian tribal governments the maximum administrative discretion possible.

c. When undertaking to formulate and implement policies that have tribal implications, agencies shall:
   1. encourage Indian tribes to develop their own policies to achieve program objectives;
   2. where possible, defer to Indian tribes to establish standards; and
   3. in determining whether to establish Federal standards, consult with tribal officials as to the need for Federal standards and any alternatives that would limit the scope of Federal standards or otherwise preserve the prerogatives and authority of Indian tribes.

Section 4. Special Requirements for Legislative Proposals.

Agencies shall not submit to the Congress legislation that would be inconsistent with the policy- making criteria in Section 3.

Section 5. Consultation.

a. Each agency shall have an accountable process to ensure meaningful and timely input by tribal officials in the development of regulatory policies that have tribal implications. Within 30 days after the effective date of this order, the head of each agency shall designate an official with principal responsibility for the agency's implementation of this order. Within 60 days of the effective date of this order, the designated official shall submit to the Office of Management and Budget (OMB) a description of the agency's consultation process.

b. To the extent practicable and permitted by law, no agency shall promulgate any regulation that has tribal implications, that imposes substantial direct compliance costs on Indian tribal governments, and that is not required by statute, unless:

1. funds necessary to pay the direct costs incurred by the Indian tribal government or the tribe in complying with the regulation are provided by the Federal Government; or

2. the agency, prior to the formal promulgation of the regulation,

    i) consulted with tribal officials early in the process of developing the proposed regulation;

    ii) in a separately identified portion of the preamble to the regulation as it is to be issued in the *Federal Register*, provides to the Director of OMB a tribal summary impact statement, which consists of a description of the extent of the agency's prior consultation with tribal officials, a summary of the nature of their concerns and the agency's position supporting the need to issue the regulation, and a statement of the extent to which the concerns of tribal officials have been met; and

    iii) makes available to the Director of OMB any written communications submitted to the agency by tribal officials.

    iv) To the extent practicable and permitted by law, no agency shall promulgate any regulation that has tribal implications and that preempts tribal law unless the agency, prior to the formal promulgation of the regulation,

    v) consulted with tribal officials early in the process of developing the proposed regulation;

    vi) in a separately identified portion of the preamble to the regulation as it is to be issued in the *Federal Register*, provides to the Director of OMB a tribal summary impact statement, which consists of a description of the extent of the agency's prior consultation with tribal officials, a summary of the nature of their concerns and the agency's position supporting the need to issue the regulation, and a statement of the extent to which the concerns of tribal officials have been met; and

3. makes available to the Director of OMB any written communications submitted to the agency by tribal officials.

    i) On issues relating to tribal self-government, tribal trust resources, or Indian tribal treaty and other rights, each agency should explore and, where appropriate, use consensual mechanisms for developing regulations, including negotiated rulemaking.

Section 6. *Increasing Flexibility for Indian Tribal Waivers.*

a. Agencies shall review the processes under which Indian tribes apply for waivers of statutory and regulatory requirements and take appropriate steps to streamline those processes.

b. Each agency shall, to the extent practicable and permitted by law, consider any application by an Indian tribe for a waiver of statutory or regulatory requirements in connection with any program administered by the agency with a general view toward increasing opportunities for utilizing flexible policy approaches at the Indian tribal level in cases in which the proposed waiver is consistent with the applicable Federal policy objectives and is otherwise appropriate.

c. Each agency shall, to the extent practicable and permitted by law, render a decision upon a complete application for a waiver within 120 days of receipt of such application by the agency, or as otherwise provided by law or regulation. If the application for waiver is not granted, the agency shall provide the applicant with timely written notice of the decision and the reasons therefor.

d. This section applies only to statutory or regulatory requirements that are discretionary and subject to waiver by the agency.

Section 7. Accountability.

a. In transmitting any draft final regulation that has tribal implications to OMB pursuant to Executive Order 12866 of September 30, 1993, each agency shall include a certification from the official designated to ensure compliance with this order stating that the requirements of this order have been met in a meaningful and timely manner.

b. In transmitting proposed legislation that has tribal implications to OMB, each agency shall include a certification from the official designated to ensure compliance with this order that all relevant requirements of this order have been met.

c. Within 180 days after the effective date of this order the Director of OMB and the Assistant to the President for Intergovernmental Affairs shall confer with tribal officials to ensure that this order is being properly and effectively implemented.

Section 8. Independent Agencies. Independent regulatory agencies are encouraged to comply with the provisions of this order.

Section 9. General Provisions.

a. This order shall supplement but not supersede the requirements contained in Executive Order 12866 (Regulatory Planning and Review), Executive Order 12988 (Civil Justice Reform), OMB Circular A–19, and the Executive Memorandum of April 29, 1994, on Government-to-Government Relations with Native American Tribal Governments.

b. This order shall complement the consultation and waiver provisions in sections 6 and 7 of Executive Order 13132 (Federalism).

c. Executive Order 13084 (Consultation and Coordination with Indian Tribal Governments) is revoked at the time this order takes effect.

d. This order shall be effective 60 days after the date of this order.

Section 10. Judicial Review.

This order is intended only to improve the internal management of the executive branch, and is not intended to create any right, benefit, or trust responsibility, substantive or procedural, enforceable at law by a party against the United States, its agencies, or any person.
William J. Clinton

Source:

Executive Order 13175, "Consultation and Cooperation with Indian Tribal Governments." *Federal Register* 65, no. 218 (November 9, 2000).

---

76   *National Governors Association Speech by Susan Masten (Yurok), President of the National Congress of American Indians (2001)*

Susan Masten, the second woman elected president of the National Congress of American Indians (NCAI), had been very active in Yurok politics for years, fighting hard for fishing rights, cultural identity, and environmental justice. She also served as Yurok Tribal Chairperson from 1997–2004. During her stint as NCAI president, one of her goals was to improve relations with two of the leading national-level organizations of state elected officials—the National Conference of State Legislatures (NCSL) and the National Governors Association (NGA).

NCAI had embarked on an impressive run of collaborative projects with NCSL through its State-Tribal Institute, and sought to do the same with NGA, as explained in this speech.

———

Statement of Susan Masten

I would like to begin today by thanking the National Governors Association for inviting NCAI to take part in this meeting. It was good of you to reach out and ask us to be a part of this Indian issues briefing. Too often, NGA and NCAI do not take the time to talk directly to each other. Instead we separately take our issues to Congress. You took the first step today in bridging that gap, and we appreciate it very much.

We recognize that you have several specific issues that you plan to discuss today. I am looking forward to staying with you and having some of our people participate in the specific panel discussions. Tribal governments have a keen interest and a lot of knowledge about the issues that you are discussing, so we would love to be a part of today's discussions. I'm hopeful that this is the first of many to come. The National Governor's Association's policy position on tribal issues states: "The governors recognize and respect the sovereignty of Indian tribal governments and support economic advancement and independence for tribes. State and tribal governments must continue to work together on many significant issues. Governors value their important relationships with tribal governments."

Given this statement from the governors, I believe that a commitment to continue to meet in the future is one of the most important things we can accomplish today.

I would like to begin by discussing the broader context within which these specific issues arise. Here at the national level, too often we act as if the relationships between states and tribes are little more than jurisdictional battles over the hot button issues, and we ignore the many similarities between states and tribes that offer great opportunities for cooperation.

At the local level, states and tribes have lots of mutual interests: law enforcement, health care, services, natural resources, to name just a few. Our front-line workers and your front-line workers are working together every day. Tribes and states also have a lot in common in other ways. Both tribal governments and state governments are confronted by limited budgets that we have to use efficiently, while trying to provide comprehensive services to our citizens. We are trying to promote economic development while at the same time protect the environment and our quality of life. In short, tribes and states have a great deal in common because we share one very unique and fundamental attribute: we are both sovereign governments.

The fact that states and tribes are both sovereign governments should be better understood than it is. Everyone knows that the U.S. Constitution set up our federal system of government, but how many people know that the Constitution also recognizes the sovereignty of Indian tribes? Far too few. Hundreds of treaties, Supreme Court decisions, federal laws and executive orders have repeatedly affirmed that Indian nations retain our fundamental and inherent powers of self-government. Most people are not aware of this because it is not taught in our schools.

Why is there so little understanding of tribal government in our country? The reason is found in our history. Indian tribes have been forcibly moved from one end of the country to another, our lands and resources have been stolen despite the guarantees of treaties and federal laws, and finally, when there was little left to take from us, our rights and needs have simply been ignored. This is a dark history we have inherited. A history which all of us need to understand better.

Indian tribes have not disappeared as so many thought we would. Despite enormous poverty, suffering and pressures to simulate, Indian people have stayed together and continued to raise our children and teach them our traditions and languages, and have struggled to maintain our sovereignty and our lands. Tribes have struggled and succeeded in establishing the federal policy of tribal self-determination that was created in 1970 by President Nixon and has been endorsed by every succeeding U.S. president including our president today, President George W. Bush. Since that time, tribes are growing stronger than ever, people are moving home to the reservations, economic development is beginning to take hold in many places, and our government structures are growing ever more effective and secure.

Why have we done this? Why did our parents and grandparents and all of the great tribal leaders work so hard to reestablish tribal sovereignty? It is not because of some abstract principle or because of a sense of entitlement. It is because tribal self-government is critical for us to maintain our cultures and our viability as distinct groups of people. It is because we want our children to grow up with the same traditions and values that we grew up with. These are reasons that everyone in America can understand because these are the basic values of cultural survival that we all share just as much as our need to breathe the air.

Although there are these common threads that run through all of our tribal history, it is really unfair to generalize because Indian tribes all over the country are so distinct and our histories and circumstances vary so widely. This is a point that I would like to emphasize: it is very difficult to generalize about tribes. Just as California is not like Rhode Island, Indian tribes have a great deal of diversity in size, culture, land base, values and economic systems. Just as states need different laws and policies so tribes need different laws and policies to fit with their unique circumstances.

Tribes and states also share social and economic systems and we are experiencing changes that can affect our relationship. A good example of this is growing suburbs and exurbs throughout the West. The 2000 census shows that the U.S. population is dramatically expanding into areas that were once very rural. Well, these same areas are where our reservations are. So on one hand it is no wonder that we are experiencing some growing pains as Americans move into Indian Country. The conflicts didn't occur as often when population densities were extremely low.

The transformations in the tribal economy are causing alarm in some places. Particularly with tribal gaming, tribes have been repeatedly challenged on their ability to raise revenue and create jobs. But tribal governmental gaming has grown at about the same rate as state gaming. Thirty-seven states and the District of Columbia now have state lotteries. Much of this growth in state-sponsored gaming was a direct result of budget deficits in the 1980s. States found state lotteries to be a good solution because it allowed them to raise revenue without raising taxes. State lotteries invest in education, environment and other important programs. Tribal governments have pursued governmental gaming for similar reasons. That is, before gaming, many Indian nations were unable to fund basic government services for their people.

Gaming in some parts of Indian Country has created jobs, provided economic growth and allowed investment in education, health care and housing, among other programs.

Moreover, tribal gaming has brought substantial beneficial economic and social impacts to surrounding communities. In fact, there is national evidence that Indian gaming results in the reduction in welfare payments and unemployment rates for Indian and non-Indian communities. I know that we will continue to argue over Indian gaming, but sometimes I can't figure out why we are having this argument in the first place.

Another relatively recent policy change that we are both experiencing is the rapid increase in state taxes on tobacco products and motor fuels. Tribes have never been subject to the state tax system and we have always had the ability to set our own taxes at whatever level we choose. Thirty years ago, when state gas taxes were only pennies and cigarette taxes were a nickel a pack, very few people bothered to drive out to rural Indian reservations to avoid the state taxes. Now that state taxes are much, much higher, and the population has moved out to where the tribes are, this issue has developed between states and tribes over the collection of taxes.

I am not a resident of Washington, DC, yet when I am here, I fully expect to pay the DC sales tax. Why should it be any different on an Indian reservation? How can tribes exist as governments and provide services to their people with this parity?

The reality is that most states and tribes have worked out tax compacts, but a few are still working on it. I think it is important to understand the social and historical context of these issues so that we can understand the role that both states and tribes have played in creating the issue, and then we sit at the table, government-to-government, and work out agreements that will be mutually acceptable. I don't believe that we want to hand this issue over to the federal government to resolve. We know that we will arrive at agreements that are much closer to what we want as state leaders and as tribal leaders by working together. We are very glad to hear that just this week the State of Washington and many of the tribes in Washington have been able to work out and pass state legislation that will authorize new cigarette tax compacts in that state.

States and tribes also have a great deal of common ground with regard to the increased decentralization or devolution of what were once federal programs. States and tribes are both great advocates of local control and the philosophy that the government functions better when it is closer to the people. In spite of some disparate treatment, state and tribal governments have many similar interests in devolutionary policies. We must collaborate to ensure that services are efficiently provided to all citizens, inside and outside of reservation boundaries, and in minimizing service overlap. And of course we both want to ensure that adequate resources are provided to implement services, particularly because fixed federal block grants may be inadequate in times of economic downturn. We also have a mutual interest in ensuring that devolved programs have sufficient flexibility and realistic performance measures and reporting requirements. In the era of devolution, collaboration between states and tribes is more important than ever.

Given all of these common issues, I want to raise a critique against the NGA's policy position on tribal issues. But I want to do this in the spirit of recognition that most national organizations, including NCAI, are subject to similar criticisms. The criticism is this: NGA's policy on tribal issues does not accurately reflect the relationships that exist between states and tribes in most places. Instead, the NGA policy is overly focused on gaming and a handful of the most difficult jurisdictional issues. This is a sour without the sweet. From this policy statement, one would think that the relationship between states and tribes is nothing but a jurisdictional battle on hard-core sovereignty issues. It is not that this view is inaccurate, but it is entirely incomplete.

Take a look at the issues that you have on the agenda today. These are real issues and difficult ones to be sure. But why are you spending a full day working only on the issues that divide us, and not on any areas where we need to build our cooperation in order to meet the needs of our citizens? Where is the discussion of issues such as law enforcement, welfare reform, wildlife management, water resources, education, health care, federal spending, child-support, economic development or transportation? I can tell you that states and tribes are busy working on these kinds of issues every day, often finding ground for cooperation, and that we need to be working on these issues at the national level as well.

The NGA may be successful this year and pushing through some legislative measure that would diminish the authority of tribes in one area or another, but this will not allow us to find creative solutions at the local level to the issues that we are facing. I know that NCAI will work very hard to make sure that our rights are not compromised. And in the long run, I do not believe that the NGA will be able to diminish or get rid of Indian tribes and their sovereign authorities. We are growing stronger, not weaker, and we have a great deal of general support from the American public. Every public survey poll shows this, and even on the most difficult issues like gaming, tribes have been able to take their issues to the voters and find support for tribal self-determination and self-reliance over the outdated notions of continued federal dependency.

States and tribes want many of the same things. I know for a fact that states do not want to push tribes back into the old cycle of poverty: the burden of that poverty will fall squarely onto the States back. We need to take a longer view of these issues and find better ways to work together and cooperate.

As I close today, I would like to challenge the National Governor's Association to rewrite its policy position on Indian issues in a way that does not overly focus on gaming alone, but that takes into account the full range of issues that states and tribes have in common. We would like to propose that we start a few joint working committees to begin to talk about the NGA policy positions and some of the key issues that we are facing. Gaming certainly merits our discussion, but we also want to talk about welfare reform reauthorization and health care issues to name a few.

As you can see from the small green booklet, we have begun to have this type of dialogue with the National Conference of State Legislatures.

The title of that book is "Government to Government," and I think that is a great theme for the future relationships that we want to have with the governors. As responsible governments, we want to sit at the table and develop cooperative relationships where states and tribes can work together for the growth and development of Indian communities and all of our neighboring communities.

Thank you very much for the opportunity to be with you this morning and we will look forward to today's discussion.

Source:

www.ncai.org.

77 Statement of Melanie Benjamin, Chief Executive, Mille Lacs Band of Ojibwe (2001)

The Midwest Alliance of Sovereign Tribes (MAST), established in 1996, is an intertribal body consisting of thirty-five member nations located within Minnesota, Michigan, Iowa, and Wisconsin. It was founded by Marge Anderson, a former leader of the Mille Lacs Band of Ojibwe in Minnesota. It is one of a number of intertribal bodies such as the United South and Eastern Tribes, Inc., Great Lakes Intertribal Council, Affiliated Tribes of Northwest Indians and Intertribal Council of California—that focuses on representing the unique needs of Native peoples in a given geographical region. MAST's own mission statement declares that it is to "advance, protect, preserve, and enhance the mutual interests, treaty rights, sovereignty, and cultural way of life of the sovereign nations of the Midwest throughout the 21st century."

At this hearing, MAST member leaders urged Congress to work with them on a number of important issues for the betterment of their communities, including topics such as education, natural resources protection, criminal and civil jurisdiction matters, economic development, and intergovernmental relations. Melanie Benjamin, who succeeded Marge Anderson as Chief Executive of the Mille Lacs Band, here offers her testimony on some of the pressing topics that required attention within her nation's borders.

Mr. Chairman and members of the committee, my name is Melanie Benjamin. I am the chief executive of the Mille Lacs Band of Ojibwe from

Onamia, Minnesota. It is an honor to present the views of the people of the Mille Lacs Band to the committee.

Today, I respectfully request that the committee introduce legislation in three different areas.

First, amendments to Title IV of Public Law 93–638, the Self-Governance Act as it applies to the Bureau of Indian Affairs and the Department of the Interior, are needed to reflect advances made in Title V.

Second, legislation relating to the transfer into trust, immunity from the exercise of local and state jurisdiction, and non-alienability of tribal fee land within reservation boundaries should be introduced.

Third, an economic development grant program should be established under Public Law 102–477 to create new jobs in Indian Country for those formerly under general assistance programs who are now attempting to achieve self-sufficiency.

Title IV Amendments and Tribal Self-Governance

The development of self-governance is probably the most significant enhancement of the United States/Tribal Government relationship since the Treaty era. Through self-governance, the Band has been able to develop economic activities to employ its members, construct facilities for education and health needs, and establish public water systems and housing. Over the past ten years, the Band has made unprecedented progress unlikely to be matched in the future by any BIA program.

As the committee knows, in 1994 Congress passed Public Law 103–413, the Tribal Self-Governance Act. This act made tribal self-governance a permanent principle of the Department of the Interior's administration of Indian affairs. Last year, Congress passed Public Law 106–260, which made self-governance a permanent part of the Indian Health Service and included a demonstration project in the Department of Health and Human Services regarding self-governance. Titles V and VI of the Self-Governance Act are vast improvements over the existing provisions in Title IV. Hence, I respectfully request that the committee consider amending Title IV.

As a member of the Rulemaking Committee on Title V, I have noted that, unlike the current version of Title IV, improvements in the Title V statute have enabled the committee to draft regulations quickly and effectively. For example, Title V contains a definition of "inherent federal function." The absence of this definition in Title IV caused a delay of several months in the rulemaking process.... In fact, the Title IV regulations took over five years to draft. It appears that the Title V regulations will be completed in the time required in the statute. Hence, various amendments to Title IV are needed. The obstinacy of the BIA in defining "inherent federal function" is indicative of their overall approach of protecting the Bureau as opposed to advancing self-governance. Failure to deal honorably with self-governance, and a delay through word games, has created a whole host of problems for self-governance tribes. A very important example deals with the very basis of self-governance: the control of dollars.

It was the belief of the Mille Lacs Band when it entered the self-governance movement that when the Bureau of Indian affairs received a budget increase, we would receive a budget increase. Based on a cursory review of the appropriations for the BIA over the past seven years, we note that the Bureau has received a substantial increase. During this same time period, the Mille Lacs Bands' base budget has declined. It is our view that our budget should reflect gains made by the BIA.

Our base funding should increase with the BIA budget. Our initial base funding was derived from tribal "638"contracts along with tribal shares from other programs. The base funding was a combination of Bureau programs compacted for and, in some cases, additional funding from a fund called "shortfall," which was determined by the Office of Self-Governance. When the Mille Lacs Band government developed its initial base funding we took all programs we were eligible for and developed a base funding amount. It was our understanding that this base funding would parallel to the funding level of the Bureau's program. However, this is not been the case.

Attached is a summary of what has happened with our funding versus what has happened with Bureau funding over the last seven years. Because the Band government compacts all eligible programs, the analysis of what has happened to funding is very clear. Under self-governance, the funding the Band received from 1993–2000 has decreased by 5% whereas the Bureau's budget has increased 20% over the same time. It is our belief that this was never the intent of the self-governance policy and that our base level funding should increase proportionally with the Bureau's budget....

Legislation on Tribally Owned Fee Lands

There are few statutes relating specifically to the status of fee-simple lands owned by the tribal government within the reservation, and this lack of guidance is generating a large number of issues. The result is that courts have to determine many matters without any guidance furthermore, because of the difficulty in moving land into trust, there are numerous problems developing out of this issue as well.

The Mille Lacs Band would like to see an improvement in the current system of transferring land from fee-simple status to federal trust status. Congress should consider the enactment of legislation that would provide a special status for tribally owned fee lands within reservation boundaries. Many of these lands are being used for tribal government purposes. In spite of this fact, these lands are subject to certain types of jurisdiction exercised by counties and states. This includes subjecting these tribal lands to taxation by another sovereign. We believe that one way to deal with these issues would be legislation that deems lands within reservations, when owned by the tribal government and used for governmental purposes, to be non-alienable and immune to the jurisdiction of any sovereign other than that of the owning tribe, except as provided by federal law.

New Economic Development Amendment

... There is a major unmet need in Indian Country for an economic development initiative which creates employment opportunities for tribal members moving from public assistance to self-sufficiency. Without job opportunities, any welfare-to-work programs will fail. The Mille Lacs Band would like to propose that Congress develop a Tribal Demonstration Project which would include economic development grants. The grant program would assist tribes in the development and implementation of management and infrastructure capability; coordinate economic development related programs and services more effectively; assist in developing tribal business ordinances; and generally encourage economic development. This demonstration project should have stable base funding and be awarded to competitively selected Indian tribes and Alaskan native villages for comprehensive economic development. The project would encourage tribes to design, improve or expand economic goals that use the available human, natural, financial, and physical resources to which the tribes have access.

Such an amendment would fight the poverty that exists on many reservations across this country. Indian families cannot move from welfare to work if there is no work.

Conclusion

The Mille Lacs Band looks forward to working with the committee on these and other issues. We believe in the preservation and protection of our land whether it is held in trust or fee as well as self-governance and economic development for ourselves and all Indian tribes. We believe that the proposed legislation I have outlined are positive steps to achieving all of these goals and therefore ask you to seriously consider adoption of legislation incorporating these measures. For this opportunity to share the views of the Mille Lacs Band, I say "Miigwetch"—thank you.

Source:

US Senate. "Goals and Priorities of the Member Tribes of the Midwest Alliance of Sovereign Tribes (MAST)." Hearing Before the Committee on Indian Affairs. 107th Cong., 1st Sess. Washington, DC: Government Printing Office, June 19 2001. http://m-a-s-t.org.

78

Charter of the Consolidated Borough of Quil Ceda Village (2001)

Quil Ceda Village was incorporated in 2001 as the first Tribal political subdivision in the United States established under the Indian Tribal Governmental Tax Status Act of 1982. That year, the Bureau of Indian Affairs approved the Tulalip Tribes' charter of the Village as a Tribal municipality and the Internal Revenue Service then recognized its designation as a political subdivision of the Tribes. Thus, it is only the second federal municipality to be created within the US— the other is Washington, DC.

Located on reservation lands, Quil Ceda Village includes a business park, shopping mall, casino, and hotel. Chartered as a consolidated borough and overseen by a council-manager government, its unique status allows the Tulalip Tribes to retain a greater portion of sales taxes collected within its boundaries. State Senator John McCoy, a member of the Tulalip Tribes and long-time chair of the National Caucus of Native American State Legislators, responsible for many positive advances in intergovernmental relations at the local, state and national levels, envisaged and led the ambitious exercise of sovereignty that greatly solidified and strengthened the nation's economic base.

Article I
Incorporation; Form of Government; Powers and Boundaries

Section One. Incorporation.

The unincorporated area of Quil Ceda on the Tulalip Indian Reservation, within the geographic limits now established herein or that may hereafter be established in the manner provided by law, shall be and is hereby declared pursuant to Tulalip Ordinance No. 111 to be the Consolidated Borough of Quil Ceda Village, a municipal body politic and corporate, in perpetuity, of the Tulalip Tribes under the name of the Consolidated Borough of Quil Ceda Village; hereinafter "the Village."

Section Two. Form of Government.

The municipal government provided by this charter shall be known as the council-manager form of government. Pursuant to the provisions of and subject only to the limitations imposed by the constitution and laws of the Tulalip Tribes of Washington and by this charter, all powers of the Village shall be vested in Village council, herein referred to as council, which shall enact local legislation, approve budgets, determine policies, and appoint the Village manager and such other officers deemed necessary and proper for the orderly government and administration of the affairs of the Village, as prescribed by the constitution, applicable laws, and ordinances hereafter adopted by the Village. All powers of the Village shall be exercised in the manner prescribed by this charter or, if the manner is not so prescribed, then in such manner as may be prescribed by ordinance. The Village shall be a political subdivision of the Tulalip Tribes as that term is defined by federal law and shall be entitled to all the powers and benefits of that designation.

Section Three. Powers of Village.

The Village shall have all general and specific powers granted to municipal and quasi municipal corporations by the various states of the United States and the laws of the Tulalip Tribes of Washington and by its Charter, including but not limited to the taxing and police powers, the powers of annexation and eminent domain, the power to protect the public safety, health and welfare of all persons within the Village, and the power to contract together with all the implied powers necessary to carry into execution all the powers herein granted. In addition, the Village shall have all the powers and privileges of a political subdivision of an Indian tribal government.

Section Four. Intergovernmental Relations.

The Village may exercise any of its powers or perform any of its functions and may participate in the financing thereof, jointly or in cooperation, by contract or otherwise, with any one or more Indian tribes, states or political subdivisions or civil divisions or agencies thereof, or the United States or any agency thereof, or with any private entity or agency.

Section Five. Boundaries.

The boundaries of the Village shall be as established in Exhibit A to the Charter, being the boundaries established at the time this charter takes effect, or such boundaries as may be established to increase or decrease the territory within the Village thereafter in the manner authorized by law.

Section Six. Debts, Immunity from Suit.

The Village is an agency, instrumentality, political subdivision and arm of the Tulalip Tribes and shall possess the same immunity from suit as is possessed by the Tulalip Tribes; provided that this immunity may be waived only by duly adopted written resolution of the Village Council; and further provided that the immunity shall not be available to the Village in any suit brought by the Board of Directors of the Tulalip Tribes; and further provided that the debts and liabilities of the Village shall not be the debts of the Tulalip Tribes.

Section Seven. Suit.

The Village shall have the power to bring suit in its own name and, where approved by resolution of the Board of Directors, in the name of the Tulalip Tribes, in any court of competent jurisdiction.

Section Eight. Purposes.

The purposes of this incorporation shall be as follows: To provide responsible local government to the Consolidated Borough of Quil Ceda Village consistent with the needs of the area of development within its borders as it now exists or shall in the future be increased within the boundaries of the Tulalip Indian Reservation and to provide the persons and enterprises located within the Village and the people of the Tulalip Indian Reservation with the opportunity to organize their human and natural resources to provide for their economic security and to provide for the health, safety and general welfare of the people of the Village and the Reservation.

Article II
Village Council

Section One. Powers of Council.

All powers of the Village not in conflict with the laws and constitution of the Tulalip Tribes and subject to the limitations of this charter, shall be vested in the Village council, which shall enact appropriate legislation and do and perform any and all acts and things that may be necessary and proper to carry out these powers or any provisions of this charter.

Section Two. Electing, Removal and Composition.

The council shall consist of a president and two council members elected by a majority vote of the Board of Directors of the Tulalip Tribes of Washington. The president and council members may be removed by the Board of Directors of the Tulalip Tribes in the same manner as they are elected.

Section Three. Term of President of Village Council.

The term of office of the president shall commence at the first regular meeting of the council following appointment, beginning in 2001, and shall be for one year.

Section Four. Terms of Council Members.

The term of office of each Village council member shall commence at the first regular meeting of the council following election, and shall be for one year.

Section Five. Qualifications.

The president and council members shall be adult citizens of the United States, shall be duly elected members of the Board of Directors of the Tulalip Tribes at the time of their appointment and shall not hold any other public or private office that in any way conflicts with the office of president or council member.

Section Six. Duties of President. The President:

(a) Shall be the chairperson of the council and preside over its meetings; the president may make and second motions and shall have a voice and vote in all its proceedings;

(b) Shall be recognized as head of the Village government for all ceremonial purposes but shall have no regular administrative authority or duties;

(c) Shall govern the Village by proclamation during times of riot, civil insurrection, major disaster, and times of great public danger.

Section Seven. President Pro-Tempore.

The council shall designate one of its members as president pro-tempore, who shall serve in such capacity at the pleasure of the council. The president pro-tempore shall perform the presidential duties during absence or disability of the president.

Section Eight. Salaries of President and Council Members.

While council members serve on the Board of Directors of the Tulalip Tribes, council members shall receive no salary for their service on the Village Council but may receive a meeting stipend as may be established by the Tulalip Board of Directors.

The annual salaries of any council president or council member who shall not be a member of the Board of Directors shall be the same salary as received by a member of the Tulalip Tribes Board of Directors annually, until changed by an Ordinance or Resolution of the Tulalip Tribes.

Section Nine. Induction of President and Council into Office.

At the first regular meeting following election, the council shall hold a meeting for the purposes of inducting a newly appointed president or council members and organizing the council.

Section Ten. Vacancies in council and office of president.

The Board of Directors by a majority vote of its members, shall within forty-five (45) days of resignation, removal, retirement, death or incapacity of a council member or president fill a vacancy, including the office of president, by electing a person to serve in the office. Prior to a Board election to fill a vacancy, the remainder of the Village council may elect, by unanimous vote, any person to act in an interim capacity any adult to serve as a replacement for the vacated position. No interim councilmember shall serve in the interim position more than 45 days.

Section Eleven. Council Meetings.

The council shall meet regularly at such times and at such places as may be prescribed by its rules, but shall hold regular meetings for which public notice has been given no less frequently than two (2) times each calendar month. All meetings of the council to conduct official business shall be open to the public; provided, that meetings involving any commercial dealings of the Village, consideration of bids, and any personnel actions of the Village may be in a closed session.

Section Twelve. Special Meetings.

Special meetings may be called by the president or two members of the council, with reasonable written notice given to all members of the council.

Section Thirteen. Rules of Procedure; Journal.

The council shall determine its own bylaws, rules and order of business subject to the provisions of this charter. It shall keep a journal of its proceedings, and the journal shall be open to public inspection during regular office hours.

Section Fourteen. Quorum; Ayes and Nays.

A majority of the members of the council shall constitute a quorum. The vote on any question shall be by ayes and nays and shall be entered in the journal. At the request of any member of the council, a roll call vote shall be taken.

Section Fifteen. Consideration of Petitions.

Any leaseholder of the Village or other person may appear before the council at any regular meeting and present a written petition; such petition shall be acted upon by the council in the regular course of business within forty-five (45) days.

Section Sixteen. Interference in Administrative Service.

Neither the council nor any of its members shall direct or request the Village manager or any of his subordinates to appoint or remove any person to or from office, or take part in any manner in the appointment or removal of officers and employees in the administrative service of the Village. Except for the purpose of inquiry, the council and its members shall deal with the administrative service of the Village solely through the Village manager, and neither the council nor any member thereof shall give orders to any subordinates of the Village manager, either publicly or privately. However, nothing in this section shall be construed as prohibiting the council while in open sessions from fully and freely discussing with or suggesting to the Village manager anything pertaining to the Village affairs or the interests of the Village. Violation of this section shall be cause for removal from office of any member of the council found, after hearing before the Board of Directors, to have committed a violation of this section. Removal shall require a majority vote of the Board of Directors.

Section Seventeen. Conduct of Council as to Powers Authorized by Charter When No Procedure Established by Law.

Whenever it is prescribed herein that any power, duty, or procedure shall or may be exercised, performed, or adopted in the manner established by any law of the Tribes, and there is no procedure established by law therefor, then the council may prescribe such procedure.

Article III
Village Manager

Section One. Appointment of Village Manager.

The council shall appoint an officer of the Village who shall have the title of Village manager and shall have the powers and perform the duties provided in this charter. No Village president or council member or member of the Board of Directors of the Tulalip Tribes shall hold the position of Village manager while at the same time holding Village or elective office.

Section Two. Qualifications; Compensation.

The Village manager shall be chosen by the council on the basis of executive and administrative qualifications, with special reference to actual experience in, or knowledge of, accepted practice in respect to the duties of the office as herein set forth. Compensation of the Village manager shall be fixed by the council.

Section Three. Powers and Duties.

The Village manager shall be the chief executive of the administrative branch of the Village government; shall be responsible to the council for proper administration of all affairs of the Village; and to that end, subject to the provisions of this charter, shall have power and/or be required to:

(a) See that all ordinances are enforced and that the provisions of all franchises, leases, contracts, permits, and privileges granted by the Village are observed;

(b) Appoint and, when he deems necessary for the good of the service, remove or suspend all officers and employees of the Village except as otherwise provided by this charter, by law, or by personnel rules adopted pursuant to this charter; and authorize the head of a department or office subject to direction and supervision of the Village manager to appoint and remove subordinates in such department or office; in selecting employees of the Village, the manager and other Village managers and supervisors shall be bound by the Indian preference laws of the United States; provided, that the Village may contract with the Tulalip Tribes to provide services to the Village without being bound by such preference laws.

(c) Prepare the annual budget estimates and submit them to the council, and be responsible for the administration of the budget after adoption;

(d) Keep the council advised at all times of the affairs and needs of the Village, and make reports annually, or more frequently if requested by the council, of all the affairs of the Village;

(e) Supervise purchasing for all departments of the Village;

(f) Perform such other duties as may be prescribed by this charter or required of the Village manager by the council, not inconsistent with this charter;

(g) Furnish a surety bond to be approved by the council, such bond to be conditioned on the faithful performance of duties; the premium of the bond shall be paid by the Village.

Section Four. Acting Village Manager.

If the Village manager is absent from the Village, is unable to perform his duties, or is suspended by the council, or if there is a vacancy in the office of Village manager, the council shall appoint an acting Village manager to serve until the Village manager returns, until the disability or suspension ceases, or until another Village manager is appointed and qualifies, as the case may be.

Section Five. Removal.

The council shall contract with the Village manager for a definite term and may remove the Village manager by a majority vote of its members. Severance pay will be at the discretion of the council. The action of the council in suspending or removing the manager shall be final and conclusive on everyone, it being the intention of this charter to vest all authority and fix all responsibility for such suspension and removal in the council.

Article IV
Administrative Departments

Section One. Administrative Departments and Officers.

The council, by ordinance not inconsistent with this charter, shall provide for the organization, conduct, and operation of the several offices and departments of the Village as established by this charter, for the creation of additional departments, divisions, offices, and agencies, and for their alteration, or abolition. These offices and departments shall include, but not be limited to administration, revenue, police, fire, and public works. The Tulalip Tribal Courts shall have jurisdiction over and provide judicial services to the Village; provided, this section shall not be interpreted to waive the immunity of the Village.

The council, by ordinance not inconsistent with this charter, may assign additional functions or duties to office, departments, or agencies. Where the positions are not incompatible, the council may combine in one person the powers and duties of two or more officers created or authorized by this charter.

The council shall provide the number, titles, qualifications, powers, duties, and compensation of all officers and employees of the Village.

Section Two. Village Clerk.

The council shall appoint an officer of the Village, with the title of Village clerk, who shall give notice of all council meetings; keep the journal of the council's proceedings, authenticate by the clerk's signature, and record in full in books kept for the purpose all ordinances and resolutions; and perform such other duties as shall be required by this charter or by ordinances. The Village clerk will serve at the pleasure of the council.

Section Three. Village Treasurer, Audits.

The council shall appoint an officer of the Village, with the title of Village treasurer, who shall receive and have custody of all the money of the Village and shall keep and save the money and dispense the same only as provided by law, and who shall always be bound by the constitution, laws, and ordinances and on whom legal garnishments and demands may be served. The Village treasurer will serve at the pleasure of the council. The council shall annually appoint a general auditor with the concurrence of the Tulalip Board of Directors. The annual audit shall be available to the Board of Directors at the same time it is made available to the Council.

Section Four. Village Attorney.

The council shall appoint a Village attorney who shall be the chief legal adviser of all offices, departments, and agencies and of all officers and employees in matters relating to their official powers and duties. It shall be the duty of the Village attorney to perform all services incident to the position as may be required by statute, by this charter, or by ordinance. The Village attorney will serve at the pleasure of the council.

Article V
Appointive Boards and Commissions

Section One. Appointive Boards and Commissions.

The council may by ordinance create, change, and abolish boards or commissions as in its judgment are required, or as are now or hereafter provided by law, and may grant to them such power and duties as are consistent with the provisions of this charter.

Section Two. Ex Officio Members.

The president and Village manager and all members of the Board of Directors shall be an ex officio member, without voting privileges, of all Village boards and commissions.

Article VI
Finance and Taxation

Section One. Fiscal Year

The fiscal year of the Village shall commence on the first day of each calendar year and end on the last day of each calendar year.

Section Two. Tax System; Use of Tribal Services.

The council may by ordinance provide a system not inconsistent with the provisions of this charter, for the assessment, levy, and collection of all Village taxes. The council shall have power to avail itself of any law of the Tulalip Tribes now or hereafter in force, and comply with the requirements thereof whereby assessments may be made by the Tribes and taxes collected by the tax collector of the Tribes for and on behalf of this Village.

Section Three. Submission of Estimates to Council; Scope of Village Manager's Estimate.

On or before the second regular council meeting in September of each year, or on such date in each year as shall be fixed by the council, the Village manager shall prepare and submit in writing to the council the estimates of each department and the Village manager's own personal report and recommendations and estimate as to the probable expenditures for the next ensuing fiscal year, stating the amount in detail required to meet all expenditures' necessary purposes, including interest and sinking funds and outstanding indebtedness, if any, an estimate of the amount of income expected from all sources in each department, and the probable amount required to be raised by taxation to cover such expenditures, interest, and sinking fund.

Section Four. Preparation and Tentative Adoption of Budget; Publication of Budget and Notice of Meeting to Fix Tax Levies.

The council shall meet annually prior to fixing tax levies where necessary and make a tentative budget of the estimated amounts required to pay the expenses of conducting the business of the Village for the ensuing fiscal year. The budget shall be prepared in such detail as provided by law, and, together with a notice that the council will meet for the purpose of making tax levies in accordance with the budget at the time and place set out in the notice, shall be published in the official public media of the Village once a week for at least two (2) consecutive weeks following the tentative adoption of such budget.

Section Five. Public Hearing and Adoption of Budget.

The council shall, at the first regular meeting in September, at the time and place designated in the notice, hold a public hearing at which any taxpayer may appear and be heard in favor of or against any proposed expenditure or tax levy. After conclusion of the public hearing, the council shall finally determine and adopt estimates of proposed expenditures for the various purposes as set forth in the published proposal, and such adopted estimates will constitute the budget for the next fiscal year. The council may insert new items or may increase or decrease the items of the budget. It may not vary the titles, descriptions, or conditions of administration specified in the budget. Before inserting any additional item or increasing any item or appropriation, the council must cause to be published, at least once in the official newspaper of the Village, a notice setting forth the nature of the proposed increase and fixing a place and time not less than ten (10) days after publication at which the council will hold a public hearing thereon.

The council shall adopt a budget on or before the Fifteenth (15th) day of November of the fiscal year currently ending. If it fails to adopt the budget by this date, the amounts appropriated for current operation for the current fiscal year shall be deemed adopted for the ensuing fiscal year on a month-to-month basis, with all items in it prorated accordingly, until such time as the council adopts a budget for the ensuing year.

Section Six. Exceeding Adopted Budget.

Nothing in this article shall be construed to limit the power of the council to appear before the Tulalip Tribes or any other duly authorized tribal body for the purpose of requesting authorization to exceed the adopted budget for emergency or unanticipated expenditures.

Section Seven. Adoption of Ordinances Fixing Tax Rates.

On the day set for making tax levies, but not later than the third Monday in October, the council shall meet and adopt an ordinance levying on the assessed valuation of certain property within the village, sales conducted within the village, business conducted within the village, and all other matters upon which taxes may be lawfully assessed within the village, the taxes which are necessary to provide for the purposes for which the Village is incorporated; provided that the tax burden borne by persons and entities for transactions within the village shall not exceed the tax burden imposed upon property, transactions, persons and entities within any incorporated municipality within Snohomish County, Washington.

Section Eight. Additional Taxes for Special Purposes.

The council shall have the power to levy and collect taxes in addition to the taxes herein authorized to be levied and collected, sufficient to pay the interest and maintain the sinking fund of the bonded indebtedness of the Village and an additional amount deemed to be advisable and necessary for any public or municipal purposes within the Tulalip Indian Reservation.

Section Nine. Tax Exemptions.

All the property, and transactions, including leaseholds, within the Village shall be subject to taxation, except these properties and transactions which are exempt from taxes under the laws of the United States and the laws of the Tribes.

Section Ten. Transfer Appropriations.

The Village manager, subject to the approval of the council, may at any time transfer any unencumbered appropriation balance or portion thereof between general classifications of expenditures within the last three (3) months of the fiscal year, the council may transfer any unencumbered appropriation balance or portion thereof from one office, department, or agency to another.

Section Eleven. Claims or Demands against the Village.

The council shall prescribe by ordinance the manner and limitations of time in which claims or demands against the Village shall be presented, audited, and paid.

Section Twelve. Transfer of Sums from any Funds to Principal and Interest Funds.

Whenever the interest or principal reduction funds for the bonded indebtedness of the Village are insufficient to pay the interest or any principal payment on the bonded indebtedness when due, the council shall direct the transfer from the general fund or any other fund having monies therein to such interest or principal funds, the necessary amounts of money to pay the interest or principal payment due on the bonded indebtedness, and the amount so transferred shall be returned to the respective funds from which the transfer was made whenever sufficient monies have accrued in the bonded indebtedness funds.

Section Thirteen. Lapse of Appropriations.

Every appropriation, except an appropriation for a capital expenditure, shall lapse at the close of the fiscal year to the extent that it has not been expended or encumbered. An appropriation for a capital expenditure shall continue in force until the purpose for which it is made has been accomplished or abandoned; the purpose of any such appropriation shall be deemed abandoned if three (3) years pass without any disbursement from or encumbrance of the appropriation.

Section Fourteen. Independent Annual Audit.

Prior to the end of each fiscal year, the council with the concurrence of the Tulalip Board of Directors shall designate certified public accountants who, as of the end of the fiscal year, shall make an independent audit of the Village government and shall submit their report to the council, the Board of Directors, and to the Village manager. All such audit reports shall be a matter of public record. Such accountants shall have no personal interest, direct or indirect, in the fiscal affairs of the Village government or of any of its officers. They shall not maintain any accounts or records of the Village business, but within specifications approved by the council, shall post audit the books and documents kept by the Village in any separate or subordinate accounts kept by any other office, department, or agency of the Village government.

Article VII
Ordinances and Resolutions

Section One. Council to Act by Resolution or Ordinance.
The Council Shall Act by Resolution or Ordinance.

Section Two. Actions Requiring an Ordinance.

In addition to those actions required by law or other provisions of this charter to be done by ordinance, the following acts of the council shall be done by ordinance:

(a) Adopting or amending an administrative code, or establishing, altering, or abolishing any Village department, office or agency;

(b) Providing for a fine or other penalty or establishing a rule or regulation for violation of which a fine or other penalty is imposed;

(c) Levying taxes, except as otherwise provided herein;

(d) Granting, renewing, or extending a franchise;

(e) Regulating the rate charged by a public utility for its services;

(f) Authorizing the borrowing of money;

(g) Conveying or leasing, or authorizing the conveyance or leasing, of any lands of the Village.

(h) Adopting, with or without amendment, ordinances proposed under the initiative power; and

(i) Amending or repealing any ordinance previously adopted, except as otherwise provided herein.

(j) Exercising the powers of eminent domain and annexation within the Tulalip Indian Reservation.

Acts other than those referred to in this section may be done either by ordinance or resolution.

Section Three. Ayes and Nays to Be Recorded.

The ayes and nays shall be taken on the passage of all ordinances and resolutions and entered in the journal of council proceedings.

Section Four. When Majority Vote Required.

A majority vote of all the members of the council shall be necessary to pass any ordinance or resolution having the effect of an ordinance.

Section Five. Enacting Style.

The enacting clause of all ordinances passed by the council shall be in these words: ["Be it ordained by the council of the Consolidated Borough of Quil Ceda Village as follows:"].

Section Six. Reading or Posting and Passage of Ordinances and Resolutions; Effective Date.

All proposed ordinances and resolutions having the effect of ordinances shall either be read in full or posted in a public place at least twenty-four (24) hours prior to their adoption. If any amendments are proposed to a posted ordinance, such amendments shall be read in full prior to adoption of the ordinance.

A measure may be placed upon final passage at the same meeting as when introduced, by unanimous consent of the council.

Measures without an emergency clause shall take effect and become operative thirty (30) days after the date of their passage.

Section Seven. Emergency Measures; Effective Date.

An emergency measure is one necessary for the immediate preservation of the public peace, health, or safety, in which the emergency is set forth and defined. An emergency measure may be placed upon its second reading and final passage at the same meeting as when first introduced, on the affirmative vote of all members of the council.

An emergency measure shall take effect immediately on its passage.

Section Eight. Signing of Ordinances and Resolutions.

All ordinances and resolutions shall be signed by the president and attested to by the Village clerk.

Section Nine. Publication of Ordinances and Resolutions.

All ordinances and resolutions having the effect of ordinances, except emergency measures, shall be published once in the official public media of the Village within twenty (20) days of their passage before they become effective and operative.

Emergency ordinances that have been passed by the necessary unanimous vote of the council shall be published one time in the official media of the Village within Fourteen (14) days after their passage.

Section Ten. Revision of Ordinances and Resolutions.

Ordinances or resolutions having the effect of ordinances shall not be revised, reenacted, or amended by reference to title only, but such ordinances or resolutions to be revised or reenacted, or the section or sections thereof to be amended, or the new section or sections to be added thereto, shall be set forth and adopted in the method provide herein for the adoption of ordinances and resolutions.

Section Eleven. Repealing or Suspending Ordinances or Resolutions.

No ordinance, or resolution having the effect of an ordinance, or section thereof shall be repealed or suspended except by ordinance or resolution adopted in the manner provided herein.

Section Twelve. Filing, Recording, and Certification of Ordinances and Resolutions.

All ordinances and resolutions shall be filed and safely kept by the Village clerk and duly recorded and certified by the Village clerk in books kept for the purpose. Recorded copies thereof certified by the Village clerk or the originals thereof shall be prima facie evidence of the contents of such ordinances or resolutions and of the due passage and publication of the same, and shall be admissible in evidence in any court or in any proceeding where the contents of such ordinances or resolutions are in question. Nothing herein contained shall be construed to prevent the proof of passage and publication of any ordinance or resolution in the manner otherwise prescribed by law.

Section Thirteen. Adoption by Reference.

The council may enact the provisions of a code or public record theretofore in existence without setting forth such provisions, but the adopting such code or public record by reference; provided, such ordinance shall be published in full. At least three (3) copies of the code or public record shall be filed in the office of the Village clerk and kept available for public use and inspection. A code or public record enacted by reference may be amended in the same manner.

No penalty clause shall be enacted by reference thereto. A penalty clause contained in a code or public record adopted by reference shall be set forth in full in the adopting reference.

Section Fourteen. Codification of Ordinances.

Any or all ordinances of the Village that have been enacted and published in the manner required at the time of their adoption, and that have not been repealed, shall be compiled, consolidated, revised, indexed, and arranged as a comprehensive code, and such code may be adopted by reference, with the same effect as an ordinance, by the passage of any ordinance for such purpose. Such code need not be published in the manner required for other ordinances, but not less than two (2) copies thereof shall be filed for use and examination by the public in the office of the Village clerk prior to the adoption thereof. Ordinances codified shall be repealed as of the effective date of the code. Amendments to the code shall be enacted in the same manner as ordinances.

Article VIII
Contracts

Section One. Execution.

All contracts shall be executed by the president in the name of the Consolidated Borough of Quil Ceda Village, except as may otherwise be provided either by this charter or by law, and must be countersigned by the Village clerk, who shall number and register the contracts in a book kept for that purpose.

Section Two. Contracts for Village Improvements.

Any Village improvement costing more than ten-thousand Dollars ($10,000.00) shall be executed by a written contract except where such improvement is authorized by the council to be executed directly by a Village department in conformity with detailed plans, specifications, and estimates. All contracts for more than twenty thousand Dollars ($20,000.00) shall be subject to Tulalip contracting preference laws and Ordinances.

Section Three. Purchases.

The Village manager shall contract for and purchase or issue purchase authorizations for all supplies, materials, equipment, and services for the offices, departments, and agencies of the Village.

No bids shall be required for any purchase not in excess of five-thousand Dollars ($5,000.00). For any purchases from five-thousand Dollars ($5,000.00) to fifty thousand Dollars ($50,000.00) inclusive, the Village manager or agents of the Village manager hereunder shall invite written bids from at least three [3] qualified bidders and keep a record of the bids and of the awards of purchase for public examination or inspection.

Every purchase exceeding the sum of fifty-thousand Dollars ($50,000.00) shall be awarded to the lowest responsible bidder after such public notice and competition as provided by law, unless the council rejects all bids.

All such purchases shall be subject to the provisions of Tulalip Tribal contracting preference laws and ordinances.

Section Four. Bids.

Advertisements for bids shall distinctly and specifically state the character of the Village improvement contemplated and/or the kind of supplies, materials, equipment, and services required. Such notice shall be published at least once in the official public media of the Village, not less than thirty (30) days prior to the opening of bids. Bidding will be by sealed proposals only and under such regulations as may be prescribed by the council.

Section Five. Transfer of Property.

The Village manager may transfer supplies, materials, and equipment to or between offices, departments, and agencies, subject to such regulations as the council may prescribe.

Section Six. Fraud and Collusion.

Any member of the council or any officer or employee of the Village who aids or assists a bidder in securing a contract to furnish labor, material, equipment, supplies, or services at a higher price than proposed by any other bidder, or who favors one bidder over another by giving or withholding information, or who willfully misleads any bidder in regard to the character of the labor, material, equipment supplies, or services called for, or the conditions under which the proposed work is to be done, or who knowingly accepts materials, supplies, or equipment of a quality inferior to that called for by any contract, or who knowingly certified to a greater amount of labor or service performed than has been actually performed or to receipt of a greater amount or different kind of material, supplies, or equipment than was actually received, shall be guilty of a misdemeanor and on condition thereof shall be removed from office or position.

Section Seven. Personal Interest.

No member of the council or any officer or employee of the Village shall have a substantial interest, direct or indirect, or by reason of ownership of stock in any corporation, in any contract or in the sale to the Village of or to a contractor supplying the Village with any land, or rights or interests in any land, or material, supplies, equipment, or services. Any willful violations of this section shall constitute malfeasance in office, and any officer or employee of the Village found guilty thereof shall thereby forfeit his or her office or position. Any violation of this section with the knowledge, express or implied, of the persons contracting with the Village shall render the contract voidable by the Village manager or the council.

Section Eight. Lease of Village Property.

The council may lease any Village land, buildings, or personal property on such terms and conditions as the council may prescribe. All leases shall be made to the highest responsible bidder, after publication of notice thereof in the official public media of the Village once a week for at least two (2) weeks, stating explicitly the terms and conditions of the proposed lease. At its discretion, the council may reject any and all bids.

Section Nine. Sale of Village Property.

The Village may not sell or convey all or any part of its real property. Personal property may be sold or conveyed in the manner provided by law.

Article IX
Franchises and Public Utilities

Section One. Franchises.

A person desiring to obtain a franchise to operate a public utility from the Village shall present the franchise desired to the Village council, and it shall be filed among Village records.

If the council deems the granting of the franchise beneficial to the Village, it shall pass a resolution, stating that fact.

A franchise shall not be granted for a longer term than 10 (ten) years.

Section Two. Establishment of Municipally Owned and Operated Utilities.

The Village shall have the power to own and operate any public utility, to construct and install all facilities that are reasonably needed, and to lease or purchase any existing utility properties used or useful for public service. The Village may also furnish service to adjacent and nearby territories that may be conveniently and economically served by a municipally owned and operated utility, subject to the limitations of the provisions of the general laws of the state. The council may provide by ordinance for the establishment of such utility and provide for its regulation and control and the fixing of rates to be charged.

The council may by ordinance provide for the extension, enlargement, or improvement of existing utilities, and provide reasonable reserves for such purpose.

Section Three. Establishment of classifications and regulation of rates of public utilities.

The Village shall have full power to and may prescribe just and reasonable classifications to be used and just and reasonable rates and charges to be made and collected by all corporations rendering public utility service within the corporate limits of the Village as now or hereafter constituted, except public service corporations.

Article X
General Provisions

Section One. Publicity of Records.

All records and accounts of every office, department, or agency of the Village shall be open for inspection by any person or any representative of the press at all reasonable times and under reasonable regulations established by the council, except the personnel records of employees and records and documents the disclosure of which would tend to defeat the lawful purpose that they are intended to accomplish.

Section Two. Official Bonds.

All elected and appointed officers, and such other employees as the council may by ordinance or resolution require to do so, shall give bond in such amount and with such surety as may be approved by the council. The premium on such bonds shall be paid by the Village.

Section Three. Oath of Office.

Every officer of the Village, whether elected or appointed under the provisions of this charter, or under any ordinance of the Village, shall, before assuming the duties of the office, take and subscribe an oath required by the Tribes.

Section Four. Short Title.

This charter, adopted pursuant to Ordinance 111 of the Tulalip Tribes, shall be known and may be cited as the Charter of the Consolidated Borough of Quil Ceda Village.

Section Five. Plenary and Implied Powers of Council.

The council shall have plenary power to enact and make all proper and necessary ordinances, resolutions, and orders to carry out and give effect to the express as well as the implied powers granted in this charter to the end that a complete, harmonious, and effective municipal government may be initiated, installed, operated, and maintained in the Village, and thereby protect and safeguard the rights, interests, safety, morality, health, and welfare of the Village and its inhabitants.

Article XI
Construction of Terms

Wherever the context of this charter so requires, the singular number includes the plural, and the plural includes the singular; the word "person" includes a corporation, company, partnership or association, or society, as well as a natural person.

Article XII
Amendments

This charter, or any part or article or section thereof, may be amended in the manner provided by the municipal government enabling legislation adopted as Tulalip Ordinance 111.

Source:

http://www.quilcedavillage.org/Government/QuilCedaVillage/VillageCharter.

79

Memorandum of Agreement between the Shoshone-Bannock Tribes and Power County (2002)

The Shoshone-Bannock Tribes inhabit the Fort Hall Reservation in southeastern Idaho. The reservation is home to two distinctive Native peoples—the Shoshone (also known as the Northern Shoshoni) and the Bannock. Signers of two treaties with the US—the Treaty of Soda Springs (1863) and the Fort Bridger Treaty (1868)—the Sho-Bans, as they are colloquially known, adopted a formal constitution in 1934 under the Indian Reorganization Act, and three years later the two Tribes ratified a corporate charter to officially create the legal entity known as the Shoshone-Bannock Tribes.

Allotment of the reservation was completed in 1914, but Tribal members and the federal government as trustee still share control of over 90 percent of the original land base. Nevertheless, interracial tensions are a concern and the

Sho-Bans are engaged with local, state, and federal officials on a number of issues. One of the major topics is civil jurisdiction. The following agreement negotiated between the Tribes' governing body, the Fort Hall Business Council, and the Power County Sheriff's Office and the county's prosecuting attorney, is one example of an intergovernmental process designed to improve relations between the parties insofar as civil enforcement of traffic laws are concerned between Natives and non-Natives.

Memorandum of Agreement: Shoshone-Bannock Tribes and Power County, Idaho

This Memorandum of Agreement is executed this 2nd day of February, 2002, by and between the Shoshone-Bannock Tribes, hereinafter "Tribes," acting by and through the Chairman of the Fort Hall Business Council, and the Power County Sheriff's Office, consisting of the Sheriff and his deputy officers, and the Power County Prosecuting Attorney, hereinafter "Power County."

Whereas, the State of Idaho, acting pursuant to a federal law known as Public Law 280,…enacted Idaho Code Sections 67–5101 through 67–5103 in 1963, by which the State acquired jurisdiction to enforce state, civil and criminal laws on the Fort Hall Indian Reservation, hereinafter "Reservation," concerning the operation and management of motor vehicles, by Indians, upon highways and roads maintained by the county or State or political subdivisions thereof; and

Whereas, Power County and the Tribes by execution of this agreement designate that the highways and roads maintained by the County or State for purposes of this agreement are those highways and roads that are currently being maintained by the County or State; and

Whereas, by virtue of Idaho Code Section 67–5102 the State's assumption of traffic jurisdiction within the Reservation was expressly declared to be "concurrent (and not exclusive) with jurisdiction in the same matters existing in Tribes or the federal government;" and

Whereas, the Idaho State-Tribal Relations Act, Idaho Code Sections 67–4001 through 67–4003, enacted in 1984, authorizes the State and its political subdivisions and public agencies as defined by Idaho Code Section 67–2327, including Power County, to execute intergovernmental agreements with designated Indian Tribes, including the Tribes, to provide for joint or concurrent exercise of jurisdictional powers consistent with Idaho Code Sections 67– 5101 and 67–5102; and

Whereas, by virtue of inherent, retained sovereign powers of the Tribes and by virtue of Article VI, Section 1 (a) of the Tribes' 1936 Constitution, the Fort Hall Business Council, acting on behalf of the Tribes, is empowered to execute intergovernmental agreements with the state and its political subdivisions, including Power County; and

Whereas, Power County's jurisdiction to enforce State traffic laws against Indians and non-Indians upon Reservation highways and roads maintained by the State or County is concurrent with the Tribes' jurisdiction to enforce civil Tribal traffic laws against Indians and non-Indians upon such Reservation highways and roads; and

Whereas, Power County and the Tribes possess independent authority to execute an intergovernmental agreement concerning the exercise of concurrent traffic law jurisdiction on the Reservation; and

Whereas, in order to coordinate traffic law enforcement involving Indians on the Fort Hall Indian Reservation and to provide enrolled members of the Shoshone-Bannock Tribes and other Indians with the option of proceeding through the Shoshone-Bannock Tribal Court system when cited by Power County law enforcement officers for on-Reservation traffic infractions or misdemeanors; and

Whereas, Power County expressly states that nothing stated in this agreement is to be construed as a waiver of any of Power County's concurrent traffic-related jurisdiction in accordance with Idaho Code §§ 67–5102 through 67–5103 over persons who travel on state and county maintained roads within Power County, and that this agreement is entered into solely for the purpose of achieving a temporary solution to jurisdictional conflicts on Fort Hall Indian Reservation roads until a permanent solution can be achieved; and

Whereas, the Tribes expressly state that nothing stated in this agreement is to be construed as a waiver of any of the Tribes' inherent powers as a sovereign tribal government under the 1868 Fort Bridger Treaty or any other provision of law or a consent to jurisdiction greater than provided by existing law, and that this agreement is entered into solely for the purpose of achieving a temporary solution to jurisdictional conflicts on Fort Hall Indian Reservation roads until a permanent solution can be achieved.

Therefore, the Power County Sheriff, the Power County Prosecuting Attorney (together "Power County"), and the Tribes hereby mutually agree as follows:

1. Whenever a Power County Sheriff's Office officer intends to issue an infraction notice or misdemeanor citation to a member of the Shoshone-Bannock Tribes or other Indian for violation of a State traffic law upon highways and roads maintained by the County or State within the Fort Hall Indian Reservation, the Power County Sheriff's Office officer shall advise the affected person, at the time of issuing the infraction notice or misdemeanor citation, of that person's option to elect to have the infraction or misdemeanor processed through the Shoshone-Bannock Tribal Court, hereinafter "Tribal Court."

2. This option to proceed in Tribal Court upon an infraction notice or misdemeanor citation shall be made available by a Power County Sheriff's Office officer to any person who is an enrolled member of the Tribes or who is able to establish status as a federally-recognized Indian. Any enrolled member of the Tribes shall be required to produce in the field a current Tribal enrollment card upon request of a Power County Sheriff's Office officer if such member indicates a desire to exercise the option to proceed through the Tribal Court. An individual claiming to be a federally-recognized Indian shall be required to produce in the field current and valid Tribal identification if such person indicates a desire to exercise the option to proceed through the Tribal Court.

3. The option to proceed through the Tribal Court upon an infraction notice or misdemeanor citation shall be made available whenever the traffic infraction or misdemeanor under State law also constitutes a violation of any applicable Tribal traffic law or whenever Tribal law permits the assimilation or incorporation of State traffic infractions or misdemeanors as Tribal traffic violations. The Power County Sheriff's Office and Power County Prosecuting Attorney and the Tribes shall cooperate to prepare an appropriate list of applicable State and Tribal laws for ready and convenient use by Power County Sheriff's Office officers in the field.

4. The Power County Sheriff's Office and Power County Prosecuting Attorney and the Tribes shall cooperatively develop a brief form for use in the field by Power County Sheriff's Office officers that clearly explains the option to proceed through the Tribal Court upon a traffic infraction notice or misdemeanor citation issued by Power County Sheriff's Office officers within the Fort Hall Indian Reservation. This notification form shall be signed by the affected Tribal member or other Indian, and it shall indicate whether the affected person desires to proceed on the infraction or misdemeanor through the Tribal Court. A copy of this notification form shall be given to the concerned Tribal member or other Indian in the field by a Power County Sheriff's Office officer at the time an infraction notice or misdemeanor citation is issued.

5. If an enrolled member of the Tribes or other Indian elects to proceed through the Tribal Court, then the Power County Sheriff's Office shall promptly thereafter forward to the Clerk of the Trial Court both a copy of the infraction notice or misdemeanor citation and a copy of the signed notification form evidencing exercise of the option to proceed through the Tribal Court. A police report shall not be required to be filed with the Tribal Court until such time as the tribal member or other Indian pleads not guilty and a trial is scheduled.

6. If an enrolled member of the Tribes or other Indian does not produce an enrollment card or other proof of Indian identity at the time of a traffic stop and the Power County Sheriff's Office officer may cite the Indian into state court. Thereafter, the Indian may request that the Power County Prosecuting Attorney transfer the infraction or misdemeanor case to the Tribal Court. The Power County Sheriff's Office and Power County Prosecuting Attorney shall not oppose a timely request for transfer to the Tribal Court where sufficient proof of Indian identity is established.

7. Promptly upon receipt of an infraction notice or misdemeanor citation and a signed notification form, the Clerk of the Tribal court shall set a date and time for appearance by the Indian defendant in the Tribal Court on the traffic infraction or misdemeanor. Power County Sheriff's Office officers shall cooperate, as necessary, in the hearing or trial on any contested infraction or misdemeanor including appearance as witnesses in the Tribal Court.

8. The Tribes shall make a special effort to see that Power County Sheriff's Office officers do not have to unnecessarily spend time in making appearances in Tribal Court in support of infraction or misdemeanor cases referred to Tribal Court.

9. Upon final disposition of an infraction or misdemeanor filed in the Tribal Court by a Power County Sheriff's Office officer the Clerk of the Tribal Court shall give prompt written notification to the Power County Sheriff's Office officer who issued the infraction notice or misdemeanor citation of the final disposition ordered by the Tribal Court.

10. The Clerk of the Tribal Court shall also send written notification of the final disposition to the Idaho Department of Transportation so that the infraction or misdemeanor violation may be included in the official driver records maintained by the State of Idaho.

11. All fines and penalties assessed in infraction and misdemeanor cases referred to Tribal Court by Power County Sheriff's Office officers shall remain in the Tribal Court system, unless specifically ordered to be otherwise disbursed by a Tribal Court Judge.

12. In any case where a Power County Sheriff's Office officer is involved in investigating or apprehending an Indian for a traffic offense, occurring on a state or county maintained road or highway on the Fort Hall Indian Reservation, which involves a serious injury, a fatality, or other aggravating circumstances, the case shall be referred to federal authorities for prosecution under the Indian Major Crimes Act or the Indian Country Crimes Act (including the Assimilative Crimes Act). The case shall also be referred to the prosecutor for the Shoshone-Bannock Tribes since prosecution by both federal and tribal authorities does not constitute a violation of constitutional protections against Double Jeopardy according to *United States v. Wheeler* (1978). If federal authorities decline prosecution of the case, then the Power County Sheriff's Office officer may refer the case to prosecuting authorities for the State of Idaho.

13. The Tribes agree that the Power County Sheriff's Office and the Idaho State Police shall have the primary responsibility for traffic patrol on I-86. The Power County Sheriff's Office, the Idaho State Police, and the Fort Hall Police Department shall have concurrent responsibility for patrolling the Arbon Highway and Big Sky Subdivision and the roads contained therein. However, in the event that a non-Tribal member is stopped by a Tribal officer on these roads, the officer will either contact a Power County Sheriff's Office Deputy immediately to handle the traffic stop or cite the individual into the Power County Court.

14. The Tribes agree to compensate Power County Sheriff's Office deputies for mileage at the then-current State-approved rate, regular hourly wage, and overtime when applicable. Likewise, in the event a Tribal officer is required to testify in a matter brought before the State courts in Power County, the Power County Prosecuting Attorney's office shall pay like expenses and compensation for witness fees.

15. The Tribes pledge to immediately undertake a thorough review of all Tribal laws relating to traffic infractions and offenses for the purpose of identifying ways of improving and updating traffic law enforcement.

Additionally, the Tribes agree to make reasonable efforts to establish an effective manual or computer reporting system for communicating with the State of Idaho's traffic citation reporting system. The Tribes furthermore agree to record and report all traffic citation dispositions of Tribal members referred under this Agreement on their internal computer system and the State of Idaho's system to facilitate consistent treatment of traffic law offenders between and among agencies and entities.

16. The Tribes and Power County agree that they will facilitate communication between law enforcement authorities and agencies to better facilitate appropriate and consistent prosecution of criminal offenders. Specifically, the Tribes agree that in the case of violation of a felony DUI statute or other provisions of traffic-related law serious enough to warrant punishment in excess of that authorized by the Shoshone-Bannock Law and Order Code, Tribal law enforcement authorities will consult with Federal authorities and the Power County Prosecuting Attorney's office to determine fair and appropriate prosecution of such violations under applicable law.

17. The parties to this Memorandum of Agreement shall only be liable for the actions of their own employees. Nothing contained herein shall be construed as creating an agency relationship between the parties as a basis for establishing liability.

18. The parties to this Memorandum of Agreement will administer this agreement and no separate entity is created to administer the agreement

19. The parties to this Memorandum of Agreement will finance the administration of this agreement through their respective regular budgets, and no additional or separate budget is established.

20. This agreement shall not be construed to prevent prosecutions consistent with *United States v. Wheeler* (1978).

21. This Memorandum of Agreement shall be in effect for a period of one (1) year from the date of its execution, and it may be extended thereafter by written mutual consent of the parties. The Power County Sheriff's Office, the Power County Prosecuting Attorney, and the Tribes may at any time revise or amend the Memorandum by written mutual consent

22. This Memorandum of Agreement shall be executed in duplicate originals, with one original to be retained by each party hereto.

Tribes: Blaine Edmo, Chairman, Fort Hall Business Council.
Power County Sheriff's Office: Howard Sprague.
Power County Prosecuting Attorney: Paul Laggis.
February 2, 2002

Source:

http://web.archive.org/web/20081128044627/https://www.ncai.org/.

80

Senator Ben Nighthorse Campbell (Northern Cheyenne), Interim Chairman Wayne Shaw (Seminole), and Chairwoman Donnamarie Potts (Buena Vista Rancheria of Me-Wuk Indians) on "Intra-Tribal Leadership Disputes and Tribal Governance" (2002)

Senator Campbell, at that time the lone Native US Senator, convened a hearing in order to afford the Bureau of Indian Affairs (BIA) and several Native leaders an opportunity to voice their concerns about intra-tribal conflicts—like disenrollment—that were creating significant internal and intergovernmental problems for the two Native nations represented below—the Seminole Nation of Oklahoma and the Buena Vista Rancheria of Me-Wuk Indians—and to define the role of the BIA when confronted with internally driven tribal conflicts.

Campbell's overview statement and the remarks of the two Native leaders reveal the conflicts and complexities inherent in this generation of tribal citizenship/membership decisions, as well as the ways in which the BIA exacerbates these tensions as it inconsistently wields profound discretional authority regarding Native identity.

Statement of Senator Ben Nighthorse Campbell

Senator Campbell: The Committee on Indian Affairs will be in session. Good morning, we welcome our witnesses this morning.

Historically, the Federal Government has determined whether and which groups of Indians exist as Indian tribes. Similarly, tribes themselves have an inherent power to fashion their own form of government, and to make membership decisions affecting their tribe.

Historically, the Federal Government does not fashion the tribal governments. It accepts the decision of the tribe, after the tribe qualifies through a very rigorous recognition process.

So the decision whether to govern themselves by traditional religious forms of government, such as the Pueblos of Mexico, or to incorporate under the Indian Recognition Act, as many tribes have done, since 1934, rests with the Indian people themselves, and that is where it ought to be.

I think rightly the Federal Government has also historically tried to tread very gingerly when it comes to getting involved with decisions of the legitimacy of a particular tribal government.

This is a very complicated process. It does not satisfy all Indian people who may or may not be tribal members. In fact, even last week, those who were watching the debates on the floor of the Senate saw one attempt to stop the recognition process altogether.

Nonetheless, the Bureau of Indian Affairs [BIA] has been called on to step into what are often very messy and unpleasant situations, and to sort things out in a way that respects tribal sovereignty, but also the rights of individual members.

In the course of my tenure on this committee, first as a member, and then as the chairman, and now as the vice chairman, I have seen an unhealthy increase in disputes and leadership challenges that are of an intra-tribal nature. That is not inter-tribal. Intra-tribal means the factions or groups within a single tribe, battling for control for the legitimacy of that tribe.

Just in the past several months, a series of such disputes has caused the Department of the Interior, as well as the Congress, to get involved. These include, but are not limited to, several instances. The BIA declined to reconsider a Regional Director decision to recognize one factor in over another in a leadership dispute with the St. Regis Mohawks in 2002.

The Bureau acknowledged the validity of a tribal constitution in the tribal election of the Crow Tribe in 2001. The Bureau got involved with a constitutional and membership question with the Seminoles of Oklahoma in 2002.

They recognized the interim leadership and Constitutional challenge for the Saginaw Chippewa Tribe in 2000, and they deferred the tribal membership decisions of the Shakopee Mdewakanton in Minnesota in 1997.

In the one that brings us here today, the BIA removed the tribal leadership in favor of a challenging faction for the Buena Vista Me-Wuks in 2002.

Today, we will hear from the department, as well as two groups who are vying for leadership of the Buena Vista Me-Wuk Tribe from Northern California.

I know something about this area. I knew many of the Me-Wuks very well. In fact, because I was born and raised in Me-Wuk Country around Auburn, CA, and I spent many years around Sacramento, I knew a number of the family members that are involved in this whole discussion. That is particularly how I got interested in this.

I certainly do not have any magic answers to the problems, but I believe we need to look at the problems, as well as potential solutions that have been offered by the Bureau.

Senator Campbell. With that, I welcome the witnesses....

Statement of Wayne Shaw, Acting Interim Chairman of the Seminole Nation of Oklahoma

Chairman Inouye, Vice Chairman Campbell, and members of the committee:

My name is Wayne Shaw. I am the acting tribal chairman of the General Council of the Seminole Nation of Oklahoma, and a member of the——band of that

382   DOCUMENTS OF NATIVE AMERICAN POLITICAL DEVELOPMENT

tribe. For——years I have served my nation in public service as band chief, tribal gaming commissioner, youth athletics organizer, and general council representative.

Your hearings today concern the issue of [intra-tribal disputes.] With your permission, I respectfully submit by the following testimony an account of the recent experiences of the Seminole Nation of Oklahoma in regards thereto.

The Seminoles of Oklahoma have a long, proud history. It goes back before the Americans, back before the British, back even before the Spanish and the jurisdiction they called La Florida. Seminole history tells us who we are, what to honor, and what to defend. It gives us our traditions and our customs, and our form of government. It transmits to us our bands and clans, and the matrilineal rules of belonging. And it establishes our General Council and the offices of principal chief and vice chief.

That's Seminole history, and that's who I am. I didn't learn that history from books, essays or articles, or from white men or from government records. I learned it at the feet of my elders, who learned in the same way from their elders. For us, the Seminole people, as for many native peoples, history is not something lost behind us. It is here in our present, and guides us toward our future.

Let me now tell you something about our contemporary history, which speaks to the topic before you today.

The Seminole Nation has finally emerged, thanks to the decision in *Seminole Nation v. Norton II*, delivered 3 days ago, from over 1 year of turmoil, uncertainty, and sorrow brought on by what the large majority of Seminoles consider to have been the unnecessary, small-minded and vindictive intrusion of the Bureau of Indian Affairs into our internal affairs. This uncompromising and deplorable interference has led directly to documented violence, the exposure of members of our community to greater risks to health and well-being, and the jeopardizing of our students' future educations.

This sad episode in an already tragic history of Seminole-United States relations began in the Nation's attempts 2 years ago to amend its Constitution and the criteria for tribal membership. Our goal was to exclude from tribal membership all persons who could not show lineal blood descent in any of the traditional Seminole clans or bands in accordance with our traditional, customary laws. Much has been made of these amendments/'96 in the courts, in the press, and in the offices of the Federal Government/'96 and of the supposedly "racist" Seminoles who enacted them. The fact remains that under the Nation's laws any person who can show matrilineal descent through a traditional band/'96 regardless of any other native or ethnic heritage which that person may proudly share/'96 is to be considered a Seminole Indian and a member of the Seminole Nation of Oklahoma. It's true that the amendments would have removed from the Nation's General Council the representatives of the Freedmen, African-American descendants of ex-slaves. That fact, however, goes not to the supposed racism of the Seminoles, but to the sad and miserable/'96 not to say denied/'96 history of the United States' own race relations with Indians and with Blacks.

In enacting the amendments in August 2000, the Seminole people sought to reassert their traditional ways and forms of government. This, we believe, is the nation's right as a federally recognized native sovereign, and is a right guaranteed to the tribe by the treaty of 1866. No law has ever been enacted nor treaty signed that requires the Seminoles to recognize or accept new or non-traditional bands into its legislative assembly. Where it was done, it was done at the sufferance of the Seminole people, acting as sovereigns. In the same way it was withdrawn.

For protecting our traditions and attempting to preserve our heritage we are attacked as racist. Yet we did not create the circumstances that prompted us to act. Nor have we been alone in acting as we did. Yet only we have been made examples of and forced to suffer the consequences of the BIA's disapproval of our traditional ways.

Immediately after the Civil War, the United States "negotiated" new treaties with each of the so-called Five Civilized Tribes. Each treaty contained similar provisions for the settlement of Freedmen among them. The ostensible reason for the settlement was, as the treaties indicate, the failure of the United States to provide civil rights for the newly freed slaves and freedmen. Over the ensuing years, each of the other Five Tribes removed the Freedmen from their tribes. What has distinguished the Seminoles, the last of the Five Civilized Tribes to attempt to confine their Council to traditional tribal members, has been the response of the United States to their attempt.

Immediately after their ratification and adoption, our constitutional amendments were disapproved by the BIA. We challenged that disapproval in court, as is our right. While the decision was pending, the Nation conducted its 4-yearly general elections in July 2001. The elections were conducted according to the un-amended and unchallenged provisions of the Nation's federally approved Constitution. The results were clear, decisive, and most importantly for the honorable members of this Committee, they were unchallenged by anyone. Later that summer, the new officers-elect of the Nation were sworn in, and the new Seminole government set about the business of the Nation.

In early October 2001 an opinion in *Seminole v. Norton I* issued, holding that the membership amendments were unlawfully adopted and therefore without effect. We respectfully disagreed with the court's reasoning and holding and immediately appealed.

In the meantime the nation's general council nevertheless took action in accordance with the court's opinion pending the outcome of its appeal. The council passed a resolution formally noting the continuing and integral presence of the Freedmen bands on the general council, notifying the Freedmen band representatives by hand of the same, and requesting the honor of their presence in the deliberations and actions of the general council. That, we thought, should have been that, at least until the outcome of the appeal (which, by the way, was ultimately denied on the grounds that the decision was non-final, and hence not appealable). It turns out that for the BIA, it was only the beginning.

It's not given to us mortals to know the thoughts of bureaucrats; but that way lies madness. The BIA, perhaps still smarting from the Seminole's challenge to its authority, seized upon *Seminole Nation v. Norton I* as a whip with which to punish the nation. Where there had been only a satisfied electorate, the BIA stepped in to create "warring factions"; where there had been only one sore loser, the BIA created an "intra-tribal dispute" by denying the existence of the nation's government and instead choosing to recognize only a former chief. Not content with that mischief, the local agency superintendent advised the Freedmen to ignore the actions of the General Council and stay away from its meetings.

Having invented fictional factions and bogus intra-tribal disputes, the BIA next informed my no-longer recognized government that if the nation wanted to continue to receive its Federal funds, and if it wished to maintain government-to-government relations with the United States, it would have to re-install a former chief (a man resoundingly and incurably voted out of office) and immediately conduct new general elections. It offered no advice, though, on how to do so in conformity with the provisions of our federally approved constitution.

Needless to say, the Seminole people, pending the outcome of the appeal of *Seminole Nation v. Norton I*, refused. In the meantime, however, the newly recognized former chief, backed by the resources and support of the BIA and its staff, traveled around Seminole County trying his best to sow seeds of confusion. He did a pretty good job. He threatened anyone doing business with the nation, he issued "executive orders" hiring staff, firing directors, and taking over assets; and he publicly attacked the Seminole government and its people at meetings in which he was joined on the podium by officials of the BIA and the National Indian Gaming Commission, all while the nation's appeal of the court decision was pending. With the tacit approval of the BIA, he even went to Federal court seeking to have the Seminole government turned out of office, an effort quickly dismissed. Despite this, the nation continued to work diligently and in good faith through its attorneys with the Department of Justice and the BIA to try and resolve what was, at best, an inter-government dispute. The road was steep and the attitude of the BIA, if not hostile, was at best indifferent.

The Bureau's initial actions suggested to us that they weren't interested in our laws or our constitution. That suspicion was confirmed at our negotiation meetings with them. At one conference at the Wewoka Agency offices, literally across the road from Seminole Tribal Headquarters, the Regional Director assigned to mediate said he'd never seen a copy of the Seminole Constitution, much less read it. We then discovered that the Wewoka Agency office didn't even have a copy. The Director asked if we would get him a copy.

Six months later, at another settlement conference, this time in Oklahoma City, the Deputy Assistant Secretary of the Interior, who'd flown in especially for the meeting, confessed she hadn't read the Seminole Constitution, didn't have a copy, and didn't know its provisions; nor was she familiar with the Seminole government's structure. She asked if we would get her a copy as soon as the meeting was finished. Members of the committee, the Seminoles are not a large tribe, and we're not a wealthy one, either. Our home is one of the poorest counties in Oklahoma, which is itself one of the poorer States in the Union. But recent years have brought us a measurable, if modest, amount of success from gaming and other businesses. Last year alone we grew to become the largest employer in Seminole County, moving ahead of the Wrangler Jeans Company. As well as jobs, these businesses provided revenues that went into the nation's treasury, where they allowed us to provide much needed services to our people and resources for their problems in ways we couldn't do before. But that is all gone now.

Events of last May scared off our gaming customers, and chased away many current and at least one prospective business partners. That was when a BIA judge issued a series of ex parte orders, each more outrageous than the previous, shutting down the nation and turning over control of the nation, its assets and its property to the BIA's anointed leader. Men /"96 many of them non-Seminoles /"96 with automatic weapons and military fatigues appeared at our government offices and our gaming facilities, demanding entry. Our General Council House seized and vandalized. Records from the nation's Business and Regulatory Commission were taken, and others destroyed. One member of the General Council was attacked and hospitalized, another arrested. Yet the Seminole people did not rise to the bait, but stood firm on their rights under law.

The BIA court orders, issued with the full knowledge and tacit approval of the Bureau itself, went so far beyond the pale of judicial responsibility that an appellate panel met in emergency session and quickly overturned them. But by then the damage to the nation, its businesses, and their reputation, was done.

Thanks to the BIA's policy of bad faith negotiations, of cutting off of Federal funds for essential services on the pretext of upholding their "solemn" trust responsibilities (the solemnity of which has certainly been called into question by the Secretary of the Interior herself), the nation's gaming operations have suffered, perhaps irreparably. Employees have now been laid off, staff hours reduced, and revenues to the nation's treasury have dwindled.

Some Seminoles have asked whether what has befallen them really has anything to do with the Freedmen at all, or whether it's really just a big game/"96 maybe of skill, maybe of chance/"96 played by folks in Washington and Oklahoma City, folks with the desire to win at any cost. But I'm sure the better informed among you can judge as to that.

As for myself, like I said at the beginning, I'm sort of a historian. All Seminoles are. Long after this committee adjourns, after this Senate's term expires, and this administration leaves office, the Seminoles will still be here making their own history. We survived the Spanish, the British, the Seminole Wars, and removal. We'll survive the New York Times, the Chicago Tribune, and all the other authorities on Seminole ways. We'll most certainly survive the Bureau of Indian Affairs, those makers of factions and ridiculers of "solemn trust." This will be true of all Indian peoples faced with the consequences of intra-tribal disputes which are, in reality, the product not of their own internal politics, but those of outsiders who continue to attempt to use the tribes as a vehicle for their own desires.

The issue for this committee, and the Government it represents, is what kind of a history you will leave behind for your people, and whether you will finally allow the Seminoles the honor of their own history.

I thank you all for having permitted me to present you with these views.

Statement of Donnamarie Potts, Chairwoman of Buena Vista Rancheria of Me-Wuk Indians

Mr. Chairman, Mr. Vice Chairman, thank you for the opportunity to appear before this committee on a matter of great importance to the future of my tribe and my family. I have a number of documents I would like to submit for the record, but would like to take my allotted time here to tell you our story. Like most California reservations, Buena Vista was created in the 1920's as a refuge for homeless Indians who were the survivors of the genocide brought upon us by first the Spanish and then the gold miners. While the origins of the Me-Wuk Indian People of the Buena Vista Rancheria go back to the late 1800's, in the interest of time I will start with more recent events.

In 1994, with the assistance of the Sacramento Office of the Bureau of Indian Affairs, my late aunt, Lucille Lucero, completed and adopted a tribal constitution. This constitution named myself and my children as Historical Members of the tribe. We have with us today photographs of the signing ceremony at the BIA office. My Elder and I worked over 10 years with no funds to assist us to reach this point.

In the early 1980's, my Elders had deeded the majority of the Buena Vista land ownership to my name as the one chosen to carry on the tribe's heritage. By early 1996, I had bought the remaining rights to the last small part of our 67 acres on the Rancheria with my own funds, earned by working in the local fields. To ensure this would remain a home for my people, I decided to donate that land to the tribe. Before doing so, I asked the BIA for confirmation of our constitution and my family's membership in the tribe. As you can see from his response, Superintendent Harold Bradford clearly states that I am a member of the tribe. In addition, he declares the constitution enacted by my aunt to be valid.

This is only one example of confirmation from the BIA. I have over 30 examples over the years of similar evidence of a government-to-government relationship between the Rancheria and the Federal Government, including participation in Self-Governance and other Federal programs available only to recognized tribes. To this day, I continue to receive weekly documents from the BIA showing our ongoing recognition and participation in programs.

Relying on that 1996 letter, I deeded all of my land to the tribe, hired tribal employees, and began exploring opportunities for economic development and other projects to benefit not only our tribe, but all Indian people in the areas. I consider this to be a right created from my property under Federal Indian law.

As you can understand, I was shocked and terrified in December of last year to receive a letter from that same BIA office informing me that the Federal Government no longer considered me and my family members of the Rancheria. They also now say that the constitution they assisted with and approved and then affirmed is no longer valid. As you will see in the materials I have submitted, this decision contradicts the legislation and Federal court ruling that established and reinstated this tribe. It also arbitrarily reverses nearly a decade of a government-to-government relationship.

Simply put: The Government told us we were a tribe. The Government assisted in preparation and approved our constitution. The Government recognized us as historic members as we were designated by our Elders. The Government recognized me as the tribe's selected leader. The Government, over and over again, told us our constitution was valid and provided Tribal Self-Governance funds.

Then, in a secretive, closed-door process, that same agency of the Government told us none of that had ever existed. There was no hearing. No opportunity to confront any accuser or decision-maker. No opportunity to challenge documents that were fraudulently used against me.

This is nothing less than termination. The Federal Government once again terminated my tribe. And, in doing so, they took my land and my family's heritage.

This proclamation was made despite the fact that each of these historical members were recognized in the tribe's constitution, a constitution prepared and executed in 1994 with the Superintendent and other BIA personnel in the BIA's Sacramento offices, and despite the fact that the BIA has affirmed its recognition of the tribe's constitution, the tribe's members, and/or the tribe's chairperson over 30 times over the past 8 years.

We have appealed this decision to the Interior Board of Indian Appeals (the "IBIA"), but we understand that it may take years for IBIA to rule on this case and that the IBIA often merely remands cases to the regional officials who made the original decision. Also, while Assistant Secretary Neal McCaleb has declined take this appeal in his office, it is clear from the regulations that he will eventually have to rule on my appeal, as the IBIA is precluded from making any membership decisions. In the meantime, my land and the tribe's property rights have been taken without due process, the tribe is being destroyed and years of work "by the book" to achieve economic development will be gone forever.

I have come to this hearing to plead with you for help. As I worry daily about the possible extinction of my tribe and my Elders' legacy, I use this opportunity for strength and resolve.

I am encouraged by the interest you have taken to discuss our tribe's history and my family. Without this venue, our fate would be entirely in the hands of people who do not know or care about the history of this tribe and my family, and do not understand the importance of our vows to our Elders. The fact that you have taken this time out of your busy schedules to listen, gives me the resolve to continue in this struggle. We will forever remember this and pass the story of this event down to our children.

It is devastating and frightening to us that the Federal Government could take our land, take our tribe's history and its future and strip us of our status as Indian people—and then make us wait years for the IBIA's version of justice, while the BIA uses economic starvation as a weapon to further weaken us. How can they have that power over a sovereign nation? Is our sovereignty and very existence so fragile that it can be taken away in an instant at the whim of a local agent? It is also amazing that the Federal Government could recognize a tribal government dozens of time and then, without a formal process, wipe it out. Is the era of termination back?

Since this action was taken, my tribe has suffered in ways I thought were a thing of the past. The local BIA office has cutoff our Self-Governance funds and has refused to reinstate them, even though their own regulations require them to continue such obligations while an appeal such as this is pending. As chairperson of the tribe, I have no income and have had to lay off all the tribal employees. All utilities for the tribal government office—power and telephone—have been shut off. The tribal government cars and even the small trailer we used for our home are being repossessed. Without assistance from our friends, we would be helpless.

As recently as last fall, this was a thriving Indian community with the opportunity for a great future ahead of us. We had worked for decades doing everything "by the book," following all the Government's regulations, to finally be ready to reach economic stability. We had established a good working relationship with the community and business vendors. Now, everything is gone.

And why? Because I, the leader of a sovereign nation, dared to explore financial opportunities available under Federal law that might create competition or jealousy? It is just my small tribe against many others. Without this opportunity to tell our story, we would be overwhelmed.

I would like to briefly address two issues I have seen raised in the news media. The first is the debate over tribes, especially in California, that some judge to be "too small." Yes, many California tribes can be considered small when compared with those in other parts of the country. That is a result of waves of European invasion, first the Spanish and then others looking for gold. The newcomers killed my ancestors, moved them around and broke them up. In the 1920's the California Rancherias were created by Congress for the benefit of the remaining Indians living without land. The situation we live in today is not our doing. It is the doing of the Federal Government.

Second, I am sure many in this room see this dispute as just being about gaming. I must point out that the Secretary of the Interior herself, in an interview with Indian Country today earlier this month, has stated that gaming should not be considered when looking at tribal governance issues. I quote: "The decision-making process on recognition is one that ought to be objective and not depend on what the motivation is for the people that are seeking approval." Secretary Norton is talking about new recognition of tribes. I am talking about the termination of mine.

Senator Campbell has often said that Indians are the only people in this country that need a card proving their heritage. Although humiliating, I got such a "card" from the Sacramento BIA many decades ago. The Federal Government has now taken that away, along with my land, my status as a tribal leader and our chance to better the lives of many Indians in the Sacramento area. I now live in fear that all we have believed in and worked for, and all that we promised our Elders will be lost forever. I know that you know all of this, but feel I should say it here for the benefit of other members of Congress.

I am convinced that this hearing will prove we are the proper Me-Wuk Indian People of the Buena Vista Rancheria, as many know us to be. I have been here, on this land, all my life, and cannot imagine that this type of arbitrary forced extinction can still occur. Centuries ago, our people were able to travel the whole valley in search of game and resources. Today, I am merely trying to protect the last 67 acres our tribe has left. This hearing, today, is our only hope.

Thank you, once again, for the opportunity to tell our story. Our Elders would want the story of our history told to this committee and would want me to fight to the end. This is our last chance to save what is left of our history, and our future.

Sources:

US Senate. "Intra-Tribal Leadership Disputes and Tribal Governance." Hearing Before the Committee on Indian Affairs. 107th Cong., 2nd Sess. Washington, DC: Government Printing Office, September 26, 2002.

Wilkins, David E., and Shelly Hulse Wilkins. *Dismembered: Native Disenrollment and the Battle for Human Rights*. Seattle: University of Washington Press, 2017.

81   *Ernest L. Stevens (Oneida) Letter to* Time *Magazine Regarding Indian Gaming (2002)*

By the first decade of the twenty-first century, Native gambling operations were generating millions of dollars for a number of Tribal nations. Such economic achievements were still the exception across Indian Country, as poverty continued to be the norm for many Nations. Nevertheless, the high-profile financial success of these Tribes elicited a powerful backlash from many non-Indians and subsequent media depictions served to alter public perceptions of how Native peoples should live and make a living.

Many Natives sensed an assumption on the part of non-Indians that "making money was inconsistent with Indian traits." And one declared that "many Americans seem to believe Indians must be poor and helpless in order to be Indian."

Ernest Stevens, the chairman of the National Indian Gaming Association (NIGA), addressed these sentiments in his strongly worded response to *Time* magazine's article on the alleged problems caused by Indian gaming operations.

———

Dear Editor:

On behalf of the 184 Tribes of the National Indian Gaming Association, I would like to express my disgust with your December 16, 2002 special report, "Indian Casinos: Wheel of Misfortune." The story begins with the word "imagine…." That is the appropriate beginning for a story twisted to the point of a fairy tale. Your reporters use isolated circumstances to write what amounts to a gossip column.

Your story is based on the false and offensive premise that "Washington" created Indian gaming as a "cheap way to wean tribes from government handouts." Indian gaming is not a federal program. Instead, it is one tool that Tribes use to generate revenue for their communities. The Federal programs that you refer to as handouts represent an attempt by the federal government to live up to thousands of treaty obligations incurred when establishing the land base for this Nation. American Indians have been victimized by federal policies supporting genocide and assimilation, which took millions of lives and millions of acres of Indian land, and caused economic and cultural destruction. Our grandfathers, Pontiac, Tecumseh, Crazy Horse, Chief Joseph, Geronimo, and so many others, fought for our rights—especially our right to self-government on our own land. The U.S. Constitution, the President, Congress, and the United States Supreme Court all recognize Indian Tribes as governments.

Indian gaming is self-reliance. Through Indian gaming, Tribes have created over 300,000 jobs nationwide. Jobs in Indian Country are precious—whether its 80 jobs on the Pine Ridge reservation, located in the poorest county in the United States, or 3,000 jobs at the Oneida Nation of New York, outside Syracuse. Yet your report completely discounts the value of jobs to our people who have historically suffered shocking unemployment rates, high levels of poverty and lack of economic opportunities on Indian homelands.

More than 200 of the roughly 340 Indian Tribes in the lower 48 states use Indian gaming to generate tribal government revenue. That is about 60 percent of Indian Tribes. So yes, Indian gaming is broadly benefiting Indian Country. Naturally, Indian Tribes that are closer to large markets are generating revenue. Is that a surprise in a market economy? If you are advocating "to each according to his need and from each according to his ability," Russia tried that and failed. On the same note, we can hardly believe that an organization led by Ted Turner can, without blushing, publish stories suggesting that others should not pursue economic ventures in America.

Indian Tribes use gaming first and foremost for tribal government programs, community infrastructure, charity, and aid to local governments. Where Indian Tribes have suffered the highest teen suicide rates in the country, Indian gaming has built schools, funded college scholarships, and given our children hope for a brighter future. The Mille Lacs Band of Ojibwe, for example, built two schools and their high school graduates are now fluent in both Ojibwe and English. Where our people suffer epidemic problems of diabetes, heart and liver disease, Indian gaming is building health clinics, dialysis centers, and fitness centers.

Indian gaming not only works for Indian Country, it works for America. Contrary to your story, Tribes are not running roughshod over our neighboring communities. Non-Indians hold 75 percent of the 300,000 jobs Indian gaming has created nationwide. Tribes have brought economic development to historically rural and undeveloped areas. It's a fact that many Indian casinos are the largest employers in their areas. In addition, Tribes have numerous service agreements with state and local governments to share revenues, contribute emergency service equipment, build roads and other infrastructure, and provide other government services to non-Indian community members. For example, the Mohegan Tribe's restaurants serve buffalo meat purchased from Plains Indian Tribes while the Agua Caliente Band of Cahuilla Indians purchased fire trucks for Palm Springs. The Forest County Potawatomi Tribe funds Milwaukee Indian School and aids the Red Cliff and Mole Lake Bands of Chippewa. Additionally, Tribes donate $68 million annually to charitable organizations.

American Indians are American taxpayers. Indian gaming revenue is 100 percent taxed—the vast majority goes directly for tribal government purposes serving as tribal tax revenue, and any remainder that is paid to tribal members is subject to Federal income taxation. In fact, through employee income, payroll, vendor taxes, and revenue sharing agreements, Indian gaming generates over $4 billion in annual revenue for the Federal Government, over $1 billion for the states, and $50 million for local governments. American Indians pay another $4 billion in personal Federal income taxes.

That the National Indian Gaming Commission [NIGC] has yet to discover any major cases of corruption is a testament to the upstanding job done by our regulatory personnel. Your article continues to perpetuate a myth that Indian gaming is not regulated. This is simply not true. President Bush has just appointed a former U.S. Attorney, former FBI agent, and former state deputy attorney general to staff the NIGC. In addition to the $164 million that Indian Tribes dedicate to tribal government regulation and the $40 plus million that tribal governments pay to states for state regulation, the NIGC has an $8 million budget. In total, that's over $212 million that Indian Tribes spend annually on regulation. This figure includes the employment of over 2,800 gaming commissioners and regulatory staff. In addition, Tribes work with the FBI within the Department of Justice, FinCEN and the IRS within Treasury, and the BIA within the Interior Department. Your suggestion that this regulatory system is less than comprehensive is just plain wrong—as a number of DOJ investigations have found.

Furthermore, your discussion of management contracts is faulty at best. Whether a Tribe chooses to employ a management company or developer is an exercise of a Tribe's individual sovereignty. Each Tribe has the right to choose what is most beneficial for its own membership and community. Whether or not a Tribe chooses a management firm is a tribal decision and the fact remains that Tribes are legal entities with the right to determine their own future as they see fit within the context of the law. Many Tribes have never had a management agreement and have operated their gaming enterprises pursuant to their own gaming ordinances, long before the Indian Gaming Regulatory Act was passed.

In conclusion, as American Indians, we find it highly offensive that TIME published an article belittling tribal self-government and the very positive attempts of tribal governments to dispossession for hundreds of years. You do not belittle Israeli or Palestinian efforts toward self-determination, but yet it cannot fathom that within the United States, Indian Tribes continue to be vital, self-governing nations working to build a life for our people. Indian gaming has positively impacted local communities, and has transformed tribal communities that were once forgotten. It provides jobs to many who never worked before, provides care for our elders, and brings hope and opportunity to our children. Manufacturing scandal to sell magazines at the cost of these advances is most dishonorable.

Ernie Stevens, Jr., Chairman, National Indian Gaming Association, December 10, 2002

Sources:

Barlett, Donald L., and James B. Steele. "Look Who's Cashing In at Indian Casinos: Hint: It's Not the People Who Are Supposed to Benefit." *Time* 160, no. 25 (December 16, 2002), 44–58.

Cramer, Renee Ann. *Cash, Color, and Colonialism: The Politics of Tribal Acknowledgment.* Norman: University of Oklahoma Press, 2005.

Stevens, Ernest L., Jr., "Letter to the Editor of *Time* Magazine," press release, December 10, 2002, http://www.indiangaming.org/info/pr/press-releases-2002/time-magazine.shtml.
    http://content.time.com/time/magazine/0 ,9263,7601021218,00.html

82

Relations between the Tohono O'odham Nation and the Bureau of Customs and Border Protection (2003)

On September 11, 2001, the United States suffered a series of devastating terrorist attacks that killed or maimed thousands of individuals. In response, Congress adopted the Homeland Security Act of 2002. This measure authorized the reorganization of existing federal agencies under a newly established Department of Homeland Security and expanded border protection policies through the National Homeland Security Reorganization Plan.

Twenty-five Native nations are located on or near the borders of Canada and Mexico, and the policy changes initiated by the 9/11 attacks had significant impacts on those nations and their peoples. However, the Native governments in these sensitive areas were never consulted during this time and did not receive direct funding for their own homeland security needs. With 28,000 citizens living on a 2.8 million–acre land base, the Tohono O'odham Nation of Southern Arizona is geographically the second-largest reservation within the US and seventy-five miles of their lands connect with the US–Mexico international border. By 2001, that stretch of territory had become a well-known avenue for both undocumented immigrants and drug trafficking activities yet they, too, were left out of Homeland Security planning and funding considerations.

The lack of consultation and consent with Tribal nations prompted Senator Daniel Inouye and others to introduce a bill, S.578, titled the "Tribal Government Amendments to the Homeland Security Act of 2002," that sought recognition of Tribal governments as having authority "to provide for the health and safety of those who reside on tribal lands," and are "necessary components of a comprehensive system to secure the homeland of the United States, among other powers." S.578 generated vigorous dissent from conservative lawmakers who alleged that Tribal governments would be empowered to strip "several million U.S. citizens of their constitutional protections," amounting to a "breathtaking example of racial tyranny."

Sen. Inouye, a long-time champion of Indigenous peoples, found those comments to be baseless. In his own words, "To suggest that Tribal governments are terrorists or that citizens of this country are subject to attack by Native people is to me one of the most outrageous assertions I have ever heard."

In response to the bill, the Tohono O'odham legislative council on July 11, 2003, adopted the following resolution urging the US and the Bureau of Customs and Border (CBP) to work proactively with the Tribe by affirming their inherent governmental authority over their own lands and persons living within or traversing them, through information and infrastructure protection, science and technology, emergency preparedness, improved communication and sharing of ideas, and direct federal funding for manpower and resource support.

Resolution of the Tohono O'odham Legislative Council

Whereas, the Tohono O'odham Nation through historical oversight and exclusion from decision-making between the United States and Mexico's treaties and agreements resulted in 75 miles of the international boundary being adjacent to the Tohono O'odham Nation; and

Whereas, due to an influx of undocumented immigrants crossing through the boundaries of the Tohono O'odham Nation, The Former United States Border Patrol as operated within the lands of the nation for over twenty years; and

Whereas, over time, due to the physical presence of the US border patrol on the nations lands, district officials and citizens of the Tohono O'odham Nation have voiced concerns regarding the disruption of their daily lives due to lack of respect for people, land, and the environment of the Nation; and

Whereas, in 2002 due to terrorism attacks on citizens of the United States, President George Bush, with the support of the United States Congress, established the United States Office of Homeland Security, effectively reorganizing the Border Patrol as the Bureau of Customs and Border Protection within the US Office of Homeland Security; and

Whereas, there exist records of United States presidential executive orders regarding respect for government to government relations and consultation on all matters, which have a direct impact on Indian tribal nations;

Whereas, Tohono O'odham Nation and the Bureau of Customs and Border Protection share a common goal of protecting the United States and its borders within the Nation's lands.

Now, therefore, be it resolved by the Legislative Council that it hereby supports the Tohono O'odham Nation's Position Paper, which outlines the Nation's stance on the Bureau of Customs and Border Protection conduct of activities within the boundaries of the nation....

Tohono O'odham Legislative Council, Dennis Ramon, Chairman. July 14, 2003

Source:

US Senate. "Tribal Government Amendments to the Homeland Security Act of 2002." Hearing Before the Committee on Indian Affairs. 108th Cong., 1st Sess. on S. 578. Washington, DC: Government Printing Office, July 30, 2003.

83   *Maltos v. Sauk Suiattle Tribe (2003)*

Since the late 1990s, both crime and revenue have increased throughout Indian Country. Civil violations and criminal activity—gang warfare, illegal drug activity, treason, and sexual violence against Native women—have led some Native governments to reintroduce banishment (physical expulsion from Tribal lands) as a form of punishment; whereas increased revenue, typically associated with high-stakes gambling activity—has been associated with the practice of disenrollment (formal political termination of a Tribal citizen's rights as a member of the nation).

Disenrollment has become a national phenomenon, with nearly eighty Native nations in at least twenty states engaging in the practice of disenfranchising members. In addition to financial incentives, two other factors have dominated the rationales used by Tribal officials to disenroll citizens: documentary errors involving those on official Tribal rolls, some of which date back to the chaotic allotment era of the 1880s, and the lack of sufficient or appropriate blood quantum.

By contrast, those who face dismemberment assert that official policy rationales are merely pretenses that conceal the real explanations for why they have been targeted by Tribal officials for disenrollment. These include efforts to purge citizenship rolls of political dissidents, attempts to consolidate economic and political power bases, or simply targeting individuals or entire families because of personal feuds or family vendettas.

In the ensuing case, the Sauk-Suiattle Tribal Court of Appeals was called upon to hear the case of Nino Maltos, who had brought suit against the Tribe and the council for having been disenrolled. He claimed personal injury and that the Tribe's action violated its own code and federal statutes. The Tribe asserted sovereign immunity. Chief Judge Martin Bohl of the Tribal Court issued an order granting the Tribe's motion to dismiss on sovereign immunity grounds, but directed notice of a rehearing for Maltos because he had been denied due process. Maltos then appealed.

The Appellate court in a 2–1 decision held that the Tribe's enrollment ordinance was "ambiguous" and that a member had the right to appeal their loss of membership. More important, the court determined that there was no discernible distinction between "loss of membership" and a "denial of membership." In conclusion, the court rejected the Tribe's sovereign immunity stance, and declared that what mattered the most was that Maltos had been denied due process by not having been informed of his right to appeal his disenrollment, a clear violation of his sovereign right as a citizen of his nation.

———

Opinion by Richard A. Woodrow, Justice

...This Court having reviewed the record and listened to the arguments of counsel, agrees that the trial court does have jurisdiction to order a rehearing.

We reached this opinion by deciding that sovereign immunity does not apply. The rehearing is an administrative remedy and as such does not constitute a suit against the Tribe....

The enrollment ordinance is ambiguous. It is unclear if a member may appeal a dis-enrollment or a relinquishment of membership in the tribe. This court holds that a member may appeal a loss of membership in which privileges of membership are revoked by the Tribal Council or the Enrollment Committee. There is no distinction that this court can find between a loss of membership and a denial of membership. This conclusion is based upon the following facts: 1) the tribal membership is a valuable property right and all members must be afforded due process when that right is taken by the tribe; 2) tribal members should have the same appeal rights as other Indians seeking to become tribal members; 3) the Enrollment Ordinance is ambiguous regarding appeals rights and this ambiguity should be resolved in favor of the tribal members; 4) there does not appear to be any appeal process or right to re-apply for membership if a member is dis-enrolled or relinquishes membership brought by the motion of the Tribal Council or the Enrollment Committee. There should always be a remedy for mistake or error....

The court concludes that tribal sovereignty was never at issue in this case. The trial court must hold a hearing to determine if the Respondent [Maltos] was given notice of his right to appeal, and if the Respondent understood that he had the right to appeal a dis-enrollment or relinquishment or if the Respondent was given his notice to appeal and waive that right by inaction and a failure to exhaust his administrative remedies....

Source:

Nino Maltos v. Sauk-Suiattle Tribe, 6 NICS App. 132 (November 2003).

---

84   *Executive Order #39: Affirmation of the Government-to-Government Relationship Between the State of Wisconsin and Indian Tribal Governments (2004)*

Wisconsin's borders contain the lands and governments of eleven sovereign Native nations: Bad River Band of Lake Superior Chippewa, Forest County Potawatomi, Ho-Chunk Nation, La Courte Oreilles Band of Lake Superior Chippewa, Lac du Flambeau Band of Lake Superior Chippewa, Menominee

Indian Tribe, Oneida Tribe of Indians, Red Cliff Band of Lake Superior Chippewa, St. Croix Chippewa, Sokaogon Mole Lake Chippewa, and Stockbridge Munsee.

These Native nations have endured the consequences of a series of devastating state and federal policies. Wisconsin was one of the five states granted criminal jurisdiction over Tribal governments by federal decree in 1953 via P.L. 280 and was home to the first Indigenous nation—the Menominee—to be politically terminated by Congress in 1954, although formal termination did not occur until 1961. [The Menominee regained full recognition in 1973.]

There were bitter, often violent, confrontations over fishing rights, as Tribes were long-denied the ability to exercise their treaty-reserved right to fish until a series of federal court cases found in their favor in the 1970s, 1980s, and 1990s.

The following sovereignty accord, modeled loosely after the Washington State Centennial Accord of 1989, charts a new, cooperative course in intergovernmental relations.

Wisconsin Governor Jim Doyle, Executive Order #39

Whereas, the State of Wisconsin has a unique legal relationship with Indian Tribes, as affirmed and set forth in state and federal law; and

Whereas, within Wisconsin there are 11 federally recognized Tribes with elected or appointed Tribal governments; and

Whereas, the State of Wisconsin, a sovereign state within the United States, recognizes the unique status of Indian Tribes and their right to existence, self-government, and self-determination; and

Whereas, state regulations and other policy statements or actions have an impact on Indian Tribes; and

Whereas, State and Tribal governments play key roles in serving all of the citizens of the State of Wisconsin and collaboration between Tribes and State agencies will ensure that services are efficiently provided to all citizens, minimize service overlap, preserve natural resources and encourage sustainable economic development;

Now therefore, I, Jim Doyle, Governor of the State of Wisconsin, by the authority vested in me by the Constitution and the laws of this State, do hereby:

1. Direct cabinet agencies to recognize the unique legal relationship between the State of Wisconsin and Indian Tribes, respect fundamental principles that establish and maintain this relationship and accord Tribal governments the same respect accorded other governments;

2. Direct cabinet agencies to recognize the unique government-to-government relationship between the State of Wisconsin and Indian Tribes when formulating and implementing polices or programs that directly affect Indian Tribes and their members, and whenever feasible and appropriate, consult the governments of the affected Tribe or Tribes regarding state action or proposed action that is anticipated to directly affect an Indian Tribe or its members;

3. In instances where the State of Wisconsin assumes control over formerly federal programs that directly affect Indian Tribes or their members, direct cabinet agencies, when feasible and appropriate, to consider Tribal needs and endeavor to ensure that Tribal interests are taken into account by the cabinet agency administering the formerly federal program; and

4. Direct cabinet agencies to work cooperatively to accomplish the goals of this order;

5. General Provisions.

   a. Nothing in this order shall require cabinet agencies to violate or ignore any laws, rules, directives or other legal requirements or obligations imposed by state or federal law.

   b. Nothing in this order shall require cabinet agencies to violate or ignore any agreements or compacts between one or more Indian Tribes and the State of Wisconsin or one or more of its agencies.

   c. If any provision in this order conflicts with any laws, rules, agreements or other legal requirements or obligations imposed by state or federal law, the state or federal law shall control.

   d. Nothing in this order prohibits or limits any cabinet agency from asserting or pursuing any action or right, or taking any position under state or federal law or any existing agreement in relation to the interests of the State of Wisconsin or any of its state agencies.

   e. Nothing in this order creates any right, benefit, or trust responsibility, substantive or procedural, enforceable at law by a party against the State of Wisconsin, its agencies, or any person.

In Testimony Whereof, I have hereunto set my hand and caused the Great Seal of the State of Wisconsin to be affixed. Done at the Capitol in the City of Madison this twenty-seventh day of February, in the year two thousand four.

Jim Doyle, Governor, Douglas La Follette, Secretary of State

Source:

Executive Order #39.
   http://witribes.wi.gov/docview.asp?docid=23379&locid=57.

---

85   *The Diné Marriage Act (2005)*

Over the past twenty years, scholars from fields related to gender identification and sexual orientation have questioned and researched traditional Judeo-Christian tenets used to justify centuries of persecution of those living outside the male/female paradigm. While this destructive worldview was endemic to colonizing powers, it is generally understood that Native peoples viewed these matters as issues of personal autonomy and, thus, people who did not conform to binary roles functioned as any other member of an Indigenous community. Many contend Indigenous peoples accepted gender and sexuality as a continuum, unbound from the two strict categories deemed the only moral options by European-based societies.

There exists historical evidence of non-binary gender identification and sexual orientation within Native societies. Some proof comes from Native oral histories, and there are also surviving accounts written by invading forces, including clerics, traders, and military observers, who describe what they considered abhorrent behaviors. There are even nineteenth-century photographs of Natives who defied strictures imposed by the colonizing culture.

Given these differences, it is understandable that Western Europeans and Native peoples also held divergent views on the concept of marriage. For colonizing societies, marriage, gender, and sexuality were inextricably linked; marriage was a spiritual and legal covenant between one man and one woman, and sexuality only expressed within the confines of that relationship. Acting outside the boundaries of this contract resulted in grave consequences, both in this life and the next. Thus, marriage was the elemental institution underpinning patriarchal structures and controls.

Traditionally, most Indigenous ideas and rules regarding marriage have been based on kinship systems that are commonly rooted in clan structures. Individuals of the same clan are prohibited from marrying so as to maintain a robust population and a logical social structure. Incest was arguably the worst taboo and many societies had methods for punishing those who committed such violations, including banishment and death. It is clear that these practical survival concerns were preeminent, and many Native societies have carried intricate instructions for maintaining health and harmony forward into the present day. In contrast, traditional societies did not pass down rules limiting or outlawing non-binary roles—an indication that, for communities working together to survive using the skills of every relative, those who identified and lived outside male/female roles were another part of the fabric of daily existence.

By the first decade of the twenty-first century, as mainstream Americans began to address these issues more openly, some Tribal nations began to confront them, as well. The two largest, the Navajo in 2005 and the Cherokee in 2004, adopted resolutions opposing same-sex marriage, notwithstanding the wealth of historical evidence showing that such unions had never been prohibited within their societies. The language and justifications used in these bans reveal the influence of colonialism and Christianity on these fundamental questions of gender, sexuality, and marriage and the extent to which Western patriarchal norms had usurped traditional ways.

In December 2016, the Cherokee Nation overturned its ban with Attorney General Todd Hembree's opinion that two sections of the 2004 Cherokee Nation Marriage and Family Act were unconstitutional: "The constitution affords these rights to all Cherokee citizens, regardless of sexual orientation and the Cherokee Nation, or any subdivision, must recognize validly issued civil unions, same-sex marriages, and same-sex domestic partnerships from other jurisdictions."

Interestingly, Hembree's rationale was, in part, based on Cherokee matrimonial traditions, "oral history teaches that since time immemorial Cherokees have recognized perpetual partnerships akin to marriage that are unique to Cherokee society. For instance, in traditional Cherokee society the basic unit of kinship was the clan. All members of the clan descend from the same individual, and although blood connection may have been long forgotten by the time of European contact, 'this relationship seem[ed] to be as binding as the ties of consanguinity.' Because of this, 'children belonging to the same clan [could] never, under penalty of death, intermarry' and young people were discouraged from marrying into their father's clan as well. And, since clan affiliation was inherited through the mother's line, clan members were encouraged to marry into either the maternal grandfather's clan or paternal grandfather's clan....Oral history also teaches that the Cherokee and Euro-American worldviews differed dramatically regarding appropriate gender roles, marriage, sexuality, and spiritual beliefs. Indeed, while the majority of Cherokees subscribed to culturally defined gender roles, evidence suggests a tradition of homosexuality or alternative sexuality among a minority of Cherokees."

By contrast, the April 22, 2005, Navajo Nation Council's unanimous approval of the following resolution outlawing same-sex marriage on the Navajo Nation remains in effect despite challenges including President Joe Shirley Jr.'s veto of the law that he viewed as an attempt to discriminate by legislating issues already settled by the Nation's cultural system. Shirley's veto was promptly overridden by a vote of 62–14.

An Action Relating to Domestic Relations Enacting the Diné Marriage Act of 2005; Amending Title 9 of the Navajo Nation Code

Be It Enacted:
The Navajo Nation Council hereby enacts the Diné Marriage Act of 2005, as follows:

Section 1. Enactment of the Diné Marriage Act of 2005

The Navajo Nation Council hereby enacts the Diné Marriage Act of 2005.

Section 2. Amendments to Title 9 Navajo Nation Code

The Navajo Nation Council hereby amends the Navajo Nation Code, Title 9, as follows:

1. Validity generally
    A. Marriages contracted outside of the Navajo Nation are valid within the Navajo Nation if valid by the laws of the place where contracted with the exception of marriages that are void and prohibited by Section 2 of this Title.

B. Marriages may be validly contracted within Navajo Indian Country by meeting the requirements of 9 N.N.C. §§3 and 4.

2. Plural Marriages Void

A. All plural marriages contracted, whether or not in accordance with Navajo custom, shall be void and prohibited.

B. Marriage between parents and children, including grandparents and grandchildren of every degree, between brothers and sisters of one-half degree, as well as whole blood, and between uncles and nieces, aunts and nephews, and between first cousins, is prohibited and void

C. Marriage between persons of the same sex is void and prohibited.

Section 3. Purposes

The purposes of marriage on the Navajo Nation are to promote strong families and to preserve and strengthen family values.

All subsequent sections shall be renumbered, as necessary.

Certification

I hereby certify that the foregoing resolution was duly considered by the Navajo Nation Council at a duly called meeting in Window Rock, Navajo Nation (Arizona) at which a quorum was present and that the same was passed by a vote of 67 in favor and 0 opposed, this 22nd day of April 2005. Lawrence T. Morgan, Speaker, Navajo Nation Council. Motion: Harry Goldtooth. Second: Alice White.

Memorandum

To: Honorable Lawrence T. Morgan, Speaker Navajo Nation Council

From: Joe Shirley, Jr., President, The Navajo Nation

Date: May 1, 2005

Subject: Resolution No. CP–29–05, Relating To Domestic Relations; Enacting The Diné Marriage Act Of 2005; Amending Title 9 Of The Navajo Nation Code.

By the authority vested in me as President of the Navajo Nation, I hereby veto Resolution No. CAP–29–05, for the following reasons:

The legislation is unnecessary and addresses issues already governed by existing law and by cultural values and our clan system. Further, the legislation seems to be focused on the prohibition of same-sex marriage and appears discriminatory.

On an issue as personal as this, it behooves us to allow the people to raise the question and address it themselves through an initiative, rather than have it decided by 67 members of the Navajo Nation Council. To do otherwise is to permit the Navajo government to unnecessarily intrude and interfere into private, personal lives.

Same-sex marriage is a non-issue on Navajo land, so why waste time and resources on it. We have more important issues to address such as impoverishment, unemployment, rampant crime, child abuse, drug abuse, diabetes and other social, environmental, and health care issues.

Resolution of the Navajo Nation Council

20th Navajo Nation Council—Third Year, 2005

An Action Overriding the Navajo Nation President's Veto of Navajo Nation Council Resolution CAP–29–05

Be It Enacted:

The Navajo Nation Council hereby overrides the Navajo Nation President's veto of Resolution CAP–29–05, An Action Relating to Domestic Relations: Enacting the Diné Marriage Act of 2005; Amending Title 9 of the Navajo Nation Code.

Certification

I hereby certify that the foregoing resolution was duly considered by the Navajo Nation Council at a duly called meeting in Window Rock, Navajo Nation (Arizona) at which a quorum was present and that the same was passed by a vote of 62 in favor and 14 opposed, this 3rd day of June 2005.

Sources:

Bushyhead, Julie. "The Coquille Indian Tribe, Same-Sex Marriage, and Spousal Benefits: A Practical Guide." *Arizona Journal of International & Comparative Law* 26 (2009): 509–546.

Fletcher, Matthew L. M. "Same-Sex Marriage, Indian Tribes, and the Constitution." *University of Miami Law Review* 61 (2006): 53–85.

Nez Denetdale, Jennifer. "Securing Navajo National Boundaries: War, Patriotism, Tradition, and the Diné Marriage Act of 2005." *Wicazo Sa Review* 24, no. 2 (2009): 131–148.

2016-CNAG-03 Cherokee Nation Opinion Attorney General (2016).

86   *Acknowledgment and Apology to Native Peoples with Response from Tex Hall, President, National Congress of American Indians (2005)*

In the latter part of the twentieth century, official apologies from colonial powers were more forthcoming than at any other time in history. Britain's Queen Elizabeth apologized to the Maori people of New Zealand, the Australian government apologized for its policy of stealing Aboriginal children, Canada apologized to First Nations and Canadian Ukrainians, and South African president F. W. de Klerk apologized to the victims of apartheid.

The US expressed regrets to several groups—Hawaiian Natives for the illegal annexation of their land, African Americans tormented by the Tuskegee syphilis experiment, and Japanese Americans forcibly interned during World

War II. Interestingly, African Americans, despite centuries of slavery and Jim Crow laws, have yet to receive a full formal governmental apology.

Native nations, while provided opportunities to sue the federal government for violations of treaties via various claims processes, did not receive an official apology for ill treatment by the US until 2009 when President Obama, as part of a defense appropriation bill, signed into law a watered-down version of a resolution authored by Senators Sam Brownback (R-KS) and Byron Dorgan (D-ND). The perfunctory nature of the process, lack of publicity, and concluding disclaimer that seemed to contradict the sentiment of the statement upset many in Indian Country.

On September 8, 2000, the 175th anniversary of the Bureau of Indian affairs, BIA Assistant Secretary Kevin Gover acknowledged the harm his agency had done to Native peoples. It is telling that such a statement was finally made when the assistant secretary position was held by a native—Gover is Pawnee—and 90 percent of BIA personnel were natives.

The originally proposed 2005 Senate resolution follows here, along with a statement in response by Tex Hall (Three Affiliated Tribes), president of the National Congress of American Indians, wherein he notes that an apology is only the first step toward true reconciliation. Nearly a decade later, Hall, a well-known Indian Country leader, was to become a controversial figure for his business practices, including alleged conflicts of interest with oil and gas companies that caused environmental damage. An independent investigative report on his activities released in 2014 found improprieties and resulted in a prepared resolution for his suspension as chairman. Although it failed to pass, questions regarding the alleged scandals remained and ultimately undermined Hall's ambitions for continued leadership.

Brownback (for himself, Dorgan, and Dodd) introduced the following joint resolution; which was read twice and referred to the Committee on Indian Affairs.

Joint Resolution

To acknowledge a long history of official depredations and ill-conceived policies by the United States Government regarding Indian tribes and offer an apology to all Native Peoples on behalf of the United States.

Whereas the ancestors of today's Native Peoples inhabited the land of the present-day United States since time immemorial and for thousands of years before the arrival of peoples of European descent;

Whereas the Native Peoples have for millennia honored, protected, and stewarded this land we cherish;

Whereas the Native Peoples are spiritual peoples with a deep and abiding belief in the Creator, and for millennia their peoples have maintained a powerful spiritual connection to this land, as is evidenced by their customs and legends;

Whereas the arrival of Europeans in North America opened a new chapter in the histories of the Native Peoples;

Whereas, while establishment of permanent European settlements in North America did stir conflict with nearby Indian tribes, peaceful and mutually beneficial interactions also took place;

Whereas the foundational English settlements in Jamestown, Virginia, and Plymouth, Massachusetts, owed their survival in large measure to the compassion and aid of the Native Peoples in their vicinities;

Whereas in the infancy of the United States, the founders of the Republic expressed their desire for a just relationship with the Indian tribes, as evidenced by the Northwest Ordinance enacted by Congress in 1787, which begins with the phrase, "The utmost good faith shall always be observed toward the Indians";

Whereas Indian tribes provided great assistance to the fledgling Republic as it strengthened and grew, including invaluable help to Meriwether Lewis and William Clark on their epic journey from St. Louis, Missouri, to the Pacific Coast;

Whereas Native Peoples and non-Native settlers engaged in numerous armed conflicts;

Whereas the United States Government violated many of the treaties ratified by Congress and other diplomatic agreements with Indian tribes;

Whereas this Nation should address the broken treaties and many of the more ill-conceived Federal policies that followed, such as extermination, termination, forced removal and relocation, the outlawing of traditional religions, and the destruction of sacred places;

Whereas the United States forced Indian tribes and their citizens to move away from their traditional homelands and onto federally established and controlled reservations, in accordance with such Acts as the Indian Removal Act of 1830;

Whereas many Native Peoples suffered and perished—

(1) during the execution of the official United States Government policy of forced removal, including the infamous Trail of Tears and Long Walk;

(2) during bloody armed confrontations and massacres, such as the Sand Creek Massacre in 1864 and the Wounded Knee Massacre in 1890; and

(3) on numerous Indian reservations;

Whereas the United States Government condemned the traditions, beliefs, and customs of the Native Peoples and endeavored to assimilate them by such policies as the redistribution of land under the General Allotment Act of 1887 and the forcible removal of Native children from their families to faraway boarding schools where their Native practices and languages were degraded and forbidden;

Whereas officials of the United States Government and private United States citizens harmed Native Peoples by the unlawful acquisition of recognized tribal land and the theft of tribal resources and assets from recognized tribal land;

Whereas the policies of the United States Government toward Indian tribes and the breaking of covenants with Indian tribes have contributed to the severe social ills and economic troubles in many Native communities today;

Whereas, despite the wrongs committed against Native Peoples by the United States, the Native Peoples have remained committed to the protection of this great land, as evidenced by the fact that, on a per capita basis, more Native people have served in the United States Armed Forces and placed themselves in harm's way in defense of the United States in every major military conflict than any other ethnic group;

Whereas Indian tribes have actively influenced the public life of the United States by continued cooperation with Congress and the Department of the Interior, through the involvement of Native individuals in official United States Government positions, and by leadership of their own sovereign Indian tribes;

Whereas Indian tribes are resilient and determined to preserve, develop, and transmit to future generations their unique cultural identities;

Whereas the National Museum of the American Indian was established within the Smithsonian Institution as a living memorial to the Native Peoples and their traditions; and

Whereas Native Peoples are endowed by their Creator with certain unalienable rights, and that among those are life, liberty, and the pursuit of happiness: Now, therefore, be it

Resolved by the Senate and House of Representatives of the United States of America in Congress assembled,

Section 1. Acknowledgment and Apology

The United States, acting through Congress—

(1) recognizes the special legal and political relationship the Indian tribes have with the United States and the solemn covenant with the land we share;

(2) commends and honors the Native Peoples for the thousands of years that they have stewarded and protected this land;

(3) recognizes that there have been years of official depredations, ill-conceived policies, and the breaking of covenants by the United States Government regarding Indian tribes;

(4) apologizes on behalf of the people of the United States to all Native Peoples for the many instances of violence, maltreatment, and neglect inflicted on Native Peoples by citizens of the United States;

(5) expresses its regret for the ramifications of former wrongs and its commitment to build on the positive relationships of the past and present to move toward a brighter future where all the people of this land live reconciled as brothers and sisters, and harmoniously steward and protect this land together;

(6) urges the President to acknowledge the wrongs of the United States against Indian tribes in the history of the United States in order to bring healing to this land by providing a proper foundation for reconciliation between the United States and Indian tribes; and

(7) commends the State governments that have begun reconciliation efforts with recognized Indian tribes located in their boundaries and encourages all State governments similarly to work toward reconciling relationships with Indian tribes within their boundaries.

Section 2. Disclaimer.

Nothing in this Joint Resolution—

(1) authorizes or supports any claim against the United States; or

(2) serves as a settlement of any claim against the United States.

Prepared Statement of Tex Hall, President, National Congress of American Indians

Dosha! Good morning Chairman McCain, Vice Chairman Dorgan, and members of the committee. My name is Tex Hall, and I am president of the National Congress of American Indians and chairman of the Mandan, Hidatsa and Arikara Nation of North Dakota.

NCAI is the oldest and largest American Indian organization in the United States. I sit before you today representing over 250 tribal governments and thousands of Indian people. NCAI was founded in 1944 in response to termination and assimilation policies that the United States forced upon the tribal governments in contradiction of their treaty rights and status as sovereign governments. Today NCAI remains dedicated to protecting the rights of tribal governments to achieve self-determination and self-sufficiency.

On behalf of NCAI, thank you for giving me the opportunity to testify in regard to S.J. Res. 15, which would acknowledge the many misdeeds of the United States in its interaction with Native Americans and recognize and honor the importance of Native Americans to this land and to our nation—in the past and today. I also want to thank Senator Sam Brownback for his leadership in introducing this resolution and Senators Boxer, Dodd, Inouye, Dorgan, Cochran, and Akaka for cosponsoring the Apology Resolution.

We all know the atrocities wrought against Native people in the United States—the holocaust, the land theft, the forced removals, the boarding school experience completely wiping out the language and cultures of our Native brothers and sisters, the broken treaties, and the attempts to undermine our status as sovereign nations. Passage of the Apology Resolution would mark the Federal Governments first effort to extend an official apology for the years of wrongdoing in interactions with Indian tribes.

It is a long-time coming.

A similar Apology Resolution enumerating the various wrongdoings of the United States Government in relation to the Native Hawaiians and the Kingdom of Hawai'i was passed and signed into law by President Clinton in 1993. The Canadian Government likewise apologized to its First peoples in 1998.

The NCAI leadership worked with Congressional leadership in the last Congress to analyze the impact of this landmark resolution, which was first introduced during the 108th Congress by Senator Brownback, for himself, Senator Ben Nighthorse Campbell, and Senator Inouye. NCAI solicited responses to the proposed language from tribal leaders and facilitated discussion among tribal leadership and Congress on the issue. Tribal leadership across Indian country continues to give a variety of responses to the Apology Resolution, and I would like to share some of those responses with you today.

First, it is important to recognize that the intensity of the reaction of tribal leaders to the Apology Resolution demonstrates that the destructive policies addressed in this resolution are not a fading distant past for Indian peoples; they are present harms that continue to be felt in very real ways every day. We continue to live with the legacy of the Federal Government's misguided policies of the past, as well as present day policies that undermine our ability to live as robust, healthy, self-determining peoples. Tribal leaders have stressed that the apology must recognize contemporary, and not just historical, problems in Indian-government relations.

Many government policies continue to reflect a reluctance to truly recognize tribes as sovereigns. For example, tribes, unlike other governments, are limited in their ability to raise money by issuing tax exempt bonds. Tribes are also left out of the funds that the Federal Government has directed to every State in this Nation for emergency response and homeland security. Tribal law enforcement agencies do not have the jurisdiction and resources they need to protect public safety, and recent Supreme Court decisions have blurred the lines of jurisdiction at the borders between state and tribal lands.

Tribal leaders have commented that an apology may be the first step in a reconciliation process between tribes and the U.S. Government, but for this to be true, the apology must be more than just words on paper. There is a lot of unfinished business that must be attended to before true reconciliation can be achieved. As one tribal leader has said, apologizing does not in any way wipe the slate clean or let anyone off the hook.

I had the opportunity recently to testify before this committee on the President's proposed budget for fiscal year 2006. As I said at the time, Indian people are deeply disappointed that this budget does not support strong tribal self-government and self-determination. The President has proposed drastic budget cuts to many of the programs that are vital to the health and well-being of our people. For example, American Indians and Alaska Natives have a life expectancy 5 years less than all other races in this country and suffer from high rates of diabetes, heart disease, suicide, cancer, and alcoholism. Despite these health disparities, the per capita expenditure for American Indian and Alaska Native medical services is less than one-third of the average annual expenditure for individual Medicaid assistance, and is even less than the Nation's per capita health expenditure for Federal prisoners. These programs are guaranteed to us by solemn treaties and tribes paid for these services by ceding about 3 billion acres of land to the Federal Government. A strong Federal commitment to make good on old promises to provide resources for services, prevention programs, and health care facilities is badly needed to turn around the troubling health statistics in Indian country and is an important step toward reconciliation.

To many, an apology rings hollow when the U.S. Government is continuing to fail to fulfill its treaty promises. Only when coupled with a continued commitment to the government to government relationship and to Federal Indian programs like health, education, and housing, can the Apology Resolution truly begin to make a meaningful difference for Indian tribes. Otherwise, as one tribal leader put it, the resolution will be like apologizing for stepping on someone's foot while you continue to stand on it.

The message I would like to leave you with today is that passage of the Apology Resolution may be an important and meaningful first step toward reconciliation. Native Americans have come through extraordinarily trying times over the past two centuries, and we have emerged strong. Native Americans are the fastest growing segment of the population by percentage—in the face of policies aimed at ensuring our destruction, we have chosen survival.

However, we have a long way to go. An apology implies a recognition that an injustice occurred. And the importance of this recognition cannot be underestimated. It also implies, however, that there is a will to try to do something about the harms that are caused by that injustice. True healing must begin with a recognition of the harm, but it cannot stop there. An apology cannot substitute for upholding the hundreds of treaties made with Indian nations and fully living up to the Federal trust responsibility. Tribal leaders have cautioned that the apology will be meaningless if it is not accompanied by actions that begin to correct the wrongs of the past and the present. Indian sovereignty is still under threat and Indian people are still being left behind in this country. We look forward to working with you as we move forward in taking the next steps toward reconciliation and securing the future for Indian peoples.

Sources:

Brooks, Roy L., ed. *When Sorry Isn't Enough: The Controversy Over Apologies and Reparations for Human Injustice.* New York: New York University Press, 1999.

US Senate. "Acknowledgment and Apology." Hearing Before the Committee on Indian Affairs." 109th Cong., 1st Sess. on S. J. Res. 15. Washington, DC: Government Printing Office, May 25, 2005.

87
Allen v. Cherokee Nation Tribal Council (2006)

The Cherokee Nation Tribal Council adopted a law in 2002 that declared that "tribal membership is derived only through proof of Cherokee blood based on the Final Rolls." This stringent and racially tinged language effectively deprived the nearly 2,800 Cherokee Freedmen of their citizenship within the Cherokee Nation. The Freedman are the descendants of African Americans who prior to the US Civil War had been enslaved by some Cherokee citizens but were subsequently freed and politically incorporated into the Cherokee Nation under Article 9 of the 1866 Treaty signed between the federal government and the Cherokee Nation. The 2002 law also appeared to directly contradict language in the Nation's 1975 Constitution that had defined Cherokee citizenship broadly to include not only those who were ethnologically Cherokee but also included African American, Shawnee, and Delaware individuals who had long been politically incorporated into the Nation.

In 2004 Lucy Allen, a descendant of individuals listed on the Dawes Commission Rolls as "Cherokee Freedmen," filed a lawsuit against the Tribal Council asking the Nation's court to declare the 2002 law unconstitutional because it was more restrictive than the membership criteria set forth in article 3 of the 1975 Constitution.

The Cherokee Nation Judicial Appeals Tribunal rendered a 2–1 decision in 2006, elaborated below, holding that the Freedmen were entitled to citizenship under the Tribe's constitution and that the Council's more restrictive membership criteria were improper and invalid. Despite this impressive ruling, the Cherokee Nation subsequently held a nation-wide referendum vote in which a majority of the nation's electorate agreed that the Constitution should be amended to include a blood requirement for Cherokee citizenship. With this action, the Cherokee Nation terminated the Freedmen's citizenship.

The Freedmen subsequently filed a class-action lawsuit that fueled several years of legal battles. Finally, in 2017 the US District Court for the District of Columbia ruled in *The Cherokee Nation v. Nash* that, "the Cherokee Nation can continue to define itself as it sees fit but must do so equally and evenhandedly with respect to native Cherokees and the descendants of Cherokee freedmen….In accordance with Article 9 of the 1866 Treaty, the Cherokee Freedmen have a present right to citizenship in the Cherokee Nation that is coextensive with the rights of native Cherokees."

The Cherokee Nation indicated its acceptance of this decision that kept the terms of the treaty intact. The question of Freedmen citizenship in the Cherokee Nation was thus finally settled.

Opinion by Stacy L. Leeds

Petitioner Lucy Allen is a descendant of individuals listed on the Dawes Commission Rolls as "Cherokee Freedmen." To become a tribal member under the current legislation, she must prove she is "Cherokee by blood." She asks this Court to declare 11 C.N.C.A. Sec. 12 unconstitutional because it is more restrictive than the membership criteria set forth in Article III of the 1975 Constitution....

The Cherokee citizenry has the ultimate authority to define tribal citizenship. When they adopted the 1975 Constitution, they did not limit membership to people who possess Cherokee blood. Instead, they extended membership to all the people who were "citizens" of the Cherokee Nation as listed on the Dawes Commission Rolls.

The Constitution could be amended to require that all tribal members possess Cherokee blood. The people could also choose to set a minimum Cherokee blood quantum. However, if the Cherokee people wish to limit tribal citizenship, and such limitation would terminate the pre-existing citizenship of even one Cherokee citizen, then it must be done in the open. It cannot be accomplished through silence.

The Council lacks the power to redefine tribal membership absent a constitutional amendment. The Council is empowered to enact enrollment procedures, but those laws must be consistent with the 1975 Constitution. The current legislation is contrary to the plain language of the 1975 Constitution.

The Cherokee Nation is a Sovereign. The Cherokee Nation is much more than just a group of families with a common ancestry. For almost 150 years, the Cherokee Nation has included not only citizens that are Cherokee by blood, but also citizens who have origins in other Indian nations and/or African and/or European ancestry. Many of these citizens are mixed race and a small minority of these citizens possess no Cherokee blood at all.

People will always disagree on who is culturally Cherokee and who possess enough Cherokee blood to be "racially" Indian. It is not the role of this Court to engage in these political or social debates. This Court must interpret the law as it is plainly written in our Constitution....

It has been argued that the Cherokee Freedmen were forced on the Cherokee Nation by the federal government and that the Cherokee Nation never voluntarily accepted the Freedmen as citizens. This is simply not the case.

In the Treaty of 1866, the Cherokee Nation agreed to extend citizenship to Freedmen and agreed to give them the same rights as "native" citizens. Although this treaty was signed at the end of the Civil War, when the Cherokee Nation was in a weaker bargaining position, it is nonetheless an agreement between two sovereign nations.

When the Cherokee Nation enters into treaties with other nations, we expect the other sovereign to live up to the promises they make. It is rightly expected that we will also keep the promises we make....

This case poses an interesting question of whether the Cherokee Nation, like other sovereigns, has the internal power to unilaterally abrogate treaties. This Court sees no reason why the Cherokee Nation must be bound by a treaty until the end of time, particularly when that treaty has been broken by the other sovereign.

However, if the Cherokee Nation is going to make a decision not to abide by a previous treaty provision, it must do so by clear actions which are consistent with the Cherokee Nation Constitution. A treaty provision cannot be set aside by mere implication....

Leach v. Tribal Election Commission and *McClain v. Cherokee Nation Election Commission* require a legislative act be held unconstitutional if it adds new requirements to a constitutional provision. 11 C.N.C.A. Sec. 12 adds a "by blood" requirement that simply does not exist in Article III [of the Constitution].

11 C.N.C.A. Sec. 12 is hereby deemed unconstitutional. This Court's decision in *Riggs v. Ummerteske* is hereby reversed.

It is so ordered this 7th day of March, 2006.

Justice Stacy L. Leeds....

Sources:

Allen v. Cherokee Nation Tribal Council, Judicial Appeals Tribunal of the Cherokee Nation, JAT–04–09 (2006).

Inniss, Lolita Buckner. "Cherokee Freedmen and the Color of Belonging." *Columbia Journal of Race and Law* 5, no. 2 (2015): 100–118.

88

The Impeachment of Oglala Lakota President Cecilia Fire Thunder (2006)

Oglala Sioux Tribal President Cecilia Fire Thunder garnered national attention when, in response to South Dakota's proposed statewide ban on abortions, she vowed to use the Tribe's sovereign authority to protect women's health and rights on Lakota lands.

In March 2006, in a blatantly political attempt to challenge the 1973 Supreme Court ruling known as *Roe v. Wade*, South Dakota Governor Mike Rounds signed into law House Bill 1215, the nation's most restrictive ban on abortions, which provided no exceptions for rape or incest, and only limited protection for a woman's life. Fire Thunder responded by declaring the Lakota would provide constitutionally protected abortion services and access to reproductive health care by creating a new, reservation-based clinic. Her defiant action boldly challenged the state's jurisdiction both over Indian lands and women's bodies. She noted that in Lakota history, "you didn't have people passing laws to control a woman's body."

Fire Thunder, the Tribe's first female president, was a former nurse who had spent years advocating for Native health. In Pine Ridge, she worked as a community organizer against domestic violence. There, she saw firsthand the disproportionate rates of sexual violence experienced by Native women. Though the media focused on abortion, Fire Thunder contended the issue was about health and well-being. She said the clinic would also serve as a haven for victims of sexual assault, as well as a venue for educating everyone about reproductive health, planned parenting, and contraception.

This strong assertion of Tribal sovereignty was met with varied responses. Indeed, there were many Native and non-Native people like her who supported the building of a clinic at Pine Ridge. In November 2006, South Dakota citizens rejected the state abortion ban at a voter referendum, with citizens in the two counties that make up the Pine Ridge Reservation voting against the ban by a substantial majority.

However, a more conservative Tribal faction, led by Fire Thunder's political opponents, supported the state of South Dakota. Fire Thunder had already faced threats of removal by the Tribal Council. The clinic controversy offered her critics another powerful line of attack. Some argued abortion services conflicted with traditional Lakota values. Others were simply unhappy that a woman was leading the people. Those who felt she had overstepped her position as president pointed out that she had solicited funds on behalf of the Tribe for building the clinic without first obtaining a sanction by the Council. On May 30, 2006, the Tribal Council officially banned abortions on the Pine Ridge Indian Reservation. They impeached Fire Thunder on June 29, 2006.

In undertaking these actions and utilizing these patriarchal rationales, the Tribal Council actually chose to limit their own sovereignty—suppressing their own powers and compromising the quality of health care on the reservation—in favor of state government interests. As a result, the opportunity to expand and strengthen sovereignty was diminished along with the chance to improve the health and well-being of Tribal citizens.

What follows are three documents: a newspaper article that provides an overview of this complex and troublesome episode, the Tribal Council's Motion to formally "suspend" Fire Thunder on May 30 that specifies the long list of allegations made against her, and finally the Council's unanimous Ordinance prohibiting the construction of any abortion clinic on Lakota lands, replete with restrictions levied on Fire Thunder.

Tribal Leader Ousted over Abortion Clinic

Pine Ridge, S.D.—The first woman ever elected to the top leadership position of the Oglala Sioux Tribe found her two-year term shortened by what she contends was an illegal impeachment proceeding by the tribal council.

Former Oglala Sioux Tribal President Cecelia Fire Thunder worked through the pressure of three impeachment attempts, the third of which was successful. She says that she was removed from office for standing up for her principles.

Fire Thunder was impeached because she proposed a women's health clinic for the Pine Ridge Reservation. The clinic idea came about when she acted in opposition to the statewide abortion ban, the most stringent in the nation, which became law earlier this year and does not include exemptions for incest, rape or the health of the mother.

Earlier attempts to remove her centered on a loan she negotiated with a sister tribe, the Shakopee Mdewakanton Dakota Community. The $38 million low-interest loan helped to pay an immediate debt and construct a new hotel and casino. She was criticized for mortgaging land and thereby putting the tribe into more debt; also, some people speculated that part of the $38 million went into many of the tribal officials' pockets—none of which was accurate, Fire Thunder has contended. A short-term debt was paid, and the new casino/hotel complex will be completed in early 2007.

Fire Thunder, under fire for most of her time in office, points out her many accomplishments in office, which was shortened by five months. A loan with the federal Farmers Home Administration was renegotiated in Congress to reduce the principal, which left an additional $500,000 a year for the tribe to pay off other debt. A complete reconciliation of tribal finances was ordered and fiscal accountability was attempted.

The OST Head Start program was in jeopardy of closure, and under Fire Thunder's administration the program was transferred to the Oglala Lakota College for administration. The program is now running successfully.

She blames the tribal council for her problems while in office and the fact that there is no separation of powers on Pine Ridge. During Fire Thunder's impeachment hearing, the council violated numerous tribal constitutional requirements and federal law by not providing proper due process.

On appeal, she was returned to office by the chief tribal judge, only to be removed again a few hours later when the judge rescinded her first order. Chief Judge Lisa Adams admitted to being pressured by the tribal council to change her order that returned Fire Thunder to office. "We know that goes on; it is a common practice to influence a judge," Fire Thunder said.

Fire Thunder said she would fight her removal from office in tribal court; however, at the urging of other tribal leaders and friends, she instead opted to seek re-election. She finished third in the primary election, which left her out of the general election. But at the last minute, front-runner President Alex White Plume was removed from the ballot and Fire Thunder was added. She lost the election to John Yellow Bird Steele.

Today, Fire Thunder proposes to work with individuals and groups on Pine Ridge to rewrite the constitution and the bylaws that govern elections and pro-cedures. "I am asking people to ask for a separation of powers. The council interferes with the court. We must ask for accountability," she said.

Fire Thunder was a nationally known figure before she was elected to lead the Oglala Sioux Tribe, and after her removal she is in as much or more demand as a speaker and consultant. She is now working tirelessly to turn around the effects of colonization in Indian country and to retain a true traditional culture to the OST and to other nations.

Fire Thunder continues to promote health care for women, and the clinic she proposed is moving forward with a board of directors in charge. The idea of the clinic was the final straw for many on the tribal council, and the abortion issue provided a new motive to remove her.

Fire Thunder's position on women's health, rape, incest and abortion is her own, and not the position of the OST. She elevated the debate to a national level, not as president of the OST, but as a person who just happened to be president.

She, like many others in South Dakota, was angry at the state Legislature for passing a bill that would ban abortion in all cases except when necessary to save the woman's life. Fire Thunder publicly joined a list of concerned state residents who opposed that legislation. Many people say her position was vindicated, and that she was right, when the voters of South Dakota rejected the ban as written. "As a female, it was my responsibility to bring this awareness using the power of my office," she said.

In the beginning of the clinic debate, Fire Thunder took the stance that it will be built to provide information to women and men, and to provide a comfortable and safe atmosphere for women to talk about and receive treatment on reproductive health. "I keep thinking about the times I've worked with women who never had a choice," Fire Thunder said. A registered nurse who worked in women's health in California, she also worked briefly at an abortion clinic there.

Working toward a healthy Indian country is on Fire Thunder's to-do list, which includes changing attitudes and removing the effects of hundreds of years of outside influences. She will continue her 20 years of work to understand and cure the effects of colonization in Indian country. "Colonization is the taking away of identities, it's the breaking away of the rules to live by as a people, and that's what colonization did," she said.

Paramount to her future work will be bringing accountability to the tribal government on Pine Ridge. Her claim is that she was ousted illegally and by a tribal council that ignored the constitution of the United States, the constitution of the Oglala Sioux Tribe and of the tribe's ordinances and resolutions when she was removed from office; she has repeatedly stated that she doesn't want any other elected official to be subjected to that type of treatment.

Summary of the Oglala Sioux Tribal Council Special Session— May 30, 2006

Motion No. 06–86:

Motion made by Garfield Steele, seconded by Lyle Jack to suspend the president of the Oglala Sioux Tribe, Cecelia Fire Thunder, without pay, and that a hearing be set up within (20) twenty days from today, for the following: 1) She invited federal and state law onto our sovereign reservation by challenging the new state abortion law, to begin her own abortion clinic, under the auspicious (*sic*) of the Oglala Sioux Tribe; 2) For using the OST e-mail, news media and post office box to solicit funds for her own endeavors; 3) For violating the OST Code; 4) For violating natural laws, cultural, traditional and spiritual laws; 5) For misrepresenting, to the world, that the Oglala Sioux Tribe is in support of abortion and this clinic; and 6) For violating the OST Constitution and by-laws, OST procurement ordinance, and OST administrative operating procedures; and to also include the following agreed-upon amendments, that she will not conduct any type of business that has to do with the Oglala Sioux Tribe, in the name of the Oglala Sioux Tribe, everything is to cease on and off the reservation, no representation and she will not go to the radio and/or media to state her case; also that it be known and sent out that the Oglala Sioux Tribe will no longer accept any contributions, sent for the abortion clinic, and all previous donations are to be sent back to the donors; and that she will not travel on behalf of the Oglala Sioux Tribe.

Roll Call Vote: Motion Carried (14) Yes, (1) No, and (2) Not Voting.

Ordinance of the Oglala Sioux Tribal Council of the Oglala Sioux Tribe: Ordinance No. 06–11

Ordinance of the Oglala Sioux Tribal Council prohibiting any healthcare facility located within the exterior boundaries of the Pine Ridge Indian Reservation as defined under Article 1 of the Oglala Sioux Tribe Constitution from performing an abortion irrespective of whether the health of the expecting mother is at risk or whether the unborn child is conceived through rape or incest.

Whereas, the Oglala Sioux Tribe has adopted its Constitution and by-laws by referendum vote on December 10, 1935, in accordance with Section 16 of the Indian Reorganization act of 1934 ... and under Article IV of the Constitution of the Oglala Sioux Tribal Council is the governing body of the Pine Ridge Indian Reservation, and

Whereas, the Oglala Sioux tribal Council is empowered pursuant to Article IV Sec. 1 (k) of the Oglala Sioux Tribe Constitution and by-laws "to promulgate and enforce ordinances governing the conduct of persons on the Pine Ridge Reservation," and

Whereas, the Oglala Sioux tribal Council is empowered pursuant to Article IV Sec. 1 (q) of the Oglala Sioux tribe Constitution and by-laws "to regulate the domestic relations of members of the tribe," and

Whereas, under Chapter 5 Sec. 1.05 of the Oglala Sioux Tribe Law and Order Code "a child conceived, but not born, is to be deemed an existing person so far as may be necessary for its interests and welfare to be protected event of its subsequent birth," now

Therefore be it ordained, that the Oglala Tribal Council prohibits any healthcare facility (i.e., health facility owned by tribal, state, or the federal government, a nonprofit organization, or a private organization) located within the exterior boundaries of the Pine Ridge Indian Reservation as defied under Article 1 of the Oglala Sioux Tribe Constitution from performing an abortion irrespective of whether the health of the expecting mother is at risk or whether the unborn child is conceived of through rape or incest, and

Be it further ordained, that no person may knowingly administer to, prescribe for, or procure for, or sell to any pregnant woman any medicine, drug, or other substance with the specific intent of causing or abetting the termination of the life of an unborn child and that no person may knowingly use or employee any instrument or procedure upon a pregnant woman with the specific intent of causing or abetting the termination of the life of an unborn human being, and

Be it further ordained, that the medical treatment provided to the mother by a licensed health care physician that results in the accidental or unintentional injury or death to the unborn child shall not be considered an abortion under this Ordinance, and

Be it further ordained, that any elected official of the Oglala Sioux Tribe who received or receives any funds for health facility to perform an abortion on the Pine Ridge Indian Reservation shall immediately return all funds to the sender, and
CERTIFICATION
I, as undersigned Secretary of the Oglala Sioux Tribal Council of the Oglala Sioux Tribe hereby certify that this Ordinance was adopted by the vote of 16 for; 0 Against; 0 Abstain; 0 Not Voting during a special session held on the 30th day of May 2006.
Rhonda J. Two Eagle, Secretary Oglala Sioux Tribe
Attest: Alex White Plume, Vice-President Oglala Sioux Tribe

Source:

Melmer, David. "Tribal Leader Ousted over Abortion Clinic." *Indian Country Today* (2006).
Oglala Sioux Tribal Council Motion and Ordinance in Author's Possession.

89 *United League of Indigenous Nations Treaty (2007)*

Native nations in the US were required by specific treaty provisions agreed upon during the major treaty era (1778–1868) to surrender the power to negotiate treaties with foreign nations. However, there are no such restrictions on their right to forge diplomatic accords with other Native nations. Thus, as Indigenous peoples began to flex their diplomatic muscles via memoranda of agreements, sovereignty accords, and the like, it made good sense for them to renew the process of negotiating international treaties with other Indigenous nations.

The first contemporary example of this type of accord was the United League of Indigenous Nations Treaty (ULIN), signed by representatives from eleven Native nations from the United States, several First Nations from Canada, the Maori of New Zealand, and the Ngawindjeri people from Australia. The ULIN was developed by the National Congress of American Indians' Special Committee on Indigenous Nation Relationships after meetings with the leaders of Native peoples in the other countries represented.

The ULIN creates a global political, cultural, and economic alliance between the parties so they will be better prepared to deal with issues like trade and commerce, cultural property, climate change, and human rights.

United League of Indigenous Nations Treaty

Preamble

We, the signatory Indigenous Nations and Peoples, hereby pledge mutual recognition of our inherent rights and power to govern ourselves and our ancestral homelands and traditional territories. Each signatory nation, having provided evidence that their respective governing body has taken action in accordance with their own custom, law and or tradition to knowingly agree to and adopt the terms of this treaty, hereby establish the political, social, cultural and economic relations contemplated herein.

Principles

Recognizing each other as self-governing Indigenous Nations, we subscribe to the following principles:

1. The Creator has made us part of, and inseparable from, the natural world around us. This truth binds us together and gives rise to a shared commitment to care for, conserve, and protect the land, air, water and animal life within our usual, customary and traditional territories.
2. Our inherent customary rights to self-governance and self-determination have existed since time immemorial, have been bestowed by the Creator and are defined in accordance with our own laws, values, customs and mores.
3. Political, social, cultural and economic relationships between our Indigenous Nations have existed since time immemorial and our right to continue such relationships are inseparable from our inherent Indigenous rights of nationhood. Indigenous Peoples have the right of self-determination and, by virtue of that right, our Peoples freely determine our political status and freely pursue our social, cultural and economic development.
4. No other political jurisdiction, including nation states and their governmental agencies or subdivisions, possess governmental power over any of our Indigenous nations, our people and our usual, customary and traditional territories.
5. Our inherent, aboriginal control and enjoyment of our territories includes our collective rights over the environment consisting of the air, lands, inland waters, oceans, seas, sea ice, flora, fauna and all other surface and sub-surface resources.
6. Our indigenous rights include all traditional and ecological knowledge derived from our relationship with our lands, air and waters from time immemorial, the exercise of conservation practices, traditional ceremonies, medicinal and healing practices and all other expressions of art and culture.

Goals

This Treaty is for the purpose of achieving the following goals:

1. To establish supportive bonds among signatory Indigenous Nations in order to secure, recover, and promote, through political, social, cultural and economic unity, the rights of all our peoples, the protection and recovery of our homelands and for the well-being of all our future generations.

2. To establish a foundation for the exercise of contemporary Indigenous nation sovereignty, without regard to existing or future international political boundaries of non-Indigenous nations, for the following purposes: (a) protecting our cultural properties, including but not limited to sacred songs, signs and symbols, traditional ecological knowledge and other forms of cultural heritage rights by collectively affirming the principle that our own Indigenous lands and customs regarding our cultural properties are prior and paramount to the application of any other sovereign's laws or jurisdiction including international bodies and agencies, (b) protecting our Indigenous lands, air and waters from environmental destruction through exercising our rights of political representation as Indigenous nations before all national and international bodies that have been charged, through international treaties, agreements and conventions, with environmental protection responsibilities, (c) engaging in mutually beneficial trade and commerce between Indigenous nations and the economic enterprises owned and operated collectively by Indigenous peoples and by individual citizens of our Indigenous nations, and, (d) preserving and protecting the human rights of our Indigenous people from such violations as involuntary servitude, human trafficking, or any other forms of oppression.

3. To develop an effective and meaningful process to promote communication and cooperation among the Indigenous Nations on all other common issues, concerns, pursuits, and initiatives.

4. To ensure that scholarly exchanges and joint study on strategies of self-determination are undertaken by Indigenous scholars.

Mutual Covenants

We, the signatory Indigenous Nations, are committed to providing the following mutual aid and assistance, to the best of our ability and in accordance with our own prior and paramount Indigenous laws, customs and traditions:

1. Exchanging economic, legal, political, traditional and technical knowledge regarding the protection of Indigenous cultural properties.

2. Collaborating on research on environmental issues that impact Indigenous homelands, including baseline studies and socio-economic assessments

that consider the cultural, social and sustainable uses of Indigenous Peoples' territories and resources.

3. Participating in trade and commerce missions to lay a foundation for business relations and the development of an international, integrated Indigenous economy and;

Each signatory Indigenous Nation shall:

1. Appoint a coordinator or responsible official for Treaty matters;
2. Identify ad establish an inter-Nation coordination office and communication network to assist in assembling data, information, knowledge and research needed to effectively address substantial issues of common concern;
3. Coordinate statements of policy and information on Treaty matters, especially information to be disseminated to the media;
4. Participate in periodic reviews and strategy planning sessions as needed.

Effective Date

The effective date of this Treaty is August 1, 2007.

Ratification

Following the effective date of this Treaty, any other Indigenous Nation may ratify this Treaty at a meeting of the United League of Indigenous Nations. Ratifying Indigenous Nations may attach explanations or clarifications expressing their respective cultural understandings associated with the provisions of the Treaty through a Statement of Understandings which must be consistent with the spirit and intent of the Treaty.

Source:

www.indigenousnationstreaty.org.

90

Statement by Chief Judge Joseph Thomas Flies-Away (Hualapai): Tribal Courts and the Administration of Justice in Indian Country (2008)

One of the first strategies used by the federal government in the late 1800s to deny Native sovereignty and self-determination was the imposition of the Western legal paradigm and its institutions over tribal lands, peoples, and cultures. Not until the

1934 Indian Reorganization Act did the United States begin to relent in its efforts to deny the expression and practice of Native legal and customary law. Since the 1930s, as Tribal governments have strengthened and stabilized, courts have been established in about 350 Native communities.

In some respects, Tribal courts are similar to local, state, and federal courts, but in others they are profoundly different. To a certain degree, many operate in a theocratic fashion, such that there is little or no separation between spiritual and state values because custom and tradition remain at the heart of the administration of justice. Also, Tribal courts and their personnel have had severe limitations placed upon them by federal decrees that constrain the degree of punishment they can mete out, as well as over whom—Native or non-native—the court can wield jurisdiction.

Hualapai Chief Judge Joseph Thomas Flies-Away here addresses these and other concerns, and argues that tribal courts require more federal resources in order to cope with the rise of crime in Indian Country. He supports his contention with robust statistics. From 2004 to 2007, the US government, which has criminal jurisdiction over fourteen major crimes, "declined to prosecute an average of 62% of reservation crimes." Within that broad figure, "78 percent of adult and child sex crimes and 50 percent of reservation homicides went unpunished in the federal system" (Statement of Sen. Byron L. Dorgan, Chairman of the Committee of Indian Affairs).

Prepared Statement of Hon. Joseph Thomas Flies-Away, Chief Judge, Hualapai Tribe

Mr. Chairperson, Madame Vice Chairperson and Members of the Committee, Kam yuu! I am honored to be invited to testify before the Senate Committee on Indian Affairs on Tribal Court Systems and the proposed Tribal Law and Order Act of 2008. Unfortunately, the timeframe for preparation did not give me the ability to fully articulate all of the prevalent issues that come to mind though I will attempt to address some of the most important issues as I and our Tribal Council sees them. Below I describe a few of these issues and comment briefly on specific sections of the Act.

First however, let me briefly introduce myself to you. I am a Hualapai Tribal Member and the Chief Judge of the Hualapai Judiciary. I have served as a Tribal Council Member and Planner for my Tribe in recent years. I have also served as a judge for the past 12 years and in total sat in 9 tribal courts throughout Indian Country and serve currently as a pro tem judge, visiting judge, and appellate justice for various tribal courts as well as consult with tribes when I have time. I have been privileged to work with many other tribal courts throughout the country, including native villages of Alaska, to help develop their judicial systems and infrastructures, perform evaluations, draft and review codes, and provide other technical assistance to Courts and tribal government. I have also taught at the university level in Indigenous Community & Nation Building and Federal Indian Law. In my travels and efforts throughout Indian Country I see a strong commitment and dedication from tribes/villages to continue to rebuild their nations taking the best of their past and culture and mingling with the advantages and innovations of the present. I see indigenous peoples take what little resources they may have and make the best of it even though the community and nation building journey is difficult and frustrating much, if not all the time.

Below is a short description of the topics that I believe are important for the Committee to hear and take into consideration in your legislating efforts. Unfortunately, as the time given to each witness for verbal testimony is only five (5) minutes, my comments to the Committee will be limited at that proceeding. I will do my best to articulate what I think is most important in the little time that I have. I imagine that there may be questions for the witnesses by the Senators on the Committee. With your questions I hope I will be able to stress other areas that require federal intervention and assistance that I do not mention in my direct comments and in this written testimony.

As requested by Senator Dorgan the primary purpose for my testimony is to discuss Tribal Courts in general and comment on the proposed Tribal Law and Order Act of 2008. Below I highlight various issues regarding tribal courts that I think are relevant, which I have written about previously and discuss with tribal folks at every opportunity. I am sure you will hear similar remarks from the other witnesses who I am honored to be sitting before you today.

Of course what our tribal leaders wanted me to emphasize up front is the need for more funding for tribal courts and the areas that support its work. Funds are required so that the need for culturally accordant conflict resolution for our Tribe and others can be accomplished more thoroughly and for benefit of those persons under our jurisdiction. The other issue my Council directed me to emphasize is the need for detention and rehabilitation resources that allow the Court to address the criminal and other negative behavior that hampers our Tribe's progress.

My final statements here regard the proposed Tribal Law and Order Act of 2008. Below I have highlighted a few sections in the Bill that our Tribe and I both have questions and/or concerns.

I will begin with general comments about Tribal Systems:

Tribal Court System (Tribal Justice System): Critical Component of Tribal Government

Tribal Courts and Tribal Court systems are critical components of tribal government. All governments must provide a means for conflict resolution for its polity, its people. Without such a forum disputes and disagreements of all sorts would negate the ability of the people to gather, ground, and grow (i.e. build and rebuild communities and nations). Prior to Anglo intervention in the Americas indigenous peoples practiced various forms of conflict and dispute resolution. While the practices may not have resembled those of Western Culture the ability of tribal members to participate in debate and defend their points of view was not just allowed, but expected (i.e. due process). Unfortunately, because tribal ways did not resemble European practices, they were thought to be savage, backward, and uncivilized. Suffice it to say the forums for indigenous people worked for native folks then as much as the methods worked for other peoples around the world.

Tribal Courts/Systems currently are the tribal forums that attempt to resolve various controversy and conflict that Tribal peoples, our governments, and other persons face. Many systems rely on written law (constitutions and codes) to direct the settlement of disputes and conflicts. Others apply customary processes, procedures, and laws to address controversy. In all the tribes/villages that I have visited thus far their Tribal Court systems were thought to be critical to the success of their governmental function to serve the needs of the people. Or, if the systems were in development tribal staff and officials would state that they wanted their Court System to provide a fundamental service that would benefit the community/nation as a whole. As are many nations around the world, each tribal or village government is at a different period of development of a justice system. Some are quite advanced, while others are just beginning to develop a judicial system under the conditions and circumstances they may face in their part of the United States. Despite the various places these tribes may be in their development journey, they each need the resources, support, and encouragement to continue to develop the best practice judicial system they can to bolster their overall governing system.

Requires the Cooperation & Collaboration of Various Sectors
(Departments and Programs) of Tribal Government
As a judicial system is an important and critical part of tribal government, it cannot function all alone and unto itself. A system to resolve conflict and dispute for any polity must include or collaborate with a number of various agencies, programs, and people of their government. A true full complement of a judicial system, though to many it is not as clear, does not only consist of a judge, clerk, probation officer, jury members, advocates, and bailiff. To fully move towards resolution or conciliation of criminal, civil, juvenile, family, and other issues brought to Court there are many others who contribute to a beneficial end; to peace.

This is not to say that Separation of Powers is not an important and necessary characteristic of good government. Separation of Power is essential to keep various branches of government from interfering with each other's work. Nevertheless, there is considerable contribution and cooperation that must exist between the branches or departments that must be present in order for resolution/concord to be reached. Individual court users, practitioners, and staff including the citizenry of a nation must be trained and provided insight of how this separation works and how parts of government must also work together.

Expression and Exercise of Tribal Sovereignty

The existence and administration of a Tribal Court-Judicial Branch is an expression and exercise of Tribal Sovereignty. As mentioned above the provision of conflict and dispute resolution is an important part of a government. Because conflict resolution is a necessary service that the Tribe must provide, the provision of such a service demonstrates the government's sovereign responsibility to address and fix its own problems, controversy, and other conflict. As a tribal court confronts conflict and listens to the parties regarding the issues raised it must develop an understanding and ruling of the law, wholly applicable to that matter and to that sovereign. The creation and development of law is unique to that nation. This practice contributes to the individuality and sovereignty of that nation. As a tribal court continues to resolve conflict, develop standards and precedent for litigants to apply, the more the Tribe is expressing and exercising its sovereignty.

Contributes to Economic Possibility

Tribal Courts further support an environment of impartiality and fair play. In doing so individuals, corporations, and others believe they can safely engage in commerce and business with the Tribe and tribal members with the assurance that wrong doing can be challenged, addressed, and corrected. Economic development and possibility become more achievable when there is a forum for legitimate legal issues to be brought and remedies sought. Whether the matter concerns a promise/contract issue of a small amount of money between tribal members or a multi-million dollar claim between a corporation and vendor, Tribal Courts can provide a competent and transparent forum for resolution.

Many tribes, however, are still developing Courts where business matters can be brought. Outside business entities are weary of tribal law and processes, which may not resemble a U.C.C. or other commercial code. Over time, however, with greater resources and further development, tribal courts will provide the necessary components and legal procedures as does any state or federal court hearing such cases. Hopefully, however, Tribes will not adopt other jurisdictions' laws full sail without assuring its efficacy for their nation. Tribes who have developed in this area can be supportive and helpful to others in their development.

Manifestation of Tribal Culture (i.e. culturally accordant conflict resolution/ peace making)

Tribal judicial systems can be fashioned into culturally accordant tribal institutions that reflect the culture and history of the tribal people it serves. Tribal Courts over the years have been grappling with the nature of the adversarial system that was more or less imposed upon them.

While some tribes find the adversarial system adequate and useful, other tribes desire to develop courts that reflect more of a restorative nature that tribal people traditionally practiced. Unfortunately, because the adversarial system is deeply ingrained in tribal court personnel, as that is what they were taught, and "outsiders" bring to the Court, it is difficult for some to reclaim the traditional method and move forward with it. Some tribes, however, have been successful at this development and produced peacemaking processes or other traditional means of bringing people to peace, and the practices are greatly appreciated by their people as they feel familiar and are comfortable with it. Tribes must be allowed to develop these processes, perhaps allow for various tracks for court users to choose from so that the greatest appreciation can be solicited.

Uphold and Protect Constitutional Rights (including due process)
Tribal Courts serve to uphold and defend the rights of all persons, not just members, who are within its jurisdiction. Individual rights as defined in tribal constitutions, codes, and federal statutes such as the Indian Civil Rights Act are best adjudicated in the Tribal forum where the tribal court judge can articulate what the law means in that jurisdiction. This is even more important when the tribal judge is a member of the tribe who can also apply or be open to applying tribal custom and tradition.

Tribes throughout the United States are actively pursuing or considering revising and amending their constitutions to articulate a more tribal perspective, rather than applying the constitutions that were basically written for them or modeled after BIA documents. What may be at issue as tribal courts continue to develop and revise their constitutions, are conflicts between rights as articulated in their constitutions and tribal government (and their subordinate entities) claims to sovereign immunity? If a tribal government does not afford due process to a person under their jurisdiction, and/or change the law on an individual after the matter was brought to Court, when the Constitution articulates various rights, does sovereign immunity completely shield the Tribe from what might be illegal or unconstitutional conduct? These claims will be brought before tribal courts and have been slowing reaching the courts of late, and outcomes may be telling as to the future of tribal sovereignty.

Requires Adequate Funding & Resources (facilities & program support)
All Tribal Courts, including the Hualapai Tribal Court, require the funding to fully meet the judicial needs of their constituents. While some tribes, such as Hualapai, have been able to put some of their own general funds into Court development, the amount is not enough to fully satisfy the need to support the growth the Tribe has had over the years. Hualapai, and I am sure others, require adequate facilities and space to perform its function and purpose for our people. Many tribal courts are housed in older buildings and required to hear cases in makeshift court rooms while at the same time endeavoring to demand the respect of Court users and others who come to Court. Offices are small and hearings sometimes must be held in them as there may be only be one court room. Funding issues, of course, are always an issue for tribal governments, but it appears that given judicial services is a primary and critical function of government that federal funding would rise to the level of support that such a need requires.

Necessitates Consistent Availability of Detention & Rehabilitation Resources

Lastly, more funds are required for both detention and rehabilitation resources. The Hualapai Tribe has put some of its own funding into building a state of the art juvenile detention facility only to have it sitting unused for almost a year. The BIA is unable to provide the funding for staffing and operating the facility and the Tribe cannot assume the responsibility alone. The Tribe initially intended to provide resources in the facility to address rehabilitation issues, however, again BIA funds do not serve this function and IHS is also unable to assist in the goals the Tribe set out to accomplish. Over time, perhaps, after many years of economic development for us and others, the Tribe(s) may be able to cover various costs for this operation, however, at this very moment, the need is huge for our young people to be not only disciplined but provided the healing services they need to someday be positive contributors to our tribal society.

Other

There is a Federal Law that prevents BIA & IHS employees from being brought to Tribal Court via a subpoena as well as denies the Court the ability to issue Order to Show Cause orders to BIA detention staff for failure to provide adequate detention services (see below).

Tribal Law and Order Act of 2008
Sec. 303—Access to National Criminal Information Databases

While criminal data collection is important in order to analyze criminal behavior and trends, this act will allow tribal law enforcement officials to enter criminal data into a national data base, presumably regarding tribal members. One question is how will the criminal information be utilized by federal, state, and tribal jurisdictions? Will it be used to augment sentencing orders in each jurisdiction? Tribal leaders in the past have been wary of sharing criminal information as it is thought to infringe on tribal sovereignty. Do tribal leaders need to approve the sharing of information in a manner and form that they prefer or is the Federal Government to do so for them?

Sec. 304—Tribal Court Sentencing Authority

Section 304 of the Act provides for increased Tribal Court sentencing authority for one charge from 1 year/$5,000.00 to 3 years/$15,000.00. Though this provision to strengthen Tribal Court sentencing power is positive, capacity issues and short falls for most Tribal or BIA detention facilities must be addressed and remedied. Many Tribes simply do not have jails and rely on the BIA to provide detention services. The supply of bed space does not meet the demand, which creates an inconsistent detention system allowing for release of inmates for lack of space, medical ailments, and swapping of more dangerous inmates for lesser dangerous ones. The need for more detention funds (both facility construction and programmatic) is required. Not only must more detention facilities on tribal lands be constructed, Tribes must have resources to staff the jails and provide treatment (healing & restoration) to tribal inmates. Though the Act states the possibility of housing tribal inmates in Federal detention facilities, the preference for tribes may be to house their tribal and native community members in a tribal detention facility.

Sec. 603—Testimony by Federal Employees in Cases of Rape and Sexual Assault
Section 603 of the Act will allow federal employees in rape and sexual assault cases to testify in tribal court. The Hualapai Tribal Court has received two letters from both Bureau and IHS officials citing 45 C.F.R. Part 2, which states that federal employees are prohibited from giving testimony unless the appropriate Director approves. How does Section 603 mesh with 45 C.F.R. Part 2?

A Hualapai Tribal Court Order to show cause on BIA detention supervisor for failure to assure that a Defendant (father) was transported to a custody Hearing, upon proper notice to him in the detention facility, caused a U.S. Solicitor to threaten the arrest of any Tribal Judge who interferes with the federal officer's duties. The Tribal Court merely issued the OSC to the BIA Supervisor for failure to perform his trust responsibility to the Tribe by bringing the inmate to Court.

A Hualapai Tribal Court Order requesting the attendance of an IHS Community Health Nurse to a hearing to develop a service plan for a Child in Need of Care was denied as the Order needed to be approved by a senior official in the area. Again a letter to the Court citing 45 C.F.R. Part 2 was sent to the Court stating the Nurse cannot provide testimony to the Court. The hearing, however, was scheduled only to solicit the input of service providers, include the Community Health Nurse, to develop a plan to provide services to the Minor Child and family to meet his needs. The Nurse was not requested to provide testimony to prove innocence or guilt in any way.

If the Act is to promote cooperation between federal agencies and the Tribes, then this area must be reviewed so that the Tribal Court's request for federal assistance is honored and any trust responsibility honored.

Sources:

Austin, Raymond D. Navajo Courts and Navajo Common Law: A Tradition of Tribal Self- Governance. Minneapolis: University of Minnesota Press, 2009.

Deloria, Vine, Jr., and Clifford M. Lytle. American Indians, American Justice. Austin: University of Texas Press, 1983.

US Senate. "Tribal Courts and the Administration of Justice in Indian Country." Hearing Before the Committee on Indian Affairs. 110th Cong., 2nd Sess. Washington, DC: Government Printing Office, July 24, 2008.

91

Testimony of Brian Cladoosby (Swinomish), President of the Affiliated Tribes of Northwest Indians, on Economic and Social Issues Affecting Northwest Tribes (2010)

The year 2010 was an eventful one for Congress with regard to important legislation affecting Native peoples. Although many questions were discussed and addressed, two laws in particular received a great deal of fanfare: the Tribal Law and Order Act and Congress's approval of the *Cobell* claims settlement act, officially known as the Claims Resolution Act.

When Congress convened a hearing in August 2010 to address "economic and social issues affecting the Northwest Tribes," many Native voices were given an opportunity to be heard. Brian Cladoosby (Swinomish) was then chairman of his Nation, but he was also president of the fifty-seven-member Affiliated Tribes of Northwest Indians, a regional body organized in 1953. His testimony covered several topics that warranted attention.

———

Testimony of Brian Cladoosby, President, Affiliated Tribes of Northwest Indians

Good morning Chairman Dorgan and members of the Committee. My name is Brian Cladoosby, and my traditional name is Speepots. I am the President of the Affiliated Tribes of Northwest Indians (ATNI) and the Chairman of the Swinomish Indian Tribe. ATNI appreciates the opportunity to testify on the economic and social issues affecting Indian tribes in the Northwest.

Founded in 1953, ATNI represents 57 tribal governments from Oregon, Idaho, Washington, western Montana, Alaska, northern California, and Nevada. Today, I am proud to be able to highlight for the Committee some of the economic and social issues affecting Northwest Tribes. The Northwest Tribes are very diverse. The Northwest is home to Tribes with large reservations and natural resource based economies and others with very little, if any, land. Despite our ranging differences Northwest Tribes stand strong together under ATNI to face the challenges of ensuring our communities are healthy, safe and sustainable.

First, I would like to share some thoughts. We, as Northwest Tribes, are learning more as we progress. We have learned that distributing income from casinos is not the answer. Indeed, just as would be imagined for any other community, free, windfall money is more likely to reduce motivation, destroy self-esteem, and aggravates the long endured and reinforced symptoms of poverty than it is to solve them. We have learned that job creation alone is not the solution. People accustomed to living outdoors, to whom hunting and fishing remain among the most valued possible human endeavors aren't necessarily drawn to windowless, smoke filed rooms lit with flashing lights or corporate style offices.

Gaming has enabled many Northwest tribes to provide basic health care, education, and housing. We address many of those by-products of poverty with childcare, provide for law and justice, care for the elders, and drug and alcohol programs. We provide these social services not only to ourselves, but in many of the remote communities that are our homes. In many cases, we are the only providers of these services and make them available to our neighbors.

Increasingly, the Northwest Tribes have been leaders in assuming direct managing of our natural resources. According to Bureau of Indian Affairs statistics, the Northwest Tribes and their enterprises support 40,000 jobs and buy over a billion dollars a year in supplies and services, much of which supports our larger local communities. We deliver a full range of government services of a complexity unsurpassed in the U.S. except by the Federal Government. And we operate businesses of a size and scale on par with almost any private business. Yet we typically do so with the human resources of a small town. The largest Tribes in our region seldom exceed 10,000 in total population and smallest tribes go as low as 700 in population.

With these observations in mind, below are some issues, concerns, and opportunities that ATNI sees with respect to economic and social issues for its membership.

Expanding Self Determination and Self Governance opportunities is a key to the future of many ATNI Tribes. Many ATNI Tribes seek to continue to restore their resources so that they can once again be contributors to their spiritual, physical, and economic health. We ask that the Federal Government actively pursue with us our lead role under the directives of the Indian Self Determination Act (P.L. 93–638). This would include making the policy of self-determination a proactive element of the Congress and the Federal Government, not just a consequence of the Tribes' insistence.

Renewable Energy Development and Climate Change: ATNI member tribes are very interested in energy development because it is a key to economic development for many Northwest Tribes, many of which are impoverished and have unemployment rates that are much higher than other areas of the country. ATNI member tribes are exploring wind, biomass, solar, geothermal, and hydroelectric energy opportunities, among others. While some Tribes have experience in those areas, most do not and seek help in building expertise and knowledge. To this end, the ability of Northwest Tribes to obtain capacity building grants to allow them to create the expertise to diversify away from a reliance on casino gaming will be critical to ensuring that these projects progress and become successful. In addition, several ATNI member Tribes, such as my own Tribe, the Swinomish Tribe, have climate change policies and are concerned about the effects of climate change in ocean, rain and snowfall, and changes in fish and wildlife, and in our culture.

Streamlining the fee-to-trust process so lands reacquired by Tribes can become productive for them more quickly is also important to ATNI. This includes breaking down unnecessary barriers and expenses that the Bureau of Indian Affairs requires of Tribes to put even on-reservation land into trust status.

The enactment of a Carcieri "fix" to ensure that all federally recognized Tribes can avail themselves of the opportunity to have land taken into trust for economic development or other purposes is a critical issue for ATNI. Although opponents have attempted to make this a gaming issue, the case negatively affects Northwest Tribes at the most fundamental levels. For example, the uncertainty caused by the decision has indefinitely delayed a fee-to-trust application submitted by the Sauk-Suiattle Indian Tribe for 1.5 acres for a housing development. A number of other Tribes in the Northwest are potentially affected by the decision.

Trust reform is an area where ATNI has been a national leader for several years. ATNI's commitment to this issue is grounded in maintaining the integrity of the United States' trust responsibility that is, as you know, based upon the historical cession of millions of acres of ancestral lands by the tribes. In return for these lands, the United States government committed itself to protecting the tribes in the possession and occupancy of their remaining homelands. ATNI believes strongly that Congress should consider a comprehensive approach to trust management. ATNI and other tribal organizations spent significant time and energy in working with both this Committee in recent years on these issues, specifically developing Title III of the Indian Trust Reform Act of 2005 (introduced as H.R. 4322 in the 109th Congress) and transitioning the Office of the Special Trustee back to the Bureau of Indian Affairs. Looking ahead, we hope that the Committee will consider these views as it considers other bills and initiatives relating to administration of Indian trust assets.

Federal and state taxation of Indian land and property is another area of concern and interest to ATNI and its member tribes. For too long, Indian tribes have been at a disadvantage in the area of taxation. For example, Thurston County, in southern Washington, is attempting to impose personal property taxes on permanent buildings on tribal trust land on the Chehalis Tribe's Reservation. Under a joint venture, the Tribe and its minority-interest non-Indian business partner use the buildings to operate a $170-million hotel, convention center, and water park known as the Great Wolf Lodge. The Tribe has invested in upwards of $86 million of its own cash, credit and sweat equity in the Great Wolf Lodge project and the project is a sterling example of the benefits of non-gaming economic development to tribal and surrounding communities.

For more than 100 years, Indian lands and property have been tax exempt. Because there is no federal statute that expressly preempts property taxes in this context, however, the Chehalis Tribe has been forced to defend its rights through expensive and burdensome litigation. This problem is not confined to the Northwest. Renewable energy projects on Indian lands, which necessarily require non-Indian partners to be viable, have also been targeted by state and local governments in the Great Plains and the Southwest for personal property taxes.

The Committee can help Tribes address these issues through legislative reforms that will bring more substantial private investment and in turn economic opportunity to Indian Country. In this regard, ATNI encourages the Committee, together with the Senate Committee on Finance, to explore opportunities to clarify that (1) Tribal majority-owned businesses should be treated like other Tribal businesses and not taxed locally; and (2) improvements to Indian Trust Land should be treated like the underlying real property for state and local tax purposes. Given the potential benefits of these clarifications for renewable energy development in Indian country, ATNI suggests that they would be candidates for inclusion in the energy package that the Senate is expected to consider next month. Unless Congress clarifies existing law in this manner, Tribes will continue to face obstacles in moving away from casinos and into green energy, hospitality, and countless other areas of non-gaming economic development.

Housing is still far more substandard than for the rest of the country. An estimated 200,000 housing units are needed immediately in Indian Country and approximately 90,000 Native families are homeless or under-housed. Overcrowding on tribal lands is almost 15 percent, and 11 percent of Indian homes lack complete plumbing and kitchen facilities. Although Economic Development produces much needed jobs it is slower to improve the housing conditions of Native Americans. ATNI recognizes that without faster results to improving housing conditions tribes continue to maintain federal funding dependency. ATNI urges congress to maintain the levels of housing funding for budget year 2011.

Natural Resources have always been at the center of our cultures for the Pacific Northwest Tribes, a fact no less true today than when many of our tribes signed agreements with the U.S. government. These resources are essential for our spiritual, economic and cultural survival as Indian people. The tribes of the Pacific Northwest depend economically on healthy salmon, wildlife, forests as well as on optimal water and air quality. Habitat destruction, pollution, unregulated water withdrawals, poor land-use planning, and many other environmental issues today threaten to make meaningless our reserved rights. ATNI asks for adequate and efficient funding of federal reserved obligations through tribal natural resources management programs, projects, and agreements. Flat funding levels and inflation have stripped us of buying power, leaving us with real funding equal to that we received 30 years ago, despite the fact that our management responsibilities have grown exponentially. Areas in critical need of funds are water resources management, hatcheries, habitat restoration, timber and wildlife management. Our reserved rights are dependent on healthy natural resources, which in turn depend on a healthy environment. Healthy environments lead to healthy communities and healthy economies.

I appreciate the opportunity to provide this testimony before the Committee. At this time, I would be happy to answer any questions that the Committee may have.

Source:

US Senate. "Economic and Social Issues Affecting the Northwest Tribes." Hearing Before the Committee on Indian Affairs. 111th Cong., 2nd Sess. Washington, DC: August 12, 2010.

92 *Shirley v. Morgan (2010)*

The Navajo Nation has been at the forefront of executing innovative political, cultural, and legal changes that have served as models for many other Indigenous peoples. As the largest nation operating without a formal written constitution, the Navajo, by the first decade of the twenty-first century, constructed a unique, sophisticated three-branch government. They did so after enduring many years of internal political conflict that compelled the people and some of the Nation's leadership to consider ways to reincorporate more traditional values and structures of governance into their organic laws. But over the years, such changes often proved difficult to implement because the legislative and executive branches were less inclined than the Navajo judicial branch to accept that direction.

By the spring of 2010, tensions were extremely high between the three branches and across the Nation. In May of that year, the Navajo Nation's Supreme Court handed down two major decisions, *Nelson v. Shirley* and *Shirley v. Morgan*. Not unlike John Marshall's *Marbury v. Madison* (1803), the decisions firmly served to remind the Diné legislators, the president, and the entire Nation of the High Court's authority to interpret the Nation's laws, especially the Fundamental Law of 2002 that incorporated unwritten Diné customs and traditions into the nation's Tribal Code. They also reminded the Diné people that the people, not the elected government officials, were the true sovereigns.

In *Nelson*, the justices unanimously held that "the Navajo people have the inherent authority reserved to them to enact laws. The People's laws are superior to the statutory laws enacted by the Council, and the referendum/initiative processes are modern acknowledgments of this authority." The court went on to note that "while the Council may limit itself in creating laws, it cannot limit the Diné when they are attempting to address the structure of their governing system."

The following case was a powerful companion to *Nelson* and issued on the same day. In *Shirley v. Morgan*, the court went even further in elaborating on the inherent authority within the people as articulated in their traditional origin accounts, values, and traditions. This decision had its origins in the Tribal Council's decision in October 2009 to strip President Joe Shirley of power by placing him on administrative leave over allegations of ethical and criminal wrongdoing in several business transactions. Shirley filed for relief in the District Court in December, asserting that the council's action was flawed as it violated his rights, was an affront to the separation of powers doctrine, and denied his right to due process under statutory and fundamental law. The District Court ruled in Shirley's favor, declaring that the council had exceeded its legislative authority. The Speaker of the Council appealed the court's ruling to the Navajo Nation's Supreme Court. With tensions at an extremely high level between the three branches of government, the justices took the opportunity to dramatically and emphatically issue a bold and precedent-setting opinion that affirmed the power of judicial review, recast the separation of powers doctrine, clarified that the People were the superior sovereign, and reminded everyone in the Nation that the Fundamental Law was superior to statutory law.

In the ruling the justices embarked on a detailed and culturally based explanation of from whence the Diné understanding of participatory democracy arose. Acknowledging that it derived from neither US law nor the Navajo Nation Council, the justices declared that instead "it comes from a deeper, more profound system of governance," the Navajo People's traditional communal governance, rooted in the Diné Life Way.

Shirley v. Morgan (2010)

Joe Shirley, Jr., in his capacity as president of the Navajo Nation and individually, filed an action for an ex parte temporary restraining order and preliminary injunction against the Navajo Nation Council and Lawrence T. Morgan, in his capacity as Speaker and individually, in the Window Rock District Court, to enjoin enforcement of Navajo Nation Council resolution CO–41–09 placing him on administrative leave. The District Court ruled that Resolution . . . is null and void and, therefore unenforceable. We affirm the judgment invalidating Resolution CO–41–09 on different grounds. . . .

This appeal concerns the clash between the executive and legislative branches of our government. On October 26, 2009, the president, Joe Shirley, Jr., was placed on administrative leave by the Navajo Nation Council (Council) by enactment of an emergency legislation. The measure was based on an investigative report returned by two law firms into the president's role in two business dealings that has never been made public, nor shared with the president. President Shirley filed for emergency injunctive relief in the District Court on December 7, 2010, claiming that the legislation putting him on administrative leave is invalid as mandatory statutory enactment procedure was not followed . . . that it violates *Diné bi beenahaz'áanii* by disabling a *naat'áanii* chosen by the people from carrying out the responsibilities entrusted to him; that it violates separation of powers; that it violates his right to due process under statutory and fundamental law; and that irreparable harm has occurred and will continue to occur in the absence of the president. . . .

This appeal comes to us at a critical time of great disharmony between the branches of the Navajo Nation government that is evident to the Navajo people. The leadership of the branches have been in conflict over governmental reform, and unable to sit down with each other and talk things out for almost two years, with the executive and legislative branches each claiming interference with their inner operations and the very structure of their respective authority.

There is obviously a great difference between the branches as to what is the source of authority to govern on the Navajo Nation. The underlying difference is about whether the authority to govern comes from the Council or the people.

The Council has become so intransigent in its position that it now purports to have authority to enact a new statute that would reduce the discretion of our courts to question the sources and complexion of our laws and governmental authority....

We have said that the primary principle that informs this Court's interpretation of procedural due process is *K'é*, which fosters fairness through mutual respect, and requires that an individual is fully informed and provided an opportunity to speak....In any dispute between the Navajo Nation leadership that is brought before our courts, we will consider and apply *k'é* as the primary principle under *Diné bi beenahaz'áanii*, which is the Fundamental Law of the Navajo people. *K'é* is the high standard which the people hold our leadership in their enactments and exercise of powers during the period they hold office, in service of the Navajo people who have chosen them, and in dealings with each other.

As we begin examining the doctrines and principles applicable to this case, we state uncategorically that the courts will not become entangled in the political maneuvering that we and the people are now serving. The court will take its proper role—that of an independent decision-maker which has been summoned by the branches and the people to move this dispute forward and bring it to an end with a final resolution consistent with our teachings, values, symbols, and tradition....

Diné bi beenahaz'áanii as acknowledged by the Council teaches that our Diné leaders are to adhere to the values and principles of *Diné bi beenahza'áanii*...[which] are the very foundational laws of Navajo culture. They are not man-made law, and may not be "enacted" by individuals or entities or the Navajo Nation Council, they may simply be acknowledged by our man-made laws. Our elders and medicine people are the keepers and teachers of *Diné bi beenahaz'áanii*....

In asserting various positions in their briefs, Appellants [Morgan et al.] have claimed that there is no separation of powers doctrine on the Navajo Nation because "there is no written constitution," therefore "no public agreement."...Appellants finally assert that, whatever the historical circumstances, "the Council is in fact the original governing body of the Navajo Nation."...

Appellants are the Speaker and Council of the Navajo Nation asserting, in the context of this lawsuit, that the Council is the absolute source of governance for the Navajo people, that there is nothing indigenous about the three branch government, and that traditional laws of the Navajo people have no relevance in modern governance. Quite frankly, this court is startled, *bik'ee dlyéés*, by the propositions being advanced by our Navajo leaders; that the Speaker and Council, the elected leaders of the *Alάąji" Naat'áji Nahat'á* component of our government, believe that the government that they have been entrusted with really is not a Diné government, and that Diné values, principles, laws, tradition and culture have nothing to do with our government structure. It is, indeed, sad to hear from our own leaders such a belief and how they propose that such a government must be maintained. It shows disrespect for oneself and the people they represent. When we hear this, we are reminded of the terrible history of colonialism and its terrible impact on all Indian Nations. Our leaders of the legislative branch apparently believe that colonialism has succeeded with the Diné. The court strongly disagrees that there is nothing indigenous to our government. The Court is obligated to respond in a blunt manner to such an outrageous proposition.

We take judicial notice that the Navajo people have long resisted the imposition of a written Constitution in the mold of the U.S. Constitution. The notion of a piece of writing, even if popularly "enacted" to serve as the higher law, has been anathema to our people for whom *Diné bi beenahaz'áanii*, the Fundamental Laws, are immutable as given to the Diné by...the Holy Ones. The history of Navajo resistance in the twentieth century to such a document is well recorded. However, we take judicial notice that the written Constitution of the United States is only one aspect of the Anglo fundamental laws and is not the only source of Anglo higher law....

As a tribal nation, we have asserted our inherent sovereignty—our historical sovereignty, our language, culture, our value system, and our legal heritage based on unwritten Fundamental Laws that form the very foundation of who we are as Diné.

We have said before that participatory democracy does not come from the non-Navajo nor does it come from the Council. It comes from a deeper, more profound system of governance: the Navajo people's traditional communal governance, rooted in the *Diné Life Way*....The ideal Navajo Nation Government is not one that is governed by perfect individuals, but which is oriented toward the public interest and recognizes fully that the power to govern comes from the people, *Hozhóójí dóó Hashkééji*.

We take judicial notice that foreign structures of government have been imposed on the Navajo people since *Hwééldih* [a prison camp for many Navajos in New Mexico, also known as Bosque Redondo or Fort Sumner—where they were held for four years in the 1860s after their military defeat by the US military]. However, our present three-branch form of government was established by our Council itself after an episode of serious governmental malfeasance in order to benefit the Navajo people, to ensure that such abuse is not repeated....

A shared leadership in which each leader performs separate functions in the proper way for the public good is an intrinsic part of our Navajo history. "Separation of functions is a concept that is so deeply rooted in Navajo culture that it is accepted without question. It is essential to maintaining balance and harmony."...[The Navajo Nation Code] acknowledges that our Fundamental Law is the premise for our principles of separation of powers and checks and balances. Section 203 acknowledges that there are four components to Diné governance—*Hozhóójí Nahat'á* (executive branch), *Naat'ájí Nahat'á* (legislative branch), *Hashkééjí Nahat'á* (judicial branch), and *Naayee'jí Nahat'á* (National Security Branch). They each have their functions. They are all *naat'aaniis* of equal stature, from the people's point of view. These components are expected to work cooperatively and cohesively together. Three of these components are reflected in the current three branches. The fourth component, the Protector/Warrior, is not established as a branch, but this component is reflected in those who protect us, e.g., police, fire department, and the rangers.

The laws, culture, and value system of the Navajo people had their genesis in the Journey of the Diné from time immemorial to the Emergence into this world. The people are taught early on about the role and responsibilities of the leader and how they are selected. Today, we are again involved in a dispute about leadership and authority.... There is a well-known episode from our Emergence that tells us how a dispute came to be and how it was resolved. The episode began when a question arose as to who would be selected as leader.

A group of the people nominated the wolf *Ma'iitsoh* and they talked about his qualities, that he would protect the people so that we would come to no harm, and he had powerful words and connection to the Holy People. Another group nominated the bluebird *Dólii*, that he was compassionate and had qualities of nurturing, which the people need because that's the way people grow. Yet another group nominated the mountain lion *Náshdóįtsoh* because he was a hunter, so the people would never go hungry, so it was about survival. Finally, the last group nominated the hummingbird *Dah yiiṭįhí*, who was swift and would go from plant to plant bringing back pollen, and pollen represents the spirituality and reverence which the people need to have honor for one another.

The people couldn't agree to choose one leader among those nominated, each wanted the one each nominated. Finally, they resolved to send the wolf towards the East and bring back something for the people that will sustain life. The bluebird was sent to the South, the mountain lion was sent to the West, and hummingbird to the North. The people waited and waited and no one came back. They kept looking into the four directions for their leader until one day, the people looked into the North and there was something white that was moving, and it was the Dawn moving towards them. They saw it was the wolf, who had brought back the Dawn... as his coat, which is thought *Nitsáhákeeses*, white shell which is used in mineral offerings, the white corn for food, and songs *Sin dóó Tsodizin*. At midday, the people looked into the South and there was something blue that was moving, and it was the blue sky moving towards them. They saw it was the bluebird, who had brought back the blue sky... as his coat, which is planning *Nahat'á*, turquoise which is used in mineral offerings, the blue corn for food, and wise words.... When the sun set, the people looked into the sunset and there was something gold that was moving, and it was the mountain lion moving towards them, who had brought back the gold of the sunset *Nihotsooí* as his coat, which is *Iína* life, abalone shell which is used in mineral offerings, yellow corn for food, and birth and development.... Finally, after dark, the people looked into the North and saw all kinds of different colors moving into each other, and it was the hummingbird moving towards them, who had brought back the night *Chaháłheeł* as his coat, which is *Sihasin* hope, jet which is used in mineral offerings, squash for food, and reverence *Hodílzin*.

The people were awed as each of these was brought out. In spite of what each group had previously assumed was vital to sustain life, the people felt that... each brought back a crucial element for life, therefore all would be leaders and must work together to sustain life. The people decided to make all of them leaders. We retell this story to emphasize that, since beyond recorded time, the people have understood the separation of functions of leaders, and that in order to survive as a people, there must be collaboration in coming together both in the community and in the leadership chosen by the people to pool skills, resources and characteristics. There is no supremacy of any one portion of the day over another, therefore there is no greater skill, resource, characteristic, or leader over the others. The people choose and challenge their leaders to give something useful and valuable to the people in equal parts, and the leaders provide.

With this episode, Fundamental Law was established that there should not be concentrated power. There are different components of government that must work together. The modern system which reflects those components must work together. . . .

We find that a clarifying opinion is necessary here, on the issue of the source of governmental authority in order to reach finality in this case, to fend off the likelihood of imminent and costly suits between the branches, and to prevent further injury to our governmental system sure to impact the public welfare.

We affirm the power of the people to choose their form of government. Egalitarianism is the fundamental principle of Navajo participatory democracy. The egalitarian principle is the ability of the people as a whole to determine the laws by which they will be governed. We elaborated on the fundamental principles of the "reserved" power of the people as it pertains to the Navajo government in *In re Navajo Nation Election* . . . (2009), and so affirm today.

Source:

Office of the Navajo Nation President and Vice-President and Joe Shirley, Jr. v. The Navajo Nation Council and Lawrence T. Morgan, No. SC–CV–02–10 (2010).

---

93   *Statement of Cedric Crowell, Chairman, Mashpee Wampanoag Tribe: The Indian Reorganization Act—Seventy-Five Years Later (2011)*

When Congress adopted the Indian Reorganization Act (IRA) in 1934, its broad intent was to halt the allotment of Tribal land, restore lands to Native communities, support legal and political reorganization of Tribal governments, and fortify the cultural sovereignty of Native peoples. This important piece of legislation, while in some aspects, controversial, is the bedrock of modern federal Indian policy and Native sovereignty.

In 2009 the Supreme Court handed down *Carcieri v. Salazar*, a problematic decision that limited the authority of the Secretary of the Interior under the Bureau of Indian Affairs. The case involved a challenge by Rhode Island to the secretary's authority to take thirty-one acres of land into trust for the Narragansett Tribe. The court declared that the term "now" in the phrase "now under federal jurisdiction and the definition of Indian" limited the Secretary's power to only take land into trust for those Native communities that were under federal jurisdiction as of June 18, 1934, the date the IRA became law.

Cedric Cromwell, chairman of the Mashpee Wampanoag—a small and recently recognized northeastern Tribal nation, like the Narragansett—gave testimony on the seventy-fifth anniversary of the IRA's enactment and urged Congress to find a way to override the *Carcieri* ruling. Various bills were introduced in the 111th, 112th, and 113th Congresses to effect the override. The effort is ongoing but, thus far, an override has yet to been enacted.

Statement of Cedric Crowell, Chairman, Mashpee Wampanoag Tribe

I thank the Committee for this opportunity to supplement the hearing record to provide additional context for the need for the 1934 enactment of the Indian Reorganization Act.

I appreciate the Committee's interest in reviewing the context of the Congress's intent when enacting the Indian Reorganization Act—to provide relief to tribes adversely affected by the prior policies that sought to dismantle tribal communities by destroying tribal land bases and traditional lifestyle.

The Mashpee Wampanoag Tribe, whose government to government relationship with the United States was reaffirmed in 2007, once occupied a large land area throughout eastern Massachusetts and into present day Rhode Island. Today, it lacks a single acre of federal trust land base. As many have stated, Congress intended, through the Indian Reorganization Act, to repudiate the process of allotting tribal land. To reach that goal, it empowered the Secretary of the Interior to acquire land in trust to begin to restore tribal land holdings. The confusion in the wake of the Carcieri decision is complicating our efforts to begin such restoration.

As others have testified, the process of allotting tribal lands was part of a massive effort to disrupt tribal common land tenure. It has its origins with the General Allotment Act of 1887, commonly referred to as the Dawes Act. Named after its principal sponsor, Massachusetts Senator Henry Dawes, the Act established the most powerful federal apparatus for dispossessing tribal communities of their lands. Senator Dawes was continuing an effort that had already proved successful in Massachusetts.

Decades before the General Allotment Act, the Mashpee Wampanoag Tribe was among the first to be harmed by allotment policy. Massachusetts was among the first states to use that strategy to separate the people from their homeland.

The Mashpee Tribe, as part of the Wampanoag Confederacy, once exercised control over a land area that extended from Cape Cod to the Blackstone River and Narragansett Bay in present day Rhode Island and up to the Merrimack River near present day Gloucester, Massachusetts. The spread of disease, colonization and English Settlement quickly decimated that base. Despite the trauma of first contact, years after the establishment of the Plymouth Colony, a remnant of tribal homeland was still protected.

For centuries after English settlement, the Mashpee Tribe still held approximately 55 square miles of land in common based on historic deeds to the Tribe. This was confirmed by deeds that the Plymouth Bay Colony reexecuted and recorded as Marshpee Plantation in 1671. The deeds provided that land could not be sold outside the Tribe without unanimous consent of the whole Tribe.

Through deed restrictions, Tribal lands were protected against alienation for two centuries, assuring that the Wampanoag had a secure, if diminished, homeland that was capable of housing our people and providing them with food from the land and the waters. The Colony and later the Commonwealth of Massachusetts respected the tribal right to possess the land until an 1842 Act of the General Court provided for the land to be divided up and then allotted in severalty to tribal members.

In 1869, two votes in Mashpee were held seeking the Tribe's consent to this allotment policy. Tribal voters twice rejected the proposal. However, in 1870, each tribal member over 18 received 60 acres of land—freely alienable and fully taxable. The effect of this law was to destroy the Tribe's reservation and deprive the Tribe of thousands of acres of tribal common lands. This single act by the Massachusetts legislature seriously wounded our Tribe.

The Mashpee experience thereafter foreshadowed the effect that the Allotment Act had throughout Indian country. Once lands were alienable, desperately poor tribal members would in short time lose their parcels. By 1871, outsiders had acquired control of the choicest plots of land in Mashpee, immediately clear-cutting much of the last remaining hardwood in Massachusetts. Speculative development soon followed. Even though the Mashpee Tribe retained political control of the Town of Mashpee as long as outsiders were not permanent residents, the die was cast. By the late twentieth century, the Tribe had lost control of its land base.

As Mashpee development accelerated, the Tribe and its members continued to lose land, the environment continued to degrade, and the tribal members, forced out of Town government, received no benefit. Today, many tribal members cannot afford to live where their ancestors are buried, and we are struggling to overcome the barriers that the Carcieri case has imposed to our ability to restore even a small portion of our homeland.

Although we believe that the Secretary of the Interior retains the ability to take land in trust for our Tribe, the uncertainty surrounding the Carcieri decision has caused confusion as well as the promise of protracted and costly litigation when our initial reservation is approved.

The Mashpee Tribe was one of the first targets of the allotment policy that Massachusetts Senator Henry Dawes brought to bear on other tribes throughout the country. We now urge this Congress to take action to finish the job it started in 1934, and provide meaningful relief—to Mashpee and to other Indian tribes that have been harmed.

The Mashpee Tribe has been here long before 1934. Despite centuries of protecting our homeland from encroachment, we were devastated by the first impact of forced allotment. In 1934 Congress recognized that allotment was a failed policy, unfairly destructive of tribal communities. We suffered that harm before 1934 and continue to suffer from it today. We ought to benefit from the actions and the assistance that Congress promised in 1934. This Congress should stand by its promise, and enact the fix necessary to avoid the further harm posed by the flawed decision of the Supreme Court.

Sources:

Indian Law Resource Center. *Native Land Law: General Principles of Law Relating to Native Lands and Natural Resources.* Toronto: Thomson Reuters, 2013. See especially chapter 12.

US Senate. "The Indian Reorganization Act—75 Years Later: Renewing Our Commitment to Restore Tribal Homeland and Promote Self-Determination." Hearing Before the Committee on Indian Affairs. 112th Cong., 1st Sess. Washington, DC: Government Printing Office, June 23, 2011.

94   Report from the Treaty Indian Tribes in Western Washington— Executive Summary of Treaty Rights at Risk (2011)

Despite a series of important judicial rulings affirming their treaty right to harvest fish and shellfish, it became incumbent on Western Washington State Tribes to challenge both state and federal officials in 2011 for their failure to live up to their commitment to protect and enhance the fragile ecosystems that support the wildlife the Native nations depend upon. The following report lays out recommendations Tribal nations believe would help alleviate their concerns about the enormous problems confronting salmon and other water-based species.

Through the treaties we reserved that which is most important to us as a people: The right to harvest salmon in our traditional fishing areas. But today the salmon is disappearing because the federal government is failing to protect salmon habitat. Without the salmon there is no treaty right. We kept our word when we ceded all of western Washington to the United States, and we expect the United States to keep its word.

—Billy Frank Jr., chairman of the Northwest Indian Fisheries Commission

This paper examines how the rights of Western Washington treaty Tribes to harvest treaty fish and shellfish, and the federal government's salmon and orca protection efforts, are at grave risk. This is being caused by a lack of coordinated federal leadership, a failure to exercise authorities, and the disparate application of salmon conservation measures. The US government must step up and provide the leadership needed to resolve these issues if salmon are to be successfully recovered and protected. In 2018, State Attorney General, Bob Ferguson (D), in a move reminiscent of his notorious predecessor Slade Gorton (R), defied Tribes, public opinion and the Governor by challenging the scope of treaty fishing rights. He appealed court decisions that compelled Washington State to complete a costly environmental clean-up of salmon stream-blocking culverts. With a rare tie decision in *Washington v. United States*, the US Supreme Court ruled in the Tribes' favor securing treaty rights and cooperative agreements.

———

Treaty Rights At Risk

Stopping habitat degradation is the cornerstone of salmon recovery, but habitat is still declining.

According to the Puget Sound Chinook Salmon Recovery Plan developed by the state and tribal salmon co-managers and adopted by the National Marine Fisheries Service (NMFS), protecting existing habitat is the most important action needed in the short term. Despite this commitment, NMFS' 2010 assessment of the Puget Sound Chinook Salmon Recovery Plan declared that habitat is still declining and protection efforts need improvement.

Tribal harvest is accountable and tribes are doing their share to promote recovery.

In 1974, the federal court decision in *United States v. Washington*—known as the Boldt decision—affirmed the tribes' treaty right to half of the harvestable salmon, and established the tribes as co-managers of Washington fisheries. Initially, this recognition of the tribes' rights led to a significant increase in treaty harvest because the tribes finally were able to catch their share. However, harvest has been and continues to be constrained dramatically by degraded habitat. As a direct result, treaty harvest has been diminished to levels not seen since before the Boldt decision.

Tribal co-management of harvest is governed by the tribes' commitment to support salmon rebuilding efforts. NMFS' own analysis of recovery plan implementation indicates that harvest is doing its share to support salmon recovery. NMFS also concedes that salmon populations in many watersheds cannot recover even if harvest were completely eliminated. Yet, while harvest is accountable for recovery, habitat degradation continues steadily, destroying the salmon resource and along with it, the cultures and communities of the treaty Indian tribes in western Washington.

NMFS is applying disparate conservation standards to harvest actions versus habitat actions, thereby threatening treaty rights and impeding salmon recovery.

NMFS holds the tribes to a different standard than all others by applying more stringent standards to tribal salmon harvest than to actions that degrade salmon habitat. In reviewing harvest decisions, NMFS expects tribal harvest plans to contribute to salmon recovery over time. In contrast, when reviewing actions affecting Puget Sound habitat, NMFS seeks merely to maintain existing habitat productivity and quantity—regardless of whether it is adequate to support recovery.

NMFS' Biological Opinion and Reasonable and Prudent Alternative (RPA) for the Federal Emergency Management Agency (FEMA) National Flood Insurance Program is a key example of this disparate treatment. This flood insurance program sets the minimum requirements for floodplain management throughout most of Puget Sound. However, NMFS does not require an increase in habitat productivity and quantity, even in watersheds where NMFS concedes that habitat conditions are the key obstacle to salmon recovery. Another example of disparate treatment is NMFS' approach to southern resident killer whales (orca). NMFS claims orca are not recovering because there are too few large chinook salmon for them to eat. But instead of addressing all activities that affect chinook abundance, NMFS looks only to harvest reductions to address the problem.

This overemphasis on harvest restricts the tribes' treaty rights, while ignoring the science that indicates that habitat loss and degradation account for an even greater take of salmon and orca. These discriminatory actions contravene the federal government's trust responsibility to the western Washington treaty Indian tribes and undermine accomplishment of federal fish and wildlife management objectives.

The federal government is not fully implementing its obligation to protect treaty rights.

Salmon recovery is based on the crucial premise that we can protect what habitat remains while we restore previously degraded habitat conditions. Unfortunately, significant investments in recovery may not be realized because the rate of habitat loss continues to outpace restoration. The resulting net decline in habitat demonstrates the federal government's failure to protect the tribes' treaty-reserved rights.

The federal government has existing tools that it could employ to better protect habitat and support salmon recovery, but in many cases those tools are either misapplied or not being implemented adequately. For example, the U.S.

Army Corps of Engineers' § 404 permitting authorizes the very same structures that salmon recovery actions seek to remove. Also, the federal government has approved and continues to fund state programs under the guise of coastal zone management that actually impede salmon recovery. For instance, the state's Shoreline Management Act also permits shoreline development for single-family residences, including bulkheads and docks that degrade habitat.

Instream flows also are under assault and need protection from excessive withdrawals. The tribes have pursued a number of approaches to define and establish the instream flows necessary to protect and restore salmon resources. Unfortunately, each of these efforts has been undermined by flawed state policies that failed to institute a comprehensive effort to establish instream flows. Therefore, federal intervention is needed to adjudicate instream flows that are protective of fish habitat, and consistent with treaty-reserved rights.

Finally, federal agencies such as NMFS have failed to use their authority to prosecute those who degrade salmon habitat. In July 2000, NMFS formally published its policy governing enforcement of the Endangered Species Act (ESA) prohibition against take, and included a series of habitat impacts that would receive "heightened scrutiny." Although shoreline armoring and riparian vegetation removal were on NMFS' priority list, there appears to be only one instance of NMFS exercising its enforcement authority over these activities during the past decade.

Salmon recovery crosses many jurisdictions, and leadership is needed to implement recovery consistently across those jurisdictional lines.

The government's piecemeal approach to recovery has resulted in a lack of agency consistency and ultimately the implementation of federal programs that serve neither to recover salmon nor protect treaty rights. For example, many federally funded environmental and conservation grant programs are not required to protect salmon. Instead, in many cases those programs rely on a planning process that ultimately lets the landowner decide what is best for salmon, even if those choices are contrary to federally approved total maximum daily loads (TMDLs) or federally-approved salmon recovery plans.

Moreover, despite ESA listing, and declining harvest and habitat, basic federal obligations remain unfulfilled. For example, the National Oceanic and Atmospheric Administration (NOAA) and U.S. Environmental Protection Agency (EPA) have failed to use their authority under the Coastal Zone Management Act (CZMA) to protect salmon and treaty rights. The CZMA obligates EPA and NOAA to assure that state nonpoint source coastal protection plans are consistent with applicable federal law, including the Clean Water Act, ESA, and federally secured treaty rights. These plans were supposed to be developed by 1995, but 17 years later, the federal agencies have failed to obtain the state of Washington's compliance.

Given the critical importance of protecting habitat, it is essential that leadership is exercised to ensure that these basic federal obligations are met, including protection of treaty rights.

**The federal government can remedy this erosion
of treaty-reserved rights by taking action:**

1. Stop the disparate treatment of Indian tribes when applying salmon conservation measures.
   a. Apply at least as stringent a conservation standard to actions affecting salmon habitat as is applied to salmon harvest.
   b. Assure that all federal actions affecting habitat contribute to recovery of salmon and orca.
   c. Develop a comprehensive and timely plan for addressing orca prey consumption needs that does not result in disparate treatment of treaty fishing and addresses all identified factors for decline.
2. Protect and restore western Washington treaty rights by better protecting habitat.
   a. Require federal funding that supports state programs and pass-through grants to be conditioned so that all funded efforts are designed to achieve consistency with state water quality standards and salmon recovery plan habitat objectives.
   b. Direct federal agencies to increase enforcement of federal obligations to protect habitat including the ESA and Clean Water Act.
   c. Direct NMFS and EPA to assure that state Shoreline Master Program updates are consistent with all federal obligations involving treaty rights.
   d. Direct the Department of Justice to initiate limited water rights adjudications to identify treaty-reserved rights for instream flows in selected watersheds.
3. Establish federal oversight and coordination to align environmental and conservation programs to achieve salmon recovery and protect treaty-reserved rights.
   a. Oversee and align funding programs to ensure achievement of recovery objectives.
   b. Unify federal agencies and resolve inter-agency conflicts to support salmon recovery.
   c. Hold federal agencies accountable for acts or omissions that lead to disparate treatment of tribes and failure to protect treaty-reserved rights.
   d. Harmonize federal actions to ensure consistency and compliance with federal obligations and treaty rights.

Sources:

http://nwifc.org.

A Report from the Treaty Indian Tribes in Western Washington— Executive Summary Treaty Rights at Risk: Ongoing Habitat Loss, the Decline of the Salmon Resource, and Recommendations for Change (2011). www.treatyrightsatrisk.org/.

Washington v. United States http://www.scotusblog.com/case-files/cases/washington-v-united-states/.

95   *Statement of Fawn Sharp, President, Quinault Indian Nation, on the Federal Trust Responsibility (2012)*

The trust doctrine, also known as the trust relationship, broadly entails the unique legal, moral, and fiduciary duty of the federal government to assist Native nations in the protection of their lands, resources, and cultural heritage. The federal government, many courts have maintained, is to be held to the highest standards of good faith and honesty in its dealings with Indigenous peoples.

Nevertheless, since the trust doctrine is not explicitly constitutionally based, it is not enforceable against Congress, although it has occasionally proven a potent source of rights against the executive branch. Importantly, the trust doctrine, also referred to as the *trustee-beneficiary relationship* (with the federal government serving as the trustee and the Tribes as the beneficiary), is not synonymous with the so-called *guardian-ward relationship* that was said to exist between Native peoples and the federal government from the 1860s to the 1930s.

Given its variety of origin points—international law, papal bulls, judicial precedent, common law, federal statutes, treaties, executive orders, federal policy directives—it is little wonder that different individuals will arrive at different definitions of what *trust* entails. At this 2012 hearing, Fawn Sharp (Quinault), along with several other Natives leaders, testified before the members of the Committee of Indian Affairs. The committee sought to learn from Tribal leaders how and why the trust relationship began, how it changed across time, and its current status in the minds of Native political elites, scholars, and federal officials.

Statement of Fawn Sharp, President, Quinault Indian Nation

Good afternoon distinguished Committee Members and esteemed witnesses joining me today to provide testimony on Fulfilling the Federal Trust Responsibility: The Foundation of the Government-to-Government Responsibility. My testimony addresses this topic from several, unified perspectives: as the President of the Quinault Indian Nation and President of the Affiliated Tribes of Northwest Indians regarding natural resources under authorities of Self-Determination and Self-Governance, and as the Chairperson of the Secretary of the Department of the Interior's National Commission on Indian Trust Administration and Reform.

First and foremost I would like to applaud this Committee for continuing such a vigilant effort to address the plethora of disparities Indian people are forced to deal with on a daily basis. It is because of these hearings and the Roundtable Sessions that Congress, the Administration and the American public are being educated about our issues. Mase' [Thank you]!

Prologue and Vision

Five centuries ago, Europeans relied upon the notion of the "Doctrine of Discovery" to provide a quasi-religious, political justification for colonialism. This Doctrine led to the expropriation and exploitation of the natural resources of this land with little regard for the impacts on the cultures and economies of the Indian peoples that had relied upon for them for countless millennia.

When the United States was founded two and a half centuries ago, alliances were sought with Tribal nations to try to free the colonies from European powers. For nearly a half century after Independence, the United States entered into treaties to formalize relations with Tribal nations. In exchange for promises to protect Tribal peoples from depredation and provide for their needs, Tribal nations relinquished claims of title to their traditional territories and agreed to relocate to small areas of land that were to be set aside for their exclusive use and occupancy. These promises, and subsequent laws such as the General Allotment Act, form the foundation of the trust responsibility, a concept that was rooted in the fundamental notion that Tribal nations are dependent on the largesse of the dominant government, somehow incompetent and incapable of managing their own affairs.

Yet, even the solemn treaty promises of the United States were broken repeatedly.

- Treachery, fraud, and corruption of Indian agents assigned to serve the needs of reservation communities were common.
- Indian children were removed from their homes and placed in boarding schools where they were forbidden to speak their native languages.
- As non-Indians coveted the land and resources such as gold which were found on reservations, Tribal nations were forced to relocate or accept diminished land bases.
- Tribal lands were flooded to create reservoirs to provide water and power and to try to protect non-Indian property.
- A policy of allotment was adopted to "civilize" Indians while opening reservations to settlement and development by non-Indians. The confused and complex ownership and occupancy of Indian reservations created a jurisdictional morass that allows developers to ignore laws and regulations intended to protect the environment and perpetrators of crimes such as rape or the manufacture and distribution of illegal substances to evade prosecution.

- Tribal lands have become dumping grounds for hazardous materials that non-Indian communities would not tolerate.
- Tribes are being required to compensate for environmental deterioration caused by non-Indian development on and off reservations, infringing upon our prerogatives to utilize reservation resources for the benefit of our own communities.
- When the duty to fulfill treaty obligations became burdensome, the United States pursued a policy of termination to try to "get out of the Indian business."

Until just a few decades ago, when a new era of Self-Determination and Self-Governance was ushered in, the Indian policy of the United States was centered on conquest, removal, dislocation, and extirpation.

The purpose of highlighting this litany of wrongs against Indians is not to dwell on the past, but to serve as a prelude to discussion of the future form and substance of relations between Indian Tribes and the United States. The trust responsibility and government-to-government relationships are central to our deliberations. I say "our" because decisions cannot be made unilaterally by the United States. Our discussion should include consideration of the implications of the United Nations Declaration on the Rights of Indigenous Peoples (UNDRIP), particularly articles relating to free, prior, and informed consent. As sovereigns, Indian Nations and the United States must engage in substantive dialogue to collectively establish a common vision and policy to guide our path to tomorrow.

In 1977, the American Indian Policy Review Commission issued a report to Congress noting, "The Relationship of the American Indian tribes to the United States is founded on principals of international law...a relationship founded on treaties in which Indian tribes placed themselves under the protection of the United States and the United States assumed the obligation of supplying such protection." This relationship is not working! The implementation of the United Nations Declaration on the Rights of Indigenous Peoples is essential, the inability to pass amendments to the DOI Self-Governance amendments and the lack of funding to allow Tribes to protect our borders and communities are but a few of the elements of the current dysfunctional trust responsibility to American Indian and Alaska Native peoples. The United States trust responsibility has not evolved with the changed political relationship between the United States government and Indian governments. It must be changed to reflect the realities in Indian Country in the 21st century.

The following comments center on Self-Determination and natural resources, the particular area on which the Committee is seeking comments from the Quinault Nation:

- A Different Kind of Trust Responsibility. Historical notions of dependency and incompetency must be abandoned. Our dialogue should be focused on the forgotten trust responsibility of the United States—the responsibility to support the capacity of Tribes to take their place alongside the American system of governments. For natural resources, recognition and acceptance of Tribes as capable, responsible resource managers will be essential to enable us to protect our cultures and economies and to work collaboratively at the local, state, regional, national, and international levels to sustain the environment.

- Self-Determination and Self-Governance. The Quinault Nation was one of the first Tribes to employ Self-Determination contracting and Self-Governance compacting to improve its ability to manage its natural resources. The devastation of our forests, salmon, lands, and waters wrought by decades of mismanagement by the United States could no longer be tolerated and spurred our determination to embark on the newly opened path to Self-Determination. For years, buy-Indian and Self-Determination contracts provided a means for us to perform activities in lieu of the Bureau of Indian Affairs (BIA). We had little latitude to establish objectives and goals, but were rather limited to those imposed and supported by the federal administration and BIA. We found it necessary to turn to Congress to enable us to establish a demonstration program for a Tribal forestry program that was designed to address resource management problems that had accumulated over decades of BIA administration. Our ability to develop our own programs and priorities for forestry, fisheries, health, and social programs has been greatly enhanced through the use of Self-Governance compacting. Quinault was in the first tier of Tribes to participate in the Self-Governance program. While Self-Governance has provided us with the flexibility to tailor programs to best fit the needs of our own communities, several improvements, noted in H.R. 2444, the Department of the Interior Self-Governance Amendments, are needed.

The Quinault Indian Nation compacted to manage our forest lands but we have not received the additional funding or increases in our formula to manage existing obligations. We are further challenged by the increased cost of fuel to perform these services.

- A New Focus for Federal Administration: Support for Tribal Self-Government. There is a need to expand our vision of the nature of the trust responsibility to see beyond the accustomed, narrow confines of fiduciary duties and obligations. In some respects, this requires the term trust responsibility to be turned on its head. Instead of a policy that perpetuates paternalism and dependency, trust responsibility should be viewed as the responsibility to administer Indian Affairs in a manner deserving of the trust of Indian Country. The time has come to transform the role of the United States from guardian to enabler, to make the primary function of the trustee that of supporting and assisting the capacity of Tribes to truly exercise Self-Determination. Tribes that are ready for this step should have the opportunity to establish relationships with the United States that move beyond tutelage to a position of sovereign equality. To make this transformation, fundamental, seminal issues must be addressed.

Paternalistic procedures, practices, and policies for management of the trust corpus that perpetuate paternalism, dependency, and bureaucracy while trying to shield the United States from financial liability for mismanagement have debilitating effects on the ability of Tribes to manage and develop their own lands and resources and greatly increased the costs of federal adminis- tration. Federal bureaucracy and administration has left Indian Country dirt poor despite the abundance of natural resources that blesses many reservations.

These administrative measures should be reformulated through a collabo- rative process between Tribal governments and the United States with the over- arching objective of strengthening the ability of Tribes to fully and exclusively exercise their inherent sovereign authorities to manage the lands and resources within reservation boundaries.

This discussion should include clarification that Indian lands are private lands that are held in trust with a fiduciary responsibility of the United States to manage the trust corpus for their beneficial owners. Trust lands are not sub- ject to the federal nexus that triggers application of laws and regulations in- tended to govern public lands, such as NEPA and the ESA.

Tribal authority to make and enforce laws and regulations of their own making, including taxation authority, against Indians, non-Indians, and non- Tribal members alike must become a reality.

Currently, the Department of the Interior is in the position of being both "pitcher" and "umpire" for trust administration; independent oversight is needed. Consideration should also be given for the need for, and value of, es- tablishing a high-level ombudsman position, to help overcome recalcitrance in federal administration of Indian Affairs.

- Land consolidation and Jurisdiction. A major focus of trust responsibility and government-to-government relations should be directed at assisting Tribes to restore the integrity of reservation land bases as permanent homelands for their peoples and to establish viable land bases for newly federally-recognized Tribes. Funding provided under the recent Cobell settlement could provide critical resources for land consolidation, but efforts and priorities must be Tribally, not administratively-driven. Chaos caused by the Supreme Court's decision in Carcieri must be rectified legislatively.
- Off-Reservation Co-Management. The ability of Tribes to co-manage re- sources within their traditional ceded territories off reservation needs and deserves support. Arbitrary restrictions, such as those employed by the EPA for development of Tribal water quality programs restrict use to on-reservation activities, failing to recognize Tribal needs to protect off- reservation resources that are essential to their ability to exercise treaty and other federally reserved rights. The United States should provide fi- nancial, technical, and political support for Tribal governments to for- mally engage and substantively participate in international deliberations involving natural resources and environment, e.g., climate change, biodi- versity.
- Consultation. Federal entity requirements for consultation with Tribal governments on matters pertaining to Tribal rights and interests should be made mandatory and enforceable. However, it is crucial, that consultation be

implemented as part of a true government-to-government process that involves respectful dialogue to identify and try to overcome differences, not as a pro-forma checklist that reserves decision-making authority solely to the federal entity.

- Formalize Trust Agreements. The foundations for trust administration of natural resources need to be poured. Consideration should be given to enacting a suite of laws pertaining to Tribal natural resources. The National Indian Forest Resources Management Act and Indian Agriculture Act enunciated the federal trust responsibility and set forth certain standards for management. Comparable laws are needed for fish and wildlife, energy, and water resources.

Fiduciary standards expressed in Section 303 of the Department of Interior manual should be cooperatively and collectively reviewed by Tribal and administrative representatives and revised as needed.

The ability to establish formal contractual intergovernmental agreements between the United States and Tribes which would clarify duties, obligations, and responsibilities should be explored. These Agreements would establish performance standards for programs operated by both Tribes and federal agencies. A variety of arrangements could be considered, such as the option for Tribes to place their lands in a special form of trust that would protect them from taxation or jurisdictional intrusions by local, state, and federal governments. This option could reduce burdens, liabilities, and costs of federal administration and remove impediments in securing financing for Tribal natural resource development.

The concept of converting Tribal trust lands to a new type of ownership, Tribal restricted fee, is presently under discussion by the House of Representatives (American Indian Empowerment Act of 2011, H.R. 3532). President Rob Porter (Seneca Nation of New York) testified at a recent hearing on this proposed legislation: "[I]t would do this by enabling Indian nations and Tribes to voluntarily convert some or all their existing Tribal lands from Tribal trust lands held by the United States to Tribal restricted fee status held by the Tribal government and thereby enjoy the enhanced flexibility that attaches to restricted fee land holdings. That flexibility should produce great savings in time and cost that otherwise would burden development on Tribal trust land." The advantages and disadvantages, pros and cons of providing such an option deserve thoughtful, serious deliberation by Tribal governments, Congress, and the Administration.

National Commission on Indian Trust Administration and Reform

The work of the National Commission on Indian Trust Administration and Reform is underway. As Chairperson I am joined by a cadre of Leadership and Academia who has listened and been engrained in the trust reform issues for many decades. Ours is a charge that we all consider very serious and with the help of this Committee, we will take the first step to improving the system that we can all agree is "not working"! We held our first meeting on March 1–2, 2012 and will begin to convene field Listening Sessions in June 2012. We are seeking the input of Indian Country regarding the Department's administration and management of trust assets and carrying out its fiduciary trust responsibility for individual Indians and Tribes.

Again, thank you to the Committee for allowing me to testify before you today on this important issue.

Sources:

Monette, Richard A. "Governing Private Property in Indian Country: The Double-Edged Sword of the Trust Relationship and the Trust Responsibility Arising Out of Early Supreme Court Opinions and the General Allotment Act." *New Mexico Law Review* 25 (Winter 1995): 35–64.

Tsosie, Rebecca. "The Conflict between the 'Public Trust' and the 'Indian Trust' Doctrines: Federal Public Land Policy and Native Nations." *Tulsa Law Review* 39 (Winter 2003): 271–311.

US Senate. "Fulfilling the Federal Trust Responsibility: The Foundation of the Government-to-Government Relationship." Hearing before the Committee on Indian Affairs. 112th Cong., 2nd Sess. Washington, DC: Government Printing Office, May 17, 2012.

96   *Opinion of the Attorney General for the Commonwealth of Virginia on Tribal Nations' Obligations to Abide by State Regulations (2013)*

The Commonwealth of Virginia is home to seven federally recognized tribes, the Pamunkey, Chickahominy, Eastern Chickahominy, Upper Mattaponi, Rappahannock, Nansemond and Monacan Nations. Most Native communities, even those that had signed covenants with the Commonwealth, were not recognized by Virginia until the early 1980s and, for many years, these severely marginalized communities suffered crippling poverty, lack of educational opportunities, and severe racial discrimination. The Pamunkey Indian Tribe, despite having signed a still-binding treaty with Virginia in 1677 and living continuously on designated reservation land since 1658, were not formally acknowledged by the federal government until January 2016. The remaining six were recognized by an act of Congress in 2018.

The Virginia Attorney General's opinion, written in response to a Virginia Department of Game & Inland Fisheries and Virginia Marine Resources Commission joint query, affirmed that Virginia Natives descended from a Nation that signed the 1677 Treaty are not required to secure a state license to fish, hunt, or trap in Virginia, a strong recognition of tribal sovereignty.

Dear Messrs. Duncan and Travelstead:

I am responding to your request for an official advisory opinion in accordance with § 2.2–505 of the Code of Virginia.

Issues Presented

You ask whether members of Virginia Indian tribes are subject to Virginia's fish and wildlife laws and regulations with respect to seasons, moratoria, minimum size limits, possession limits, and method of take. If they are, you ask if there are any geographical limits to the application of those laws and whether there is any distinction among subsistence, recreational and commercial hunting, trapping and fishing. You also ask whether members of these tribes are required to obtain a fishing license from the Virginia Marine Resources Commission to fish in tidal waters. Finally, you seek guidance as to which Virginia Indian tribes are formally recognized by the Commonwealth.

Response

It is my opinion that an Indian who habitually resides on an Indian reservation or an Indian that is a member of a Virginia recognized tribe who resides in the Commonwealth is not required to obtain a license to fish in Virginia's inland waters, or to hunt or trap in Virginia. It is also my opinion that members of the Virginia tribes that were parties to the Treaty of 1677 with England are not required to obtain a license to fish or oyster in Virginia's tidal waters provided the activity is limited to harvesting for sustenance. Finally, it is my opinion that Virginia Indians are bound by the trapping, hunting and fishing laws and regulations of the Commonwealth regardless of whether they are on or off a reservation.

Applicable Law and Discussion

Generally, it is unlawful to hunt, trap or fish in the Commonwealth without a license. Nonetheless, there is an exception to the license requirement that provides that "[n]o license to hunt, trap or fish shall be required of any Indian who habitually resides on an Indian reservation or of a member of the Virginia recognized tribes who resides in the Commonwealth." The fishing license exception is based on Indian heritage and is limited to fishing in Virginia's inland waters. Nonetheless, members of any Virginia tribe that was a party to the Treaty of 1677 are not required to have a license to fish or oyster in Virginia's tidal waters provided they are doing so for their sustenance. The Treaty of 1677 states in pertinent part that "the said Indians have and enjoy theire wonted conveniences of Oystering, fishing, and Gathering anything else for their natural Support not useful to the English." Because the Commonwealth stands as the successor to the English Crown in the Treaty of 1677, it respects the spirit and intent of the treaty. Therefore, the Commonwealth still recognizes this exception.

Despite these exceptions, Virginia Indians must follow fish and wildlife laws and regulations with respect to seasons, moratoria, minimum size limits, possession limits, and method of take. The term " '[l]icense' has generally been defined as conferring a right to do something which otherwise one would not have the right to do. . . ." The statutory license exception, based on heritage and the exemption that comes from the Treaty of 1677, places Virginia Indians on equal footing with all others who are exempt from the licensing requirement, such as landowners hunting, fishing and trapping on their own property. Virginia Indians, along with all other exempt hunters, anglers and trappers, must comply with applicable fish and wildlife laws and regulations with respect to seasons, moratoria, minimum size limits, possession limits, and method of take to the same extent as anyone required to obtain a license. Additionally, Virginia Indians are subject to regulations promulgated by the Department of Game and Inland Fisheries and the Virginia Marine Resources Commission provided that the regulations are not written or applied in a discriminatory manner against Indians.

Additionally, the gaming and fishing laws and regulations are as applicable on a reservation as they are elsewhere in the Commonwealth. While Virginia Indians have the exclusive right of use and occupancy of reservation land, the Commonwealth owns the land. There is nothing in place that limits the Commonwealth's jurisdiction. Therefore, the laws and regulations of the Commonwealth apply on a reservation.

Conclusion

Accordingly, it is my opinion that an Indian who habitually resides on an Indian reservation or an Indian that is a member of a Virginia recognized tribe who resides in the Commonwealth is not required to obtain a license to fish in Virginia's inland waters, or to hunt or trap in Virginia. It is also my opinion that members of the Virginia tribes that were parties to the Treaty of 1677 with England are not required to obtain a license to fish or oyster in Virginia's tidal waters provided the activity is limited to harvesting for sustenance. Finally, it is my opinion that Virginia Indians are bound by the trapping, hunting and fishing laws and regulations of the Commonwealth regardless of whether they live on or off a reservation.

With kindest regards, I am
Kenneth T. Cuccinelli, II
Attorney General

Sources: Author has copy of this opinion.

Cook, Samuel R. *Monacans and Miners: Native America and Coal Mining Communities in Appalachia.* Lincoln: University of Nebraska Press, 2000.
    Roundtree, Helen C. *Pocahantas's People: The Powhatan Indians of Virginia Through Four Centuries.* Norman: University of Oklahoma Press, 1990.

97

Statement by the Pamunkey Tribe upon Receiving Federal Recognition (2014)

The Pamunkey Nation, direct descendants of the Powhatan peoples, signed two treaties with foreign powers. First, an accord with Great Britain in 1646, and then the 1677 Treaty of Middle Plantation with the Virginia Colony. While the 1677 treaty contained fairly liberal language toward the Pamunkey, it did require that tribal leaders "acknowledge to have their immediate dependency on, and own all subjection to the Great King of England." In addition, tribal leaders were to annually deliver to the governor certain animal pelts, wild game, and three arrows as a form of tribute. That ceremony has been performed every year since 1677.

The Pamunkey secured a 1,200-acre reservation in 1658 in King William County that has been continuously occupied since that time. Notwithstanding these two important facts, the federal government had not formally acknowledged the Pamunkey as a recognized Native Nation until 2016. The assistant secretary of Indian affairs issued a "proposed finding" to acknowledge them in 2014, but it took two more years before that finally became law.

Statement by the Pamunkey Tribe

We have been working towards this point for decades, and are very pleased to have received a positive preliminary determination. We look forward to continuing our government-to-government relationship with the United States.

Today, after years of research and preparation, culminating on October 14, 2010 in the filing of a fully documented petition for federal acknowledgment with the Assistant Secretary of Indian affairs (AS–IA), U.S. Department of the Interior, AS–IA published a proposed finding to acknowledge the Pamunkey Indian tribe as a federally recognized Indian tribe on January 17, 2014.

The Pamunkey Indian tribe, located on the Pamunkey Indian Reservation, Virginia has a rich and well-documented history. In the course of collecting evidence for the federal acknowledgment petition, researchers compiled thousands of documents recording the Tribe's existence and enduring presence from the period of first European contact to the present. These documents comprise numerous colonial documents, official government censuses, correspondences between the Pamunkey Indian Tribe and officials of the Commonwealth and US governments, numerous newspaper stories, church and school records, books by prominent scholars, popular authors, and federal officials, memoirs and much more. Because of these rich resources, continuous and detailed genealogies have been created for the Pamunkey Tribal members. Moreover, this documentation demonstrates the continuity of the tribe as a distinct political and cultural group since well before the advent of the United States.

The Pamunkey Indian Tribe played a vital role in the Europeans' first contact with the New World. Documents have been preserved in the archives of the United States and England that clearly show the continual existence of the Pamunkey Indian tribe as an independent sovereign since the first visit of Captain John Smith in 1607, when the English settled Jamestown. The Pamunkey still honor the treaty relationship formed between the Tribe and Great Britain in 1646, and reasserted through the Treaty of Middle Plantation in 1677. One expression of the perseverance of this treaty relationship, performed as recently as November 2013, is the annual tribute ceremony where deer and other wild game are presented to the Governor of Virginia by the Pamunkey chief and members of the Tribal Council in Richmond, Virginia. The continuity of the Tribe's community and political authority has helped the Tribe preserve its cultural traditions and a tightknit community through nearly four centuries. Federal acknowledgment will serve to strengthen these bonds for the future.

Sources:

Pollard, John Garland. *The Pamunkey Indians of Virginia*. Bureau of American Ethnology. Bulletin 17. Washington, DC: Government Printing Office, 1894.

Roundtree, Helen C. *Pocahontas's People: The Powhatan Indians of Virginia Through Four Centuries*. Norman: University of Oklahoma Press, 1990.

98

Northern Tribes Buffalo Treaty (2014)

For millennia, Native peoples throughout much of North America had an intimate relationship with buffalo. The massive animals were viewed as relatives, not merely as resources, and they played a crucial role in many origin accounts and subsistence patterns. They significantly shaped the ecosystem that linked various species—including humans—to the land. The deliberate and systematic slaughter of nearly all buffalo in the nineteenth century by whites had devastating consequences for all those nations, other species, and the fragile prairie lands that depended upon the herds. Fortunately, buffalo survived and by the 1970s some efforts began to establish and manage new herds.

The InterTribal Bison Cooperative (ITBC), with a current membership of fifty-six Native nations, was founded in 1992 with the mission to promote buffalo restoration in a manner that would support "spiritual revitalization, ecological restoration, and economic development." In ensuing years it became evident that a broader vision was required, thus, on September 23, 2014, an international agreement, the Northern Tribes Buffalo Treaty, was signed in Blackfeet territory, Montana. Signatory nations included eight Native peoples from the US and Canada who own and manage some 6.3 million acres of prairie grassland—nearly three times the size of Yellowstone National Park. The Blackfeet, Blood Tribe, Siksika Nation, Piikani Nation, Assiniboine & Gros Ventre, Assiniboine & Sioux Tribe, Salish & Kootenai, and the Tsuut'ina Nation collectively agreed to pursue ecological restoration of the buffalo on their lands and to renew and strengthen international relations with one another.

The Buffalo Treaty

Since time immemorial, hundreds of generations of the first peoples of the First Nations of North America have come and gone since before and after the melting of the glaciers that covered North America. For all those generations Buffalo has been our relatives. Buffalo is part of us and We are part of Buffalo culturally, materially, and spiritually. Our ongoing relationship is so close and well embodied in us that Buffalo is the essence of our holistic ecocultural life ways.

Purpose and Objectives of the Treaty

To honor, recognize, and revitalize the time immemorial relationship We have with Buffalo, it is the collective intention of We, the undersigned nations, to welcome Buffalo to once again live among us as creator intended by doing everything within our means so We and Buffalo will once again live together to nurture each other culturally and spiritually. It is our collective intention to recognize Buffalo as a wild free-ranging animal and as an important part of the ecological system; to provide a safe place and environment across our historical lands, on both sides of the United States–Canada border, so together We can have our brother, the Buffalo, lead us in nurturing our land, plants and other animals to once again realize The Buffalo Ways for our future generations.

Parties to the Treaty

We, the undersigned, include but not limited to Blackfeet Nation, Blood Tribe, Siksika Nation, Piikani Nation, the Assiniboine and Gros Ventre Tribes of Fort Belknap Indian Reservation, the Assiniboine and Sioux Tribes, The Salish and Kootenai Tribes of the Confederated Salish and Kootenai Indian Reservation, Tsuut'ina Nation and the Nakoda Nation.

Article I—Conservation

Recognizing Buffalo as a practitioner of conservation, We, collectively, agree to:
    Perpetuate conservation by respecting the interrelationships between us and "all our relations" including animals, plants, and mother Earth;
    Perpetuate and continue our spiritual ceremonies, sacred societies, and sacred objects and bundles as a means to bring about ecological balance; and
    Perpetuate and practice our sacred languages as a means to embody the thoughts and beliefs of ecological balance.

Article II—Culture

Realizing Buffalo ways as a foundation of our ways of life, We, collectively, agree to perpetuate all aspects of our respective cultures related to Buffalo including customs, practices, harvesting, beliefs, songs, and ceremonies.

Article III—Economics

Recognizing Buffalo as the centerpiece of our traditional and modern economies, We, collectively, agree to perpetuate economic development revolving around Buffalo in an environmentally responsible manner including food, crafts, ecotourism, and other beneficial by-products arising out of Buffalo's gifts to us.

Article 4—Health

Taking into consideration all the social and health benefits of a Buffalo ecology, We, collectively, agree to perpetuate the health benefits of Buffalo.

Article V—Education

Recognizing and continuing to embody all the teachings We have received from Buffalo, We, collectively, agreed to develop programs revolving around Buffalo as a means of transferring intergenerational knowledge to the younger and future generations and sharing knowledge amongst our respective nations.

Article VI—Research

Realizing that learning is a lifelong process, We, collectively, agree to perpetuate knowledge gathering and knowledge sharing according to our customs and inherent authorities revolving around Buffalo that do not violate our traditional ethical standards as a means to expand our knowledge base regarding the environment, wildlife, plant life, water, and the role Buffalo played in the history, spiritual, economic, and social life of our nations.

Article VII—Adhesions

North American Tribes and First Nations, and nations, states, and provinces may become signatories to this treaty providing they agree to the terms of this treaty.

Article VIII—Partnerships and Supporters

We, collectively, invited non-governmental organizations, corporations and others of the business and commercial community, to form partnerships with the signatories to bring about the manifestation of the intent of this treaty.

Organizations and individuals may become signatories to this treaty as partners and supporters providing they perpetuate the spirit and intent of this treaty.

Article 8 amendments

This treaty may be amended from time-to-time by a simple majority of the signatories.

Sources:

Braun, Sebastian Felix. *Buffalo Inc. American Indians and Economic Development*. Norman: University of Oklahoma Press, 2008.

Isenberg, Andrew. "Toward a Policy of Destruction: Buffaloes, Law, and the Market, 1803–83." *Great Plains Quarterly* 12 (Fall 1992): 227–241.

99

Ho-Chunk Nation Proposed Constitutional Provision to Provide for the Rights of Nature (2016)

According to Vine Deloria Jr., a fundamental premise upon which most Indigenous peoples historically lived was that the natural world and all species inhabiting that world, including even so-called "inanimate" objects like rocks and mountains, were alive and entitled to utmost respect as autonomous and unique entities. Terms of kinship were used to signify this living, organic relationship, such as Mother Earth, Father Sun, Buffalo Brother, and Grandmother Moon.

Europeans' arrival in North America precipitated dramatic and profound changes, as many species were exterminated or reduced to near extinction levels. While colonies, states, and the federal government occasionally enacted laws to combat animal cruelty, there has been little broad recognition that the natural world or the species and beings of the world have any inherent rights as sovereign entities.

Nature's lack of legal standing and the need for that status to be recognized was powerfully raised by Christopher Stone in a law review essay in 1971, "Should Trees Have Standing? Toward Legal Rights for Natural Objects," written in an effort to influence US Supreme Court justices who had been asked to review a Ninth Circuit Court of Appeals decision, *Sierra Club* v. *Hickel*. While Stone's arguments to extend legal rights to the natural world did not carry the day, three justices thought enough of his theory to at least grant "standing" to natural beings and accord them with a measure of legal rights.

It was not until the first decade of the twenty-first century that some governments—domestically and internationally—began to adopt laws or amend their constitutions to grant legal rights to nature. In 2006, Tamaqua Borough, Pennsylvania, banned the dumping of toxic waste as a violation of the rights of nature, thus becoming the first governmental entity to recognize this concept in law. Two years later, Ecuador became the first international state to enshrine the rights of nature in its constitution. And in 2010, Bolivia, led by an Indigenous president, Evo Morales, adopted the "Law of the Rights of Nature." New Zealand, Australia, India, Switzerland, Sweden, Germany, and a few other national bodies have also moved to accord legal rights to certain lands, species, and waterways.

In October 2017, the Ponca Nation became the first Tribe located within the boundaries of the US to officially recognize the rights of nature after years of enduring pollution and earthquakes caused by fracking processes that have become ubiquitous throughout the state of Oklahoma.

The ensuing document, a proposed constitutional amendment approved by the Ho-Chunk General Council in 2016, recognizes the inherent rights of nature. If ultimately adopted by their nation, the Ho-Chunk will join the Ponca Nation in their fight to protect the land, sky, and water from those who seek to profit from irreversibly destructive extraction processes.

Excerpt from the preamble to the proposed Ho-Chunk Constitution amendment:

> *Whereas, in the tradition of the Nation's relationship with Mother Earth, from which we came and upon which we depend... we recognize that to protect Mother Earth, we must place the highest protections on nature, through the recognition of rights in the Nation's highest law, our Constitution....*

Press Release: Ho-Chunk Nation General Council Approves Rights of Nature Constitutional Amendment, September 2018

Mercersburg, Pa: On Saturday, the General Council of the Ho-Chunk Nation voted overwhelmingly to amend their tribal constitution to enshrine the Rights of Nature. The Ho-Chunk Nation is the first tribal nation in the United States to take this critical step. A vote of the full membership will follow.

Bill Greendeer, a member of the Ho-Chunk Nation and the Deer clan, proposed the amendment which establishes, "Ecosystems and natural communities within the Ho-Chunk territory possess an inherent, fundamental, and inalienable right to exist and thrive." Further it prohibits frac sand mining, fossil fuel extraction, and genetic engineering as violations of the Rights of Nature.

Resolution 09—19–15

Whereas, on November 1, 1994, the Secretary of the Interior approved a new Constitution for the Ho-Chunk Nation ("Constitution"), formerly known as the Wisconsin Winnebago Nation; and

Whereas, the Ho-Chunk Nation ("Nation") is a federally recognized Indian Tribe, organized pursuant to the Indian Reorganization Act of 1934; and

Whereas, pursuant to Article IV, Section 1 of the Constitution, the People of the Ho-Chunk Nation hereby grant all inherent sovereign powers to the General Council; and

Whereas, pursuant to Article IV, Section 3 (a), the General Council retains the power to set policy for the Nation; and

Whereas, pursuant to Article IV, Section 3 (f), action by the General Council shall be binding; and

Whereas, pursuant to Article IV, Section 5, and Article VI Section 2 (i), an Annual meeting has been duly called and notice duly given by the President; and

Whereas, pursuant to Article IV, Section 7, twenty (20) percent of the eligible voters of the Nation present in General Council shall constitute a quorum; and

Whereas, the Nation has a desire to protect the environment and the rights of nature from commercial activities that pollute the environment, which has caused climate a loss of natural resources necessary for continued survival.

Whereas, the Nation wants to provide constitutional rights to protect the rights of nature and add a provision to the Constitution under the Bill of Rights as follows:

Article X—Bill of Rights

Section 2. *Rights of Nature.*

(a) The Ho-Chunk Nation, in exercising its powers of self-government, shall:

(1) Respect the rights of Nature, life cycles, structures, functions and protect the rights of all living plants, animals and the environment in which all living entities and organisms reside, and promote and protect maintenance and regeneration of its life cycles, structure, functions.

(2) All Ho-Chunk people can call upon Elected and Appointed Officials to enforce the rights of nature under the following principles:

(i) Nature has the right to be restored. This restoration shall be separate and apart from the obligation of the Nation and natural persons or legal entities to compensate individuals and communities that depend on affected natural systems.

(ii) In those cases of severe or permanent environmental impact, including those caused by the exploitation of nonrenewable natural resources, the Nation shall establish the most effective mechanisms to achieve the restoration and shall adopt adequate measures to eliminate or mitigate harmful environmental consequences.

(iii) The Nation shall apply preventive and restrictive measures on activities that might lead to the extinction of species, destruction of ecosystems and permanent alteration of natural cycles.

(iv) People shall have the right to benefit from the environment and the natural wealth enabling them to enjoy the good way of living.

(v) The Nation shall give incentives to natural persons and legal entities and to communities to protect nature and to promote respect for all the elements comprising an ecosystem.

(vi) The Nation shall apply preventive and restrictive measures on activities that might lead to the extinction of species, destruction of ecosystems and permanent alteration of natural cycles.

(vii)   The introduction of organisms and organic and inorganic material that might definitively alter the Nation's genetic assets is forbidden.

(viii) Persons, communities, and people shall have the right to benefit from the environment and the natural wealth enabling them to enjoy the good way of living.

(ix)   Environmental services shall not be subject to appropriation; their production, delivery, use and development shall be regulated by the Nation.

Now Therefore Be It Resolved that the Ho-Chunk Nation Constitution be amended as stated above adding the above provision to the Constitution as Section 2 of the Bill of Rights.

Be It Resolved General Council Agency shall request a Secretarial Election to amend the Constitution as provided above, if necessary, on an expedited basis, and the General Council Agency can take any and all action necessary to implement this resolution. General Council Agency is vested with a full power of attorney as provided under the General Council Power of Attorney Resolution, and is expressly authorized to call for a Secretarial Election, appoint members to the Secretarial Election Board, and request an appropriation of funds from the Bureau of Indian Affairs to conduct this election.

Sources:

Deloria, Vine, Jr. *The Metaphysics of Modern Existence.* Golden, CO: Fulcrum Publishing, 2013.

   Stone, Christopher D. "Should Trees Have Standing? And Other Essays on Law, Morals, and the Environment." Dobbs Ferry, NY: Oceana Publishers, 1996.

100

Northwest Tribes' Response to the Treaty-Affirming Denial of a Construction Permit for a Coal Export Terminal (2016)

The Lummi Nation resides on a reservation situated at the mouth of the Nooksack River that was fashioned by the 1855 Treaty of Point Elliott. Like many Native peoples in Western Washington, the Lummi have long depended on fishing, shell fishing, and plant gathering to sustain themselves. The Point Elliott Treaty contains a singular clause that has been the basis for litigation over the years:

"The right of taking fish, at all usual and accustomed grounds and stations, is further secured to said Indians, in common with all citizens of the Territory."

Despite the clarity of this clause, Lummi and other Native fishers were generally denied the rights to fish until they were affirmed by a series of court cases in the 1970s, the most notable, *U.S. v. Washington* (1974). This and other positive rulings fueled the Nation's development of a sophisticated aquaculture project that produces salmon and other species for release in the local rivers. The Lummi have been vigilant in protecting and enhancing their treaty fishing rights throughout the contemporary era.

When Pacific International Terminal sought to build a massive coal export terminal at Cherry Point in a treaty-protected region, the Lummi and a multitude of allies mustered a campaign to convince the US Army Corps of Engineers to deny the company's application. The Corps agreed with the Lummi Nation in a decision rendered May 9, 2016. The Lummi and their many allies were ecstatic with the ruling as the following comments from Tribal leaders attest.

———

Statements from Tim Ballew II, chairman of the Lummi Indian Business Council and Other Northwest Tribal Leaders: *Response to U.S. Army Corps of Engineers' Decision to Deny Pacific International Terminals' Application to Build North America's Largest Coal Export Terminal in the Lummi Nation's Treaty-Protected Fishing Waters.*

This is a historic victory for treaty rights and the constitution. It is a historic victory for the Lummi Nation and our entire region. We are pleased to see that the Corps has honored the treaty and the constitution by providing a decision that recognizes the terminal's impacts to our fishing rights. This decision is a win for the treaty and protects our sacred site. Our ancient ones at Xwe'chieXen, Cherry Point, will rest protected.

Because of this decision, the water we rely on to feed our families, for our ceremonies and for commercial purposes remains protected. But this is more than a victory for our people; it's a victory for treaty rights.

Treaty rights shape our region and nation. As tribes across the United States face pressures from development and resource extraction, we'll continue to see tribes lead the fight to defend their treaty rights, and protect and manage their lands and waters for future generations.

The impact of a coal terminal on our treaty fishing rights would be severe, irreparable and impossible to mitigate.

Today's victory is monumental and the Corps followed a fair process defined by law to make the right decision. The Corps has honored the treaty between Lummi and the United States.

We will always fight to protect Xwe'chieXen.

Tim Ballew, Chair, Lummi Nation

The Corps of Engineers made the right decision today. We have lived along these rivers and shores for millennia. Just as it is the Corps' duty to uphold our treaty rights, so it is our duty to fight for and protect these waters for future generations. —Frances Charles, Chair, Lower Elwha Klallam

The Corps' decision is a victory for the Yakama Nation and all other treaty tribes. The proposed terminal could have destroyed the way of life for the Lummi and all indigenous people who depend on the Salish Sea for their livelihood and culture. The increased shipment of coal that this terminal would have triggered was a direct and dire threat to the Yakama Nation, our lands and waters, and our people. By denying the permit, the Corps upheld its duty to the tribes to protect treaty rights. The fight, however, is not over. The threat of the coal movement remains, and the Yakama Nation will not abide these threats. We will not negotiate or accept mitigation for destruction or infringements upon the rights our ancestors secured for us and our people. —JoDe L. Goudy, Chair, Yakama Nation

As a Washington tribe whose way of life is being threatened by the development and expansion of three oil terminals, the Quinault Indian Nation rejoices today with our Lummi brothers and sisters. The danger that the terminal posed to the culture, lifestyle and economy of the Coast Salish people was unacceptable, and we're pleased the Corps did its duty to uphold Lummi's treaty rights. —Tyson Johnston, Vice President, Quinault Indian Nation

Today, the Army Corps of Engineers honored the treaty signed by Lummi elders more than a century ago to protect their people and their way of life. Today, we unite with Lummi to celebrate this momentous news. —Dave Brown Eagle, Vice-Chair, Spokane Tribe

Our ancestors sacrificed so much to protect these waters and our way of life. Thanks to them, the treaty reserved our rights to harvest fish and shellfish and draw from the abundance of the sea. The Tulalip Tribes applauds the Army Corps of Engineers for its decision to deny the permit for the Gateway Pacific Terminal and protect treaty rights. —Melvin R. Sheldon Jr., Chair, Tulalip Tribes

This has been a long journey and the Nooksack Indian Tribe is happy to be able to share in the joy and success of the Lummi Nation. A coal terminal at Cherry Point would violate treaty rights, and today the Corps affirmed that position and protected the Salish Sea for generations to come. —Lona Johnson, Councilmember, Nooksack Indian Tribe

Washington tribes have fought long and hard to protect our natural resources—for our people and for all people. By denying the permit, the Corps recognizes the potentially disastrous consequences of a coal terminal on the health of the Salish Sea and our tribal economies. —Kevin Lenon, Vice-Chair, Sauk-Suiattle Tribe

Source:

Memorandum, CENWS–OD–RG, 9 May 2016, subject: Gateway Pacific Terminal Project and Lummi Nation's Usual and Accustomed Treaty Fishing Rights at Cherry Point, Whatcom, County.

101

*Treaty Alliance Against
Tar Sands Expansion (2016)*

International treaty making continued in 2016 when fifty Native nations from Canada and the United States hammered out this strongly worded accord in which the nations categorically rejected expansion of the production of the Alberta Tar Sands, including the transportation of that resource via railroads, tankers, or pipelines. Three major projects were targeted: Kinder Morgan, Inc.; TransCanada Corporation; and Enbridge, Inc. The nations were deeply concerned about the environmental damage possible if the Tar Sands expansion were allowed to go forward with installation of their proposed projects.

———

Treaty Alliance Against Tar Sands Expansion Treaty

We have inhabited, protected and governed our territories according to our respective laws and traditions since time immemorial. Sovereign Indigenous Nations entered into solemn treaties with European powers and their successors but Indigenous Nations have an even longer history of treaty making amongst themselves. Many such treaties between Indigenous Nations concern peace and friendship and the protection of Mother Earth.

The expansion of the Alberta Tar Sands, a truly massive threat bearing down on all of the Indigenous Peoples of Turtle Island and beyond, calls now for such a treaty between Indigenous Nations:

Plans for major increases in the production of the Tar Sands have led to many new projects aimed at building, converting or expanding pipelines as well as introducing or increasing oil train and tanker traffic, all of which threaten many Indigenous Nations' territories, waterways, shores and communities with the very real risk of toxic and hazardous oil spills.

The expansion of the Tar Sands would also lead to increased destruction and poisoning of the lands, waters and air of the Indigenous Peoples directly on the frontlines and downstream of the Tar Sands.

In addition, every single Indigenous Nation on Turtle Island will suffer terrible harm if such pipeline, rail and tanker projects move ahead because, by leading to the expansion of the Tar Sands, such projects will unquestionably fuel catastrophic climate change. Climate change has already started to endanger our peoples' way of life and now threatens our very survival.

Tar Sands expansion is a collective threat to our Nations. It requires a collective response.

Therefore, our Nations hereby join together under the present treaty to officially prohibit and to agree to collectively challenge and resist the use of our respective territories and coasts in connection with the expansion of the production of the Alberta Tar Sands, including for the transport of such expanded production, whether by pipeline, rail or tanker.

As sovereign Indigenous Nations, we enter this treaty pursuant to our inherent legal authority and responsibility to protect our respective territories from threats to our lands, waters, air and climate, but we do so knowing full well that it is in the best interest of all peoples, Indigenous and non-Indigenous, to put a stop to the threat of Tar Sands expansion.

We wish to work in collaboration with all peoples and all governments in building a more equitable and sustainable future, one that will produce healthier and more prosperous communities across Turtle Island and beyond, as well as preserve and protect our peoples' way of life.

Source:

www.treatyalliance.org.

102   *The Grizzly Treaty (2016)*

The US Fish and Wildlife Service attempted many times to remove the grizzly bear from the federal endangered and threatened species list where it had been placed in 1975. Delisting had first been proposed in 2005, but federal court rulings halted that attempt. Still, the agency continued to argue protections were not necessary because the population had recovered.

These decades of threats to weaken protections for the grizzly prompted the creation of another major international accord, this one negotiated between more than fifty federally recognized Native nations and Canada's Assembly of First Nations, which advocates for over 900,000 natives in Canada. The treaty united the Nations around their shared understanding of the sacredness of the bear and its relation to cultural and spiritual life. The Nations found allies with prominent environmental groups.

Although the Treaty Nations faced a formidable, well-funded coalition of ranchers, Fish and Wildlife personnel, and state and federal officials, their efforts, which included an appeal to President Obama for intervention, held the delisting process at bay. However, when Donald Trump became president in January 2017, pressure intensified for the bears' removal.

On June 22, 2017, Secretary of the Interior Ryan Zinke announced that as the grizzly bear population was no longer considered imperiled, protections provided by the Endangered Species Act were no longer needed. The secretary's cited measure of success was the increase of the grizzly population from 138 bears in 1975 to 700 in 2017. Thus, authority for the bears' management was handed over to the Tribes and the states of Idaho, Montana, and Wyoming.

———

Grizzly Treaty

Since time immemorial, hundreds of generations of the first peoples of the First Nations of North America have come and gone since before and after the melting of the glaciers that covered North America. For all those generations the Grizzly has been our ancestor, our relative. The Grizzly is part of us and We are part of the Grizzly culturally, spiritually and ceremonially. Our ancient relationship is so close and so embodied in us that the Grizzly is the spirit of our holistic eco-cultural life-ways.

Purpose and Objective of the Treaty

To honor, recognize, and revitalize the ancient relationship we have with the Grizzly, it is the collective intention of We, the undersigned Nations, to welcome the Grizzly to once again live beside us as Creator intended and to restore the balance where We are the stewards and Grizzly is the guardian of our lands. We will do everything within our means so that with Grizzly, We will once again live in the sacred cycle of reciprocity to nurture each other culturally and spiritually. It is our collective intention to recognize the Grizzly as an umbrella species, central to the ecological system; and to provide a safe space and environment across our historic homelands we once shared with the Grizzly where biologically suitable habitat still exists in the United States and Canada, so together We can have our grandparent, the Grizzly, guide us in nurturing our land, plants and the other two-legged, four-legged and winged beings to once again realize the Grizzly Medicine Ways for our future generations and recognize that Our Drumbeat is the Heartbeat of the Grizzly. In our collective Nations' efforts to protect and preserve the Grizzly—and by doing so protect, preserve and perpetuate indigenous cultures—this treaty is analogous to the UN Declaration on the Rights of Indigenous People (UNDRIP).

Parties to the Treaty

We, the undersigned, including the Piikani Nation and Tribal Nations from the four sacred directions of Turtle Island.

Article 1—Conservation

Recognizing the Grizzly as a practitioner of conservation, We, collectively, recognize that our ancestors were conservationists before the term existed in the Western lexicon, and that in their honor we agree to perpetuate their principals of caring for Mother Earth that is today called conservation. Fundamental to that is respecting the interrelationships between us and "all our relations" including animals, plants and all living and growing things that are shapes, as are We, of Mother Earth. We commit to perpetuate and continue our spiritual ceremonies, sacred societies, sacred languages and sacred bundles in which the Grizzly has a unique place, and to perpetuate and practice as a means to embody the thoughts and beliefs of ecological balance.

Article II—Culture

Realizing the Grizzly is a foundation of our traditional ways, We, collectively, agree to perpetuate all aspects of our respective cultures related to the Grizzly including customs, practices, healing and curing rituals, naming, beliefs, songs, and ceremonies.

Article III—Economics

Recognizing the Grizzly as a traditional teacher and guardian of our lands and people, We, collectively, agree to pursue economic development revolving around the Grizzly in an environmentally and culturally compatible manner, including eco-tourism models with Grizzly watching, photography and culturally oriented educational tourism, traditional crafts, publishing and literacy materials inspired by traditional narratives to which the Grizzly is central, and other beneficial by-products arising out of Grizzly's gifts to us.

Article IV—Health

Taking into consideration all the social and health benefits the Grizzly has shared with our people for millennia, We, collectively, agree to follow and develop the traditional Grizzly Bear Medicine Teachings that introduced our ancestors to our first healing and curing practices.

Article V—Education

Recognizing and continuing to embody all the teachings we have received from the Grizzly, We, collectively, agree to develop programs revolving around Grizzly as a means of transferring intergenerational knowledge to the younger and future generations and sharing knowledge amongst our respective Nations.

Article VI—Hunting

Understanding that the Grizzly is an ancestor, a grandparent, and a relative, no hunting of the Grizzly—be that categorized as sport or trophy hunting—will be permitted or licensed on any lands our Nations hold jurisdiction over. The Grizzly will enjoy full protections on all tribal land.

Article VII—Management

Recognizing that our collective objective is to see the Grizzly returned to areas of biologically suitable habitat on tribal lands within the Grizzly's historic range pre-colonial contact, and for linkage zones to be established between the existing, fragmented populations, Grizzly management plans for our Nations will be formulated from a cultural foundation, while accommodating the "best available science." We, collectively, recognize that our ancestors practiced the "best available science" in their stewardship of the land, as they lived in balance with our Mother Earth when the biomass was at its height. Our Nations will not adopt state, provincial or federal plans, as all are infringements of our sovereignty. We, collectively, will formulate vocational and educational programs for our people, so that on our lands, they will be the leaders of our culturally compatible Grizzly management programs. Upon the signing of this Treaty, any management removal of a Grizzly will be undertaken with ceremony, and such parts of the Grizzly that have always been kept in sacred bundles or used for traditional healing practices will be provided to such persons qualified. No Grizzly will be removed from the population before all other options have been exhausted.

Article VIII—Research

Recognizing that learning is a life-long process, We, collectively, agree to perpetuate knowledge-gathering and knowledge-sharing according to our customs and inherent authorities revolving around the Grizzly that do not violate our traditional ethical standards as a means to expand our knowledge base regarding the environment, wildlife, plant life, water, and the role Grizzly played in the history, spiritual, economic, and social life of our Nations. We, collectively, agree to consult with the leading, independent biologists qualified in the study of the Grizzly to ensure that our Nations continue to lead in the preservation and recovery of the Grizzly.

Article IX—Threats

THE CROWN OF THE CONTINENT

We, collectively, recognize that the Grizzly in the Crown of the Continent is threatened, as are the Grizzly bears attempting to live in arterial habitats connecting with populations elsewhere in the Rocky Mountains. Only a limited portion of the Crown of the Continent is productive enough and safe enough to produce Grizzly bears in excess of the numbers that die. These favored areas include Glacier and Waterton National Parks, the North and Middle Forks of the Flathead River, and western portions of the Blackfeet Reservation. Most other areas, including central and southern portions of the Bob Marshall Wilderness, the East Front, and portions of the Flathead Valley, produce lethal human interactions that kill Grizzly bears at a greater rate than they can reproduce. In addition, the Grizzly in the Crown of the Continent has suffered from devastating environmental changes. On the west side, a 15-year berry famine lasted from 1996 through 2010. Between 1985 and 2012 some 25 percent of Grizzly habitat in the United States burned, including around 40 percent of core Grizzly distribution. Many of these burns have come back as unproductive habitats, including dog hair regeneration of lodge pole pine. Between the 1970s and 2012, most mature white bark pine in the Crown was killed by white pine blister rust. Human populations in the Flathead and Swan Valleys have concurrently exploded. Not surprisingly, Grizzly bear deaths increased between the early 1990s and early 2010s by 2–10 times as much as any plausible increase in population size. We, collectively, recognize that the Grizzly is seeking habitats on the plains and elsewhere not because of increasing numbers, but because of the need to find new food sources.

GREATER YELLOWSTONE

All evidence indicates that the Grizzly population in Greater Yellowstone has been stationary since the early part of the twenty-first century, and repopulation of historic range is due to Grizzly seeking alternative foods. The catastrophic loss of Grizzly's dietary staples in this region, including white bark pine, which has been reduced by some 85 percent, and cutthroat trout, are well documented. One of Grizzly's remaining protein-rich food sources, the army cutworm moth, is vulnerable to climate change and pesticides. If as a result of wasting disease or otherwise the region's elk population suffers significant reduction the impact on Grizzly would be similarly devastating. A greater reliance on meat for survival increases the potential for conflicts. No alternative food sources exist in this ecosystem that provide caloric equivalency to those that are rapidly disappearing. Grizzly in Greater Yellowstone is an island population, genetically isolated, and with no present opportunity to establish critical linkage zones with the Crown of the Continent population. An island population is forever a threatened population.

THE GREAT BEAR RAINFOREST

In common with those in the Crown of the Continent and Greater Yellowstone, the Grizzly in the Great Bear Rainforest faces significant threats from climate change, including deforestation and declining salmon runs. Grizzlies are abandoning areas where they were once supposed to be abundant, and seeking sustenance on islands where they have never been seen before. As salmon stocks dwindle, the Grizzly is searching for alternative food sources, and consequently having fewer cubs, replicating the pernicious cycle in Yellowstone and the Crown. The Grizzly population in the Great Bear Rainforest is unknown, but irrespective, in contravention of ordinances passed by the Coastal First Nations, authorities issue batches of trophy hunting tags every year based only on population guesstimates. Grizzlies are commonly spotted from planes, chased down in boats, or shot as they walk by camouflaged blinds. They are hunted in the fall when they come down to feed on salmon, and then hunted in the spring when they emerge from hibernation. There are no rules against trophy hunting mothers, and a third of the Grizzlies killed in BC are female.

Grizzly has been an integral part of human culture since time before memory, and factors into the songs, dances, and crests of every First Nation on the coast. Grizzly is more than a neighbor; in many families, Grizzlies are considered relatives, because bears move fluidly between the worlds in First Nations oral histories, transforming into people, and even marrying humans. Grizzly is a teacher, healer, and protector. Killing a Grizzly for no reason represents a grave breach of protocol and traditional law.

As the original stewards of this land, our Nations commit to act to aid our sacred relative, the Grizzly.

Article X—Conflict Reductions

Following the precedent set by some of our sister Nations, We, collectively, recognize the need to establish seasonal closures to areas that offer the Grizzly sensitive habitat, be that for food gathering, reproduction, or the rearing of young. In the spirit of our ancestors, We will introduce culturally compatible conflict reduction programs on our Nations, that are inclusive and educational, and reconnect our people with Grizzly and traditional precepts of tribal society and responsibility.

Article XI—Adhesions

North American Tribes and First Nations, and Nations, States, and Provinces may become signatories to this treaty providing they agree to the terms of this treaty.

Article XII—Partnerships and Supporters

We, collectively, seek to be true partners with federal authorities in the reintroduction and future management of the Grizzly, in a relationship of reciprocity and equality. We, collectively, invite Non-Governmental Organizations, Corporations and others of the business and commercial community to form partnerships with the signatories to bring about the manifestation of the intent of this treaty. Organizations and individuals may become signatories to this treaty as partners and supporters providing they perpetuate the spirit and intent of this treaty.

Article XIII—Amendments

This treaty may be amended from time-to-time by a simple majority of the signatories.

Sources:

Department of the Interior. Fish & Wildlife Service. 50 CFR. Part 17. [Docket No. FWS–R6–ES–2016–0042] (2017).

https://www.nps.gov/yell/learn/nature/bearesa.htm.

103

Presidential Memorandum Regarding the Dakota Access Pipeline and a Declaration from Standing Rock Sioux Chair Dave Archambault (2017)

Thousands of miles of oil-carrying underground and above-ground pipelines crisscross the United States and link the United States with Canada. Some of these pipelines lie upon, crossover, or are buried underneath Native lands. As climate change has intensified, an ever-shifting and expanding coalition has developed, comprising Native peoples and segments of the US population who stand steadfastly against industrial pollution and for environmental sustainability and renewable energy alternatives.

Thus, it was no surprise in 2014 when a major conflict arose pitting a fossil fuel industrial party, Dakota Access, LLC, a Native nation, the Standing Rock Sioux, and a federal agency—the Army Corps of Engineers—against one another. The galvanizing event was the effort by Dakota Access to secure permission from the Army Corps for an easement to allow for completion of the construction of a 1,104-mile-long oil pipeline from North Dakota to Illinois. Although the original plan had called for the line to pass near Bismarck, a majority white city, the route was changed to avoid potential conflict with that constituency.

The revision called for the pipeline to burrow under the Missouri River very near the present-day boundaries of the Standing Rock Sioux Reservation, which straddles the border between North Dakota and South Dakota. The pipeline would therefore be situated on land the Lakota view as "unceded Indian territory" under the tenets of two treaties: the 1851 Fort Laramie Treaty and an 1868 treaty of the same name.

A majority of the pipeline, most of it under state or private land, had already been completed, but three percent of the route was slated to cross under the river, defined as a navigable waterway per the Clean Water Act, the Rivers and Harbors Act, and the National Environmental Policy Act. Because of this designation, the Missouri River section of the pipeline required a federal permit from the Corps of Engineers before construction could be completed.

The Corps claimed initially that the Standing Rock Sioux government had been properly "consulted" before initial authorization for the pipeline's completion was granted. Standing Rock disagreed and sued in federal court. They also sent out a call for support from others opposed to DAPL. This set in motion a series of back-and-forth events, culminating in a massive gathering of allies—some 10,000 strong by late 2016. Supporters from around the world answered the Standing Rock call for help and descended upon their lands in solidarity. This was arguably the greatest demonstration of support for a Native nation in US history.

With President Barack Obama's prodding, the Army Corps reversed policy course on December 4, 2016, and postponed approval of the easement. This was hailed as a major victory by Standing Rock and their thousands of supporters. But when Donald Trump assumed the presidency in January 2017 one of his first acts was to issue a presidential memorandum directing the Corps to reverse course and issue the easement. The Corps complied and granted the easement but Standing Rock sued again, and in June 2017 a federal judge determined that the Corps permits authorizing the pipeline violated federal law in certain respects.

The two ensuing documents—Trump's executive memorandum urging the easement and a February 9, 2017, declaration by Standing Rock Chairman Dave Archambault II—together lay out in broad strokes what Standing Rock continues to fight for and why the struggle is so important. The Archambault statement is a "Second Declaration" seeking an injunction because he provided an initial declaration on August 4, 2016, written for the same purpose.

Donald Trump Memorandum

Subject: Construction of the Dakota Access Pipeline

Section 1. Policy. The Dakota Access Pipeline (DAPL) under development by Dakota Access, LLC, represents a substantial, multi-billion-dollar private investment in our Nation's energy infrastructure. This approximately 1,100-mile pipeline is designed to carry approximately 500,000 barrels per day of crude oil from the Bakken and Three Forks oil production areas in North Dakota to oil markets in the United States. At this time, the DAPL is more than 90 percent complete across its entire route. Only a limited portion remains to be constructed.

I believe that construction and operation of lawfully permitted pipeline infrastructure serve the national interest.

Accordingly, pursuant to the authority vested in me as President by the Constitution and the laws of the United States of America, I hereby direct as follows:

Section 2. Directives. (a) Pipeline Approval Review. The Secretary of the Army shall instruct the Assistant Secretary of the Army for Civil Works and the U.S. Army Corps of Engineers (USACE), including the Commanding General and Chief of Engineers, to take all actions necessary and appropriate to:

   (i) review and approve in an expedited manner, to the extent permitted by law and as warranted, and with such conditions as are necessary or appropriate, requests for approvals to construct and operate the DAPL, including easements or rights-of-way to cross Federal areas under section 28 of the Mineral Leasing Act, as amended, 30 U.S.C. 185; permits or approvals under section 404 of the Clean Water Act, 33 U.S.C. 1344; permits or approvals under section 14 of the Rivers and Harbors Act, 33 U.S.C. 408; and such other Federal approvals as may be necessary;

(ii) consider, to the extent permitted by law and as warranted, whether to rescind or modify the memorandum by the Assistant Secretary of the Army for Civil Works dated December 4, 2016 (Proposed Dakota Access Pipeline Crossing at Lake Oahe, North Dakota), and whether to withdraw the Notice of Intent to Prepare an Environmental Impact Statement in Connection with Dakota Access, LLC's Request for an Easement to Cross Lake Oahe, North Dakota, dated January 18, 2017, and published at 82 Fed. Reg. 5543;

(iii) consider, to the extent permitted by law and as warranted, prior reviews and determinations, including the Environmental Assessment issued in July of 2016 for the DAPL, as satisfying all applicable requirements of the National Environmental Policy Act, as amended, 42 U.S.C. 4321 et seq., and any other provision of law that requires executive agency consultation or review (including the consultation or review required under section 7(a) of the Endangered Species Act of 1973, 16 U.S.C. 1536(a));

(iv) review and grant, to the extent permitted by law and as warranted, requests for waivers of notice periods arising from or related to USACE real estate policies and regulations; and

(v) issue, to the extent permitted by law and as warranted, any approved easements or rights-of-way immediately after notice is provided to the Congress pursuant to section 28(w) of the Mineral Leasing Act, as amended, 30 U.S.C. 185(w).

(b) Publication. The Secretary of the Army shall promptly provide a copy of this memorandum to the Speaker of the House of Representatives, the President pro tempore of the Senate, the Majority Leader of the Senate, and the Governors of each State located along the Dakota Access Pipeline route. The Secretary of the Army is authorized and directed to publish this memorandum in the Federal Register.

(c) Private Property. Nothing in this memorandum alters any Federal, State, or local process or condition in effect on the date of this memorandum that is necessary to secure access from an owner of private property to construct the pipeline and facilities described herein. Land or an interest in land for the pipeline and facilities described herein may only be acquired consistently with the Constitution and applicable State laws.

Section 3. General Provisions. (a) Nothing in this memorandum shall be construed to impair or otherwise affect:

(i) the authority granted by law to an executive department or agency, or the head thereof; or

(ii) the functions of the Director of the Office of Management and Budget relating to budgetary, administrative, or legislative proposals.

(b) This memorandum shall be implemented consistent with applicable law and subject to the availability of appropriations.

(c) This memorandum is not intended to, and does not, create any right or benefit, substantive or procedural, enforceable at law or in equity by any party against the United States, its departments, agencies, or entities, its officers, employees, or agents, or any other person.

Donald J. Trump

Second Declaration of Dave Archambault, II

February 9, 2017
    In the United States District Court for the District of Columbia
    Standing Rock Sioux Tribe, Plaintiff, v. US Army Corps of
Engineers, Defendant.

    I, Dave Archambault II, declare as follows:

1. My name is Dave Archambault, II and I am the Chairman of the
   Standing Rock Sioux Tribe. I have served as Chairman since 2013.
   I also served as a member of the Tribal Council from 2007 until 2011.
2. Since the Tribe first learned that the Dakota Access pipeline planned to
   cross Lake Oahe immediately upstream from the Standing Rock Sioux
   Reservation, the Tribe's position has been clear—we oppose the pipeline crossing Lake Oahe at that location. Our fundamental interest is to
   protect the waters of Lake Oahe from the risks associated with oil spills
   and to protect sacred sites along the pipeline's proposed path from
   destruction and desecration.
3. The waters of Lake Oahe have great significance to my people and to me.
   They are the waters that we drink, that we rely on for irrigation and other
   economic pursuits, and that sustain us spiritually. It is the drinking water
   supply for our homes, as well as the hospital, schools, and all public
   buildings on the Reservation. We have seen so many oil spills in North
   Dakota and around the country, and we are aware of the devastating impacts such spills have had in the past and continue to have today. As a
   fundamental part of our belief system, which is the belief system that
   guides my life, we have an obligation to our children, and to future generations, to protect against the contamination of these precious waters.
4. There is an important historic dimension to our concerns about the
   Dakota Access pipeline. The United States entered treaties with the
   Sioux Nation in 1851 and 1868, promising that we would have our
   homeland forever and that they would protect us against depredations.
   But, after gold was found and immigrants came into our territory, the
   United States broke its promises to us. The United States even tried to
   starve my people, in an effort to get us to consent to the taking of our
   lands. But we did not consent. Nevertheless, the United States dispos-
   sessed us from large amounts of land promised to us.
5. In modern times, this pattern continued—as our lands were taken and our
   way of life destroyed, to benefit others. In 1958, Congress enacted the
   Oahe Taking Act which took away 56,000 acres of land on our Reservation.
   These were fertile, wooded bottomlands—the best lands of the
   Reservation. These lands were permanently flooded, requiring the forced
   relocation of my people from their protected lowlands to the harsh and
   windswept uplands. This was a devastating event in the life of the Tribe,
   causing vast economic and social hardship that continues to this day.
6. The Tribe has a strong interest in making sure that this historic pattern
   does not continue. In every era, when the United States responds to

demands from those seeking to advance particular economic interests—for gold in the Black Hills, for land for non-Indian homesteaders on our Reservation, or for navigation or hydropower—it has always been the Tribe that has borne the heavy burdens, through the loss of our lands and harm to our way of life. While so much has been taken away by the misdeeds of the federal government, the Tribe has survived, and we have an obligation to protect what remains for the good of our children. We must take positive steps to see that our rights are not ignored by the federal government. That is why we have stressed the importance of meaningful consultation regarding the Dakota Access pipeline.

We must see that the federal government, which has solemn obligations under our Treaties and under the trust responsibility, hears our voices, and protects our Reservation and our way of life. As Chairman of the Tribe, I have done all I can to advance these principles.

7. There is also an important spiritual dimension to our concerns about the Dakota Access pipeline. Water plays a central role in our spiritual beliefs and our religious ceremonies. Our creation stories include stories of the importance of water. In our world view, everything is connected—people, animals, the land, and the water—and our belief system requires maintaining water in a pure form. Water is the critical element that nourishes and sustains all life. And water itself has a spirit that connects us all. When we say "mni wiconi," it means that water is a source of life—that water gives life. Water provides the foundation and basis for all living things. That is a core religious belief that sustains me and our people.

8. The waters of Lake Oahe have a particular religious significance to me and to the Tribe. Certain religious ceremonies, such as the sundance, have historically taken place on the banks of Lake Oahe right near where Dakota Access proposes to cross. Other ceremonies continue to this day. For example, each year when the ice begins to break up after the winter, families from our Tribe have prayer ceremonies on the banks of Lake Oahe at the site of the proposed crossing. Other ceremonies are also connected with Lake Oahe—although our ancestors have taught us that certain ceremonies should not be disclosed to outsiders. Nevertheless, there is a significant connection between the waters of Lake Oahe and the religious practices of my people.

9. One of the teachings of our ancestors, which is central to our belief system, is that to understand the interconnected nature of all things, one must look up to the heavens and down to the center of the earth. Along with our precious waters, the earth, the air and the sun are also sources of life. All of these four sources are connected, and all four are necessary for all beings to exist. We do not look at the sky and the ground as separate things—they are part of the unity of all of nature. This means that we must protect and conserve not only things on the surface, but in the sky and under the ground as well. Our ceremonies reflect the interconnectedness of water, earth, air and the sun (fire), and our spiritual life depends on the integrity of this understanding.

10. Another important teaching of our ancestors is to honor those who have come before us and in particular to ensure that their final resting places are not harmed or desecrated. In Lake Oahe, directly in the path of the proposed Dakota Access pipeline crossing, there is an island. Before the federal government built the Oahe Dam and Reservoir, this was not an island, but dry land along the Missouri River. It is my understanding that there are ancestors buried on this island and so this is a site of great religious and cultural significance to us.

11. Consistent with our history and our spiritual knowledge and understanding, the Tribe has worked hard to address its concerns regarding the Dakota Access pipeline in a good way. On behalf of the Tribe I have expressed our concerns in innumerable meetings with federal officials, I have spoken with all who would listen, and I have written to all those who had a role in the decisions to be made.

12. Throughout the process, we emphasized three things. First, we have a right to be heard—so meaningful consultation must be afforded to us consistent with the federal trust responsibility. Second, our Treaties must be honored, our sacred places protected, and our waters preserved. Third, the decision-making process must be fair—which means that an environmental impact statement is required. These positions have never changed.

13. The Army's December 4, 2016 decision and the January 18, 2017 notice in the Federal Register regarding the Army's intent to proceed with an Environmental Impact Statement was a significant development. After all of our efforts to be heard regarding oil spill risks, alternative routes and Treaty rights, the Army determined that it does have an obligation to take a closer look at these matters through an EIS. I felt that this was a significant vindication of the Tribe's position that we have a right to be heard and to have the Army address our concerns in a fair and comprehensive way. That has not happened before. While not guaranteeing any particular outcome, the Army's decision to do an EIS provided us with hope—as the process would open the door to meaningful consideration of our rights. The Tribe wrote to the Army, expressing our intent to participate fully in the EIS process, and asking to be a cooperating agency.

14. The Army's recent decision granting the easement to cross Lake Oahe immediately upstream from our Reservation indicates that, once again, the federal government feels that it can ignore the interests of the Tribe. In granting the easement, the Army did not consider our Treaty rights to hunt and fish on our Reservation or our *Winters* doctrine reserved water rights which sustain us. An oil spill would be devastating to those rights, and to the lives of my people, but none of that has been considered by the Army in granting the easement.

15. It is vitally important to our people that our rights be heard by this Court before Dakota Access drills under Lake Oahe.

16. Undertaking HDD drilling to place a major crude oil pipeline under Lake Oahe would interfere with important religious practices of the Tribe. The area where Dakota Access proposes to drill is a sacred

area, where numerous religious rituals are undertaken, as described above. The construction of the pipeline would harm the integrity and spiritual nature of the area, which extends under the ground. Our rituals could never be undertaken in those locations again. The proposed route would also go directly under the burial sites of ancestors in the island in Lake Oahe, and this would desecrate those graves—in much the same manner as placing a pipeline under a formal cemetery. Overall, the drilling under Lake Oahe would be a substantial burden to the exercise of religion by our people in that area.

17. The HDD drilling under Lake Oahe would also have a significant impact on the well-being of our people. Throughout the course of our history, we have suffered historic trauma. This has taken many forms—the devastating loss of lands, the destruction of the buffalo and our way of life, the efforts by the federal government to take away our language and culture, the impacts of poverty, and the ravages of racism. All of this has been endured with great dignity by my people. But over time this history takes a significant toll on our physical and mental health. Many of the health challenges that we face today have been linked, in significant scientific studies, to the historic traumas that we have faced. The traumas of our ancestors are passed down across the generations and impact us today.

18. While I am not a psychologist or social worker, as Chairman I know many Tribal members, and I understand how our history of trauma affects us and creates challenges for us today. One of those challenges today involves the Dakota Access pipeline. Our history tells us that the federal government does not listen to the voices of our people and does not care about our rights or interests. Our Tribe has been subject to terrible misdeeds and abuse at the hands of the federal government, and this has been so in Treaty times, at the time our lands were taken for the Oahe project, and up until the present. This pattern of ignoring Tribal interests continued with respect to the Dakota Access pipeline, until the Army finally determined that our position has merit and that an environmental impact statement was required. That step suggested, perhaps for the first time ever, that the voices of the Tribe do matter and that the federal government was willing to at least consider, in a meaningful way, our rights. The decision to undertake an EIS signified a recognition that we have a right to be heard.

19. The Army's decision to grant the easement basically strips the Tribe of the right to be heard. Once again, we are told that Tribal interests do not matter. If Dakota Access is allowed to drill under Lake Oahe before this Court hears the Tribe's position and rules on it, that would cause deep and lasting harm to our people. We have faced historic trauma and mistreatment across generations, which instilled in us the view that our rights do not matter to the federal government. But we have managed to overcome that here, when the Army determined that our concerns merited an EIS. Having come this far, there will be a deep and harmful impact on us if we are told that, not only has the Army changed its mind, but that the Court will not hear us until after the drill-

ing is done and the oil is flowing. If that happens, it would reinforce the deeply held understanding that the historic wrongs committed by the United States against us will continue and that our voices will not be heard in ways that matter by those who have the power to stop the harm to our people. In my view, that would be a terrible blow to our people, and it would have major and lasting physical and emotional consequences. As Chairman, I have a responsibility to provide for the health and welfare of our people, and if there is drilling under Lake Oahe, I will need to bear the additional burden of addressing the increased needs of our people who are adversely impacted.

20. The adverse consequences to our people of permitting Dakota Access to drill under Lake Oahe before our rights have been addressed by the Court would be profound. The drilling itself would violate our religious tenets and practices and would reinforce the federal government's intent to continue its pattern of wrongdoing against the Tribe. And if the drilling is permitted to go forward to completion, and if oil is actually transported through the pipeline under Lake Oahe, the harm to the Tribe and our people would be magnified. In that event, we would be living under the risk of an oil spill that would harm the waters that sustain our people, our economy and our spiritual lives. An oil spill would foul the water that we drink, that we rely upon for our Treaty protected, subsistence hunting, fishing and traditional plant gathering, and that provides irrigation for our farming and other economic ventures. The risk of an oil spill by the pipeline was significant enough that the original route of the pipeline—which was supposed to cross the River north of Bismarck—was changed. That risk is now placed squarely on the Tribe, as our Reservation is immediately downstream from the proposed crossing of Lake Oahe. We are entitled to be heard on this risk, particularly in light of the history of federal wrongdoings against us, the promises made to us in the Treaties, and the government's trust responsibility to protect our rights and resources from harm.

21. In conclusion, allowing Dakota Access to proceed to drill under Lake Oahe before this Court rules on the legality of the Army's actions would cause irreparable harm to the Tribe and our people. And if Dakota Access is allowed to complete the drilling and transport oil under Lake Oahe before the Court rules on the legality of the Army's actions that would cause further and even more profound irreparable harm to the Tribe and our people.

I declare under penalty of perjury that the foregoing is true and correct to the best of my knowledge. Executed on February 9, 2017, at Fort Yates, North Dakota.

Sources:

Biolsi, Thomas. "Settler Colonialism and the Treaty Imaginary." *Red Ink* 19, no. 1 (Spring 2017): 170.

http://earthjustice.org/cases/2016/the-dakota-access-pipeline.

104

Documents Related to the Indian Child Welfare Act (2017)

In 1978, after decades of study and testimony regarding disproportionate representation of Native children in the US child welfare system and the devastating consequences, Congress enacted The Indian Child Welfare Act (ICWA), "... to protect the best interest of Indian Children and to promote the stability and security of Indian tribes and families by the establishment of minimum Federal standards for the removal of Indian children and placement of such children in homes which will reflect the unique values of Indian culture...."(25 U.S. C. 1902). Essentially, the act codifies federal requirements for state child custody proceedings involving children who are members of, or eligible for, membership in federally recognized tribes.

However, as the act provided neither dedicated federal oversight nor consistent enforcement mechanisms, states were able to slowly adopt, or altogether ignore, the new rules. Native children and families thus continued to be unjustly swept into the child welfare system. The record is replete with examples of instances where states removed children and placed them with non-Indian families without regard to the rules or respect for due process, let alone any recognition of the sovereignty of Tribal governments who should have had the authority over such decisions. The phenomenon appears to have been driven by a combination of ignorance, racism, and a particularly insidious incentive—the more Native children in the system, the more federal funding for the state coffers.

After three decades of lackluster compliance, the issue resurfaced in mainstream media through several high-profile cases, most famously, the 2013 US Supreme Court opinion in *Adoptive Couple v. Baby Girl*. Later that year, a National Public Radio investigative report on abuses with South Dakota child welfare agencies exposed major ongoing problems, The resultant attention and confusion led to some attempts at reform. In 2016, states received clarification and guidelines, including the Bureau of Indian Affairs' *Guidelines for State Courts in Indian Child Custody Proceedings* and, importantly, comprehensive, legally binding federal regulations regarding implementation for state courts and agencies, both public and private.

The following article by respected legal scholar Steven Pevar, here speaking on behalf of the American Civil Liberties Union (ACLU), provides an overview of an important ICWA case, *Oglala Sioux Tribe and Rosebud Sioux Tribe v. Fleming*. It is followed by an amicus brief filed jointly by the Cherokee Nation and Navajo Nations, ICWA Law Center, National Indian Child Welfare Association (NICWA) and National Congress of American Indians (NCAI) in support of that lawsuit. These documents offer insights into an issue that has long tormented Native Nations. The philosophies and incentives underpinning some of today's Indian child welfare systems reveal them to be, in effect, modern manifestations of the boarding school system. Intent language and tactics may be different, but the result is the same: Native children removed from their homes, estranged from their cultures and left vulnerable to potential abuse and assimilation.

———

"In South Dakota, Officials Defied a Federal Judge and Took Indian Kids Away From Their Parents in Rigged Proceedings." Article by Stephen Pevar from the ACLU blog, February 22, 2017.

During the mid-1970s, Congress confirmed what Indian tribes had been saying for decades: State and local social workers and judges were aggressively using child custody hearings to take Indian children away from their families and tribes and place them in foster or adoptive homes, more often than not with white families. According to a congressional investigation, between 25 and 35 percent of all Indian children in the U.S. had been taken from their homes—a rate that jeopardized tribal culture if not the very survival of the tribes. Investigators determined that many removals were unwarranted and unnecessary. In 1978, Congress responded by passing the Indian Child Welfare Act [2] (ICWA), which established minimum federal standards to guide when and how state agencies could remove Native American children from their parents' custody and their cultural environment.

Nearly four decades later, state and local social workers and judges in Rapid City, South Dakota, are violating the rules in open defiance of ICWA, the Constitution, and now a federal judge. The reason for their noncompliance is unclear but the consequences are striking. Since 2010, more than 1,000 Native-American children in Pennington County, home to Rapid City, have been removed from their families by state welfare workers and placed in foster care, disproportionately in non-Indian homes.

In addition, statistics compiled by the South Dakota Department of Social Services (DSS) show that although American Indians comprise less than 9 percent of South Dakota's population, 52 percent of the children in the state's foster care system are American Indians. An Indian child is 11 times more likely to be placed in foster care than a white child in South Dakota. The child custody hearings typically lasted fewer than five minutes—some were done in 60 seconds—and the state won 100 percent of the time.

In 2013, the ACLU agreed to help challenge this. We filed [3] a class action lawsuit on behalf of two South Dakota tribes, the Oglala Sioux and Rosebud Sioux Tribes, and on behalf of all Indian families living in Pennington County South Dakota, challenging the state's child removal procedures of Indian children. The defendants are the presiding state court judge, the state director of DSS, the Pennington County director of DSS, and the state attorney filing the removal petitions.

In March 2015, Chief Federal District Court Judge Jeffrey L. Viken confirmed [4] what our complaint had alleged: State employees were removing children from their homes and then holding hearings in state court within

48 hours, in which parents were not assigned counsel to represent them, were not given a copy of the petition accusing them of wrongdoing, and no state employee was called to testify. Moreover, the parents were not permitted to testify, call witnesses, or cross-examine any state employee. The hearings typically lasted fewer than five minutes—some were done in 60 seconds—and the state won 100 percent of the time. That's right, 100 percent.

Often, Judge Viken found children would remain in foster care for two months or longer before their parents were given an opportunity to challenge the removal at a subsequent hearing. The judge held that the removal hearings violated ICWA as well as the Due Process Clause of the 14th Amendment to the Constitution. He invited both the plaintiffs and the defendants to suggest remedies for the violations. However, the defendants not only failed to submit any proposed remedies but largely ignored Judge Viken's ruling.

In August 2016, Viken convened a compliance hearing, which revealed the scope of the defendants' inaction. He followed in December 2016 with a 27-page decision [5] finding that the defendants "continue to disregard his prior rulings" and ordered "an immediate halt" to further violations. This time his ruling was accompanied by a formal injunction, which means that failure to comply could result in a contempt of court citation.

During the 1970s inquiry that led to the establishment of ICWA, Congress found that state officials, including judges and social workers, often removed Indian children based on biased and culturally insensitive grounds. To many Anglo-Americans, for example, leaving a child for extended periods of time with a grandparent or other relative may seem like abandonment, but such conduct is accepted and even encouraged on many Indian reservations. It's worth noting that in his December 2016 ruling, Judge Viken cited the 1954 Supreme Court decision in *Brown v. Board of Education*, which required the integration of public schools. As we know, that decision was met with explicit and orchestrated defiance from some state officials who opposed it. Judge Viken's reference to Brown is fitting.

Since the defendants never drew up their own remediation plan, in his recent ruling Judge Viken specified the actions they needed to take in order to rectify past procedural violations and to fully comply with ICWA and the Constitution. But the defendants prefer to dig in their heels: They are appealing Viken's injunctions to the U.S. Court of Appeals for the Eighth Circuit in St. Louis. Their briefs are due March 10th.

The South Dakota officials who are resisting Viken's orders are the ones most responsible for ensuring that Native American children and their families are treated fairly and properly. To that end, they must obey federal law. We intend to make sure that they do.

Motion for Leave to Brief Of Amici Curiae Cherokee Nation of Oklahoma, Navajo Nation, ICWA Law Center, National Congress of American Indians, National Indian Child Welfare Association

Appellate Case: 17–1135 Date Filed: 06/08/2017 Entry ID: 4545429

Summary of the Argument

The Indian Child Welfare Act is the culmination of hundreds of years of federal and state policies that decimated Indian families. Starting with the devastating federal boarding school era, and through the mid-1970s, Indian child welfare was the purview of the federal and state governments. After the end of the federal boarding school era, states stepped in to take control over Indian families and children.[1] In Minnesota, for example, seven years after the boarding schools closed, American Indian children made up 9.2 percent of the child welfare caseload, despite being only .5 percent of the population.[2] Across the country, state social workers routinely removed Indian children from their homes and schools based on vague allegations of poverty and neglect.[3] By the time Congress passed ICWA in 1978, 25–35 percent of all Indian children had been taken from their families and placed in adoptive, foster, or institutional care.[4]

Congress enacted the Indian Child Welfare Act (ICWA) in response to this wholesale removal of Indian children from their families by State and private child welfare agencies at rates far disproportionate to those of non-Indian families. Studies and Congressional testimony revealed the devastating impact of this displacement on Indian tribes and families and identified significant and pervasive abuses in state child welfare practices contributing to these harms. As a result, ICWA was carefully crafted to protect the rights of Indian children, families, and tribes by establishing minimum federal standards to govern state child welfare proceedings involving Indian children. In passing ICWA, Congress intended to combat the deliberate, collaborative abuse of the child welfare system, to recognize tribes' inherent authority to determine the best interest of their children, and to restore the integrity of Indian families.

Despite ICWA's passage, the abuse of Indian children and families continues to the present. In this case, the district court found a South Dakota state judge and the State Department of Social Services "failed to protect Indian parents' fundamental rights to a fair hearing by not allowing them to present evidence to contradict the State's removal documents. The defendants failed by not allowing the parents to confront and cross-examine DSS witnesses. The defendants failed by using documents as a basis for the court's decisions which were not provided to the parents and which were not received in evidence at the 48-hour hearings."[5] This lawsuit, brought by the Oglala Sioux and Rosebud Sioux Tribes is vital to ensuring courts follow the minimum federal requirements established in ICWA, adjust their state practice accordingly, and allow for tribes to enforce due process violations against their citizens. Therefore, Amici agree with Plaintiffs-Appellees that this Court should affirm the decision below.

---

1. Margaret Jacobs, A Generation Removed: The Fostering and Adoption of Indigenous Children in the Postwar World 6 (2014).

2. Id.

3. Id. at 97–103.

4. 25 U.S.C. § 1901(4); H.R. Rep. No. 95-1386 at 10 (1978).

5. *Oglala Sioux Tribe v. Van Hunnik*, 100 F.Supp.3d 749, 772 (D.S.D., 2015).

Argument

I. Congress Enacted ICWA Pursuant to its Trust Responsibility and in Response to the Widespread Abuses Committed by State Child Welfare Systems Against Indian Children and Families.

The United States has a "distinctive obligation of trust" to federally recognized tribes.[6] (ICWA) explicitly recognizes this obligation in no uncertain terms: Congress, through statutes, treaties, and the general course of dealing with Indian tribes, has assumed the responsibility for the protection and preservation of Indian tribes and their resources ... there is no resource that is more vital to the continued existence and integrity of Indian tribes than their children ... the United States has a direct interest, as trustee, in protecting Indian children who are members of or are eligible for membership in an Indian tribe.[7] This obligation of trust extends specifically to Indian children and families.[8] ICWA's findings explicitly recognize Congress's exclusive constitutional authority to legislate in the area of Indian affairs.[9]

These findings are a result of years of Congressionally commissioned reports and wide-ranging testimony taken from "the broad spectrum of concerned parties, public and private, Indian and non-Indian."[10] The legislative testimony wove together a chilling narrative—state and private child welfare agencies, with the backing of many state courts and, at times in collaboration with the federal government, had engaged in the systematic removal of Indian children from their families without evidence of harm or due process of law. By the time of ICWA's passage, state agencies had removed between 25 and 35 percent of all Indian children nationwide from their families, placing about 90 percent of those removed children in non-Indian homes.[11] Of those removals, 99 percent were cited for vague reasons of "neglect" or "social deprivation" and the emotional damage the children might be subject to by continuing to live with their Indian families.[12]

For states within the Eighth Circuit, the situation was particularly dire. In South Dakota, one out of every eighteen Indian children were adopted, almost always out of their communities, compared with one out of every 28.7

---

6. *Seminole Nation v. United States*, 316 U.S. 286, 296–97 (1942) and the Indian Child Welfare Act 25 U.S.C. §§ 1901 et. seq.

7. 25 U.S.C. §§ 1901(2)–(3).

8. See Matthew L.M. Fletcher and Wenona T. Singel, Indian Children and the Federal-Trust Relationship, forthcoming, Neb. L. Rev. (2017), https://papers.ssrn.com/sol3/papers.cfm?abstract_id=2772139.

9. 25 U.S.C. § 1901(1); see also U.S. Const. art. I, § 8, cl. 3 (charging Congress with the exclusive authority to "regulate commerce...with the Indian Tribes"); *Seminole Tribe v. Fla.*, 517 U.S. 44, 62 (1996) (summarizing the Indian Commerce Clause's broad grant of authority to Congress over Indian affairs); *Rice v. Cayetano*, 528 U.S. 495, 519 (2000) ("Congress may fulfill its treaty obligations and its responsibilities to the Indian tribes by enacting legislation dedicated to their circumstances and needs.").

10. H.R. Rep. 95–1386 at 4 (1978), as reprinted in 1978 U.S.C.C.A.N. 7530 http://www.narf.org/nill/documents/icwa/federal/lh/hr1386.pdf ("1978 House Report").

11. *Miss. Band of Choctaw Indians v. Holyfield*, 490 U.S. 30, 32–33 (1989) (citing Problems that American Indian Families Face in Raising their Children and how these Problems are Affected by Federal Action or Inaction: Hearings Before the Subcomm. on Indian Affairs of the S. Comm. On Interior and Insular Affairs, 93rd Cong. 2nd Sess. 3 (1974) http://www.narf.org/nill/documents/icwa/federal/lh/hear040874/hear040 874.pdf (statement of William Byler) ("1974 Senate Hearings")).

12. 1978 House Report at 10.

non-Indian children.[13] Worse, one out of every 22 Indian children were in foster care, as opposed to one out of every 492 non-Indian children.[14] Other states in the Eighth Circuit had similar numbers. In both Minnesota and North Dakota, Indian children were 5.2 times more likely to be removed and placed in either adoptive or foster care than non-Indian children.[15]

In addition, the removals were often done with no respect for due process, and with no legal standards at the initial removal hearing. As in the case at bar, the initial removal and subsequent emergency or initial hearing involved some of the worst violations of fundamental due process. In the testimony of Cheryl DeCoteau, describing the removal and hearings of her children in South Dakota, Ms. DeCoteau testified she did not receive notice of two hearings regarding the removal and placement of her son.[16] During her testimony her attorney interjected that the process was the "grossest violations of due process" he had ever seen.[17] In conducting removals of Indian children, not only did state officials, agencies, and procedures "fail . . . to take into account the special problems and circumstances of Indian families and the legitimate interest of the Indian tribe in preserving and protecting the Indian family as the wellspring of its own future,"[18] they also failed to prove up basic standards of unfitness against Indian parents.[19] ("It was never proven in court that she was unfit. We had a hearing in the district county court. . . . The burden of proof was very clearly shifted on Mrs. DeCoteau to prove that she was fit, rather than the State proving she was unfit.").

In fact, Congress found that "many social workers, ignorant of Indian cultural values and social norms, make decisions that are wholly inappropriate in the context of Indian family life and so they frequently discover neglect or abandonment where none exists."[20] Further, Congress found that "the decision to take Indian children from their natural homes is, in most cases, carried out without due process of law. For example, it is rare for either Indian children or their parents to be represented by counsel or have the supporting testimony of an expert witness. . . . The conflict between Indian and non-Indian social systems operates to defeat due process."[21] Abusive child welfare practices also proved harmful to Indian children. In ICWA, Congress was concerned about "the placement of Indian children in non-Indian . . . based in part on evidence of the detrimental impact on the children themselves of such placement outside their culture."[22] Congress heard manifold examples of Indian children placed in non-Indian homes later suffering from identity crises when they reached

13. Task Force Four, Report on Federal, State, and Tribal Jurisdiction, Final Report to the American Indian Policy Review Commission, 231 (1976) http://www.narf.org/nill/documents/icwa/federal/lh/76rep/76rep.pdf ("Task Force Four Report").

14. Id. at 232.

15. Id. at 210, 221.

16. 1974 Senate Hearings at 67 (statement of Cheryl DeCoteau).

17. Id.

18. 1978 House Report at 19,

19. 1974 Senate Hearings at 67 (Testimony of Bertram Hirsch)

20. 1978 House Report at 10.

21. Id. at 11.

22. Holyfield, 490 U.S. at 499–500.

adolescence and adulthood.[23] Such evidence led Congress to conclude that "[r]emoval of Indians from Indian society has serious long-and short-term effects...for the individual child...who may suffer untold social and psychological consequences."[24] More recent studies have also shown the harm of putting children in foster care[25] The higher standard Congress adopted in ICWA for removing Indian children not only addresses the cultural bias of state social workers, but also the harm caused to children by the removal.

Congress explicitly recognized and attempted to remediate this national crisis through ICWA—a statute designed to establish "minimum Federal standards for the removal of Indian children from their families and the placement of such children in foster or adoptive homes"[26] ICWA thus contains protections that provide notice, court-appointed counsel, and require the testimony of a qualified expert witness to place a child in foster care.[27] One of the most important provisions of ICWA, the notice provision, ensures that parents know when the state is going to have a hearing about their child, and ensures the tribe knows the state has removed or otherwise has exercised jurisdiction over a tribal child.[28]

Uniquely, ICWA must be implemented by state and private agencies and applied by state courts with the intention "to promote the stability and security of Indian tribes and families."[29] The Congressional findings further "make clear that the underlying principle of the bill is in the best interest of the Indian child."[30] At its core, ICWA "seeks to protect the rights of the Indian child as an Indian and the rights of the Indian community and tribe in retaining its children in its society...by establishing 'a Federal policy that wherever possible, an Indian child should remain in the Indian community.' "[31]

II. Because ICWA is Implemented by State Court Systems, State Laws Must Work Alongside ICWA, Not in Conflict With It.

A. State Child Welfare Systems Overwhelmingly Address Cases of Neglect, and ICWA Provides the Gold Standard for Supporting Children and Families.

Children removed by state child welfare systems, are, in the vast majority of cases, removed for neglect, which usually involves poverty, mental health or

    23. See, e.g., 1974 Hearings at 114 (statement of James Shore, former Chief, Mental Health Office, Portland Area Indian Health Service, and William Nicholls, Director, Health, Welfare and Social Services, Confederated Tribes of The Warm Springs Reservation.).
    24. S. Rep. No. 95–597 at 43 (1977).
    25. See Joseph J. Doyle Jr., Child Protection and Child Outcomes: Measuring the Effects of Foster Care, 97 Amer. Eco. Rev. 1583 (2007)("Large marginal treatment effect estimates suggest caution in the interpretation, but the results suggest that children on the margin of placement tend to have better outcomes when they remain at home, especially older children.").
    26. 25 U.S.C. § 1902.
    27. 25 U.S.C. 1912(a), (b), (e); see also 1978 House Report at 22.
    28. 5 U.S.C. § 1911(a).
    29. 25 U.S.C. § 1902.
    30. 1978 House Report at 19; 25 U.S.C. § 1902 ("Congress hereby declares that it is the policy of this Nation to protect the best interests of Indian children...").
    31. Holyfield, 490 U.S. at 37 (quoting 1978 House Report at 23) (emphasis added).

chemical dependency issues of the parents.[32] This means that for the vast majority of children, real wrap-around, in-home care and services, the kind ICWA envisions in 25 U.S.C. § 1912(d), may alleviate the need for an emergency removal of a child, because she is not facing imminent physical damage or harm required by ICWA.[33]

The history of Indian child welfare policies indicated to Congress that Indian children and families in particular needed federally ensured, heightened standards before a child could be removed. ICWA provides the framework for its application, defining to whom it applies and under what circumstances. It also provides various procedural and substantive provisions to protect Indian families and children under the jurisdiction of state court systems.[34] The law applies only to child custody proceedings involving an "Indian child."[35] ICWA's application is directly tied to the child's membership or eligibility for membership in a federally recognized tribe.[36] ICWA's provisions apply to four defined types of state child custody proceedings: (1) foster care placement; (2) termination of parental rights; (3) preadoptive placement; and (4) adoptive placement.[37] These include any "emergency proceedings."[38] Any proceeding that could end up with a child placed in foster care is an ICWA proceeding.[39]

The Act also delineates the division of jurisdiction in proceedings between tribal and state courts,[40] and provides explicit protections for families in state court proceedings that involve the involuntary removal of an Indian child from her parent or Indian custodian,[41] (requiring that the party seeking to place a child in foster care prove to a court that "active efforts have been made to prevent the breakup of the Indian family" and prove that the continued custody of the child by the parent or Indian custodian is "likely to result in serious emotional or physical damage" through the testimony of a qualified expert witness.). ICWA requires that "[i]n any involuntary proceeding in a State court, where the court knows or has reason to know that an Indian child is involved, the party seeking the foster care placement of, or termination of parental rights to, an Indian child shall notify the parent or Indian custodian and the Indian child's tribe...."[42] In situations where children are removed due to an immediate emergency, ICWA mandates they should be returned to their homes once the emergency has passed.[43] That standard, addressed at length in the principal briefs, requires the removal be terminated immediately when the removal is no

32. Child Trends, Child Maltreatment Indicators of Child and Youth Well-Being (September, 2016), www.childtrends.org/wpcontent/uploads/2016/09/40_Child_Maltreatment.pdf ("In 2014, 7.1 per thousand children were reported victims of neglect, compared with 1.6 for physical abuse, 0.8 for sexual abuse, and 0.6 for psychological or emotional abuse.").

33. 25 U.S.C. § 1922.

34. Holyfield, 490 U.S. at 36.

35. 25 U.S.C. § 1903(4).

36. Id.

37. 25 U.S.C. § 1903(1).

38. Indian Child Welfare Act Final Rule, 81 Fed. Reg. 38,868, (to be codified at 25 C.F.R. pt. 23.103(a)(2)).

39. Id. at 38,799.

40. See 25 U.S.C. § 1911(a)-(b),

41. See, e.g. 25 U.S.C. § 1912(d) and (e).

42. 25 U.S.C. § 1912(a).

43. 25 U.S.C. § 1922.

longer necessary to prevent imminent physical damage or harm to the child.[44] This standard is consistent with social science research finding long-term harm of non-kin foster care.[45] This is a standard higher than that of most state child welfare codes, but it has not prevented other states from ensuring this standard is met for Indian children.

The standards required by ICWA are considered the gold standard for protecting children and families.[46] Similarly, Casey Family Programs and twelve other child welfare organizations argued in their amicus brief in support of a motion to dismiss a challenge to ICWA that, "although the protection of children is paramount, children's well-being is best served if they are removed from their families only when necessary to protect them from serious harm"[47]

B. Unlike South Dakota, Other Eighth Circuit States Have Adopted ICWA's Heightened Standards at the Initial Emergency Proceeding.

As federal law, ICWA provides the minimum floor from which states must operate.[48] States can adopt higher protections for families, and ensure that families in child welfare proceedings receive both due process protections and the highest levels of reunification efforts and kinship placement.[49] Multiple states in the Eighth Circuit have state ICWA laws, to guarantee the state laws interact smoothly with ICWA's federal requirements. These laws provide the heightened standard of section 1922 along with ensuring a prompt ending to the emergency removal, notice to the parents and tribes, and ensuring that the standards of 25 U.S.C. § 1912 are applied as early as possible in the proceedings.

Minnesota, Nebraska, and Iowa all have comprehensive state ICWA laws providing heightened protections to Native children and families.[50] In addition, other states in this Circuit provide some kind of evidentiary standard for determining if the placement should continue at the first hearing, and a timeframe for hearings.[51] South Dakota's assertion of having an "informal proceeding" within forty-eight hours and then keeping the child in foster care up to another 60 days without a hearing is contrary to best practices in child welfare as well as other state practices in this Circuit.[52]

44. Id.

45. See Delilah Bruskas, Children in Foster Care: A Vulnerable Population at Risk, 21 J. of Child and Adolescent Psychiatric Nursing 70 (2008); Doyle Jr., Child Protection and Child Outcomes at 1584.

46. See Brief of Casey Family Programs & Child Welfare League of America, et al. as Amici Curiae Supporting Respondent, Adoptive Couple v. Baby Girl, 133 S.Ct. 2552 (2013) 2013 WL 1279468 at *1 ("Amici are united in their view that, in the Indian Child Welfare Act, Congress adopted the gold standard for child welfare policies and practices that should be afforded to all children...").

47. Brief of Casey Family Programs and Twelve Other National Child Welfare Organizations as Amici Curiae Supporting Defendants, Carter v. Washburn, 2017 WL 1019685, 4 (Ariz. Dist. Ct. Oct. 23, 2015) (No. CV–15–01259).

48. 25 U.S.C. § 1902.

49. See Minn. Indian Family Preservation Act, Minn. Stat. §§ 260.751–260.835 (2015).

50. Minn. Stat. §§260.751–260.835 (2015); Neb. Rev. Stat. §§431501–43–1517 (2015); Iowa Code Ann. §§232B.1–232B.14 (2003).

51. See Mo. Sup. Ct. R. 123.05(f)("at the protective custody hearing, the court shall determine and make findings on the following issues: whether the juvenile can safely return home immediately..."); Mo. Sup. Ct. R. 124.01(a)(a protective custody hearing shall happen within 3 days, and an adjudication hearing within 60 days).

52. See Oglala Sioux Tribe, 100 F.Supp.3rd. at 770–772.

Iowa, for example, requires the court to determine whether there is an "imminent risk to the child's life and health" to keep the child out of the house.[53] Iowa also limits the time frame of an emergency proceeding to 30 days. Iowa Code Ann. § 232B.6(4). In addition, Iowa's ICWA law has extensive direction on emergency procedures for Indian children. In fact, the newly issued Federal Regulations on ICWA implementation closely mimic Iowa's ICWA law.[54]

Iowa's law requires that: "in a case of emergency removal of an Indian child, regardless of residence or domicile of the child, the state shall ensure that the emergency removal or placement terminates immediately when the removal or placement is no longer necessary to prevent imminent physical damage or harm to the child and shall expeditiously initiate a child custody proceeding subject to the provisions of this chapter, transfer the child to the jurisdiction of the appropriate Indian tribe, or restore the child to the child's parent or Indian custodian, as may be appropriate."[55]

In addition, Iowa law requires the: "emergency removal or placement of an Indian child shall immediately terminate, and any court order approving the removal or placement shall be vacated, when the removal or placement is no longer necessary to prevent imminent physical damage or harm to the child. In no case shall an emergency removal or placement order remain in effect for more than fifteen days unless, upon a showing that continuation of the order is necessary to prevent imminent physical damage or harm to the child, the court extends the order for a period not to exceed an additional thirty days. If the Indian child's tribe has been identified, the court shall notify the tribe of the date and time of any hearing scheduled to determine whether to extend an emergency removal or placement order."[56]

Nebraska also requires the emergency removal of Indian children to meet the ICWA standard of preventing "imminent physical damage or harm to the child."[57] In addition, there "must be a nexus between the State ground for removal and the ICWA requirement that such removal or placement is necessary in order to prevent imminent physical damage or harm to the child."[58] Nebraska state law fully adopts 25 U.S.C. § 1922 into state law.[59]

An example of Nebraska's child welfare timeline can be found in In re Interest of Shayla H. 764 N.W.2d 119 (Neb. Ct. App. 2009). In that case, when the children were removed from the home, the first hearing was scheduled within five days of the state's ex parte temporary custody petition.[60] That hearing was continued for a week, and at the temporary custody hearing, among other things, the court "heard testimony from [Department's safety worker],

53. Iowa Code Ann. § 232.79(4)(b).
54. 81 Fed. Reg. 38,872, (to be codified at 24 C.F.R. §23.113).
55. Iowa Code Ann. § 232B.6(1).
56. Iowa Code Ann. § 232B.6 (4).
57. Neb. Rev. St. §43–1514 (2015).
58. Neb. Juv. Ct. Law and Practice, Emergency removal of the child § 13:7 (2016).
59. Neb. Rev. St. §43–1514 (2015).
60. Id. at 122.

[the father], and children's mother."[61] An adjudication hearing happened within 60 days of the temporary custody hearing.[62]

Minnesota may have the best practice in the Eighth Circuit, as codified in state law and in practice. In Minnesota, tribes and parents receive notice of the hearing prior to the emergency hearing, which must be held within 72 hours of the child's removal.[63] This practice is likely one of the reasons Minnesota's numbers of Indian children in care is so high, as they are one of the very few states accurately identifying their Native children at such an early stage. At that hearing, active efforts are discussed, as is the placement of the child to ensure she is close to home and with family when possible.[64] The standard to keep the child out of her home at that hearing is the standard of section 1922—that she is in imminent physical danger if she is returned home.[65]

Finally, there is very little case law on the intersection of the emergency proceedings and ICWA and there are none in this Circuit—outside of South Dakota. While the South Dakota Supreme Court held in *Cheyenne River Sioux v. Davis* that the emergency standards of ICWA did not apply at the initial hearing, the decision misreads section 1922.[66] If the initial emergency hearings regarding Indian children are subject to jurisdiction under section 1922, then they are necessarily also subject to the heightened standards.[67] The Department of the Interior, in its agency commentary preceding the ICWA regulations, emphasized the "immediacy of the threat is what allows the State to temporarily suspend the initiation of a full 'child-custody proceeding' subject to ICWA. Where harm is not imminent, issues…may be addressed either without removal, or with a removal on a non-emergency basis."[68]

III. When States Refuse to Follow ICWA, Tribes Have the Ability to Sue on Behalf of Their Families to Enforce the Law.

In ICWA cases, tribes have an interest distinct from, but on par with, Indian parents.[69] These interests include the protection of the child, the relationship of the child to the tribe, and in addition, the protection of vulnerable citizen parents. This last prong is evident by section 1914 of ICWA, which allows tribes to "petition any court of competent jurisdiction" to invalidate an action that "violated any provisions of 1911, 1912, and 1913 of this title."[70] These sections are the bulk of ICWA's procedural and substantive provisions, but importantly for this discussion, they include the notice provision and the appointment of

61. Id.

62. Id.

63. Minn. Stat. Ann. § 260.761 Subd. 2 (c).

64. Minn. Stat. Ann. 260.762 Subd. 3.

65. 25 U.S.C. § 1922.

66. 822 N.W.2d 62 (S.D. 2012)(distinguished by *Oglala Sioux Tribe v. Hunnik*, No. Civ 13–5020–JLV (D.S.D., Feb. 9, 2016)).

67. 81 Fed. Reg. 38,872 (to be codified at 25 C.F.R. pt. 23.113); see In re T.S., 315 P.3d 1030 (Okla. Ct. App. 2013)("The second sentence of § 1922 contains two mandates for State,… '[the State] shall insure that the emergency removal or placement terminates immediately when such removal or placement is no longer necessary to prevent imminent physical damage or harm to the child.'; In re Esther V., 248 P.3d 863 (N.M. 2011); In re S.B., 30 Cal. Rptr. 3d 726 (Cal. Ct. App. 2005); *D.E.D. v. State*, 704 P.2d 774 (Alaska, 1985).

68. 81 Fed. Reg. 38,794.

69. Holyfield at 51 (quoting In re Adoption of Hallowell, 732 P.2d 962, 969–970 (Utah 1986)).

70. 25 U.S.C. § 1914.

counsel to indigent parent provision.[71] This means the tribe has the right to petition a court to address practices that violate parents' rights, not just tribal rights. In this case, the tribes rightly used the parens patriae doctrine to appeal those violations.

Parens patriae allows a sovereign entity to protect its citizens by bringing litigation on their behalf. The doctrine is recognized by the Supreme Court as the inherent power of every sovereign "to be exercised in the interest of humanity, and for the prevention of injury to those who cannot protect themselves."[72] Under parens patriae, the sovereign entity acts an advocate for its injured citizens.[73] Native American tribes, as federally recognized sovereigns, have the inherent right to bring parens patriae suits.[74] When a tribe is suing in its parens patriae capacity it needs to meet three requirements. First, the tribe must articulate a separate interest from private parties in the suit. *Alfred L. Snapp & Son, Inc. v. Puerto Rico ex rel. Barez*, 458 U.S. 592, 601–08 (1982). Tribes have an interest in the application of ICWA in state courts based on their own rights under ICWA, separate and apart from individual tribal members.

Second, the tribe must express a quasi-sovereign interest concrete enough to meet the actual controversy requirement of constitutional standing. –While the determination of a quasi-sovereign interest "is a matter for a case-by-case development," the Supreme Court has recognized certain characteristics of a quasi-sovereign interest which it has split into two categories: 1) a state's interest in the physical and economic health and well-being of its residents, and 2) a state's interest in securing its rightful place in the federal system.[75] ICWA cases fall into the first category as they raise concerns of the health, welfare, and family integrity of tribal members.[76] As discussed above, Congress passed ICWA to prevent the unnecessary removal of Indian children. In doing so Congress recognized the importance of children to the survival of a Tribe and created rights for tribes in state court custody proceedings. Tribes have a sovereign interest in ensuring the rights afforded under ICWA are enforced and that ICWA is followed by state courts.

Third, the tribe must be acting on behalf of a substantial number of its citizens and not just a special interest.[77] The Supreme Court has held this number may vary, such as when the absolute number of affected citizens was small but the effect on the State as a whole could be substantial.[78] The Court has not attempted to draw any definitive limits on the proportion of the population of the State that must be adversely affected by the challenged behavior. Although more must be alleged than injury to an identifiable group of individual residents, the indirect effects of the injury must be considered as well in determining whether the State has alleged injury to a sufficiently substantial segment of its population. One helpful indication in determining whether

71. 25 U.S.C. § 1912(a), (b).

72. *Late Corp. of Church of Jesus Christ v. United States*, 136 U.S. 1, 57 (1890).

73. See *Kan. v. Utilicorp United, Inc.*, 497 U.S. 199, 219 (1990).

74. *Standing Rock Sioux Indian Tribe v. Dorgan*, 505 F.2d 1135, 1137 (8th Cir. 1974)(granting the tribe parens patriae standing to recover state taxes illegally collected from its members).

75. Id.

76. Id.

77. Id.

78. Id.

an alleged injury to the health and welfare of its citizens suffices to give the State standing to sue as parens patriae is whether the injury is one that the State, if it could, would likely attempt to address through its sovereign lawmaking powers.[79]

Unfortunately, federal district courts have imposed a more stringent standard of this rule on tribes. The court in *Assiniboine & Sioux Tribes v. Montana*,[80] and courts in subsequent cases, have ruled that tribes lack standing to bring parens patriae suits because they were not representing the interest of all its members.[81] However, these holdings are in contradiction with the Supreme Court's decision in Snapp and the decision below. The district court below properly held, and Defendant-Appellees do not contest, that tribes have a right of parens patriae standing for ICWA cases.

Conclusion

For the foregoing reasons, Amici Curiae respectfully request the Court affirm the district court's holdings.

Respectfully submitted this 8th day of June, 2017.

Kathryn E. Fort, Indian Law Clinic, Michigan State University College of Law, Lansing, MI

Katherine Belzowski, Navajo Nation, Window Rock, AZ

Chrissi Nimmo, Cherokee Nation, Tahlequah, OK

Sources:

American Civil Liberties Union Blog (https://www.aclu.org).
https://turtletalk.files.wordpress.com/2017/06/17-1135_proposedamicibrief.pdf.

105

Bears Ears Inter-Tribal Coalition Letter to the Secretary of Interior (2017)

Native peoples' organic relationship with the lands of North America date back tens of thousands of years. Such a lengthy tenure ensures that specific sites within Native territories and formerly held territories possess a special, sacred

---

79. 458 U.S. at 607.
80. 568 F. Supp. 269 (D. Mont. 1983),
81. See *Kickapoo Tribe of Okla. v. Lujan*, 728 F. Supp. 791, 795 (D.D.C. 1990); *Alabama & Coushatta Tribes of Tex. v. Tr. Of the Big Sandy Independent School Dist.*, 817 F. Supp. 1319, 1327 (E.D. Tex. 1993).

status. Some, like Pipestone Quarry in southwestern Minnesota, were visited and revered by many nations. Bears Ears is such a place.

Located in southern Utah, north of the Navajo Nation and west of the Ute Mountain Ute Reservation, Bears Ears is 1.9 million acres replete with sacredness and cultural vitality. Five nations, the Hopi, Navajo, Ute Mountain Ute, and Zuni, hold the area as a critically important place. For more than a decade, they have united to lobby the federal government to designate the area as a national monument and thus protect it from mining, looting, and off-road vehicle use.

In 2015, their persistence was rewarded when President Barack Obama declared Bears Ears a national monument. But, when Donald Trump became president, he issued an executive order directing Secretary of the Interior Ryan Zinke to revisit Obama's decision. The five Nations, through the Bears Ears Intertribal Coalition, wrote the following letter to Secretary Zinke urging him not retract the Bears Ears' designation. Their request was in vain, as Trump, at Zinke's recommendation, signed two orders in December 2017 slashing the size of Bears Ears and Grand Staircase-Escalante national monuments by 85 percent making it the largest rollback of federal land protection in the nation's history. Tribes and environmental advocacy groups have since filed lawsuits challenging these orders, but plans to exploit and extract resources are underway.

———

Dear Secretary Zinke,

The Bears Ears Inter-Tribal Coalition, a partnership of the Hopi, Navajo, Ute Indian Tribe, Ute Mountain Ute, and Zuni Tribal governments, is deeply troubled by the Executive Order directing the Department of Interior to review and propose changes to national monuments, and by your statements that Bears Ears will undergo such a review within 45 days. The designation of the Bears Ears National Monument was a long overdue moment in the protection of our cultural and spiritual heritage. Our Tribal governments have made it clear that any change to the monument would undermine the efforts of so many, and would disrespect our deep and enduring connections to this place.

During your confirmation hearing, you said "tribal sovereignty should mean something," and "our nation should better equip our Indian Tribes with the ability for self-determination." The establishment of the Bears Ears Commission, consisting of elected delegates from each of the five tribes, is a step in that direction. The Bears Ears National Monument proclamation is very clear that the Secretary must work with the Bears Ears Commission. We urge you to honor your statements, the proclamation, and our sovereignty as Tribal nations and leave Bears Ears National Monument as it is. The national monument has taken more than 80 years to designate, and finally acknowledges a cultural landscape rich in antiquities, with hundreds of thousands of archaeological and cultural sites sacred to dozens of tribes. The land is powerful medicine for healing—of the land, of plants and animals and for all people.

Our letters to your office from each of our Tribal nations, the Bears Ears Inter-Tribal Coalition, and the Bears Ears Commission requesting meetings with you have gone unanswered. It seems illogical that letters sent nearly 100 days ago have not been answered, yet there will be review of Bears Ears within the next 45 days. The fact that you have not met with us is evident in your statement yesterday to the press. You said: "The administration has heard from Congress.... The designation of monuments may have cost jobs, wages, and public access.... It is the opinion of the West that it is abused." Please do not forget—our Tribes are the original inhabitants of the West long before the United States was a nation, and we do not view Bears Ears National Monument as an abuse. To the contrary, it is a fulfillment of both our duty to preserve our cultures and our ancestral lands, and its designation was the result of a long, deliberative process with your predecessor to further our self-determination. To that end, we reiterate our requests for you to meet with each of the Tribes, and the Bears Ears Tribal Commission.

Bears Ears National Monument is more than just mere federal land to us, as it may be to many other stakeholders—it is a living landscape; it has a pulse. "Bears Ears" translates literally from all of our Native languages—Diné, Hopi, Ute, and Zuni. We have known this place since time immemorial. Bears Ears is a place where certain herbs, medicines, and ceremonial materials exist that are not found anywhere else on Earth.

For the Navajo, the monument is rich with places of great power tied to mythological cosmology, as well as the birthplace of important leaders from modern history. For the Ute, much of the monument was actually proposed as our reservation in the early 20th century, and in the monument is a location where a prophecy foretells that all the nations of the world will come together to heal. For the Hopi, Zuni, and other Pueblos, the monument is a place that bears ample evidence of migrations over centuries that lead the to the center places where we now reside.

Our ancestors are buried here, and we all practice pilgrimage to sacred locations throughout the monument. It means different things to each of our Tribes, but we all share in a desire to see it remain protected as a national monument. So great is its power that we have agreed, for the first time in history, to set aside our differences to work together to see it protected and defended. The significance and importance of our unity cannot be overstated.

The Bears Ears National Monument is the first national monument to be protected at the behest of sovereign Tribal Nations. Its proclamation recognizes Native American Traditional Knowledge as both a value to be protected by the monument and a resource to be used in its management. The proclamation also established a Tribal commission to work with the U.S. Government to help plan for and manage the lands. The Bears Ears Commission has been formalized and has already began meeting with federal land managers. In addition to sitting down with our Tribal Councils, we invite you to join the next Bears Ears Commission meeting on May 19th, 2017. This will give you the opportunity to witness for yourself the substantial progress we have made in building relationships with your staff on-the-ground, and to learn of the inspiring plans we jointly have for what will surely be America's best national monument—one which invites and involves all who wish to share in our knowledge systems and our cultures in a landscape unmatched in beauty.

Once again, we invite you to meet with the Bears Ears Inter-Tribal Coalition at your earliest convenience. We are more than mere stakeholders—we are sovereign governments with a strong commitment to the future of Bears Ears, and we must be an integral part of your review of the Bears Ears National Monument. Our Tribal nations came together and worked closely with the U.S. Government to finally recognize Bears Ears as a cultural and historic landscape that carries deep meaning for our peoples. The permanent protection of Bears Ears is long overdue, and has finally given us a strong voice in how these lands are to be managed. We advocated for the Bears Ears National Monument, and we remain strongly committed to its defense. We insist that our concerns be given the utmost respect in your upcoming review of Bears Ears National Monument.

Sincerely,

Alfred Lomahquahu, Co-Chair, Bears Ears Inter-Tribal Coalition, Vice Chairman, Hopi Tribe

Carleton Bowekaty, Co-Chair, Bears Ears Inter-Tribal Coalition, Council Member, Zuni Tribe

Shaun Chapoose, Chairman, Ute Indian Tribe Business Committee

Harold Cuthair, Chairman, Ute Mountain Ute Tribe

Davis Filfred, Navajo Nation Council Delegate, Utah Navajo Nation Council

Source:

http://www.bearsearscoalition.org/wp-content/uploads/2015/10/Bears-Ears-Inter-Tribal-Coalition-Proposal-10-15-15.pdf.

106   *Joint Petition from Five Anishinaabe (Ojibwe) Nations Regarding Enbridge Pipeline 3 (2018)*

For several years, Anishinaabe (Ojibwe or Chippewa) nations have battled the state of Minnesota's Departments of Commerce and Transportation and the private firm Enbridge Energy, which has designs on constructing a new $2.6 billion, 340-mile-long pipeline (Line 3) that would carry Canadian oil to Enbridge's station in Superior, Wisconsin, and then through Minnesota across territory deemed vital by the Anishinaabe nations of Fond du Lac, Mille Lacs, Leech Lake, White Earth, and Red Lake. While the proposed route would not go through existing Native reservations lands, it would run through treaty-recognized territory that includes sacred lands, lakes, watersheds, and important cultural sites. In addition to these substantial environmental and cultural impacts, the influx of temporary workers necessary to build such a pipeline would pose a danger to vulnerable Native populations, as spikes in criminal activity, particularly instances of violence against women and sex trafficking, are well documented dark consequences of these projects.

Led by the Fond du Lac Band, five nations representing nearly 50,000 Natives united to submit the ensuing brief. They contend the State of Minnesota ignored Nations' expressed concerns about potential environmental and social problems associated with such pipelines, disregarded treaty rights, and paid no heed to the analyses provided by both the State Historic Preservation Office and the Minnesota Indian Affairs Council, which represents the interests of all Native nations located within the boundaries of the state.

The Nations request the Public Utilities Commission halt the process until (1) a comprehensive survey of cultural resources is completed for the entire proposed route and alternative routes, (2) an additional Environmental Impact Statement of potential effects on the treaty resources of all five nations is conducted, and (3) the state creates an organizational structure that includes all Tribal nations in planning, scheduling, and implementation.

Joint Petition Regarding Enbridge Pipeline 3

Introduction

On behalf of their 48,000 enrolled members, intervenors Fond du Lac Band of Lake Superior Chippewa, Mille Lacs Band of Ojibwe, Leech Lake Band of Ojibwe, White Earth Band of Ojibwa, and Red Lake Band of Chippewa (collectively the "Tribes") jointly move the Public Utilities Commission ("Commission") to reconsider and amend its December 14 Order Finding Environmental Impact Statement Inadequate ("December 14 Order"). The state's historic properties work on the Line 3 Replacement project (the "Project") to date has been so inadequate that it could be used as a "what not to do" example in future guidance. The lead state agency, the Department of Commerce—Energy Environmental Review and Analysis Unit ("DOC"), has all but ignored its obligations under state historic properties law. The DOC has disregarded the explicit advice and direction of the State Historic Preservation Office ("SHPO") and the Minnesota Indian Affairs Council ("MIAC"). The DOC has ignored the guidance of its own tribal liaison—who was hired for the express purpose of coordinating with tribes on the Project. Given the track record, perhaps it goes without saying that the DOC is also discounted extensive comments from the Tribes, other intervenors, and members of the public. The DOC's approach violates a host of state laws, including the Minnesota Environmental Policy Act ("MEPA"), the Minnesota Field Archaeology Act, and the Minnesota Historic Sites Act.

The DOC has taken the position that it can rely entirely on whatever tribal historic properties work the US Army Corps of Engineers ("Corps"), the federal permitting agency on the Project, may conduct in the future as part of federal National Environmental Policy Act ("NEPA") and Nationally Historic

Preservation Act ("NHPA") Section 106 compliance. Section 106 review does require tribal consultation, survey, and evaluation of impacts on historic properties of importance to tribes, including a survey of tribal traditional cultural properties ("TCPs"), a subtype of historic property protected by both state and federal law. And it is true that a state agency can sometimes meet the requirements of state historic properties law by adopting federal work product. But that only works where there is a joint state-federal EIS— or at least better coordination of state and federal work than has been conducted on this Project. Because Enbridge suspended its federal permit applications during the current iteration of the Project, Section 106 work was suspended, too (although, due to tribal insistence, Section 106 work has now restarted). But there is far more work to do to meet Section 106 requirements, including additional interviews, fieldwork, and other analysis that remains to be done to fully assess TCPs on the Project. The Fond du Lac Band explained this in the "Interim Report: Line 3 Corridor Tribal Cultural Survey."

Instead of adjusting for the suspension of the federal section 106 process, DOC dropped an incomplete historic properties analysis into the FEIS [Final Environmental Impact Statement] and called it a day. This approach falls far below the requirements of state law. Similarly, the DOC ignored calls for the FEIS to fully cover impacts to treaty resources, and evaluation that overlaps with TCP analysis.... Whatever the reason, refusing to include a full historic properties review in the FEIS, the DOC has both ignored state law and continued an ugly legacy of state and federal agencies ignoring tribal interests despite devastating consequences. As the Commission knows, in 2017, the state Department of Transportation failed to conduct full historic properties review and consult with tribal governments in the area of the Highway 23 road and bridge project in Duluth. The result was destruction of the tribal burial site. There is no substitute for full and timely historic evaluation.

Furthermore, this is one of the same, avoidable errors that the Corps made on the Dakota Access Pipeline ("DAPL") in North Dakota. Permitting that project on an incomplete record has meant the destruction of tribal sacred sites, irreversible impacts to treaty resources, and extensive litigation— litigation in which the Corps is not being held accountable and where additional environmental review is even now being conducted. Moreover, the mass civil disobedience, protest caps, and worldwide demonstrations opposing DAPL are well-documented. The Commission has every reason to do a better job for Minnesota.

Therefore, the Tribes together take the earliest opportunity to brief this matter and to petition the Commission to reconsider its December 14 Order. The Tribes expressly ask that the Commission amend the Order to direct that full historic properties review the completed as part of the FEIS. Specifically, the Tribes request that the December 14 Order at Deficiency 4 be amended to read: "The FEIS must include a completed TCR Survey along the entire Applicant's Preferred Route and the alternate routes before any routing or need decision will be made. Additionally, cumulative impacts to treaty resources must be evaluated and included here, including evaluation data." At Section V below, the Tribes propose a structure for accomplishing the work. The Tribes asked for both a reply and oral argument on this Petition.

Factual Background

There is no dispute regarding the tribal background and historic properties work performed (or not performed) to date. The relevant facts are all in the record (or are subject to judicial notice, in the case of news articles and state policy guidance), with appropriate exhibits attached hereto.

1. Tribal historic properties in Minnesota

Ojibwa, Dakota, and other tribal people have for millennia occupied the land now recognized as Minnesota. There is extensive evidence of this habitation throughout Northern Minnesota in the form of TCP's. TCPs in northern Minnesota take many different forms...such as "cultural corridors" including waterways, portages, and trails; historic villages and counts; grave sites; wild rice water; maple sugarbush; essential animal habitats; sites where medicinal plants grow; and other sacred places. Many of these places are not recorded in a written record but are part of the confidential knowledge passed down through tribal elders.

It is undisputed that permitting agencies must conduct appropriate evaluation and plan mitigation impacts to TCP's through and with tribes as the experts regarding both locations and preservation needs. Even Enbridge's own consulting archaeologist Dr. Christopher Bergman testified in the evidentiary hearing that tribes are the "experts" who must identify tribal TCP's. Furthermore, asked whether it would be "best management practice to do a full traditional resources survey along the entire scope of this pipeline on the preferred route," Dr. Bergman agreed that it was "absolutely essential."

There is no question that off reservation hunting, fishing, and gathering resources...will be impacted by the Project, regardless of route.... Correspondingly, the Tribes repeatedly asked for inclusion of appropriate cumulative impacts analysis on treaty issues of the APR and the alternatives, but the FEIS contain these data. The FEIS omits any evaluation for the projected or potential loss to any wild rice waters or wildlife habitat in the seated territories where the APR and alternatives would run.

Argument

1. The Commission can and should grant a petition to reconsider here because it is the earliest and most effective way to address defects in the FEIS.

In the December 14 Order, the Commission found the FEIS is inadequate—included only the minimal requirement that the FEIS must state that the TCR Survey needs to be completed "before construction." The Commission has effectively excused the DOC's failure to make reasonable efforts to undertake a full historic properties survey and to include the results in the FEIS. In another way, the Commission has decided that it will make routing and need decisions on one of the state's largest ever construction projects without ever considering a full record of the impacts on historic properties. This violates MEPA and the state law....Acting now is also in keeping with the purpose of

MEPA to ensure timely and complete EIS work. Minnesota courts recognize that MEPA requires early environmental review, just as in NEPA does....By far the most efficient way for the Commission to address this serious omission in the FEIS is reconsideration of the Order....

Conclusion

There is no legal basis upon which the Commission can waive the DOCs failure to undertake full historic properties and treaty impacts review on this Project. Work must be done now and included in the FEIS before the Commission makes the routing or need decisions and the work must include a full TCR Survey along the APR, SA–04, and all other alternatives. Therefore, the Tribes respectfully ask that the Commission reconsider its December 14 Order to include this requirement as part of the work the DOC is already doing to revise the FEIS.

Dated: January 2, 2018

Sources:

Brown, Alleen, "Tribal Liaison in Minnesota Pipeline Review Is Sidelined After Oil Company Complains to Governor" (August 12, 2017). And see https://theintercept.com/2017/08/12/tribal-liaison-in-minnesota-pipeline-review-is-sidelined-after-oid-company-complains-to-governor.

In the Matter of the Application of Enbridge Energy, Limited Partnership for a Certificate of Need for the Line 3 Replacement Project in Minnesota from the North Dakota Border to the Wisconsin Border. OAH 65–2500–32764 MPUC PL–9/CN–14–916.

In the Matter of the Application of Enbridge Energy, Limited Partnership for a Routing Permit for the Line 3 Replacement Project in Minnesota from the North Dakota Border to the Wisconsin Border. OAH 65–2500–33377 MPUC PL–9/PPL–15–137.

107

Regarding the Crisis of Missing and Murdered Native Women (2018)

Since the first contact with invading powers Native Women have suffered horrific levels of physical, emotional, and sexual violence. It is only recently that significant public outcry has driven the creation of policies and laws needed to address these profound problems. Two recent federal laws, the 2010 Tribal Law and Order Act and the reauthorization of the Violence against Women Act (VAWA) in 2013, are important steps aimed at addressing violence against Native women, particularly with regard to prosecution of non-Indian perpetrators. Amendments to VAWA in 2013 that became effective in 2015 returned a measure of jurisdictional power back to Tribal courts, but only under certain conditions: the non-Indian defendant must have ties to the Tribe and the Tribe must apply for the authority to prosecute.

A 2016 National Institute of Justice report found 84 percent of Native women have experienced violence and 56 percent have suffered sexual violence. They experience the highest per capita rate of rape in the US and are ten times more likely to be murdered. Thirty-nine percent of Native women will be subject to violence by an intimate partner as compared to 27 percent of white women. Sixty-seven percent of Native victims of sexual violence describe their attacker as non-Native. In 2016, according to the National Crime Information Center, more than 125 Native women went missing in the state of North Dakota, alone.

What makes these figures even more disturbing is the fact that they are likely scaled down because of chronic underreporting of violence and sexual assault across Indian Country. Even when a Native woman reports a violent attack to the authorities—who are typically federal officials because of the nature of the crimes—prosecutors frequently decline to pursue the case.

On May 5, 2017, with the support of nearly two hundred Tribal, national, and state organizations, the US Senate adopted S. Res. 60 designating the "National Day of Awareness for Missing and Murdered Native Women and Girls" to honor the lives of those missing and murdered and to show solidarity with them and their families. While Congress was willing to raise awareness of the issue, no substantive policy changes were proposed.

That September, the United Tribes of North Dakota sent a letter to North Dakota's congressional delegation seeking justice for the family of Savanna LaFontaine-Greywind, a Spirit Lake tribal member who had gone missing the month prior and was found dead a few days later. In October 2017, Senator Heidi Heitkamp (D-ND) introduced Savanna's Act, which would require an annual data report to Congress on missing and murdered Native women, improve Tribal law enforcement access to federal crime databases, and create standardized case protocols.

Although that federal action failed to progress, other actions moved forward. In March 2018, Washington governor Jay Inslee signed into law a measure requiring the State Patrol, working in coordination with Tribes, local law enforcement, and the Department of Justice, to find ways to improve criminal protections for reporting and identifying missing Native American women. The Minnesota Legislature considered a similar measure sponsored by Rep. Mary Kunesh-Podein, a descendant of the Standing Rock Sioux Tribe, to create a Governor's Task Force on Missing and Murdered Indigenous Women. In April 2018, the US Congress designated May 5, 2018, as the "National Day of Awareness for Missing and Murdered Native Women and Girls."

The resolutions that follow, one from the National Congress of American Indians and the other passed by the US Senate, graphically describe the situation in Indian Country.

———

National Congress of American Indians Resolution

Whereas, we, the members of the National Congress of American Indians of the United States, invoking the divine blessing of the Creator upon our efforts and purposes, in order to preserve for ourselves and our descendants the inherent sovereign rights of our Indian nations, rights secured under Indian treaties and agreements with the United States, and all other rights and benefits to which we are entitled under the laws and Constitution of the United States, to enlighten the public toward a better understanding of the Indian people, to preserve Indian cultural values, and otherwise promote the health, safety and welfare of the Indian people, do hereby establish and submit the following resolution; and

Whereas, the National Congress of American Indians (NCAI) was established in 1944 and is the oldest and largest national organization of American Indian and Alaska Native tribal governments; and

Whereas, on some reservations American Indian and Alaska Native women face murder rates that are more than 10 times the national average; and

Whereas, according to the Centers for Disease Control and Prevention, homicide is the third leading cause of death among American Indian and Alaska Native women between 10 and 24 years of age and the fifth leading cause of death for American Indian and Alaska Native women between 25 and 34 years of age; and

Whereas, Hanna Harris of the Northern Cheyenne Indian Tribe was 21 years old when she went missing on July 4, 2013 and, due to the inadequate response of the justice system, her family and friends searched for Hanna, led a march for justice for Hanna's murder and for other unresolved murders of American Indian women; and

Whereas, Roy Lynn Rides Horse of the Crow Tribe was beaten, burned and left for dead, and walked several miles before collapsing and due to inadequate response of the justice system to investigate RoyLynn's case, the Crow Tribe also led a march for justice on June 16, 2016; and

Whereas, on the day RoyLynn Rides Horse passed over the Montana congressional delegation introduced a resolution to designate May 5, 2017 as National Day of Awareness for Missing and Murdered Native Women and Girls, which seeks to commemorate the lives of missing and murdered American Indian and Alaska Native women; and

Whereas, over 175 tribal, state, regional, and national organizations have joined with the National Indigenous Women's Resource Center in support of the resolution to create a National Day of Awareness for Missing Native Women and Girls; and

Whereas, the Violence Against Women Act of 2005, and 2013, directed the Attorney General, acting through the National Institute of Justice (NIJ), to conduct a program of research to develop a more comprehensive understanding of violence against Native women, specifically including murder of Native women.

Now Therefore Be It Resolved, that the National Congress of American Indians does hereby support the congressional resolution creating a National Day of Awareness for Missing and Murdered Native Women and Girls; and

Be It Further Resolved, that the NCAI does hereby resolve to call upon the Department of Justice to fully implement the VAWA 2005 program of research and specifically provide Indian tribes information regarding the disappearance and murder of Native women; and

Be It Further Resolved,that the NCAI does hereby resolve to advocate for changes to increase safety for Native women to address the crisis of missing and murdered Native women and girls by the federal government, with agencies including but not limited to the Departments of Justice, Interior, and Health and Human Services including actions, such as:

1. To review, revise, and create law enforcement and justice protocols appropriate to the disappearance of Native women and girls, including inter-jurisdictional issues; and
2. To provide increased victim services to the families and community members of the disappeared or murdered Native women such as counseling for the children of the disappeared, burial assistance and community walks and healing ceremonies; and
3. Coordination of efforts across federal departments to increase the response to the disappearance or murder of Native women and girls; and
4. Coordinate in consultation with Indian tribes efforts to increase the response of state governments, where appropriate, to cases of disappearance or murder of Native women or girls; and

Be It Finally Resolved that this resolution shall be the policy of NCAI until it is withdrawn or modified by subsequent resolution.

Certification

The foregoing resolution was adopted by the General Assembly at the 2016 Annual Session of the National Congress of American Indians, held at the Phoenix Convention Center, October 9th–14th 2016, with a quorum present.

Brian Cladoosby, President
Aaron Payment, Recording Secretary

Senate Resolution Designating May 5, 2018, as the "National Day of Awareness for Missing and Murdered Native Women and Girls."

Whereas, according to a study commissioned by the Department of Justice, in some tribal communities, American Indian women face murder rates that are more than 10 times the national average murder rate;

Whereas, according to the most recently available data from the Centers for Disease Control and Prevention, in 2015, homicide—

(1) ranged from the second to seventh leading cause of death for American Indian and Alaska Native females between 1 and 39 years of age; and

(2) remained a leading cause of death for most American Indian and Alaska Native females between 40 and 64 years of age;

Whereas little data exist on the number of missing American Indian and Alaska Native women and girls in the United States;

Whereas, on July 5, 2013, Hanna Harris, a member of the Northern Cheyenne Tribe, was reported missing by her family in Lame Deer, Montana;

Whereas the body of Hanna Harris was found 5 days after she went missing;

Whereas Hanna Harris was determined to have been raped and murdered, and the individuals accused of committing those crimes were convicted;

Whereas the case of Hanna Harris is an example of many similar cases; and

Whereas Hanna Harris was born on May 5, 1992: Now, therefore, be it

Resolved, That the Senate—

(1) designates May 5, 2018, as the "National Day of Awareness for Missing and Murdered Native Women and Girls"; and

(2) calls on the people of the United States and interested groups—

(A) to commemorate the lives of missing and murdered American Indian and Alaska Native women and girls whose cases are documented and undocumented in public records and the media; and

(B) to demonstrate solidarity with the families of the victims in light of those tragedies.

Sources:

Casselman, Amy L. *Injustice in Indian Country: Jurisdiction, American Law, and Sexual Violence Against Native Women.* New York: Peter Lang, 2016.

Deer, Sarah. *The Beginning and End of Rape: Confronting Sexual Violence in Native America.* Minneapolis: University of Minnesota Press, 2015.

Heitkamp, Heidi. "Savanna's Act," https://www.congress.gov/bill/115th-congress/senate-bill/1942.

https://www.congress.gov/bill/115th-congress/senate-resolution/401/text.

108

Alaska Legislative
Concurrent Resolution
Urging Recognition of a
Linguistic Emergency (2018)

Both chambers of the Alaska State Legislature agreed to send this unique
resolution to Governor Bill Walker asking that he officially recognize the
urgent need to protect and fortify Alaska Native Languages. The resolution was
originally sponsored by Rep. Dan Ortiz (I-Ketchikan) in response to a recommendation from the Alaska Native Language Preservation and Advisory
Council. The week-long Senate debate prior to passage centered on the use of
the word "emergency," considered controversial by some, but the description
was ultimately retained.

―――――

For House Concurrent Resolution No. 19: Urging
Governor Bill Walker to Issue an Administrative Order
Recognizing a Linguistic Emergency.

Be It Resolved by the Legislature of the State of Alaska:

Whereas the state is home to 20 officially recognized Alaska Native lan-
guages, Inupiaq, Siberian Yupik, Central Alaskan Yup'ik, Alutiiq, Unangax^,
Dena'ina, Deg Xinag, Holikachuk, Koyukon, Upper Kuskokwim, Gwich'in,
Tanana, Upper Tanana, Tanacross, H?n, Ahtna, Eyak, Tlingit, Haida, and
Tsimshian, alongside English; and

Whereas House Bill No. 216, enacted as ch. 116, SLA 2014, signed into
law by Governor Sean Parnell, adding the 20 Alaska Native languages to the
official languages of the state, was the culmination of hundreds of hours of
effort by legislators, Alaska Natives, and others; and

Whereas Senate Bill No. 130, enacted as ch. 48, SLA 2012, signed into
law by Governor Sean Parnell, established the Alaska Native Language
Preservation and Advisory Council to advise both the governor and legislature
on programs, policies, and projects to provide for the cost-effective preservation, restoration, and revitalization of Alaska Native languages in the state; and

Whereas the state is in critical danger of losing those languages and,
according to the Alaska Native Language Preservation and Advisory Council,
the state may lose the last fluent speakers of all 20 Alaska Native languages by
the end of the 21st century if currentrates of language loss continue as they
have since the 1970s; and

Whereas one Alaska Native language, Eyak, lost its last fluent speaker in 2008; and Whereas 50 years of research shows that early, total language immersion education for English speakers increases academic proficiency in both English and the immersion language, as well as in other academic subjects; and

Whereas indigenous peoples should be able to provide education in the peoples' own languages in a manner that is appropriate to the peoples' cultural methods of teaching and learning; and

Whereas language is an important element of culture, and the use of Alaska Native languages can strengthen Alaska Native culture in a mutually reinforcing cycle;

Be It Resolved that the Alaska State Legislature urges the Governor, the Alaska Native Language Preservation and Advisory Council, and other state agencies to work expeditiously and actively with the legislature and Alaska Native organizations to ensure thesurvival and continued use of all 20 of the state's Alaska Native languages; and be it

Further Resolved that the Alaska State Legislature encourages the Governor, in cooperation with the legislature, to work with Alaska Native organizations to initiate and strengthen, as appropriate, legislative and policy measures that prioritize the survival and continued use of Alaska Native languages; and be it

Further Resolved that the Alaska State Legislature urges Governor Bill Walker to issue an administrative order recognizing a linguistic emergency.

Source:

http://www.akleg.gov/basis/Bill/Text/30?Hsid=HCR019C.

Bibliographic Essay

THE 573 INDIGENOUS peoples inhabiting the US today occupy a singular political niche within the larger society. Recognized as original sovereigns, they enjoy an extra-constitutional relationship with the federal and state governments, having never been incorporated into the US or state constitutions. Tribal governments today retain their inherent sovereign status and small remnants of their lands, although their authority as governing bodies and as proprietary landholders has been substantially diminished by federal and state statutes, presidential decrees, court cases, and administrative activities—chiefly within the Department of the Interior.

Still, the nearly 400 ratified treaties that were negotiated between 1778 and 1871 affirmed Native sovereignty and established a close, if uneven, enduring political relationship with the US. Complicating this unique government-to-government arrangement is the reality that federal lawmakers have attempted at various times to forcibly assimilate Native individuals via boarding schools, individualization of tribal property, imposition of Western legal institutions and values, and Christian missionary activity. One such attempt was passage of the Indian Citizenship Act of 1924, granting US citizenship with the goal of absorbing Natives into the larger society. Interestingly, this action positioned these people as rights holders in three polities: their tribal nation, state of residence, and the US.

Even with treble citizenship, Native political, property, and cultural rights still lack fundamental protection from the federal government despite ratified treaties and constitutional acknowledgment in the commerce clause. Notwithstanding the longevity and legitimacy of Indigenous peoples as self-governing communities, there is a dearth of literature by political scientists examining the political institutions and politics generated by or affecting them.

Although the literature on Indigenous politics and governance in the US is meager, there exists sufficient data to provide a sample of commentary in several critical areas, including studies that examine constitutionalism in Indian

Country, political activism, governmental reform and development, intergovernmental relations, and political identity, among other topics.

Despite the length of tenure of these nations and their diverse governing arrangements, there have been a limited number of texts that broadly examine their political and governing systems. Francis Svennson had an early take on Native politics in the short but lively work *The Ethnics in American Politics: American Indians* (Burgess Publishing Co., 1973) that examined the persistence and value of Tribal nationalism. Sharon O'Brien's *American Indian Tribal Governments* (University of Oklahoma Press, 1989) and Donald Grinde's edited collection *Native Americans* (Congressional Quarterly Press, 2002) employed a policy and case study approach that emphasized the history and vitality of Native governments.

David E. Wilkins and Heidi K. Stark's *American Indian Politics and the American Political System*, 4th ed. (Rowman & Littlefield, 2018) and Jerry Stubben's *Native Americans and Political Participation: A Reference Handbook* (ABC-CLIO, 2006) were broader studies that described and evaluated how Native politics was being conducted internally and intergovernmentally.

Native nations and inspired Native individuals and their works, such as those by Hazel Hertzberg, specifically *The Search for an American Indian Identity: Modern Pan-Indian Movements* (Syracuse University Press, 1971), and Joane Nagel, *American Indian Ethnic Renewal: Red Power and the Resurgence of Identity and Culture* (Oxford University Press, 1996) attest, have been actively engaged in all manner of political activism since precolonial times. While this statement also applies to the members of other racial, ethnic, and gender groups, the situation of Indigenous peoples is, arguably, far more complicated because of the unique extra-constitutional place these nations inhabit.

For much of US history, the general goal of most other minority groups' members has been inclusion within the American social contract. In contrast, most Native nations have fought to retain their political and cultural independence—based on their treaties and sovereignty—resisting absorption into the American polity. This is well described by Vine Deloria Jr.'s *Behind the Trail of Broken Treaties: An Indian Declaration of Independence* (University of Texas Press, originally published in 1974, reprinted in 1985), an account that details the factors leading to the major native demonstrations in the early 1970s and critiques the legal doctrines of "discovery" and "plenary power" that provide the federal government with significant leverage over Native peoples.

However, the Indian gaming phenomenon has begun to change this dynamic, as many Native peoples are economically incorporated on a scale never before witnessed, even as they retain a strong cultural awareness, as Jessica Cattelino's work *High Stakes: Florida Seminole Gaming and Sovereignty* (Duke University Press, 2008) on the Seminole Nation of Florida shows. John Sayers's important book on the American Indian Movement (AIM) and media depictions of the group and its leadership, *Ghost Dancing the Law: The Wounded Knee Trials* (Harvard University Press, 1997) focuses on ways Indigenous peoples organized outside regular paths of political influence in order to leverage meaningful policy changes.

Notwithstanding their historic and ongoing pre-constitutional and extra-constitutional status, some Native nations and an ever-increasing number of Native individuals have pursued direct political participation in the states and the federal electoral systems. Daniel McCool was the first political scientist to scrutinize Native voting patterns and his co-authored book *Native Vote: American Indians, the Voting Rights Act, and the Right to Vote* (Cambridge University Press, 2007) is an account of Natives insisting on their right to vote in non-native elections and it provides a thorough examination of the methods used by states and federal officials to limit their voting rights at that time. Jean Schroedel and Artour Aslanian in "Native American Vote Suppression: The Case of South Dakota" (*Race, Gender, and Class* 22, nos. 1 and 2 [2015]) focus on that state's systematic efforts to suppress the Native vote.

Generally, the relations between Native nations and other political powers have been defined as political, rooted as they are in treaties and other forms of diplomacy. Little academic attention has been given to other integral dimensions of these interactions, such as race, economics, property, or religion. Tom Biolsi's *Organizing the Lakota: The Political Economy of the New Deal on Pine Ridge and Rosebud Reservations* (University of Arizona Press, 1992) and Loretta Fowler's *Arapaho Politics: 1851–1978: Symbols in Crisis of Authority* (University of Nebraska Press, 1982) detail the efforts of the Lakota and the Arapaho as those nations reformulated their governing mechanisms.

Felix S. Cohen's *On the Drafting of Tribal Constitutions* (University of Oklahoma Press, 2006) and Eric Lemont's edited volume *American Indian Constitutional Reform and the Rebuilding of Native Nations* (University of Texas Press, 2006) critically examine how formal constitution-making and reform are carried out in Indian Country. The distinctive state corporate status of Alaskan natives is the focus of Caroline M. Brown's work, "Political and Legal Status of Alaska Natives," in *A Companion to the Anthropology of American Indians*, ed. Tom Biolsi ([Blackwell Publishers, 2004], 248–267). And Hawaiian Natives' de facto sovereignty and proprietary rights are addressed by Noenoe K. Silva's excellent book *Aloha Betrayed: Native Hawaiian Resistance to American Colonialism* (Duke University Press, 2004), that relies on previously unknown Hawaiian language texts to chart the intents and sustained political, economic, and cultural resistance by Native Hawaiians to US imperialism, thereby refuting the persistent myth that Native Hawaiians passively accepted their loss of land and culture.

The most well-known and studied Native political relationships are those between those nations and the federal government. However, in addition to the US, Native nations have politically engaged one another, European colonial powers, individual colonies/states, and other polities and corporate groups throughout history. A majority of pre-contact Indigenous peoples forged diplomatic relationships with encroaching foreign powers and later the US government via bilateral and multilateral treaties. Within the US system, Congress is explicitly authorized to oversee trade and commerce with Native peoples. Arguably of equal importance, though woefully under-studied, are the relationships between Native nations and state governments. Tribal nations and states share some citizens and lands. In their relations as quasi-sovereign entities they have each jealously, and sometimes violently, guarded their collective rights to political powers, natural resources, and cultural histories. Only in recent years have they begun to find common ground to improve intergovernmental relations, as the following works show.

Jeffrey S. Ashley and Secody Hubbard's *Negotiated Sovereignty: Working to Improve Tribal-State Relations* (Praeger, 2004) uses six case studies of Tribal-state relations to argue that negotiation rather than litigation is the more favorable approach for improved relations. While each case is unique, there are common themes of checkerboard land, conflictual history, and the need for non-adversarial dispute resolution. Brad Bay and Erin Fouberg, in *The Tribes and the States: Geographies of Intergovernmental Interaction* (Rowman & Littlefield, 2002), provide a useful set of essays by a diverse group of scholars examining the complicated relationship, through geographical lens, on topics such as taxation, criminal jurisdiction, gaming and environmental policy. The writers urge the parties to negotiate rather than litigate.

Laura E. Evans, *Power from Powerlessness: Tribal Governments, Institutional Niches, and American Federalism* (Oxford University Press, 2011) is a detailed case-based analysis, featuring twelve Native nations, that delineates how Tribal governments, many short on political power and resources, effectively utilize expertise, funding, networking, and incrementalism to achieve some policy successes in their relations with state and local governments.

Andrea Wilkins's *Fostering State-Tribal Collaboration: An Indian Law Primer* (Rowman & Littlefield, 2016) presents a concise and accessible overview of the political-legal relationship that encourages parties to engage in collaborative policy development as a means to ease tensions and improve delivery of services.

Issues of feminism, gender, and sexuality are beginning to receive serious attention by scholars in Native Studies. Throughout history, while the roles of Indigenous women and men varied, their statuses were of equal importance, as Jennifer Denetdale points out in her study, *Reclaiming Dine History: The Legacies of Navajo Chief Manuelito and Juanita* (University of Arizona Press, 2007). The arrival of Europeans and the inculcation of some of their religious, social, and economic values—especially patriarchy and sexism—led to a profound degradation of respect for gender and sexual dynamic features, affecting the governance of Native societies. Sarah Deer's illuminating study, *The Beginning and End of Rape: Confronting Sexual Violence in Native America* (University of Minnesota Press, 2015) provides ample evidence of how colonialism morphed with shifting Indigenous values, culminating in devastating sexual violence against Native women into modern times. Mark Rifkin's *When Did Indians Become Straight? Kinship, the History of Sexuality and Native Sovereignty* (Oxford University Press, 2011) focuses on Native sexuality and how the federal government sought to intervene in the most intimate of relationships and activities. *Critically Sovereign: Indigenous Gender, Sexuality, and Feminist Studies*, (Duke University, 2017), edited by Joanne Barker offers important perspectives.

In describing the basis of Indigenous knowledge, Vine Deloria Jr. said that two of the most important concepts were power and place. He defined power as the living energy that inhabits and composes the universe, and places the relationships of different entities with one another. Deloria summarized it thus: "Power and place produce personality." For Native peoples this simple but profound statement means the universe is alive and has a personal relationship with each human being. This metaphysical viewpoint is evidenced by the actions of Native nations and their citizens, as they stand on the front lines to fight against the powers precipitating the environmental and climate crisis that is affecting the entire globe.

These instances are well documented in the following: Daniel Wildcat, *Red Alert!: Saving the Planet with Indigenous Knowledge* (Fulcrum, 2009); Randall S. Abate and Elizabeth Ann Kronk Warner, *Climate Change and Indigenous Peoples: The Search for Legal Remedies* (Edward Elgar Publishing, 2013); Julie Koppel Maldonado et al., *Climate Change and Indigenous Peoples in the United States: Impacts, Experiences and Actions* (Springer International Publishing, 2014); Joshua Reid's history, *The Sea Is My Country: The Maritime World of the Makahs* (Yale University Press, 2015); and by Zoltan Grossman in, *Unlikely Alliances: Native Nations and White Communities Join to Defend Rural Lands* (University of Washington Press, 2017).

Indigenous communities are frequently the first to experience the negative effects of climate change. They also suffer the indignity of being denied access to their most sacred sites or the power to adequately defend those areas, as Bruce G. Miller described in "Culture as Cultural Defense: An American Indian Sacred Site in Court" (*American Indian Quarterly* 22 [1998]: 83–97). Many lack the political muscle needed to shield their lands and resources from corporate, governmental, and private exploitation, as argued by Jeffrey Ostler in *The Lakotas and the Black Hills: The Struggle for Sacred Ground* (Penguin Group, 2010), with a sweeping historical and legal overview of the efforts of the Lakota people to defend and reacquire the Black Hills.

Finally, scholars continue to challenge the notion that Native peoples are only historical actors, as in Sherry Smith and Brian Frehner's *Indians and Energy: Exploitation and Opportunity in the American Southwest* (School for Advanced Research Press, 2010), where authors from a variety of disciplines explain how Indigenous peoples have engaged energy resources as owners, lessees, and consumers. Kim Tallbear offers important research in identity in *Native American DNA: Tribal Belonging and the False Promise of Genetic Science* (University of Minnesota, 2013); and Mark Rifkin uses the concept of time to examine the impacts of colonization in *Beyond Settler Time: Temporal Sovereignty and Indigenous Self-Determination* (Duke University, 2017).

Index